To Form A More Perfect Union

Copyright © 1987 by Willard A. Weiss
All rights reserved.

Published by Daring Books,
Box 526, Canton, Ohio 44701

Library of Congress Cataloging-in-Publication Data

Weiss, Willard A.
  "To form a more perfect union."
  Bibliography: p.
  1. United States--Politics and government--1981- Miscellanea.   I. Title.
JK289.W4   1987   320.973   86-24377
ISBN 0-938936-60-3

Printed in the United States of America.

To Form A More Perfect Union

by
Willard Weiss

Daring Books
Canton • Ohio

CONTENTS

FOREWORD .... vii - xv

Thursday, February 12, 1987
CONGRESS APPOINTS COMMISSION TO STUDY CONSTITUTION 18

Wednesday, May 13, 1987
COMMISSION DINES AT THE CITY TAVERN 24

Thursday, May 14, 1987
OPENING SESSION.. 42

Monday, May 25, 1987
STATE OF THE UNION - I....................................... 58

Thursday, May 28, 1987
STATE OF THE UNION - II 71

Friday, May 29, 1987
STATE OF THE UNION - III 79

Monday, June 1, 1987
STATE OF THE UNION - IV 97

Tuesday, June 2, 1987
COMMISSION'S THOUGHTS ON PRESIDENCY 127

Wednesday, June 3, 1987
TESTIMONY OF PRESIDENTS: JOHN QUINCY ADAMS
TO JAMES BUCHANAN 144

Thursday, June 4, 1987
PRESIDENT ABRAHAM LINCOLN TESTIFIES...................... 156

Friday, June 5, 1987
TESTIMONY OF PRESIDENTS: ANDREW
JOHNSON TO BENJAMIN HARRISON 169

Monday, June 8, 1987
TESTIMONY OF PRESIDENTS: THEODORE ROOSEVELT TO
FRANKLIN DELANO ROOSEVELT 182

Tuesday, June 9, 1987
TESTIMONY OF PRESIDENTS: HARRY S. TRUMAN TO
JOHN F. KENNEDY 215

Tuesday, June 16, 1987
COMMISSION REVIEWS TESTIMONY 231

Wednesday, June 17, 1987
BENJAMIN FRANKLIN'S CONCEPTS ON CONSTITUTION 239

Thursday, June 18, 1987
PROBLEMS UNDER OUR FIRST CONSTITUTION 273

Friday, June 19, 1987
COMMISSION DISCUSSES PREFERENCES ON
GOVERNMENT STRUCTURE 310

Monday, June 29, 1987
THE "UNNECESSARY" VICE PRESIDENT 328

Tuesday, June 30, 1987
THE HOUSE OF REPRESENTATIVES 342

Wednesday, July 1, 1987
CONSTITUTIONAL COUNCIL TO PRESIDENT 357

Thursday, July 2, 1987
THE SENATE 375

Friday, July 3, 1987
THE CHADHA CASE 406

Monday, July 6, 1987
THE PRESIDENT AND THE SENATE:
SHARING OF POWERS 422

Tuesday, July 7, 1987
THE SENATE AS COUNCIL TO THE PRESIDENT 454

Monday, July 13, 1987
BENJAMIN FRANKLIN PROPOSES EIGHT
AMENDMENTS TO CONSTITUTION 469

Monday, July 27, 1987
COMMISSION ACCEPTS BENJAMIN
FRANKLIN'S PROPOSALS 488

Thursday, August 6, 1987
ORIGIN OF PRESIDENTIAL FOUR-YEAR TERM 489

Monday, August 10, 1987
ORIGIN OF METHOD OF ELECTION OF PRESIDENT 509

Monday, August 24, 1987
COST OF PRESIDENTS TO TAXPAYERS 551

Wednesday Evening, August 26, 1987
BENJAMIN FRANKLIN MEETS WILL ROGERS 565

Thursday, August 31, 1987
GENERAL DOUGLAS MACARTHUR TESTIFIES 577

Monday, September 7, 1987
BENJAMIN FRANKLIN PROPOSES
"NO CONFIDENCE VOTE" BY PEOPLE 598

Thursday, September 17, 1987
COMMISSION MAKES RECOMMENDATIONS
TO CONGRESS 621

Monday, June 15, 1988
CONGRESS APPROVES AND TRANSMITS PROPOSED
AMENDMENTS TO STATES FOR RATIFICATION 633

Monday, July 4, 1988
CONCERT ON INDEPENDENCE MALL IN PHILADELPHIA:
JOHN PHILLIP SOUSA CONDUCTING 635

Bibliography 644

Source References 648

Index 665

FOREWORD

What did we gain in two hundred years of America? Two hundred million people?

Did we "establish justice" or just tolerate injustice?

Did we "promote the general welfare" or demote ourselves to a state of welfare?

Did we elevate human values or deflate values of humans?

Did "We the People . . . secure the blessings of liberty" envisioned in the Constitution or has that vision been obscured by false illusions?

Is not America the land of Plenty — with Japanese cars on American streets while America's unemployed are millions deep?

Is not America a country invincible — withholding its wheat, expecting Russia to go down in defeat?

Is not America the home of the Brave — leaving American hostages in Iran and America in a frustrating jam; leaving it to our good neighbor Canada to hit a jackpot for the U.S. in a hot spot. Can we forget this merciful coup, for which we said merci beaucoup? Or, has America changed course in the wake of the Achille Lauro tide of events?

Is not America's Creed, "Give me your tired, your poor, your huddled masses yearning to breathe free, the wretched refuse of your teeming shore, send these . . ." — along with thousands of Cuban criminals?

Or doesn't anybody care?

Where are the Washingtons, the Jeffersons, and the Lincolns who gave us their loving care?

Did not Henry David Thoreau say, "If man does not keep pace with his companions, perhaps it is because he hears a different drummer"? Where is that different drummer who can set a different pace for America?

Or doesn't anybody care?

What about the "drummer" in the office of the president of the United States? It has been said that the presidency is not a prize to be won by glittering promises. It is not a commodity to be sold by high pressure salesmanship. The presidency is a most sacred trust. Yet, consider the voices of a few past presidents on the burdens of that office. Are these sentiments compatible with that sacred trust?

John Adams: "At the mid term of my single term I felt that the business of the office was so oppressive that I could hardly support it two years longer . . . had I been chosen President again, I am certain I could not have lived another year."

Thomas Jefferson: "I am tired of an office where I can do no more good . . . it brings nothing but increasing drudgery. . . ."

John Quincy Adams: "The four most miserable years of my life were my four years in the presidency."

Andrew Jackson: "I can with truth say mine was a situation of dignified slavery."

Rutherford Hayes: "Nobody ever left the Presidency with less regret . . . than I . . . The escape from bondage into freedom was grateful indeed to my feelings. . . . The burden has not been a light one. . . ."

James Garfield: "Four years of this intellectual dissipation may cripple me for the rest of my life. . . . I do not know that I shall ever become reconciled to this office. . . . My God! What is there in this place that a man should ever want to get in it."

Grover Cleveland: "The office of the president has not, to me personally, a single allurement. . . . It involves a responsibility beyond human strength . . . the Presidency has cost me so much health and vigor that I have sometimes doubted if I could carry the burden to the end. . . ."

Woodrow Wilson: "The amount of work a President is supposed to do is preposterous . . . a man who seeks the Presidency of the United States is an audacious fool. . . ."

Warren Harding: "The White House is a prison . . . I am in jail. . . . I knew this job would be too much for me. . . . God, what a job!"

Harry Truman: "There is no exaltation in the office of the President of the United States—sorrow is the proper word."

John F. Kennedy: "When I ran for the Presidency of the United States . . . I could not realize—nor could any man realize who does not bear the burdens of this office—how heavy and constant would be those burdens."

These sad expressions of past presidents are like a haunting refrain that reveals a general mood that should be of deep concern to us all. Are these expressions compatible with Franklin Delano Roosevelt's statement that the presidency is a most sacred trust? Are they compatible with the constitutional oath taken by a president before entering his office? The burden of the office of the president is one of the many issues which this book addresses.

Consider just one more thought about the office of the president. George Mason, a delegate to the Federal Convention of 1787, which drafted the Constitution, refused to sign the Constitution, saying,

> The President of the United States has no Constitutional Council, a thing unknown in any safe and regular government. He will therefore be unsupported by proper information and advice and will generally be directed by minions and favorites . . . or a Council of State will grow out of the principal officers of the great departments; the worst and most dangerous of all ingredients for such a Council in a free country, for they may be induced to join in any dangerous or oppressive measures, to shelter themselves, and prevent an inquiry into their own misconduct in office.

That was two hundred years ago.

And, that is exactly what happened. Perhaps George Mason was a prophet. Perhaps he could envision "all the president's 'yes' men." Perhaps he feared the assemblage of "minions and favorites," such advisors as H. R. Haldeman, aide to President Richard Nixon, who, a White House tape tells us, suggested in 1971 that "thugs" and "murderers" be used against antiwar protesters to "knock their heads off." Then there was Bert Lance, director of the Office of Management and Budget in Jimmy

Carter's administration, who was indicted by a federal grand jury on charges that he and three of his business associates conspired to obtain twenty million dollars in loans for their own benefit from 41 banks from 1970 to 1978. Add to the list David Stockman, budget director to president Ronald Reagan, who, in a highly controversial article in *The Atlantic*, criticized an economic program he himself had helped design. Assistant Senate Democratic leader Alan Cranston said of Stockman,

> The President will have a hard time convincing the Congress and the American people they should have confidence in a budget that was put together by a man who admits he is guilty of poor judgment and loose talk! . . . The country needs to know who else in the executive branch knew that the budget was composed of "snap judgements and technical bloopers" and that it was based on figures pulled out of thin air.

And when the House Budget Committee began hearings on President Reagan's 1983 budget and its projected deficit, Representative David Obey, Democrat from Wisconsin, zeroed in on Stockman: "There is nothing funny about what happens to the country when people who run the government don't level with the country and don't level with Congress. . . . I have no questions for you because, very frankly, I would not believe the answers you would give me."

For good or bad, others in this category include Louis McHenry Howe of "mess kit" fame, advisor and secretary to President Franklin Roosevelt, reputed to have arranged for the sale of 200,000 mess kits to Civilian Conservation Corps boys for a high price through a friend of Roosevelt's; Howe apparently received nothing. Add Sherman Adams of "vicuna" coat fame, assistant to President Dwight D. Eisenhower, forced out of office after accepting the coat as a gift from a manufacturer; Hamilton Jordan of "stuff like snuff" fame, assistant to President Carter; and Richard V. Allen, former assistant to the president for national-security affairs, forced out of the Reagan administration after a $1,000 "misunderstanding" that arose when three Japanese tried to hand the cash to Nancy Reagan after an interview Allen helped to arrange.

And then there were the ten of Watergate infamy: H. R. Haldeman, John D. Ehrlichman, Charles W. Colson, John W. Dean III, E. Howard Hunt, Jr, G. Gordon Liddy, Dwight L. Chapin, Egil Krough, Jr., Jeb Stuart Magruder, and Herbert L. Porter.

The common thread here is that all these persons were in positions to give advice to the president for action, or in positions from which action could be taken in the name of the president, even without the president's knowledge. They were "minions and favorites, the worst and most dangerous of all ingredients . . . in a free country," just as George Mason had predicted.

Something is terribly wrong in the United States and in the office of the president of the United States. We can no longer afford to be in a position where government of the people, by the people, and for the people, hands that government over to "minions and favorites."

This book asserts the claim that the structure of government under the Constitution of the United States no longer meets the needs of the nation — no longer renders it possible for one person to take the helm and guide our ship of state through rough seas. Anyone can hold the helm when the sea is calm.

This book is intended to show the People and the Congress how "to form a more perfect Union."

The two-hundredth anniversary of the United States Constitution is in 1987. In this book, in that year, Congress appoints George Washington, John Adams, Thomas Jefferson, James Madison, and Benjamin Franklin to a Commission whose purpose is to hold hearings on the Constitution to determine whether any changes should be made. The book treats all people who lived at any time during the last 225 years as though they are still alive. Thus, we find Benjamin Franklin having dinner with Will Rogers at the City Tavern in Philadelphia, which was in existence then and is in existence today. The hearings of the Commission which begin May 14, 1987 and end September 17, 1987, are all held in the Assembly Room in the Old State House in Philadelphia, which we know as Independence Hall.

The Commission calls witnesses to testify on the State of the Union during the last two centuries. Most of the presidents are called to testify, and it is determined that there is a common thread imbedded in the testimony which requires the Commission to go back and determine what went wrong in the Federal Convention of 1787, and the Constitution it produced. When the Commission terminates its sessions exactly two hundred years after the Constitution was signed, it recommends to the Congress of the United States nine very specific substantive and practical amendments to the Constitution. The proposals sent to Congress are debated over a period of several months, approved, and sent to the states for ratification.

Is this book fiction or nonfiction? I would like it to be considered nonfiction, since most of the words used in the book are the actual words spoken or written at some point in history by the persons testifying. The fictional creation of a Commission by Congress and the assumption that all people who lived at any time during the last few centuries are still alive, merely create the framework within which the story can unfold.

The source for each piece of testimony or dialogue appears at the end of the book. I strived to achieve an adaptation of the material without changing the intent of the document's author. In a great many instances material is used without quotation marks since to do otherwise would be intrusive. Silent editorial emendations have been made as required to render the text intelligible whether or not the material has quotation marks. For example, spelling has been modernized; omitted words have been inserted at appropriate places; obvious slips of the pen and inadvertent repetitions are usually corrected; capitalization and punctuation have been standardized; tenses have been changed where necessary; doubtful cases have been resolved in favor of current usage. Yet, in many cases the material is preserved and presented as in the original.

In researching the material for this book, I spent much time in Philadelphia — truly the City of Brotherly Love — where I received the ultimate in cooperation from the Pennsylvania Historical Society, the National Park Service, the historian for the City of Philadelphia, and the archivist of the State of Pennsylvania. I poured through thousands of bits of information in the National Park Service Library in Philadelphia and received the generous assistance of its historians, both active and retired.

Philadelphia, where the Declaration of Independence and the Constitution were drafted and signed, is the situs of this book. Here in this milieu I walked along the paths of George Washington, John Adams, Thomas Jefferson, James Madison, and Benjamin Franklin and tried to reach the unreachable, their very state of mind.

One may justifiably ask whether this book is in the form of a script for a play or perhaps for television. Actually, it is neither. The format follows that of the Congressional Record of the Congress of the United States, which records the proceedings on the floor of the House and the Senate, the same format as that recording the proceedings of any Commission or Committee established or appointed by Congress today, the same as that of the Journals of the Continental Congress (1774 to 1789) which recorded our separation from England, the Declaration of Independence, the Revolutionary War, the Articles of Confederation, and the transmittal of the Constitution for ratificaton to the states in 1787. The format is the same as that of James Madison's notes of the debates in the Federal Convention of 1787, where the Constitution was designed and signed.

Who am I to deviate from this time-honored format?

I am an attorney and an actuary. As an attorney my professional field is limited to Federal practice in the area of pension trusts. As an actuary, my professional field is in the area of providing actuarial services under the provisions of the Employee Retirement Income Security Act, sometimes called ERISA, and I am licensed by the Federal government for this purpose as an Enrolled Actuary.

What is an actuary? An actuary is a person skilled in the mathematics of probabilities and interest as applied to the risks of life or living. For example, a person who develops the premiums for your life insurance policy is an actuary.

Now — why is an actuary writing a book about the Constitution? As an actuary I sense that connections and relationships are found in almost any seemingly disparate set of historical facts. This is best illustrated by an example of how my mind works. A few days after the American hostages were released from Iran I woke my wife at 4 a.m. and told her this story: There is a connection between the freeing of the hostages and the freedom sought by the Colonies in the Declaration of Independence on July 4, 1776. It is as simple as adding, dividing and multiplying, I said:

The word "hostage" contains seven letters and the word "freedom" contains seven letters. July is the seventh month of the year.

There were 52 hostages and there were 13 Colonies. Divide 52 by 13 and we have 4. Now we have July 4th.

The hostages were in captivity for 444 days. The Declaration was signed on the 4th. Multiply 4 times 444 and we have 1776.

Hence — July 4, 1776.

And when my mind works like that, sometimes I think I am Benjamin Franklin.

I trust you will tolerate my imagination and grant me an exemption from a non compos mentis status.

But the serious question remains: Did our founders flounder?

Gouverneur Morris, one of the delegates to the Federal Convention of 1787, was concerned about it: "Fond, however, as the framers of our National Constitution were of republican government, they were not so much blinded by their attachment as not to discern the difficulty, perhaps impracticability, of raising a durable edifice from crumbling materials. History, the parent of political science, has told them that it was almost as vain to expect permanency from democracy as to construct a palace on the surface of the sea. But it would have been foolish to fold their arms and sink into despondence because they could neither form nor establish the best of all possible systems. . . . We did the best we could; leaving it with those who should come after us to take counsel from experience, and exercise prudently the power of amendment, which we had provided."

And on the subject of amending the Constitution, Thomas Jefferson said, "Some men look at Constitutions with sanctimonious reverence and deem them like the ark of the covenant, too sacred to be touched. They ascribe to the men of the preceding age a wisdom more than human, and suppose what they did to be beyond amendment. . . . Laws and institutions must go hand in hand with the progress of the human mind. . . . As new discoveries are made, new truths disclosed and manners and opinions change with the change of circumstances, constitutions must advance also, and keep pace with the times. . . ."

Two hundred years are gone now, and "Constitutions must advance also, and keep pace with the times."

"The treasure of time once lost, can never be recovered; yet we squander it as tho' 'twere nothing worth, or we had no use for it. . . . Be wise to-day, 'tis madness to defer. . . . Procrastination is the thief of time," wrote Benjamin Franklin in 1751.

Perhaps we now have our last chance, an opportunity to correct the course of the ship of state, to amend the system, or as Gen. Douglas MacArthur cautioned, "if we will not devise some greater and more equitable system, our Armageddon will be at our door."

Time is like a stream of water. Presidents, senators, representatives, good men and bad may step into the stream and stir up the water, but let them step out and soon the stream will look just as it did before. The stream rolls on, and brings with it always, hope.

Of hope, perhaps my father said it best —
"And the world goes on.
I shall think of nothing gloomy.
I shall think only of the happy things.
If you don't think of where you are going, you're nothing but an animal."

This book is dedicated to the American Public, "to form a more perfect Union."

Willard A. Weiss

ACKNOWLEDGEMENTS

I am grateful to many for their assistance in the preparation of this book.

My thanks to my granddaughter, Jill Robin Weiss, whose contribution is emblazoned across the cover, for she suggested the title. Jill was twelve years old when, as a student at Hawken School, she was assigned the task of memorizing the Preamble to the Constitution. It was on this repetitious assignment in my presence that she extracted the words "To Form a More Perfect Union" for the title. Thanks, Jill.

Many guided me in this project in one way or another. My thanks go to them:

Bernard Goodman, assistant superintendent of Independence National Historic Park; and to Martin Yoelson, former chief historian; and David Dutcher, current chief historian of Independence National Historic Park, who allowed me to use the Independence National Historic Park Library.

The late Roman Kos, librarian of the Independence National Historic Park Library, who was of great assistance.

Richard Tyler, historian for the Philadelphia Historic Commission, who made available to me his unpublished manuscript, "The Common Cause of America: A Study of the First Continental Congress."

Peter Parker and Bruce Laverty of the Historical Society of Philadelphia.

Clarence Wolf of George S. MacManus Co., Philadelphia.

Henry E. Brown, associate archivist, Bureau of Archives and History, William Penn Memorial Museum, Harrisburg.

John D. R. Platt, retired historian from the National

Park Service at Independence National Historic Park, who gave most generously of his knowledge, experience, and time.

Laura L. Nagy, former senior editor at the Kent State University Press, who served as my editor, and whose contributions are immeasurable.

Thelma Rivin, who gave unstintingly of her time in typing the manuscript, and her husband, Ray, for his patience with her long hours of hard work.

Irving Kaplan, my golfing partner, who contributed to the concept in the early stages of the manuscript.

The late Richard Felber.

My wife, Bobbi, for her reviews of the various drafts of the manuscript and her support.

My sons, James, Richard, and Kenneth for cheering me on.

Yet, despite all the assistance and encouragement, all errors and oversights belong to me.

CONGRESS APPOINTS COMMISSION TO STUDY CONSITUTION

On February 12, 1987, on the ensuing occasion of the two hundredth anniversary of the Constitution of the United States, the Congress of the United States appointed a Commission to hold hearings for the purpose of recommending to the Congress such amendments as may render the Constitution more adequate to the present-day needs of this nation. The text of those hearings and of related events follow.

PUBLIC LAW 100 - 87

ONE HUNDREDTH CONGRESS OF THE UNITED STATES OF AMERICA

AT THE FIRST SESSION

Begun and held at the City of Washington on Thursday the twelfth day of February, one thousand nine hundred and eighty-seven

AN ACT

To establish a Joint Commission for the purpose of considering and recommending amendments to the Constitution of the United States on the occasion of the Bicentennial of the Constitution.

Be it enacted by the Senate and House of Representatives of the United States of America in Congress assembled, that:

(a) There is established a Commission to be known as the Bicentennial Constitutional Commission for the purpose of devising, deliberating on, and recommending to the Congress of the United States, such amendments to the Constitution as may be necessary or advisable to render such Constitution more adequate to the exigencies of this nation.

(b) The Commission shall be composed of five members as follows:

> Gen. George Washington, former president of the United States
> Mr. John Adams, former president of the United States
> Dr. Benjamin Franklin, former president of the state of Pennsylvania
> Mr. Thomas Jefferson, former president of the United States

Mr. James Madison, former president of the United States

(c) The Chairman of the Commission shall be General George Washington.

(d) Meetings and hearings of the Commission shall be held in the Assembly Room of the old Pennsylvania State House, currently known as Independence Hall, located in Philadelphia, Pennsylvania, such room being the same room in which the Declaration of Independence in the year 1776, and the Constitution of the United States in the year 1787, were deliberated and signed.

(e) Formal meetings and hearings of the Commission shall commence on May 14, 1987 and end on September 17, 1987, such period being the same period in which the Federal Convention devised, deliberated, and concluded the provisions of the Constitution of the United States in the year 1787.

(f) The Commission shall submit to the Congress not later than December 31, 1987, a final report together with such recommendations, including recommendations for legislation, as the Commission deems advisable.

(g) The Commisison shall cease to exist on July 4, 1988.

(h) The biography of each member of the Commission, aforesaid, is set forth as follows:

(1) For General George Washington:
George Washington was born at Wakefield, near Popes Creek, Westmoreland County, Virginia, February 22, 1732; attended an "old field" school; engaged in the surveying of lands; was appointed adjutant general of a military district in Virginia with the rank of major in 1751; served in the French and Indian War, becoming aide-de-camp to General Braddock in 1755; engaged in agriculture at Mount Vernon; served as a magistrate and as a member of the colonial House of Burgesses 1758 to 1774; was Member of the First and Second Continental Congresses in 1774 and 1775; was unanimously chosen June 15, 1775, as commander-in-chief of all the forces raised or to be raised; commanded

the armies throughout the War for Independence and received the special thanks and recognition of Congress upon eight separate occasions; resigned his commission December 23, 1783, and returned to private life at Mount Vernon; was delegate to, and president of, the national convention that framed the Federal Constitution in Philadelphia in 1787; was unanimously elected as the first president of the United States, being inaugurated April 30, 1789 in New York City; was unanimously reelected in 1792; retired March 3, 1797, after declining a renomination; issued his farewell address to the people of the United States in September 1796; was again appointed as lieutenant general and commander of the United States Army, July 3, 1798.

(2) For Mr. John Adams:
John Adams (father of John Quincy Adams and grandfather of Charles Francis Adams) was born in Braintree, Massachusetts, October 30, 1735; was graduated from Harvard College in 1755; studied law, was admitted to the bar in 1758 and commenced practice in Suffolk County, Massachusetts; served as member of the First Continental Congress 1774-78; signed the Declaration of Independence and proposed George Washington of Virginia for general of the American Army; was head of the War Department, commissioner to the Court of France; Minister Plenipotentiary to Holland; was first Minister to England, serving from 1785 until 1788; was elected in 1788 as the first vice-president of the United States on the Federalist ticket with George Washington as president; was reelected in 1792; was elected president of the United States as a member of the Federalist party and served from March 4, 1797 to March 3, 1801; his last act in office was to appoint John Marshall as chief justice of the United States.

(3) For Dr. Benjamin Franklin:
Benjamin Franklin was born in Boston, Massachusetts, January 17, 1706; attended the Boston Grammar School one year; was instructed in elementary branches by a private tutor; was employed in a tallow chandlery for two years;

learned the art of printing, and after working at his trade in Boston, Philadelphia, and London, established himself in Philadelphia as a printer and publisher; founded the *Pennsylvania Gazette* in 1728, and in 1732, began the publication of *Poor Richard's Almanack*; was postmaster of Philadelphia in 1737; was member of the provincial assembly 1744-54; was member of several Indian commissions; was elected a member of the Royal Society for his scientific discoveries; was deputy postmaster general of the British North American Colonies 1753-74; was agent of Pennsylvania in London 1757-62 and 1764-75; was member of the Continental Congress in 1775 and 1776; signed the Declaration of Independence; was president of the Pennsylvania constitutional convention of 1776; was sent as a diplomatic commissioner to France by the Continental Congress and, later, was minister to France 1776-85; was one of the negotiators of the treaty of peace with Great Britain; was president of Pennsylvania 1785-88; was president of the trustees of the University of Pennsylvania; was a delegate to the convention which framed the Federal Constitution in 1787.

(4) For Mr. Thomas Jefferson:
Thomas Jefferson was born in Old Shadwell, Virginia, April 13, 1743; attended a preparatory school conducted by the Rev. Mr. Maury; was graduated from William and Mary College, Williamsburg, Virginia, in 1762; studied law; was admitted to the bar and commenced practice in 1767; was a member of the Continental Congress in 1775 and 1776; was chairman of the committee that drew up the Declaration of Independence; made and presented the first draft of the Declaration that was submitted to the Congress July 2, 1776; signed the Declaration of Independence August 2, 1776; resigned soon after and returned to his estate, Monticello; was governor of Virginia 1779-81; was again a member of the Continental Congress, 1783-85; was appointed a minister plenipotentiary to France May 7, 1784, and then sole minister to the King of France March 10, 1785,

for three years; was appointed secretary of state of the United States September 26, 1789, and served until December 3, 1793; was elected vice-president of the United States and served from March 4, 1797, to March 3, 1801; was elected president of the United States in 1801, by the House of Representatives on the thirty-sixth ballot; was reelected in 1805, and served from March 4, 1801, to March 3, 1809; retired to Monticello; was active in founding the University of Virginia at Charlottesville.

(5) For Mr. James Madison:

James Madison was born in Port Conway, King George County, Virginia, March 16, 1751; studied under private tutors and was graduated from Princeton College in 1771; studied law at Princeton College one year; returned to Virginia and continued the study of law; was admitted to the bar; was a member of the committee of safety from Orange County in 1774; was a member of the Continental Congress, 1780-83 and 1786-88; was a prominent delegate in the Federal Constitutional Convention at Philadelphia, Pennsylvania, in 1787; was elected as a Democrat to the first and to the three succeeding Congresses (March 4, 1789 - March 3, 1797); was appointed by President Jefferson as secretary of state March 5, 1801; entered upon the duties of that office May 2, 1801, and served until March 4, 1809; was elected as a Democratic president of the United States, was reelected, and served from March 4, 1809 to March 3, 1817; retired to his estate, Montpelier, Orange County, Virginia; was rector of the University of Virginia at Charlottesville and visitor to the College of William and Mary, Williamsburg, Virginia.

WEDNESDAY, MAY 13, 1987

COMMISSION DINES AT THE CITY TAVERN

Mr. Willard A. WEISS (author, standing in front of the City Tavern, in Philadelphia). The past is past, the present is present, and never the times shall meet; except in the minds of those who make believe they sit in God's great Judgment seat.

An eighteenth-century tavern was much more than a place to quench one's thirst. Food and drink were, of course, served, but social functions were equally important: taverns were the cities' central meeting places. Taverns hosted dinners for fraternal societies, meetings of political friends and foes, gatherings of local military companies, dancers, musical concerts, and all sorts of entertainment. News from afar reached taverns more quickly than it did the newspapers.

Such was the City Tavern, located on Second Street near Walnut, in Philadelphia. When John Adams arrived in Philadelphia in August of 1774, to attend the First Continental Congress, he was greeted by leading citizens and immediately taken to the tavern he would call "the most genteel one in America." A few months earlier Paul Revere had ridden up to the tavern with the news of the closing of the port of Boston by the British government. For over a decade the City Tavern would be a familiar sight to leading figures working in the cause of the Revolution or working on the clauses of the Constitution.

The City Tavern knew the patronage of the great and the near-great. It became the practice of the members of the Second Continental Congress to dine together there each Saturday. In addition, eight of the delegates, Gen. George Washington, Edmund Randolph, Richard Henry Lee, Benjamin Harrison, John Alsop, Samuel Chase, Caesar Rodney, and George Read, formed a "table" and dined there daily.

The City Tavern comprised several levels. The basement housed the kitchen, the first and second floors contained the public areas, and the third floor was devoted to lodging rooms. On the first floor was the Subscription Room, the Bar Room, the Coffee Room, and the Southwest Dining Room. On the second floor was the Long Room, the scene of elegant balls and brilliant entertainments. It was in the Long Room that Congress held the first Fourth of July celebration in 1777.

In 1854, the City Tavern was demolished to make way for new brownstone stores. A newspaper of the time noted that in a generation or two "the City Tavern will not be remembered except by some curious delver into the past."

It was remembered.

In 1975, the National Park Service rebuilt the City Tavern. Today, the Tavern appears essentially as it did two hundred years ago, even down to the front awning which shielded the Tavern from the summer sun.

It is Wednesday evening, May 13th, 1987. Gen. George Washington, John Adams, Benjamin Franklin, Thomas Jefferson, and James Madison, all members of the Bicentennial Constitutional Commission, are dining in the Southwest Dining Room of the City Tavern. Gen. George Washington is speaking. . . .

* * *

Gen. WASHINGTON. It was two hundred years ago, Monday, September 17, 1787, the last day of the Federal Convention. The Constitution had received the unanimous assent of eleven states and was subscribed to by every member present except Gov. Edmund Randolph of Virginia, Col. George Mason of Virginia, and Mr. Elbridge Gerry of Massachusetts. The business of the Convention being then closed, the members adjourned to the City Tavern, dined together and took a cordial leave of one another. I returned to my lodgings, received the papers from the Secretary of the Convention, and retired to meditate on the momentous week which had been executed. I had been in attendance not less than five, for a large part of the time six, and sometimes seven hours sitting every day, excepting Sundays and a ten-day adjournment to give a Committee the opportunity and time to arrange the business of the Convention. This went on for more than four months. That is substantially what I wrote in my diary for September 17, 1787.

Dr. FRANKLIN. I was there.

Mr. MADISON. I was there.

Mr. JEFFERSON. I was in France.

Mr. ADAMS. I was in England. Jemmy, why was the Constitution approved by only eleven states in the Federal Convention?

Mr. MADISON. John, Rhode Island never did send delegates, and after July 10, 1787, New York was not able to vote because it never had sufficient delegates present.

Mr. JEFFERSON. But twelve and not eleven states signed the Constitution. . . .

Mr. MADISON. Well, Col. Alexander Hamilton signed for New York, but he probably ought not to have done it. You see, his credentials and authority from the state of New York were "for the sole and express purpose of revising the Articles of Confederation." And, here we were, signing a brand new constitution.

Gen. WASHINGTON. I had wanted Hamilton at the Convention. He had attended and left on June 29th. Two other delegates from New York, John Lansing and Robert Yates, attended and left July 10th. On that day I wrote Alexander Hamilton, "the state of the Councils which prevailed at the period you left this City . . . are now, if possible, in a worse train than ever; you will find but little ground on which the hope of a good establishment can be formed. In a word, I almost despair of seeing a favorable issue to the proceedings of the Convention, and do therefore repent having had any agency in the business.

"The men who oppose a strong and energetic government are, in my opinion, narrow-minded politicians, or are under the influence of local views. The apprehension expressed by them that the people will not accede to the form proposed is the ostensible, not the real cause of the opposition — but admitting that the present sentiment is as they prognosticate, the question ought nevertheless to be, is it, or is it not, the best form? If the former, recommend it, and it will assuredly obtain meager opposition.

"I am sorry you went away. I wish you were back . . . ."

Dr. FRANKLIN. Speaking of the signers of the Constitution, was there not an incident relating to John Dickinson's signature?

Mr. MADISON. Indeed. John Dickinson's name is appended to the Constitution, but he did not sign his name. You see, he left town and asked George Read to sign for him. Read signed his own name and that of Dickinson to the Constitution.

Mr. ADAMS. Can we find these explanations in the Journal of the Federal Convention?

Mr. MADISON. No. Major William Jackson, Secretary to the Federal Convention, was responsible for the preparation of its journal. I once received a letter from Jared Sparks, who was preparing a history of the period; in it he said, "It seems to me that your secretary of the Convention was a very stupid secretary, not to take care of those things better, and to make a better journal than the dry bones which now go by that name."

Gen. WASHINGTON. Allow me to relate what happened to me immediately after I left the Convention. I finished what private business I had on Tuesday, September 18th and took leave of the families with which I had been most intimate — Mr. and Mrs. Robert Morris and Gourverneur Morris. I left Philadelphia in the afternoon reaching Chester where I lodged, in company of Mr. Blair, whom I had invited to a seat in my carriage until we should reach Mount Vernon.

The next day, Wednesday, the 19th, rain prevented our

setting off till about eight o'clock, when it ceased and promising to be fair, we departed. We fed the horses at Wilmington, dined at Christiana bridge, and lodged at the head of the Elk. At the bridge we had a narrow escape. The rain had fallen the preceding evening and swelled the water considerably. There was no fording it safely.

I was reduced to the necessity therefore of remaining on the other side or of attempting to cross an old, rotten and long disused bridge. Being anxious to get on I preferred the latter. In the attempt to cross, one of my two horses fell fifteen feet at least, the other very near following, which, had it happened, would have taken the carriage with baggage along and destroyed the whole effectually. However, by prompt assistance of some people at a mill just by, and great exertion, the first horse was disengaged from his harness, the second prevented from going through, and the carriage was drawn off and rescued from hurt.

Dr. FRANKLIN. Incredible!

Gen. WASHINGTON. Well, it was a harrowing experience. I finally arrived at Mount Vernon on Saturday, the 22nd, after an absence of four months and fourteen days.

Mr. MADISON. George Mason also had a bad incident on his journey home from the convention. As you indicated, he was one of three who declined to sign the Constitution.

He left Philadelphia in an exceeding ill humour indeed. A number of little circumstances arising in part from the impatience which prevailed towards the close of the business, conspired to whet his acrimony. He returned to Virginia with a fixed disposition to prevent the adoption of the plan if possible. I recall him saying, "They have done what they ought not to have done, and have left undone what they ought to have done."

Anyway, the accident occurred near Baltimore as Mason and Dr. James McHenry were returning from Philadelphia. It was reported that the driver overturned the coach and "they were both hurt — the Colonel most so — he lost blood at Baltimore and is well." You recall Dr. McHenry. He not only signed the Constitution, they named Fort McHenry at Baltimore, where the "Star Spangled Banner" was inspired, after him.

Gen. WASHINGTON. I remember that — Mason had written me from his home, Gunston Hall, in Virginia, which, incidentally, was separated only by ridges from Mount Vernon, saying: "I got very much hurt in my neck and head, by the unlucky accident on the road; it is now wearing off; tho' at times still uneasy to me."

Mr. ADAMS. A most fortunate recovery for both of you. Tell me, General, just where are you staying?

Gen. WASHINGTON. At the Valley Forge Hilton.

Mr. ADAMS. And you, Ben?

Dr. FRANKLIN. The Franklin Plaza.

Mr. ADAMS. Tom?

Mr. JEFFERSON. The George Washington Motor Lodge. The Hilton was filled. What about you?

Mr. ADAMS. I am with Ben over at the Franklin Plaza. What about you, Jemmy?

Mr. MADISON. I haven't decided yet — you see, they have a Madison Avenue in New York City . . .

Dr. FRANKLIN. But no Madison Hotel in Philadelphia. In the early days we had no hotels or motels, just lodgings, taverns, and inns. I recall that in those early days when I went into an inn every individual had a question or two to propose to me and there was no possibility of procuring any refreshment. I learned to counter these encounters from the moment I went into any of these places by speaking first, in this manner: "Worthy people, I am Benjamin Franklin of Philadelphia; I have some relations locally, with whom I am going to visit; my stay will be short and I shall then return to Philadelphia and follow my business, as a prudent man ought to do. This is all I know of myself, and all I can possibly inform you of; I beg therefore that you will have pity upon me and my horse, and give us both some refreshment."

Mr. ADAMS. I recall those early days well. I remember a day in June, 1774, a few months before I came to Philadelphia. The Essex Supreme Court, sitting at Ipswich, Massachusetts had adjourned. I took a long walk through the Neck as they called it, a fine tract of land — corn, rye, grass interspersed in great perfection this fine season. I wandered alone and pondered. I mused, I moped, I ruminated. I was often in reveries. The objects before me were too grand and multifarious for my comprehension. We had not men fit for the times. We were deficient in genius, in education, in travel, in fortune — in everything. I felt unutterable anxiety. God, grant us Wisdom, and fortitude! Should the opposition be suppressed, should this Country submit, what, Infamy and Ruin! God forbid.

And then, it was August 29, 1774. A number of carriages and gentlemen came out of Philadelphia to meet us. We then rode into town, and dirty, dusty and fatigued as we were, we could not resist the importunity to go to the tavern, "the most genteel one in America." Here we had a fresh welcome to the city of Philadelphia, and after some time spent in conversation, a curtain was drawn, and in the other half of the chamber a supper appeared as elegant as ever was laid upon a table. The following morning, at ten, the delegates met at the City Tavern, and walked to the Carpenters' Hall, where they took a view of the room, and of the Chamber where there is an excellent library; there was also a long entry where the gentlemen may walk, and a convenient chamber opposite the library. Mr. Lynch arose, and said there was a gentleman present who had presided with great dignity over a very respectable society, greatly to the advantage of America, and he therefore proposed that the Honorable Peyton Randolph, Esquire, one of the delegates from Virginia, and the late Speaker of their House of Burgesses, should be appointed Chairman, and he doubted not it would be unanimous.

The question was put, and he was unanimously chosen.

Gen. WASHINGTON. And so the First Continental Congress started on the long and arduously travelled road of the Second Congress, the Federal Convention, and the Congress of the United States, leading one day to Constitution Avenue, Washington, D.C. Tomorrow we commence meetings as the Bicentennial Constitutional Commission, appointed by the One hundredth Congress of the United States for the purpose of considering and recommending to the Congress such amendments to the Constitution of the United States of America as may be necessary or advisable to render such Constitution more adequate to the exigencies of this Nation.

Dr. FRANKLIN. Gentlemen, a toast to General Washington! That you may long possess happiness, that you may be ever hailed The Deliverer of your Country, and enjoy, every Blessing Heaven can bestow, is the sincere and ardent prayer of all, and of one who professes himself to be, with every sentiment of regard and all possible attachment, your friend.

Mr. ADAMS. Do you remember how we used to feast upon "Philadelphia Beer and Porter," while putting down "ten thousand delicasies?" Then there was punch — the deadliest perhaps—the infamous "Fish House Punch." By the time you consumed one, you had forgotten the ingredients. But, punch in all its several variations was a hospitable offering. A little lemon, some sugar, wine, rum, and hot water could quench a fair thirst, or perhaps one sour, two sweet, four strong, and eight weak, mixed in a burnt china punchbowl. Ratafia, an almond-flavored liqueur, was a favorite of the ladies. And beer and cider were used by everyone, rich and poor, and little wonder.

Anything was preferable to the water. Philadelphia's water system was less than perfect. Several community pumps were available on every block, but a fire in the neighborhood could exhaust them. Some households had private wells in the yard, all located perilously near the "necessary." Moreover, the city was bounded by two rivers and had a fairly high water table. A few days' rain would create a sodden swamp in every low spot in town. On the whole, there was probably good reason for the popularity of beer and cider.

Mr. JEFFERSON. Our physical and eating habits in the 1780s were much different from that of today.

Dr. FRANKLIN. Eat few suppers, and you'll need few medicines.

Mr. JEFFERSON. Aye, your Poor Richard spoke the truth of that. I myself lived so much like other people, that I might refer to ordinary life as the history of my own. Like my friend, the Doctor, I lived temperately, eating little animal food, and that not as an aliment so much as a condiment for the vegetables, which constituted my principal diet. I drank three glasses of wine, and added a glass and a half when with a friend but halved its effects by drinking the weak wines only. The ardent wines I could not drink, nor did I use ardent spirits in any form. Malt liquors and cider were my table drinks, and my breakfast, like that also of my friend, was of tea and coffee. I have been blest with organs of digestion which accept and concoct, without every murmuring whatever the palate chooses to consign to them, and I have not yet lost a tooth by age. I am not so regular in my sleep, devoting to it from five to eight hours, according as my company or the book I am reading interests me; and I never go to bed without an hour or half hour's previous reading of something moral, whereon to ruminate in the intervals of sleep. But whether I retire to bed early or late, I rise with the sun. I use spectacles at night, but not necessarily in the day, unless in reading small print. I have the habit of bathing my feet in cold water every morning for sixty years past. A fever of more than twenty-four hours I have not had above two or three times in my life. A periodical headache has affected me occasionally, which seems now to have left me; and, except on a late occasion of indisposition, I enjoy good health. . . .

Mr. MADISON. Your mention of strong spirits reminds me that the Count de Moustier, Minister Plenipotentiary of France, once asked me whether brandy could supplant rum in the states, and how much French wine was consumed in Virginia. I told him that it would be very difficult for brandy entirely to supplant run. The brandies, doubtless from France, with very trifling exceptions, entered on the Custom House books between September 1, 1786, and July 20, 1787, amounted to 10,630 gallons. The rum entering within that period amounted to 499,083 gallons; the gin to 9,102 half gallons; and the cordials and other spirits to 4,169 half gallons.

The wines entered within the above periods amounted to 109,948 gallons, on which quantity about 40,000 gallons were French. . . .

Dr. FRANKLIN. I'll drink to that! A typical studious Madisonian response! John, what did you order?

Mr. ADAMS. Broiled Chesapeake Bay Oysters, and for the main course, Salmagundy.

Mr. JEFFERSON. Baked Clams, and my main fare is tile fish stuffed with hazel nuts and baked and served with a creamy sauce. For dessert, it will be carrot cake.

Dr. FRANKLIN. In our time, in Philadelphia, in my home, our table was plain and simple. For instance, my breakfast was for a long time bread and milk, no tea, and I ate it out of a two-penny earthen Porringer with a pewter spoon. But mark how luxury will enter families and make Progress, in spite of principle. Being called one morning to breakfast, I found it in a china bowl with a spoon of silver. They had been bought for me without my knowledge by my wife and had cost the enormous sum of three and twenty shillings, for which she had no other excuse or apology to make, but that she thought her husband deserv'd a silver spoon and china bowl as well as any of his neighbors.

Mr. MADISON. Yes, in those times, at the dining table, as in matters of dress, colonists followed the British lead. The main meal of the day was a dinner, served at midday, followed by a lighter supper about seven o'clock in the evening. In wealthier homes, the dinner hour was gradually pushed back; by the beginning of the nineteenth century, today's luncheon and dinner hours generally prevailed.

Where money was scarce, the staples were bread, grain porridge or gruel, and salt pork or fish, supplemented by whatever fruits and vegetables were cheap and easy to grow. On the other hand, when the financial situation was comfortable, no Philadelphian would hesitate to treat his family and guests to as much culinary elegance and volume as he could provide. Breakfasts were hearty; eggs and coffee were served with a full complement of meats, including beef, ham, stewed kidneys, or even salt fish. Small portions of everything that pleased were the rule. One could expect two or three courses at dinner, with a dessert of fruit and cheese. Wine was almost always served throughout the meal, causing numerous interruptions for toasts or "drinking of healths." A Frenchman visiting in the 1780s grumbled that the toasting made dinners "extremely long."

Dr. FRANKLIN. I remember well that the moment the men announced they preferred Bacchus to Venus the women departed.

Mr. ADAMS. The system of toast in vogue in our time was rather arduous. For example, the Pennsylvania Packet reported for July 4, 1778, Saturday the fourth of July, the glorious Anniversary of the Independence of America, was celebrated by the Honorable Congress with a grand festival at the City Tavern in this metropolis. The principal civil and military officers and strangers in town were present at it by invitation. After dinner the following toasts were given by the Honorable President of Congress:

1. The United States of America
2. The Protector of the Rights of Mankind
3. The Friendly European Powers
4. The happy era of the Independence of America
5. The Commander in Chief of the American Forces
6. The American Arms by land and sea
7. The Glorious 19th of April, 1775
8. The Glorious 20th of December, 1776
9. The Glorious 16th of October, 1777
10. The 28th of June, twice Glorious 1776-1778
11. May the Arts and Sciences flourish in America
12. May the People continue free forever
13. May the Union of the American States be perpetual.

I remember that I approved the patriotic toasts, but disliked the tiresome exchange of "individual healths," where they called upon each individual in turn to drink his health. It was enough to make the actor of this ridiculous comedy die of thirst while trying to remember the names of all around a table of twenty-five or thirty persons. It was also enough to make the unfortunate whom he addressed die of impatience because he could not give proper attention to what he was eating and what they were saying to him, being incessantly called at from right to left by cruelly charitable men anxious that he should notice the compliment he was receiving.

Gen. WASHINGTON. On that very subject of compliments, I must make an admittance concerning a matter of significance to me which has bothered me for some time now. I realize that with my "Cherry tree" background, I am known as "Honest George" . . .

Dr. FRANKLIN. Begging your pardon, General, but you are known as the man who could not tell a lie. Perhaps you are thinking of Abraham Lincoln. He was known as "Honest Abe."

Gen. WASHINGTON. So be it. Anyway, in 1786, I received a letter from Henry Lee of Virginia, then a delegate in the Continental Congress, to use my "unbounded influence" in bringing back peace and reconciliation among the seditious in Massachusetts. I responded that "You talk, my good sir, of employing influence to appease the present tumults in Massachusetts. I know not where that influence is to be found, or, if attainable, that it would be a proper remedy for the disorders. Influence is no government."

I violated my principle that "Influence is no government" when I wrote to George Mason on November 4, 1787. Despite the fact that he had declined to sign the Constitution, I asked him to use his influence in getting certain legislation through the Virginia General Assembly, at which he was a delegate: "In consequence of a resolution which passed at the last meeting of the Potomk Company, and in behalf of the Directors, I transmit the enclosed petition to you, for the consideration of your Honorable House. The Petition is short. We therefore rely on you, if the sentiment shall meet your approbation, for argument in support of it . . . With very great esteem and regard I am - your most obedient servant. George Washington."

The petition sought help from the Virginia legislature through a specific enactment that would compel shareholders in the Potomack Navigation Company to pay their levies promptly. Predictably my prestige brought a prompt response from the lawmakers, who, on December 1, 1787, passed "An act giving a more speedy remedy against delinquent subscribers to the Potowmack and James River companies."

Dr. FRANKLIN. How do you spell "Potomac"?

Mr. MADISON. General, in the course of our lives we all encountered situations where on later reflection our actions may have been otherwise. I recall when I was in the House of Representatives—it was January, 1794—we were considering a memorial from the Relief Committee of Baltimore for the Relief of St. Domingo Refugees. I remarked before the House that "the government of the United States is a definite government, confined to specified objects. It is not like the state governments, whose powers are more general. Charity is no part of the legislative duty of the government. . . . It would puzzle any gentleman to lay his finger on any part of the Constitution which would authorize the government to interpose in the relief of the St. Domingo Sufferers. . . ." The motion to grant relief to the St. Domingo sufferers lost.

Yet, when I became president of the United States, the House of Representatives in May 1812, passed "An Act for the relief of the citizens of Venezuela" authorizing me to expend $50,000 to purchase provisions for that object. I did not object, though I was no angel.

If men were angels, no government would be necessary. If angels were to govern man, neither external nor internal controls in government would be necessary.

Mr. ADAMS. Society was not at that time what it is at present. We had not yet learned to ape the manners of the Aristocracy of other countries, or to aim at their expensive and showy pleasures. Everything was then in the plain Republican style. A few private balls were given in the course of the season; dinner parties were sociable, their fare was simple, but the wines excellent, and they flowed in abundance.

Evening visits were in fashion and most of the houses at that time were open to visitors in the evening. The lady sat at her tea-table; the tea and cakes were handed round, and sometimes fruit and a glass of wine. When the company was small they all sat round the table. After tea, music began, but not such music as you now hear at our evening parties; it was of a much more simple character. Every gentleman and lady who could sing was called on in turn for a song, and it was immediately performed without instrumental accompaniment. The gentlemen sang hunting songs and the ladies Scotch ballads and some popular English airs.

As for myself, I had no pleasure or amusements which had any charms for me. Balls, assemblies, concerts, cards, horses, dogs, never engaged any part of my attention or concern. Nor was I ever happy in large and promiscuous companies. Business alone, with the intimate unreserved conversation of a few friends, books, and familiar correspondences, engaged all my time, and I had no pleasure, no ease in any other way. In Philadelphia I had no opportunity to meddle with books, only in the way of business. The conversation I had here was all in the ceremonious, reserved, impenetrable way. Thus, I sketch a character for myself as a morose philosopher and a surly politician.

Dr. FRANKLIN. As long as John is talking about custom, General, is there any dress code to be adhered to during the course of our sessions?

Gen. WASHINGTON. I defer to Mr. Madison on that question.

Mr. MADISON. I would personally prefer the genteel dress of the day, something stylish but not pretentious. Perhaps the members might have their hair combed out, powdered and tied in a long queue; it would be fitting, for example, that they wear a plaited white stock; a shirt ruffled at the bosom and over the hands, and fastened at the wrist with gold sleeve buttons; a peach bloom coat and white buttons, lined with white silk, and standing off at the skirts with buckram; a figured silk vest divided at the bottom, so that the pockets extend on the thighs; black silk small breeches with large gold or silver knee buckles; white cotton or silk stockings; large shoes with short quarters and buckles to match; a full bottomed wig; a red roquelaure, and that they carry a gold headed cane.

Dr. FRANKLIN. General, such garb is garbage! I refuse to attend a session in that ridiculous, decorous dress!

Mr. ADAMS. Ben, as always, you will wear what you please. Tom, what about the currency? Do you think we ought to make recommendations on this subject?

Mr. JEFFERSON. Did you know that in the 1780s I had hopes that we would preserve the pound as a money unit and its subdivisions into 20ths, 240ths, and 960ths? Certain innovators had been wishing to banish all this cunning learning, to adopt the dollar for our unit, to divide that into 120ths, 100ths, etc. and to have a gold coin of the value of 10 dollars, a silver coin of the value of a dollar, another of the value of 1/10 of a dollar or the Spanish Bit, and a copper one equal to 1/100th of a dollar, and of course very near the value of a New York penny. Intermediate silver coins were also proposed for convenience, to wit, the half dollar or five tenths, the Pistereen .2 and the half bit .05. Thus, in a sum of money expressed in these figures, 34.72, every figure expresses the number of pieces of the several coins which will pay off the sum, to wit, 3 golden pieces, 4 units 7 bits and 2 coppers. This was surely an age of innovation and America the focus of it!

Dr. FRANKLIN. The currency-makers have done right by us, though. Look, General, the one-dollar bill has your portrait on it.

Gen. WASHINGTON. Really? Pass the buck, I want to see it.

Dr. FRANKLIN. And Tom, the two-dollar bill has your portrait on it . . . but, I understand it is not used much.

Then there's the one-hundred-dollar bill circulating with my own countenance on it. On the back side is Independence Hall, as they came to call it. My Poor Richard once said, "The use of money is all the advantage there is in having money. For six pounds a year you may have use of one hundred pounds, if you are a man of known prudence and honesty."

And Jemmy, they used your visage on a five-thousand-dollar note, but that bill has not been printed in years. Be content, though. "Who is rich? He that rejoices in his portion."

But, John, it doesn't appear that you have a portion of the action. To my knowledge, in the last two centuries I do not think the government minted a lead cent for you. But, then, again, "He that hath a Trade, hath an Estate," and certainly that you hath. Which reminds me of a tradesman, a certain Jacob Hiltzheimer, keeper of the Continental stables, who in 1781, presented a complaint to the Continental Congress President of the shortage of feed for horses of members of Congress: "I take the liberty to inform your Excellency that the horses in my care belonging to members of the Hon'ble the Continental Congress have been without grain some time and now without hay too. Sometime ago, I bought hay on credit to the amount of about twenty thousand dollars with a promise to pay in a short time but could not comply for want of money wherefore it is out of my power to purchase any more without paying for it at the time."

Mr. ADAMS. Let me match your story with this one. In September 1774, I was dining one evening at the home of the Judge Thomas Willing, who was then an associate of the Supreme Court of Pennsylvania. We had a most splendid feast—turtle and all the trimmings. Judge Willing had asked a lawyer why the lawyers were so increased. The lawyer responded,

>You ask me why Lawyers so much are increased
>The most of the Country already are fleec'd
>The reason I'm sure is most strikingly plain
>Tho sheep are of't sheered yet the wool grows again
>And tho you may think e'er so odd of the matter
>The oft'ner fleeced, the wool grows the better.

Mr. JEFFERSON. Incidentally, I think that at that time there were about one hundred and twenty-five lawyers in America out of a total population of about three million.

Gen. WASHINGTON. Gentlemen, if I may introduce a more serious tone to our festivities, tomorrow we meet on an auspicious occasion. We have undertaken these assigned tasks and undergone these experiences before. I look back at our efforts in writing the Constitution of the United States, which we are today called upon to evaluate in the test of elapsed time, and, I can only say, as I did previously that "Although there were some things in the Constitution recommended by the Federal Convention to the determination of the People, which did not fully accord with my wishes; yet, having taken every circumstance seriously into consideration, I was convinced it approached nearer to perfection than any government hitherto instituted among men. I was fully convinced, that nothing but a genuine spirit of amity and accommodation could have induced the members to make those mutual concessions and to sacrifice, at the shrine of enlightened liberty, those local prejudices, which seemed to impose an insurmountable barrier, to prevent them from harmonizing in any system whatsoever."

Dr. FRANKLIN. Yet, it is well to remember that all the members of the Federal Convention did not put up their horses in the same stable.

Gen. WASHINGTON. True. It appears to me little short of a miracle that the delegates from so many different states, which states you know were also different from each other, in their manners, circumstances, and prejudices, should have united in forming a system of national government, so little liable to well-founded objections.

Mr. MADISON. And today, the palladium of constitutional liberty rests with the people. The people, who are the authors of this blessing, must also be its guardians. Their eyes must be ever ready to mark, their voice to pronounce, and their arms to repel or repair aggressions on the authority of their constitutions, the most sacred part of their property.

Mr. JEFFERSON. You will probably hear me say many times before our Commission that some men look at constitutions with sanctimonious reverence and deem them like the ark of the covenant, too sacred to be touched. They ascribe to the men of the preceding age a wisdom more than human, and suppose what they did to be beyond amendment. I knew that age well; I belonged to it and labored with it. I am certainly not an advocate for frequent and untried changes in laws and constitutions. I think moderate imperfections had better be borne with because, when once known, we accommodate ourselves to them and find practical means of correcting their ill effects. But I know also, that laws and institutions must go hand-in-hand with the progress of the human mind. As that becomes more developed, more enlightened, as new discoveries are made, new truths disclosed and manners and opinions change with the change of circumstances, institutions must advance also, and keep pace with the times.

Dr. FRANKLIN. The Constitution may be likened to a pump. If it runs dry—and fails to sustain liberty and the pursuit of happiness—sensible people will give a bucket or two to prime it, in the form of amendments, that they may afterwards get from it all they have occasion for.

Mr. ADAMS. I often wondered who would write the history of our Union. Who could write it? Now I wonder, who will write the history of our re-union?

Mr. MADISON. I am not so much concerned with that as I am with how we will come to be known. Then, we were called founders. Today . . .

Dr. FRANKLIN. We probably will be known as The Spirits of '76.

Gen. WASHINGTON. Gentlemen, the hour is late . . .

Dr. FRANKLIN. May I propose a toast? (Raises glass.)

May the Great Disposer of all human events animate and guide our councils, and enable us to determine, that we may not only re-establish our own temporal peace and happiness, but those of our posterity.

Mr. ADAMS. Good night all. Early to bed and early to rise . . .

Dr. FRANKLIN. That's my line, John.

Mr. MADISON. Gentlemen, how shall we split the bill?

Gen. WASHINGTON. Get Alexander Hamilton to pay it. He's always had a talent for handling money. He's seated right over there. Good night, all. Tomorrow dawns early.

OPENING SESSION

HEARINGS

before the

BICENTENNIAL CONSTITUTIONAL COMMISSION

of the

ONE HUNDREDTH CONGRESS

---------- * ----------

A REVIEW OF THE CONSTITUTION OF THE UNITED STATES OF AMERICA FOR THE PURPOSE OF RECOMMENDING TO THE CONGRESS OF THE UNITED STATES SUCH AMENDMENTS AS MAY BE NECESSARY OR ADVISABLE TO RENDER SUCH CONSTITUTION MORE ADEQUATE TO THE NEEDS OF THIS NATION.

---------- * ----------

Held in the Assembly Room of the Old Pennsylvania State House (Independence Hall) in Philadelphia, Pennsylvania

May 14 to September 17, 1987

THURSDAY, MAY 14, 1987

The Commission met at 10 a.m. pursuant to notice, in the Assembly Room of the Old Pennsylvania State House in Philadelphia, Pennsylvania, now called Independence Hall, Gen. George Washington serving as Chairman and presiding.
      Present: Gen. George Washington, Mr. John Adams, Dr. Benjamin Franklin, Mr. Thomas Jefferson and Mr. James Madison.

OPENING STATEMENT

      Gen. WASHINGTON (Chairman). The Bicentennial Constitutional Commission today begins hearings to determine whether the Constitution of the United States should be amended to render it more adequate to the needs of our nation.

      Within these hallowed walls the Declaration of Independence and the Constitution of the United States were signed.

      Here, the shot heard round the world was responded to, for in this room the Revolutionary War was planned and from this room directed.

      Here, I was appointed General to command all the Continental forces for the defense of American Liberty.

      Here, the departments of government were devised, developed and tested.

      Here resided the powers delegated to the United States, in Congress assembled.

      Here, in this room, was created the United States of America.

      Two hundred years ago today, Mr. James Madison and I sat down in this Assembly Room to begin the journey from which the Constitution of the United States emerged four months and three days later. Dr. Benjamin Franklin joined us and took his seat on May 28, 1787, and served with us in the Federal Convention until the Constitution was signed on September 17, 1787. During our deliberations in 1787, Mr. John Adams was in London serving as our first Minister to England, and Mr. Thomas Jefferson was in Paris serving as Minister to the king of France.

On a personal note, among the vicissitudes incident to life, no event could have filled me with greater anxieties than that of notification of the creation of this Commission. On the one hand, I was summoned by my country, whose voice I can never hear but with veneration and love, on the other hand, the magnitude and difficulty of the trust to which the voice of my country called me could not but overwhelm with despondence, one who, inheriting inferior endowments from nature and unpracticed in the duties of civil administration, ought to be peculiarly conscious of his own deficiencies. All I dare hope is that if, in executing this task, I have been too much swayed by a grateful remembrance of former instances, my error will be palliated by the motives which misled me and its consequences be judged by my country, with some share of the partiality in which they originated.

Such being the impressions under which I have, in obedience to the public summons, repaired to the present station, it would be peculiarly improper to omit in this first official act, my fervent supplications to that Almighty Being who rules over the universe—who presides in the councils of nations—and whose providential aids can supply every human defect, that his benediction may consecrate to the liberties and happiness of the people of the United States. In tendering this homage to the great author of every public and private good, I assure myself that it expresses your sentiments not less than my own, nor those of my fellow citizens. No people can be bound to acknowledge and adore the invisible hand, which conducts the affairs of men, more than the people of the United States.

I dwell on our prospects with every satisfaction which an ardent love for my country can inspire. The preservation of the sacred fire of liberty and the destiny of the republican model of government are justly considered as deeply staked on the experiment entrusted to the hands of the American people.

With respect to the task mandated to this Commission, the Fifth Article of the Constitution reads in part as follows:

The Congress whenever two-thirds of both Houses shall deem it necessary, shall call a Convention for proposing Amendments, which, in either Case, shall be valid to all Intents and Purposes, as part of this Constitution, when ratified by the Legislatures of three-fourths of the several States, or by Conventions in three-fourths thereof, as the one or the other Mode of Ratification may be proposed by the Congress. . . .

It will remain with the judgment of the people to decide, how far an exercise of the occasional power delegated by the Fifth Article of the Constitution is rendered expedient at the present juncture by virtue of any recommendations this Commission may see fit to make. While they should carefully avoid every alteration which might endanger the benefits of a united and effective government or which ought to await the further future lessons or experience, a reverence for the characteristic right of free men and a regard for the public harmony, will sufficiently influence their deliberations on the question how far the constitution can be more impregnably fortified.

To the preceding observations I have one to add, which will be as brief as possible. When I was first honored with a call into the service of my country, then on the eve of an arduous struggle for its liberties, the light in which I contemplated my duty required that I should renounce every pecuniary compensation. From this resolution I have in no instance departed. And being still under the impressions which produced it, I must decline, as inapplicable to myself, any share in personal emoluments, and must accordingly pray that the pecuniary estimates for the station in which I am placed, may, during my continuance in it, be limited to such actual expenditures as the public good may be thought to require.

Dr. FRANKLIN. I believe we can all concur in the statements of Gen. Washington and I would like to add a few thoughts of my own.

There is nothing in which mankind reproach themselves more than in their diversity of opinions. Every man sets himself above another in his own opinion and there are not two men in the world whose sentiments are alike in every thing; like lawyers, who with equal force of argument, can plead either for the plaintiff or defendant.

And so it came to pass in the Federal Convention in 1878.

I confess that there were several parts of the Constitution which I did not then approve, and I was not sure I would ever approve them. For having lived long, I had experienced many instances of being obliged by better information, or fuller consideration, to change opinions even on important subjects, which I once thought right, but found to be otherwise. It was therefore that, the older I grew, the more apt I was to doubt my own judgment, and to pay more respect to the judgment of others.

Though many private persons think highly of their own infallibility, few express it so naturally as a certain French lady, who, in a dispute with her sister, said, "I don't know how it happens, sister, but I meet with nobody but myself, that is always in the right."

In these sentiments, I agreed to the Constitution, with all its faults, if they were such; because I thought a general government necessary for us.

When you assemble a number of men to have the advantage of their joint wisdom, you inevitably assemble with those men all their prejudices, their passions, their errors of opinion, their local interests and their selfish views. From such an assembly can a perfect production be expected? It therefore astonishes me to find this system approaching so near to perfection. Thus I consented to the Constitution because I expected no better, and because I was not sure that it was not the best.

On the subject of opinion, I take leave to conclude with an old Fable, which some have heard before, and some have not.

A certain well-meaning man and his son were traveling towards a market town, with an ass which they had to sell. The road was bad; and the old man therefore rode, but the son went afoot. The first passenger they met asked the father if he was not ashamed to ride by himself and suffer the poor lad to wade along through the mire; this induced him to take up his son behind him. He had not travelled far, when he met others, who said they were two unmerciful lubbers to get both on the back of that poor ass, in such a deep road. Upon this the old man got off and let his son ride alone. The next they met called the lad a graceless, rascally young jackanapes, to ride that manner through the dirt, while his aged father trudged along on foot, and they said the old man was a fool, for suffering it. He then bid his son come down, and walk with him; and they travelled on leading the ass by the halter till they met another company, who called them a couple of blockheads, for going both on foot in such a dirty way, when they had an empty ass with them, which they might ride upon. The old man could bear it no longer. "My son," said he, "it grieves me much that we cannot please all these people: Let us throw the ass over the next bridge and be no further troubled with him."

Had the old man been seen acting this last resolution, he would probably have been called a fool for troubling himself about the different opinions of all who were pleased to find fault with him. I consider the variety of humors among men, and despair of pleasing everybody. In the same sense, we are not going to destroy all vestige of good in our Constitution—as the old man did in his own way—on account of differences of opinion of men on the same subject.

Much of the strength and efficiency of any government, in procuring and securing happiness to the people, depends on opinion—on the general opinion of the goodness of the government as well as of the wisdom and integrity of its governors.

It is within this framework, that we meet again in this great Assembly Room to obtain opinion as to whether our government is well administered and whether the Constitution continues to meet the needs of the nation.

Since presumption ruins many, I cannot help expressing a wish that every member of this Commission, and all persons testifying before it, may, along with me, doubt a little of his own infallibility.

Gen. WASHINGTON. Thank you, Dr. Franklin. .ving thus imparted to the members of the Commission my sentiments as they have been awakened by the occasion which brings us together, and having heard the sentiments of Dr. Franklin, this Commission will proceed to the next order of business. I propose that we proceed according to the following schedule:

    The selection of a secretary.

    The drawing up of rules to be observed as the standing orders of the Commission.

    The drafting of an initial agenda for the conduct of meetings.

    Let us proceed. Mr. Madison.

    Mr. MADISON. I propose that this Commission have two secretaries: namely, Mr. Charles Thomson and Maj. William Jackson. Mr. Thomson would serve as secretary keeping minutes of our proceedings, as well as our point of reference with respect to matters arising under the Journals of the Continental Congress, of which he was secretary. Major Jackson would serve as assistant secretary and be used as our point of reference with respect to matters arising in the Federal Convention of 1787, of which he was secretary. I propose that he be reelected today to serve our Commission in the capacity stated.

    Gen. WASHINGTON. Gentlemen, are we agreed on Maj. Jackson's role? (Members nod assent.) Proceed, Mr. Madison.

    Mr. MADISON. Thank you, General. As for Mr. Thomson, for the benefit of the attending public and the record let me give a short sketch of his considerable public service.

    For fifteen years, Mr. Thomson was secretary to the government that joined the thirteen former British colonies together into the United States. He was the only person associated with the First Continental Congress that convened in 1774, the Continental Congress that gave way to the government under President George Washington in 1789, and all the Congresses in between. Mr. Thomson's services bridged the period that included the Declaration of Independence, the successful war with Great Britain, the depression of the 1780s and the framing of the federal Constitution. As secretary to the United States in Congress Assembled from 1774 until 1789, Charles Thomson was indeed secretary to a nation in the making.

As secretary to Congress, Mr. Thomson recorded its minutes and edited its journals; he handled much of its correspondence and kept his office as a repository of records, books, laws of the various states, newspapers, paper, ink, quills, and all the other materials necessary for the conduct of a legislative body. As the most effective executive officer the Congress possessed, Mr. Thomson corresponded with the states to urge their compliance with the laws and requisitions from Congress. At times he even had to plead for the states to send representatives to Congress in order that a quorum might be present to transact business. He issued passports, letters of marque and reprisal, news releases, and public proclamations. He presided over Congress for brief periods, served as secretary of foreign affairs in addition to performing the duties of his own office, and maintained an extensive correspondence with Washington, Jefferson, Franklin, Jay and John Adams. He served the Revolution from its inception to its conclusion. It is significant to recall that only John Hancock and Charles Thomson signed the Declaration of Independence on July 4, 1776. Charles Thomson attested as secretary.

But his record does not stop here. After his retirement from public life in 1789, Mr. Thomson devoted himself almost exclusively to caring for his estate near Philadelphia, and to the translation of the Bible from the Greek. To obtain the most accurate available version of the Old Testament, Mr. Thomson made his translation from a copy of the Septuagint published at Cambridge, England, in 1665, by John Field. This publication was descended from the Sixtine edition based on Codex Vaticanus, the earliest known manuscript, which as the name implies, is today in the Vatican Library in Rome.

It is fitting perhaps that we look in at the first and last moments of the Continental Congress, a Congress which for the most part operated under the Articles of Confederation, which immediately preceded the present Constitution of the United States.

For this purpose I have taken the liberty of asking Mr. Thomson to give in his own words a narrative of his officiating as Secretary of the first Congress. Mr. Thomson.

Mr. Charles THOMSON. Thank you, Mr. Madison. I was married on Thursday, September 1, 1774. On the next Monday, I can to town to pay my respects to my wife's aunt and the family. Just as I alighted on Chestnut Street the doorkeepers of Congress, then first meeting, accosted me with a message from them requesting my presence. Surprised at this and not being able to divine why I was wanted, I bade my servant put up my horses, and followed the messenger to Carpenter's Hall and I entered Congress. Here was, indeed, an august assembly. Deep thought and solemn anxiety were observable on their countenances. I walked up the aisle, and standing opposite the president, I bowed, and told him I awaited his pleasure. He replied, "Congress desires a favour of you, Sir, to take their minutes." I bowed in acquiescence, and took my seat at the desk. After a short silence, Patrick Henry rose to speak. I did not then know him; he was dressed in a suit of parson's grey, and from his appearance I took him for a Presbyterian clergyman, used to haranguing the people. He observed, "We are here met on an occasion of great difficulty and distress. . . ." One would propose one thing and another a different one, whilst perhaps a third would think of something better suited to his unhappy circumstances, which he would embrace, and think no more of the rejected schemes with which he would have nothing to do. I thought that this was very good instruction to me, with respect to the taking of the minutes: What Congress adopted, I commited to writing; with what they rejected, I had nothing further to do, and even this method led to some squabbles with the members, who were desirous of having their speeches and resolutions, however put to rest by the majority, still preserved upon the minutes.

I well remember the day of the Declaration of Independence; the boldness of the measure frighted and appalled even its well wishers. The citizens mostly kept aloof—the crowd that assembled at the state house was not great, and those among them who joined the acclamation were not of the highest order, or the most sober and reflecting. But its decisive character soon firmly united its supporters, convinced that in case Britain should prove victorious, they had nothing to hope from her clemency. It was indeed a time of deep anxiety and momentous doubt.

Mr. MADISON. Thank you, Mr. Thomson. That was the beginning of the Continental Congress and Mr. Thomson's services. And the end? Well, the end was perhaps best discussed by Mr. Edmund Cody Burnett, who wrote an eight-volume treatise on the Continental Congress. Mr. Burnett.

Mr. BURNETT. In the early days of January 1789, the members who had been hanging around and drifting in and out conceived the delusive hope that the Continental Congress was about to assemble, choose itself a president, and proceed to business. Some of them indeed had urgent business that they were anxious to lay before the assembled Congress, business that in some cases was as chestnuts in the fire, in others as irons that they would fain heat in the Congressional furnace and have hammered into the desired shape of the Congressional anvil. And so, as one member after another trudged into town in the early days of the new year, hopes began to take the place of anxieties.

The days slid by, with no "Congress assembled," while a goodly number of members wandered about the city or journeyed back to their homes, apparently too indifferent, most of them, even to report their presence to Secretary Thomson, who, it is safe to assume, sat in his office, pen in hand, the book of the chronicles of Congress open on his desk, eager to record them one and all as attending, happy if perchance he might be privileged to write "Congress assembled." But it was not to be. From the 19th of February to the 2nd of March not even one lone delegate thrust his head inside the door of the secretary's office. On the notable 2nd of March, however, two days before the time set for the new Congress to assemble, Mr. Thomson recorded, "Mr. Philip Pell from New York" attended. Peradventure, Mr. Thomson had buttonholed Mr. Pell on the street and enticed him into his office for this express purpose—but it sufficed. The faithful secretary had fought the good fight to preserve the visible head of the Union; he had perservered to the end; he had won the victory. The spark of life had been kept in the body of the dying Continental Congress until its heir and successor was crossing the threshold.

In an important sense it is not correct to assume that the old Congress was even now defunct. There remained Secretary Thomson himself as a connecting link between the old and the new; and there were other links besides. Most of the executive departments of the old Congress were passed over to the new government intact and continued to function for several months. The secretary himself, having served Congress faithfully throughout the whole of its life of fifteen years, fondly hoped that he would be given a suitable place in the new order. He soon discovered, however, that, along with much else of that old order, the place for which he was destined was the place called discard. It came about therefore that, on the 23rd of July, 1789, Charles Thomson transmitted to President Washington his resignation of the office of secretary of Congress; on the 24th the president accepted the resignation and on the 25th, in accordance with President Washington's direction, "the books, records and papers of the late Congress, the Great Seal of the Federal Union and the Seal of the Admiralty" were delivered over to Roger Alden, deputy secretary of Congress, who had been designated by President Washington as custodian for the time being. It was then and only then that the Continental Congress really came to an end. Mr. Thomson was more than Secretary. He was the heart of America.

Gen. WASHINGTON. Thank you, Mr. Burnett.

Mr. JEFFERSON. (Aside to Mr. Adams) I can recall when Thomson told me that his time and thoughts were so entirely engrossed with the duties and business of his office that he had no leisure to prosecute those philosophical researches he once was fond of. And from what he could see, Congress was disposed rather to increase than diminish his duties.

Mr. ADAMS. (Aside to Mr. Jefferson) Indeed. And, I recall Bishop William White once mentioned that during the war the Congress was on many occasions reduced to great pecuniary difficulties of which he had occasion to see very singular proofs. He said that adjoining the room in which Congress sat, which was later to become the Supreme Court Room, there was a small antechamber used by Thomson which was connected by a flight of steps outside with a room upstairs where Thomson's clerks sat and wrote habitually. One day in the winter he saw the clerks bringing their books and papers downstairs into Thomson's room and, on enquiring the cause of this removal, he found that the janitor of Congress refused to make a fire in the clerk's room for fear that Congress would not be able to pay him for it, and the clerks were therefore obliged to come into the secretary's office and write by his fire.

Mr. MADISON. Mr. Chairman, I move for the selection by this Commission of Mr. Charles Thomson as secretary and Maj. William Jackson as Assistant secretary of this Commission.

Dr. FRANKLIN. I second the motion.

Gen. WASHINGTON. Is it agreed? (Members murmur assent.) Any opposed? (No response.) It is so agreed.

The next order of business is the development of rules to be observed by the Commission. As you know, like the Senate and the House of Representatives, Committees and Commissions established by Congress can set their own rules.

Mr. JEFFERSON. I should know. I wrote the Manual of Parliamentary Practice for my own guidance when I was president of the Senate during the years of my vice-presidency from 1797 to 1801.

It is interesting to me that the manual I drafted is still printed today in the Rules of the House of Representatives. Why are the rules I wrote for the Senate used in the House? Well, in 1837, the House agreed that the provisions of the Manual should "govern the House in all cases to which they are applicable and in which they are not in conflict with the standing rules and orders of the House."

Dr. FRANKLIN. Do you want to tell us about how you came to draft the Declaration of Independence?

Mr. JEFFERSON. Not especially.

Mr. MADISON. Or shall we discuss the subject now as to why some of us opposed a vice-presidency?

Gen. WASHINGTON. Out of order.

Mr. JEFFERSON. I was a *working* vice-president.

Mr. MADISON. The same work could have been accomplished by a president of the Senate who was not a vice-president.

Gen. WASHINGTON. Out of order, gentlemen.

Mr. JEFFERSON. I do want to make one further comment on the subject of rules and the importance of adhering to rules. We felt rules were important in protecting the minority.

Mr. Onslow, the ablest among the Speakers of the House of Commons, in England, used to say it was a maxim he had often heard when he was a young man, "from old and experienced Members, that nothing tended more to throw power into the hands of administration, and those who acted with the majority of the House of Commons, than a neglect of, or departure from, the rules of proceeding; that these forms, as instituted by our ancestors, operated as a check and control on the actions of the majority, and that they were, in many instances, a shelter and protection to the minority, against the attempts of power." The maxim is certainly true, and is in good sense. It is always in the power of the majority, by their numbers, to stop any improper measures proposed on the part of their opponents. The only weapon by which the minority can defend themselves is by strict adherence to the forms and rules of proceeding.

And whether these forms be in all cases the most rational or not is really not of so great importance. It is much more material that there should be a rule to go by than what that rule is. It is very material that order, decency, and regularity be preserved in a dignified public body."

Gen. WASHINGTON. And so it is today. Let us proceed with our own rules. It is intended that our sessions be open to spectators to the extent possible. Since the history of America runs deep in the memory of the members of this Commission, I express the wish that each member feel free to explain, expand or comment on any matter under discussion, in such manner as he thinks will contribute to a better or clearer understanding or perspective of our sessions. Are there suggestions as to how this might best be accomplished?

Mr. JEFFERSON. (Aside to Mr. Adams) You know, I served with Gen. Washington in the Legislature of Virginia before the Revolution, and during it, with Dr. Franklin in Congress. I never heard either of them speak ten minutes at a time nor to any but the main point which was to decide the question. They laid their shoulders to the great points, knowing that the little ones would follow of themselves.

Gen. WASHINGTON. Mr. Madison.

Mr. MADISON. I propose to the Commission that with respect to matters before the Commission to be voted on by its members that we follow the same rules observed by the Federal Convention in 1787 to the extent applicable.

Mr. ADAMS. Since neither Mr. Jefferson nor I attended the Federal Convention, would it not be appropriate to restate the key rules for our consideration?

Mr. MADISON. Certainly. The key rules were as follows:

Every member, rising to speak, shall address the Chairman; and whilst he shall be speaking, none shall pass between them, or hold discourse with another, or read a book, pamphlet, or paper, printed or manuscript - and of two members, rising at the same time, the Chairman shall name him who shall be first heard.

A member may be called to order by any other member, as well as by the Chairman, and may be allowed to explain his conduct or expressions, supposed to be reprehensible—and all questions of order shall be decided by the Chairman without appeal or debate.

The foregoing rules to be observed as standing Orders of the Commission were adopted May 28, 1787.

On May 29, 1787, the following rule, among others, was added:

That a motion to reconsider a matter, which had been determined by a majority, may be made, with leave unanimously given, on the same day in which the vote passed, but otherwise, not without one day's previous notice; in which last case, if the Commission agree to the reconsideration, some future day shall be assigned for that purpose.

Mr. THOMSON. (To the Spectators) Interestingly, this last rule generated an incredible repetition of subject matter, perhaps at times detrimental to our national interests. A subject could never be considered concluded with this rule in effect.

Mr. MADISON. I move that the foregoing rules as proposed be adopted as standing Orders of the Commission.

Dr. FRANKLIN. I second the motion.

Gen. WASHINGTON. Any discussion?

Mr. ADAMS. We are not the fifty-five delegates who attended the Federal Convention and we do not require this form of regimentation. I am of the opinion that only a rule relating to quorums and voting is necessary and that all other matters of rules and orders be left to the Chairman to be decided according to equitable practice without appeal or debate. I would much prefer to see the Commission act on an informal basis, if possible, particularly in view of the caliber of person expected to testify before it.

Mr. THOMSON. After debate, the rules as agreed to by the Commission would thus read as follows:

The Commission, to do business, shall consist of not less than three members; and all questions shall be decided by the greater number of those in attendance; but a lesser number than three shall adjourn from day to day.

All other questions of rules or order shall be decided by the Chairman without appeal or debate.

Dr. FRANKLIN. So we wind up with two, instead of fourteen, rules. This reminds me of my own rules. I had made it a rule, whenever in my power, to avoid becoming the draftsman of papers to be reviewed by a public body. I took my lesson from an incident which I will relate to you. When I was a journeyman printer, one of my companions, an apprentice hatter, having served out his time, was about to open shop for himself. His first concern was to have a handsome signboard with a proper inscription. He composed it in these words: "John Thompson, hatter, makes and sells hats for ready money" with a figure of a hat subjoined. But he thought he would submit it to his friends for their amendments. The first he showed it to thought the word "hatter" tautologous, because it was followed by the words "makes hats" which showed he was a hatter. It was struck out. The next observed that the word "makes" might as well be omitted, because his customers would not care who made the hats. If good, they would buy, by whomsoever made. He struck it out. A third said he thought the words "for ready money" were useless, as it was not the custom of the place to sell on credit. Everyone who purchased expected to pay. They were parted with, and the inscription now stood: "John Thomson sells hats." "Sells hats?" says his next friend. "Why, nobody will expect you to give them away. What then is the use of that word?" It was stricken out, and "hats" followed it, as there was one painted on the board. So his inscription was reduced ultimately to "John Thomson" with the figure of a hat subjoined.

So be it with our rules.

Gen. WASHINGTON. The Commission is in agreement, then? (Members nod and murmur assent)

Thus we have completed the day's duties as set before us. This Commission will adjourn until 10 a.m. on Monday, May 25, 1987, at which time we will undertake to discuss the conditions and occurrences within these United States that have occasioned the necessity of our presence here.

We are adjourned.

MONDAY MAY 25, 1987

STATE OF THE UNION - I

The Commission met, pursuant to notice, at 10 a.m., in the Assembly Room of Independence Hall, Gen. George Washington presiding.

        Present: Gen. George Washington, Mr. John Adams, Dr. Benjamin Franklin, Mr. Thomas Jefferson and Mr. James Madison.

        Gen. WASHINGTON. The Commission will come to order.

        Gentlemen, as set before you at the close of our last meeting, I propose that it is not only fitting but essential that this Commission examine the state of this Union and the conditions that have served to generate our presence here and our duties. Which of the members would like to initiate this self-examination? Mr. Madison.

        Mr. MADISON. Mr. Robert Sherrill is a prize-winning reporter, author of an article entitled "The Government of the Living Dead," and is the author of several books on government. I have asked Mr. Sherrill to give us a panoramic sketch of our government in the 1980s. Mr. Sherrill.

        Mr. SHERRILL. Thank you Mr. Madison. I thank you for the opportunity to appear before the Commission, and I hope my remarks do not offend your concepts of posterity. I have to be blunt, however, and tell you that we are living under the biggest patchwork government the world has ever seen. More patches would just make matters worse. It's time simply to throw out most of the bungled apparatus and start over again. It's time to simplify. It's time to reduce the operation to a scale that the average American can understand and cope with.

Our government is so big that it boggles. And its rate of growth is even more boggling. For the first 140 years of our nation's life, federal spending never exceeded 3 percent of the gross national product. But all that ended with the fantastic pump-priming of the economy in the 1930s, so that by the mid-1950s total federal spending was running about 18 percent of the gross national product. Today it is 23 percent. In other words, one out of every four dollars spent in this country is spent by the federal government.

In the early 1930s, there was one government worker for every ten in industry. Today the ratio is one to four. In the first year of President Kennedy's administration, the federal government spent $81 billion. Two decades later, the government was budgeted to spend $613 billion—an increase of more than 700 percent.

How does one make sense out of $613 billion? What does a "billion" mean? In a rare moment of insight, one of our U.S. senators recently tried to put it in perspective by pointing out that "a billion minutes ago, St. Peter was ten years dead."

It would take 613,000 persons working 100 years at $10,000 a year and giving all their income to the government to pay for this one year's operation. Or let's spread it a little thinner: every American—every one of the 220 million men and women and children in this country—would have to chip in $2,800 to pay this budget. And that's for just one year, remember. They would have to come up with even more the following year.

The worst part, the truly incalculable part, is the amount of waste—improper fund disbursements, useless programs, double payments, uncollected bills, mismanagement, carelessness.

We spent at least $143 billion—more than one out of every four tax dollars—for a Defense Department that cannot keep eight helicopters in the air at the same time on a botched rescue mission and admits it could not launch a major offensive overseas with less than three weeks' notice.

The federal budget is full of brainwashing funds. It includes $30 million for Department of Energy propaganda to persuade us that there is an energy crisis. It wasted another $2.5 million on a failed campaign to convince us that we should love the metric system.

Two of our ex-presidents—Mr. Ford, who was never elected to the office, and Mr. Nixon, who left it in disgrace—currently cost us $800,000 a year. We paid $2,242 for plants for Mr. Ford's office and $1,200 a year for somebody to come by and water them. Mr. Nixon charged $45,461 for writing paper and envelopes.

We spend about $64 million a year on Department of Justice lawyers who haven't won a major antitrust lawsuit against oil companies in sixty years.

We pay about $350 million a year to an Immigration and Naturalization Service that had been unable to prevent 8 million illegal immigrants from sneaking into the United States.

Federal officials spend nearly $100 million a year of our money for special economic advice. And yet at no time within living memory has Congress or the president, acting on the advice of these experts, correctly predicted the inflation rate, the unemployment rate, or the nation's economic growth rate.

The 42,000-mile interstate highway system, which will cost us more than $100 billion before it is completed, is the world's biggest public works project. Yet our federal highway engineers have bungled the construction job so badly and our highway administrators have allowed the system to be so abused by overweight trucks that already some 28,000 miles are obsolete by modern road standards. The Federal Highway Administration admits that our total highway system is falling apart 50 percent faster than it is being built. All told, we spend more than $8 billion a year in federal funds on our roads of all kinds and on our bridges. We've been spending that kind of money on them for many years. Yet the FHA estimates that more than 100,000 bridges are obsolete or are actually in danger of falling down.

In the name of "national security," federal bureaucrats have spent $16 billion to stockpile stuff like opium (72,000 pounds), sapphires and rubies (16 million carats), and tons upon tons of tannin, mica, and shellac. The bureaucrats say that they hope to buy and stockpile 6.5 million pounds of feathers in the near future.

The list of failures and bad judgments could go on for hours. It could be repeated every year. There will be no end to it—unless we get rid of the people and governmental apparatus responsible for this mess. Let me give you some examples.

Over the years our generous politicians have given the railroads 94,300,000 acres of our land, a total area three times the size of New York State, an area nearly equal to California. A tenth of California, a tenth of Arizona, a sixth of Montana, a seventh of Nebraska, a fifth of Washington, a tenth of Wyoming and a fourth of North Dakota have been turned over to the railroads. Our land, gone forever.

And what did we get in return? We got rate gouging and exploitation. In the first quarter of 1980, the profits of Burlington Northern jumped nearly 80 percent—largely because of income from the sale of oil and coal from those lands that once belonged to us and were given to Burlington by politicians. Burlington Northern owns 11 billion tons of western coal—20 percent of the world's known reserves.

Gen. Washington, as you yourself may recall, when you were president there was only one federal bureaucrat per 31,000 Americans (including slaves). The ratio was maintained, more or less, until the Civil War which, as all wars do, threw everything out of balance. By the end of that affair, the bureaucracy was swollen to one federal worker per 5,555 citizens, and the inflation of government continued without interruption thereafter. At the turn of the century, the ratio had drifted to an ominous one bureaucrat per 2,534 citizens. In 1940, after seven years of the agency-crazy New Deal, the bureaucracy had started to gallop; the ratio was now one bureaucrat per 720 Americans. Then came World War II, the Korean War, the Vietnam War, and the Great Society—and today the ratio stands at an alarming one federal bureaucrat per 73 citizens.

That comes down to about 3 million bureaucrats, nearly one-third of whom—991,000—work for the Defense Department.

Dr. FRANKLIN. Just one comment. You mention 3 million bureaucrats. It is interesting to note that we have working for the government in the 1980s the same number of persons as we had total population in the 1780s! Please continue, Mr. Sherrill.

Mr. SHERRILL. Today the federal government owns 406,494 buildings (at last count), containing 2.6 billion square feet. That's enough square footage to make 300 World Trade Centers or 1,250 Empire State Buildings. The world's largest office building is the Pentagon, which alone is as big as three Empire State Buildings. Its corridors run for 18 miles—nearly the width of the English Channel.

On top of that we spend $1 billion to lease buildings. The General Services Administration, the federal landlord, admits that $2.6 million a year is wasted on rent for office space it isn't using.

Why do the bureaucrats think they need so much room? One reason might be the millions of forms they send citizens and businesses to fill out. When those forms come back in, they have to be filed away somewhere. Thus, each year the bureaucracy is inundated with 4.5 million cubic feet of new records that cost $8 billion to print, shuffle, sort, and file. There are 8,000 record systems scattered throughout the bureaucracy, and buried within them are data ranging from how many soldiers were hospitalized in World War I for trenchmouth to how many cows died of bloat in North Dakota in 1927 to how many navy reservists have been issued toothbrushes.

We will give $1.6 billion to a Postal Service that, with a great deal of luck, may move a letter one city block in three days. Its idea of efficiency is to require the public to memorize nine-number zip codes.

The federal government owns a half million vehicles—sedans, station wagons, buses, trucks. If you lined up the federal vehicles bumper to bumper, they would stretch from New York City to Jacksonville, Florida.

One of the most symptomatic examples I can give you involves a subsidy administered by the Department of Agriculture, the $3.2 million Beekeeper Indemnity Fund. It allows the government to buy just what this country needs—dead bees. Five beekeepers in Arizona collected $1 million from that fund to give their bees a proper funeral.

Amtrack, the allegedly "independent" passenger railroad service, was put together by the bureaucrats as a way to relieve the railroad industry of its responsibilities to the riding public. Far from being independent, Amtrak is subsidized with nearly a billion dollars every year. To put that in perspective, just bear in mind that when an Amtrak lobbyist climbs aboard an Amtrak train in New York to come to Washington to squeeze more subsidies from the government, he pays only 40 percent of the cost of his trip. The other 60 percent is subsidized—as it is for every Amtrak rider—by the American public.

At least two states should be eliminated from the Union: Alaska, where the federal government owns nearly 91 percent of the land, and Nevada, where it owns nearly 88 percent. There is no logic to their existence. Why shouldn't they revert to being federal territories? It is absurd to have the American people burdened with the four senators and two congressmen from two states that hardly exist. It is also absurd to let the 400,000 people of Alaska pocket $4 billion a year in oil royalties, a bonanza that recently allowed them to abolish their state income tax and pocket a couple of thousand bucks per adult; that oil belongs to all of us.

It might also be a good idea to consider wiping out Idaho (where the federal government owns 64 percent of the land) and Utah (65 percent).

Maybe it would be a good idea to have a rotating "national capital"—this year in Atlanta, next year in San Francisco, the following year in Detroit, and so forth. Make Congress a traveling three-month or, at most, six-month show, meeting in a different "capital" every year. And let the congressmen do their legislating where American Legion conventions and livestock shows and boxing matches are normally held, where the atmosphere is permanently permeated with the odors of sweat and sawdust and stale popcorn. It will encourage them to get their work done fast and get out of town. And it will help put a modest touch and a realistic grass-roots price tag on the legislation that emerges.

Before there was a presidency, there was a Congress. Before there was a Supreme Court, there was a Congress. Before there was a bureaucracy, there was a Congress. It was the first branch of government in existence. It was there to count the electoral votes for the first president and to help George Washington organize his administration.

And just as Congress created our original political sins, it can also bring about their end. If we can win Congress over to our way of thinking, the rest will be easy. Congress has the power to unmake everything it has made or any fraction thereof.

Gentlemen, thank you.

Mr. MADISON. Allow me to interject here that at one time we had a travelling Congress, sometimes not even by choice.

From 1774 to 1776, Congress was active in Philadelphia. When the British occupied Philadelphia in 1776, Congress moved to Baltimore. When the British left, Congress moved back to Philadelphia. On September 27, 1777, Congress met for one day in Lancaster, Pennsylvania, and from September 30, 1777 to June 27, 1778, it resided at York, Pennsylvania. It then removed to Philadelphia, residing there from 1778 to June 21, 1783, on which date a meeting of federal soldiers threatened to attack Congress, whereupon Congress moved to Princeton, New Jersey, then known as Prince Town. From November 1783 to December 1784, Congress was in Trenton, New Jersey and from January 11, 1785 to March 3, 1789, in New York City. Under the new Constitution, from March 4, 1789 to August 12, 1790, Congress met in New York City. From December 6, 1790 to May 14, 1800, Philadelphia was the meeting place. Since November 17, 1800, Washington D.C. has been the meeting place. So, between 1774 and 1800, Congress moved eleven times.

Dr. FRANKLIN. Mr. Sherrill, may I ask, your article—"The Government of the Living Dead" wasn't it—where did it appear?

Mr. SHERRILL. In the January 1981 issue of Penthouse Magazine.

Dr. FRANKLIN. I am not acquainted with that publication. I assume it keeps on top of affairs.

Mr. SHERRILL. No comment, please.

Dr. FRANKLIN. Your profusion of itemization brings to mind Ed McMahon of the Johnny Carson Show, who, if here would say—"That represents the most complete list of government operations. Everything you want to know about government affairs is on that list." And Johnny Carson would respond—"You are wrong, Mr. Misfact."

Well, I have a list of my own to show that times have not changed that much. Yes, we had our own share of boondoggles and mind-boggling situations.

"The Treasury of the United States is totally exhausted without the hope of its soon being replenished," wrote the Maryland Delegates in Congress on June 3, 1781.

"No Journals of Congress have been printed since December for want of money to pay the expense," wrote the Connecticut Delegates on June 12, 1781. One can liken that to not publishing the Congressional Record in the 1980s.

"We suggested to Congress the propriety of recommending to the States a general Thanksgiving but as there were but seven States on the Floor and one or two of them against it, the measure could not be adopted," wrote the Massachusetts Delegates on November 2, 1785.

Hugh Williamson wrote to James Iredell in 1783, "The framers of our Confederation, with reverence be it said, were not infallible. . . . We borrow money, and have not the means of paying sixpence. There is no measure, however wise or necessary, that may not be defeated by any single State, however small or wrong-headed. The cloud of public creditors, including the army, are gathering about us; the prospect thickens. Believe me, that I would rather take the field in the hardest military service I ever saw, than face the difficulties that await us in Congress within a few months. . . ."

Mr. MADISON. Dr. Franklin, Jacob Read wrote to me in 1785, "Congress is thin and I am sorry to say that the States seem averse to do any Act that has in prospect to assert the dignity of the federal Government. We debate, make and hear long and often Spirited Speeches, but when the Moment arrives for a Vote we Adjourn and thus the feeling of Individuals and the Welfare of the Union is trifled with. . . . We have in short nothing Pleasing in prospect and if in a short time the States do not enable Congress to act with some vigour and put the power of compulsion into the hand of the Union I am free to Confess I think it almost time to give over the farce of what I cannot consider as an efficient Government."

Dr. FRANKLIN. Thomas Rodney wrote in his diary in April 1781, "It is to be lamented that Congress is so deficient in the abilities of financing that no member is capable of offering a system that is worthy of the establishment of Congress, none whose ideas are at the same time both simple and systematical enough for this purpose." Perhaps we needed a man of a different stock—a David Stockman.

David Ramsay wrote to Dr. Benjamin Rush in February, 1786: "There is a languour in the States that forebodes ruin. The present Congress for want of more States has not power to coin a copper. In 1775 there was more patriotism in a village than there is now in the thirteen states."

Mr. ADAMS. Allow me to add to this list. John Hancock was president of Congress when he signed the Declaration of Independence on July 4, 1776. He was elected president of Congress again on November 23, 1785. On November 30, 1785, he wrote Mr. Thomson acknowledging that Congress had appointed him president: "I feel myself exceedingly honor'd by this Appointment and wish my abilities were more equal to the complete execution of the duties of that office. . . . As soon as I can arrange my affairs here, I will proceed to New York; I am not able to fix the precise time, but will undertake the journey as speedily as possible, and by the next post will write you more explicitly."

But President John Hancock, in his second term around, never showed up!

Dr. FRANKLIN. . . . and they named an insurance company after him?

I recall that in 1776, John Hancock, as president of Congress, wrote to William Palfrey: "It is my opinion you had better hire a clerk immediately and run the risk of Congress making an allowance for him."

Mr. MADISON. I once noted that the most precarious of all occupations which give bread to the industrious are those depending on mere fashion, which generally changes so suddenly, and often so considerably, as to throw whole bodies of people out of employment.

As an illustration I pointed to the change in fashion from buckles and buttons to strings and straps. The effect? Twenty thousand persons in the buckle trade in England became unemployed, in consequence of the change in fashion to shoestrings and slippers. What lesson did we learn? Twenty thousand persons were to get or go without their bread, as a wanton youth may fancy to wear his shoes with or without straps, or to fasten his straps with strings or with buckles.

The condition of those who receive employment and bread from the precarious source of fashion and superfluity, is a lesson to nations as well as to individuals. In proportion as a nation depends on external commerce, it is dependent on the consumption and caprice of other nations. Dependence in the case of nations is greater than among individuals of the same nation; for besides the mutability of fashion, which is the same in both, the mutability of policy is a source of danger.

So we had our economic problems and you have yours. You may have imagined differently. It is just not so.

Dr. FRANKLIN. Mr. Sherrill referred to the massive number of cars used by the government. Well, we had our transportation excesses, too. In 1777, the Executive Committee of Congress wrote to President John Hancock: "We mentioned sometime ago the waste and destruction that were going forward in the Continental stables here. The more we enquire into that matter the more ruinous we find it, and the business is now in such a state of confusion that we hardly know how to remedy it. Our opinion is that no such thing as a Continental stable should ever have existed . . . The horses, after being worked to the bone, become neglected because it is nobody's business to take care of them, the feed is stolen, wasted and destroyed, because nobody can tell who is entitled to it and who is not; every officer in the service crams his horses into the public stables and calls him Continental; every team that is hired and ought to find their own feed say they are Continental and demand it as a right from the public. Mr. Hiltzhimier, our stable master, does all he can to prevent waste, imposition and abuses, but they threaten his life and to burn his stables. We sent him a guard and they were as bad as the wagoners. . . . We should think it would be best to sell all the Continental horses and wagons, shut up the stables, and encourage private people to provide the public with them on hire by good prices, for then the horses would be taken care of and the feed not be wasted. . . .''

I would like now to spend a moment on the subject of the post office, which Mr. Sherrill referred to.

From 1753 until 1774, I was the king's deputy postmaster-general for the American Colonies. I was dismissed from office in 1774 because I was charged with procuring and making public certain letters which were supposed to be slurring on Colonial men and measures. When the postal rates increased, William Goodard, an editor adversely affected by the change, built up an independent postal system. This, however, soon gave way to a Congressional post.

On May 29, 1775, the Continental Congress, feeling that the "critical situation of the colonies" made it "highly necessary that ways and means should be devised for the speedy and secure conveyance of intelligence from one end of the Continent to the other," resolved that a committee be appointed "to consider the best means of establishing posts for conveying letters and intelligence through this continent." I was made chairman of the committee. The committee brought in a report on July 25, and the next day the Post Office Department was organized. The postmaster-general was to maintain his office at Philadelphia and receive a salary of $1,000; the secretary and comptroller was to be appointed by the postmaster-general and was to receive a salary of $340; and the deputy postmasters, who likewise were to be appointed by the postmaster-general as he felt they were needed, were to be paid on a commission basis: Twenty percent on sums collected and paid into the general office not exceeding $1,000, and ten percent on all collections above that sum, constituted their remuneration.

Any deficits in the system were to be discharged by the United Colonies. A line of posts was to be established from New England to Georgia, and such cross posts as the postmaster-general might think fit.

The system was modified and enlarged from time to time as need arose. On July 5, 1776, Congress resolved that the postmaster-general be directed to have expresses established between Philadelphia and New York and that Gen. Washington "be desired" to send dispatches to Congress daily. Three days later, action was taken to relieve postmasters, while on duty, from military services. On August 30, Congress, having received the report of a Committee appointed for the purpose, resolved that there should be a rider on the post-roads for every twenty-five or thirty miles, the route to be traveled three times a week; that it be recommended to the state assemblies that postmasters be relieved of some of their public duties; that three advice boats be established to ply between Philadelphia and North Carolina, South Carolina, and Georgia; and that these boats be under the Secret Committee, freight and postage rates being used to help defray their expenses.

On November 7, 1776, Richard Bache—my son-in-law—who had been comptroller of the system, was appointed postmaster-general in my place, as I was absent on a French mission. The postal system, never as successful in operation as people had hoped it would be, began to be warmly criticized.

The postal authorities encountered many difficulties, but probably the most vexing one, as in the case of other branches of the government, was financial. The hope of Congress that postage rates might be put at a lower figure than the late royal ones ended in disappointment, for experience soon showed that even with high rates it was not easy to make the system pay for itself. By the close of 1779, funds were not sufficient to pay the riders.

Due to chaotic conditions, bad roads and lack of bridges, mails were likely to be delayed or not arrive at all. On June 17, 1782, the postmaster-general, now Ebenezer Hazard, communicated to the president of Congress the discouraging news: "The Southern Post has this moment arrived;—I am sorry to add, without the mails." The reason for this was that the rider had been robbed within five miles of Hartford Town, Maryland. Riders were sometimes taken by the enemy, for due to lack of forage and for other reasons, guards could not always be maintained. In February 1784, it appears to have been found that mails from the southwards had arrived but twice in seven weeks and then only from Virginia; and from the eastward but once in three weeks. If people could cover these distances on horseback and in carriages, it seemed to some that there was no valid excuse for this poor service. But two years later, delays continued, due to inability to get across ferries or for other reasons.

In 1786, the postmaster-general complained that while in earlier years there had been three surveyors, a comptroller, and an inspector of dead letters, all these officials were now dismissed for financial reasons, leaving the work of the department to himself and one assistant.

Mr. ADAMS. I can recall writing to Mr. Jefferson that "A Committee on the Post Office have found a thousand difficulties. The Post comes but once a week. It is not easy to get faithful Riders to go oftener. The expense is very high, and the profits (so dear is everything, and so little correspondence is carried on, except in franked letters), will not support the office."

Dr. FRANKLIN. So you see, Mr. Sherrill, we didn't solve our post office problems and you haven't solved yours.

Mr. SHERRILL. I thank you, your Excellency.

Dr. FRANKLIN. The word "excellency" does not belong to me, and Doctor will be sufficient to distinguish me from my grandson.

Gen. WASHINGTON. I see that the hour is late. For that reason the Commission will adjourn until Thursday, May 28th at 10 o'clock a.m.

THURSDAY, MAY 28, 1987

STATE OF THE UNION - II

The Commission met, pursuant to notice, at 10 a.m. in the Assembly Room of Independence Hall, Gen. George Washington presiding.

>Present: Mr. John Adams, Dr. Benjamin Franklin, Mr. Thomas Jefferson, Mr. James Madison and Gen. George Washington.

OPENING STATEMENT

Gen. WASHINGTON. The Commission has listened to testimony relative to the state of the union in modern times and has placed such times in juxtaposition to our former times to better see the changing times. Whether we talk about your time or our time, the real underlying question is, have our national goals been satisfied? In 1776 we said, "We hold these truths to be self evident, that all men are created equal, that they are endowed by their creator with certain unalienable Rights, that among these are Life, Liberty and the pursuit of Happiness." Have we secured these goals unto ourselves?

In 1787, we created the Constitution of the United States in order to establish Justice, insure domestic tranquility, provide for the American defense, promote the general welfare, and secure the blessings of Liberty to ourselves and our posterity. Have we received unto ourselves these goals? If we have not, it is the right of the people to alter or abolish its form of government and to institute a new one, laying its foundations on such principles and organizing its powers in such form, as to them shall seem most likely to effect their safety and happiness. Prudence, indeed, will dictate that governments long established should not be changed for legal and transient causes; and accordingly all experience has shown that mankind are more disposed to suffer, while evils are sufferable, than to right themselves by abolishing the forms to which they are accustomed. But when a long train of abuses and usurpations evinces an adverse design . . . it is our right . . . to provide new guards for our future security.

These were our declarations, for the benefit of ourselves and posterity; and in support thereof, with a firm reliance in the protection of divine Providence, we mutually pledged to each other our lives, our fortunes and our sacred honor.

What have we today secured for ourselves and posterity? What have we mutually pledged to one another . . . our lives? our fortunes? . . . our sacred honor?—or is that all hogwash . . . in modern times. Mr. Madison.

Mr. MADISON. It is my opinion that before a well-defined agenda is set, we continue to examine the structure and State of the Union. Among over thirteen hundred government reports, my attention has been directed to the so-called Hoover Commission Reports.

The Hoover Commission was created by The Lodge Brown Act by unanimous vote of the Congress in July, 1947. The Commission was bipartisan, with six members from each party. Four Commissioners each were chosen by the president of the senate, the Speaker of the House of Representatives, and President Truman. Mr. Herbert Hoover was chosen as chairman.

Mr. Hoover has been rated among the ablest administrators of all times. He was acclaimed for his humanitarian efforts during World War I, served as Secretary of Commerce in the Harding and Coolidge administrations and as the thirty-first president of the United States from 1929 to 1933.

The Hoover Commission made a characteristically

thorough and thoughtful approach to its mighty task. It began by defining some twenty-four of the principal problems of government and management. These included such things as personnel, budgeting and accounting, the Post Office, the National Security Organization, the State Department, and many other matters bearing on the assignment.

The Commission created special research committees called "task forces." These comprised some of the most eminent specialists available in each field. The task forces were given time, opportunity, and staffs with which to pursue their inquiries until they got to the "heart" of each problem. Then, after periods of ten to fourteen months they returned to the Commission with their findings in each field.

The result was the most imposing collection of facts, figures, and opinions on government that has ever been assembled. It amounted, in fact, to some two and a half million words of basic data of the most valuable sort.

From this massive bulk the Commission then prepared to carve out the model of a streamlined, modern government.

On a business basis alone, the Hoover Commission Report promised cash savings estimated at more than $3 billion a year.

A new Hoover Commission was created in 1953. During the period 1953 to 1955, the Commission studied and made recommendations in nineteen areas of Federal government operations. It presented 314 recommendations in reports totalling 1,632 pages, plus task force reports of several million words.

Why two Commissions to cover the same subject?

The major difference between the method of operation of the two Commissions was that the first Commission concerned itself chiefly with reorganization of departments and agencies and their relations with each other. That Commission's proposals were directed toward removing roadblocks to more effective organizaton and the reduction of expenditures.

The second Commission dealt more extensively with functional organization and with questions of policy.

It is to be noted that by Congressional authority both

Commissions studied the organization of the executive branch of the government.

Mr. ADAMS. Why is it that Congress will usually study the executive department and not its own house—the Congress?

Mr. MADISON. Actually, I note there are many reports covering the operations of Congress. Congress does attempt to oversee its own activities. But apparently the overwhelming thrust of activity has been in the Executive Department. We will probably find out more about this as we proceed.

Now, getting to the Hoover Commission, we are privileged to have Mr. Herbert Hoover here to furnish us with information concerning the operation of the Federal government in his time and as of today. Mr. Hoover, we welcome you and invite you to sit with our Commission.

Mr. HOOVER. I genuinely appreciate this opportunity to appear before your Commission.

No man can be president without looking back upon the effort given to the country by the thirty presidents who in my case had preceded me. No man of imagination can be president without thinking of what shall be the course of his country under the thirty more presidents who will follow him. He must think of himself as a link in the long chain of his country's destiny, past and future.

The presidency is more than executive responsibility. It is the symbol of America's high purpose. The president must represent the Nation's ideals, and he must also represent them to the nations of the world.

The nature of the presidential office as it has evolved through the history of the Republic is somewhat puzzling. Since the Founding Fathers, we have grown from three million to two hundred twenty-five million in population and from thirteen to fifty states. We have grown from an agricultural country to a complex industrial nation. We have risen in power to the first stature among nations. The original constitutional concept of the president's office has certainly been enlarged. He has become a broader policy-maker in legislation, foreign affairs, economic concerns, and social life than the Founding Fathers ever contemplated.

The president is, by his oath, one of the protectors of the Constitution. As "Chief Executive" he is administrator of the government. As "Commander-in-Chief" he has a responsibility in national defense. As "Chief Magistrate" he is the chief Federal law enforcement officer. Through his responsibility for foreign relations, he must keep the peace in a world of increasing perplexities. With the growth of the two-party system, he has become the leader of his party, bearing the responsibility to carry out the platform on which he was elected and to keep the party in power. As advisor to the Congress on the state of the nation, he must demonstrate constant leadership by proposing social and economic reforms made necessary by the increasing complexity of American life. He must be the conserver of national resources, and he must carry forward the great public works in pace with public need. He must encourage all good causes. Presidents have given different emphasis to these functions, depending upon the man and the times. In the end, the president has become increasingly the depository of all national ills, especially if things go wrong.

Dr. FRANKLIN. (Aside to Mr. Jefferson) And things did go wrong. The greatest depression ever in America started in 1929, in his term of office. Do you know what Will Rogers told me about Mr. Hoover and his times? He said, "I always felt there was only one thing that could possibly defeat Mr. Hoover's capable management of our affairs and that was when he runs out of practical men to put on commissions. Everyone was a college professor. Knowing college professors he gave them three years to agree on an answer.

I could have told him before sundown what's changed our lives: buying on credit, waiting for relief, Ford cars, too many Republicans, Notre Dame coaching methods and two-thirds of the Americans, both old and young, thinking they possessed 'it'."

Mr. ADAMS. Mr. Hoover, it would be helpful if you reviewed key portions of your reports and tried to relate some of the items to the present time.

Dr. FRANKLIN. (Aside to Mr, Jefferson) You know, few government reports are best sellers. It is unfortunately one of the elementary truisms of government at every level that the reports of study commissions are to be seen, not read, and certainly not to be acted upon.

Mr. HOOVER. The necessity for reorganization of the executive branch of the government was clearly recognized by the Congress when it created the Commission, with the full approval of the president. Congress assigned the Commission the duty of examination and recommendation under the following statement from the act creating the Commission:

"It is hereby declared to be the policy of Congress to promote economy, efficiency, and improved service in the transaction of the public business in the departments, bureaus, agencies, boards, commission, offices, independent establishments, and instrumentalities of the executive branch of the government by

> 1. Limiting expenditures to the lowest amount consistent with the efficient performance of essential services, activities, and functions;
> 2. Eliminating duplication and overlapping of services, activities, and functions;
> 3. Consolidating services, activities, and functions of a similar nature.
> 4. Abolishing services, activities, and functions not necessary to the efficient conduct of Government.
> 5. Defining and limiting executive functions, services and activities."

This concern of Congress for economy and efficiency reflected the overwhelming interest of every thoughtful citizen and taxpayer in the land.

The writing and adoption of the Federal Constitution proved that a republic could deliberately analyze its political institutions and redesign its government to meet the demands of the future. The broad pattern that America then selected is sound. Today we must deal with the infinitely more complicated government of the twentieth century.

As a result of depression, war, new needs for defense, and our greater responsibilities in the foreign field, the Federal Government has become the most gigantic business on earth. In the twenty-year period preceding 1950, the number of its civil employees rose from 570,000 to over 2,100,000. The number of bureaus, sections, services, and units increased fourfold to over 1,800. Annual expenditures increased from about $3.6 billion to over $42 billion. The national debt per individual citizen increased from about $130 to about $1,700. Such rapid growth could not take place without causing serious problems.

Mr. ADAMS. Mr. Hoover, just how do those figures look when carried forward to the 1980s?

Mr. HOOVER. Today the number of federally paid employees total about 2,900,000. The number of bureaus, sections, services, and units remains over 1,800.

Annual Federal expenditures today are over $600 billion, an increase of about fifteen times from the issuance of our original report, an increase of 166 times in a little over fifty years. During this same period—1929 to 1980—our population went from 121,767,000 to over 225,000,000 persons, an increase of less than two times in about fifty years. The transition of our national debt is likewise of interest. In 1929, it was $16.9 billion. In 1980, it was about $900 billion, an increase of over fifty-three times in about fifty years. Today that amounts to about $4,000 for every man, woman and child in the United States.

Mr. ADAMS. I just want to point out that in 1791, our national debt was $75,463,000. In 1835 and 1836, our national debt was only $38,000, the lowest in American history!

Mr. MADISON. Andrew Jackson was president then.

Dr. FRANKLIN. Let's resurrect and reelect that man!

Mr. ADAMS. Mr. Hoover, just how are the nearly 3 million federal employees allocated among the executive, legislative, and judicial branches of our government?

Mr. HOOVER. About 2,845,000 are in the executive branch, including the independent agencies; 40,000 in the legislative branch; and 15,000 in the judicial branch.

Mr. ADAMS. And how are annual expenditures allocated among these branches?

Mr. HOOVER. The legislative branch is budgeted for $1.3 billion. The judicial branch, $650 million and the executive branch over $600 billion.

Mr. ADAMS. So the bulk of the problem structurally, personnel-wise, and dollar-wise appears to rest in the executive branch.

Mr. Hoover, did your studies include recommendations as to Constitutional amendments needed to effect changes in the executive branch?

Mr. HOOVER. No. Our Commission found that the United States is paying heavily for a lack of order, a lack of clear lines of authority and responsibility, and a lack of effective organization in the executive branch. We recommended reorganization in the executive branch. We recommended reorganization of the executive branch to give it the simplicity of structure, the unity of purpose, and the clear line of executive authority that was intended under the Constitution. But, we did not have the authority to make recommendations of a constitutional nature. In the second report, we did indicate the major type of action needed for each recommendation, whether legislative or executive, and we did indicate where further study was needed. But we made no specific recommendation for amendment of the Constitution.

Mr. JEFFERSON. What did the work of your Commission cost the federal government?

Mr. HOOVER. The cost of the two reports was probably in excess of $3 million.

Mr. JEFFERSON. What would the cost be today?

Mr. HOOVER. Probably over $15 million.

Mr. ADAMS. Mr. Hoover, what were your findings and what action was taken thereon?

Gen. WASHINGTON. Excuse me, Mr. Adams. Because of the extensive nature of the question, I am of the opinion that we should adjourn until tomorrow, when we will continue this testimony.

The Commission will adjourn until tomorrow, May 29th at 10 o'clock a.m.

FRIDAY, MAY 29, 1987

STATE OF THE UNION - III

The Committee met, pursuant to notice, at 10 a.m. in the Assembly Room of Independence Hall, Gen. George Washington presiding.

Present: Mr. John Adams, Dr. Benjamin Franklin, Mr. Thomas Jefferson, Mr. James Madison, and Gen. George Washington.

Gen. WASHINGTON. The Commission has under discussion the organization of the Federal Departments and agencies. Mr. Herbert Hoover, former president of the United States, has been testifying and will continue his testimony today. Mr. Madison.

Mr. MADISON. Before proceeding with your testimony, Mr. Hoover, I would like to make a few observations of my own, based on a review I made of the table of organization of federal executive departments and agencies. I note that associated with the executive office of the president, which employs about two thousand, there are thirteen executive departments employing over 1.7 million persons. Over and above this there are sixty-two independent agencies employing over 1.1 million persons. For the benefit of future discussions let me read a list of executive departments of the United States. They are:

Department of Agriculture
Department of Commerce
Department of Defense
Department of Education
Department of Energy

Department of Health and Human Services
Department of Housing and Urban Development
Department of the Interior
Department of Justice
Department of Labor
Department of State
Department of Transportation
Department of Treasury

These executive departments consist of over five hundred agencies, services, bureaus, divisions, branches, sections, or units and have offices at about twelve thousand locations. Technically, all 1.7 million persons in the executive departments are directly responsible to the president of the United States—plus, of course, the two thousand persons in the executive office of the president—his immediate family, so to say.

In addition, the sixty-two independent agencies and commissions of the federal government have at least five hundred divisions, branches, sections, and units located in thousands of offices.

Mr. HOOVER. As we left the matter yesterday you asked me to discuss the findings of the Hoover Commission and what action was taken in connection with those findings.

At the end of World War II the government had leveled off to some eighteen hundred agencies employing three and a half million persons, housed in five thousand office buildings (not including post offices), with expenditures by the executive branch of over 40 billion annually. Somewhere between seventy and a hundred agencies, boards, and commissions reported, in theory, directly to the president; others were accountable to Congress, yet more to various cabinet heads; not a few apparently accounted to no one, the line of authority having been blurred or broken. The government owned more than a million cars and trucks. It was spending a billion dollars a year just to maintain its records. Different bodies in the government doing the same or similar work were competing for the tax dollar in a welter of duplicating activities.

Congress had concerned itself with the problem repeatedly, but little had been accomplished. Two world wars and eleven years of depression had compounded the confusion. Congress again began to worry about the snowballing executive agencies, some of them "temporary" bodies tottering with age.

I was consulted by legislative leaders in the spring of 1947. I outlined a project for a twelve-man bipartisan commission with wide powers to examine the tangle and propose methods for unknotting it. I hoped that the job wouldn't end in my lap and feared that it would.

In July, Congress adopted my proposal and everyone took it for granted that it would be Hoover's "baby." What I never realized was that this "last public assignment" would engage me, with one interval, until I was eighty-one years old.

For some twenty months our team painstakingly gathered and analyzed basic facts, delving into the incredibly complex and overlapping mechanisms of government operations. Members of the force roamed the length and breadth of the land in field trips, examining files, asking questions. With few exceptions they had the cooperation of officialdom. The raw notes that were compiled, mountains of them, eventually ended up on my desk. I supervised a staff of hundreds, sat in on task force meetings, and presided over sixty-nine of the seventy commission meetings.

The first of the nineteen sections of our sections of our report was submitted to Congress on February 7, 1949, and thereafter came in at the rate of about three a week. I wrote sixteen of the reports and, of course, the overall covering report, and edited the other three.

Congress now had before it some two and a half million words of concrete data. The commission offered 280 detailed individual recommendations.

Mr. MADISON. Mr. Hoover, is there one, just one, key finding that stands out in your mind?

Mr. HOOVER. Yes, very definitely. Our very first and most important finding was that the executive branch was not organized into a workable number of major departments and agencies which the president could effectively direct, but was cut up into a large number of agencies, which divided responsibility and which were too great in number for effective direction from the top.

We found that of sixty-four federal agencies, the president had an unavoidable direct responsibility for about thirty-one.

Definite authority at the top, a clear line of authority from top to bottom, and adequate staff aids to the exercise of authority did not exist. Authority was diffused, lines of authority confused, staff services were insufficient. Consequently, responsibility and accountability were impaired.

The president, and under him his chief lieutenants, the department heads, we found, must be held responsible and accountable to the people and the Congress for the conduct of the executive branch.

Dr. FRANKLIN. And after two and a half million words and 280 recommendations this was your main theme.

Mr. HOOVER. Yes.

Mr. MADISON. What was done with the 1949 report?

Mr. HOOVER. On February 7, 1949, the very day when it received the initial report, the House of Representatives, by a vote of 356 to 9, gave the president broad powers to carry out administrative reforms indicated by the Commission.

Mr. MADISON. Did you say "the very day"?

Mr. HOOVER. Yes, I did. Some of the changes could be made by Executive Order under existing authority over agencies directly accountable to the president, others by Congress.

Despite loud opposition, an estimated 70 percent of the recommendations had been adpoted by the end of the Truman term and in the first Eisenhower year. "Even the least of the Hoover recommendations," the Saturday Evening Post wrote, "has been enacted over the dead body of some bureaucrat who screamed that any change in his agency would result in a national calamity. No calamities and a great deal of good have resulted."

Dozens of agencies were eliminated or combined. The State Department was wholly reorganized. Under the Military Unification Act, some impressive savings were achieved.

Mr. ADAMS. Was the main frame of your report—a clear line of authority, responsibility and accountability—solved and resolved?

Mr. HOOVER. I would say, no.

Dr. FRANKLIN. I would say, definitely no. What we have today is a big unworkable, ramshackle house, distorted by random additions, by corridors that go nowhere and rooms that don't connect, a house loosely expanded through the years.

I realize that we didn't promise you a rose garden, but we didn't expect a garden full of weeds. I once wrote to my sister Jane Mecom of Boston. I was in London, England, then; it was 1758. I quoted an ancient poet whose works we have all studied and copied at school long ago:

A man of words and not of deeds

Is like a garden full of weeds.

And so it was with this report—it taught nothing that this nation really bought. And it left us with the echo of an empty canting harangue. As I wrote Sister Jane, inverting the good old verse

A man of deeds and not of words

Is like a garden full of —

I have forgot the rhyme, but remember t'was something the very reverse of perfume.

Mr. MADISON. Mr. Hoover, is there anything further you wish to note about the 1947-49 report?

Mr. HOOVER. Yes. The members of the cabinet are the primary advisors to the president. He is free to select them to decide the subjects on which he wishes advice, and to follow their advice or not as he sees fit.

The cabinet as a body, however, is not an effectve council of advisors to the president and it does not have a collective responsibility for administration policies. That responsibility rests upon the president. The cabinet members, being chosen to direct great specialized operating departments, are not all fitted to advise him on every subject.

Mr. MADISON. I suppose the key statement here is that the cabinet members are the primary advisors to the president but the cabinet is not an effective council.

Mr. HOOVER. That is true.

Mr. MADISON. Now let's get to the 1953-55 Report.

Mr. HOOVER. By 1953, the intensifying cold war, the Korean struggle, and massive rearmament had again expanded government and its costs. The budget stood at $72 billion and the federal payroll had increased by half a billion. Congress therefore reestablished the commission. Dwight D. Eisenhower was president then.

The second Commission turned out to be more difficult and demanding than the first. Besides, it proved far more controversial and thus involved debate on many of its issues. Whereas the first Commission dealt with governmental practices, its successor also examined policies and functions.

On September 29, 1953, the initial meeting of the second commission, its membership mostly new, was held in the White House with the president attending. Actual work was begun by mid-November. To overcome obstructions met in the first round, Congress gave us the authority to subpoena witnesses and administer oaths.

This time the Commission dealt not only with how things were done but whether they should be done at all by government. We lived out of suitcases, had dozens of task force meetings. I wrote or rewrote all but two of the twenty reports on sixty government agencies. After one year of working on the report, I told the West Side Association of Commerce in New York City in a speech that the government was engaged in about a thousand business enterprises competitive with private enterprises. This estimate later had to be almost tripled.

Later I noted that we had undertaken a study of paperwork in the government. We found that aside from some hundreds of tons of printed matter, the federal government circulated about twenty-five billion pieces of paper each year, at a cost of about $4 billion to prepare, send, and then file the materials when they came back. Some eighteen million of these were forms.

We examined 328 forms and found 51 were duplicates.

The field of budget and accounting seemed to be especially important. Few citizens will understand the intricacies of an activity as huge as that needed to plan for, allocate, and account for annual expenditures. Every citizen, however, should realize that planning the size of the budget—and the way in which funds are allocated - involves major decisions with respect to government policy.

The findings of our Commission showed that it was difficult to determine just what the government owned and what it owed.

Dr. FRANKLIN. But they sure know what the taxpayer owns and what he owes!

Mr. HOOVER. In our time, the budget of the United States contained over twelve hundred pages and weighed more than five pounds.

It was estimated that ninety thousand full-time employees were needed to compile the financial facts needed by government agencies to assure the public of integrity in government spending.

It was impossible to determine the total cost of budgeting and accounting. The cost of preparing the budget of the Department of Defense alone was estimated at about $30 million, while in the Executive Branch, salaries of full-time employees in the accounting and fiscal fields were estimated at $316 million.

I note that today the Office of Management and Budget employs 630 of the total of 1,998 employees in the Executive office of the president. This office is budgeted for over $32 million a year.

In 1970, during the first term of President Richard Nixon, the Office of Management and Budget was established. In our report we stated that the budget and accounting functions are basic to the whole conduct of government; that in the preparation of the budget lies not only the control of departmental expenditures but also the power to insist on efficient methods of management in the spending agencies. And within an effective budgeting system lies the restoration of the full control of the national purse to the Congress—yes, the restoration of full control of funding to Congress, where it belongs constitutionally.

Dr. FRANKLIN. And President Nixon established

Budget Control in the White House!

Mr. HOOVER. Yes.

Mr. MADISON. You spoke of government operation of businesses. Can you expand on that?

Mr. HOOVER. The government creates business-type enterprises in economic emergencies, in the emergencies of war, and for the development of projects which are not adapted to private enterprise because of their nature or their magnitude. One of the major problems before us is the continuation of these government business enterprises after the emergency that engendered them terminated. All too often they continue to function long after the original need has passed and even though the operation of many of them is not in the public interest.

A precise estimate of the extent of these enterprises could not be made. We found, however, that the total number of government commercial and industrial-type facilities within the Department of Defense alone probably exceeded twenty-five hundred.

As of December 31, 1954, the Commission's Subcommittee on Business Enterprises in the Department of Defense found forty-seven categories of such activities. Included were manufacturers of clothing, paint, ice cream, and eye glasses; companies specializing in furniture repair, cement mixing, and coffee roasting; some tree and garden nurseries, air lines, steamship lines, and a railroad.

Probably about a thousand of the twenty-five hundred individual facilities could be eliminated without injury to our national defense or to any essential government function.

Among civilian agencies, also, there existed no definitive list of publicly owned enterprises. The total amount of capital invested in them was unknown as was the number of their employees, the gross value of goods and services produced by them annually, and the profit or loss to the government resulting from their operations. Further, a few enjoyed a monopoly position since private enterprise in effect was excluded from the field when the government contracted only with its own "company" for the goods and services it needed.

The genius of the private enterprise system is that it generates initiative, ingenuity, inventiveness, and unparalleled productivity. With the normal bureaucratic rigidities that accompany any government, obviously, the same forces that produce excellent results in private industry do not do so in government business enterprises.

Mr. MADISON. Can you be a little more specific?

Mr. HOOVER. Some of these business enterprises were self-supporting with regard to their administrative expenses. Some were not and appropriations from the Congress were required for administration. Business enterprises having administrative expenses paid entirely or partly by the taxpayer included the Federal Housing Administration, certain components of the Public Housing Administration, the Federal Crop Insurance Corporation, the Farmers Home Administration, and the Rural Electrification Administration.

We recommended that Congress require these agencies either to conduct their business so as to recover their administrative expenses or, alternatively, to set out such subsidies as part of their annual request to the Congress for appropriations.

Certain agencies provided direct or indirect subsidies to their clientele even aside from their failure to earn administrative expenses. Included were the Public Housing Administration, the Commodity Credit Corporation, the Postal Service, the Bureau of Reclamation, and the United States Maritime Commission.

We recommended that both incorporated and unincorporated business enterprises report specifically to Congress each year the extent to which earned income failed to cover (a) interest on capital furnished by the government, (b) losses on loans or investments, and (c) operating expenses. Otherwise, through the exhaustion of capital, there is a hidden subsidy and the real financial results of government operations are obscured. These subsidies may not be disclosed until liquidation. Losses and subsidies should be made clear each fiscal year and passed upon by Congress.

It would take days to cover or uncover the scope and

extent of such federally operated enterprises.

Mr. MADISON. What about the 1980s?

Mr. HOOVER. Most of these units still exist. Many more have been created—as witness Amtrak, a billion-dollar boondoggle. If you don't mind, I would like to postpone comment on the 1980s until I finish my discussion of the last Hoover report.

Mr. MADISON. That is quite satisfactory.

Mr. HOOVER. While I am on the subject of transportation—such as Amtrak—the same situation prevailed in my time and probably still prevails with respect to air transport.

Our report showed the Military Air Transport Service operated in fiscal year 1954 at a recorded cost of $481,400,000. Most of its routes paralleled those of commercial United States airlines, but we found that the Air Transport Service of our government flew 13,000 pounds of furniture from Bermuda to the United States, flew 25,000 pounds of cement to Bermuda, and flew an Air Force band about once a month from Westover, Massachusetts to Bermuda as a "morale booster" because there was no band in Bermuda. The worthiness of the project was not challenged. However, two United States certificated airlines had regularly scheduled flights along the same route. The task force suggested that they could have "readily accommodated the band" at "less cost" to the government.

With respect to stockpiling and the disposal of surplus property by the military we disclosed some interesting facts: At the Warner Robins Air Material Area depot in Georgia, a sampling was made of the inventory of twenty-five standard items. Stock on hand represented zero to seventy-nine years' supply. Authorized retention stock levels ranged from six months' to more than nine years' supply. At the Navy Ship Parts Control Center in Mechanicsburg, Pennsylvania, stock on hand for twenty-five items showed from sixteen months to 128 years' supply. The latter item was gear drives. The Army Signal Corps had an authorized stock level of almost 1.5 million dry-cell flashlight batteries. This is an 8.5 years' supply of this short shelf-life item.

With respect to clothing the Commission found "too

many depots and tremendous quantities of depot stocks which far exceeded the operating levels set by the Services." The Army bought clothing for 30,000 women. However, since World War II, there had never been more than 15,000 women in the service. Consequently, in 1954 the operating stock of clothing showed a 10.6 years' supply of women's uniforms and 9.9 years' supply of women's shirts. In Wilmington, California, the General Services Administration and the Veterans' Administration had separate subsistence stores on the same reservation "side by side in identical buildings."

When surplus property were disposed of the average returns for such property were low, usually about 5 to 7 percent of acquisition cost.

Lastly, in this category, there is the case of the Army hauling 807,000 pounds of canned tomatoes from California to New York and the Navy hauling 775,000 pounds of canned tomatoes from the East to California. The net effect of this cross-hauling was tantamount to the Armed Services routing twenty carloads of tomatoes from Sacramento to San Francisco via New York.

A word about independent regulatory agencies. The independent regulatory commission was a comparatively new feature of the federal government in my time. It consisted then and consists today of a board or commission, not within an executive department, engaged in the regulation of some form of private activity.

Beginning in 1887 with the Interstate Commerce Commission, the number of independent regulatory commissions has increased materially. Besides the ICC, a few of the many such commissions are the Federal Trade Commission, the Securities and Exchange Commission, the Civil Aeronautics Board, the Federal Reserve Board, and the National Labor Relations Board. Thousands of pages of regulations guide private activity within these areas. Controversial issues of the greatest significance to the nation's economic development are disposed of each year by these commissions. It is clear that their efficient operation is of vital significance to the entire nation.

These commissions were created not only to provide for the orderly dispatch of complicated controversies of bodies deemed expert in their respective fields, but also to eliminate abuses that had crept in and, at the same time, to promote an adequate and healthy development of the activities subject to their control.

We believed that the independent regulatory commissions had a proper place in the machinery of our government, a place very like that originally conceived, but that the role of these commissions as originally established had not been adequately fulfilled.

Administrative direction had not developed with the commissions. Their chairmen were too frequently merely presiding officers at commission meetings. No one had been responsible for planning and guiding the general program of commission activity. Unnecessary red tape had crept into their procedures, causing useless delay and expense. Coordination between these commissions and the general program of the executive departments was often loose and casual and sometimes nonexistent.

In essence the independent regulatory agencies generally operated beyond the realm and policies of the executive department—all too frequently, as separate entities. Thus, purely executive functions had been entrusted to these independent regulatory agencies. The consequences have not been too happy, for a plural executive is not the most efficient device.

Some of the data in our second report with respect to the Department of Defense raised what is possibly the most crucial question of all: How long will bureaucrats be permitted to continue to ignore the intent of the Congress? In our form of government the Congress through legislation expresses the desires of the people. If it does not do so, there are opportunities to make periodic changes in the personnel of the Congress. No such opportunity exists to alter the actions of the vast majority of the personnel in the executive branch, who are charged with administering these laws. Some of the facts brought out by this report made it quite clear that this defiance of the intent of the

Congress is not only expensive in terms of dollars, but it may also weaken our defense.

The wise division of powers in the Constitution assigns the executive power to the president in unequivocal language: "The executive power shall be vested in a president of the United States of America."

But the president has many other constitutional responsibilities: "He shall take care that the laws be faithfully executed." He is commander-in-chief of the armed forces; he must conduct foreign relations; he must make legislative recommendations and approve or disapprove of legislative enactments. He is chief of state, and he is the political symbol of the American people."

Has the growth of the administrative process been at the expense of the constitutional separation of powers? Is not the increasing delegation of authority by Congress to administrative agencies creating inevitable problems for a governmental system designed to assure a separation of powers?

Congress declares policy, prescribes standards limiting agency action, and entrusts to the executive branch the function of completing the process of control.

Ours is a government of law and not of men. The concept of supremacy of the law is that certain established precepts should rule the actions of men and of governments. It is the basis of the protection of individual rights and it prevents the servants of the people from becoming masters of the people. Arbitrary actions by governments or men are inconsistent with law.

It would seem proper now for the Bicentennial Commission to examine the growth of this delegated authority, the objective being to reestablish the Constitutional authority of the Congress as well as our traditional concepts of separation.

Mr. ADAMS. It is significant to point out here that, as a matter of organization, the Department of Justice is not a part of the judicial branch. It is a part of the executive branch. Is that correct?

Mr. HOOVER. Yes.

Mr. ADAMS. Can you give us further insight into this development?

Mr. HOOVER. Legal staffs exist in almost every entity of the executive branch. Their operations are conducted without effective coordination. Since the establishment of the Department of Justice in 1870, attempts have been made to overcome the problems which inevitably result from the lack of coordination.

When the department was set up, Congress provided that attorneys in the other departments be transferred to it. They did not, however, repeal laws permitting independent legal staffs. In 1918, and again in 1933, Executive Orders were issued to strengthen the Department of Justice by making it the chief employer of attorneys and the center for handling all government litigation.

The expiration of Executive Orders and the continued authorization of independent legal staffs prevented the development of the Department of Justice as the government's chief law office. In my time, the size of the legal staffs varied. There were approximately 5,300 attorney positions in fifty-four departments and agencies of the executive branch exclusive of the Department of Defense, while in the Department of Defense there were about 1,300 civilian attorneys and 3,100 military personnel who performed exclusively legal duties.

Thus, almost 9,000 individuals were responsible for furnishing legal advice, drafting legal instruments, and performing other legal services at every level of the executive branch. Only 1,773 of these were employed in the Department of Justice.

According to the table of organization in the 1980s, the picture looks like this. The Department of Justice today employs over 56,000 persons, 18,000 of whom are in the FBI. These are not necessarily all attorneys, of course, but they are persons associated with the legal process of the executive department. At least an additional 10,000 persons are engaged in legal activity in the executive departments other than the Department of Justice. In the independent agencies, each agency has its own Office of Counsel and it appears that there are in excess of five thousand persons employed in all such general counsel offices.

Mr. ADAMS. And these are the persons who legislate

by issuing regulations?

Mr. HOOVER. The Department does more than that, of course. As the largest law firm in the nation, the Department of Justice serves as counsel for its citizens. It represents them in enforcing the law in the public interest. Through its thousands of lawyers, investigators, and agents the department plays the key role in protection against criminals and subversion, in ensuring healthy competition of business in our free enterprise system, in safeguarding the consumer, and in enforcing drug, immigration, and naturalization laws. The department also plays a significant role in protecting citizens through its efforts for effective law enforcement, crime prevention, crime detection, and prosecution and rehabilitation of offenders.

Moreover, the department conducts all suits in the Supreme Court involving the United States. It represents the government in legal matters generally, rendering legal advice and opinions, upon request, to the president and to the heads of the executive departments. The attorney general supervises and directs these activities, as well as those of the U.S. Attorneys and U.S. marshals in the various judicial districts around the country.

Mr. ADAMS. Mr. Hoover, you have made some critical statements respecting administrative agencies, such as as their ignoring the intent of Congress. You have implied that actions of governmental agencies are at times inconsistent with law.

Mr. Hoover, we want a specific illustration supporting the implication that government agencies legislate and that they at times legislate in a manner inconsistent with law.

Mr. MADISON. I would like to consider having some outside person support Mr. Hoover's statement, in the presence of Mr. Hoover.

Gen. WASHINGTON. Your request is accepted, Mr. Madison. Mr. Adams has arranged for support of this point at our next session, is that correct?

Mr. ADAMS. Yes it is.

Gen. WASHINGTON. Then, Mr. Hoover, would you conclude your fine testimony by relating to us the disposition of your second report?

Mr. HOOVER. Twenty reports were submitted to the Congress by June 30, 1955, included 314 recommendations based on inquiry into seventeen functional activities of the executive branch.

Sixty of the sixty-four executive agencies were studied. These agencies accounted for over 95 percent of the expenditures of the executive branch.

Our reports estimated annual savings at $6 billion.

Mr. ADAMS. What did the federal government pay for the second Hoover Commission Reports?

Mr. HOOVER. I believe it was around 2.8 million. I predicted that some people would not like the second commission report. This was an understatement. But I managed to console myself with the thought, "Old Reformers never die; they get thrown out." I thought the final box score on this commission's recommendations would be as good as the first one had been—over 70 percent of them adopted and put into effect.

But the second report did not fare that well. A generous estimate made several years later put the acceptance at around 30 percent and possibly it was not that high—the medicine prescribed was far too bitter for the bureaucratic palate.

Mr. MADISON. What would you characterize as most important in your second report?

Mr. HOOVER. Most significantly, the Commission pointed to ways of recovering billions by the Treasury through liquidation of useless functions and withdrawals from enterprises in flagrant competition with private business. Supposedly "temporary" institutions created in times of national emergency, some had developed an extraordinary longevity. One of them lasted thirty-six years and lost money every year.

We debunked the claims that certain of the federal businesses were earning profits. They were exempt from federal taxes, and their accounting in many cases did not include overhead, personnel, pensions, and other obligations shouldered by private competitors. Our Commission remarked that this was "a strange proceeding in a government pledged to fair competition. . . . The loss is not wholly the taxpayers' money. It is also a loss by injury to the vitality of the private enterprise system. It is a destruction of freedom."

The Hoover Commission urged that the government retire in favor of private business.

Mr. ADAMS. Mr. Hoover, are you acquainted with President Reagan's Private Sector Survey on Cost Control conducted by Mr. J. Peter Grace?

Mr. HOOVER. Of course. The president's report on cost control—let's call it the Grace Report for its chairman, Mr. Grace—was set up by President Reagan in 1982 for the purpose of doing on-site studies of all the major departments and agencies that make up the executive branch. The Grace Report was entirely a voluntary effort. The government did not contribute a cent. Civic-minded corporations donated money and materials and many of their best management talents. One hundred and sixty chief executives of the nation's leading corporations made up the executive committee. A staff of over two thousand volunteers was assembled.

Mr. ADAMS. How did the Hoover Reports differ from the Grace Report?

Mr. HOOVER. The Hoover Commission was established by an act of Congress and directed its activities primarily to the deficiencies of the executive department. The Grace Commission, on the other hand, was set up by President Reagan and directed its activities substantially to the inadequacies of Congress. Seventy-three percent of the Grace report recommendations required direct Congressional action. The Grace Report listed 2,478 specific ways to cut spending.

Mr. ADAMS. Do you have any further comments on the Grace Report, Mr. Hoover?

Mr. HOOVER. We can dramatize Pentagon purchases of three-cent screws for $91, nine-cent batteries for $114, and sixty-cent light bulbs for $511, but how do we dramatize the import of Mr. Grace's specter of a thirteen trillion dollar national debt by the year 2,000, representing an average of $50,000 for every man, woman and child currently living in the United States, if government spending follows its current pattern?

Dr. FRANKLIN. That reminds me of Senator Everett Dirksen's epithet, which could become our national epitaph: "A billion here, a billion there, and pretty soon we're talking about real money."

Mr. HOOVER. Mr. Grace concluded that we need to let our elected representatives know that we can no longer tolerate their continued fiscal irresponsibility and that like the character in the movie Network, "We're mad as hell, and we're not going to take it anymore!"

Gen. WASHINGTON. Mr. Hoover, this Commission extends to you its sincere thanks for your testimony.

Taken together, the two Hoover Commission reports probably represent the most thorough and uninhibited examination of federal machinery and functions in the nation's history. The imprint of your thinking on government, as an ex-president, will remain large and deep. You faced a problem which many a president and a Congress had dealt with ineffectively for at least a century. The reports will continue to serve as a guiding light—a beacon—for future presidents. Mr. Hoover, we thank you.

The Commission will adjourn until Monday, June 1st at 10 o'clock a.m.

MONDAY, JUNE 1, 1987

STATE OF THE UNION - IV

The Commission met, pursuant to notice, at 10 a.m. in the Assembly Room of Independence Hall, Gen. George Washington presiding.

        Present: Mr. John Adams, Dr. Benjamin Franklin, Mr. Thomas Jefferson, Mr. James Madison and Gen. George Washington.

Gen. WASHINGTON. Mr. Hoover's testimony raised serious questions about the tendency of governmental agencies to ignore the intent of Congress. The subject to be developed today concerns the extent to which federal regulations are being promulgated by executive departments on a basis inconsistent with law. At our last session Mr. Madison suggested having an outside person testify on this practice. Mr. Madison has arranged for this testimony. Mr. Adams.

Mr. ADAMS. We are pleased to have with us today Mr. Willard A. Weiss of Cleveland, Ohio. Mr. Weiss is an actuary and an attorney. He is a member of the Ohio Bar, a Fellow of the Conference of Actuaries in Public Practice, a member of the American Academy of Actuaries and an Enrolled Actuary licensed by the federal government to perform actuarial services under the Employees' Retirement Income Security Act of 1974.

Mr. Weiss, what we are most interested in is a very specific example or illustration of how existing departments can issue regulations inconsistent with law. I understand that your testimony will be based on your own professional experience in law and actuarial science. Will you please proceed with your testimony.

Mr. WEISS. In presenting an actual case of regulations being issued containing provisions inconsistent with law, let me give the applicable law, the regulations involved, the case, and the court decision. The federal agency involved was the Internal Revenue Service. The applicable law was Section 23(p) of the Revenue Act of 1942. Without engaging in the high technicalities of Section 23(p), for the purpose of simplification, the section set forth three limitations applying to tax deductions an employer can take for contributions he makes to a pension plan for his employees. The limits of the law were generally as follows:

(i) Formula A, "plus" (ii) Formula B, "or"

(iii) "in lieu of the amounts allowable under (i) and (ii) above," Formula C. Let me emphasize that this consistuted the law of the land, as acted upon and approved by Congress.

But regulations which applied to this law were later issued by the IRS Commissioner and contained in Section 29.23(p)-6 of Regulations 111, in part, the following: ". . . clause (ii) must be construed in the light of its obvious relationship to clauses (i) and (iii) and the interplay of clauses (i), (ii), and (iii). Each employer desiring to fund under clause (ii) shall submit the proposed method to the Commissioner and receive approval of such method before the results will be acceptable. Any method which does not fund the cost of past service more rapidly than that permitted under clause (iii) will be acceptable, and the approval of the Comissioner will not be necessary in such a case. . . ." Thus read the regulations, neither acted upon nor approved by Congress.

Dr. FRANKLIN. Mr. Adams, if you don't mind, I would like to interject and make a point on the subject of regulations. Over two hundred years ago, I said that perhaps it would be better if government meddled no further with trade than to protect it, and let it take its course. Most of the statutes or acts, edicts and placards of parliaments, princes and states for regulating and directing trade, have, I think, been either political blunders or jobs obtained by artful men for private advantage under the pretense of public good.

Mr. ADAMS. Thank you, Dr. Franklin. Mr. Weiss, will you continue?

Mr. WEISS. (Continuing) Thus the commissioner said in his regulations that deductions for employer contributions to a pension plan calculated under clauses (i) and (ii) cannot exceed an amount calculated under clause (iii). But note that the language of the law said that the employer would be allowed deductions calcuated under clause (i) plus (ii) or in lieu thereof, under clause (iii), without establishing any relationship between (i) and (ii) on the one hand, and (iii) on the other hand. In other words, the law says one thing and the commissioner says another. This is the essence of inconsistency between law and regulations.

On June 1, 1945, the commissioner promulgated what he called a Bulletin on Section 23(p)(1)(A) and (B). This bulletin purported to further delineate the commissioner's regulations on the subject.

We now come to a case situation.

Mr. MADISON. Mr. Weiss, may I interrupt before you proceed with your case illustration? I am looking at the preamble to the section of the law you quoted. I just cannot believe what I am reading. For the benefit of the Commission and the record, will you please read the preamble following the words "General Rule."?

Mr. WEISS. Yes, sir. The paragraph reads as follows: "If contributions are paid by an employer to or under a stock bonus, pension, profit-sharing, or annuity plan, or if compensation is paid or accrued on account of any employee under a plan deferring the receipt of such compensation, such contributions or compensation shall not be deductible under subsection (a) but shall be deductible, if deductible under subsection (a) without regard to this subsection, under this subsection but only to the following extent . . ."

Mr. MADISON. Who wrote that?

Mr. WEISS. Mr. Madison, on that question you are in good company. I doubt if the *Readers Digest* realizes to this day that this section of the law, which resulted in a court case, was the subject of an article in its January 1944 issue. The article was entitled "The Looming Nightmare of March 15" and was written by Sylvia F. Porter, a financial editor at that time for the *New York Post*. The article included the following which I believe will answer your question:

> Complicated laws are contrived in the attempt to plug loopholes through which tax evaders might slip. For decades, Congress and our shrewdest lawyers have been playing a game to see which will uncover a loophole first. But no justification in all the world can be found for this little gem, surely penned by a comma mad fugitive from Harvard Law School: "If contributions are paid by an employer to or under a stock bonus, pension, profit-sharing or annuity plan, or if compensation is paid or accrued on account of any employee under a plan deferring the receipt of such compensation, such contributions or compensation shall not be deductible under subsection (a) but shall be deductible if deductible under subsection (a) without regard to this subsection, under this subsection but only to the following extent . . .

When you've read it through a half dozen times, give up. All it means is that an employer may deduct from his income reasonable payments made under a pension plan.

Mr. Madison, does that answer your question?

Mr. MADISON. It does indeed! Thank you. Please proceed.

Mr. WEISS. Proceeding with the law case. The particular case is that of *The Saalfied Publishing Company* v. *Commissioner,* a Tax Court case. The Court's decision was promulgated November 1, 1948. The facts are briefly as follows: The petitioner filed its tax return for 1943 and among other items claimed a tax deduction for its contributions to its pension plan. The commissioner allowed a certain portion of the contribution as a tax deduction and disallowed the balance. The only issue for decision was whether the commissioner erred in his disallowance. The petitioner claimed his deduction under Section 23(p)(1)(A) and (B), which I referred to before. The commissioner claimed the allowances calculated under its regulations and its Bulletin were lower than the amount calculated by the petitioner, and hence the disallowance.

The problem for the court was to determine whether there was in the statue, or in any interpretation thereof contained in the regulations, any justification for the limitation which the commissioner placed upon the deduction claimed by the petitioner. I will now quote from the court's opinion:

> It is stipulated that the Commissioner made his determination under his regulation and subpart B of Part II of a "Bulletin on Section 23(p)(A) and (B)" promulgated by him on June 1, 1945. It is not at all clear from this statement or an examination of the Bulletin just how the Commissioner arrived at the amount which he allowed as a deduction, but it is, of course, clear that he did not allow as a deduction the entire amount actuarially necessary to provide the remaining unfunded cost of the employees' past and current service credits distributed as a level amount. The Bulletin to which reference has been made contains the following foreword:
>> "This Bulletin contains information from which taxpayers and their counsel may obtain the best available indication of the trend of official opinion in the administration of provisions of Section 23(p)(1)(A) and (B) of the Internal Revenue Code, as amended by the Revenue Act of 1942, relating to deductions for contributions of an employer under pension and annuity plans in taxable years beginning after December 31, 1941. It does not have the force and effect of a Treasury Decision and does not commit the Department to any interpretation of the law which has not been formally approved and promulgated by the Secretary of the Treasury.
>> (Signed) Joseph D. Nunman, Jr. June 1, 1945, Commissioner of Internal Service."
>
> This Bulletin does not purport to be a regulation or even a binding rule of the Bureau. Apparently it has never been printed by the Government Printer, included in the Federal Register, or approved by the Secretary of the Treasury. The only copy of the Bulletin which this court has been able to

obtain was one printed by one of the tax services. It is 21 pages long, not counting advertising matter, and contains many complicated statements, tables, tests and computations. The tax year involved herein is 1943 while the Bulletin is dated June 1, 1945. No good purpose would be served by discussing this Bulletin further. Suffice to say that no such document could have any binding effect upon the Court in deciding this case. . . . It seems wholly inconsistent for the Commissioner to place a further and more severe limitation upon clause (ii) than the one which Congress expressly provided therein. There is nothing in the Congressional Reports indicating any intention on the part of the Congress that the deduction allowed under clauses (i) and (ii) should be thus . . . limited.

The Court then goes on to state and hold that the regulations "along with some method set forth in the Bulletin mentioned above, has produced a result in this case which finds no support in the statute. They do not provide a reasonable and proper interpretation of the law enacted by Congress but attempt to write into the law something which Congress did not place there or intend to place there. It is therefore held that, as so applied, they are unreasonable and null and void. . . . The petitioner's method is sound and results in no abuse contemplated by Congress. The petitioner is entitled to the entire decution which it claimed and the Commissioner erred in limiting the deduction . . ."

Mr. ADAMS. Mr. Weiss, do you know to what extent this kind of situation prevails? In other words, to what extent are regulations written contrary to law?

Mr. WEISS. I do not believe this information is available to me under the Freedom of Information Act, and I have never undertaken the legal research necessary to determine its prevalence.

Mr. MADISON. That's all right, Mr. Weiss; the information is available to us.

Mr. Weiss, in brief, what is your opinion relative to federation regulations?

Mr. WEISS. In my opinion the substantive portion of

regulations should be drafted by Congress and not delegated to the executive departments or the administrative agencies. These agencies should be left to develop administrative regulations only, not substantive ones. If regulations are not written in this manner, the Congress should be required to approve all regulations and most assuredly Congress should be required to monitor all regulations.

Mr. MADISON. Mr. Weiss, before you leave, I am interested in the answer to one question. The section you quoted from the *Readers Digest*, the one penned by a comma-mad fugitive from Harvard Law School, was from the Revenue Act of 1942. Can you tell us how that same section reads today?

Mr. WEISS. Yes, Dr. Franklin. Just a moment . . . here it is. It is now Section 404 of the Internal Revenue Code and the comparable section reads as follows: "If contributions are paid by an employer to or under a stock bonus, pension, profit-sharing, or annuity plan, or if compensation is paid or accrued on account of any employee under a plan deferring the receipt of such compensation, such contributions or compensation shall not be deductible under section 162 (relating to trade or business expenses) or section 212 (relating to expenses for the production of income) but, if they satisfy the conditions of either of such sections, they shall be deductible under this section, subject, however, to the following limitations as to the amounts deductible in any year."

Dr. FRANKLIN. Incredible!

Gen. WASHINGTON. Thank you, Mr. Weiss. Mr. Adams, who is our next speaker?

Mr. ADAMS. Our next speaker will be Dr. Donald Lambro. Mr. Lambro is author of the book *Fat City*, published in 1980 by Regnery/Gateway, Inc. This book should be read by every member of this Commission. Mr. Lambro will give us his appraisal of government affairs in the 1980s. Mr. Lambro.

Mr. LAMBRO. Gentlemen. I appreciate the opportunity to appear before you. My research has led me to many situations and incidents, the revelation of which may provide some assistance to the Commission.

The federal government is a wasteland, losing $100 billion a year. Tens of billions of tax dollars disappear each year from the federal government through fraud, mismanagement, abuse, waste, error, and sheer extravagance. No one in Washington knows what the actual total is. What is even worse, the government doesn't want to know, for if it did, the total would be so unbelievably enormous that it would destroy whatever faith, if any, remained among taxpayers in Washington's ability to spend our money wisely.

Over the last several years, the government has lost more than $3.5 billion as the result of debts written off as uncollectable. These bad debt losses had been rising at a rate of $500 million a year. By the end of 1978, a staggering $140 billion in loans and accounts receivable were owed to the government, an increase of $22 billion from the previous fiscal year.

What I would like to relate are actual incidents which have occurred in certain of the federal agencies.

Let's start with the OSHA—The Occupational Safety and Health Administration. This agency was established pursuant to the Occupational Safety and Health Act of 1970. It develops and promulgates occupational safety and health standards; develops and issues regulations; conducts investigations and inspections to determine the status of compliance with safety and health standards and regulations; and issues citations and proposes penalties for noncompliance with safety and health standards and regulations. It employs 2,962 persons. It is budgeted for over $200 million a year.

A survey by the National Association of Manufacturers computed the cost of complying with OSHA's requirements at an average of $35,000 for firms of between one and a hundred workers, $73,500 for companies of up to five hundred employees, and $350,000 for firms of up to a thousand workers.

An OSHA inspector told a Florida meat-packing company that a safety railing had to be put up around its loading dock to keep workers from falling off. After the company installed the railing, an Agriculture Department inspector ordered it removed as an obstacle to sanitation.

The Agricultural Stabilization and Conservation Service employs 2,970 persons. This service maintains a Beekeeper Indemnity Program. This program, begun in 1970, essentially pays beekeepers in the event their bees are killed, through no fault of the beekeepers, by federally registered and approved pesticides.

Dr. FRANKLIN. I understand that since payments began there was not a single case of a bee dying from natural causes.

Mr. LAMBRO. The average claim has been $3,000. In all, $23.8 million has been paid out since the program began.

Let's look at the federal advisory boards, committees, commissions and councils. The federal government is drenched in advisory comittees—more than eight hundred of them at the end of 1978, costing over $75 million a year. Here is a sampling of what agencies remain securely tucked away in the bureaucracy:

Secretary of the Navy's Advisory Committee on Naval History; Theatre Advisory Panel; National Boating Safety Advisory Council; National Advisory Council for Career Education; National Professional Standards Review Council; National Council on the Humanities; National Council on the Arts; National Public Advisory Committee on Regional Economic Development; National Arboretum Advisory Council; National Advisory Research Resources Council; Music Advisory Panel; Model Adoption Legislation and Procedures Advisory Panel; Media Arts Advisory Panel; National Mobile Home Advisory Council; Social Sciences and Population Study Section; Travel Advisory Board; Visual Arts Advisory Panel; National Advisory Council on Women's Educational Programs; National Commission on Neighborhoods; and the Small Business Advisory Committee.

Most of these committees and other advisory panels meet very rarely, sometimes once or twice a year, and few of them have any permanent staff. Some of these committees, such as those dealing with health and diseases, as well as military matters, are obviously important and should be preserved—though no doubt a number of them could be consolidated. The rest, however, should be abolished. An arm of government has evolved where none was ever intended.

Let's look at the National Board for the Promotion of Rifle Practice. This board was budgeted for $425,000 in 1981. The board trains civilians to shoot small-caliber military weapons so that in the event of war these gun enthusiasts will be prepared to defend their homeland against enemy invaders. To a large degree, however, it is really a program that provides many happy hours of pleasure for people who just like to go out on a range and shoot. It is hard to imagine why the government is financing this kind of activity, particularly in time of peace, but it has been doing so since 1903. That was the year when Elihu Root, the secretary of war, first organized the board.

The Carter administration sought to abolish the Board in fiscal 1980, but Congress resisted this effort as it has previous efforts to terminate the agency. In fiscal 1979 Congress provided the Board with $375,000 in operating funds which is the only figure usually used to identify its cost. But an additional $329,000 is also appropriated annually for ammunition. Thirty-eight million rounds were given out in 1978.

Let's look at the Franklin Delano Roosevelt Memorial Commission. The estimated outlay in 1980 was $45,000. This Commission was established in 1955 to develop plans for a permanent memorial to FDR. Its unsuccessful search for a suitable monument has been marked by endless dispute and bickering. By the end of 1981 no memorial had been erected, despite the expenditure of hundreds of thousands of dollars over a quarter of a century.

Now let's turn to the Consumer Products Safety Commission. The purpose of this Commission is to protect the public against unreasonable risks of injury from consumer products; to assist consumers to evaluate the comparative safety of consumer products; to develop uniform safety standards for consumer products and minimize conflicting state and local regulations; and to promote research and investigation into the causes and prevention of product-related deaths, illnesses, and injuries.

This commission is budgeted at about $43 million a year. Created by Congress in 1973 as an independent regulatory agency, the commission has been a case-book example of excessive federal regulation. The commission has spread its regulatory net over everything, concerning itself with products from skateboards to television antennas. It has instructed skiers to tighten their bindings and to keep their ski equipment in tip-top shape while on the slopes. It has advised people on the do's and don'ts of bicycling.

The Safety Commission's actions regarding skateboards is a good case in point. On October 26, 1978, the Commission received a petition from the Consumer Affairs Committee of the Americans for Democratic Action requesting the issuance of a ban on skateboards. The petition contended that skateboards have been associated with many serious injuries and that the design of the skateboard cannot be improved in any way to make it safe. The commission indicated that twenty-five deaths from skateboards had occurred between 1975 and 1977, and that injuries from skateboards had decreased from 140,000 in 1977 to about 87,000 in 1978. It stated that the main factors found to cause injuries were, in order of prominence, irregular riding surface; loss of balance; slipping from the board; jumping from the board; falling while turning; striking an obstacle, and the board slipping out from under the victim. The Commission indicated that skateboard breakage such as broken decks or wheels falling off was involved in less than 2 percent of skateboard injuries. The Commission therefore denied the petition to ban skateboards on the basis that skateboarding injuries were primarily "use related" rather than "product related."

Dr. FRANKLIN. Sounds like an exercise by a useless Skate Board?

Mr. LAMBRO. The Smithsonian Institution is currently budgeted for about $120 million a year. There is no question tht some of the Smithsonian grants are going to highly worthy projects, but consider these: a study of the semen of the Ceylon elephant; editing and translating Ali ibn Ridwan's "On the Prevention of Bodily Ills in Egypt," which deals with epidemic diseases in eleventh-century Egypt; and how about an "Ethnographic film study of a nomadic herbing society, the Pashtoon people of Afghanistan, some of whom have settled in India."

Consider the Federal Trade Commission. The basic objective of the FTC as stated in the United States Government Manual is the maintenance of strongly competitive enterprise as the keystone of the American economic system. Although the duties of the Commission are many and varied under law, the foundation of public policy underlying all these duties is essentially the same: to prevent the free enterprise system from being stifled, substantially lessened or fettered by monopoly or restraints on trade, or corrupted by unfair or deceptive trade practices.

In brief, the Commission is charged with keeping competition both free and fair.

The FTC is currently budgeted at $72 million a year. It has two thousand persons in its employ. Here are examples of what the FTC has been doing with your money.
- $41,900 for a survey on the effectiveness of corrective advertising for Listerine
- $19,000 for a survey of households to determine the products eaten by children as snacks
- $4,000 for an analysis of Piaget's theory of children's cognitive development
- $3,000 for a follow-up telephone census on the three-day cooling-off rule for door-to-door sales

Dr. FRANKLIN. Are you sure that wasn't followed up with a door-to-door census of the cooling-off rule for door-to-door sales?

Mr. LAMBRO. No comment. This is just a small sampling of the FTC's fiscal 1978 and 1979 program contracts, but it vividly illustrates that this agency is researching subjects and conducting projects that are a million light-years away from the real problems and everyday concerns of most Americans.

Then there's the Food and Drug Administration. This group employs 8,400 persons. It is currently budgeted at over $300 million a year. The FDA's activities are directed toward protecting the health of the nation against impure and unsafe foods, drugs and cosmetics, and other potential hazards. Just one illustration of its authority. In 1979 the Food and Drug Administration published in the Federal Register an advance notice of proposed rulemaking on the subject of lead in food and requested information and data from the public. The FDA said that it planned to reduce the level of lead intake by humans. We are exposed to lead from a variety of sources—in the air we breathe, in the food we eat, and in the water we drink. Lead is widely recognized as a toxic substance, and has been a matter of concern to the FDA and other public health agencies for some time because of the possibility of cancer in humans.

The most important source of additional lead in the food supply, the administration said, is the method of packaging and holding food, with the popular tin can as the foremost offender. Thirty-three billion tin cans are used each year to package food and approximately twenty-five billion more are used annually to package carbonated beverages. The source of the added lead is not the can itself, but the lead solder used in the can seams. Lead from tin can solder contributes about 14 percent of the total lead ingested by humans. The FDA has concerned itself with lead for six years now.

Dr. FRANKLIN. I suppose, this is Your Government at Work, getting the lead out of your can.

Mr. ADAMS. Perhaps future lead-seamed cans will contain the phrase "The Surgeon General has determined that use of this can may be hazardous to your health. This can contains lead which has been determined to cause cancer in laboratory animals."

Mr. LAMBRO. Let's take another look at your government at work. On Wednesday, May 28, 1980, for example, the Fish and Wildlife Service of the Department of the Interior issued a "Proposed Rule" in the Federal Register proposing to set up a "Critical Habitat for the Coachella Valley Fringe-Toed Lizard" under the Endangered Species Act.

The proposed rule notes that "The Coachella Valley fringe-toed lizard, eight to eleven centimeters in snoot-vent length, is whitish in color with many closely set black marks forming a network of outlined circular whitish areas." The proposed rule went on to state that "Comments from the public must be received by July 28, 1980. Comments from the governor of California must be received by August 26, 1980. A public meeting on this proposal will be held on June 20, 1980, and a public hearing will be held on July 7, 1980."

Dr. FRANKLIN. The Governor of California was probably too busy with the California "medfly" problem to attend this meeting on the Coachella Valley fringe-toed lizard.

Mr. LAMBRO. Just imagine the paperwork needed to research these subjects and to implement controls. And while on the subject of paperwork, in 1974 Congress created the Federal Paperwork Commission, which churned out a considerable amount of paperwork of its own and even produced a movie about the problem. The Commission made over 770 paper-cutting recommendations designed to save more than $10 billion.

In March 1978, President Carter issued Executive Order No. 12044 requiring agencies to evaluate their rules periodically, revising them to reduce paperwork burdens. In January 1980 proposed rules attempting to control the paperwork burden on the public were reported in the Federal Register. At that time, the Office of Management and Budget estimated that there were 175 federal employees responsible for overseeing the Federal Reports Act, at a cost of $10 million annually. The Paperwork Commission was allocated zero dollars in the 1981 budget. The effort appears to rise and fall depending on the political climate, but the "heat" on the public continues.

The government's own statistics on its paperwork demands are staggering. The Agriculture Department, for example, annually spends $150 million producing various forms—forms that have produced 989,224 cubic feet of records, filling almost 37,000 file drawers. The Labor Department estimates that respondents annually complete 44.8 million of its forms, requiring 17.2 million hours of effort. The General Accounting Office reports that Americans fill out 424.8 million federal forms each year—consuming 127.7 million hours of work.

Translating this time into money, the best available estimates are that business annually spends $32 billion to comply with the paperwork demands of Washington—but experts say this official figure is probably underestimated by a factor of four. It costs individuals nearly $9 billion a year to meet their own paperwork requirements, primarily tax forms. Eventually this total overall cost of paperwork is borne by every American, in the form of higher taxes and rising prices.

For example, a leading pharmaceutical firm, Eli Lilly, spends more time filling out government forms than doing heart-disease and cancer research. A single report from The Exxon Corporation to the Federal Energy Agency runs 445,000 pages, the equivalent of a thousand volumes. Another major oil company estimates that it has to file more than four hundred reports (excluding tax forms) each year with at least forty-five different federal agencies.

One government agency sought to buy about $4,000 worth of fire-fighting equipment. The agency's solicitation bid was 155 pages long and included 23 pages of foldout diagrams. Forty-one firms were solicited, but only two responded. The successful bid, grotestquely swollen by the cost of filling out the required forms, was $15,497 or about four times the estimated cost of the equipment.

After Congress enacted the Employee Retirement Income Security Act (ERISA), the mandatory reports became so intolerable that firms began terminating existing plans and refusing to establish new ones, thereby jeopardizing the pensions of thousands of workers. In one case, said a government report, "Fifteen employees lost their pension plan because the small company could not handle the paperwork."

This penchant for paper generates an increasingly impenetrable mesh of rules—45,000 pages of complex new regulations a year. Twenty-seven different government agencies monitor some 5,600 federal regulations that pertain to the manufacture of steel alone.

As my last point, I would like to discuss the subject of revenue sharing. Since 1972 the federal government has had a revenue-sharing program with the states by which it gives the states, cities, and towns about $7 billion annually to spend as they wish. In 1980, the Office of Revenue Sharing gave away $6.8 billion at an administrative cost of $6.2 million.

But this revenue sharing does not represent total federal aid to the states. Other federal agencies, such as the Department of Transportation, the Department of Education, the Environmental Protection Agency, the Department of Housing and Urban Development, and the Employment and Training Administration, gave the states $76 billion, making the total giveaway $83 billion. Our federal debt is well over a trillion dollars and, incidentally, we have a Bureau of the National Debt employing over twenty-two hundred. Just the interest on this debt amounts to over $80 billion a year. In other words, what we give away annually is equal to the interest we pay on our national debt. In 1957 the total federal income was only $80 billion. We give away, then, what our total federal income was in 1957. The debt of all the states combined is only a third that of the federal government. We just ask ourselves the question, What is there really left to share? The cupboard is bare.

Mr. MADISON. Mr. Lambro, we certainly thank you for your testimony.

Gen. WASHINGTON. We will recess for ten minutes.

(Mr. Jefferson and others exit. Gen. Washington remains.)

Gen. WASHINGTON. (To the spectators) Mr. Jefferson, my long-time friend and colleague, is of a temperament and bearing that befits his role on this Commission. He is a man of lofty stature, with a noble face, with a Scotch-Irish cast of feature, and with curly hair of a reddish tint, although greatly mixed with gray. His mouth is large and firm set, while his nose is of the true Scottish type and unusually wide at the nostrils. As to his eyes, I would say that they are of a grayish and light blue tint mixed, and steely in expression. His brow is broad and white and very free from wrinkles. His whole appearance denotes a man of vigorous actions. One would judge him to be a gentleman of landed property, with all the inclinations of a foxhunting squire.

Mr. Jefferson maintained a decalogue of canons for

conduct in practical life. His own list reads like some of Dr. Franklin's own proverbs, but wherever they came from, this is what Mr. Jefferson wrote:
1. Never put off till tomorrow what you can do today.
2. Never trouble another for what you can do yourself.
3. Never spend your money before you have it.
4. Never buy what you do not want because it is cheap; it will be dear to you.
5. Pride costs us more than hunger, thirst, and cold.
6. We never repent of having eaten too little.
7. Nothing is troublesome that we do willingly.
8. How much pain have cost us the evils which have never happened.
9. Take things always by their smooth handle.
10. When angry, count ten before you speak; if very angry, a hundred."

My friend, Mr. Jefferson, wrote that list for Thomas Jefferson Smith, who was the son of Mr. Samuel Harrison Smith, one of Mr. Jefferson's old friends. It was written on February 21, 1825.

Well, the Commission members are returning. . . . This session will now resume its proceedings. Mr. Madison.

Mr. MADISON. Dr. Franklin has requested the floor. I yield to Dr. Franklin.

Dr. FRANKLIN. While listening to Mr. Lambro talk about millions of officeholders—and that in essence is what this is all about, people—I was reminded of the time I was deputy postmaster general for North America, serving under the king of England. Efforts were made to deprive me of my office when I defended American rights. When rumors of these attempts reached Boston, my sister, Jane Mecom, wrote me, worried about the loss and embarrassment I might suffer. I replied setting down my standard of independence for officeholders. I said, "I have heard of some great Man, whose rule it was, with regard to offices, never to ask for them, and never to refuse them; to which I have always added, in my own practice, never to resign them. As I told my friends, I rose to the office through a long course of service in the inferior degrees of it. Before my time, through bad management, it never produced the salary annex'd to it; and when I received it, no salary was to be allowed, if the office did not produce it." I repeat, no salary was to be allowed, if the office did not produce it. During the first four years it was so far from defraying itself, that it became nine hundred and fifty pounds sterling in debt to me.

How many officeholders today would work under these pecuniary conditions? I am afraid those practices would be considered pecuniarily puny.

It may be imagined by some that this is a Utopian idea, and that we can ever find men to serve us in the executive department without paying them well for their services. I conceive this to be a mistake. Some facts present themselves to me, which incline me to a contrary opinion. The high-sheriff of a county in England was an honorable office, but it was not a profitable one. It was rather expensive and therefore not sought for. But yet, it was executed and well executed, and usually by some of the principal gentlemen of the county. In France, the office of counsellor, or member of their judiciary parliament, was even more honorable. It was therefore purchased at a high price; there were indeed fees on the law proceedings, which were divided among them, but these fees did not amount to more than three percent on the sum paid for the place. Therefore, as legal interest was there at five percent, they in fact paid two percent for being allowed to do the judiciary business of the nation, which was at the same time entirely exempt from the burden of paying them any salaries for their services. I do not, however, mean to recommend this as an eligible mode for our judiciary department. I only bring the instance to show that the pleasure of doing good and serving their country and the respect such conduct entitles them to are sufficient motives with some minds to give up a great portion of their time to the public, without the mean inducement of pecuniary satisfaction.

But all this is not the mainstay of what I would like to know now. I want to know just how everything that happens or is to happen in government is told to the public. How are the things that Mr. Hoover and Mr. Lambro spoke about communicated to the people of the United States? You see, in the early days I was a printer. I started publishing the *Pennsylvania Gazette* in 1729.

A writer once observed in the *Gazette* that "However little some may think of Common News-Papers, to the wise man they appear the ark of God, for the safety of the people." In 1731 I founded the Library Company of Philadelphia, which is still in existence today. And from 1733 to 1758, I published *Poor Richard's Almanack*. In colonial America, *Poor Richard's Almanack* was read by one out of every hundred citizens. It enjoyed a popularity second only to the Bible. In France, the publication went through fifty-six editions.

Louis Wright, a scholar of American colonial history and culture, once said of me that for the past two centuries my homely aphorisms and observations have influenced more Americans than the learned wisdom of all the formal philosophers put together. I mention this not out of a sense of egotism—after all, I am the only member of this Commission who was not a president of the United States; I was only president of the State of Pennsylvania—but, rather to establish my credentials in the area of communicating with the public.

Mr. MADISON. Dr. Franklin, we have asked Mr. William S. Fairhill to discuss with us certain matters relating to that very subject, communication. Mr. Fairhill was formerly deputy director in the Office of Management and Budget. Mr. Fairhill is a graduate of Harvard Law School and the Harvard School of Business Administration, and he served in the administration of President Carter. Mr. Fairhill.

Dr. FRANKLIN. (Aside to Mr. Jefferson) I heard this fellow Carson on the "Tonite Show" say that when a dentist asked President Reagan to cut back on jelly beans because they were bad for the teeth, Reagan said he didn't care. Carter had great teeth and it didn't do the country any good.

Mr. JEFFERSON. (Aside to Mr. Franklin) I must watch that program.

Dr. FRANKLIN. Mr. Fairhill, would you please

enumerate for us the various ways in which the federal government communicates its acts and proposed acts, its actions and proposed actions, and how the public may act in advance or react in response thereto?

Mr. FAIRHILL. Certainly, Dr. Franklin. During the past decade, numerous pieces of legislation have been enacted which help provide citizens with greater access to government information. Two important laws permitting such access to information are the Freedom of Information Act and the Sunshine Act.

The Freedom of Information Act (5 U.S.C. 552) requires that information held by Federal agencies be made available to the public unless it comes within one of the specific categories exempt from public disclosure, such as matters involving national security, foreign policy interests, the internal management of an agency, or an individual's right to privacy. Agency decisions to withhold records requested under the act are subject to judicial review.

Virtually all agencies of the executive branch of the federal government have issued regulations implementing the Freedom of Information Act. These regulations inform the public where certain types of information may be readily obtained, how other information may be obtained on request, and what internal agency appeals are available if a member of the public is refused requested information.

The Sunshine Act declares that the public is entitled to the fullest possible information about the decision-making processes of the federal government. The act provides for making this information known by requiring that all meetings of government agencies be open to the public unless they come within one of the specific categories exempt from public disclosure. The government in the Sunshine Act requires that public announcement be made of the time, place, and subject matter of each agency meeting, whether it is open or closed to the public, and the name and telephone number of the official designated to answer questions about the meeting. Each issue of the Federal Register, which I will describe, has a special section containing these agency notices of "Sunshine Act Meetings." The minutes or a transcript of each meeting must be made promptly and conveniently available to the public. Virtually all agencies of the federal government have issued regulations to implement the Sunshine Act, including procedures to be followed in closing meetings to the public.

The daily Federal Register provides a uniform system for publishing presidential and executive agency documents. These documents include executive orders and proclamations as well as rules, proposed rules, and notices of the federal agencies. The rules and proposed rules published in the Federal Register cover a wide range of government activities affecting all aspects of life—consumer product safety, education, environmental protection, food and drug standards, housing and occupational health and safety, transportation, and many more areas of concern to the public.

The proposed rules portion of the Federal Register invites citizens or groups to participate in the consideration of the proposed rule through the submission of written data, views, or arguments, and sometimes by oral presentation. In addition, the Federal Register publishes nonregulatory public interest announcements, such as advisory committee meetings, grant application deadlines, and availability of environmental impact statements. Through the publication of these proposed rules and notices, citizens are given the opportunity to be informed of and participate in the workings of their government.

Dr. FRANKLIN. Mr. Fairhill, what is the daily circulation of the Federal Register?

Mr. FAIRHILL. To my knowledge, during a recent five-year period, the annual number of subscriptions for daily circulation was about 52,000. In addition, certain libraries, about 1,350 of them, are designated as depository libraries for the Federal Register and other government publications.

Dr. FRANKLIN. Do you mean to tell me that in a country such as the United States, with a population of over 225 million people, that only 52,000 copies of this information are available to the public each day?

Mr. FAIRHILL. That is correct, Dr. Franklin.

Dr. FRANKLIN. Please proceed. I will get back to the Federal Register later.

Mr. FAIRHILL. Acts of Congress are communicated through publication of Slip Laws and United States Statutes at Large. Slip Laws are pamphlet prints of each public and private law enacted by Congress and are issued a few days after becoming law. Later, they are bound as part of the statutes volumes. Listings of newly enacted laws appear in the Reminders section of the daily Federal Register and in the Weekly Compilation of Presidential Documents.

United States Statutes at Large are issued annually, in bound volumes, and contain all public and private laws and concurrent resolutions enacted during a session of Congress, reorganization plans, proposed and ratified amendments to the Constitution, and presidential proclamations.

The Code of Federal Regulations (CFR) is an annual culmination of the general and permanent rules published in the daily Federal Register by the agencies of the federal government. The CFR is divided into fifty titles that represent broad areas subject to federal regulation. Each title is revised at least once each calendar year. The CFR is kept up-to-date by the individual issues of the Federal Register. Therefore, the Federal Register and the CFR must be used together to determine the latest version of any given rule.

Federal regulations implement Acts of Congress and actions of the executive department.

Presidential documents are found in the Weekly Compilation of Presidential Documents which serves as a timely, up-to-date report of the public policies and activities of the president. It contains the remarks, news conferences, messages to Congress, statements, and other presidential material of a public nature issued by the White House Press Office during the week reported.

There is a codification of the Presidential Proclamations and Executive Orders which provides in one convenient reference source proclamations and Executive Orders which have general applicability and continuing effect. Each codified document is assigned to one of the fifty chapters, representing broad subject areas similar to the title designations of the Code of Federal Regulations and the United States Code.

In addition to the foregoing, there are Federal Information Centers. Persons interested in information on various aspects of the federal government, including programs and services, may visit, phone, or write Federal Information Centers, maintained throughout the country by the General Services Administration.

Mr. MADISON. Mr. Fairhill, you have noted that proposed regulations are communicated to the public by publication in the Federal Register, and the public thereby is given the opportunity to present its view. This procedure apparently applies to the executive department. You have not indicated, however, how the public gets to testify on proposed legislation in Congress.

Mr. FAIRHILL. All proposed legislation, and nearly all formal actions by either of the two Houses of Congress, take the form of a bill or a resolution. Legislation originates in several ways. The Constitution provides that the president "shall from time to time give the Congress information of the state of the Union, and recommend to their consideration such measures as he shall judge necessary and expedient."

The president fulfills this duty either by personally addressing a joint session of the two Houses or by sending messages in writing to the Congress or to either body thereof, which are received and referred to the appropriate committees. The president usually presents or submits his annual message on the state of the Union shortly after the beginning of a session.

The right of petition is guaranteed the citizens of the United States by the Constitution, and many individual petitions and memorials from state legislatures are sent to Congress. They are laid before the two Houses by their respective presiding officers or submitted by individual members of the House and Senate in their respective bodies, and are usually referred to the appropriate committees of the house in which they were submitted.

Bills to carry out the recommendations of the president are usually introduced by the chairman of the various committees or subcommittees thereof which have jurisdiction of the subject matter. Sometimes the committees themselves may submit and report to the Senate "original bills" to carry out such recommendations.

The ideas for legislative proposals may come from an individual representative or senator, from any of the executive departments of the government, from private organized groups or associates, or from any individual citizen. However, they can be introduced in their respective Houses only by senators and representatives. When introduced they are referred to the standing committees, which have jurisdiction of the subject matter.

Members frequently introduce bills that are similar in purpose, in which case the committee considering them may take one of the bills and add the best features of the others for reporting to the parent body, or draft an entirely new bill and report it (known as an "original bill") in lieu of the others.

Mr. MADISON. Mr. Fairhill, this still does not answer the question as to how the public gets involved in the detail of proposed legislation.

Mr. FAIRHILL. Committees or subcommittees of each house generally hold hearings on all major or controversial legislation before drafting the proposal into a final form for reporting to its respective house. The length of hearings and the number of witnesses testifying vary, depending upon the time element, the number of witnesses wanting to be heard, the desires of the committee to hear witnesses, and so on.

A subcommittee makes reports to its full committee, and the latter may adopt such reports without change, amend them in any way it desires, reject them, or adopt an entirely different report.

After consideration of any bill, the full committee may report it favorably with or without amendments, submit an adverse report thereon, or vote not to report anything.

Mr. MADISON. The question is still not answered.

Mr. Fairhill, just how does the public know that hearings are going to be held on certain proposed legislation?

Mr. FAIRHILL. Each hearing is generally open to the public except when the committee determines that the testimony to be taken at that hearing may relate to a matter of national security, may tend to reflect adversely on the character or reputation of the witness or any other individual, or may divulge matters deemed confidential under other provisions of law or government regulation.

With respect to any hearing open to the public, public announcement must be made of the date, place, and subject matter of the hearing at least one week before the commencement of the hearing. Any announcement made must be published in the *Daily Digest*.

Mr. MADISON. And what is the *Daily Digest*?

Mr. FAIRHILL. The *Daily Digest* is part of the *Congressional Record*. The *Congressional Record* is printed each day that the Senate or House is in session, and with rare exceptions consists of a section devoted solely to the proceedings of the Senate and a section devoted solely to the proceedings of the House, which together embody all the proceedings of both houses for the said day.

There is also a section entitled "Daily Digest" which is printed in the back of the daily issue of the *Congressional Record* devoted to a resume of committee meetings and actions taken by the two houses, and a listing of Committee meetings for the following day giving subject matter, location, and time. There is also a listing of Committee meetings scheduled ahead.

Mr. MADISON. What is the circulation of the *Congressional Record*?

Mr. FAIRHILL. The number of paid subscriptions is currently 4,769. In addition, there is an official distribution of 24,936, making a total distribution of 29,805.

Mr. MADISON. So, for 225 million persons, only about 30,000 copies of the *Congressional Record* are circulated?

Mr. FAIRHILL. Yes. You must take into account that it is available for reading to all persons through depository libraries.

Mr. MADISON. And again, how many depository libraries are there?

Mr. FAIRHILL. It is my understanding that there are 1,353 depository libraries. There are also 36 regional depositories which agree to keep a complete collection permanently.

Mr. MADISON. That certainly does not appear to me to be adequate communication of government matters.

Mr. ADAMS. Mr. Fairhill, you have been poring and pondering over various issues of the Federal Register, which you previously referred to as covering regulations and proposed regulations of the executive branch—a wide range of activities affecting all aspects of life and of concern to the public. Would you please furnish us with some actual examples of such regulations and proposed regulations.

Mr. FAIRHILL. The *Federal Register* is an official publication of the United States government, published daily, Monday through Friday, excepting holidays. In addition to regulations, it publishes presidential proclamations and federal agency documents and activities. People have the right in most instances to express their own opinion in writing or in person before a proposal becomes final. Where such privilege exists, appropriate instructions are given.

In 1979, for example, the National Aeronautics and Space Administration—NASA—issued a proposed rule covering the authority of the Space Transportation System Commander. The Space Commander is the person responsible for maintaining order and discipline of all personnel aboard a space shuttle flight, the testing for which started in 1981. In the past all persons launched into outer space had been employees of the United States government. On future flights of the space shuttle it was expected that some personnel would be flown who would be neither United States nationals nor employees of the United States government. The proposed regulation was intended to make clear that all those participating in the space shuttle flight would be subject to the authority of the Space Commander. Written comments of the public were requested. The public was assumed capable of making adequate comments on this area of government activity.

Here is another example: the Department of Interior and the Department of State announced in the *Federal Register* that they would hold a public meeting on September 11, 1979, to discuss the preparation of an environmental impact statement on a proposed Caribou Convention. A problem apparently arose since caribou herds that migrate between Alaska and Canada have substantially declined in the past quarter century. Joint management of this resource by the United States and Canada was considered essential to insure its conservation since these caribou migrate thousands of miles and frequently cross the international boundary.

Mr. ADAMS. Who would actually participate in meetings or consultation on matters of this type?

Mr. FAIRHILL. In this particular case, the secretary of the interior of the United States, the Canadian environment minister, the state department of the United States, the department of external affairs of Canada and the United States Fish and Wildlife Service were all represented in consultation on how joint management could best be implemented by international agreement between the two nations.

Dr. FRANKLIN. The committees are certainly not becoming extinct!

Mr. FAIRHILL. Look at one more example of regulations issued. In 1979 the Agricultural Marketing service issued Lemon Regulation 211. The regulation established the quantity of fresh California-Arizona lemons that may be shipped to market during a certain period. The regulation was based on recommendations and information submitted by the Lemon Administrative Committee. The Lemon Administrative Committee met on August 7, 1979 to consider supply and marketing conditions and other factors affecting the need for regulation and recommended a quantity of lemons deemed advisable to be handled during a specific week.

Dr. FRANKLIN. In whose administration was that regulation issued? President Carter's?

Mr. FAIRHILL. Yes, sir.

Dr. FRANKLIN. They used to refer to Carter's peanut administration. It apparently was changed to Carter's lemon administration!

Mr. FAIRHILL. Let's turn to a presidential proclamation. President Carter designated Monday, October 8, 1979 as Columbus Day. In his proclamation he said that 487 years had passed since an Italian navigator in the service of Spain left the Old World to find the New. Christopher Columbus, he said, was determined to test an audacious theory: to reach the East, sail west. As a nation which has always striven for the same qualities as the Great Navigator, we must continue the search for new horizons.

Mr. ADAMS. Go West, young man, the oil is in the East. That's where we erred, we should have gone east instead of west.

Dr. FRANKLIN. I think it sounds more like the three C's - Wrong Way Columbus, Wrong Way Corrigan, and Wrong Way Carter.

Mr. FAIRHILL. Another Presidential Proclamation. This one appears on page 49,235 of the August 22, 1979 issue of the *Federal Register*, as Proclamation 4674.

Mr. ADAMS. Did you say page 49,235?

Mr. FAIRHILL. Yes, sir.

Mr. ADAMS. How many pages are there in the *Federal Register* in a typical year?

Mr. FAIRHILL. Could easily run eighty to ninety thousand pages.

Dr. FRANKLIN. Incredible!

Mr. ADAMS. Please continue, Mr. Fairhill.

Mr. FAIRHILL. In the proclamation, President Carter proclaimed August 26, 1979 as Women's Equality Day. He reiterated his commitment to make the Equal Rights Amendment a part of our Constitution. He said that the Equal Rights Amendment did not legislate that men and women are the same; it simply said that the law cannot penalize women because they are female. Nor does the Equal Rights Amendment impose new, unwanted roles on women, he said; rather it safeguards their opportunity to develop their full potential in the direction they choose. He said that as women are free from arbitrary barriers and stereotypes, men are liberated as well.

President Carter's proclamation went on to say that the Equal Rights Amendment was first introduced in Congress in 1923, and that "after lengthy and careful debate," Congress submitted it to the states for ratification on March 22, 1972. In 1979, all but three of the necessary thirty-eighty states had ratified it. By the deadline date of June 30, 1982, the amendment failed of ratification.

Dr. FRANKLIN. That was quite a lengthy and careful debate. My calculation is that there were 49 years of "lengthy and careful debate" by Congress!

Mr. FAIRHILL. Just one more example and I will conclude my testimony on the question. From time to time the Federal Insurance Administration lists in the *Federal Register* locations eligible for flood insurance and gives the elevations at such locations. As a matter of background, the government maintains a National Flood Insurance Program which enables property owners to purchase flood insurance at rates made reasonable through a federal subsidy. In return, communities agree to adopt local flood management measures aimed at protecting lives and new construction from future flooding. Periodically the Federal Insurance Administrator establishes base flood elevations based on 100-year records of flood experience. These elevations are the basis for the flood management measures that a community is required to adopt in order to participate in the National Flood Insurance Program. A few of the scores of locations eligible for flood insurance and their flood elevations as reported by the Federal Insurance Administration in the Federal Register on September 4, 1979 are as follows:

Rancocas Creek, New Jersey	11 feet
Palo Alto Municipal Airport San Francisco Bay, California	7 feet
Big Timber Creek, New Jersey	10 feet
Hams Fork, Wyoming	6,917 feet

Mr. ADAMS. Mr. Fairhill, did you say flood insurance at 6,917 feet?

Mr. FAIRHILL. Yes sir.

Dr. FRANKLIN. Noah, get the ark!

Mr. MADISON. Mr. Fairhill, we thank you for your enlightening testimony today. I am certain you will contribute much before this Commission terminates its hearings.

Mr. JEFFERSON. Gentlemen, we have had a long day. The Commission will therefore adjourn until Tuesday, June 2, at 10 o'clock a.m.

TUESDAY, JUNE 2, 1987

COMMISSION'S THOUGHTS ON PRESIDENCY

The Committee met, pursuant to notice, at 10 a.m. in the Assembly Room of Independence Hall, Gen. George Washington presiding.

        Present: Mr. John Adams, Dr. Benjamin Franklin, Mr. Thomas Jefferson, Mr. James Madison and Gen. George Washington.

Gen. WASHINGTON. We have listened to testimony relating to the growth of the government of this nation over a period of about two hundred years. In our time the Constitution provided for three branches of national government: legislative, executive, and judicial. The legislative, to make the laws; the executive to "take care that the laws be faithfully executed"; and the judicial, to adjudicate cases and controversies arising out of the Constitution. The Constitution still provides for three branches of national government. It has not changed in this respect. But as we listen to testimony we learn that the government has grown to gargantuan dimensions, and that it has, in effect, cross-pollinated. By this I mean that each of the branches has assumed some of the characteristics of the other. For example, we have heard testimony that agencies of the executive branch "legislate" by issuing regulations. The Supreme Court, in *Marbury* v. *Madison* in 1803, claimed the right to examine the constitutionality of acts performed by the other two branches. Congress has established independent regulatory agencies which take care that the laws are faithfully executed. There is therefore a tremendous interplay between the branches and a large measure of overlapping of activity.

In terms of sheer size, we note that we have gone from a population of 3.9 million in 1790 to over 225 million today. We note that the executive branch has grown from 4,479 persons in 1816, the first year for which statistics of this type are available, to over 2.8 million today. It is interesting to note that the 4,479 persons employed in the executive branch in 1816 consisted of 3,341 in the post office, 190 in defense, and 938 in other departments of the executive branches. In Congress, the Senate has grown from 26 to 100; the House of Representatives, from 65 to 435. In 1790 each congressman represented an average of about 60,000 constituents. Today, each congressman represents an average of over 500,000 constituents. In the judicial branch, the original six-member Supreme Court has grown to nine and an entire federal judiciary consisting of 132 judges in the United States Courts of Appeals, 485 judges in the United States District Courts, plus judges in Territorial Courts and special courts, such as the United States Customs and Patent Appeals and the United States Tax Court. It seems to me that we must reflect and ask ourselves, is this what we expected? Is this what we intended? Was this our vision of a future America? Let us examine our own thoughts and visions in our time, of this time, at this time.

The Commission will proceed. Mr. Jefferson.

Mr. JEFFERSON. While I tend to agree with the course of discussion taken by you, General, I would like to remind you, sir, that we are yet without an agenda, and that if we proceed in this manner and follow the course of testimony it would appear to me that we should narrow our discussions to where we have been taken by the testimony—namely, the executive department, and then the office of the president itself.

You asked the question, General, what was our vision of a future America?

I believed, then, that our country was too large to have all its affairs directed by a single government. Public servants at such a distance, and away from under the eye of their constituents, must, from the circumstance of distance, be unable to administer and overlook all the details necessary for the good government of the citizens. The same circumstances, by rendering detection impossible to their constituents, invites the public agents to corruption, plunder and waste. And I verily believed, that if the principle were to prevail, of a common law being in force in the United States . . . it would become the most corrupt government on earth.

I believed that an augmentation of the field for jobbing, speculating, plundering, office-building and office-hunting would be produced by an assumption of all the state powers into the hands of the general government.

The true theory of our constitution is surely the wisest and best, that the states are independent as to everything within themselves, and united as to everything respecting foreign nations.

I believed that the general government should be reduced to foreign concerns only . . . and our general government reduced to a very simple organization, and a very inexpensive one; a few plain duties to be performed by a few servants.

Mr. ADAMS. And when did you make these beliefs known?

Mr. JEFFERSON. In 1800.

Mr. MADISON. I do not believe we are here today to reargue the issue of states rights, but in what you say, you appear to tend toward a different separation of government than that which actually eventuated. Can you elaborate?

Mr. JEFFERSON. It is a fatal heresy to suppose that either our state governments are superior to the federal, or the federal to the states. The people, to whom all authority belongs, have divided the powers of government into two distinct departments, the leading characters of which are foreign and domestic; and they have appointed for each a distinct set of functionaries. These they have made co-ordinate, checking and balancing each other, like the three cardinal departments in the individual states: each equally supreme as to the powers delegated to itself, and neither authorized ultimately to decide what belongs to itself, or its coparcener in government.

I saw . . . the rapid strides with which the federal branch of our government advanced toward the ursurpation of all the rights reserved to the states, and the consolidation in itself of all powers, foreign and domestic.

In essence, I was for preserving to the states the powers not yielded by them to the Union . . and I was not for transferring all the powers of the states to the general government . . .

I was for a government rigorously frugal and simple, applying all the possible savings of the public revenue to the discharge of the national debt; and not for the multiplication of officers and salaries merely to make partisans and for increasing by every device, the public debt, on the principle of its being a public blessing.

Mr. MADISON. I was not unaware that in a country wide and expanding as ours is, and in the anxiety to convey information to the door of every citizen, an unforseen multiplication of offices may add a weight to the executive scale, disturbing the equilibrium of the government. I should therefore see with pleasure a guard against the evil, by whatever regulations having that effect may be within the scope of legislative power; or, if necessary, even by an amendment of the Constitution when a lucid interval of party excitement shall invite the experiment.

Mr. Jefferson, you have assigned domestic affairs to the states and foreign affairs to the federal government. The fact is, that's what we spend most of our time on in the Federal Convention of 1787—states' versus federal rights. The states were granted representation and equal voting in the Senate under the original Constitution, which provided in Section 3 that "The Senate of the United States shall be composed of two Senators from each State chosen by the Legislature thereof . . ." The Seventeenth Amendment changed all that in 1913. The amendment provided that "The Senate of the United States shall be composed of two Senators from each State elected by the people thereof. . . ." So the format of representation originally agreed to, which gave to the states great power, was lost in the Seventeenth Amendment. How did this come about?

The ratification of the Seventeenth Amendment was the outcome of increasing popular dissatisfaction with the operation of the originally established method of electing senators. As the franchise became exercisable by greater numbers of people, the belief became widespread that senators ought to be popularly elected in the same manner as representatives. Acceptance of this idea was fostered by the mounting accumulation of evidence of the practical disadvantages and malpractices attendant upon legislative selection, such as deadlocks within legislatures resulting in vacancies remaining unfilled for substantial intervals, the influencing of legislative selection by corrupt political organizations and special interest groups through purchase of legislative seats, and the neglect of duties by legislators as a consequence of protracted electoral contests. Prior to ratification, however, many states had perfected arrangements calculated to afford the voters more effective control over the selection of senators. State laws were amended to enable voters participating in primary elections to designate their preference for one of several party candidates for a senatorial seat, and nominations unofficially effected thereby were transmitted to the legislature. Although their action rested upon a stronger foundation than common understanding, the legislatures generally elected the winning candidate of the majority, and, indeed, in two states, candidates for legislative seats were required to promise to support, without regard to party ties, the senatorial candidate polling the most votes. As a result of such developments, at least twenty-nine states by 1912, one year before ratification, were nominating senators on a popular basis, and, as a consequence, the constitutional discretion of the legislatures had been reduced to little more than that retained by presidential electors.

With all this in mind, Mr. Jefferson, I do not believe we should reargue this issue. However, I do believe that there is much to what you say when you divide national functions into two parts—namely, domestic and foreign. It would almost appear as though you need a president for each part—or perhaps, a vice-president for each part.

Mr. ADAMS. All of which brings us back to the weight of government affairs on the office of the president.

Dr. FRANKLIN. Before Mr. Adams pursues any course of discussion on the presidency, I would like to make a few remarks continuing the subject Mr. Jefferson and Mr. Madison were addressing themselves to, relative to the structure of Congress.

At the time of and after the Federal Convention, I was of the opinion that the two chambers were not necessary. I knew I would have nothing to do with the execution of it, being determined to quit all public business with my then present employment. At eighty-three one certainly had a right to ambition repose.

As to the two chambers, I was of the opinion that one alone would be better; but my dear friends, nothing in human affairs and schemes is perfect; and perhaps that is the case of our opinions.

When I wrote the first draft of the Articles of Confederation in 1775, I provided for a unicameral legislature. The Pennsylvania Constitution, adopted in 1776 and which I helped draft, provided for a unicameral legislature. The Articles of Confederation under which the United States of America functioned until 1789 provided for a unicameral Congress.

Mr. MADISON. I might add, in your behalf, Dr. Franklin, that my notes of the Federal Convention for Thursday May 31, 1787 read that the resolution "that the National Legislature ought to consist of two branches was agreed to without debate or dissent, except that of Pennsylvania, given probably from complaisance to Doctor Franklin, who was understood to be partial to a single house of legislation."

Dr. FRANKLIN. A two-branched legislature? Has not the famous political Fable of the Snake, with two heads and one body, some useful instruction contained in it? She was going to a brook to drink and on her way was to pass through a hedge, a twig of which opposed her direct course; one head chose to go on the right side of the twig, the other on the left; so that time was spent in the contest, and, before the decision was completed, the poor snake died with thirst. So then, what purpose does a dual-branched legislature serve today, particularly where its original purpose had been scuttled by the Seventeenth Amendment?

Mr. ADAMS. Why a second chamber? I'll tell you

why. There is a story that, on his return from France, Mr. Jefferson called General Washington to account at the breakfast table for having agreed to a second chamber. "Why," asked Washington, "did you pour that coffee into your saucer?" "To cool it," quoth Mr. Jefferson. "Even so," said Gen. Washington, "we pour legislation into the senatorial saucer to cool it."

Gen. WASHINGTON. Dr. Franklin, I am of the opinion that we should reserve discussion of the structure of Congress to a later time and resume discussion of Mr. Jefferson's topic—namely, the office of the president. In approaching this subject it would appear that each of us, excepting Dr. Franklin, having served as president of the United States—in fact, we are the first four presidents—have had experiences in the office which we should discuss frankly at this time. In other words, how did we feel, individually, about the office?

Dr. FRANKLIN. (Aside to Mr. Adams) Sounds like this is going to be the "Face to Face" program on T.V.—only it's "President to President."

Mr. JEFFERSON. Let's see, I was the third president of the United States and I served from 1801 to 1809. In January, 1807 I received a letter from my ancient friend, John Dickinson. . .

Mr. ADAMS. (Aside to Dr. Franklin) His ancient friend, John Dickinson! He wasn't a friend of mine, that piddling genius.

Dr. FRANKLIN. (Aside to Mr. Adams) Nor mine.

Mr. JEFFERSON. In it he advised me that the people settled in the territory ceded by France to the United States— the territory of Orleans—were universally dissatisfied with our government. In the same month, I answered his letter advising him that I was already aware of the great discontents existing among the French inhabitants of the territory of Orleans and I cited the sources of their discontent. The reasons are not important for our discussion here, but in my closing lines I did make these comments upon the presidency: "I have tired you, my friend, with a long letter. But your tedium will end in a few lines more. Mine has two years to endure. I am tired of an office where

I can do no more good, than many others who would be glad to be employed in it. To myself, personally, it brings nothing but increasing drudgery and daily loss of friends. My only consolation is in the belief that my fellow citizens at large give me credit for good intentions. I will certainly endeavor to merit the continuance of that good will which follows well-intended actions, and their approbation will be the dearest reward I can carry into retirement." Gentlemen, those were my thoughts, expressed privately.

Mr. ADAMS. Mr. Jefferson, did you have a solution in mind?

Mr. JEFFERSON. Yes, my opinion originally was that the president of the United States should have been elected for seven years, and forever ineligible afterwards. I have since become sensible that seven years is too long to be irremovable, and that there should be a peaceable way of withdrawing a man in midway who is doing wrong. The service for eight years, with a power to remove at the end of the first four, comes nearly to my principle as corrected by experience; and it is in adherence to that, that I was determined to withdraw at the end of my second term. General Washington set the example of voluntary retirement after eight years. I followed it.

Gen. WASHINGTON. Thank you, Mr. Jefferson. Mr. Madison had the papers on my own conflict with thoughts of standing for reelection for a second term and I have asked him to relate this information to this Commission.

Mr. MADISON. In consequence of a note I received from President Washington, requesting me to call on him, I did so on May 5, 1792. He opened the conversation by observing that, having some time ago communicated to me his intention of retiring from public life on the expiration of his four years—that is, at the end of his first term—he wished to advise with me on the mode and time most proper for making known that intention. He had, he said, spoken with no one yet on those particular points, and took this opportunity of mentioning them to me, that I might consider the matter, and give him my opinion before the adjournment of Congress, or my departure from

Philadelphia.

His disinclination to continue as president was becoming every day more and more fixed; so that he wished to make up his mind as soon as possible. I held it a duty to offer my opinion that his retiring at the present juncture might have effects that ought not to be hazarded; that I was not unaware of the urgency of his inclination, or of the peculiar motives he might feel to withdraw himself from a situation into which it was so well known to myself he had entered with a scrupulous reluctance.

He could not believe or conceive himself any wise necessary to the successful administration of the government; that, on the contrary he had from the beginning found himself deficient in many of the essential qualifications, owing to his inexperience in the forms of public business, his unfitness to judge of legal questions, and questions arising out of the Constitution; that others more conversant in such matters would be better able to execute the trust; that he found himself, also, in the decline of life, his health becoming sensibly more infirm, and perhaps his faculties also; that the fatigues and disagreeableness of his situation were in fact scarcely tolerable to him; that he only uttered his real sentiments when he declared that his inclination would lead him rather to go to his farm, take his spade in his hand, and work for his bread, than remain in his present situation.

I was led by this explanation to remark to him, that however novel or difficult the business might have been to him, it could not be doubted that, with the aid of the official opinions and informations within his command, his judgment must have been as competent in all cases as that of anyone who could have been put in his place, and, in many cases, certainly more so; that in the great point of conciliating and uniting all parties under a government which had excited such violent controversies and divisions, it was well known that his services had been in a manner essential; that with respect to the spirit of party that was taking place under the operations of the government, I was sensible of its existence, but considered that as an argument for his remaining, rather than retiring, until the public opinion, the character of the government, and the course of its administration, should be better decided.

I could not forbear thinking that although his retirement might not be fatal to the public good, yet a postponement of it was another sacrifice exacted by his patriotism.

On Wednesday evening, May 9, 1972, understanding that the president was to set out the ensuing morning for Mount Vernon, I called on him to let him know that, as far as I had formed an opinion on the subject he had mentioned to me, it was in favor of a direct address of notification to the public, in time for its proper effect on the election; which I thought might be put into such form as would avoid every appearance of presumption or indelicacy, and seemed to be absolutely required by his situation. I observed that no other mode deserving consideration had occurred. I added, that if on further reflection I should view the subject in any new lights, I would make it the subject of a letter, though I retained my hopes that it would not yet be necessary for him to come to any opinion on it. He begged that I would do so and also suggest any matters that might occur as proper to be included in what he might say to Congress at the opening of their next session, passing over the idea of his relinquishing his purpose of retiring in a manner that did not indicate the slightest assent to it.

On Friday, May 25, 1792, I met the president on the road returning from Mount Vernon to Philadelphia, when he handed me a letter dated the 20th of May, 1792. I request that the contents of the letter be entered upon the record at this place. I quote:

> As there is a possibility, if not a probability, that I shall not see you on your return home; or, if I should see you, that it may be on the road and under circumstances which will prevent my speaking to you on the subject we last conversed upon, I take the liberty of committing to paper the following thoughts and requests.
>
> I have not been unmindful of the sentiments expressed by you in the conversations just alluded to; on the contrary I have again, and again revolved them, with thoughtful anxiety; but without being able to dispose my mind to a longer continuation in the office I have now the

honor to hold. I therefore still look forward to the fulfillment of my fondest and most ardent wishes to spend the remainder of my days (which I cannot expect will be many) in ease and tranquility.

Nothing short of conviction that my dereliction of the Chair of Government (if it should be the desire of the people to continue me in it) would involve the country in serious disputes respecting the chief magistrate, and the disagreeable consequences which might result therefrom in the floating, and divided opinions which seem to prevail at present, could, in any wise, induce me to relinquish the determination I have formed. . . .

Under these impressions then, permit me to reiterate the request I made to you at our last meeting—namely—to think of the proper time and the best mode of announcing the intention; and that you would prepare the letter.

I would fain carry my request to you farther than is asked above, although I am sensible that your compliance with it must add to your trouble; but as the recess may afford you leisure, and I flatter myself you have dispositions to oblige me, I will, without apology desire . . . that you would turn your thoughts to a Valedictory address from me to the public; expressing in plain and modest terms—that having been honored with the Presidential Chair, and to the best of my abilities contributed to the organization and administration of the government—that having arrived at a period of life when private walks in the shade of retirement become necessary and will be most pleasing to me; and the spirit of the government may render a rotation in the elective officers of it more congenial with their ideas of liberty and safety, that I take my leave of them as a public man. . . .

I answered President Washington's letter on June 21, 1792 and enclosed a draft of a farewell address but repeated my ardent wish and hope that our country may not, at this important conjuncture, be deprived of the inestimable advantage of having him at the head of its counsels. I now request that portions of the draft of the formal address I prepared for President Washington for use at the end of his first term be included in the record. It reads, in part:

    Substance of farewell address drafted by James Madison for use by President Washington at the end of his first term.

    The period which will close the appointment with which my fellow-citizens have honored me being not very distant, and the time actually arrived at which their thoughts must be designating the citizen who is to administer the executive government of the U.S. during the ensuing term, it may be requisite to a more distinct expression of the public voice that I should apprise such of my fellow-citizens as may retain their partiality towards me, that I am not to be numbered among those out of whom a choice is to be made.
. . .

    The impressions under which I entered on the present arduous trust were explained on the proper occasion. In discharge of this trust, I can only say that I have contributed toward the organization and administration of the government the best exertions of which a very fallible judgment was capable. For any errors which may have flowed from this source, I feel all the regret which an anxiety for the public good can excite; not without the double consolation, however, arising from a consciousness of their being involuntary, and an experience of the candor which will interpret them. If there were any circumstances which could give value to my inferior qualifications for the trust, these circumstances must have been temporary. In this light was the undertaking viewed when I ventured upon it. Being, moreover, still farther advanced into the decline of life, I am every day more sensible that the increasing weight of years renders the private walks of it in the shade of retirement as necessary as they will be acceptable to me. May I be allowed to add that it will be among the highest, as well as the purest enjoyments that can sweeten the remnant of my days, to partake in a private station, in the midst of my fellow-citizens, of that benign influence of good laws under a free government which has been the ultimate object of all our wishes, and in which I confide as the happy reward of our cares and labors? May I be allowed further to add, as a consideration far more important, that an early example of rotation in an office of so high and delicate a nature may equally accord with the republican spirit of our Constitution, and the ideas of liberty and safety entertained by the people. . . .

We have established a common government, which, being free in its principles, being founded in our own choice, being intended as the guardian of our common rights and the patron of our common interests, and wisely containing within itself a provision for its own amendment as experience may point out its errors, seems to promise everything that can be expected from such an institution; and if supported by wise counsels, by virtuous conduct, and by mutual and friendly allowances, must approach as near to perfection as any human work can aspire, and nearer than any which the annals of mankind have recorded.

With these wishes and hopes I shall make my exit from civil life, and I have taken the same liberty of expressing them which I formerly used in offering the sentiments which were suggested by my exit from military life.

Of course, as history knows, this address was never given. Mr. Alexander Hamilton and Mr. Thomas Jefferson were among the friends of the president who urged that he run for another term. When the electors met early in 1793, the only contest was between John Adams, who received seventy-seven votes for vice-president, and George Clinton, who got fifty. Gen. Washington once again was the unanimous choice for president.

First REPORTER. (From the *Washington Post*) Do you think anyone will believe us if we report that George Washington never wanted a second term, and that the alleged precedent for a two-term president was really a legend?

Second REPORTER. (From the *Washington Post*) They'll never believe us! They'll all think we are two-timing history if we say he never wanted to be a two-termer.

Dr. FRANKLIN. As a matter of interest, since President Washington did not draft this farewell address, did he draft the farewell address he delivered in 1797?

Mr. MADISON. In August, 1796, Mr. Hamilton prepared the first draft of the president's farewell address. We should say that the president prepared a farewell address with Mr. Hamilton's help. Contrary to what you suggest, that address was never delivered, but was instead widely published, first in Philadelphia in the *American Daily Advertiser* on September 19, 1796. The reason it wasn't delivered personally by the president is evident from its contents. It apprised the citizens of his resolution to decline consideration of his name for the further administration of the executive government. He wanted to do this well in advance of the new election to enable the citizens sufficient time to consider designating the person who was to be clothed with that important trust.

Dr. FRANKLIN. In other words, President Washington had at least two ghost writers.

Mr. ADAMS. Frankly, the discussion on authorship serves no further purpose. The point has already been made that by virtue of President Washington's desire to vacate his office at the end of his first term, as discussed with Mr. Madison, he had disclosed his feelings about the office.

Gen. WASHINGTON. That is correct, and shortly after my reelection in 1793 I wrote my old and close friend Gov. Henry Lee of Virginia, telling him, "to say I feel pleasure from commencing another tour of duty would be a departure from the truth; for however it might savor of affection in the opinion of the world . . . my particular, and confidential friends well know, that it was after a long and painful conflict in my own breast, that I was withheld . . . from requesting, in time, that no vote might be thrown away upon me; it being my fixed determination to return to the walks of private life at the end of my term."

Lastly, I must admit that before my first term as president I wrote my good friend the Marquis de Lafayette, telling him that the presidency had no enticing charms, and no fascinating allurements for me.

Gentlemen, these were my sentiments concerning the office of the president of the United States. Mr. Adams, would you continue this discussion?

Mr. ADAMS. Certainly. Let me say first that I was never an idolater and never one to mince words, and I am sure my friend Gen. Washington will tolerate and perhaps accept my apologies for my thoughts in 1790 about the growing Washington legend. I remember saying,

> The History of our Revolution will be one continued lie from one end to the other. The essence of the whole will be that Dr. Franklin's electrical rod smote the earth and out sprung General Washington. That Franklin electrified him with his rod—and thence forward these two conducted all the policy, negotiations, legislatures, and war. ... If this letter should be preserved and read one hundred years hence the reader will say, "the envy of this John Adams could not bear to think of the Truth! He ventured to scribble . . . blasphemy that he dared not speak when he lived. But barkers at the sun and moon are always silly curs." But this . . . is the fate of all ages and nations . . . No nation can adore more than one man at a time. It is a happy circumstance that the object of our devotion is so well deserving of it; that he has virtue so exquisite and wisdom so consummate. There is no citizen of America who will say that there is in the world so fit a man for the head of the nation. From my soul I think there is not; and the question should not be who has done or suffered most, or who has been the most essential and indispensable cause of the Revolution, but who is the best qualified to govern us?

As I look back at my own term as president—and I had only one term—I can recall several incidents appropriate to this subject.

The people elected me to administer the government, it is true. I administered it from Quincy, Massachusetts, as readily as I could do it at Philadelphia. The secretaries of state, treasury, war, navy, and the attorney-general transmitted me daily by the post all the business of consequence, and nothing was done without my advice and direction, any more than when I was in the same city with them. The post went very rapidly, and I answered by the return of it, so that nothing suffered or was lost.

At the mid-term of my single term I felt that the business of the office was so oppressive that I could hardly support it two years longer. I thought that if I could have my wish, there should never be a show or a feast made for the president while I held office. Lastly, had I been chosen president again, I am certain I could not have lived another year. Gentlemen, these were my sentiments.

Mr. MADISON. It may be difficult for me to describe the presidency in terms of a burden. It is perhaps easier to talk of embarrassment. Who else was president when the City of Washington was captured by the British, when the capitol was burned, when the White House was substantially burned, when we fought a battle after the war was over—the Battle of New Orleans, in January 1815. I was president, to my chagrin . . . It was the War of 1812, as they call it today. Then it was known as the Second War of Independence. America found itself threatened with national extermination . . . her people torn by dissension . . . her treasury empty . . . her economy in ruins . . . her coasts blockaded and defenseless . . . her army bogged down . . . her navy bottled up. And yet within eight months all changed. America was at peace, her people unified, her economy mending, her army and navy bursting with pride.

Mr. ADAMS. Wasn't the Gilbert Stuart portrait of George Washington saved by your wife, Dolley?

Mr. MADISON. Yes. The full-length portrait was hanging on the west wall of the dining room in the White House. It was the showpiece of the mansion. Ironically, nobody could get it down. It was screwed too tightly to the wall. Dolley ordered the frame broken and the canvas taken out. It was done and placed in the hands of two gentlemen from New York, for safekeeping.

Gen. WASHINGTON. Thank you. My unequivocal thanks.

Mr. ADAMS. Mr. Madison, are there any personal thoughts of yours on the office of the president?

Mr. MADISON. No, but the advice nearest to my heart and deepest in my convictions is that the Union of the States be cherished and perpetuated. Let the enemy to it be regarded as a Pandora with her box opened; and the disguised one, as the Serpent creeping with his deadly wiles into Paradise.

Dr. FRANKLIN. (Aside to Mr. Jefferson) How typically Jemmy! He hasn't changed a bit. I was scanning through Thomas Rodney's diary and noted his description of Madison at the time he was a delegate to the Continental Congress in 1781. It read, "I take notice of a Mr. Madison of Virginia, who with some little reading in the Law is just from the College and possesses all the self-conceit that is common to youth and inexperience in the like cases—but it is unattended with that gracefulness and ease which some times makes even the impertinence of youth and inexperience agreeable or at least not offensive."

Nor has his stature altered. His one-time private secretary, Edward Coles, later governor of Illinois, described him as "about five feet, six inches, of a small and delicate form, of rather a tawny complexion, bespeaking a sedentary and studious man. His hair was dark brown, his eyes were bluish, but not of a bright blue."

Gen. WASHINGTON. It seems to me . . .

Dr. FRANKLIN. Mr. Chairman, just a word, please. As the only member of this commission who was not a president of the United States, I feel somewhat left out. However, without casting a stone, or laying claim to envy I say—of learned fools I have seen ten times ten; of unlearned wise men I have seen a hundred.

Mr. JEFFERSON. When did you first say that? . . .

Dr. FRANKLIN. In my *Poor Richard's Almanack* in 1735.

Gen. WASHINGTON. It seems to me that three out of four of us who served as president of the United States had definite negative feelings about the job. If we, who are all considered founders of this country, had this disposition toward the position, how did our successors feel? Were we alone in our sentiments or were other presidents of the same ilk? It seems to me that we ought to invite some of the successor presidents to sit with us and candidly discuss this matter and such other matters as may be deemed advisable.

Mr. ADAMS. Aye.

Mr. JEFFERSON. Aye.

Mr. MADISON. Aye.

Dr. FRANKLIN. Aye.

Gen. WASHINGTON. Accordingly, this Commission is adjourned until Wednesday June 3rd at 10 o'clock a.m.

WEDNESDAY, JUNE 3, 1987

TESTIMONY OF PRESIDENTS: JOHN QUINCY ADAMS TO JAMES BUCHANAN

The Committee met, pursuant to notice, at 10 a.m. in the Assembly Room of Independence Hall, Gen. George Washington presiding.

    Present: Mr. John Adams, Dr. Benjamin Franklin, Mr. Thomas Jefferson, Mr. James Madison and Gen. George Washington.

    Gen. WASHINGTON. Today we continue our session by inviting various past presidents to discuss with us their personal feelings toward the office of the presidency, an office which, as we have already determined, three members of the Commission did not relish. The question which we have agreed to explore today relates to the extent to which any of the presidents who followed us into the office had similar thoughts of the office.

    With this object we welcome at this session today former presidents John Quincy Adams, Andrew Jackson, Martin Van Buren, James K. Polk, and James Buchanan. Gentlemen, we welcome you all.

    Our first speaker will be John Quincy Adams. Mr. Adams—John Quincy—has the distinction of being the only president who was the son of another. He served as president, like his father, for one term only . . .

    Dr. FRANKLIN. I am compelled to interrupt for just a moment to advise John Quincy that he and his father should not be perturbed at having served only one term each. After all, we only allow two terms to a family.

Mr. JOHN QUINCY ADAMS. Is that true?

Mr. MADISON. No, he is just jesting.

Mr. JEFFERSON. I don't think that jest just.

Dr. FRANKLIN. But my jest is just a gesture. . .

Gen. WASHINGTON. Gentlemen, please allow me to continue.

As a matter of background, John Quincy Adams was the sixth president of the United States; he was born in Braintree, Massachusetts, July 11, 1767; acquired his early education in Europe; attended the University of Leyden; was graduated from Harvard University in 1788; studied law; was admitted to the bar and commenced practice in Boston, Massachusetts. He was elected to the United States Senate and served from March 4, 1803, until June 8, 1808, and was secretary of state, in the cabinet of President Monroe (1817-25). In 1925, the election of the president of the United States fell upon the House of Representatives, as neither of the candidates had secured a majority of the electors chosen by the states. Mr. Adams, who stood second to Andrew Jackson in the electoral vote, was chosen and served from March 4, 1825 to March 3, 1829; he was later elected as a Whig to the twenty-second and to the eight succeeding Congresses.

Mr. Adams, we are pleased to have you among us.

Mr. MADISON. Mr. Adams, we are discussing the burden of the presidency and would like you to share with us your thoughts of the office you held.

Mr. J. Q. ADAMS. I can give it to you in a nutshell. The four most miserable years of my life were my four years in the presidency.

Mr. MADISON. I am certain this is not all you have to say. Did you express or suppress those feelings?

Mr. J. Q. ADAMS. No one knows, and few can conceive, the agony of mind that I suffered from the time that I was made by circumstances, and not by my volition, a candidate for the presidency till I was dismissed from that station by the failure of my reelection. They were feelings to be suppressed; and they were suppressed.

I could never be sure of writing a line that would not some day be published by friend or foe. Nor could I write a sentence susceptible of an odious misconstruction but it will be seized upon and bandied about like a watchword for hatred and derision. This condition of things gave style the cramp.

But it was not limited to my administration. The most popular of all the objections to the Constitution had been the accumulation of power in the office of the president. In President Washington's term, exercise of those powers was watched with a jealous and suspicius eye—his personal deportment and his domestic establishment were treasured up and doled out in whispers and surmises that he was affecting the state, and adopting the forms of a monarchy.

Mr. MADISON. Any other thoughts about the job?

Mr. J. Q. ADAMS. I can scarcely conceive a more harassing, wearying, teasing condition of existence than the office of the presidency. It literally renders life burdensome. It was perpetual motion and crazing cares. The weight grew heavier from day to day.

Mr. MADISON. In what other way can you characterize the office?

Mr. J. Q. ADAMS. I do have a pet subject. The example of President Washington retiring from the presidency after a double term of four years was followed by Mr. Jefferson, against the urgent solicitations of several state legislatures. This second example of voluntary self-chastened ambition by the decided approbation of public opinion has been held obligatory upon their successors and had become a tacit subsidiary Constitutional law. Every change of a president of the United States has exhibited some variety of policy from that of his predecessor. In more than one case, the change has extended to political and even to moral principle, but the policy of the country has been fashioned far more by the influences of public opinion and the prevailing humours in the two Houses of Congress, than by the judgment, the will, or the principles of the president of the United States. The president himself is no more than a representative of public opinion at the time of his election; and as public opinion is subject to great and frequent fluctuations, he must accomodate his policy to them; or the people will speedily give him a successor; or either House of Congress will effectually control his power. It is thus that the government of our country, instead of being the most simple democracy, is the most complicated government on the face of the globe.

Gen. WASHINGTON. Thank you Mr. John Quincy Adams. We would most appreciate if you would remain with us for today's session and feel free to enter into our discussion.

Our next speaker will be Mr. Andrew Jackson. Mr. Jackson was the seventh president of the United States; he was born in such obscurity on March 15, 1767, that two states have claimed his birthplace, though he himself stated that he had been told it was in the Maxhaw settlement, now Lancaster County, in South Carolina. During the Revolution he was captured by the British and confined in a stockade at Camden, South Carolina; he studied law in Salisbury, North Carolina. He was a delegate to the convention that framed a constitution for Tennessee and upon the admission of Tennessee as a state into the Union, he was elected to the Fourth Congress and served from December 5, 1796, to March 3, 1797; he was elected to the United States Senate for the term commencing March 4, 1797. He served in the Creek War of 1813 and was commissioned brigadier general in the United States Army April 19, 1814, and major general, May 1, 1814. He led his army to New Orleans, where he defeated the British January 8, 1815, for which he received the thanks of Congress and a gold medal. He later commanded an expedition which captured Florida in 1817, was governor of Florida, and was elected president of the United States in 1828 and reelected in 1832, serving from March 4, 1829 to March 3, 1837.

Andrew Jackson was the first president from west of the Alleghenies, and the first other than from Virginia or Massachusetts. We welcome the charismatic "Old Hickory," former President Andrew Jackson.

Mr. ADAMS. The question before us, as you know, is the extent, if any, to which the presidency became a burden to the president holding office. Your reaction? Your recollection?

Mr. JACKSON. I can with truth say mine was a situation of dignified slavery.

Dr. FRANKLIN. All you presidents seem to characterize the office in a nutshell—as a nut-house.

Gen. WASHINGTON. Dr. Franklin!

Mr. ADAMS. Is there no salvation in the presidency?

Mr. JACKSON. I thought that if I could restore to our institutions their primitive simplicity and purity, could succeed in banishing extraneous corrupting influences which tend to fasten monopoly and aristocracy on the constitution and make the government an engine of oppression to the people intead of the agent of their will, I might then look back to the honors conferred upon me with feelings of just pride—with the consciousness that they have not been bestowed altogether in vain.

Mr. ADAMS. Do you have any specific recommendations?

Mr. JACKSON. It was a leading object with you, the framers of the Constitution, to keep as separate as possible the actions of the legislative and executive branches of the government. To secure this object nothing is more essential than to preserve the former from all temptations of private interest, and therefore so to direct the patronage of the latter as not to permit such temptations to be offered. Experience abundantly demonstrates that every precaution in this respect is a valuable safeguard of liberty, and one which my reflections upon the tendencies of our system incline me to think should be made still stronger.

The agent most likely to contravene this design of the Constitution is the chief magistrate. In order, particularly, that his appointment may as far as possible be placed beyond the reach of any improper influences, I can not too earnestly invite your attention to the propriety of promoting an amendment of the Constitution as will render him ineligible after one term of service. In connection with such an amendment it would seem advisable to limit the service of the chief magistrate to a single term of either four or six years.

Gen. WASHINGTON. Thank you Mr. Jackson. We would be most pleased if you would remain with us for the balance of today's session. Please feel free to enter into our discussion.

Next we have on the agenda Mr. Martin Van Buren. Mr. Van Buren was the eighth president of the United States. Interestingly, Mr. Van Buren was the first president born after the Declaration of Independence.

Mr. Van Buren was born in Kinderhook, New York, December, 1782, attended the district schools and Kinderhook Academy, studied law, was admitted to the bar in New York City and commenced practice in Kinderhook, New York in 1803. A member of the state senate from 1813 to 1820, he was attorney general of New York from 1815 to 1819, was elected to the United States Senate and reelected in 1827, serving from March 4, 1821 until December 20, 1828. He served as governor of New York from January 1 to March 12, 1829, was appointed secretary of state in the cabinet of President Andrew Jackson and served from March 28, 1829, until his resignation, effective May 23, 1831, when he was commissioned minister to Great Britain; the Senate rejected his nomination January 25, 1832, and he returned to the United States. Elected vice-president of the United States on the ticket with Andrew Jackson, he served from March 4, 1833 to March 3, 1837. He was elected president of the United States and served from March 4, 1837 to March 3, 1841.

Dr. FRANKLIN. (Aside to Mr. Jefferson) Tom, Van Buren was a sagacious lawyer—a very clever lawyer—in fact, so clever he was called the "Red Fox of Kinderhook." General Washington and I are the only members of this Commission who are non-lawyers. I think I know you well enough to tell you what I thought of lawyers. The course of the Courts is so tedious and the expense so high that the remedy, "Justice," is worse than "Injustice," the "Disease." In my travels, I once saw a sign called "The Two Men at Law"; one of them was painted on one side, in a melancholy posture, all in rags, with this Scroll, "I have lost my Cause." The other was drawn capering for joy, on the other side, with these words, "I have gained my suit"; but he was stark naked.

Gen. WASHINGTON. Gentlemen, Mr. Van Buren.

Mr. VAN BUREN. I must not be understood by anything I say here as undervaluing the honor, dignity, and usefulness of the presidential office. No American citizen can fail to regard that position as, in every respect, the most exalted, as it is the most responsible public trust that can be conferred on man, for the acquisition of which no sacrifices, on the part of one competent to discharge its duties, can be deemed too great which do not include the sacrifice of honor or morality. But the extent to which personal happiness and enjoyment will be promoted by its possession is a question to be solved by the taste and temperament of the incumbent. There are men, and not a few, who derive so much pleasure from the mere possession of great power that any degree of dissatisfaction caused by its exercise is not too dear a price for the coveted indulgence, and the personal adulation which is sure to follow the footsteps of authority while it last fills the measure of their satisfaction. Those better regulated minds, however, whose gratification on reaching that high office is mainly derived from the consciousness that their countrymen have deemed them worthy of it and from the hope that they may be able to justify that confidence and to discharge its duties so as to promote the public good, will save themselves from great disappointments by postponing all thoughts of individual enjoyment to the completion of their labors. If those whose sense of duty and whose dispositions are of the character which alone can fit them for that station look to secure much personal gratification while swaying the rod of power, they will find in that as in all other human calculations and plans "begun on earth below," that, "The ample proposition that hope makes, Fails in the promis'd largeness."

Dr. FRANKLIN. (Aside to Mr. Jefferson) What is that arse talking about!

Mr. MADISON. Mr. Van Buren. You are somewhat floating over our heads—at least mine. Can you be a little clearer—maybe even *much* clearer?

Mr. VAN BUREN. At the very head of presidential disappointments is the experience truly described by Mr. Jefferson when he said that the two happiest days of his life were those of his entrance upon his office and of his surrender of it. The truth of the matter may be stated in a word: whilst to have been deemed worthy by a majority of the people of the United States to fill the office of chief magistrate of the Republic is an honor which ought to satisfy the aspirations of the most ambitious citizen, the period of his actual possession of its powers and performance of its duties is and must, from the nature of things, always be, to a right-minded man, one of toilsome and anxious probation.

Dr. FRANKLIN. (Aside to Gen. Washington) Let us get this fellow out of here.

Gen. WASHINGTON. Thank you Mr. Van Buren. We thank you for your testimony. You are welcome to sit with us for the balance of today's session, if you wish.

Mr. ADAMS. Mr. Chairman, if you please, I have a question or two I would like to ask Mr. Van Buren.

Gen. WASHINGTON. Proceed.

Mr. ADAMS. The panic of 1837 occurred toward the beginning of your term—when it was only three months old. It initiated a five-year long national depression. What steps did you take to avert that depression?

Mr. VAN BUREN. It was my belief that business recklessness and overextension of credit were the cause. I undertook to reduce government spending, particularly aid for internal improvements, and I used other deflationary tactics.

Mr. ADAMS. Did they succeed?

Mr. VAN BUREN. None succeeded.

Mr. ADAMS. Thank you.

Gen. WASHINGTON. We have asked Mr. James K. Polk, our eleventh president, to say a few words about the office of the presidency. Regrettably, Mr. Polk can be with us just briefly, as he has other appointments.

Mr. Polk was born near Little Sugar Creek, North Carolina on November 2, 1795; he attended the common schools and was tutored privately, was graduated from the University of North Carolina at Chapel Hill in 1818, studied law, was admitted to the bar in 1820 and commenced practice in Columbia, Tennessee. He was elected to the Nineteenth and to the six succeeding Congresses, March 4, 1825 to March 3, 1839; was governor of Tennessee from 1838 to 1841; was elected president in 1844 on the Democratic ticket with George M. Dallas as vice-president, was inaugurated on March 4, 1845, and served until March 3, 1849. He declined to be a candidate for renomination. Mr. Polk.

Mr. POLK. Thank you Gen. Washington. I will be brief. To the members of this Commission, I say that it is emphatically true that the presidency is "no bed of roses." In truth, though I occupied a very high position, I was the hardest-working man in the country. No president who performs his duty faithfully and conscientiously can have any leisure. If he entrusts the details and smaller matters to subordinates constant errors will occur. I preferred to supervise the whole operation of the government myself rather than entrust the public business to subordinates, and this made my duties very great.

Gentlemen, thank you.

Gen. WASHINGTON. Thank you, Mr. Polk, for giving us your time today. Our next and last speaker for the day will be Mr. James Buchanan, our fifteenth president. Mr. Buchanan was born at Cove Gap, near Mercersburg, Pennsylvania, April 23, 1791; he was privately tutored, then attended the village academy, and was graduated from Dickinson College, Carlisle, Pennsylvania in 1809. He studied law, was admitted to the bar in 1812, and practiced in Lancaster. He was one of the first volunteers in the War of 1812 and served under Judge Shippen in the defense of Baltimore. A member of the State House of Representatives in 1814 and 1815, he was elected to the Seventeenth and to the four succeeding Congresses, serving from March 4, 1821 to March 3, 1831; he was one of the managers appointed by the House of Representatives in 1830 to conduct the impeachment proceedings against James H. Peck, judge of the United States District Court for the District of Missouri. Elected to the United States Senate to fill the vacancy caused by the resignation of William Wilkins, he served from December 6, 1834, until resigning on March 5, 1845, to accept a cabinet portfolio; he was secretary of state in the cabinet of President Polk from March 6, 1845 to March 7, 1848 and was elected president in 1856 as a Democrat, serving from March 4, 1857 to March 3, 1861.

Mr. Buchanan, the floor is yours.

Dr. FRANKLIN. (Aside to Mr. Jefferson) Did you know that Mr. Buchanan was the only Chief Executive who was never married?

Mr. BUCHANAN. From the very nature of the office and its high responsibilities, the president must necessarily be conservative. The stern duty of administering the vast and complicated concerns of this government affords in itself a guarantee that he will not attempt any violation of a clear constitutional right.

After all, he is no more than the chief executive officer of the government. His province is not to make but to execute the laws. . . .

Mr. MADISON. Mr. Buchanan, do you really believe that this principle has been adhered to?

Mr. BUCHANAN. As I said, the responsibility and true position of the Executive is that he is bound by solemn oath, before God and the country, to "take care that the laws be faithfully executed," and from this obligation he cannot be absolved by any human power. What you really ask is what if the performance of this duty, in whole or in part, has been rendered impracticable by events over which he could have exercised no control? Such was my case throughout the state of South Carolina. All the federal officers within its limits, through whose agency alone our laws could be carried into execution, had already resigned. We no longer had a district judge, a district attorney or a marshal in South Carolina. In fact the whole machinery of the federal government necessary for the distribution of remedial justice among the people had been demolished, and it would have been difficult, if not impossible, to replace it.

The only acts of Congress on the statue book bearing upon this subject are those of February 28, 1795 and March 3, 1807. These authorized the president, after he shall have ascertained that the marshal, with his "posse comitatus," was unable to execute civil or criminal process in any particular case, to call forth the militia and employ the army and navy to aid him, in performing this service, having first by proclamation commanded the insurgents "to disperse and retire peaceably to their respective abodes within a limited time." This duty could not possibly be performed in a state where no judicial authority existed to issue process, and where there was no marshal to execute it, and where, even if there were such an officer, the entire population would constitute one solid combination to resist him.

Mr. MADISON. And this type of event, I assume, prevented you, as Chief Executive, from exercising your constitutional duty of assuring the execution of the laws of the United States? And what you are referring to, of course, was a prelude to the Civil War between the States.

Mr. BUCHANAN. That is correct.

Mr. ADAMS. What were your personal feelings towards the job of Chief Executive?

Mr. BUCHANAN. I was in my 69th year in 1859 and heartily tired of my position as president. I said then that, should a kind Providence prolong my days until March, 1861, I shall leave the office with much greater satisfaction than when entering on the duties of the office.

Mr. ADAMS. Wasn't there some special remark you made to President Lincoln when you showed him the White House?

Mr. BUCHANAN. Yes, when I parted from President Lincoln, on introducing him to the Executive Mansion, I said to him, "If you are as happy, my dear sir, on entering this house as I am in leaving it and returning home, you are the happiest man in this country!"

Gen. WASHINGTON. Mr. Buchanan, we thank you.

I wish to announce that tomorrow, Thursday, June 4th, the Commission will have the privilege and honor of spending a full session with former President Abraham Lincoln. Mr. Lincoln is coming from Washington, D.C. especially to be with us. We look forward to his session. Accordingly, this Commission is adjourned until Thursday, June 4th at 10 o'clock a.m.

First SPECTATOR (To Second SPECTATOR). Did you know that President Buchanan supported a proposal to buy Cuba for $300 million?

Second SPECTATOR (To First SPECTATOR). Boy, would that have solved—or prevented—problems with Castro!

THURSDAY, JUNE 4, 1987

PRESIDENT ABRAHAM LINCOLN TESTIFIES

The Committee met pursuant to notice, at 10 a.m. in the Assembly Room of Independence Hall, Gen. George Washington presiding.

        Present: Mr. John Adams, Dr. Benjamin Franklin, Mr. Thomas Jefferson, Mr. James Madison and Gen. George Washington.

        Gen. WASHINGTON. (Standing) It is with much pleasure that we express our thanks to Mr. Abraham Lincoln, our sixteenth president, for his presence here today. We are deeply honored and invite him to a seat among us.

        Born in Hardin County, Kentucky, February 12, 1809, Mr. Lincoln attended a log-cabin school at short intervals and was self-instructed in elementary branches; he read the principles of law and various works on surveying, was admitted to the bar in 1836 and moved to Springfield, Illinois in 1837 where he engaged in the practice of law. Elected as a Whig to the Thirtieth Congress (March 4, 1847-March 3, 1849), he was chosen by the Republican party to oppose Stephen A. Douglas for the United States Senate in 1858, and the debates between the candidates made ½memorable the campaign in which Douglas was final victor. Elected as the first Republican president, Mr. Lincoln was inaugurated March 4, 1861, was unaminously renominated in the convention of June 8, 1864, and was inaugurated for a second term March 4, 1965, which he served until April 15, 1865.

        At this point of our session today, I ask Mr. Frederick Douglass, the foremost Negro leader in nineteenth-century

America, to introduce Mr. Lincoln. Mr. Douglass was born a slave on the Eastern Shore of Maryland. Upon his escape to the North in 1838, he dedicated his energies to the destruction of the system of slavery and rapidly became its outstanding black abolitionist. During and after the Civil War, he played a distinguished role as leader of and for his people. In 1847, he moved to Rochester, New York where he began publication of his newspaper, the *National Star*. Mr. Frederick Douglass.

Mr. DOUGLASS. Black Americans fully comprehend the relation of Abraham Lincoln both to ourselves and to the white people of the United States. It must be admitted, truth compels me to say, that Abraham Lincoln was not, in the fullest sense of the word, either our man or our model. In his interest, in his associations, in his habits or thought, and in his prejudices, he was a white man.

He was preeminently the white man's president, entirely devoted to the welfare of white men. He was ready and willing at any time during the first years of his administration to deny, postpone, and sacrifice the rights of humanity in the colored people to promote the welfare of the white people of this country. In all his education and feeling he was an American of the Americans. He came into the presidential chair upon one principle alone, namely, opposition to the *extension* of slavery. His arguments in furtherance of this policy had their motive and mainspring in his patriotic devotion to the interests of his own race. To protect, defend, and perpetuate slavery in the states where it existed, Abraham Lincoln was not less ready than any other president to draw the sword of the nation. He was ready to execute all the supposed guarantees of the United States Constitution in favor of the slave system anywhere inside the slave states. He was willing to pursue, recapture, and send back the fugitive slave to his master, and to suppress a slave rising for liberty, though his guilty master were already in arms against the government. The race to which we belong were not the special objects of his consideration. You and yours were the objects of his deepest affection and his most earnest solicitude. You are the children of Abraham Lincoln. We are at best only his step-children; children by adoption; children by forces of circumstances and necessity. To you it especially belongs to sound his praises and commend his example, for to you he was a great and glorious friend and benefactor. While Abraham Lincoln saved you a country, he delivered us from a bondage, one hour of which, according to Mr. Jefferson, was worse than ages of the oppression your fathers rose in rebellion to oppose.

Yet, the name of Abraham Lincoln was near and dear to our hearts in the darkest and most perilous hours of the Republic. We were no more ashamed of him when shrouded in clouds of darkness, of doubt, and defeat than when we saw him crowned with victory, honor, and glory. Our faith in him was often taxed and strained to the uttermost, but it never failed. When he tarried long in the mountain; when he strangely told us that we were the cause of the war; when he still more strangely told us that we were to leave the land in which we were born; when he refused to employ our arms in defense of the Union; when after accepting our service as colored soldiers, he refused to retaliate our murder and torture as colored prisoners; when he told us he would save the Union if he could with slavery; when he revoked the Proclamation of Emancipation of Gen. Fremont; when he refused to remove the popular commander of the Army of the Potomac, in the days of its inaction and defeat, who was more zealous in his efforts to protect slavery than to suppress rebellion; when we saw all this, and more, we were at times grieved, stunned, and greatly bewildered; but our hearts believed while they ached and bled. Nor was this, even at that time, a blind and unreasoning superstition. Despite the mist and haze that surrounded him; despite the tumult, the hurry, and confusion of the hour, we were able to take a comprehensive view of Abraham Lincoln, and to make reasonable allowance for the circumstances of his position. We saw him, measured him, and estimated him; not by stray utterances to injudicious and tedious delegations, who often tried his patience; not by isolated facts torn from their connection; not by any partial and imperfect glimpses, caught at inopportune moments; but by a broad survey, in the light of the stern logic of great events, and in view of that divinity which shapes our ends, rough hew them how we will, we came to the conclusion that the hour and the man of our redemption had somehow met in the person of Abraham Lincoln. It mattered little to us what language he might employ on special occasions; it mattered little to us, when we fully knew him, whether he was swift or slow in his movements; it was enough for us that Abraham Lincoln was at the head of a great movement and was in living and earnest sympathy with the movement.

Though he loved Caesar less than Rome, though the Union was more to him than our freedom or our future, under his wise and beneficient rule we saw ourselves gradually lifted from the depths of slavery to the heights of liberty and manhood; under his wise and beneficient rule, and by measures approved and vigorously pressed by him, we saw that the handwriting of ages, in the form of prejudice and proscription, was rapidly fading away from the face of our whole country; under his rule, and in due time, about as soon after all of the country could tolerate the strange spectacle, we saw our brave sons and brothers laying off the rags of bondage, and being clothed all over in the blue uniforms of the soldiers of the United States; under his rule we saw two hundred thousand of our dark and dusky people responding to the call of Abraham Lincoln, and with muskets on their shoulders, and eagles on their buttons, timing their high footsteps to liberty and union under the national flag.

Can any colored man, or any white man friendly to the freedom of all men, ever forget the night which followed the first day of January, 1863, when the world was to see if Abraham Lincoln would prove to be as good as his word? I shall never forget that memorable night, when in a distant city I waited and watched at a public meeting, with three thousand others not less anxious than myself, for the word of deliverance.

I have said that President Lincoln was a white man and shared the prejudices common to his countrymen towards the colored race. Looking back to his times and to the condition of his country, we are compelled to admit that this unfriendly feeling on his part may be safely set down as one element of his wonderful success in organizing the loyal American people for the tremendous conflict before them and bringing them safely through that conflict. His great mission was to accomplish two things: first, to save his country from dismemberment and ruin; and second, to free his country from the great crime of slavery. To do one or the other, or both, he must have the earnest sympathy and the powerful cooperation of his loyal fellow countrymen. Without this primary and essential condition to success his efforts must have been vain and utterly fruitless. Had he put the abolition of slavery before the salvation of the Union, he would have inevitably driven from him a powerful class of the American people and rendered resistance to rebellion impossible. Viewed from the genuine abolition ground, Mr. Lincoln seemed tardy, cold, dull, and indifferent; but measuring him by the sentiment of his country, a sentiment he was bound as a statesman to consult, he was swift, zealous, radical and determined.

Upon his inauguration as president of the United States, an office, even when assumed under the most favorable conditions, fitted to tax and strain the largest abilities, Abraham Lincoln was met by a tremendous crisis. He was called upon not merely to administer the government, but to decide, in the face of terrible odds, the fate of the Republic.

A formidable rebellion rose in his path before him; the Union was already practically dissolved; his country was torn and rent asunder at the center. Hostile armies were already organized against the Republic, armed with the munitions of war which the Republic had provided for its own defense. The tremendous question for him to decide was whether his country should survive the crisis and flourish, or be dismembered and perish.

Happily for the country, happily for you and for me, he brought his strong common sense, sharpened in the school of adversity, to bear upon the question. He did not hesitate, he did not doubt, he did not falter; but at once resolved that at whatever peril, at whatever cost, the union of the states should be preserved. He calmly and bravely heard the voices of doubt and fear all around him; but he had an oath in heaven, and there was not power enough on earth to make this honest boatman, backwoodsman, and broadhanded splitter of rails evade or violate that sacred oath. The trust that Abraham Lincoln had in himself and in the people was surprising and grand, but it was also enlightened and well founded. He knew the American people better than they knew themselves, and his truth was based upon this knowledge.

There is little necessity on this occasion to speak at length and critically of this great and good man, and of his high mission in the world. Any man can say things that are true of Abraham Lincoln, but no man can say anything that is new of Abraham Lincoln. His personal traits and public acts are better known to the American people than are those of any other man of his age. He was a mystery to no man who saw him and heard him. Though high in position, the humblest could approach him and feel at home in his presence. Though deep, he was transparent; though strong, he was gentle; though decided and pronounced in his convictions, he was tolerant towards those who differed from him and patient under reproaches. Even those who only knew him through his public utterance obtained a tolerably clear idea of his character and personality. The image of the man went out with his words, and those who read them knew him.

No man who knew Abraham Lincoln could hate him—but because of his fidelity to union and liberty, he is doubly dear to us.

I end as I began. In doing honor to our friend and liberator, we have been doing highest honors to ourselves and those who come after us; we have been fastening ourselves to a name and fame imperishable and immortal; we have also been defending ourselves from a blighting scandal. When now it shall be said that the colored man is soulless, that he has no appreciation of benefits or benefactors; when the foul reproach of ingratitude is hurled at us, and it is attempted to scourge us beyond the range of human brotherhood, we may calmly point to our friend, Abraham Lincoln.

Gen. WASHINGTON. Thank you, Mr. Douglass, for your inspiring introduction. The Commission will recess for ten minutes.

First SPECTATOR (To Second SPECTATOR). Have you ever stopped to think about the differences between presidents Lincoln, Nixon, and Carter?

Second SPECTATOR (To First SPECTATOR). Character, man, character.

(Assembly Hall clears. After some moments, Commission members resume their seats.)

Gen. WASHINGTON. As Mr. Lincoln in his time may have placed the issue of "Union" first and "emancipation" second, we, as the so-called "fathers," in our time, placed the issue of a "Constitution" first and "slavery" second. The principal difference is that Abraham Lincoln accomplished in his time what we could not accomplish in ours—a resolution of the issue of slavery.

At this point I want to restate something I said in 1786: "There is not a man living who wishes more sincerely than I do to see a plan adopted, for the abolition of slavery. But there is only one proper way and effectual mode by which it can be accomplished, and that is by legislative authority."

Gentlemen, we now turn our attention to the man who accomplished what we could not—Mr. Abraham Lincoln.

Mr. LINCOLN. Some six score and four years ago I said that four score and seven years ago our fathers brought forth on this continent a new nation, conceived in liberty and dedicated to the propositon that all men are created equal. The "fathers" I referred to included Gen. Washington, John Adams, Dr. Franklin, Mr. Jefferson, and Mr. Madison. To be with you today is like walking through history. I count this rendezvous as a blessing of Divine Providence.

At my point of history, a duty devolved upon me which was, perhaps, greater than that which devolved upon any other man since the days of Gen. Washington. He never could have succeeded except for the aid of Divine Providence, upon which he at all times relied. I feel that I could not have succeeded without the same Divine Aid which sustained him.

But the support of Divine Providence which I required was no different from that of my opposition. We both read the same Bible and prayed to the same God, and each invoked His aid against the other. It may seem strange that any men should dare to ask a just God's assistance in wringing their bread from the sweat of other men's faces, but let us judge not that we be not judged. The prayers of both could not be answered. The Almighty has His own purposes.

It must be said, as was said three thousand years ago, that the Judgments of the Lord are true and righteous altogether. And so, with malice toward none, with charity for all, with firmness in the right as God gives us to see the right, we resolved in our time that this nation, under God, shall have a new birth of freedom; and that government of the people, by the people, for the people, shall not perish from the earth.

First SPECTATOR. My what an impressive character! Just looking at him commands respect.

Second SPECTATOR. He certainly has perfect composure and coolness, an uncouth height, complete black dress, stove pipe hat pushed back on the head, dark brown complexion, seamed and wrinkled yet canny-looking face, bushy head of hair, disproportionately long neck, and y'know—he holds his hands behind when he stands and speaks.

First SPECTATOR. To sketch Lincoln properly, inside and out, would require the eyes and brains and finger-touch of Michelangelo, assisted by Rabelais!

Washington Post REPORTER. (On overhearing the conversation) In an mock biography, intended to wrap up Lincoln as entirely ridiculous, a writer with a genius for nonsense once let himself go:

"Mr Lincoln stands six-feet twelve in his socks, which he changes once every ten days. His anatomy is composed mostly of bones, and when walking he resembles the offspring of a happy marriage between a derrick and a windmill. When speaking he reminds one of the old signal-telegraph that used to stand on Staten Island. His head is shaped something like a rutabaga, and his complexion is that of a Saratoga trunk. His hands and feet are plenty large enough, and in society he has the air of having too many of them. The glove-makers have not yet had time to construct gloves that will fit him. In his habits he is by no means foppish, though he brushes his hair sometimes, and is said to wash. He swears fluently. A strict temperance man himself, he does not object to another man's being pretty drunk, especially when he is about to make a bargain with him. He is fond of fried liver and onions and is a member of the church. He can hardly be called handsome, though he is certainly much better looking since he had the small-pox.''

Someone once told William Allen White that he had seen Lincoln sitting in a chair with his legs crossed and both feet flat on the floor.

(Spectators laugh.)

Gen. WASHINGTON. Order, please. Pardon the interruption, Mr. Lincoln. Please continue, Mr. Madison.

Mr. MADISON. Mr. Lincoln, as president of the United States, in what manner did you view the Constitution in your time?

Mr. LINCOLN. This country, with its institutions, belongs to the people who inhabit it. Whenever they shall grow weary of the existing government, they can exercise their constitutional right of amending it, or their revolutionary right to dismember or overthrow it. The chief magistrate derives all his authority from the people, and they confer no authority upon him to dismember the country. The people themselves can do this if they choose; but the executive, as such, has nothing to do with it. His duty is to administer the government as it came into his hands, and to transmit it, unimpaired by him, to his successor.

In my judgment, as long as the people retain their virtue and vigilance, no administration, by any extreme of wickedness or folly, can very seriously injure the government in the short space of four years.

Dr. FRANKLIN. It is doubtful that your last statement applies to today's nuclear world, Mr. Lincoln.

Mr. MADISON. Mr. Lincoln, you stated that it is the president's duty to administer the government as it came into his hands, and then to transmit it to his successor "unimpaired by him." What was the national debt in the year before you took office; let's see, that was 1860.

Mr. LINCOLN. Almost $65 million.

Mr. MADISON. What was the national debt in your first year in office?

Mr. LINCOLN. $90 million.

Mr. MADISON. What was the national debt at the end of your first term, in 1865?

Mr. LINCOLN. Almost $2.7 billion.

First SPECTATOR. (Aside to Second SPECTATOR.) Did you know that it was during Lincoln's first term in 1863, that the national debt first went over one billion dollars?

Mr. MADISON. In other words, the government turned over to your successor was "impaired" to the extent of over two and a half billion dollars.

Mr. LINCOLN. That was the price of preserving the Union, Mr. Madison. After all, the new government started in 1789 with a national debt of over $75 million, a heritage of the War for Independence. Can we really use the word "impaired?" Was not the national really "spared" in both instances?

Dr. FRANKLIN. Impaired—unimpaired—spared. Each generation values an era or event according to its own standards. The only point of consistency is that "The Golden Age is never the present Age."

Mr. LINCOLN. In our time I valued the Union above all other considerations. "Save the Union," was my oft-repeated statement. Everything else was subsidary to that objective—which reminds me of a story. There was an Illinois farmer who for years had prized and loved a soaring elm tree that spread its majestic branches near his house. Chasing a squirrel one day, the farmer saw the little animal scurry up the giant elm's trunk and suddenly disappear in a hole. Looking farther, the farmer found the great tree to be hollow, the whole inside rotten, the tree ready to fall at the next heavy storm wind. The farmer moaned to his wife, "My God! I wish I had never seen that squirrel!" And I hope that this Commission after its chores are finished does not have to say about the branches of government: "And I wish we had never seen what we have seen."

Mr. ADAMS. There is no question that the Constitution was strained to the ultimate during your administration. Please tell us in your own words how you handled your relationship to the Constitution.

Mr. LINCOLN. As a basic premise, what was the presidency to me if I had no country?

In that sense the Constitution was secondary. I told Salmon P. Chase, my secretary of the treasury, that I would violate the Constitution, if necessary, to save the Union; and I suspected that our Constitution was going to have a rough time of it before we got done with our row. After all, the rebels were violating the Constitution to destroy the Union. I can no more be persuaded that the government can constitutionally take no strong measures in time of rebellion, because it can be shown that the same could not be lawfully taken in time of peace, than I can be persuaded that a particular drug is not good medicine for a sick man because it can be shown to not be good food for a well one. Nor am I able to appreciate the danger that the American people will by means of military arrests during a rebellion lose the right of public discussion, the liberty of speech and the press, the law of evidence, trial by jury, and *habeas corpus* throughout the indefinite peaceful future, any more than I am able to believe that a man could contract so strong an appetite for emetics during temporary illness as to persist in feeding upon them during the remainder of his healthful life.

Mr. JEFFERSON. How do you justify what you consider acts for the public safety? Can you override the guaranteed rights of individuals?

Mr. LINCOLN. The Constitution contemplates the question as likely to occur for decision, but it does not expressly declare who is to decide it. By necessary implication, when rebellion or invasion comes, the decision is to be made from time to time; and I think the man whom, for the time, the people have, under the Constitution, made the commander-in-chief of their army and navy, is the man who holds the power and bears the responsibility of making it. If he uses the power justly, the same people will probably justify him; if he abuses it, he is in their hands to be dealt with by all the modes they have reserved to themselves in the Constitution.

Dr. FRANKLIN. We may have been somewhat uselessly anticipatory when we apologized, in effect, for not having accomplished in our time what you accomplished in your time with respect to the issue of slavery. If the question were put to you, as it was put to us, would you have saved the Union and accepted the continuance of the institution of slavery?

Mr. LINCOLN. I would save the Union. I would save it in the shortest way under the Constitution. The sooner the national authority could be restored, the nearer the Union would be the Union as it was. If there be those who would not save the Union unless they could at the same time save slavery, I do not agree with them. If there be those who would not save the Union unless they could at the same time destroy slavery, I do not agree with them. My paramount object in that struggle was to save the Union, and was not either to save or to destroy slavery. If I could have saved the Union without freeing any slave, I would have done it; and if I could have saved it by freeing all the slaves, I would have done it; and if I could have saved it by freeing some and leaving others alone, I would also have done that. What I did about slavery and the colored race, I did because I believed it helped to save the Union.

I have here stated my purpose according to my view of official duty; and I intend no modification of my oft-expressed personal wish that all men everywhere could be free.

Dr. FRANKLIN. And what about your personal thoughts about the job of being president, Mr. Lincoln?

Mr. LINCOLN. It was seventy-two years since the first inauguration of a president under our national Constitution. During that period fifteen different and greatly distinguished citizens in succession, administered the executive branch of the government. They conducted it through many perils, and generally with great success. Yet, with all this scope of precedent, I entered upon the same task for the brief constitutional term of four years under great and peculiar difficulty. A disruption of the Federal Union, theretofore only menaced, was not formidably attempted.

In my position, I was environed with difficulties. Yet they were scarcely so great as the difficulties of those who upon the battlefield were endeavoring to purchase with their blood and their lives the future happiness and prosperity of this country.

From my boyhood up my ambition was to be president. I was, for a time, president of one part of this divided country at least; but I wished I had never been born! It was a white elephant on my hands and hard to manage. With a fire in my front and rear; having to contend with the jealousies of the military commanders, and not receiving that cordial co-operation and support from Congress which could reasonably be expected; with an active and formidable enemy in the field threatening the very life-blood of the government, my position was anything but a bed of roses.

In God's name, I said, if any one can do better in my place than I have done, or am endeavoring to do, let him try his hand at it, and no one will be better contented than myself.

I could not fly from my thoughts—my solicitude for this great country followed me wherever I went. I did not think it personal vanity or ambition, though I was not free from these infirmities.

I could not run this thing, the presidency, upon the theory that every officeholder must think I am the greatest man in the nation, and I did not.

At the end of my first term, I felt I had enough to look after without giving much of my time to the consideration of the subject of who shall be my successor in office. The position was not an easy one; and the occupant, whoever he may be, for the next four years, I thought, would have little leisure to pluck a thorn or plant a rose in his own pathway.

I had hoped, however, that I would never have another four years of such anxiety, tribulation, and abuse. My only ambition had been to put down the rebellion and restore peace; after which I wanted to resign my office, go abroad, take some rest, study foreign governments, see something of foreign life, and in my old age die in peace with the good will of all of God's creatures.

FRIDAY, JUNE 5, 1987

TESTIMONY OF PRESIDENTS: ANDREW JOHNSON TO BENJAMIN HARRISON

The Committee met pursuant to notice, at 10 a.m. in the Assembly Room of Independence Hall, Gen. George Washington presiding.

  Present: Mr. John Adams, Dr. Benjamin Franklin, Mr. Thomas Jefferson, Mr. James Madison and Gen. George Washington.

  Gen. WASHINGTON. Today the Bicentennial Constitutional Commission will hear from former presidents Andrew Johnson, Rutherford B. Hayes, James A. Garfield, Grover Cleveland, and Mr. Benjamin Harrison.

  Our first speaker will be Mr. Andrew Johnson, the seventeenth president of the United States.

  Born in Raleigh, North Carolina on December 29, 1808, Mr. Johnson was self-educated, never having attended school a day in his life; he received instruction in elementary English branches from the woman who would eventually become his wife on May 27, 1826. He was a member of the Tennessee House of Representatives from 1835 to 1837 and 1839 to 1841, served in the state Senate in 1841, was elected to the Twenty-eighth and to the four succeeding Congresses (March 4, 1843 to March 3, 1853), and was governor of Tennessee (1853-57). Mr. Johnson was elected to the United States Senate and served from October 8, 1857 to March 4, 1862; he was then appointed military governor of Tennessee by President Lincoln with the rank of brigadier general.

He was elected vice-president of the United States on the Republican ticket headed by Lincoln in 1864 and was inaugurated March 4, 1865. Mr. Johnson became president on April 15, 1865. Wide differences arising between the president and the Republican Congress, a resolution for his impeachment passed the House of Representatives February 24, 1868; eleven articles were set out in the resolutions and the trial before the Senate lasted three months; at its conclusion he was acquitted (May 16, 1868) by a vote of thirty-five for conviction to nineteen for acquittal, the necessary two-thirds vote for impeachment not having been obtained; he retired to his home in Tennessee upon the expiration of the presidential term, March 3, 1869.

Gentlemen, we welcome Mr. Andrew Johnson.

Mr. THOMSON. (aside to Mr. Thomson). Did you know that "Andy" Johnson was a tailor by trade and made his own clothes until he went to Washington as a Congressmen? When he was governor of Tennessee he made a suit of clothes for the governor of Kentucky and received a homemade shovel and pair of tongs in return.

You should also be interested in knowing that while "Andy" Johnson was preoccupied with the turmoil of Reconstruction, his able Secretary of State, William H. Seward, purchased Alaska from Russia for $7.2 million.

Mr. JOHNSON. I am most pleased to be here with you today. The subject matter of this Commission—the Constitution—is a most important consideration to this nation. The triumphant success of the Constitution is due to the wonderful wisdom with which the functions of government were distributed between the three principal departments—the legislative, the executive, and the judicial—and to the fidelity with which each has confined itself or been confined by the general voice of the nation within its peculiar and proper sphere. While a just, proper, and watchful jealousy of executive power constantly prevails, as it ought ever to prevail, yet it is equally true that an efficient executive, capable, in the language of the oath prescribed to the president, of executing the laws and, within the sphere of executive action, of preserving, protecting, and defending the Constitution of the United States, is an indispensable security for tranquility at home and peace, honor, and safety abroad. Governments have been erected in many countries upon our model.

Yet, during my term, legislation of Congress attempted to strip the executive department of the government of some of its essential powers. This interference with the constitutional authority of the executive department was an evil that would inevitably sap the foundations of our federal system. I vetoed that legislation. It was my removal of Mr. Edwin M. Stanton, my secretary of war, who in my judgment consistently disagreed with me and actively resisted my policies, that led to my impeachment.

You no doubt are aware that in my administration certain evil-disposed persons formed a conspiracy to depose me, as president of the United States, and to supply my place by an individual of their own selection. Their plan of operation seemed to contemplate certain accusations against the president, which were to take the form of Articles of Impeachment and that, before hearing or trial, he would be under color of law, placed under arrest, and suspended or removed from office.

The persons engaged in this scheme discovered that, to accomplish their purpose, they must resort to a revolution changing the whole organic system of our government. The temptation to join in a revolutionary enterprise for the overthrow of our institutions was extremely strong at that moment. A combination of men directing the operations of government without regard to law, or under a Constitution, would be absolute masters of all the wealth of the country, the richest in the world, and they could hold at their mercy the life and liberty of every individual within our territorial limits. Supreme and irresponsible power is always dangerous and seductive; but with our large army and powerful navy and vast resources, it is a prize so dazzling that we cannot wonder that the desire to grasp it should overcome the public virtue of some ambitious men. The coveted power, once usurped, would easily find means to make itself perpetual.

In the end the impeachment of me failed—it lost by

one vote.

In my own case, I feel, and I felt, I was justified in doing what I did. Why do I delve into this episode? Simply because America, within the last fifteen years, travelled the road toward a somewhat similar experience, where the president himself was the interloper and his Watergate became his Waterloo, potentially opening the gates of treachery to the threshold of impeachment. Yes, that was Richard Milhouse Nixon. These two eipsodes should provide a lesson for this Commission to consider. It should lead to a resolution as to what constitutional provisions are needed to monitor the activities of the coordinate branches of government to protect the public against treason, bribery and high crimes in government.

Gen. WASHINGTON. Thank you, Mr. Johnson. We invite you to stay with us for the remainder of today's session.

We now proceed to our next speaker, Mr. Rutherford B. Hayes, the nineteenth president. Born in Delaware, Ohio, October 4, 1822, Mr. Hayes attended the common schools, the Methodist Academy in Norwalk, Ohio, and the Webb Preparatory School in Middletown, Connecticut; he was graduated from Kenyon College, Gambier, Ohio, in August 1842 and from Harvard Law School in January 1845. He was admitted to the bar May 10, 1845, and commenced practice in Lower Sandusky (now Fremont, Ohio); during the Civil War he entered the Union Army and was brevetted major general of volunteers, March 3, 1865, "for gallant and distinguished services during the campaign of 1864 in West Virginia, and particularly at the battles of Fishers Hill and Cedar Creek Virginia"; governor of Ohio from 1868 until 1872, Mr. Hayes was elected president in 1876 and served until March 3, 1881.

I am pleased to introduce Mr. Hayes.

Dr. FRANKLIN. (Aside to Mr. Adams). President Hayes was sometimes called "His Fraudulency," and sometimes "Rutherfraud B. Hayes." The name-calling stemmed from the fact that some politicians felt he had not won the election of 1876 fairly and that Samuel J. Tilden had really won. The complication was that a few states each submitted two different sets of electoral votes. Tilden needed to win only one vote; Hayes needed all the disputed votes. To settle the impasse, Congress created a special commission of fifteen members. It consisted of five from each House of Congress and five from the Supreme Court. The commission finally accepted the returns favoring Hayes by a partisan vote of 8 to 7. The issue was resolved only two days before the inauguration.

Mr. HAYES. Presidents in the past have always been better than their adversaries have predicted. I take, of course, only those who are so far removed by time that no one's sensibilities will be shocked or even touched by allusions to them—say, from Washington to Jackson inclusive. All were free from the least taint of personal corruption. All were honest men. All were in the best sense, gentlemen.

Mr. ADAMS. George Washington thanks you, Thomas Jefferson thanks you, James Madison thanks you, and I thank you.

Dr. FRANKLIN. I regret I had only one life to give to my country—and that was not as president of the United States.

Mr. ADAMS. Mr. Hayes, what were your personal feelings toward being president?

Mr. HAYES. I was not liked as a president by the politicians in office, in the press, or in Congress. But I was content to abide by the judgment—the sober second thought—of the people. But as I got rid of the cares and troubles which make the incessant and almost intolerable strain of the job, I found myself valuing more and more friends and relationships which dated back.

A common burden of the presidency was, then and now, the national pastime of appraising presidents' wives. Mrs. Hayes was regarded as a determined women. The *Boston Post* once said, "Mr. Hayes will, during the absence of Mrs. Hayes, be acting President!"

Nobody ever left the presidency with less regret, less disappointment, fewer heartburnings, or more general content with the result of his term than I did.

The escape from bondage into freedom was grateful

indeed to my feelings. The burden, even with my constitutional cheerfulness, had not been a light one. I was glad to be a freed man.

Mr. JEFFERSON. Mr. Hayes, do you have any recommendations to make to this Commission?

Mr. HAYES. Yes, James Parton in an article in the *Magazine of American History* said that George Washington was in favor of a single presidential term of seven years. Parton wrote, "The term of seven years is probably as long as any man can advantageously hold the presidency. The strain upon the faculties of a good man is too severe to be long borne and a young country needs to grow faster than an elderly mind."

This is true. The strain is hard to bear. It grows harder as time passes.

My idea is that the constitution should be amended to lengthen the term of the president to six years and render him ineligible for a second term.

Gen. WASHINGTON. Thank you, Mr. Hayes. We are pleased to have as our next speaker Mr. James A. Garfield. Mr. Garfield served as our twentieth president during the year 1881.

He was born in Orange, Ohio, November 19, 1831, and his boyhood was spent working on a farm, aiding in the support of his widowed mother. Graduated from Williams College, Williamstown, Massachusetts in 1858, he became professor of ancient languages and literature at Hiram College, Hiram, Ohio and later its president. He was a member of the state Senate in 1859, studied law, and was admitted to the bar in 1860. During the Civil War he entered the Union Army, attaining the rank of major general; he served in the Thirty-eighth and the eight succeeding Congresses, from March 4, 1863 until November 8, 1880, when he resigned, having been elected president of the United States.

Gentlemen, Mr. Garfield.

Mr. GARFIELD. On the personal side, I loved to deal with doctrines and events, but my days were frittered away with the personal seeking of people, when they ought to have been given to the great problems which concerned the whole country. Four years of this kind of intellectual dissipation could have crippled me for the remainder of my life. I thought, what might not a vigorous thinker do if he could be allowed to use the opportunities of a presidential term in vital useful activity!

I did not know that I would ever become reconciled to the office. I saw few signs that I would. The prospect was a struggle with personal wishes and a painful series of deciding between men.

Once or twice I felt like crying out in the agony of my soul against the greed for office and its consumption of my time. I thought my services ought to be worth more to the government than to be spent thus. I was vexed with the thought that I was wholly unfit for this sort of work. I would say, My God! What is there in this place that a man should ever want to get in it?

Dr. FRANKLIN. (Aside to Mr. Jefferson) . . . and we planned a government to have that effect on presidents!

Gen. WASHINGTON. Thank you, Mr. Garfield.

Our next speaker will be Mr. Grover Cleveland. Mr. Cleveland was our twenty-fourth president, serving terms from 1885 to 1898 and 1893 to 1897. Mr. Cleveland was born in 1837 at Caldwell, New Jersey, the fifth of nine children sired by a Presbyterian pastor; in 1841, he moved to Fayettville in central New York, where he received his education at home and in village schools, until he was 13 years old. Due to family financial problems, he was forced to work as a clerk; from 1853 to 1854 he taught at Gotham's New York Institution for the Blind. He was admitted to the bar in 1859, was mayor of Buffalo, governor of New York, then president of the United States. Mr. Cleveland.

Mr. JEFFERSON. (Aside to Mr. Madison). I understand that the Panic of 1893 occurred during the Cleveland presidency. The panic touched off a long and harrowing depression, accompanied by widespread unemployment. President Cleveland was unable to grasp the social realities. He was narrow and unimaginative. According to a popular story, a lean and hungry man came to the White House one day, got down on his hands and knees and began chewing the grass. "What are you doing?" asked Cleveland, seeing him from a window. "I'm hungry and have to eat grass," replied the man. "Why don't you go around to the back yard?" suggested Cleveland. "The grass is longer there."

Mr. CLEVELAND. In the scheme of our national government, the presidency is preeminently the people's office. To the citizens, I say, watch well this high office, the most precious possession of American citizenship. Demand for it the most complete devotion on the part of him to whose custody it may be intrusted, and protect it not less vigilantly against unworthy assaults from without.

Thus will you perform a sacred duty to yourselves and to those who may follow you in the enjoyment of the freest institutions which Heaven has ever vouchsafed to man.

The world does not afford a spectacle more sublime than is furnished when millions of free and intelligent American citizens select their Chief Magistrate.

It is a high office, because it represents the sovereignty of a free and mighty people. It is full of solemn responsibility and duty, because it embodies, in a greater degree than any other office on earth, the suffrage and the trust of such a people. I was president of all the people, good, bad, or indifferent.

Mr. MADISON. Mr. Cleveland, what do you think was the most important benefit you conferred on the country during your administration?

Mr. CLEVELAND. I believe the most important benefit that I conferred on the country by my presidency was to insist upon the entire independence of the executive and legislative branches of the government and compel the members of the legislative branch to see that they have responsibilities of their own, grave and well-defined, which their official oaths bind them sacredly to perform.

Mr. MADISON. Former President Hayes said in his testimony that he favored lengthening the term of the president to six years and making him ineligible for a second term. Do you have any thoughts on this?

Mr. CLEVELAND. Do you remember that I opposed

a second term on the ground that, human nature being what it is, the president would work for his reelection instead of for the country's good? That position still stands.

Mr. MADISON. But you yourself were elected to a second term.

Mr. CLEVELAND. Yes, after a gap of four years.

Mr. MADISON. Mr. Cleveland, do you have thoughts on the usefulness of ex-presidents?

Mr. CLEVELAND. It has always seemed to me that, beyond the greatness of the office and the supreme importance of its duties and responsibilities, the most impressive thing connected with the presidency is the fact that after its honor has been relinquished, and after its labor and responsibility are past, we simply see that a citizen whom the people had selected from their ranks, has returned again to the people, to resume at their side the ordinary duties which pertain to everyday citizenship.

But it must be admitted that our people are by no means united in their ideas concerning the place which our ex-presidents ought to occupy, or the disposition which should be made of them. Of course the subject would be relieved of all uncertainty and embarrassment if every president would die at the end of his term. This does not seem, however, to meet the view of those who under such an arrangement would be called on to do the dying; and so some of them continue to live, and thus perpetuate the perplexity of those who burden themselves with plans for their utilization or disposition.

Dr. FRANKLIN. What about the job of being president, from a personal standpoint?

Mr. CLEVELAND. The office of president had not, to me personally, a single allurement. I did not want the office. It involved a responsibility beyond human strength to a man who brings conscience to the discharge of his duties.

I suffered many perplexities and troubles and my term of the presidency cost me so much health and vigor that I sometimes doubted if I could carry the burden to the end. Sometimes I believed I would buy or rent a house where I could go and be away from the cursed constant grind.

In my second term I felt that I was on a treadmill again and looked forward to the time when another respite should be due me. It's a curious state of mind to be in, when the natural desire to live for the sake of living and enjoying life is nearly gone.

I often thought how solemn a thing it is to live and feel the pressure of duties which life—the mere existence in a social state—imposes; but I never appreciated the thought in its full solemnity until I became president. It seemed to me that I was as much consecrated to a service, as the religionist who secludes himself from all that is joyous in life and devotes himself to a sacred mission.

I was comforted by the thought that someday the end would come; and if on that day I could retire with a sure consciousness that I had done my whole duty according to my ability, there would be some corner for me where I could rest.

And so, you cannot imagine the relief which came to me with the termination of my official term. I fast took the place which I desired to reach—the place of a respectable private citizen.

Gen. WASHINGTON. Mr. Cleveland, we all thank you for your testimony. We now reach the last person to testify this day, Mr. Benjamin Harrison, our twenty-third president.

Mr. Harrison was a great-grandson of Benjamin Harrison of Virginia, a signer of the Declaration of Independence, and grandson of President William Henry Harrison. Born in North Bend, Ohio, August 20, 1833, he was graduated from Miami University, Oxford, Ohio in 1852, studied law in Cincinnati and moved to Indianapolis, Indiana in March 1854, where he was admitted to the bar and practiced. He served during the Civil War and was brevetted brigadier general on January 23, 1865. Elected to the United States Senate, he served from March 4, 1881, to March 3, 1887; he was elected president and was inaugurated on March 4, 1889, and served until March 3, 1893.

Mr. Harrison, what is your concept of the presidency?

Mr. HARRISON. The presidency? The most comprehensive power of the president is given in these words: "He shall take care that the laws be faithfully executed." This is the central idea of the office. The president cannot go beyond the law, and he cannot stop short of it. His duty and his oath of office take it all in and leave him no discretion, save as to the means to be employed. Laws do not execute themselves. Somebody must look after them. It is the duty of the president to see that every law passed by Congress is executed.

A word about the cabinet. In all important matters the president is consulted by all the secretaries. He is responsible for all executive action, and almost everything that is out of the routine receives some attention from him. Every important foreign complication is discussed with him, and the diplomatic note receives his approval. The same thing is true of each of the departments. Routine matters proceed without the knowledge or interference of the president; but if any matter of major importance arises, the secretary presents it for the consideration and advice of the president. Only matters of importance affecting the general policy of the administration are discussed in the cabinet meetings—according to my experience—and votes are of rare occurrence. Any secretary desiring to have an expression upon any question in his department presents it, and it is discussed; but usually questions are settled in a conference between the president and the head of the particular department. If there is that respect and confidence that should prevail between a president and his cabinet officers, this consultation is on equal terms, and the conclusion is one that both support. There should be no question of making a "mere clerk" of the cabinet officer; there is a yielding of views, now on one side, now on the other; but it must, of course, follow that when the president has views that he feels he cannot yield, those views must prevail, for the responsibility is his, both in a Constitutional and popular sense. The cabinet officer is a valued advisor, and it does not often happen that his views and those of the president cannot be reconciled.

Mr. MADISON. Mr. Harrison, you have heard testimony given today relative to the possibility ot extending the term of the president and making him ineligible for reelection. Do you have any thoughts on this?

Mr. HARRISON. The fears of those who said that the power of the office was such as to enable an ambitious incumbent to secure an indefinite succession of terms have not been realized. In practice the popular opinion has limited the eligibility of the President to one reelection. But some of our leading and most thoughtful public men have challenged the wisdom of the four-year term, and have advocated six years, usually accompanied with a prohibition of a second term. I think it would be wise to give the president, by extending the term, a better chance to show what he can do for the country. It must be admitted, also, that ineligibility to a second term will give to the executive action greater independence.

Mr. MADISON. Now that you have expressed your thoughts on what we should do, what should we *not* do?

Mr. HARRISON. A distinguished public man is reported, perhaps erroneously, to have expressed the opinion that each cabinet officer should be independent in the administration of his department, and not be subject to control by the president. The adoption of this view would give us many chief executives, exercising, not a joint but a separate, control of specified subdivisions of the executive power, and would leave the president, in whom the Constitution says "the executive power shall be vested," no function save that of appointing these presidents. It would be a farming-out of his Constitutional powers. A many-headed executive must necessarily lack that vigor and promptness of action which is often a condition of public safety.

Two presidents or three, with equal powers, would as surely bring disaster as three generals of equal rank and command in a single army. I do not doubt that this sense of single and personal responsibility to the people has strongly held our presidents to a good conscience and to a high discharge of their great duties.

Mr. MADISON. Your point is significant, Mr. Harrison, since this issue was debated when we drafted the Constitution at the Federal Convention in 1787.

Any remarks on the personal aspect of the presidency?

Mr. HARRISON. It was a rare piece of good fortune during the early months of my administration if I got one wholly uninterrupted hour at my desk each day. My time was so broken into bits that I was often driven to late night work or to set up a desk in my bedroom.

Gen. WASHINGTON. Thank you, Mr. Harrison, for your testimony. Any further questions from the Commission? Gentlemen, this session is adjourned until Monday, June 8, at 10 o'clock a.m.

MONDAY, JUNE 8, 1987

TESTIMONY OF PRESIDENTS: THEODORE ROOSEVELT TO FRANKLIN DELANO ROOSEVELT

The Committee met pursuant to notice, at 10 a.m. in the Assembly Room of Independence Hall, Gen. George Washington presiding.

        Present: Mr. John Adams, Dr. Benjamin Franklin, Mr. Thomas Jefferson, Mr. James Madison and Gen. George Washington.

        Gen. WASHINGTON. We are resuming our session with the testimony of various former presidents of the United States. Today we have with us former Presidents Theodore Roosevelt, William Howard Taft, Woodrow Wilson, Warren Gameliel Harding, Calvin Coolidge, Herbert Hoover, and Franklin Delano Roosevelt.

        We will begin with our twenty-sixth president, Mr. Theodore Roosevelt. Mr. Roosevelt was born in New York City, October 27, 1858, attended the public schools, was graduated from Harvard University in 1880, and studied law. Appointed assistant secretary of the navy in April 1897, he served until 1898, when he resigned to enter the war with Spain, during which he organized the First Regiment, United States Volunteer Cavalry, popularly known as Roosevelt's Rough Riders; he was appointed lieutenant colonel and later colonel of this regiment. During 1899 and 1900 he was governor of New York, until his election as vice-president of the United States on the Republican ticket headed by William McKinley in 1900. He was inaugurated president on March 4, 1901, and served until March 3, 1905; elected president with Charles W. Fairbanks as vice-president in 1904, he was inaugurated March 4, 1905, and served until March 3, 1909. Mr. Theodore Roosevelt.

Mr. ROOSEVELT. Gentlemen, from the outset, I want to state that I do not share the personal views of my predecessors on the subject of the presidency.

A president has a great chance; his position is almost that of a king and a prime minister rolled into one; once he has left office he cannot do very much; and he is a fool if he fails to realize it at all and to be profoundly thankful for having had the great chance. No president ever enjoyed himself in the presidency as much as I did; and no president after leaving the office took as much joy in life as I did.

But even a president has feelings.... I had eight years of the presidency; I know all the honor and pleasure of it and all of its sorrows and dangers. I was in a perfect whirl of work and had every kind of worry and trouble—but that's what I was there for and down at the bottom I enjoyed it all.

Every day, almost every hour, I had to decide very big as well as very little questions, and in almost each of them had to determine just how far it was safe to go in forcing others to accept my views and standards and just how far I must subordinate what I deemed expedient, and indeed occasionally what I deemed morally desirable, to what it was possible under the given conditions to achieve. Hay and Nicolay's *Life of Lincoln* has been to me a great comfort and aid. I had read it and profited by it, and often when dealing with some puzzling affair I found myself thinking what Lincoln would have done. It was very wearing, but I thoroughly enjoyed it, for it was fine to feel one's hand guiding great machinery, with at least the purpose, and I hoped the effect, of guiding it for the best interests of the nation as a whole.

Mr. ADAMS. Mr. Roosevelt, you have heard mention of a six- or seven-year term for the president. Do you have any thoughts on this?

Mr. ROOSEVELT. I don't know anything about seven years. But this I do know—I would rather be full President for three years than half a president for seven years.

Mr. ADAMS. On that theme, what are your thoughts about reelection?

Mr. ROOSEVELT. Any strong man fit to be president would desire a renomination and reelection after his first term.

The presidency is a great office, and the power of the president can be effectively used to secure a renomination, especially if the president has the support of certain great political and financial interests. Therefore, the American people wisely established a custom—and then adopted a constitutional amendment—against allowing any man to hold that office for more than two consecutive terms.

Mr. ADAMS. In your time, which preceded the constitutional amendment limiting the term of the presidency to two terms, did you not favor a third term?

Mr. ROOSEVELT. If I had said that I did not believe in a third consecutive term, it would have been accepted by all my enemies and a large number of my friends as an actual announcement of candidacy after one term had expired and would have had a thoroughly unhealthy effect. What I said was that I was loyal to the substance and not to the form of the tradition. Of course, the objection to a third term was merely that a president could perpetuate himself in office. When he is out of office, it is simply preposterous that the fact that he has been in office is of any consequence, for the whole immense machinery of patronage is in the hands of someone else.

Therefore the reasoning on which the anti-third term custom was based had no application whatever to an ex-president, and no application whatever to anything except consecutive terms.

I thoroughly enjoyed the job. I never felt more vigorous so far as the work of the office was concerned, and if I had followed my own desires I should have been only too delighted to stay as president. I had said that I would not accept another term. However, for the very reason that I believe in being a strong president and making the most of the office and using it without regard to the little, feeble snarling men who yell about executive usurpation, I also believe that it is not a good thing that any one man should hold it too long.

If I am repetitious, I want to be emphatic.

There inheres in the presidency more power than in any other office in any great republic or constitutional monarchy of modern times. It can only be saved from abuse by having the people as a whole accept as axiomatic the position that no man hold it for more than a limited time. I don't think that any harm comes from the concentration of power in one man's hands, provided the holder does not keep it for more than a certain, definite time, and then returns to the people from whom he sprang.

I think that the president should be a strong man, and that he should make the presidency the strongest kind of office; but because of this very belief, I feel that he should also make it evident that he has not the slightest intention to grasp at permanent power.

Mr. ADAMS. What about being a strong president?

Mr. ROOSEVELT. While president, I was president, emphatically; I used every ounce of power there was in the office and I did not care a rap for the criticisms of those who spoke of my "usurpation of power", for I knew that the talk was all nonsense and that there was no usurpation. I believe that the efficiency of this government depends upon its possessing a strong central executive. Where I could, I established a precedent for strength in the executive. I did it, for instance, by sending the fleet around the world, taking Panama, settling affairs of Santo Domingo and Cuba; settling the anthracite coal strike, keeping order in Nevada when the Federation of Miners threatened anarchy, and in bringing the big corporations to book. Why, in all these cases I felt not merely that my action was right in itself, but that in showing the strength of, or in giving strength to, the executive, I was establishing a precedent of value. I believe in a strong executive; I believe in power; but I believe that resonsibility should go with power, and that it is not well that the strong executive should be a perpetual executive. Above all and beyond all, I believe that the salvation of this country depends upon

Washington and Lincoln representing the type of leader to which we are true. I hope that in my acts I have been a good president, a president who has deserved well of the Republic. I may be mistaken, but it is my belief that the bulk of my countrymen, the men whom Abraham Lincoln called the "plain people"—the farmers, mechanics, small tradesmen, hard-working professional men—believed that I represented the democracy in somewhat the fashion that Lincoln did, that is, not in any demagogic way but with the sincere effort to stand for a government by the people and for the people.

To me there is something fine in the American theory that a private citizen can be chosen by the people to occupy a position as great as that of the mightiest monarch, and to exercise a power which may for the time being surpass that of Czar, Kaiser, or Pope, and that then, after having filled this position, the man shall leave it and go back into the ranks of his fellow citizens with entire self-respect, claiming nothing save what on his own individual merits he is entitled to receive. But it is not in the least fine, it is vulgar and foolish, for the president or ex-president to make believe, and of all things in the world, to feel pleased if other people make believe, that he is a kind of second-rate or imitation king. The effort to combine incompatibles merely makes a man look foolish. The positions of president and king are totally different in kind and degree; and it is silly, and worse than silly, to forget this. It is not of much consequence whether other people accept the American theory of the presidency; but it is of very much consequence that the American people, including especially any American who has held the office, shall accept the theory and live up to it.

In closing, when I finished my career in public life, I could truthfully say I enjoyed it to the full. I achieved a large proportion of what I set out to achieve; and I am almost ashamed to say that I did not mind in the least retiring to private life. Of course, if I had felt that I could conscientiously keep on in the presidency I should have dearly liked to have tried again; and I missed a very little having my hands on the levers of the great machine; but I was really almost uneasy to find that I did not mind the least bit in the world getting out.

Dr. FRANKLIN. (Aside to Mr. Adams). I understand that Mr. Roosevelt had a fetish about physical exercise. Four times he had broken bones in falls with horses. But he did little boxing, because, as he said, "it seemed rather absurd for a president to appear with a black eye or a swollen nose or a cut lip."

Gen. WASHINGTON. Thank you, Mr. Roosevelt. We appreciate your testimony. Please remain with us, if you can, and we welcome you to participate further, if you wish. Thank you.

The next person to testify will be Mr. William Howard Taft, our twenty-seventh president. He was born in 1857 at Mount Auburn, now part of Cincinnati, Ohio; he graduated second in his class from Woodward High School and second in his class from Yale Unviersity (1878), and then graduated from Cincinnati Law School, gaining admission to the bar in 1880. He was judge of the Ohio Supreme Court; U.S. solicitor general; federal judge for the Sixth Circuit, 1892-1900; dean of the Cincinnati Law School; and governor general of the Philippines. In 1904 he became secretary of war and later was provisional governor of Cuba. President of the United States March 4, 1909 to March 3, 1913, Mr. Taft later held a chair in Constititional Law at Yale University (1913-1921) and was chief justice of the Supreme Court of the United States from 1921 to 1930. Mr. Taft.

Mr. TAFT. Gentlemen, I am most pleased to testify before your Commission today and to give my views of the executive functions. I conceive it the true view of the executive function that the president can exercise no power which cannot be fairly and reasonably traced to some specific grant of power or justly implied and included within such express grant as proper and necessary to its exercise. Such specific grant must be either in the federal Constitution or in an act of Congress passed in pursuance thereof. There is no undefined residuum of power which he can exercise because it seems to him to be in the public interest.

Mr. THEODORE ROOSEVELT. Mr. Taft, I would be most appreciative if, with the permission of the Chairman,

I may interrupt for a moment and remark on your viewpoint, since it reflects on statements I just made.

Gen. WASHINGTON. You have one minute, Mr. Roosevelt.

Mr. ROOSEVELT. Thank you. I declined to adopt the view that what was imperatively necessary for the nation could not be done by the president unless he could find some specific authorization to do it. My belief was that it was not only his right but his duty to do anything that the needs of the nation demanded unless such action was forbidden by the Constitution or by the laws. Under this interpreation of executive power I did and caused to be done many things not previously done by the president and the heads of the departments. I did not usurp power, but I did greatly broaden the use of executive power. In other words, I acted for the public welfare, I acted for the common well-being of all our people, whenever and in whatever manner was necessary unless prevented by direct constitutional or legislative prohibition.

Mr. TAFT. The Constitution gives the president wide discretion and great power, and it ought to do so. It calls from him activity and energy to see that within his proper sphere he does what his great responsibilities and opportunities require.

But there is little danger to the public weal from the tyranny or reckless character of a president who is not sustained by the people. The absence of popular support will certainly in due course withdraw from him the sympathetic action of at least one House of Congress, and by the control that that House has over appropriations, the executive arm can be paralyzed, unless he resorts to a coup d'etat, which means impeachment, conviction, and deposition. The only danger in the action of the executive under the present limitations and lack of limitation of his powers is when his popularity is such that he can be sure of the support of the electorate and therefore of Congress, and when the majority in the legislative halls respond with alacrity and sycophancy to his will. This condition cannot probably be long continued. We have had presidents who felt the public pulse with accuracy, who played their parts upon the political stage with histrionic genius and commanded the people almost as if they were an army and the president their commander-in-chief. Yet in all these cases, the good sense of the people has ultimately prevailed and no danger has been done to our political structure and the reign of law has continued. In such times when the executive power seems to be all prevailing, there have always been men in this free and intelligent people of ours, who apparently courting political humiliation and disaster have registered protest against this undue executive domination and this use of the executive power and popular support to perpetuate itself.

Mr. JEFFERSON. While you are on the subject of presidential discretion, I would appreciate your commentary on the exercise of this discretion by a president in his capacity as commander-in-chief. In this connection, I have in mind many incidents of recent origin such as . . .

The entry of the United States into the Korean War during President Truman's administration.

The sending of the United States Marines to Lebanon during President Eisenhower's administration.

The U-2 incident during the Eisenhower administration.

The Bag of Pigs incident and the Cuban Missile Crisis during President Kennedy's administration.

The Gulf of Tonkin incident during President Johnson's administration.

The bombing of Cambodia during President Nixon's administration.

The Mayaguez incident during President Ford's administration.

The hostage crisis and the aborted helicopter rescue mission during President Carter's administration.

The Lebanon crises, the Grenada "invasion," and the interception of the Egyptian plane carrying terrorists who hijacked the *Achille Lauro*;—all during President Reagan's administration.

Mr. Taft.

Mr. TAFT. The president, of course, is the commander-in-chief of the army and navy, and the militia when called into the service of the United States. Under this, he can order the army and navy anywhere he will, if the appropriations furnish the means of transportation. Of course, the instrumentality which this power furnishes gives the president an opportunity to do things which involve consequences that it would be quite beyond his power under the Constitution directly to effect. Under the Constitution, only Congress has the power to declare war, but with the army and the navy, the president can take action such as to involve the country in war and leave Congress no option but to declare it or to recognize its existence. I discuss this subject without recognition of the War Powers Resolution of the 1970s, which, of course, had no effect, in my time. In my time, there was a wide exercise of the authority by the Executive in his capacity as commander-in-chief. There was nothing new or startling in the principle of a temporary enlargement of executive functions. Its novelty was in the great volume of power which the circumstances thrust on him and the extent of the responsibilities and the wide discretion which he had to exercise.

Mr. MADISON. Mr. Taft, do you think that the scope of appointments assigned to the president as a function of his office is too broad?

Mr. TAFT. I hated to use the patronage as a club unless I had to. Yet, one of the functions which in a practical way gives the president more personal influence than any other is that of appointments. The prestige that a president has in the outset of his administration is in part due to this power. Even in the case of the most popular president, his prestige wanes with Congress as the term wears on and the offices are distributed.

In my judgment, the president should not be required to exercise his judgment to make appointments except to fill the most important offices. In the Executive department, he should be limited to the selection of those officers, the discharge of whose duties involves discretion in the carrying out of the political and governmental policy of his administration. He therefore ought to have the appointment of his cabinet officers, and he ought also to have the appointment of a political under-secretary in each department to take the place of the head of the department when for any reason the head of the department is not able to discharge his usual duties.

The president of course should appoint the supreme judges, as the Constitution requires, and the inferior judges of the federal judiciary. He ought, too, to appoint the general officers of the army and the flag officers to the navy, and he ought also to appoint the leading ambassadors and ministers. Other appointments, it seems to me, might well be left to a system of promotion, to be carried on under civil service rules as interpreted and enforced by a Commission and the heads of departments.

Mr. ADAMS. The danger of physical harm to our national leaders at all levels of government has reached epidemic proportions. Do you care to comment on this trend?

Mr. TAFT. The assassination of three presidents led Congress to provide that the chief of the Secret Service should furnish protection to the president as he moves about either in Washington or in the country at large. While president, I never was conscious of any personal anxiety in large crowds, and I have been in many of them. Yet the record is such that Congress would be quite derelict if it disregarded the danger. Those guards are a great burden to the president. He never can go anywhere that he does not have to inflict upon those whom he wishes to visit the burden of their presence. It is a little difficult for him to avoid the feeling after a while that he is under surveillance rather than under protection.

Mr. MADISON. Various testimony has been given regarding potential changes in the length of the term of the president. What are your thoughts?

Mr. TAFT. I am strongly inclined to view that it would have been a wiser provision, as it was at one time voted in the Convention, to make the term of the president six or seven years, and render him ineligible thereafter. Such a change would give to the executive greater courage and independence in the discharge of his duties.

Dr. FRANKLIN. And what about the job of the presidency from your personal viewpoint?

Mr. TAFT. I'll be damned if I did not get tired of it. It seemed to be the profession of a president simply to hear other people talk. One trouble was no sooner over in this office than another arose. I came to the conclusion that the major part of the work of a president was to increase the gate receipts of expositions and fairs and bring tourists into town.

I thought I would rather be chief justice of the United States. A quieter life than that which comes at the White House is more in keeping with my temperament. But, when taken into consideration that I go into history as a president, and my children and children's children are the better placed on account of that fact, I am inclined to think that to be president well compensates one for all the trials and criticisms he has to bear and undergo. In the end, I was glad to be going—it was the loneliest place in the world.

Gen. WASHINGTON. Thank you, Mr. Taft. We now proceed to our next speaker, Mr. Woodrow Wilson, our twenty-eighth president. Mr. Wilson was born in 1856 at the manse of the First Presbyterian Church, Staunton, Virginia, where his father was pastor. He received a B.A. from Princeton University in 1879, graduated from the University of Virginia Law School in 1882, was admitted to the Georgia Bar and received a Ph.D. in political science from Johns Hopkins University. Mr. Wilson held a professorship in history at Bryn Mawr College and was later professor of jurisprudence and political economy at Princeton University. By 1902 he had authored nine books and twenty-two articles and was chosen president of Princeton in 1902. In 1910 he was elected governor of New Jersey and served as president of the United States from March 4, 1913 to March 3, 1921.

Members of the Commission, Mr. Wilson.

Mr. WILSON. The office of president requires the constitution of an athlete, the patience of a mother, the endurance of an early Christian. It is not a new feeling on my part, but one which I entertain with a greater intensity than formerly, that a man who seeks the presidency of the United States for anything that it will bring to him is an audacious fool. The responsibilities of the office ought to sober a man even before he approaches it.

I was constantly reminded of the personal inconvenience of being president of the United States. Sometimes, when

I was most beset, I seriously thought of renting a pair of whiskers or of doing something else that would furnish me with an adequate disguise, because I had to sail under false colors if I was going to sail incognito. The amount of work a president is supposed to do is preposterous.

I never dreamed such loneliness and desolation of heart possible. The very magnitude and fatefulness of the task I had every day to face dominated me and held me steady to my duty. The president is a superior kind of slave, and must content himself with the reflection that the kind is superior. When I thought of the number of men who were looking to me as the representative of a party, with the hope for all varieties of salvage from the things they were struggling in the midst of, it made me tremble. It made me tremble not only with a sense of inadequacy and weakness, but as if I were shaken by the very things that were shaking them and, if I seem circumspect, it was because I was so diligently trying not to make any colossal blunders. If you just calculate the number of blunders a fellow can make in twenty-four hours, if he is not careful and if he does not listen more than he talks, you would see something of the feeling that I had.

Mr. MADISON. Your administration was most characterized by problems related to foreign affairs, and in turn, by your relationship to Congress. Can you comment on these?

Mr. WILSON. I am confident that I am supported by every competent Constitutional authority in the statement that the initiative in directing the relations of our government with foreign governments is assigned by the Constitution to the executive and to the executive only. Only one of the two houses of Congress is associated with the president by the Constitution in an advisory capacity, and the advice of the Senate is provided for only when sought by the executive in regard to explicit agreements with foreign governments and the appointment of the diplomatic representatives who are to speak for this government at foreign capitals. The only safe course, I am confident, is to adhere to the prescribed method of the Constitution. We might go very far afield if we departed from it.

Mr. JEFFERSON. You were born in 1856, so that as

a boy you lived through Abraham Lincoln's most crucial years. As a matter of curiosity, Mr. Wilson, did that knowledge, that experience, direct or indirect as it was, affect your views toward the presidency?

Mr. WILSON. I have read many biographies of Lincoln; I have sought out with great interest the many intimate stories that are told of him, the narratives of nearby friends, the sketches at close quarters, in which those who had the privilege of being associated with him have tried to depict for us the very man himself "in his habit as he lived"; but I have nowhere found a real intimate of Lincoln's. I nowhere get the impression in any narrative or reminiscence that the writer had in fact penetrated to the heart of his mystery, or that any man could penetrate to the heart of it. That brooding spirit had no real familiars. I get the impression that it never spoke out in complete self-revelation and that it could not reveal itself completely to anyone. It was a very lonely spirit that looked out from underneath those shaggy brows and comprehended men without fully communing with them, as if, in spite of all its genial efforts at comradeship, it dwelt apart, saw its visions of duty where no man looked on. There is a very holy and very terrible isolation for the conscience of every man who seeks to read the destiny in affairs for others as well as for himself, for nation as well as for individuals. That privacy no man can intrude upon. That lonely search of the spirit for the right perhaps no man can assist.

Mr. JEFFERSON. No further questions, Mr. Chairman.

Gen. WASHINGTON. Thank you, Mr. Wilson. We will recess for twenty minutes.

[Recess]

Gen. WASHINGTON. The Commission will come to order. Mr. Warren G. Harding is our next speaker. Our twenty-ninth president was born in Blooming Grove, Ohio, November 2, 1865; he attended public schools in and near Caledonia, Ohio and Ohio Central College at Iberia, then studied law for a short time, taught school, engaged in the insurance business and became editor and publisher of the **Marion Star** in 1884. He was a member of the state senate from 1899 to 1903 and served as lieutenant governor before his election as a Republican to the United States Senate. Elected president on the Republican ticket with Calvin Coolidge as vice-president, he was inaugurated March 4, 1921, and served until August 2, 1923.

Mr. Harding has indicated he will limit his remarks to his personal observations of the burden of the office of the presidency.

Mr. HARDING. Thank you, Gen. Washington. I will be brief. Gentlemen, if there is anything wrong with the White House job, it is the inability to be a human being. The job of being president is one that makes almost inordinate demands upon a man's time. The White House is a prison. I could not get away from the men who dogged my footsteps. I was in jail. I was not worried about my enemies. I could take care of them. It was my friends who were giving me trouble. I knew that the job would be too much for me. Oftentimes, as I sat there I didn't seem to grasp that I was president.

God, what a job!

Thank you, gentlemen.

Gen. WASHINGTON. Thank you, Mr. Harding.

Dr. FRANKLIN. (Aside to Mr. Jefferson) These hearings are beginning to look like "cameo" appearances by former Presidents—like "walk ons" in a broadway show.

Mr. JEFFERSON. But one wonders if it is a comedy—or a tragedy?

Gen. WASHINGTON. We proceed next to Mr. Calvin Coolidge, our thirtieth president.

Mr. Coolidge was born in Plymouth, Vermont, July 4, 1872; he attended public schools, the Black River Academy and St. Johnsbury Academy and was graduated from Amherst College, Massachusetts, in 1895. He studied law, was admitted to the bar in 1897, and commenced practice in Northampton, Massachusetts. A member of the state senate, he served as president of that body in 1914 and 1915. Lieutenant governor of Massachusetts and governor in 1919 and 1920, he was elected vice-president of the United States on the Republican ticket headed by Warren G. Harding in 1920. Mr. Coolidge became president on August 3, 1923, and was elected president in 1924 for the term expiring March 3, 1929; he was not a candidate for renomination in 1928.

Gentlemen, Mr. Coolidge.

Mr. COOLIDGE. The presidency is primarily an Executive office. It is placed at the apex of our system of government. It is a place of last resport to which all questions are brought that others have not been able to answer. While it is wise for the president to get all the competent advice possible, final judgments are necessarily his own. An unofficial advisor to a president of the United States is not a good thing and is not provided for in our form of government.

Dr. FRANKLIN. Mr. Coolidge, would you please repeat that last statement?

Mr. COOLIDGE. I said that an unofficial advisor to the president is not a good thing and is not provided for in our form of government.

Dr. FRANKLIN. Thank you.

Mr. COOLIDGE. The president gets the best advice he can find, uses the best judgment at his command, and leaves the event in the hands of Providence. No one can share with him the responsibility. No one can make his decisions for him. He stands at the center of things where no one else can stand. If others make mistakes, they can be relieved, and oftentimes a remedy can be provided. But he cannot retire. His decisions are final and usually irreparable. This constitutes the appalling burden of his office. Not only the welfare of millions of his countrymen, but oftentimes the peaceful relations of the world are entrusted to his keeping. At the turn of his hand the guns of an enormous fleet would go into action anywhere in the world, carrying the iron might of death and destruction. His appointment confers the power to adminster justice, inflict criminal penalties, declare acts of state legislatures and of the Congress void, and sit in judgment over the very life of the nation. Practically all the civil and military authorities of the government, except the Congress and the courts, hold their office at his discretion. He appoints, and he can remove. The billions of dollars of government revenue are collected and expended under his direction. The Congress makes the laws, but it is the President who causes them to be executed. A power so vast in its implications has never been conferred upon any ruling sovereign.

Mr. ADAMS. Mr. Coolidge, did you ever think of yourself as a great president?

Mr. COOLIDGE. It is a great advantage to a president, and a major source of safety to the country, for him to know that he is not a great man. When a man begins to feel that he is the only one who can lead in this republic, he is guilty of treason to the spirit of our institutions.

Mr. MADISON. Can you expand on the subject of presidential powers?

Mr. COOLIDGE. The president exercises his authority in accordance with the Constitution and the law. He is truly the agent of the people, performing such functions as they have entrusted to him. The Constitution specifically vests him with the executive power. Some presidents have seemed to interpret that as an authorization to take any action which the Constitution, or perhaps the law, does not specifically prohibit. Others have considered that their powers extended only to such acts as were specifically authorized by the Constitution and the statutes. This has always seemed to me to be a hypothetical question, which it would be idle to attempt to determine in advance. It would appear to be the better practice to wait to decide each question on its merits as it arises. My colleague, Mr. Jefferson, is said to have entertained the opinion that there was no constitutional warrant for enlarging the territory of the United States, but when the actual facts confronted him he did not hesitate to negotiate the Louisiana Purchase. For all ordinary occasions the specific powers assigned to the president will be found sufficient to provide for the welfare of the country. That is all he needs.

Mr. JEFFERSON. What were your personal thoughts about the burden of being president?

Mr. COOLIDGE. The duties of the presidency are exceedingly heavy. The responsibilities are overwhelming. But it is my opinion that a man of ordinary strength can carry them if he will confine himself very strictly to a performance of the duties that are imposed upon him by the Constitution and the law. If he permits himself to be engaged in all kinds of outside enterprises, in furnishing entertainment and amusement to great numbers of public gatherings, undertaking to be the source of inspiration for every worthy public movement, . . . he will last in office about ninety days.

 It is of course obvious that the president should not burden himself with details. Those should be attended to by his departments and his office staff. He should not do any work that he can have done by others. Such energy as he has should be directed not so much towards doing work as making certain that the work is being well done.

 In the discharge of the duties of the office, then, there is one rule of action more important than all others. It consists in never doing anything that someone else can do for you.

 Mr. ADAMS. We have heard testimony recommending extending the terms of the presidency from four to six or seven years. To get at perhaps an outside limit, would ten years be appropriate?

 Mr. COOLIDGE. Ten years is too long for one man to be president.

 Dr. FRANKLIN. Mr. Coolidge, the practice among presidents in more recent times has been to send former presidents to foreign countries to represent him in one matter or another. Do you favor this practice?

 Mr. COOLIDGE. I know that when I was in Washington I wouldn't have wanted an ex-president poking around Europe. I had enough trouble with amateur diplomats.

 Gen. WASHINGTON. Thank you, Mr. Coolidge. We now return to former President Herbert Hoover. Mr. Hoover testified a few days ago on the report of the Hoover Commission on the organization of the government. He now returns to give us other glimpses of his activities. Gentlemen, Mr. Herbert Hoover.

Mr. HOOVER. The structure of our government makes the resonsibility of the president and the legislative body entirely independent, and for good reasons. Our cabinet, in fact, is only a body of operating vice-presidents, in charge of administrative departments, and meets for purposes of coordinating administrative action. It has no power over the president. It has no power to originate presidential politics. It is sometimes an advisory body, depending on the president. An American Coalition Cabinet would have no effective part in formulating presidential policies even in war, unless the president would bind himself to abide by the joint and collective vote of the cabinet. That he would not do.

The whole genius of the American people has demonstrated . . . that when we come to executive action, including the office of the president of the United States, we must have single-headed responsibility. It is just as foolish to set up a board to conduct munitions business as it would be to set up a board to conduct the presidency of the United States.

Mr. ADAMS. Mr. Hoover, what would you say are the first requisites of a president?

Mr. HOOVER. The first requisites of a president of the United States are intellectual honesty and sincerity.

Mr. MADISON. What about presidential privileges?

Mr. HOOVER. There are some valuable privileges attached to being president—among them the duty and right to terminate all interviews, conferences, social parties, and receptions. Therefore, he can go to bed whenever he likes.

Dr. FRANKLIN. Any other presidential privileges worthy of comment?

Mr. HOOVER. Yes. Believe it or not, fishing. I was quite a fisherman in my day. Fishing seems to be the sole avenue left to presidents through which they may escape to their own thoughts and may live in their own imaginings and find relief from the pneumatic hammer of constant personal contacts, and refreshment of mind in the babble of rippling brooks.

Moreover, it is a constant reminder of the democracy of life, of humility and of human frailty—for all men are equal before fishes. And it is desirable that the president of the United States should be periodically reminded of this fundamental fact—that the forces of nature discriminate for no man. Many years ago I concluded that the president differs only from other men in that he has a more extensive wardrobe.

Dr. FRANKLIN. We have talked about the privileges of the presidency; what about its burdens?

Mr. HOOVER. A useless exhaustion which had always plagued presidents was signing routine papers. No man could read them even in a twenty-four hour shift. They comprised all military officers' commissions, many appointments of civil servants, treasury orders, documents relating to the guardianship of individual Indians, pension authorities, etc., all of which the president could only sign on the dotted line and trust to Heaven and his cabinet officers that they were all right.

Dr. FRANKLIN. Mr. Hoover, is there any other subject you would like to address for the Commission's benefit?

Mr. HOOVER. Why yes, I feel very strongly about the topic of communism. Communism is an evil thing. It is contrary to the spiritual, moral and material aspirations of man. These very reasons give rise to my conviction that it will decay and die of its own poisons. But that may be many years away and, in the meantime, we must be prepared for a long journey.

What the world needs today is a moral mobilization against the hideous ideas of the police state and human slavery. The world needs mobilization against this creeping Red imperialism. The United States needs to know who are with us and whom we can depend on in the cold war.

I suggest that the United Nations be reorganized without the communist nations in it. If that is impractical, then a definite New United Front should be organized of those peoples who disavow communism, who stand for morals and religion and who love freedom.

This nation needs a rebirth of that great spiritual force which has been impaired by cynicism and weakened by foreign infections. Call it nationalism if you will. There is an American kind of nationalism, which is neither isolationism nor aggression.

Never after victory did we ask for an acre of territory, except a few military bases to protect the free nations. We have never asked for reparations or economic privileges. On the contrary, we made gigantic gifts and loans to aid nations in war and reconstruction, including Communist Russia. There is no imperialism either in our hearts or in our government.

Gen. WASHINGTON. Thank you Mr. Hoover. Please remain with us. You may be able to contribute more, particularly in view of your long "former" presidential status.

We turn now to former President Franklin Delano Roosevelt. Our thirty-second president, Mr. Roosevelt served from 1933 to 1945, longer than any other president. He was born in 1882 on a Hudson River estate at Hyde Park, New York; he attended Groton, a prestigious preparatory school in Massachusetts, from 1896 to 1900, then attended and graduated from Harvard University with an A.B. in history in 1903. He passed the bar examination in 1907, leaving school without a law degree. Elected to the state senate in 1910, he was appointed assistant secretary of the navy in 1913, and was the running mate of presidential candidate James M. Cox, in 1920. He was stricken with infantile paralysis in 1921, setting off a lifetime fight to overcome the ravages of the disease, and inspired as well as directed the March of Dimes program that eventually funded an effective vaccine. Governor of New York from 1929 to 1933, he was inaugurated president on March 4, 1933 and served until April 12, 1945.

Gentlemen, before we proceed with Mr. Roosevelt's testimony, we will recess for twenty minutes.

First SPECTATOR. I know that FDR was a heavyweight as far as presidents go, but he was before my time.

Second SPECTATOR. Mine, too. I've just heard my parents rave about him.

Mr. THOMPSON. (Overhearing, then addressing two SPECTATORS.) Perhaps I can be of some help. Some perspective is needed of the period immediately preceeding the presidential reign of Franklin D. Roosevelt to comprehend what he faced from the day he took office on March 4, 1933. Four years earlier, the peaceful year of 1929 turned out to be one of the most unforgettable in American history. This was the year of "The Great Crash."

Earlier, in the mid 1920s, just about everyone was talking about "The Stock Market." Stock prices were rising steadily. Then, early in 1929, stocks no longer were being bought and sold on the basis of intrinsic value. Instead, speculation became dominant. The Big Bull Market began in March 1928. Hoover's election in November was followed by a new boom in prices. RCA went up to 420 from 85. Du Pont was 525, up from 310. Much of the buying was being done "on margin," which meant with borrowed money. At the end of 1928, brokers' loans totaled $5.7 billion. Customer loan interest rates were 5.4 percent. The national debt was over $16 billion.

On September 3, 1929, stocks reached an all-time high. This was the day the Big Bull Market of the 1920s ended. On Black Thursday, October 24, 1929, panic struck the stock market. Oddly, one of the visitors to the Stock Exchange on that day was Winston Churchill, who had recenty been the British Chancellor of the Exchequer.

In the course of the fall season, sheaves of stock, like the autumn leaves, fell $30 billion in value. In three years, General Motors went from 73 to 8, and U.S. Steel went from 262 to 22.

The Great Depression was in motion and like a steamroller it crushed the country. It was devastating. From 1929 to 1933, it rolled on and on and in its wake, and like a wake, between 1929 and 1933 . . .

- The Gross National Product fell from $103 bilion to $55.6 billion.

- 129,230 businesses failed.

- Unemployment went from 1,550,000 to 12,830,000. One out of every four persons in the civilian labor force was out of work.

- Average family personal income dropped from $2,335 to $1,631 (1935).

- Pork chop prices were chopped from 37 to 19 cents a pound.

- Butter slid from 55 to 27 cents a pound.
- Egg prices cracked, going from 52 to 28 cents a dozen.
- Orange prices were peeled from 44 to 27 cents a dozen.
- And coffee dripped—I mean, dropped—from 47 to 26 cents a pound.
- There were 979,800 real estate foreclosures of non-farm properties.
- Over 4,000 banks failed.
- There were 9,765 bank suspensions. A "bank suspension" is defined as closing a bank to the public, either temporarily or permanently, by supervisory authorities or by the bank's boards of directors, because of financial difficulties, but does not include special banking holidays declared by civil authorities.

At the end of October 1932, Nevada proclaimed a bank holiday; in February, 1933, Louisiana suspended all bank activities; and then days later Michigan did the same.

On the day Franklin Delano Roosevelt was inaugurated, Gov. Herbert H. Lehman of New York closed all banks in the state and the country was without banking services. In the last two weeks of Herbert Hoover's regime, depositors had withdrawn more than a billion dollars and hoarded it in cash!

In his first inaugural address President Roosevelt confidently stated, "Our Constitution is so simple and practical that it is possible always to meet extraordinary needs by changes in emphasis and arrangement without loss of essential form . . . I shall ask the Congress for . . . broad executive power that would be given to me if we were in fact invaded by a foreign foe."

The day after he took office he proclaimed a four-day bank holiday and called Congress into a special session. On the first day that Congress convened, it passed an Emergency Banking Act after forty minutes' debate; the Senate followed, and in less than eight hours in all, the bill was signed into law by President Roosevelt. Half the banks, representing 90 percent of all banking resources, opened by March 15, 1933. One bank in twenty never did business again. In the first three weeks after banks reopened, more than a billion dollars was redeposited.

On March 5th Will Rogers said, "America hasn't been as happy in three years as they are today—no money, no banks, no work, no nothing. . . ." And then he later said that the president took the complicated subject of banking and made even the bankers understand it.

During "The Hundred Days" ending June 15, 1933, when the special session adjourned, Congress passed fifteen major "New Deal" laws, far-reaching in scope and significance.

The Federal Deposit Insurance Corporation (FDIC) safeguarded bank deposits. The Home Owners' Loan Corporation (HOLC) provided direct government loans for mortgages to homeowners and farmers. The Civilian Conservation Corps (CCC) put thousands of young men to work on conservation projects. The Federal Emergency Relief Act (FERA) granted funds to states and municipalities for aid to the unemployed.

The Agricultural Adjustment Act (AAA) paid subsidies to farmers for curtailing production of certain livestock and crops and guaranteed parity prices for them. The Tennessee Valley Authority (TVA) put the government into the power business in a major way and marked the beginning of intensified regional planning.

The omnibus National Industrial Recovery Act (NIRA) created the National Recovery Administration (NRA) and the Public Works Administration (PWA). Respectively, these agencies promulgated voluntary business and industrial codes geared toward increasing wages and maintaining prices and reducing unemployment and employed laborers on newly created construction projects. The NIRA also guaranteed labor's right to organize and bargain collectively.

The president had said in his inaugural address that "The people of the United States have . . . registered a mandate that they want direct, vigorous action. . . ."

They got it. Franklin Roosevelt was the catalyst. He gave it—for twelve years.

Gen. WASHINGTON. This session will resume. Thank you for appearing today, Mr. Roosevelt. Mr. Adams will begin the questioning.

Mr. ADAMS. Whatever impelled you to act so decisively in the expansion of government services?

Mr. ROOSEVELT. I received a great shock. I had been away from my home town of Hyde Park during the winter time and when I came back I found that a tragedy had occurred. I had had an old farm neighbor who had been a splendid old fellow—supervisor of the town, highway commissioner of his town, one of the best of our citizens. Before I had left, around Christmas time, I had seen the old man, who was eighty-nine, his old brother, who was eighty-seven, his other brother, who was eighty-five, and his "kid" sister, who was eighty-three.

They were living on a farm; I knew it was mortgaged to the hilt; but I assumed that everything was all right, for they still had a couple of cows and a few chickens. But when I came back in the spring, I found that in the severe winter that followed there had been a heavy fall of snow, and one of the old brothers had fallen down on his way out to the barn to milk the cow and had perished in the snow drift. The town authorities had come along and had taken the two old men and had put them into the county poorhouse; and they had taken the old lady and sent her down, for want of a better place, to the insane asylum, although she was not insane but just old.

That sold me on the idea of social justice through social action.

I saw tens of millions of our citizens denied the necessities of life.

I saw millions of families trying to live on incomes so meager that the pall of family disaster was over them day by day.

I saw millions who lived in cities and on farms under conditions labeled indecent by a so-called polite society half a century ago.

I saw millions denied education, recreation, and the opportunity to better their lot and the lot of their children.

I saw millions lacking the means to buy the products of the farm and factory.

I saw one-third of a nation ill-housed, ill-clad, and ill-nourished.

And **that** sold me on the idea of social justice through social action.

Mr. ADAMS. Mr. Roosevelt, your "social action" was often quite sweeping in nature. Do you believe that you always acted within the framework of the Constitution?

Mr. ROOSEVELT. The presidency is a most sacred trust and it ought not to be dealt with on any level other than an appeal to reason and humanity. In spite of what some people have said, I sought always to be a constitutional president.

Mr. ADAMS. What was your relationship with Congress?

Mr. ROOSEVELT. To carry out my responsibility as president, it was clear that if there was to be success in our government there ought to be cooperation between members of my own party and myself—cooperation in other words, within the majority party, between one branch of government, the legislative branch, and the head of the other branch, the executive. That is one of the essentials of a party form of government.

Within this process, the members of Congress realized that the method of normal times had to be replaced in the emergency by measures which were suited to the serious and pressing requirements of the moment. There was no actual surrender of powers; Congress still retained its constitutional authority, and no one had the slightest desire to change the balance of their power. The function of Congress is to decide what has to be done and to select the appropriate agency to carry out its will. To this policy it strictly adhered. The only thing that happened was that it designated the president as the agency to carry out certain of the purposes of the Congress. This was constitutional and in keeping with the past American tradition.

Dr. FRANKLIN. (Aside to Mr. Jefferson) I wonder how Franklin D. Roosevelt reconciles what he just said with another statement he once made: "My relative, Theodore Roosevelt, once clenched his fist and said, 'Sometimes, I wish I could be president and Congress too.' Well, I suppose if the truth were told, he is not the only president that has had that idea."

Mr. MADISON. Mr. Roosevelt, from 1933 to 1939 a vast change took place in the conduct, administration, and expense of government. The national debt, which had remained constant during Mr. Hoover's term at about $19.5 billion, more than doubled, reaching $40.4 billion. Today it is over one trillion dollars. The annual administration expense of government in your administration went from $4.6 billion to $8.8 billion. Today it is approaching $800 billion. The number of federal agencies, departments, bureaus, and commissions then stood at about a hundred. Today there are over 1,500. Federal employment went from about 600,000 employees to about one million. Today it is about 3 million.

The point is that the pattern for this tremendous expansion of government services began in your administration and has continued to this very day. Can you address yourself to this question?

Mr. ROOSEVELT. Henry Steel Commager once wrote about my administration: "Roosevelt himself, though indubitably a leader, was an instrument of the popular will rather than a creator of, or a dictator to, that will. . . . Precedents for the major part of New Deal legislation were to be found in earlier periods. . . . Eventually Roosevelt came to exercise powers far vaster than those contemplated by the Fathers of the Constitution, as vast, indeed, as those exercised by the head of any democratic state in the world. Yet it cannot fairly be asserted that any of these powers were exercised arbitrarily, or that the liberties of Americans are not so safe today as at any other time. . . ."

Mr. JEFFERSON. You have told us what Henry Steele Commager said of your administration. But what do **you** think? Did you think of yourself as a dictator?

Mr. ROOSEVELT. History proves that dictatorships do not grow out of strong and successful governments, but out of weak and helpless ones. If by democratic methods people get a government strong enough to protect them from fear and starvation, their democracy succeeds; but if they do not, they grow impatient. Therefore, the only sure bulwark of continuing liberty is a government strong enough to protect the interests of the people, and a people strong enough and well-enough informed to maintain its sovereign control over its governments.

Mr. HOOVER. Mr. Chairman, is there any single person in America who is so unaware that he does not know the gigantic growth of the personal power of the president during the administration of President Roosevelt? Arthur Schlesinger, Jr. said of President Roosevelt:

> His favorite technique was to keep grants of authority incomplete, jurisdiction uncertain, charters overlapping. The result of this competitive theory of administration was often confusion and exasperation on the operating level; but no other method could so reliably insure that in a large bureaucracy filled with ambitious men eager for power the decisions, and the power to make them, would remain with the president.

The genius of our Founding Fathers which preserved this Republic longer than any Republic in history was the concept of the limitation of powers within our government. One of their strong purposes was to protect free men by restriction of presidential power. We have seen constant attrition of those Constitutional safeguards of free men in Mr. Roosevelt's administration. I need not recall for you the "Rubber Stamp Congress"; the packed Supreme Court; war without approval of Congress; and a score of dire secret international commitments without consent of the Senate. And now comes a new discovery in presidential power. That is an "inherent" power to seize anything, at any time. All Republican presidents were densely ignorant of those inherent powers.

No man has been elected by the people to have such powers. If freedom is to live, we can no more have economic tyranny than we can have political tyranny. Representative government has not been maintained in the mastery of its own house.

Mr. ROOSEVELT. Now see here, Herbert. As far as powers go, there is not a single power I had that you and Mr. Coolidge did not have. Can anyone name any power I had that

Hoover and Coolidge did not have?

Mr. ADAMS. Mr. Roosevelt, you once stated that "The presidency as established in the Constitution has all of the powers that are required. In spite of the timid souls in 1787, who feared effective government, the presidency was established as a single, strong chief executive office in which was vested the entire executive power of the national government. . . ."

Who were those "timid souls" you referred to, Mr. Roosevelt?

Mr. ROOSEVELT. It should be evident, Mr. Adams, the reference was not to you or Mr. Jefferson, since neither of you was at the Federal Convention in 1787.

Mr. ADAMS. Then the reference was to Gen. Washington, Mr. Franklin, and Mr. Madison?

Mr. ROOSEVELT. I honored these men when I said, "The men who wrote the Constitution were the men who fought the Revolution. . . . when these men planned a new government, they drew the kind of agreement which men make when they really want to work together under it for a very long time.

For the youngest of nations they drew what is today the oldest written instrument under which men have continuously lived together as a nation.

The Constitution of the United States was a layman's document, not a lawyer's contract."

I have also said that what counts is not so much the methods of the moment as the pathways that are marked out down the years. I like to think of my administration as the expression of an enduring principle carved in stone by a nation which has come to maturity—a nation which has forever left behind the old irresponsible ways of its youth, a nation facing the realities of today and prudently taking thought for the morrow. Methods and machinery may change, but principles go on.

Mr. MADISON. In the "Hoover Commission Report" on the organization of the executive branch of the government, Mr. Hoover said that the executive branch is a chaos of bureaus and subdivisions; that the gigantic and sudden growth of the executive branch has produced great confusion within the departments and agencies as well as in their relations to the president and to each other; that there are too many separate agencies and that consequently, there are overlaps, duplications, and inadequacies in determination of policies; that the federal government has failed to develop an aggressive program for building a corps of administrators of the highest level of ability; that it is not quantity of administrators that is required, it is quality; that many statutes and departmental regulations that control the department's procedures are unduly complicated; that they set up such rigid patterns that the execution of a congressional purpose is inefficient and wasteful.

Mr. Hoover then proposed about $9 billion in annual savings for the government.

The executive branch under Mr. Hoover cost $4 billion a year to operate, and employed 600,000 persons. Lacking proper organization, it laid even then a great burden upon the executive. In 1939, for example, the executive branch cost almost $9 billion a year. When Mr. Hoover wrote the report in the fifties, the executive branch required an annual budget of $42 billion and employed 2,100,000 persons in an intricate structure of 1,816 assorted departments, bureaus, sections, divisions, administrations, etc.

Mr. Roosevelt, these are startling statistics and we have not had the opportunity prior to this time to obtain your comments on this report. Can you comment on it now?

Mr. ROOSEVELT. For many years we have all known that the executive and administrative departments of the government in Washington are a higgledy-piggledy patchwork of duplicate responsibilities and overlapping powers.

In my time, the Committee on Administrative Management pointed out that no enterprise can operate effectively if set up as our government was. There were over 100 separate departments, boards, commissions, corporations, authorities, agencies, and activities through which the work of the government was being carried on. Neither the president nor the Congress could exercise effective supervision and direction over such a tangle of establishments nor could overlapping, duplicating, and contradictory policies be avoided.

It was common knowledge that the president could not adequately handle his responsibilities; that he was overworked; that it was humanly impossible, under the system which we had for him, fully to carry out his Constitutional duty as chief executive because he was overwhelmed with minor details and needless contacts arising directly from the bad organization and equipment of the government. My predecessors have said the same thing over and over again.

The plain fact was that the organization and equipment of the executive branch of the government defeated the Constitutional intent that there be a single responsible chief executive to coordinate and manage the departments and activities in accordance with the laws enacted by the Congress. Under these conditions the government could not be thoroughly effective in working under popular control, for the common good.

Mr. ADAMS. (Aside to Mr. Jefferson) I believe that the demands for better management in government persisted into the Truman, Eisenhower, and subsequent administrations and that the conditions were not corrected by the efforts of the Hoover Commission and their recommendations on reorganization. I believe this has been borne out by testimony to date before this Commission.

Mr. JEFFERSON. (Aside to Mr. Adams) Yes, that is quite correct.

Mr. ROOSEVELT. In 1899, President McKinley could deal with the whole machinery of the executive branch through eight cabinet secretaries and the heads of two commissions; and there was but one commission of the so-called quasi-judicial type in existence. He could keep in touch with all the work through eight or ten persons.

Now not only do some thirty major agencies, to say nothing of the minor ones, report directly to the president, but there are several quasi-judicial bodies which have enough administrative work to require them also to see him on important executive matters.

It has become physically impossible for one man to see so many persons, to receive reports directly from them, and to attempt to advise them on their own problems which they submit. In addition the president today has the task of trying to keep the programs in step with each other or in line with the national policy laid down by the Congress. And he must seek to prevent unnecessary duplication of effort.

To the president of the United States there come every day thousands of messages of appeal, of protest, of support, of information and advice, messages from rich and poor, from businessman and farmer, from factory employee and relief worker, messages from every corner of our wide domain.

There were many people who came forward with the thought, verbally expressed, that the government should take over all the troubles of the country, that we could, well, as we used to say in the old days, "Let George do it," and I began to think sometimes that my first name was George.

My working day averaged about fifteen hours. Even when I went to Hyde Park or to Warm Springs, the White House office, the callers, and the telephones all followed me.

Mr. HOOVER. My I interject here that numerous are the temptations to turn aside from our true national purposes and from wise national policies and fundamental ideals of the men who built our Republic. Never was the lure of the rosy path to every panacea and of easy ways to imagined security more tempting.

For the energies of private initiative, of independence, and a high degree of individual freedom of our American system we are offered alluring substitutes with the specious claim that everybody collectively owes each of us individually a living rather than an opportunity to earn a living—and the equally specious claim that hired representatives of scores of millions of people can do better than the people themselves, in thinking and planning their daily life.

We must not be misled by the claim that the source of all wisdom is in the government. Wisdom is born out of experience, and most of all out of precisely such experience as is brought to us by the darkest moments. It is in meeting such moments that are born new insights, new sympathies, new powers, new skills. Such conflicts cannot be won by any single stroke, by any one strategy sprung from the mind of any single genius. Rather must we pin our faith upon the inventiveness, the resourcefulness, the initiative of every one of us. That cannot fail us if we keep the faith in ourselves and our future, and in the constant growth of our intelligence and ability to cooperate with one another.

The principal thing we can do if we really want to make the world over again is to try the word "old" for awhile. There are some "old" things that made this country.

There is the Old Virtue of religious faith. There are the Old Virtues of integrity and the whole truth. There is the Old Virtue of incorruptible service and honor in public office. There are the Old Virtues of economy in government, of self-reliance, thrift, and individual liberty. There are the Old Virtues of patriotism, real love of country, and willingness to sacrifice for it.

These "old" ideas are very inexpensive. They even would help win hot and cold wars. I realize such suggestions will raise that cuss word, "reactionary." But some of these things are slipping badly in American life. And if they slip too far, the lights will go out of America, even if we win these cold and hot wars. Think about it . . .

I have lived a long life. I have witnessed, and even taken part in, many great and threatening crises. With each time they have been surmounted, the American Dream has become more real. If the American people are guided aright, there will be no decline and fall in American civilization.

Mr. ROOSEVELT. Civilization cannot go back; civilization must not stand still. We have undertaken new methods. It is our task to perfect, to improve, to alter when necessary, but, in all cases to go forward.

If we do not allow a democratic government to do the things which need to be done, and if we hand down to our children a deteriorated nation, their legacy will be not a legacy of abundance or even a legacy of poverty amidst plenty, but a legacy of poverty amidst poverty.

Dr. FRANKLIN. We have just listened to two

diametrically opposing views. We, here on the Commission, are trying to determine whether changes in the Constitution are needed to make it more adequate to the exigencies of this nation. Hoover chose inaction. Roosevelt chose action, and today every man, woman and child in this country pays dearly for it—$4,350 each to be exact. The National Debt at over a trillion dollars is more than 25 percent of the personal wealth of all persons in the United States. And this is the legacy of gargantuan government. With this kind of debt, "A long life may not be long enough." As to the office of the president, evidence is "You may give a man an office, but you cannot give him discretion." Well, "When the well's dry, we know the worth of water."

Gen. WASHINGTON. Mr. Roosevelt and Mr. Hoover, we thank you both. This session will adjourn until tomorrow, Tuesday, June 9th at 10 o'clock a.m. We are adjourned.

TUESDAY, JUNE 9, 1987

TESTIMONY OF PRESIDENTS: HARRY S. TRUMAN TO JOHN F. KENNEDY

The Committee met pursuant to notice, at 10 a.m. in the Assembly Room of Independence Hall, Gen. George Washington presiding.

    Present: Mr. John Adams, Dr. Benjamin Franklin, Mr. Thomas Jefferson, Mr. James Madison and Gen. George Washington.

    Gen. WASHINGTON. We continue today our meetings with former presidents of the United States. Today we have on the agenda Mr. Harry S Truman, Gen. Dwight D. Eisenhower, and Mr. John F. Kennedy.

    Our first speaker will be former President Harry S Truman. Our thirty-third president was born in Lamar, Missouri, May 8, 1884, and attended public schools in Independence, Missouri. During the First World War, he was commissioned a first lieutenant and later a captain and served with Battery D, 129th Field Artillery, United States Army, with service overseas, until his discharge as a major on May 6, 1919. On return he engaged in the haberdashery business and studied law at Kansas City (Missouri) Law School. He served as judge of the Jackson County Court from 1922 to 1924 and presiding judge from 1926 to 1934; elected as a Democrat to the United States Senate in 1934, he was reelected in 1940 and served from January 3, 1935 until his resignation on January 17, 1945. In 1944 he was elected vice-president on the Democratic ticket with Franklin Delano Roosevelt, and on April 12, 1945 became president. He was elected in 1948 for the term ending January 20, 1953. Gentlemen,

Mr. Harry S Truman.

Mr. TRUMAN. There's never been an office—an executive office—in all the history of the world with the responsibility and the power of the presidency of the United States. That is the reason in this day and age that it must be run and respected as at no other time in the history of the world because it can mean the welfare of the world or its destruction.

When the founding fathers outlined the presidency in Article II of the Constitution, they left a great many details out and vague. I think they relied on the experience of the nation to fill in the outlines. The office of the chief executive has grown with the progress of this great republic. It has responded to the many demands that our complex society has made upon the government. It had given our nation a means of meeting our greatest emergencies. Today, it is one of the most important factors in our leadership of the free world.

Many diverse elements entered into the creation of the office, springing as it did, from the parent idea of the separation of powers.

In the first place, the president became the leader of a political party. The party under his leadership had to be dominant enough to put him in office. This political party leadership was the last thing the Constitution contemplated. The president's election was not intended to be mixed up in the hurly-burly of partisan politics.

I am glad some of you are here to see how it worked. In your day, the people were expected to choose wise and respected men who would meet in calm seclusion and choose a president and the runner-up would be vice-president.

All of this went by the board—though most of the original language remains in the Constitution. Out of the struggle and tumult of the political arena a new and different president emerged—the man who led a political party to victory and retained in his hand the power of party leadership. That is, he retained it, like the sword Excalibur, if he could wrest it from the scabbard and wield it.

Another development was connected with the first. As

the president came to be elected by the whole people, he became responsible to the whole people. I used to say the only lobbyist the whole people had in Washington was the president of the United States. Our whole people looked to him for leadership, and not confined within the limits of a written document. Every hope and every fear of his fellow citizens, almost every aspect of their welfare and activity, falls within the scope of his concern—indeed, it falls within the scope of his duty. Only one who has held that office can really appreciate that. It is the president's responsibility to look at all questions from the point of view of the whole people. His written and spoken word commands national and often international attention.

These powers which are not explicitly written into the Constitution are the powers which no president can pass on to his successor. They go only to him who can take and use them. However, it is these powers, quite as much as those enumerated in Article II of the Constitution, which make the presidential system unique.

For it is through the use of these great powers that leadership arises, events are molded, and administrations take on their character.

And so a successful administration is one of strong presidential leadership. Weak leadership—or no leadership—produces failure and often disaster.

The president is responsible for the administration of his office, and that means for the administration of the entire executive branch. It is not the business of Congress to run the agencies of government for the president.

Unless this principle is observed, it is impossible to have orderly government. The legislative power will ooze into the executive offices. It will influence and corrupt the decisions of the executive branch. It will affect promotions and transfer. It will warp and twist policies.

Not only does the president cease to be a master in his own house, but the whole house of government becomes one which has no master. The power of decision then rests only in the legislative branch, and the legislative branch by its very nature is not equipped to perform these executive functions.

To this kind of encroachment it is the duty of the president to say firmly and flatly, "No, you can't do it." The investigative power of Congress is not limitless. It extends only so far as to permit the Congress to acquire the information that it honestly needs to exercise its legislative functions. Exercised beyond these limits, it becomes a manifestation of unconstitutional power. It raises the threat of a legislative dictatorship and that's the worst dictatorship in the world.

Today the tasks of leadership falling upon the president spring not only from our national problems but from those of the whole world. Today that leadership will determine whether our government will function effectively, and upon its functioning depends the survival of each of us and also on that depends the survival of the free world, if I may be so bold as to say that.

And today our government cannot function properly unless it follows the provisions of the Constitution. Our government cannot function properly unless the president is master in his own house and unless the executive departments and agencies of the government, including the armed forces, are responsible only to the president. Thank you.

Mr. ADAMS. There are intimations in what you say which seem to call up a ghost, your relationship with Gen. Douglas MacArthur. Am I correct in this inference?

Mr. TRUMAN. Let me just make it plain that the president of the United States, and not the second or third echelon in the State Department, is responsible for making foreign policy, and furthermore, that no one in any department can sabotage the president's policy. The civil servant, the general or admiral, the foreign service officer has no authority to make policy. They act only as servants of the government, and therefore they must remain in line with the government policy that is established by those who have been chosen by the people to set that policy.

Of course, I would never deny Gen. MacArthur or anyone else the right to differ with me in opinions. The official position of the United States, however, is defined by the decisions and declarations of the president. There can be only one voice in stating the position of this country in the field of foreign relations. This is of fundamental constitutional significance.

Mr. MADISON. How would you characterize the delegation of presidential functions or duties?

Mr. TRUMAN. The presidency is so tremendous that it is necessary for a president to delegate authority. To be able to do so safely, however, he must have people around him who can be trusted not to arrogate authority to themselves.

The difficulty with many career officials in the government is that they regard themselves as the men who really make policy and run the government. They look upon the elected officials as just temporary occupants. Every president in our history has been faced with this problem: how to prevent career men from circumventing presidential policy.

Under the Constitution the president of the United States is alone responsible for the faithful execution of the laws. Our government is fixed on the basis that the president is the only person in the executive branch who has the final authority. Everyone else in the executive branch is an agent of the president. There are some people, and sometimes members of the Congress and the press, who get mixed up in their thinking about the powers of the president. The important fact to remember is that the president is the only person in the executive branch who has final authority, and if he does not exercise it, we may be in trouble. If he exercises his authority wisely, that is good for the country. If he does not exercise it wisely, that is too bad, but it is better than not exercising it at all.

MR. JEFFERSON. Apparently you have very specific thoughts concerning advisors. Can you delineate?

Mr. TRUMAN. The president cannot function without advisors or without advice. But just as soon as he is required to show what kind of advice he has had, who said what to him, or what kind of records he has, the advice he receives will become worthless.

Mr. ADAMS. And what about your relationship with Congress?

Mr. TRUMAN. As a practical proposition, the executive branch of the government can no more operate by itself than can the Congress. There have always been a few congressmen who act as if they would like to control everything on the executive side, but they find out differently when the responsibility of administration is on their shoulders. But no president has ever attempted to govern alone. Every president knows and must know that the congressional control of the purse has to be reckoned with.

Congressional criticisms are heard, not infrequently, concerning deficiencies in the executive branch of the government. I should be less than frank if I failed to point out that the Congress cannot consistently advance such criticisms and at the same time deny the president the means of removing the causes at the root of such criticisms.

Dr. FRANKLIN. Very few, if any, of the presidents testifying here discussed the role of the vice-president. You were both a vice-president and a president. How do you characterize the role of the vice-president?

Mr. TRUMAN. The president is the man who decides every major domestic policy, and he is the man who makes foreign policy and negotiates treaties. In doing these things it would be very difficult for him to take the second man in the government—the vice-president—completely into his confidence. The president, by necessity, builds his own staff, and the vice-president remains an outsider, no matter now friendly the two may be. There are many reasons for this, but an important one is the fact that both the president and vice-president are, or should be, astute politicians, and neither can take the other completely into his confidence.

Dr. FRANKLIN. In other words, unless he becomes president, the vice-president is a nonentity.

Mr. TRUMAN. I did not say that. But I will say that I think it is an omission in our political tradition that a retiring president does not make it his business to facilitate the transfer of the government to his successor.

Mr. MADISON. Mr. Truman, what are your personal feelings concerning the presidency?

Mr. TRUMAN. I felt as if I had lived five lifetimes in my first five days as president. Within the first few months, I discovered that being a president is like riding a tiger. A man has to keep on riding or be swallowed.

I learned in a very short time that the president of the United States all too often has to act in ways that please others and which are very different from the personal wishes and feelings of the president himself. The presidency of the United States has become a highly complicated and exacting job.

There is no exaltation in the office of the president of the United States—sorrow is the proper word. To be president of the United States is to be lonely, very lonely, particularly at times of great decisions.

I have said it time and again, and I will keep on saying it, that I would rather have a Medal of Honor than be president of the United States.

No one who has not had the responsibility can really understand what it is like to be president, not even his closest aides or members of his immediate family. There is no end to the chain of responsibility that binds him, and he is never allowed to forget that he is president.

I had learned that one of the hardest things for the president to do is to find time to take stock. I have always believed that the president's office ought to be open to as many citiztens as he can find time to talk to; that is part of the job, to be available to the people, to listen to their troubles, to let them share the rich tradition of the White House. But it raises havoc with one's day. Even though I always got up early, usually was at work ahead of the staff, and would take papers home with me at night to read, there always seemed to be more than I could do.

I do not know of any easy way to be president. It is more than a full-time job, and the relaxations are few.

Mr. JEFFERSON. Mr. Truman, we have been discussing the possibility of extending the term of the president, making it a single term of six, seven, eight, or ten years. Do you have any thoughts or suggestions?

Mr. TRUMAN. In my opinion eight years as president is enough, and sometimes too much, for any man to serve in that capacity.

Gen. WASHINGTON. Thank you, Mr. Truman. We now proceed to our next speaker, former President Dwight D. Eisenhower, our thirty-fourth president. He was born on October 14, 1890, in Denison, Texas. In 1911 he was appointed to West Point and during World War I engaged in training duties, rising to major in 1920. In 1926 he graduated at the top of his class from the Command and General Staff School, Fort Leavenworth, Kansas, and two years later he graduated from the Army War College; he served in the Philippines under Gen. Douglas MacArthur. Promoted to temporary brigadier general in September 1941, he was called to the War Plans Division of the army's staff headquarters in Washington after the Japanese attack on Pearl Harbor and was promoted to temporary major general in April 1942. In 1943 he became supreme commander, Allied Expeditionary Forces; in that post he oversaw the D-Day landing on June 6, 1944, and the subsequent campaigns leading to the surrender of Germany nearly a year later. He was promoted to the five-star rank of general of the army in December 1944, and in February 1948 he retired to become president of Columbia University. He served as president of the United States from January 20, 1953 to January 20, 1961. Members of the Commission, Gen. Eisenhower.

Gen. EISENHOWER. The president is the Constitutional Commander-in-Chief of our Armed Forces and is constantly confronted with major questions as to their efficiency, organization, operations, and adequacy.

The right of self-preservation is just as instinctive and natural for a nation as it is for the individual.

When the push of a button may mean obliteration of countless humans, the president of the United States must be forever on guard against any inclination on his part to impetuosity; to arrogance; to headlong action; to expediency; to facile maneuvers; even to the popularity of an action as opposed to the rightness of an action.

He cannot worry about headlines; how the next opinion poll will rate him; how his political future will be affected.

He must worry only about the good—the long-term, abiding, permanent good—of all America.

Dr. FRANKLIN. (Aside to Mr. Jefferson) . . . or good-bye, America!

Mr. MADISON. Do you have any thought on the Twenty-second Amendment limiting the term of the president to two terms?

Gen. EISENHOWER. I was opposed to the Twenty-second Amendment. By and large, the United States ought to be able to choose for its president anybody it wants, regardless of the number of terms he has served.

That is what I believe. Now, some people have said "You let him get enough power and this will lead toward a one-party government." That I don't believe. I have got the utmost faith in the long-term common sense of the American people.

Therefore, I don't think there should be any inhibitions other than those that were in the thirty-five-year age limit and so on. I think that was enough myself.

Mr. ADAMS. General, what about your personal thoughts on the job of the presidency?

Gen. EISENHOWER. The duties of the president are essentially endless. No daily schedule of appointments can give a full timetable—or even a faint indication— of the president's responsibilities. Entirely aside from the making of important decisions, the formulation of policy through the National Security Council, and the cabinet, cooperation with the Congress, and with the states, there is for the president a continuous burden of study, contemplation, and reflection.

Of the subjects demanding this endless study, some deal with foreign affairs, with the position of the United States in the international world, her strength, her aspirations, and the methods by which she may exert her influence in the solution of world problems and in the direction of a just and enduring peace. These—all of them—are a particular Constitutional responsibility of the president.

All these matters, among others, are with a president always: in Washington, in a summer White House, on a weekend absence, indeed, even at a ceremonial dinner and in every hour of leisure. The old saying is true, "A president never escapes from his office."

There are many things about the office and the work, the work with your associates, that are, well, let's say, at least intriguing, even if at times they are very fatiguing. But it is a wonderful experience.

Every problem that you take up has inevitably a terrific meaning for many millions of people so there is no problem that comes up in the presidency—even some that appear trivial—that is handled as easily as you would handle your own daily living, or even something in the military, or in other activities in which I have been engaged.

I would say that the presidency is probably the most taxing job, as far as tiring of the mind and spirit; but it also has, as I have said before, its inspirations which tend to counteract each other.

Mr. ADAMS. General, can you quite compare your career in the military to that as president?

Gen. EISENHOWER. Oh, yes, beyond question. You see, the nakedness of the battlefield when the soldier is all alone in the smoke and the clamor and the terror of war is comparable to the loneliness—at times—of the presidency. These are the times when one man must conscientiously, deliberately, prayerfully, scrutinize every argument, every proposal, every prediction, every alternative, every probable outcome of his action and then—all alone—make his decision.

In that moment he can draw on no brain trust; no pressure group; no warehouse of trick phrases; no facile answers. Even his most trusted associates and friends cannot help him in that moment. He can draw only upon the truths and principles responsible for America's birth and development, applying them to the problem immediately before him in the light of a broad experience with men and nations.

He will be face to face with himself, his conscience,

his measure of wisdom. And he will have to pray for Divine guidance from Almighty God.

Thank you for inviting me before your Commission.

Gen. WASHINGTON. Thank you, General Eisenhower. We now turn our attention to former President John F. Kennedy, our thirty-fifth president. Born in Brookline, Massachusetts, May 29, 1917, Mr. Kennedy attended the public schools, then Choate School, Wallingford, Connecticut, the London School of Economics at London, England, and Stanford University; he was graduated from Harvard University, 1950. During World War II he served as a lieutenant in the United States Navy from September 1941 to April 1945; he was a PT boat commander in the South Pacific and was awarded the Navy and Marine Corps Medal and the Purple Heart. Elected as a Democrat to the Eightieth, Eighty-First, and Eighty-Second Congresses, Mr. Kennedy was also elected to the United States Senate in 1952. He served as president from January 20, 1961 to November 22, 1963. Mr. Kennedy.

Mr. KENNEDY. I am most honored to be able to speak in the City of Philadelphia before this Commission. Each of you has through your own political service given lasting validity to the aims of our country. Your own political service carried you onward and upward to the presidency, with one exceptional exception. As for my own political service, I must say that it is a tremendous change to go from being a senator to being president. The first months are very difficult—but . . . a president with the powers of the office and responsibilities placed on it, if he has the judgment and something needs to be done, . . . can do it, depending of course on the makeup of the Congress. The fact is that, as president, I thought the Congress looked more powerful than it did when I was there in the Congress. But that's because when you're in Congress you're one of a hundred in the senate or one of 435 in the House, so that your power is divided. I look at the collective power of the Congress, particularly to block action; it is substantial power.

Our Constitution wisely assigns both joint and separate roles to each branch of the government; and a president and a

Congress who hold each other in mutual respect will neither permit nor attempt any trespass.

But there is bound to be conflict. They must cooperate to the degree that's possible. But that's why no president's program is ever put in. The only time a president's program is put in quickly and easily is when the program is insignificant. But if it's significant and affects important interests and is controversial, then there's a fight and then the president is never wholly successful.

Mr. ADAMS. Can you say something about the relationship between the president and regulatory agencies, which, as this Commission has revealed, are somewhat in the gray area between the president and Congress?

Mr. KENNEDY. The president also has his responsibilities with respect to the operation of these regulatory agencies. In addition to a constitutional duty to see that the laws are faithfully executed, and other inherent executive powers granted to him, it is his duty to staff the regulatory agencies with men and women competent to handle the responsibilities vested in them and dedicated to the goals set forth in the legislation they are appointed to implement. The president, moreover, is charged in many instances by the Congress with the specific responsibility of removing agency members for misfeasance, inefficiency, or the neglect of duty. Coupled with this is the discretionary exercise of his duty to reward faithful public service by the reappointment of agency members, which requires him to form opinions as to the capability of his or his predecessor's appointees to handle the affairs that the Congress has entrusted to them. In short, the president's responsibility requires him to know and evaluate how efficiently these agencies dispatch their business, including any lack of prompt decision on the thousands of cases which they are called upon to decide, to know of any failure to evolve policy in areas where they have been charged by the Congress to do so, or any other difficulties that militate against the performance of their statutory duties.

Mr. ADAMS. What were your thoughts on the administrative functions of the president?

Mr. KENNEDY. I've heard the testimony here and I think sometimes we overstate the administerial difficulties of the presidency. I think really, in many ways, it is a judicial function, where alternatives are suggested which involve great matters, and finally the president must make a decision. That is really the most onerous and important part of the burdens of being president. President Truman used to have a sign on his desk which said, "The buck stops here"—these matters which involve national security and other national strength finally come to rest here—but the matter of our staff, therefore, should serve only to make sure that these important matters are brought here in a way which permit a clear decision after alternatives have been presented. Occasionally, in the past, I think the staff has been used to getting a prearranged agreement, which is only confirmed at the president's desk, and that I don't agree with.

Mr. ADAMS. On the subject of staff, what about the use of advisors by presidents?

Mr. KENNEDY. I bore the responsibility of the presidency of the United States, and it was my duty to make decisions that no advisor and no ally could make for me. It was my obligation and responsibility to see that these decisions were as informed as possible, that they were based on as much direct, first-hand knowledge as possible.

The responsibilities placed on the United States are greater than I imagined them to be, and there are greater limitations upon our ability to bring about a favorable result than I had imagined it to be. And I think that's probably true of anyone who becomes president, because there's such a difference between those who advise or speak, or legislate, and the man who must select from the various alternatives proposed and say that this shall be the policy of the United States. It's much easier to make the speeches than it is to finally make the judgments, because unfortunately your advisors are frequently divided. If you take the wrong course, and on occasion I have, the president bears the burden, responsibility, quite rightly. The advisors may move on to new advice.

Congressmen are always advising presidents to get rid

of presidential advisors. That's one of the most constant threads that run through American history, and presidents ordinarily do not pay attention.

Dr. FRANKLIN. Will you repeat that?

Mr. KENNEDY. Congressmen are always advising presidents to get rid of presidential advisors . . .

Dr. FRANKLIN. Thank you.

Mr. ADAMS. You mention that on occasion you have taken the wrong course, as president. What do you think of that?

Mr. KENNEDY. I know that when things don't go well, they like to blame the president, and that is one of the things presidents are paid for. I must say that the presidency is not a very good place to make new friends.

Mr. MADISON. Mr. Kennedy, can you add your thoughts on the burden of the presidency?

Mr. KENNEDY. When I ran for the presidency of the United States, I knew that this country faced serious challenges, but I could not realize—nor could any man realize who does not bear the burden of this office—how heavy and constant would be those burdens.

President Eisenhower once said to me that, "No easy matters will ever come to you as President. If they're easy they will be settled at a lower level. The matters that finally come to you as president are always the difficult matters, matters which carry with them large implications." So this contributes to some of the burdens of the office of the presidency, which other presidents have commented on.

And finally, no man who enters upon the office can fail to recognize how every president of the United States has placed special reliance upon his faith in God.

Mr. JEFFERSON. Mr. Kennedy, what do you regard as the greatest possible danger to the United States?

Mr. KENNEDY. With all of the history of war, and the human race's history, unfortunately there has been a good deal more war than peace; with nuclear weapons distributed all through the world, and available, and the strong reluctance of any people to accept defeat, I see the possibility of the president of the United States having to face a world in which fifteen or twenty or twenty-five nations may have these weapons. I regard that as the greatest possible danger and hazard.

Every president must endure a gap between what he would like and what is possible.

We must look to . . . a new world of law, where the strong are just, and the weak secure, and the peace preserved.

All this will not be finished in a hundred days. Nor will it be finished in a thousand days, . . . nor even perhaps in our lifetime on this planet. But, as I said once before, let us begin.

Gen. WASHINGTON. Mr. Kennedy, we thank you. You may be excused. I would like to conclude this session by posing this question to my colleagues on the Commission. In the light of the testimony to date, by the presidents, is it necessary or advisable for us to proceed with testimony beyond that of former President Kennedy? Should we continue by receiving testimony from presidents Johnson, Nixon, Ford, Carter and Reagan?

Mr. MADISON. If it be the disposition of the other members, I believe we can dispense with further testimony of presidents, and if the course of our sessions require, we can always ask for their testimony at a later date. My rationale is as follows: Mr. Nixon resigned his office as president—the only president to do so—thus making President Ford's only term a derived presidency. Mr. Carter had only one term. Mr. Reagan's term may be too recent or current to evaluate properly. Under the circumstances I am of the opinion that we ought to interview such omitted presidents only when and if the occasion arises.

Mr. ADAMS. Do you not think that the testimony of Mr. Nixon—as the only president to resign—would serve a purpose, since one of our objects is to protect the public against a recurrence of what transpired?

Mr. MADISON. Again, I am of the opinion that if we require Mr. Nixon's testimony we can obtain it at a later date.

Mr. JEFFERSON. I am not so keen on receiving the testimony of a former president whose acts affected the credibility and respectability of the office of the president of the United

States by debasing its status and demeaning its character. Mr. Nixon was, as the factors bore out, a derelict president whose words were not in truth. I do not want to undermine the credibility of this Commission by his testimony. His testimony can serve no purpose to this Commission in my judgment. I stand by Mr. Madison's suggestion.

Mr. ADAMS. Mr. Jefferson referred to Mr. Nixon as a derelict president. Perhaps we ought to call his a "derelected" presidency, to coin a word. I am in favor of Mr. Madison's proposal.

Gen. WASHINGTON. On the basis of this expression of opinions, the Commission will not ask for the testimony of presidents Johnson, Ford, Carter, or Reagan unless circumstances warrant the same. In addition, the question as to whether Mr. Nixon's testimony will be requested, even if circumstances warrant, will be reserved until an issue arises in connection therewith, if at all, at which time the matter may be reappraised.

Having reached the end of the testimony of most former presidents from myself to President Kennedy, it is incumbent upon this Commission to review such testimony with a view toward its shedding some light on the next course of testimony to come before the Commission. Tuesday, June 16th is assigned for this review. Accordingly this session is adjourned until 10 o'clock a.m. on such date.

TUESDAY, JUNE 16, 1987

COMMISSION REVIEWS TESTIMONY

The Committee met pursuant to notice, at 10 a.m. in the Assembly Room of Independence Hall, Gen. George Washington presiding.

>Present: Mr. John Adams, Dr. Benjamin Franklin, Mr. Thomas Jefferson, Mr. James Madison and Gen. George Washington.

Gen. WASHINGTON. We have reached a turning point in our sessions. Today we begin a review of the testimony already presented, with the view of its shedding some light on the agenda this Commission should follow in its future sessions. On the subject of the affairs of government we have heard the testimony of Mr. Robert Sherrill, Mr. Donald Lambro, Mr. Herbert Hoover, and others. On the subject of the office of the president we have heard the thoughts of most presidents, beginning with myself and ending with Mr. John F. Kennedy.

The basic questions appear to be . . .

First, does the Constitution of 1987, which, in substance, resulted from the efforts of the members of this Commission, among others, still meet the needs of America? The reason for the establishment of this Commission is couched in that question. Second, if the answer to the first question is negative, then in what areas has the Constitution failed to keep up with the times?

Mr. JEFFERSON. It would appear to me that we should proceed from the general to the specific. In general, in my judgment, the Constitution no longer meets the needs of

America. The testimony given to date leads me to believe that, irrespective of who the president might be, the structure of the American government can no longer cope with domestic or foreign problems or crises. The key, in my judgment, is "structure" of government. You can have the finest astronaut or pilot in the world or cosmos, but if the space vehicle is structurally unsound, the pilot will not succeed. The same applies to the structure of American government today, in 1987. As Gen. Washington stated, we should review the testimony. I agree. However, I believe that the specifics of the problems and potential solutions should come from a reexamination and reassessment of the Federal Convention of 1787, which, after all, drafted the Constitution.

Mr. MADISON. There appear to be certain categories of subjects which predominate the testimony given so far. The most repeated thought, I believe, related to the burden of the office of the president. The second most repeated thought related to conflict between the Congress and the president. The third related to the structure of government—with particular reference to the executive departments. I think our review might well utilize these categories.

Dr. FRANKLIN. It would avoid a helter-skelter discussion.

Mr. JEFFERSON. The voices of the presidents concerning the burden of the presidency presents us with a haunting refrain that repeats and repeats; singly at first and then, as in a choir, their voices merge into a resounding voice—listen!

A man who seeks the presidency is an audacious fool. Could any man realize how heavy and constant would be those burdens? The amount of work is preposterous. Responsibilities enough to kill any man. Increasing drudgery. The White House is a prison. A president never escapes from his office. Mine is a situation of dignified slavery. I'll be damned if I am not getting tired of this . . . tired of an office where I can do no more good. I had enough of it, Heaven knows. In God's name! If any can do better . . . let them try. I could not have lived another year. God, what a job! No bed of roses. The office has not a single allurement. Nobody ever left with less regret. I am glad to be going—this is the loneliest place in the world. I leave it with greater satisfaction than when entering. It is an escape from bondage into freedom. I am glad to be a freed man.

Dr. FRANKLIN. (Aside to Mr. Madison) You know, Jemmy, I'm beginning to think I am glad indeed I did not become president of the United States.

Mr. JEFFERSON. I daresay that John Adams, Gen. George Washington, and I are numbered among those voices. Before entering on the execution of the office, all of us took the oath, saying: "I do solemnly swear that I will execute the office of president of the United States, and will to the best of my ability, preserve, protect, and defend the Constitution of the United States."

Are the expressions I have repeated disloyal to that oath?

The sad expressions of presidents reveal a general mood concerning the office which should be of deep concern to us all.

Mr. Franklin Roosevelt once said that the presidency is not a prize to be won by glittering promises. It is not a commodity to be sold by high-pressure salesmanship. The presidency is a most sacred trust. Are these expressions incompatible with that trust?

These men whose voices we heard are the men to whom "the People" delegated the highest office in the land. It is an office from which we expect momentous decisions. It is an office from which singlehandedly one man can ignite the world into conflagration. It is an office where one man is given control over two million servants of government. It is an office where one man is given control over our national destiny. Yet, is is an office where a president can say pathetically: "There is no exaltation in the office—sorrow is the word."

Mr. MADISON. We gave him that job. We designed it. We were not psychiatrists. We were not psychologists. We never even discussed the capability of a human being to cope with the office of the president.

We assumed he or she could.

Separation of powers—states rights versus federal rights—these were the key issues upon which we focused. Not the mind, not the emotion of a potential candidate. Our qualifications for the presidency were simple—citizenship, age, and residence—not mental or emotional adaptability.

Mr. JEFFERSON. At this time it does not seem appropriate to discuss the relationship of the president to Congress; or presidential powers, or the cabinet or presidential advisors—at least not for the present.

I believe the questions for us to consider are these. If the amount of work is "preposterous," how can we expect a president to have the patience to cultivate a proper relationship with Congress? Can we expect him to have the time to develop and monitor our national direction and foreign policy?

If the responsibilities are "enough to kill any man," how can we expect a president to exercise his presidential powers with vigor?

If the man who seeks and becomes the president is an "audacious fool," how can we expect an intellectually honest performance?

And if the office is one of "increasing drudgery," how can we expect the president to take care that the laws be faithfully executed, as required by the Constitution?

There is a fundamental paradox between the man and the job. Something does not mesh. There is an inconsistency between the aptitude of the candidate and the required attitude for the office.

Something went wrong—someplace, at some time. As I said before, perhaps it occurred in the Federal Convention of 1787. I think it behooves us to find out.

Mr. Chairman, whereas this Commission has been mandated to determine whether the Constitution meets the exigency of this nation, and whereas the Commission has determined there may be structural flaws in the constitutional design of the presidency of the United States, I move that this Commission reexamine and reassess the debates in the Federal Convention of 1787, with particular reference to the development and creation of the office of the president of the United States.

Dr. FRANKLIN. I second the motion.

Gen. WASHINGTON. The chair submits the motion to the consideration of the Commission.

Mr. MADISON. I strongly object. I would consider such a procedure as an affront to my character. After all, history has referred to me as the Father of the Constitution. Mr. Jefferson, you are known as Author of the Declaration of Independence. How would you like it if the Declaration were now amended and restated? How will I look to posterity? How will posterity look upon me?

While I believe they give me credit to which I have no claim, since this was not, like the fabled Goddess of Wisdom, the offspring of a single brain; nonetheless, I decline to distort history by now raising the specter of an ill-founded Constitution with me as its alleged author.

Dr. FRANKLIN. Your position does not appear to be consistent. You acknowledged before this Commission that you wrote a farewell address for Gen. Washignton at the end of his first term as president. It was an address which he never rendered, simply because he was induced to run again. However, in that address, you wrote, and I quote, that the Constitution wisely contained within itself "a provision for its own amendment as experience may point out its errors." And experience has borne this out. The Constitution has been amended twenty-six times. We have not moved to amend. We have only moved to reconsider. Would it be so bad if you changed your mind at least once in two hundred years?

Gen. WASHINGTON. Why not refer also to an address I actually made, Dr. Franklin, my inaugural address? I have mentioned it earlier in our sessions. Briefly, I said that the exercise of the "occasional" power to amend "ought to wait the future lessons of experience." Which is apparently what has occurred.

Mr. JEFFERSON. I am certainly not an advocate for frequent and untried changes in laws and constitutions. I think moderate imperfections had better be borne with; because, when once known, we accommodate ourselves to them, and find practical means of correcting their ill effects. But I know also, that laws and institutions must go hand in hand with the progress of the human mind. As that becomes more developed, more enlightened, as new discoveries are made, new truths disclosed, and manners and opinions change with the change of circumstances, institutions must advance also, and keep pace with the times. We might as well require a man to wear still the coat which fitted him when a boy, as civilized society to remain ever under the regimen of their barbarous ancestors. Let us . . . avail ourselves of our reason and experience to correct any crude essays of our first and inexperienced although wise, virtuous, and well-meaning councils. Each generation has a right to choose for itself the form of government it believes most promotive of its own happiness. This corporeal globe, and everything upon it, belong to its present corporeal inhabitants, during their generation. They alone have a right to direct what is the concern of themselves alone and to declare the law of that direction; and this declaration can only be made by their majority.

These are my opinions of the governments we see among men and of the principles by which we may prevent our own from falling into a dreadful track. In short, the constitution is not too sacred to be touched, Mr. Madison.

Mr. MADISON. Mr. Jefferson, I pray you, do not draw conclusions too hastily. Allow me to explain myself, if you will. I favor the propriety of resorting to the sense in which the Constitution was accepted and ratified by the nation. In that sense alone it is the legitimate Constitution. And if that be not the guide in expounding it, there can be no security for a consistent and stable, more than for a faithful, exercise of its powers. If the meaning of the text be sought in the changeable meaning of the words composing it, it is evident that the shape and attributes of the government must partake of the changes to which the words and phrases of all living languages are constantly subject. What a metamorphosis would be produced in the code of law if all its ancient phraseology were to be taken in its modern sense! The language of our Constitution is already undergoing interpretations unknown to its founders. Give to the Constitution that just construction which, with the aid of time and habit, may put an end to the more dangerous schisms otherwise growing out of it. It would be wrong, however, to detract from the talents or integrity of the opponents of the Constitution.

The propriety of resorting to the sense in which the Constitution was accepted and ratified by the nation is my first priority.

I am not so immutable as I am suspect.

The Constitution with its wise provisions for its improvement under the lights of experience will not be undervalued by any who compare the distracted and ominous condition from which it rescued the country, with the security and prosperity so long enjoyed under it, with the bright prospects which it has opened on the civilized world. It is a proud reflection for the people of the United States, proud for the cause of liberty, that history furnishes no example of a government producing like blessings in an equal degree and for the same period.

When we consider amendments to the Constitution, bear in mind that theories are the offspring of the closet; exceptions and qualifications the lesson of experience.

Experience seems to have shown that whatever may grow out of future stages of our national career, there is as yet a sufficient control in the popular will over the executive and legislative departments of the government. How far this structure of the government of the United States be adequate and safe for its objects, time alone can absolutely determine.

In the light of these beliefs, I would accept the motion on the floor if Mr. Jefferson would amend and restate it without attaching any conditions. Also, I would ask Mr. Jefferson to withdraw the whereas clauses which state that the Commission has determined that there may be structural flaws in the constitutional design of the presidency, as the Commission has reached no such decision, or any decision.

Mr. JEFFERSON. I respectfully amend my motion to read simply: I move that this Commission reexamine and reassess the debates in the Federal Convention of 1787, and the debates in the states applicable to the ratification of the Constitution of the United States.

Mr. MADISON. I second the motion.

Gen. WASHINGTON. Any further discussion?

Dr. FRANKLIN. I call for the question.

Gen. WASHINGTON. The question is the adoption of the motion as amended by Mr. Jefferson. As many as are in favor of the motion say "aye."

Dr. FRANKLIN. Aye.

Mr. ADAMS. Aye.

Mr. JEFFERSON. Aye.

Mr. MADISON. Aye.

Gen. WASHINGTON. The motion is agreed to. Members of the Commission, this session is adjourned until tomorrow, Wednesday, June 17th at 10 a.m.

WEDNESDAY, JUNE 17, 1987

BENJAMIN FRANKLIN'S CONCEPTS ON CONSTITUTION

The Committee met pursuant to notice, at 10 a.m. in the Assembly Room of Independence Hall, Gen. George Washington presiding.

Present: Mr. John Adams, Dr. Benjamin Franklin, Mr. Thomas Jefferson, Mr. James Madison and Gen. George Washington.

Gen. WASHINGTON. It has been the unanimous agreement of this Commission that it reexamine and reassess the debates in the Constitutional or so-called Federal Convention of 1787. In order to discuss this subject properly it is essential that we sketch the political climate that served as a foundation for the work of the Federal Convention.

Two hundred years ago this year, the Federal Convention concluded its work in Philadelphia and signed what would become the Constitution of the United States. Ours is the oldest continuing written constitution in the world. It is a covenant between the people and their government that has carried us through territorial expansion, civil war, industrialization, two world wars, the nuclear age, and now into the space age.

The main origins of the United States Constitution lie in centuries of experience in government, the lessons of which were brought here from England and further developed through the practices of over a century and a half in the colonies, in the early state governments, and in the struggles of the Continental Congress.

Its roots are deep in the past; and its endurance and the obedience and respect it has won are mainly the result of the slow growth of its principles from before the days of Magna Carta, up through the philosophy of John Locke, "The Spirit of the Laws" by Montesquieu, the writings of Rousseau and others.

The Constitution does not give us our rights and liberties. It only guarantees them. The people had all their rights and liberties before they created the Constitution. The Constitution was created, among other things, in order to make the people's liberties secure, not only against foreign attack but also against oppression by their own government.

Our Constitution has survived so long that we tend to forget the existence of an earlier government of the United States. The first united action of protest in the preliminaries of the Revolutionary War was the Stamp Act Congress of 1765, which framed petitions to the king and to Parliament. It was held at New York and nine of the thirteen colonies sent delegates. The voting was by colonies, one vote accorded to each.

Following the efforts by the British government to coerce Massachusetts into obedience of British measures, the colonies took action that led to the present Union.

The first Continental Congress met on September 5, 1774, in Carpenters' Hall at Philadelphia. Delegates from all the colonies, except Georgia, attended. As in the case of the Stamp Act Congress, the Continental Congress adopted the rule of one vote for each colony, regardless of population or size. This rule often hindered the competency of the general government and frequently impeded congressional action.

The Second Continental Congress met at Philadelphia on May 10, 1775. This organ of union did not possess the power to enforce its measures. The only instruments for enforcement were the states. Congress could recommend, but the states could do as they pleased, and in many instances they did nothing at all.

The Virginia Convention adopted a resolution on May 15, 1776, which instructed the colony's delegates to propose independence and gave approval to whatever measures were considered proper and necessary by the Congress "for forming foreign alliances, and a Confederation of the Colonies. ...." Richard Henry Lee introduced legislation on June 7, 1776, providing "that a plan of confederation be prepared and transmitted to the respective colonies for their consideration and approbation." In 1777, the Articles of Confederation were agreed to by Congress and submitted to the states, but the Articles did not become law until Maryland became the last state to ratify, on March 1, 1781. The Articles remained in effect until the inauguration of the new government under the Constitution in March of 1789. The Articles created the expression "The United States of America."

The Articles of Confederation reflected the suspicions that early Americans had of a centralized government. Having just freed themselves from the rule of a king, they were not about to accept strong executive leadership, either in the states or in the nation as a whole. The Articles, therefore, created a unicameral national legislature—the Continental Congress—with a president elected by the Congress.

These were our predecessors as presidents—the presidents of the Continental Congress of the United States of America—upon whose success, we, the successor presidents, assumed our status.

John Adams once said in perhaps the most critical moment that America ever saw: "There is a tide in the affairs of Men—and consequences of infinite moment depend upon the colonies assuming government at this time. ... Governments must be assumed or anarchy reign, and God knows the consequences."

And the government was assumed, and we know the consequences. And the men who served as presidents at the helm of the Congresses during those stark revolutionary and evolutionary days were Peyton Randolph of Virginia, Henry Middleton of South Carolina, John Hancock of Massachusetts, Henry Laurens of South Carolina, John Jay of New York, Samuel Huntington of Connecticut, Thomas McKean of Delaware, John Hanson of Maryland, Elias Boudinot of New Jersey, Thomas Mifflin of Pennsylvania, Richard Henry Lee of Virginia, Nathaniel Gorham of Massachusetts, Arthur St. Clair of Pennsylvania, and Cyrus Griffin of Virginia. But just what was the nature of that ship they guided?

Under the Articles of Confederation, Congress represented more than just a league of sovereign states. It was a national government, burdened with legislative and administrative responsibilities unprecedented in the colonial past. Congress had the authority to determine foreign policy, to coin and borrow money, to requisition the states for men and money, to regulate Indian affairs, and to mediate disputes between the states. On minor matters a simple majority of seven votes was necessary, with each state having one vote; but on major matters of war, finance, and treaty making, a majority of nine votes was required. Amendments to the Articles required the unanimous consent of the states. Because there was so much disagreement between the states, north and south, large and small, merchant and agrarian, a majority of nine was extremely difficult to achieve on major issues, and unanimity among the states was almost impossible.

Administrative leadership under the Articles came from its president and more particularly from Congressional committees. But these were hobbled by a rule which prohibited members from serving in Congress for more than three out of every six years, thus restricting seniority and making it difficult for committee members to build up sufficient expertise. The proliferation of standing and special committees also proved a drain on the legislative functions of the Congress. As for the presidency, the Articles of Confederation stated that the United States in Congress assembled shall have authority "to appoint one of their number to president, provided that no person be allowed to serve in the office of president more than a year in any term of three years."

The government under the Articles of Confederation was not without its achievements—such as winning the war with Great Britain and establishing the Northwest Ordinance of 1787, which organized the vast American territories which now comprise the states of Ohio, Indiana, Illinois, Michigan, and Wisconsin.

But the Confederation, under the Articles, had great weaknesses. It had no means of revenue independent of that received through its requisitions on the states, which were nothing more than requests that the states could and did disregard; and it had no control over foreign or interstate commerce. Besides these deficiencies was its inability to compel the states to honor their national obligations. It could make treaties but had no means to compel obedience to them or to provide for the payment of the foreign debt. It had responsibility but no power as a national government, no means of coercing the states to obedience. Its greatest weakness was that it had no direct origin in, or action on, the people themselves.

In June of 1786, the Congress debated a motion by Charles Pinckney of South Carolina to amend the Articles to create a federal appeals court and to strengthen the power of Congress to raise taxes from the state governments. In February of that year the state of New Jersey had simply refused to pay a tax which the Congress had levied. But since a unanimous vote was clearly impossible, Congress did not even bother to submit Pinckney's proposals to the states.

Instead, in September 1786, nine states accepted the invitation of Virginia to meet in Annapolis, Maryland, ostensibly to discuss interstate commercial activities. The Annapolis conference, however, recognized the broader nature of the problem and proposed that all of the states send delegates to a new convention, to be held at Philadelphia the following year to discuss all matters necessary "to render the constitution of the Federal government adequate to the exigencies of the Union."

The legislatures of all of the states except Rhode Island appointed deputies to the 1787 Convention, seventy-four in all, of which nineteen declined to serve or did not attend. Of the fifty-five who attended, fourteen left before the Convention closed, and three more refused to sign the final draft. Only thirty-eight signed, with the added signature of an absent deputy, John Dickinson of Delaware, making thirty-nine.

Mr. ADAMS. (Aside to Dr. Franklin) Here we go again! George Read, delegate from Delaware, signed his own and

John Dickinson's name to the Constitution. Drat that Dickinson!

Gen. WASHINGTON. Of the fifty-five men who, in varying degrees, framed the Constitution, forty-seven were natives of the colonies. The oldest was Dr. Benjamin Franklin of Pennsylvania, at eighty-one; the youngest was Jonathan Dayton of New Jersey, at twenty-six. Twenty-one delegates were under forty, fourteen were fifty or over.

Twenty-five were college educated. Eighteen had been officers in the Continental Army, and one had been a British Army officer prior to the Revolution. Thirty-four were lawyers, or had at least studied the law. Eight were merchants or financiers. Six were planters, three were physicians, two were former ministers of the gospel, and several were college professors. Dr. Franklin represented the Fourth Estate.

Forty-six had been members of one or both houses of colonial or state legislatures. Ten had attended state constitutional conventions. Several had been governors or presidents of states, and several had been state attorneys general, while several had served as justices of state courts.

Eight were signers of the Declaration of Independence. Thirty-nine or forty had been delegates to the Continental Congress. Six had signed the draft of the Articles of Confederation, seven had attended the Annapolis Convention, three had been executive officers under the Congress, and one had been a minister abroad.

The man who deserved the title of "Father of the Constitution" was thirty-six-year-old James Madison, who was honored in 1980 with the dedication of the new Madison Building of the Library of Congress. For those who have not yet visited the Madison Building, it contains a handsome hall which houses a white marble statue of Madison, surrounded by selected quotations from his writings inscribed on the wood-paneled walls. This is certainly a fitting—if belated—tribute to a man who contributed so significantly to our system of government.

Mr. Madison had served in Congress under the Articles but had to retire in 1783 because of the three-year limitation on service. During his years out of office he became increasingly concerned over the mounting sectional tensions and the inability of the central government to respond. Mr. Madison was an advocate of the new convention and became one of Virginia's delegates. He did his homework and was able to cut through the maze of complicated issues facing the convention with a sharpness of mind and a degree of preparedness that deeply impressed the other delegates. He was a man who seized the initiative when he spotted it, and thus was able to shape the course of the convention. It was Madison, also, who kept the minutes of the debates, which were conducted in secret, and so it is to him that we are indebted, for the most part, for our knowledge of the inside deliberations which produced the Constitution.

The Convention was set for May 14, 1787, a Monday, but a necessary quorum did not develop until the 25th, when seven states were represented. Before the end of May, ten states were in attendance and voting. Maryland participated on June 2nd, New Hampshire, the twelfth state, was present on July 23. Rhode Island did not participate.

The meeting was held in Independence Hall where the Declaration of Independence had been adopted and signed and where the Continental Congress had sat—the same room in which this Commission now sits.

I served as president of the Convention. Each state had one vote. Complete secrecy was the rule as in the case of the Continental Congress.

The formal journal of the convention was kept by Maj. William Jackson. The notes on the debates kept by Mr. Madison constitute the most important record thereof, and they were not made public as a whole until 1840. Notes were also kept by various other members.

Of the 116 days between May 25 and September 17, inclusive, meetings were conducted on 87 or 88 days. The Constitution was signed on September 17, 1787, by all the members except for Mr. Elbridge Gerry of Massachusetts, and Mr. George Mason and Mr. Edmund Randolph, both of Virginia.

It was at this point in the proceedings that James Madison closed his minutes to the Constitutional Convention, but he added this final anecdote, one which encapsulated the entire history of the debates:

"Whilst the last members were signing it, Doctor Franklin, looking toward the president's chair, at the back of which a rising sun happened to be painted, observed to a few members near him, that painters had found it difficult to distinguish in their art, a rising, from a setting sun. 'I have,' said he, 'often and often, in the course of the session, and the vicissitudes of my hopes and fears as to its issue, looked at that behind the president, without being able to tell whether it was rising or setting; but now at length, I have the happiness to know, that it is a rising, and not a setting sun'."

And so two hundred years later we choose to conclude that Dr. Franklin was entirely correct; that it was, and still is, a rising sun. The Constitution still stands.

Gentlemen, I ask Mr. Charles Thomson, our secretary, to have printed at this place in the record of this Commission, the names of the signers of the Constitution of the United States.

Mr. THOMSON. The names so ordered to be printed in the record are as follows:

From New Hampshire - John Langdon, Nicholas Gilman.

From Massachusetts - Nathaniel Gorham and Rufus King.

From Connecticut - William Samuel Johnson and Roger Sherman

From New York - Alexander Hamilton.

From New Jersey - William Livingston, David Brearley, William Paterson and Jonathan Dayton.

From Pennsylvania - Benjamin Franklin, Robert Morris, Thomas Fitzsimons, James Wilson, Thomas Mifflin, George Clymer, Jared Ingersoll and Gouverneur Morris.

From Delaware - George Read, John Dickinson, Jacob Broom, Gunning Bedford, Jr. and Richard Bassett.

From Maryland - James M'Henry, Daniel Carroll and Daniel of St. Thomas Jenifer.

From Virginia - John Blair, James Madison, Jr., and

George Washington, President.

From North Carolina - William Blount, Hu. Williamson, Richard Dobbs Spaight.

From South Carolina - J. Rutledge, Charles Cotesworth Pinckney, Charles Pinckney and Pierce Butler.

From Georgia - William Few and Abraham Baldwin.

Gen. WASHINGTON. I also ask to have printed in the record of the Commission, at this point, the names of those who attended the Federal Convention but did not sign the Constitution, having left the Convention before its sessions were completed; it being understood that Mr. John Dickinson's name was signed by Mr. George Read, in the absence of Mr. Dickinson.

Mr. THOMSON. The names so ordered to be printed in the record are as follows:

From Massachusetts - Caleb Strong.

From Connecticut - Oliver Ellsworth.

From New York - Robert Yates and John Lansing.

From New Jersey - William C. Houston.

From Maryland - John Francis Mercer and Luther Martin.

From Virginia - George Wythe and James M'Clurg.

From North Carolina - Alexander Martin and William R. Davie.

From Georgia - William Pierce and William Houston.

Gen. WASHINGTON. I now ask to have printed in the record of the Commission at this point, the names of those who attended the Federal Convention to the day of its closing but declined to sign the Constitution.

Mr. THOMSON. The names so ordered to be printed in the record are as follows:

From Massachusetts - Elbridge Gerry.

From Virginia - George Mason and Edmund Randolph.

Gen. WASHINGTON. In setting forth the names of those fifty-five attending the Convention, both signers and non-signers, I do so for the purpose of refreshing our minds as to who were the players in the story of the debates we are about to unfold.

I have presented this morning but a capsule of the nature of the Federal Convention of 1787, and I next ask my colleagues on the Commission to share some of their thoughts of the Convention. We will take a ten-minute recess.

[Gen. Washington leaves the Assembly room; others stay]

Dr. FRANKLIN. [Addresses Mr. Thomson] The General's regal demeanor has not changed at all over the years. Do you remember, Charles, when the Convention to form a Constitution was sitting in Philadelphia in 1787, of which Gen. Washington was president, he had stated evenings to receive the calls of his friends? At an interview between Alexander Hamilton, the Morrises, and others, Hamilton remarked that Washington was reserved and aristocratic even to his intimate friends, and allowed no one to be familiar with him. Gouverneur Morris said that was a mere fancy, and he could be as familiar with Washington as with any of his other friends. Hamilton replied, "If you will, at the next reception evening, gently slap him on the shoulder and say, 'My dear General, how happy I am to see you look so well!' A supper and wine shall be provided for you and a dozen of your friends." The challenge was accepted. On the evening appointed, a large number attended; and at an early hour Gouverneur Morris entered, bowed, shook hands, laid his left hand on Washignton's shoulder, and said, "My dear General, I am very happy to see you look so well!" Washington withdrew his hand, stepped suddenly back, fixed his eye on Morris for several minutes with an angry frown, until Morris retreated abashed, and sought refuge in the crowd. The company looked on in silence. At the supper, which was provided by Hamilton, Morris said, "I have won the bet, but paid dearly for it, and nothing could induce me to repeat it."

Mr. THOMSON. (Laughs) Aye, I remember it well.

[Gen. Washington returns]

Gen. WASHINGTON. This session will resume. Mr. Jefferson will you begin?

Mr. JEFFERSON. I do not particularly share the patriotic theme of Gen. Washington — that all goes well with the Constitution. Today with our overlapping federal and state bureaus, our national commissions for regulating much that could be better done in other ways, our federal assumption of powers that should belong to the states, we have run far beyond the Federalism of George Washington. In large measure we have ceased to be a representative Republic such as Washington fathered, and we have far outrun the Democracy which Lincoln saved. We have gotten away from the national constitution. It is a period of chaos. Whether we are entering upon the static condition prophesied by Henry Adams, where we shall have reached the limit of energy, or whether from the precepts and example of Washington and Lincoln our ship of state can be guided into safer seas, no man can foresee. Our national history is marked by false prophecies uttered by Americans not unknown to fame. Herbert Spencer once said that in due course some dreams come true, because the millions of dreams every night cover the whole range of human experience. Of the thousands of prophecies as to the future of our country, one here or there may possibly hit the mark. Our ship of state now seems to be in the doldrums, the outcome of ignoring Washington's warning against entangling foreign alliances. In this maelstrom, perhaps we should grasp onto the words of Franklin Delano Roosevelt: The only thing we have to fear is fear itself.

Dr. FRANKLIN. I believe we are off the course of our intended discussion, but we are probably also off the course of our national destiny and our personal destinies.

Look round the world and see the millions employed in doing nothing, or in something that amounts to nothing, when the necessaries and conveniences of life are in question. What is the bulk of commerce, for which we fight and destroy each other, but the toil of millions for superfluities? How much labor is spent in building and fitting great ships to go to China and Arabia for tea and coffee, to the West Indies for sugar, to America for tobacco, to Japan for autos, to the Middle East for oil? These things cannot be called the necessaries of life, for our ancestors lived very comfortably without them.

It has been computed by some political arithmetician,

that, if every man and woman would work for four hours each day on something useful, that labor would produce sufficient to procure all the necessaries and comforts of life. Want and misery would be banished out of the world, and the rest of the twenty-four hours might be leasure and pleasure.

It is wonderful how preposterously the affairs of this world are managed. Individuals manage their affairs with so much more application, industry, and address, than the public do theirs. We assemble parliaments and councils, to have the benefit of their collected wisdom; but we necessarily have, at the same time, the inconvenience of their collected passions, prejudices, and private interests. By the help of these, artful men overpower their wisdom, and dupe its possessors; and if we may judge by the acts, arrets and edicts, all the world over, for regulating commerce, an assembly of great men is the greatest fool upon earth.

I have not, indeed, yet thought of a remedy. I am not sure, that in a great state it is capable of a remedy.

'Tis however, some comfort to reflect, that, upon the while, the quantity of industry and prudence among mankind exceeds the quantity of idleness and folly.

Gen. WASHINGTON. Gentlemen, my opening statement was intended to be introductory to our subject matter. I really did not intend that its contents be debated. Therefore, shall we return to the subject at hand?

Mr. MADISON. Of course, General. I would like to pick up the theme you initiated in your opening statement and examine before this Commission those principles from predecessor constitutions that found their way to that document which we now propose to study. I would be so bold as to follow several of Dr. Franklin's political concepts — some of which, as those of us on this Commission are well aware, became essential tenets of the Constitution of 1787 — as they first found expression in the Albany Plan and later in his draft of the Articles of Confederation.

As early as 1754 delegates from New Hampshire, Massachusetts Bay, Connecticut, Rhode Island, New York, Pennsylvania, and Maryland met at Albany, New York, to treat with the Iroquois and lay plans to resist more effectively French encroachments on the British colonies in North America. Dr. Franklin took the lead in seeking a closer union of the colonies, and his proposals were the basis for the Albany Plan of Union approved by the delegates. What was the fate of the plan, Dr. Franklin?

Dr. FRANKLIN. The Crown disapproved it, as having placed too much weight in the democratic part of its Constitution — the Grand Council; and every provincial assembly rejected it as having allowed too much prerogative in the president general. So it was rejected.

Mr. MADISON. It nevertheless was an important step in the moves toward union which culminated in the Federal Constitution of 1787, and shows Dr. Franklin's persistent belief in the value of human accord. The Plan called for a union of the several colonies of "Massachusets-bay," New Hampshire, Connecticut, Rhode Island, New York, "New Jerseys," "Pennsylvania," Maryland, Virginia, North Carolina, and South Carolina. The purpose was mutual defense and security, and extension of the British settlements in North America.

Application was made for an Act of the Parliament of Great Britain to allow one "General Government" to be formed in America, each colony to retain its then Constitution, except in certain particulars. The General Government was to be administered by a president general, to be appointed by the Crown, and a Grand Council, to be elected every three years by the representative of the people in the assemblies of the colonies.

The Grand Council was to meet, at least for the first time, in Philadelphia, and would thereafter meet yearly, and oftener as required. The assent of the president general was requisite to all acts of the Grand Council, and it was the president general's duty to cause the acts to be carried out.

The president general, with the advice of the Grand Council, could direct the making of Indian Treaties, declare war with the Indian nations, or make laws regulating all Indian trade. The president and council could raise and pay soldiers, build forts for the defense of any of the Colonies, and equip vessels to guard the coasts and protect trade on the waterways, but could not enlist men in any colonies, without the consent of its legislature. For these purposes, the "General Government" had the power to make such laws and to levy such taxes as appeared most equal and just. From time to time funds could be ordered from the colonies into the General Treasury or special payments could be levied; no money was to be issued, however, but by joint orders of the president and Council.

A quorum of the grand council impowered to Act with the president general consisted of twenty-five members, among whom there was to be one or more from a majority of the Colonies. The laws made by them were to follow in spirit the laws of England, and would be approved by the Crown.

In essence, the government under the plan consisted of two branches: an appointed president general and an elected council. The council could effect nothing without the consent of the president general; through its power to appoint the president general, the Crown possessed therefore a full one half of the power of this constitution.

But the Albany Plan was not acceptable to the colonial assemblies or the British government. None of the colonies ratified it and the Connecticut Assembly declared it "a very extraordinary thing and against the rights and privileges of Englishmen." The New Jersey Assembly adopted a report stating that they were "sorry to say we find things in it which if carried into practice would affect our constitution in its very vitals." Even in Pennsylvania the Assembly, in Franklin's absence, rejected a motion to refer the plan to the next Assembly. This act of discourtesy hurt Franklin as he felt it was done behind his back. The English government took no action.

Dr. FRANKLIN. The plan was disliked by the colonies because they felt it emphasized too much the prerogative of the king and by the English ministry because it was too democratic. I was obviously disappointed by its failure. Everybody cried, a Union was absolutely necessary, but when they came to the manner and the form of the Union their weak noddles were perfectly distracted. There was no need to fear that the colonies would unite against their own nation, which it was well known they all loved much more than they loved one another. The fact was the colonies were not only jealous of the British government but of each other.

Mr. MADISON. If the Albany Plan had been adopted it would have provided for a much stronger and more complete government than the later Articles of Confederation. It anticipated several features that were incorporated into the Constitution of the United States and several that were not but should have been. And several constitutional concepts from the Albany Plan reappeared in Dr. Franklin's political thoughts throughout his life. First, the separation of the functions of the president and legislative branch or council, with each having a check on the activities of the other. Second, a unicameral legislature. Dr. Franklin has already told us of his objection to a bicameral legislature, the two-headed serpent. Third, a council to advise the president, and fourth, a three-year term for members of the legislature.

Twenty-one years would elapse before Dr. Franklin would again draft a proposed Constitution for America.

Mr. Thomson, would you kindly read the first entry you made in Papers of the Continental Congress for June 21, 1775.

Mr. THOMSON. Sir, for June 21, 1775, the entry reads: "Agreeably to Order the Congress resolved itself into a Committee of the whole to take into consideration the State of America, when Doctor B. Franklin submitted to their Consideration the following sketch of Articles of Confederation."

Mr. MADISON. I do not believe it necessary to read into the record of this session the Articles of Confederation so prepared by Dr. Franklin. However, to understand Dr. Franklin's contribution to constitutional concepts, it behooves us to note portions of his draft which will later affect our considerations here.

The name of the confederacy would have been "The United Colonies of North America," a firm league of friendship whose purpose was their common defense and their mutual and general welfare.

Delegates were to be elected annually in each Colony to meet in General Congress. Each Congress was to be held annually in a different Colony. The Congress would declare war and make peace, send and receive ambassadors, enter into alliances, and establish new colonies. The Congress could also make general laws relating to the general welfare, commerce, currency, and the military. The Congress would also appoint all general officers, civil and military. A common treasury would be established from funds supplied by each colony in proportion to the number of male votes between ages sixteen and sixty although the taxes for paying the funds were to be determined by each Colony.

The number of delegates to be elected and sent to the Congress by each colony would also be determined by the number of male voters. At every meeting of the Congress one half of the members were necessary to make a quorum, and each delegate at the Congress was to have a vote.

An executive council would be appointed by Congress out of their own body, consisting of twelve persons. The term of each member would be three years with one third of the members being changed annually. Each person who served three years as counsellor would wait three years before he could be elected again. The council was to act in the recess of Congress; manage the general continental business; receive applications from foreign countries; prepare matters for the consideration of the Congress; fill continental offices that fell vacant; and draw monies for necessary expenses.

Article XII is of particular interest. I quote: "As all new institutions have imperfections which only time and experience can discover, it is agreed, that the General Congress from time to time shall propose such Amendments of this Constitution as may be found necessary; which being approved by a majority of the Colony Assemblies, shall be equally binding with the rest of the Articles of this Confederation."

Well, Dr. Franklin concluded his draft in the following terms: "These Articles shall be proposed to the several provincial conventions or assemblies, to be by them considered, and if approved they are advised to impower their Delegates to agree to and ratify the same in the ensuing Congress. After which the Union thereby established is to continue firm till the terms of reconciliation in the petition of the last Congress to the King are agreed to. . . ."

Mr. Thomson, did you endorse the draft I just read from?

Mr. THOMSON. Yes sir.

Mr. MADISON. Will you please read your endorsement?

Mr. THOMSON. Yes sir. It reads "Sketch of Articles of Confederation. July '75. This sketch in handwriting of Doct. Franklin. Read before Congress July 21, 1775."

Mr. MADISON. Mr. Thomson, in the Papers of the Continental Congress is a page in the writing of Benjamin Franklin, giving certain resolutions on trade. The endorsement reads: "Article of Confederation . . . read July 21, 1775. On motion, postponed for further consideration."

Was any further consideration given to Dr. Franklin's draft by the Continental Congress?

Mr. THOMSON. To my knowledge, none.

Mr. MADISON. Do you know why not?

Mr. THOMSON. No sir.

Mr. MADISON. Again, there are certain recurring constitutional concepts in Dr. Franklin's draft of 1775 that should be pinpointed for our purposes. First, a unicameral Congress; second, delegates to Congress to be elected by the people according to proportional representation; third, a one- or two-year term for members of Congress; fourth; a census; fifth, perpetual rotation of the seat of Congress among all the colones; sixth, defined powers of Congress; seventh, an executive council appointed by Congress out of their own members; eighth, a three-year term in the council, with one-third rotation, so that in effect there was to be an election every year of one third of the council.

The next major progress toward a constitution occurred one year later, in June 1776.

Dr. FRANKLIN. (Aside to group of nearby spectators) I suppose I should have all this attention. But, you know, no morning sun lasts a full day. I do not pretend to the gift of prophecy. Yet, there were some scribes who ascribed to me power that could only be achieved by the scribe above.

This reminds me of a true story.

On December 31, 1776, the *Cumberland Chronicle*, a provincial weekly edited and published by J. Dunn of Whitehaven, England, printed the bulletin that I had sailed for France: "We are well informed that Dr. Franklin sailed for France from Philadelphia on Sunday, the 27th ult." Henceforth, all my movements and sayings, even my dress, household, and amusements, were to be of the greatest interest to the readers of the *Chronicle*. And, since I was so closely watched by Lord Stormont's very effective secret agents, all intelligence was relayed to England and Whitehaven, with surprising expedition.

Some of the *Chronicle's* correspondents were doubtful as to whether my errand in France was entirely diplomatic; sinister and diabolical schemes were suggested. On March 4, 1777, an alarmed agent of Lord Stormont sent an agitated report from Paris:

> We now entertain no doubt that the motive of Doctor Franklin's journey hither was entirely philosophical and that he is consulted daily by our own Ministry. Know then, that upon the principle of Archimedes, the Doctor, with the assistance of French mechanics, is preparing a great number of reflecting mirrors which will reflect so much heat from the sun as will destroy anything by fire at a very considerable distance.
>
> This apparatus is to be fixed at Calais on the French coast so as to command the English shore, whereby they mean to burn and destroy the whole navy of Great Britain in our harbors.
>
> During the conflagration the Doctor proposes to have a chain carried from Calais to Dover. He, standing at Calais, with a prodigious electrical machine of his own invention, will convey such a shock as will entirely overturn our whole island.

The truth is that I was sent to France by the Continental Congress to negotiate and sign a treaty of Alliance with France, which I accomplished in 1778.

[Spectators chuckle]

Gen. WASHINGTON. Can we have order please? Order in the hall. Mr. Madison, please continue.

Mr. MADISON. Certainly. As I was saying, on June 11, 1776, Congress resolved to appoint a committee "to prepare and digest the form of a confederation to be entered into between these colonies," and on June 12, 1776, Congress appointed a committee consisting of one member from each colony to prepare and digest the form of a confederation.

The task of framing the Articles of Confederation fell to John Dickinson of Pennsylvania, a member of the committee. One month later, July 12, 1776, the committee presented to Congress a draft in Dickinson's handwriting.

Mr. JEFFERSON. Also on June 11, 1776, a committee was appointed to prepare a Declaration of Independence. The Committee members were Mr. Adams, Dr. Franklin, Mr. Roger Sherman, Mr. Robert A. Livingston, and me. Mr. Adams, Dr. Franklin, and I were not on the committee drafting the Articles. But Mr. Sherman and Mr. Livingston were on both committees.

Mr. ADAMS. Mr. Jefferson, the sequence of your testimony appears important, simply from the standpoint that the committee appointed on June 12, 1776 "to prepare and digest the form of a confederation," had entrusted the work of drafting the instrument to John Dickinson at the moment when as I recall he was opposing a declaration of independence.

Mr. JEFFERSON. (Aside to Mr. Adams) John, are you going to crucify Dickinson?

Mr. ADAMS. (Aside to Mr. Jefferson) No, but we have been made to appear foolish or stupid by the mere placement of Dickinson in such strategic posts. After all, Congress — including you and me — had some control over what happened. Just let me develop my theme.

Mr. JEFFERSON. (Aside to Mr. Adams) As you wish.

Mr. ADAMS. On the face of things it would appear

that Dickinson was drafting a plan — the Articles — for a union in which he did not believe and for political units which he still hoped would not become free and independent states.

    The choice of Dickinson to be draftsman of the instrument of union may have had in it something of a political maneuver, to draw Mr. Dickinson into the fold of independence, or the converse, to prevent him from interfering with the drafting of the Declaration of Independence. Or, that John Dickinson, who had led the successful attempt to defeat consideration of Franklin's plan of confederation, was now in the fore of those demanding a union before a declaration of independence. Another way to defer independence. But, there was at least one other sufficient reason: of all the members of that committee Dickinson had scarcely an equal as a facile wielder of the pen. It needs nevertheless to be borne in mind that Dickinson's participation in the formation of the Articles of Confederation was for the most part limited to the process of drafting and to participation in such deliberations of the committee as took place prior to July 4. For on that day he appears to have taken his departure from Congress and to have sat no more with us until after the Articles of Confederation had been framed. Dickinson did not sign the Declaration of Independence.

    Of what took place in Dickinson's Committee but few revelations have come down to us, but those few are significant of the difficulties encountered. I will relate just one piece of discord revealed about the Committee's actions. It was Edward Rutledge, a delegate from South Carolina and a member of that Committee, who left the clearest indication that all was not harmony in the Committee. On June 29, 1776, he wrote to John Jay: "I have been much engaged lately upon a plan of a Confederation which Dickinson has drawn; it has the vice of all his productions to a considerable degree; I mean the vice of refining too much. Unless it is greatly curtailed it never can pass, as it is to be submitted to men in the respective provinces who will not be led or rather driven into measures which may lay the foundation of their ruin. If the plan now proposed should be adopted nothing less than ruin to some colonies will be the consequence of it. The idea of destroying all provincial distinctions and making everything of the most minute kind bend to what they call the good of the whole . . . I dread. . . . I am resolved to vest the Congress with no more power than that is absolutely necessary and, to use a familiar expression, to keep the staff in our own hands, for I am confident if surrendered into the hands of others a most pernicious use will be made of it."

Now mind you, I had my own opinions on Mr. Dickinson's place in the course of events, as I reflected later in life.

It was on November 12, 1813, that I wrote to Mr. Jefferson, "In the Congress of 1774 there was not a man, except Patrick Henry, who appeared to me to be sensible of the precipice or rather the pinnacle on which he stood, and had candor and courage enough to acknowledge it. . . . There was a little Aristocracy, among us, of talents and letters. Mr. Dickinson was primus inter pares; the bell weather; the leader of the aristocratical flock . . . Mr. John Jay was of this privileged order . . . The credit of most if not all those compositions — letters to his majesty, the King — was often if not generally given to one or the other of these choice spirits . . . Indeed I never bestowed much attention on any of those Addresses; which were all but repetitions of the same things; the same facts and arguments. Dress and ornament rather than body, soul and substance."

The fact of the matter is that Mr. Dickinson was the author of most of the state papers of the Continental Congress drafted prior to July 4, 1776, except the Declaration of Independence; and he was one of several who framed the Articles of Confederation. Included among the papers he drafted were the Declaration of Rights and Grievances, the first and second petitions to the king, the address to the people of Canada, the Declaration of and the Causes of Taking up Arms, and the Answer to the King's Proclamation. All of these compositions of Dickinson were aimed at reconciliation with the British. And on July 1, 1776, he made a speech in Congress *against* independence.

And this man was designated to prepare, and did prepare, the first draft of our first Constitution — the Articles of Confederation.

A puzzlement. Here was a man who eleven years later attended the Federal Convention of 1787, entering extensively into the secret debates and assisting in making decisions in committees which left little-known notes of their proceedings — a convention which produced our present-day Constitution, without amendments — the Second Constitution of the United States. A puzzlement.

Mr. JEFFERSON. Yes, he had refused to sign the Declaration of Independence, and that cost him his popularity. Perhaps he was almost our undoing. He was stilted. Some years later, November 6, 1781, he was elected president of Delaware by the Council and House of Assembly by a vote of 25 to 1, for a term of three years. On November 13 he was sworn in his new office and addressed the General Assembly in what the scribe of that body called a "pathetic speech." Samuel Adams of Boston thought Dickinson had caused an "utter loss of every power of manly sentiment of liberty and virtue."

He was immutable, as witness his refusal to call up the militia to protect Congress when he was President of the State of Pennsylvania and Congress resided in Philadelphia. He pleaded that "We cannot act with too much caution in our disputes. Anger produces anger; and differences, that might be accommodated by kind and respectful behaviours may, by imprudence, be enlarged to an incurable rage."

Mr. ADAMS. Like mine. It is incredible how this man could have threaded his way through history, rising and falling as though he controlled the tide. He was, after all, a colonial revolutionary hero, but he suffered when he refused to sign the Declaration of Independence.

The situation leading to my break with John Dickinson began with an incident which occurred somewhere between June 3 and July 24, 1775.

Congress had assembled one day and proceeded to business, and the members appeared to me to be of one mind, and that mind after my own heart. I dreaded the danger of disunion and divisions among us, and much more among the people. It appeared to me that all petitions, remonstrances, and negotiations, for the future, would be fruitless, and only occasion a loss of time and give opportunity to the enemy to sow dissension among the States and the people.

At one point, Mr. Dickinson made or procured to be made a motion for a second petition to the King, to be sent by Mr. Richard Penn, who was then bound on a voyage to England. The motion was introduced and supported by long speeches. I was opposed to it, of course, and made an opposition to it in as long a speech as I commonly made. . . . When I sat down, Mr. John Sullivan arose and began to argue on the same side with me, in a strain of wit, reasoning, and fluency, which although he was always fluent, exceeded everything I had ever heard from him before. I was much delighted, and Mr. Dickinson, very much terrified at what he said, began to tremble for his cause. At this moment I was called out to the State House yard, very much to my regret, by some one who had business with me. I took my hat, and went out of the door of Congress Hall. Mr. Dickinson observed me and darted out after me. He broke out upon me in a most abrupt and extraordinary manner; in as violent a passion as he was capable of feeling, and with an air, countenance, and gestures, as rough and haughty as if I had been a school boy and he the master. He vociferated, "What is the reason, Mr. Adams, that you New Englandmen oppose our measures of reconciliation? There now is Sullivan in a long harangue, following you in a determined opposition to our petition to the King. Look ye! If you don't concur with us in our pacific system, I and a number of us will break off from you in new England, and we will carry on the opposition by ourselves in our own way." I own I was shocked with this magisterial salutation. I knew of no pretentions Mr. Dickinson had to dictate to me, more than I had to catechize him. I was, however, as it happened, at that moment, in a very happy temper, and I answered him very coolly. "Mr. Dickinson, there are many things that I can very cheerfully sacrifice to harmony, and even to unanimity; but I am not to be threatened into an express adoption or approbation of measures which my judgment reprobates. Congress must judge, and if they pronounce against me, I must submit, as, if they determine against you, you ought to acquiesce." These were the last words which ever passed between Mr. Dickinson and me in private. We continued to debate, in Congress, upon all questions publicly, with all our usual candor and good humor. But the friendship and acquaintance was lost forever by an unfortunate accident, which I will explain.

On July 24, 1775, in a letter to Mr. James Warren, I wrote of Dickinson:

"A certain great fortune and piddling genius, whose fame has been trumpeted so loudly, has given a silly cast to our whole doings." I went on to say that: "We are between hawk and buzzard. We ought to have had in our hands a month ago the whole legislative, executive, and judicial of the whole continent, and have completely modeled a constitution; to have raised a naval power and opened our ports wide; to have arrested every friend to royal government on the continent and held them as hostages for the poor victims of Boston, and then opened the door as wide as possible for peace and reconciliation. . . . Is all this extravagant? Is it wild? Is is not the soundest policy?" Well, that letter, together with one to Mrs. Adams, entrusted to one Benjamin Hichborne for delivery, was intercepted by the British, and Gen. Gage had it published in *Draper's Massachusetts Gazette* on August 7, 1775.

Then, one day in September, while walking to the State House, I met Mr. Dickinson, on foot, in Chestnut Street. We met and passed near enough to touch elbows. He passed without moving his hat or head or hand. I bowed and pulled off my hat. He passed haughtily by. The cause of his offense, no doubt, was the letter which Gen. Gage had printed in Draper's paper. I said then to myself, that "I shall for the future, pass him in the same manner; but I was determined to make my bow, that I might know his temper. We are not to be upon speaking terms or bowing terms for the time to come. . . ." And that was my split with Mr. Dickinson.

Dr. FRANKLIN. I, too, felt no little ire over Mr. Dickinson. On October 26, 1764, by a vote of 19 to 11, the Pennsylvania Assembly appointed me as an additional agent to act for the Colony in London. Among those who dissented were eight who united in protesting my appointment. The protest was not printed as a dissent in the minutes of the Assembly; but rather it was published for the public to read in the *Pennsylvania Journal* on November 1, 1764. The author and first signatory was none other than Mr. John Dickinson. Among seven items of protest was a personal one. In protesting my appointment, it said, "The gentleman proposed, as we are informed, is very unfavorably thought of by several of his majesty's ministers; and we are humbly of opinion, that it will be disrespectful to our most gracious sovereign, and disadvantageous to ourselves and our constituents, to employ such a person as our agent."

You know, I once wrote in *Poor Richard*:
If you wou'd not be forgotten
As soon as you're dead and rotten,
Either write things worth reading,
or do things worth the writing."

In my book, John Dickinson neither wrote things worth reading nor did things worth the writing.

Mr. JEFFERSON. I must agree with your assessment. I recall when you and I were together, and the Jays, and the Dickinsons, and other anti-independents were arrayed against us. They cherished the monarchy of England; and we the rights of our countrymen.

Finally, Mr. John Jay, you know, had been in constant opposition to our laboring majority. Our estimate, at the time, was that he, Dickinson, and Johnson of Maryland, by their ingenuity, perseverance, and partiality to our English connection, had constantly kept us a year behind where we ought to have been in our preparation and proceedings. This perturbed me.

Mr. ADAMS. I have always imputed the loss of Quebec and Gen. Montgomery to Dickinson's unceasing, though finally unavailing, efforts against independence. These impeded and paralyzed all our enterprises.

Gen. WASHINGTON. Please let us return now to Mr. Madison's discussion of the Articles of Confederation. Mr. Madison.

Mr. MADISON. Let me summarize: On June 12, 1776 Congress appointed a committee to prepare a form of confederation; the task of framing the Articles of Confederation fell to John Dickinson; one month later, on July 12, 1776, the Committee presented to Congress a draft in the handwriting of John Dickinson; Mr. Dickinson was then no longer in attendance in Congress, having made a speech against independence on July 1, 1776, and having refused to sign the Declaration of Independence.

Congress debated and amended the Articles from July 22 to August 20, 1776.

The pressure of military disaster forced Congress to abandon the debate. On April 8, 1777, Congress voted to spend two days a week upon the plan of Confederation, but Congress was unable to move toward completion until October 1777. On November 15, 1777, Congress adopted the Articles of Confederation and then sent them to the states for approval. The articles were approved by the states on March 1, 1781, the state of Maryland being the last state to approve and sign.

There should be no question that the Franklin draft submitted to Congress on June 21, 1775, was used as a reference by the Dickinson Committee drafting the articles. The Dickinson draft I would like to refer to now is that submitted to Congress on July 12, 1776, and not the draft which became effective March 1, 1781. The former was in Dickinson's handwriting. The major points where the Franklin concepts parallel and diverge from the Dickinson draft are:

First, the question of frequency of elections and the length of a delegate's term. Each plan provided that the delegates should be chosen annually by the respective colonies. Franklin offered no limitation upon a delegate's term, presumably leaving that question to be determined by each colony, whereas Dickinson's plan stipulated that "No person shall be capable of being a Delegate for more than three years in any term of six years."

Second, the question of proportional representation. Franklin would have had the number of delegates from each colony regulated by the number of male votes between sixteen and sixty years old, one delegate for every 5,000 voters. Dickinson would leave the number to the discretion of the colony.

Third, the question of the manner of voting was all important. Franklin proposed that each delegate should have one vote. Dickinson's plan, on the contrary, provided that "in determining questions each colony shall have one vote."

Thus, the stage was set for the critical debates on states' rights eleven years later, when these issues were resolved by the creation of a House of Representatives and a Senate, a House with proportionate representation, and a Senate with equal states rights.

Mr. JEFFERSON. Perhaps at this point I should summarize some of my notes of the debates of July 30, 31, and August 1, 1776, on this critical issue in the Articles of Confederation.

Mr. MADISON. Please do.

Mr. JEFFERSON. The Dickinson article with which we were concerned stated that "In determining questions each colony shall have one vote."

Gen. WASHINGTON. Will you please state why you consider these debates significant for the purpose of this Commission?

Mr. JEFFERSON. First, I believe, as Mr. Madison stated, they are important because they are a link in the chain of debates that led to the eventual creation of a Senate and a House of Representatives and will lead this Commission to a discussion as to the true utility of the Senate. Second, these were probably the first debates in Congress on this issue. Third, the debates are of interest because they represented the third time Dr. Franklin's concepts were submerged and scuttled, a situation that this Commission should be vitally interested in.

Gen. WASHINGTON. I think it would suffice if you simply state the outcome of the debates.

Mr. JEFFERSON. The final vote of Congress was that each state should have one vote. A compromise had been reached in which it was agreed that on certain measures the votes of nine states should be necessary for passage. This was a concession to the interests of the larger states. While no one really knew, this was just a calm before the storm clouds of 1787.

Mr. MADISON. Thank you, Mr. Jefferson. There is one point I would like to add to your statement. I understand that on the 1st of August, 1776, Mr. Robert Sherman offered a new suggestion. He took his stand firmly upon the proposition that "we are representatives of states, not individuals"; nevertheless he suggested that "The vote should be taken two ways; call the Colonies and call the individuals, and have a majority of both." This, though vague in form, is possibly the germ of that compromise in the Constitution, credited to Sherman, whereby the states were given equal representation in the Senate and proportional representation in the House.

Continuing now on my comparison of the Franklin and Dickinson drafts of Articles of Confederation.

Fourth, as to an executive council. Under Franklin's plan, this Council was to consist of twelve members of Congress, chosen by that body and put into three groups of four in such a manner that one-third of the members would be changed annually; and further providing for three years between terms of serving on the council. The chief business of the executive council was "to manage the general continental business in the recess of Congress." In the Dickinson plan the name is changed to Council of State and its composition changed to one delegate from each state, "to be named annually by the Delegates of each colony, and where they cannot agree, by the United States assembled."

There is no constitutional council in the present-day Constitution. The executive council is perhaps the forerunner of the present-day cabinet system. And I would suspect that we will hear more on this particular subject before these sessions run their course.

Fifth, Franklin recognized that "all new institutions may have imperfections which only time and experience can discover" and therefore stipulated that Congress might propose amendments to the Constitution that, when approved by a majority of the colonial assemblies, should be "equally binding with the rest of the Articles of this Confederation." The Dickinson plan, on the contrary, provided that no alteration should be made "unless such alteration be agreed to in an assembly of the United States and be afterwards confirmed by the legislatures of *every* colony."

Note that Dickinson's plan called for the approval of "every" colony. Our present-day Constitution is a sort of cross between the two, requiring ratification "by the legislatures of three fourths of the several states, or by conventions in three-fourths thereof, as the one or the other mode of ratification may be proposed by the Congress." The present-day Constitution still contains the provision requiring the ratification of conventions of nine states for its establishment. Since the Dickinson Articles required approval of every colony for its amendment, major debates occurred on this issue, both in the Federal Convention and in the ratifying states, as to the legality of the procedures employed in creating the present-day Constitution.

Finally, Franklin nearly went to the limit of his imagination when he again proposed, in addition to the thirteen colonies, the possible inclusion of other colonies in the Confederation. He proposed that "any and every Colony from Great Britain upon the Continent of North America" not at present "engag'd in our Association" might join the Association and be received into the Confederation and thereby become "entitled to all the Advantages of our Union, mutual Assistance and Commerce"; and he specified the West India Islands, Quebec, St. Johns, Nova Scotia, Bermudas, and the East and West Floridas. On second thought, he would even open the door to Ireland. Dickinson and his committee left the door open only for Canada to come into the Confederation. Just imagine, Canada could have come into the Confederation without the approval of any of the states or of England! This open door remained in effect from March 1, 1781 to March 4, 1787.

Mr. ADAMS. With Canada's problem in the 1980s, maybe we should open the door again? But this matter is beyond the scope of our discussion here.

Mr. MADISON. I believe I am now at the point where

I can summarize the key provisions of the Articles of Confederation finally adopted by the States on March 1, 1781.

Gen. WASHINGTON. Mr. Madison, I will interrupt you first by suggesting we take a ten-minute recess.

First SPECTATOR (Aside to Second SPECTATOR). What is Mr. Adams doing?

Second SPECTATOR (Aside to First SPECTATOR). That's snuff.

First SPECTATOR. (Aside to Second Spectator) Thank God. I thought it was some other stuff.

Mr. JEFFERSON. (Aside to Mr. Adams) John, do you know who read the Declaration of Independence to the public in Independence Square on July 8, 1776?

Mr. ADAMS. No.

Mr. JEFFERSON. Do you, Ben?

Dr. FRANKLIN. No. Who?

Mr. JEFFERSON. John Nixon.

Mr. ADAMS. And that opened the dam through which independence flowed.

Dr. FRANKLIN. A dam is a watergate.

Mr. ADAMS. Aye, what's in a name?

Dr. FRANKLIN. I believe that question has been asked by poets greater than ourselves. I am reminded of a passage included in the Dickinson and final drafts. The final draft, in Article Six, said in effect that no person shall accept any title nor shall the United States, in Congress assembled, or any of them, grant any title of nobility.

Since I had had a lifelong disdain for pomp, ceremony, and titles of honor, other than my own contributions to the Articles of Confederation, Mr. Dickinson's additions, though not in exactly the words I quoted, may be the only words that were agreeable to me, for the reason I will now tell.

In olden times it was no disrespect for men and women to be called by their own names: Adam, was never called Master Adam; we never read of Noah Esquire, Lot Knight and Baronet, nor the Right Honourable Abraham, Viscount Mesopotamia, Baron of Carran; no, no, they were plain men, honest country grasiers, that took care of their families and their flocks. Moses was a great prophet, and Aaron a priest of the Lord; but we never read of the Reverend Moses, nor the Right Reverend Father in God, Aaron, by Divine Providence, Lord Arch-Bishop of Israel. You never saw Madam Rebecca in the Bible, my Lady Rachel, nor Mary, though a Princess of the Blood after the death of Joseph, called the Princess Dowager of Nazareth; no, plain Rebecca, Rachel, Mary, or the Widow Mary, or the like. It was no incivility then to mention their naked names as they were expressed.

(Members reenter the hall)

Mr. THOMSON. (Aside to Gen. Washington) General I have recorded in the Journal a recess of eighteen minutes. May I ask, sir, why an odd gap of eighteen minutes?

Gen. WASHINGTON. (Aside to Mr. Thomson) Mr. Thomson, that was the testimony of former President Richard Milhouse Nixon. The session will resume. Mr. Madison?

Mr. MADISON. The Articles of Confederation finally ratified on March 1, 1781 contained the following concepts:

First, the Confederation was called "The United States of America."

Second, each "colony" was called a "state."

Third, delegates were to be appointed annually.

Fourth, delegates were to be appointed by the legislature of each state, in such manner as each should direct.

Fifth, no person could be a delegate for more than three years in any period of six years.

Sixth, each state was to have one vote.

Seventh, a unicameral congress was provided for.

Eighth, "A Committee of the States," consisting of one delegate from each state, appointed by the Congress, was to sit in recess of Congress.

Ninth, such "Committee of the States" was to "appoint one of their number to preside, provided that no person be allowed to serve in the office of president more than one year in any term of three years."

Tenth, Canada, on acceding to the Confederation, was

to be admitted into the union.

Eleventh, "alterations" in the articles had to be confirmed by the legislatures of "every" state.

These provisions, among others, constituted the first constitution of the United States. These provisions remained in effect until March 4, 1789, when our present-day Constitution became effective. I would now like to present the conditions which led to the demise of the Articles of Confederation and the calling of the Federal Convention of 1787.

Gen. WASHINGTON. Mr. Madison, I would like you to continue your presentation tomorrow. However, before we adjourn, I give Mr. Adams the floor.

Mr. ADAMS. In the Journals of Congress for August 20, 1776, is the draft report of the Committee considering the Articles of Confederation. Mr. Thomson, will you please read the order of business next taken up on this same day by Congress?

Mr. THOMSON. I believe you are referring to this portion: "The Committee appointed to prepare a device for a great seal for the United States, brought in the same, with an explanation thereof."

Mr. MADISON. Who was on that committee?

Dr. FRANKLIN. (Answering) Mr. Adams, Mr. Jefferson, and little ol' me.

Gen. WASHINGTON. Dr. Franklin!

Mr. ADAMS. I had proposed Hercules resting on his club. Virtue pointing to her rugged mountain on one hand and persuading him to ascend. Sloth, glancing at her flowery paths of pleasure. Want only reclining on the ground, displaying the charms both of her eloquence and person, to seduce him into vice. But this was too complicated for a seal or medal, and it was not original.

Mr. JEFFERSON. I had proposed the children of Israel in the wilderness, led by a cloud by day, and a pillar of fire by night, and on the other side Hengist and Horsa, the Saxon Chiefs, from whom we claim the honour of being descended and whose political principles and form of government we have assumed.

Mr. ADAMS. The original idea for the Coat of Arms of the United States which we did adopt was formed by Du Simitiere, a gentleman of French extraction, a painter by profession, whose designs were very ingenious, and his drawings well executed. This Mr. Du Simitiere was a very curious man. . . .

Gen. WASHINGTON. Mr. Adams, this subject has no bearing on the activities of this Commission.

Dr. FRANKLIN. Mr. Chairman, if I may have your indulgence for just one more moment on this subject. For my own part, I wish the Bald Eagle had not been chosen as the representative of our country; he is a bird of bad moral character; he does not get his living honestly; you may have seen him perched on some dead tree, near the river where, too lazy to fish for himself, he watches the labour of the fishing-hawk; and when the diligent bird has at length taken a fish and is bearing it to his nest for the support of his mate and young ones, the Bald Eagle pursues him and takes it from him. Like those men who live by sharping and robbing, he is generally poor, and often very lousy. Besides, he is a rank coward; the little kingbird, not bigger than a sparrow, attacks him boldly and drives him out of the district.

The Turkey is in comparison a much more respectable bird, and withal a true original native of America. Eagles have been found in all countries, but the turkey is peculiar to ours; the first of the species seen in Europe was brought to France by the Jesuits from Canada and served at the wedding table of Charles the Ninth. He is, though a little vain and silly, it is true, not the worse emblem for that, a bird of courage, since he would not hesitate to attack a Grenadier of the British Guards who should presume to invade his farm yard with a red coat on.

Gen. WASHINGTON. Gentlemen, it seems clear that this Commission can benefit from a period of reflection and restoration. This session will adjourn until tomorrow at 10 a.m.

(Crowds exits Assembly Rooms and filters in entrance way of Independence Hall)

Mr. WENDELL WILLKIE. (Recognizing Mr. Menachim Begin in crowd) Mr. Begin, may I introduce myself?

I am Wendell Willkie.

    Mr. BEGIN. Oh, yes Mendel . . .

    Mr. WILLKIE. No, Mr. Begin, my name is Wendell, Wendell.

    Mr. BEGIN. Mendel, Wendel, Schmendel — what's the difference — it's all ONE WORLD. And speaking of one world, if you are free tonight I would enjoy having dinner with you and discussing your ONE WORLD concept.

    Mr. WILLKIE. Certainly. Where? When?

    Mr. BEGIN. How about 8 o'clock at the City Tavern.

    Mr. WILLKIE. Fine. See you there.

THURSDAY, JUNE 18, 1987

PROBLEMS UNDER OUR FIRST CONSTITUTION

The Committee met pursuant to notice, at 10 a.m. in the Assembly Room of Independence Hall, Gen. George Washington presiding.

Present: Mr. John Adams, Dr. Benjamin Franklin, Mr. Thomas Jefferson, Mr. James Madison and Gen. George Washington.

Gen. WASHINGTON. At this session, we will continue to trace the origin of constitutional concepts which preceded the drafting of the Constitution at the Federal Convention in 1787. Mr. Madison has traced certain constitutional concepts beginning with Dr. Franklin's Albany Plan of 1754, and his proposed Articles of Confederation in 1775, and Mr. Dickinson's proposed Articles of Confederation in 1776.

As we all recall, the Articles took effect on March 1, 1781. Just six days later, Mr. John Sullivan, then a member of Congress, wrote me and said, among other things, that "Congress ought to have more power, but I also think that the old members should be in Heaven or at Home before this takes place. . . ."

At this juncture, Mr. Madison and others are prepared to discuss the events which gave rise to the demise of the Articles and fed the federalists with fodder for thoughts of a Federal Convention. Mr. Madison.

Mr. MADISON. In a similar vein, Mr. Chairman, the same John Sullivan also wrote to Meshech Weare, president of New Hampshire, a few months before he wrote to you. Permit me to read a portion of his letter:

"Our political affairs are so deranged as to prevent my giving you any tolerable account respecting them and was I to attempt it the task would be disagreeable to me and painful to you. The members of Congress are mostly new and I believe in general honest. Most of those who were governed by party spirit are recalled. I am sorry to say that in my opinion they had greater wisdom than the present members possess . . . Our confederation is not in force and, even if acceded to, would be found weak and perhaps far from answering the designs. Our treasury is empty, our credit low, our finances deranged and the people at large are suspicious of every species of our paper emissions. Particular states, and even among those who have acceded to the Confederation, comply with or reject the requisitions of Congress as their own opinion or interest seem to direct. Congress, of course, becomes a body without power, and the states, . . . a monster with thirteen heads. How we are to obtain relief is the important inquiry. This can be done only in one way that I can possibly conceive which is to call a convention of the several states to declare what powers Congress is to possess and to vest them with authority to use coercive measures with those states which refuse to comply with reasonable requisitions . . ."

Mr. JEFFERSON. Mr. Madison, may I read a letter, again in the same vein, from a gentleman of the same vintage?

Mr. MADISON. Please do.

Mr. JEFFERSON. Mr. James Mitchell Varnum, a member of Congress, wrote to William Greene, governor of Rhode Island, on April 2, 1781, just one month after the Articles took effect, saying: "There are two obstacles to that energy and vigor which are absolutely necessary in the United States. In the first place, the United States have not vested Congress, or any other body, with the power of calling out effectually the resources of each state. The Articles of Confederation give only the power of apportioning. Compliance in the respective states is generally slow, and in many instances does not take place. The consequence is disappointment and may be fatal. In the second place, an extreme, though perhaps well-meant jealousy, in many members of Congress, especially those of a long standing, seems to frustrate every attempt to introduce a more efficacious system. . . . My duty, or a mistaken idea of it, obliges me to hazard a conjecture: That the time is not far distant when the present American Congress will be dissolved, or laid aside as useless, unless a change of measures shall render their authority more respectable. . . . I know of but one eligible resort in the power of the United States. That is to form a Convention not composed of members of Congress, especially those whose political sentiments have become interwoven with their habits, from a long train of thinking in the same way. It should be the business of this convention to revise and reframe the Articles of Confederation; to define the aggregate powers of the United States in Congress assembled; fix the executive departments, and ascertain their authorities. . . . This plan, if rational and necessary, must be recommended by the legislature of some one state . . . ."

Mr. Varnum's advocacy of a constitutional convention was one of several expressions on the subject at this period. The most comprehensive proposal for a convention to create a strong central government, one backed by military power and public creditors, was made by Alexander Hamilton on September 3, 1780.

The concept stemmed from the debate over the creation of state governments in 1776. In several states citizens argued that the revolutionary bodies that had taken the place of the colonial governments could not write constitutions. They insisted that only conventions elected for the purpose could do so and that the constitutions could not go into effect until they had been approved by the people.

Thank you, Mr. Madison.

Mr. MADISON. What were the conditions, then, which generated the need for change? The public debt, rendered so sacred by the cause in which it had been incurred, remained without any provision for its payment. . . .

Dr. FRANKLIN. (To the spectators.) So what's new?

Mr. MADISON. . . . The reiterated and elaborate efforts of Congress to procure from the states a more adequate power to raise the means of payment had failed. The effect of the ordinary requisitions of Congress had only displayed the inefficiency of the authority making them, none of the states having duly complied with them, some having failed altogether, or nearly so; while in one instance, that of New Jersey, a compliance was expressly refused.

The want of authority in Congress to regulate commerce had produced in foreign nations, particularly Great Britain, a monopolizing policy, injurious to the trade of the United States and destructive to their navigation; the imbecility and anticipated dissolution of the Confederacy extinguished all anticipations of a countervailing policy on the part of the United States. The same want of a general power over commerce led to an exercise of the power, separately, by the states, which not only proved abortive but engendered rival, conflicting, and angry regulations. The states having ports for foreign commerce taxed and irritated the adjoining states trading through them. Some of the states, as Connecticut, taxed imports from others, as from Massachusetts.

In sundry instances, as in New York, New Jersey, Pennsylvania, and Maryland, the navigation laws treated the citizens of other states as aliens.

In certain cases the authority of the Confederacy was disregarded, such as violations not only of the Treaty of Peace with Britain, but the treaties with France, and Holland, which violations were complained of to Congress by the foreign entities. In other cases the federal authority was violated by the making of treaties and war with Indians, as by Georgia; by troops raised and kept up without the consent of Congress, as by Massachusetts; by compacts between states without the consent of Congress, as between Pennsylvania and New Jersey and between Virginia and Maryland. From the Legislative Journals of Virginia, it appears that a vote refusing to apply to Congress for a sanction of a compact was followed by a vote against the communication of the compact to Congress.

In the internal administration of the states, violations of contracts had become familiar; depreciated paper was made a legal tender, and property was substituted for money.

Among the defects which had been severely felt was the want of uniformity in the laws of naturalization and bankruptcy, a coercive authority operating on individuals, and a guarantee of the internal tranquility of the states.

As a natural consequence of this distracted and disheartening condition of the union, the federal authority had ceased to be respected abroad, and dispositions were shown, particularly in Great Britain, to take advantage of its imbecility and to speculate on its approaching downfall. At home it had lost all confidence and credit; the unstable and unjust career of the states had also forfeited the respect and confidence essential to order and good government, involving a general decay of confidence and credit between man and man. It was found, moreover, that those least partial to popular government, or most distrustful of its efficacy, anticipated with an increase in confusion a government that might be more suitable to their opinions. Those most devoted to the principles and forms of Republics were alarmed for the cause of liberty itself, at stake in the American experiment, and anxious for a system that would avoid the inefficiency of a mere confederacy, without passing into the opposite extreme of a consolidated government.

It was known that there were individuals who had betrayed a bias toward monarchy, and there had always been some not unfavorable to a partition of the Union into several confederacies; either from a better change of figuring on a sectional theater, or that the sections would require stronger governments, or by their hostile conflicts lead to a monarchial consolidation. The idea of dismemberment had made its appearance in the newspapers.

Such were the defects, the deformities and the ominous prospects for which the Convention was to provide a remedy and which ought never to be overlooked in expounding and appreciating the constitutional charter, the remedy that was provided.

Mr. ADAMS. With respect to the debt to which you refer, for the record, what was the debt at the end of the revolutionary war?

Mr. MADISON. A staggering debt of about $40 million had accumulated by the end of the war, not including the debts of the various states.

Mr. ADAMS. And what efforts were made to collect revenues to pay these debts?

Mr. MADISON. Repeated requests would be made of the states, sometimes in the following form: "We, the United States in Congress assembled by virtue of the powers vested in us by the Confederation, do call on you as members of the Confederacy to pay into the general Treasury at the time stipulated your respective quotas, the present requisition for the support of the general Government." Or a notice would appear in the *New York Packet*, terse and to the point: "The SUBSCRIBER has received nothing on account of the quota of this State for the present year. (Signed) Alexander Hamilton, Receiver of Continental Taxes."

Superintendent of Finance Robert Morris had found that asking the states for money was "like preaching to the dead."

Central to the fiscal problems of Congress was the fact that under the Articles of Confederation it had no power to tax. It had two alternative ways of raising money. The first was to continue its practice of requisitioning funds from the states, in effect pleading for money. The second was to amend the Articles to give it a taxing power, but such an amendment required unanimity; one state could block it.

In 1781, Congress sought to amend the Articles to permit a 5 percent federal duty on imports to pay the interest and principal on the national debt, but Rhode Island refused to approve the plan. Two years later, Congress again made the proposal in a modified form. This time New York, which derived the bulk of its revenue from imports, blocked it. Henry Knox, then secretary of war, was incensed. "Every liberal good man," he exclaimed, "is wishing New York in Hell!" British merchants took advantage of the war's end to unload their heavy inventory of manufactured goods on the American markets.

Congress lacked the power to regulate commerce.

Retaliatory action by individual states proved ineffectual. Thus, when Massachusetts tried to prevent dumping, New Hampshire absorbed the imported goods.

Interstate trade restrictions accentuated the problem. States like New Jersey and Connecticut erected trade barriers for their own advantage. For example, New Jersey's citizens exported most of their produce directly, but their imports were funneled through Philadelphia and New York City. Yielding to the pressures of local businessmen, New Jersey levied a duty on foreign goods not clearing directly through her ports. In retaliation, New York charged a discriminatory entrance and clearance fee on foreign goods from Connecticut and New Jersey. Pennsylvania enacted a protective tariff in 1785, taxing both foreign goods and products made in other states.

As business continued its downward course to the year 1787, public policy was increasingly focused on currency instability and debtor-creditor issues. As a result of a scarcity of hard money, businessmen were forced to transact affairs in goods rather than in coin. Paper money issued by the states to ease the situation depreciated rapidly. In no area did the monetary problems cause so much alarm as in New England.

Hardest hit by debt was Massachusetts, for here the conservative state government refused to introduce any remedial measures. By the close of 1786, mortgage foreclosures reached a record high. The jails of the central and western parts of the state were crowded with debtors. Still other debtors were sold into service to satisfy judgments against them. The plight of these debtor farmers touched off a wave of popular indignation, targeted against both the lawyers, who were pressing the claims of the creditors, and the courts, which enforced them. The crushing burden of debt, hitting both individuals and whole communities, spurred calls for tax reduction. "We are almost ready to cry out under the burden of our taxes as the children of Israel did in Egypt when they were required to make bricks without straw," exclaimed the people of Coxhall, for "we cannot find that there is money enough to pay." Critics of the Massachusetts government argued that the state, by rapidly amortizing its debt, had shifted the tax burdens from the commercial interests to the farmer.

When the Massachusetts legislature adjourned on July 8, 1786, without heeding the farmers' petition for paper money or stay laws, discontent escalated to violence. Armed men broke up the courts at Worcester and Northampton. Militiamen confronted the Supreme Court sitting at Springfield and forced the court to adjourn.

The discontented had found a leader in Daniel Shays, a debt-ridden farmer and veteran of the Revolutionary War. Shays moved against the Springfield arsenal, but he and his followers were routed by a whiff of grapeshot from Gen. Shepherd's defending forces. Gen. Benjamin Lincoln with some 4,400 troops then took over. The morale of the insurgents weakened, and Shays retreated. At Petersham, after a forced thirty-mile march through a blinding snowstorm, the militia surprised the rebels, captured 150 of their number, and scattered the rest. Shays himself fled to Vermont and, by the end of February 1787, the uprising had been completely crushed. The voters, however, repudiated the state administration for its uncompromising stand, and a newly elected legislature of 1787 enacted laws lowering court fees and exempting clothing, household goods, and the tools of one's trade from debt process and also refrained from imposing any direct tax that year.

During Shay's rebellion Edward Carrington, a member of Congress, wrote to his governor of Virginia, Edmund Randolph: "How far the contagion of Eastern disorders will spread, it may not be so proper to conjecture from the present quiet state of the other parts of the Empire, as from the experience of human nature, and the constitutions of our governments. . . . Here is felt the imbecility, the futility, the nothingness of the federal powers; the U.S. have no troops, nor dare they call into action what is called the only safeguard of a free government, the militia of the state, it being composed of the very objects of the force; neither can reliance be placed upon that of the neighbouring states; New Hampshire has already shown her kindred to the revolters; Connecticut is not free from the infection; and the

Legislative Acts of Rhode Island have discovered that an opposition to baseness can be expected from no order of people there.

"This instance, terminate however it may, will doubtless teach the necessity of efficiency in government, and perhaps it would be best placed in the federal head. Indeed if this cannot be got in the present form, some other ought immediately to be devised. A change of choice, will, probably, be one of wisdom. If it is left to accident, we cannot account for the result.. . ."

I think this illustrates well the tenor and tempo of the times.

Mr. ADAMS. Is this Edward Carrington not the same person who was foreman of the jury during the trial of Aaron Burr in 1807?

Mr. JEFFERSON. I believe that is correct. In fact, in January 1787 I wrote to Mr. Carrington and Mr. Madison, separately, on the subject of Daniel Shay's activities. In essence, I held it that "a little rebellion now and then is a good thing and as necessary in the political world as storms in the physical. Unsuccessful rebellions indeed generally establish the encroachments on the rights of the people which have produced them. . . . The people are the only censors of their governors; and even their errors will tend to keep these to the true principles of their institution. To punish these errors too severely would be to suppress the only safeguard of the public liberty. The way to prevent these irregular interpositions of the people is to give them full information of their affairs through the channel of the public papers and to contrive that those papers should penetrate the whole mass of the people. The basis of our government being the opinion of the people, the very first object should be to keep that right; and were it left to me to decide whether we should have a government without newspapers or newspapers without a government, I should not hesitate a moment to prefer the latter. . . . Cherish therefore the spirit of our people and keep alive their attention. Do not be too severe upon their errors, but reclaim them by enlightening them."

Mr. MADISON. I believe that General Washington

and I were worried about the trend toward anarchy that the rebellion exemplified. We viewed it as a striking example of the dangerous disorder that stemmed from having an impotent central government.

Gen. WASHINGTON. I did not conceive we could long exist as a nation without having lodged somewhere a power which would pervade the whole Union in as energetic a manner as the authority of the state governments extended over the several states.

Mr. MADISON. These hearings today lead us into the key subject of the Federal Convention of 1787. I have made a brief outline of topics we may consider at today's session. They are:

1. More details on the problems of the period.
2. British, French, and American attitudes during the period.
3. Constitutional questions raised during this period.
4. The Annapolis Convention.

In order to crystalize and focus in on the problems, let me summarize the vices of the political system of the United States as I have already noted them.

First, there was the failure of the states to comply with the Constitutional requisitions.

Second, there were encroachments by the states on the federal authority, for example, the wars and treaties of Georgia with the Indians.

Third, there were violations of the laws of nations and of treaties. The Treaty of Peace wth Britain, the Treaty with France, and the Treaty with Holland had each been violated.

Fourth, there were trespasses by the states on the rights of each other; the issuance of paper money by a state may be deemed an aggression on the rights of other states, as may the laws of Maryland in favor of vessels belonging to her "own citizens."

Fifth, there was a want of concert in matters where common interest required it, such as in laws concerning naturalization.

Sixth, there was a want of guaranty to the states of their constitutions and laws against internal violence. The Articles of Confederation were silent on this point, and therefore by the second article, whereby each state retained every power not expressly delegated to the United States, the hands of the federal authority were tied.

Seventh, there was a want of sanction to the laws and a want of power of coercion in the government of the Confederacy. A sanction is as essential to the idea of law as coercion is to that of government. A federal system destitute of both lacks the great vital principles of a political constitution. Such a constitution is in fact nothing more than a treaty of amity, of commerce, and of alliance between independent and sovereign states. From what cause could so fatal an omission have happened in the Articles of Confederation?

Mr. ADAMS. Could it have been that Mr. Dickinson planned it that way?

Gen. WASHINGTON. The question is out of order, Mr. Adams.

Mr. MADISON. In answering my own question, the omission may have arisen from a mistaken confidence that the justice, the good faith, the honor, the sound policy of the several legislative assemblies would render superfluous any appeal to the ordinary motives by which the laws secure the obedience of individuals. A confidence which does honor to the enthusiastic virtue of the compilers, as much as the inexperience of the crisis, apologizes for their errors.

Mr. ADAMS. Confidence, Mr. Madison, is not a substitute for law.

Mr. MADISON. In that, I agree, Mr. Adams.

Eighth, there was a want of ratification of the Articles of Confederation by the people.

Mr. Chairman, Mr. Alexander Hamilton is in the audience, and I understand he would appreciate the opportunity of making a statement on this point of want of ratification.

Gen. WASHINGTON. Please let him do so.

Mr. MADISON. Mr. Alexander Hamilton.

Mr. HAMILTON. I will just take a moment. It had not a little contributed to the infirmities of the Articles of Confederation that it never had a ratification by the people. Resting on no better foundation than the consent of the several legislatures, it had been exposed to frequent and intricate questions concerning the validity of its powers, and had in some instances given birth to the enormous doctrine of a right of legislative repeal. Owing its ratification to the law of a state, it had been contended that the same authority might repeal the law by which it was ratified. However gross a heresy it may have been to maintain that a party to a compact has a right to revoke that compact, the doctrine itself had respectable advocates. The possibility of a question of this nature proved the necessity of laying the foundations of our national government deeper than in the mere sanction of delegated authority. The fabric of American empire ought to rest on the solid basis of the consent of the people. The streams of national power ought to flow immediately from that pure, original fountain of all legitimate authority. Thank you.

Mr. MADISON. What Mr. Hamilton alludes to is the possibility, arising under the doctrine of compacts, that a breach of any of the articles of the Confederation by any of the parties to it absolved the other parties from their respective obligations and gave them a right, if they chose to exert it, of dissolving the Union altogether.

Now continuing—

Ninth, there was a multiplicity of laws in the several states. Insofar as laws are necessary to make with precision the duties of those who are to obey them and to take from those who are to administer them a discretion which might be abused, their existence is the price of liberty. As far as laws exceed this limit they are a nuisance; a nuisance of the most pestilent kind. The short period since independence had filled as many pages with laws as the century which preceded it. Every year, almost every session, in every state a new volume was added. A review of the Codes of the states showed that every necessary and useful part of the least voluminous of them might be compressed into one-tenth of the compass, and at the same time be rendered ten-fold as perspicuous.

Tenth, there was an instability in the laws of the states. This evil deserves a distinct notice as it emphatically denotes a vicious legislation. We daily saw laws repealed or superseded before any trial could have been made of their merits, and even before a knowledge of them reached the remoter districts within which they were to operate. In the regulations of trade, this instability became a snare not only to our citizens but to foreigners also.

Eleventh, there was an injustice in the laws of the states. If the multiplicity and mutability of laws exposed a want of wisdom, their injustice betrayed a defect still more alarming, not merely because it was a greater evil in itself but because it brought into question the fundamental principle of republican government: that the majority who rule in such governments are the safest guardians both of public good and private rights.

The great desideratum in government is such a modification of the sovereignty as will render it sufficiently neutral between the different interests and factions to control one part of the society from invading the rights of another, and, at the same time, sufficiently controlled itself from setting up an interest adverse to that of the whole society.

These were my own notes. But the complaints of others were legion.

William Grayson, a member of Congress, wrote to me in March 1786: "There has been some serious thought in the minds of some of the members of Congress to recommend to the states the meeting of a general Convention to consider an alteration of the Confederation, and there is a motion to this effect now under consideration. It is contended that the present Confederation is utterly inefficient, and that if it remains much longer in its present state of imbecility, we shall be one of the most contemptible nations on the face of the Earth. For my own part, I have not yet made up my mind on the subject. I am doubtful whether it is not better to bear those ills we have than fly to others that we know not of. I am, however, in no doubt about the weakness of the federal government . . . the federal Government is weak but the individual states are strong. It is no wonder our Government should not work well. . . ."

On the other hand, Rufus King, also a member of Congress, had written earlier, "We are for increasing the power of Congress as far as it will promote the happiness of the people; but at the same time we are clearly of the opinion that every measure should be avoided which would strengthen the hands of the enemies to a free government. . . . An Administration of the present Confederation, with all its inconveniences, is preferable to the risk of general dissentions and animosities, which may approach to anarchy and prepare the way to a ruinous system of government."

Mr. ADAMS. Mr. King wrote to me in May 1786, while I was in England, saying: "It has undoubtedly been said in England that the act of Congress. . . . relative to the federal revenues, is full proof that the United States are in the utmost confusion and that the Union is nearly dissolved. That there exists a criminal neglect of several of the states in their most important duties to the confederacy cannot be denied. I hope a reform will take place. . . . We are at a crisis. . . . and a proposition has originated in Virginia for a convention of delegates, in September, from the several states, to agree on such commercial regulations as shall extend the American navigation and promote the trade of the Union. The most important states have already appointed delegates for this purpose to assemble in Maryland. And if anything can be concluded from the general reputation of the delegates already appointed, there is reason to hope that wisdom will govern their deliberations and that their result will produce a union of opinions on the subject of commercial regulations through all the states . . . ."

Mr. MADISON. And from the Rhode Island delegates to the governor of Rhode Island in September, 1786: "It is now agreed by all that our federal government is but a name, a mere shadow without any substance; and we think it our duty to inform the states that it is totally inefficient for the purposes of the Union, and that Congress, without being vested with more extensive powers, must prove totally nugatory."

Dr. FRANKLIN. How would you like to have been president of the United States in the 1980s, instead of the 1780s, and to have given Congress a State of the Union address?

Mr. JEFFERSON. I was in France at this critical point. The French minister of foreign affairs to the United States gave this view of the American crisis in February 1786: "All the members are acutely affected by the present crisis; the most brilliant talk among themselves is of quitting Congress if the states continue in their refusal to a 5 percent tax. This period, Monseigneur, is perhaps one of the most important which has occurred since the peace; . . . And one hears nothing on one side but the apprehensions of bankruptcy and the moans of good citizens, and from the other the cry of cabal and of avarice which pierces even into the sanctuary of the laws."

Mr. ADAMS. The British, regrettably, were actively adverse to our interests. Nathan Dane, a member of Congress, wrote in March, 1787: "I should be very sorry to see great numbers of our people moving to Canada. It would much affect the strength and honor of the United States, but I fear such an event. Great encouragement is given by the British government to tempt them to do it. The British are very busy on our frontiers, and our frontier inhabitants from New Hampshire to Georgia in my opinion will give us much trouble in a few years if we do not treat and govern them with much prudence and good policy."

Mr. JEFFERSON. I thought then that the British king, ministers and nation were more bitterly hostile to us than at any period since the Revolutionary War. Our enemies, for such they were in fact, had for the twelve years past followed but one uniform rule, that of doing exactly the contrary of what reason pointed out. Having early during our contest observed this in the British conduct, I governed myself by it in all prognostications of their measures; and I can say with truth it never failed me but in the circumstance of their making peace with us.

Mr. MADISON. Let us now dispose of some of the Constitutional questions of the time.

Gen. WASHINGTON. Let us first take a twenty-minute recess.

Mr. ADAMS. (Soliloquizing) America was yet in her infancy, or at least but lately arrived to manhood, and inexperienced in the perplexing mysteries of policy, as well as the dangerous operations of war. Those of us who tread the public stage in characters the most extensively conspicuous met with so many embarrassments, perplexities, and disappointments, that they have often reason to wish for the peaceful retreats of the clergy. Who would not wish to exchange the angry contentions of the forum for the peaceful contemplations of the closet? . . . Statesmen may plan and speculate for Liberty, but it is religion and morality alone which can establish the principles upon which freedom can securely stand. The only foundation of a free Constitution is pure virtue, and if this cannot be inspired into our people, in a greater measure, they may change their rulers and the forms of government, but they will not obtain a lasting liberty. They will only exchange tyrants and tyrannies.

Mr. JEFFERSON. (Soliloquizing) From events then passing in Europe, our young republic could learn many useful lessons: never to call on foreign powers to settle their differences; to guard against hereditary magistrates; to prevent their citizens from becoming so established in wealth and power as to be thought worthy of alliance by marriage with the nieces, sisters, etc. of kings; and in short to besiege the throne of heaven with eternal prayers to eradicate from creation this class of human lions and tigers, called kings.

Gen. WASHINGTON. (Soliloquizing) When America stood alone against one of the most powerful nations of the earth, the spirit of liberty seemed to animate her sons to the noblest exertions, and each man cheerfully contributed his aid in support of her dearest rights. When the hand of tyranny seemed to bear its greatest weight on this devoted country, their virtue and perseverance appeared most conspicuous and rose superior to every difficulty. If then, such patriotism manifested itself throughout all ranks and orders of men among us, shall it be said at this day that America has grown tired of being free?

Mr. MADISON. (Soliloquizing) The Union — who were its real friends? Not those who charged others with not being its friends whilst their own conduct wantonly multiplied its enemies.

Not those who favored measures which, by pampering the spirit of speculation within and without the government, disgusted the best friends of the Union.

Not those who promoted unncesssary accumulations of the debt of the Union instead of the best means of discharging it as fast as possible, thereby increasing the causes of corruption in the government and the pretext for new taxes under its authority; the former undermining the confidence, the latter alienating the affection of the people.

Not those who studied, by arbitrary interpretations and insidious precedents, to pervert the limited government of the Union into a government of unlimited discretion, contrary to the will and subversive of the authority of the people.

Not those who avowed or betrayed principles of monarchy and aristocracy, in opposition to the republican principles of the Union and the republican spirit of the people, or who espoused a system of measures more accommodated to the depraved examples of those hereditary forms than to the true genius of our own.

Not those, in a word, who would force on the people the melancholy duty of choosing between the loss of the Union and the loss of what the Union was meant to secure.

The real friends of the Union were those who were friends to the authority of the people, the sole foundation on which the Union rests.

Mr. ADAMS. (Soliloquizing) I thought, then, that after govenments shall be assumed and a Confederation formed, we would have a long, obstinate and bloody war to go through and all the intrigues of our enemies as well as the weakness and credulity of our friends to guard against.

A mind as vast as the ocean or atmosphere was necessary to penetrate and comprehend all the intricate and complicated interests which composed the machine of the Confederate

Colonies. It required all the philosophy I was master of, and more than all, at times to preserve that serenity of mind and steadiness of heart which is necessary to watch the motions of friends and enemies, of the violent and the timid, the credulous and the dull, as well as the wicked.

But if I can contribute, I thought, ever so little towards preserving the principles of virtue and freedom in the world, my time and life would not be ill spent.

A man had to have a wider expansion of genius than had fallen to my share to see to the end of those great commotions. But, I thought, on such a full sea as we were then afloat, that we must be content to trust to winds and currents, with the best skill we had, under a kind Providence to land us in a Port of Peace, Liberty, and Safety.

Gen. WASHINGTON. Gentlemen, this session will now resume. Mr. Madison.

Mr. MADISON. At this point the session is open to a discussion of constitutional questions which preceded the Federal Convention of 1787. We have discussed some of these matters but perhaps there are others.

Mr. ADAMS. It appears to me that Congress held the weapons of war and the palms of peace, but the respective states held the purse strings of the Union, the power to create Congress annually by its appointment of members, and the power to defeat Congress by recall of its members.

Mr. JEFFERSON. Today, gentlemen, not one word has been said about presidential problems. Most of the experiences here stated have related to weaknesses in Congress.

Mr. THOMSON. Mr. Chairman, as secretary to Congress at the time, and even as acting president of Congress on occasion, I would appreciate if I may have the opportunity to respond to Mr. Jefferson on the point he raises.

Gen. WASHINGTON. When were you acting president in Congress?

Mr. THOMSON. In the Journals of the Continental Congress, Volume IX, page 846, for October 29, 1777, it was "Resolved, that the Secretary officiate as President until a new choice is made." That was I, Sir.

Gen. WASHINGTON. You may proceed, Mr. Thomson.

Mr. THOMSON. On September 27, 1784, I wrote to Jacob Read, then a member of Congress: "I have waited from day to day for something to occur worth the trouble of writing. But I find myself in the situation of the country man who stopped at a brook and waited till the stream would run out and he might walk over dry. The sun rises and sets as usual. Our assembly goes on squabbling and our newspapers to disseminate scurrility. . . . Whatever little politicians may think, time will evince that it is of no small consequence to save appearances with foreign nations, and not to suffer the federal government to become invisible. A government without a visible head must appear a strange phenomenon to European politicians and will, I fear, lead them to form no very favorable opinion of our stability, wisdom, or Union. . . ."

I believe this relates to Mr. Jefferson's point. I think leadership was the issue. Please excuse my intrusion.

Mr. JEFFERSON. That is a very good point, Mr. Thomson. In retrospect, the Declaration of Independence, which I wrote. . .

Dr. FRANKLIN. We know.

Mr. JEFFERSON. . . . wrought a fundamental change in the problem of writing a constitution for the thirteen states. All earlier plans of union, such as the Albany Plan . . .

Dr. FRANKLIN. Which you did not write.

Mr. JEFFERSON. . . . contemplated the superior authority of the British government. The new system of government created under the Articles of Confederation was designed in part to remedy those defects which radical leaders saw in the British connection. The central government became the agent of the states which created it and remained superior to it. It was perhaps in the sense of an abhorrence to any authority above their own — such as a king — that the states created no authority above their own.

To correct the stalemate created by state machination

required a reapportionment of power between the states and the central government. Under the Articles of Confederation, the balance of power was given to the states. There would have to be a shifting in the balance of political power within the thirteen states to shift the balance of power to a central government. That is, of course, what eventually happened.

It was not precisely to my liking, but that is another story.

Dr. FRANKLIN. All this sounds like a dance — the two-step — first the Continental Congress, then the Federal Congress.

Mr. ADAMS. With the failure of the Articles, a centralized government that would take the place of the British government was needed.

Dr. FRANKLIN. Our Constitution — under the Articles of Confederation — seems not to have been well understood. If the Congress were a permanent body, there would have been reason to be jealous of its powers. But its members were chosen annually, could not be chosen more than three years successively nor more than three years in seven; and any of them could be recalled at any time, whenever their constituents were dissatisfied with their conduct. They were of the people and returned again to mix with the people, having no more durable preeminence than the different grains of sand in an hourglass. Such an assembly could not easily become dangerous to liberty. They were the servants of the people, sent together to do the people's business and promote the public welfare; their powers had to be sufficient, or their duties could not be performed. They had no profitable appointments but a mere payment of daily wages, such as were scarcely equivalent to their expenses; so that having no chance for great places, and enormous salaries or pensions, as in some countries, there was no intriguing or bribing for elections. . . .

Mr. MADISON. Mr. Chairman, Mr. Alexander Hamilton has some further remarks.

Gen. WASHINGTON. Please proceed, Mr. Hamilton.

Mr. HAMILTON. The insufficiency of the Confederation to preserve the union was critical. I thought at the time we may indeed with propriety be said to have reached almost the last stage of national humiliation. There was scarcely anything that could wound the pride or degrade the character of an independent motion which we did not experience. Ours was at the lowest point of declension. The United States had an indefinite discretion to make requisitions for men and money; but they had no authority to raise either. The consequence of this was that though in theory their resolutions concerning those objects were laws, constitutionally binding on the members of the Union, yet in practice they were mere recommendations which the states observed or disregarded at their option.

In our case, the concurrence of thirteen distinct sovereign wills was requisite under the Confederation to the complete execution of every important measure that proceeded from the Union. What happened was to have been forseen. The measures of the Union were not executed; the delinquencies of the states, step by step, matured themselves to an extreme which had at length arrested all the wheels of the national government and brought them to an awful stand.

Each state, yielding to the persuasive voice of immediate interest or convenience, had successively withdrawn its support, till the frail and tottering edifice seemed ready to fall upon our hands and to crush us beneath its ruins. The government of the Union, like that of each state, had to be able to address itself immediately to the hopes and fears of individuals and to attract to its support those passions which have the strongest influence upon the human heart. It had to possess all the means, and have a right to resort to all the methods, of executing the powers with which it seemingly was entrusted but which in reality were possessed and exercised by the governments of the particular states.

Lastly, the right of equal suffrage among the states was an exceptionable part of the Confederation. Every idea of proportion and every rule of fair representation conspired to condemn a principle which gave to Rhode Island an equal right in the scale of power with Massachusetts, or Connecticut, or New

York; and to Delaware an equal voice in the national deliberations with Pennsylvania, or Virginia, or North Carolina. Its operation contradicted the fundamental maxim of republican government, which requires that the sense of the majority should prevail. Sophistry may reply that sovereigns are equal and that a majority of the votes of the states constitute a majority of confederated America. But this kind of logical legerdemain could never counteract the plain suggestions of justice and common-sense.

Mr. ADAMS. We ambled through those scrambled times. I do not think we feared fear, as Mr. Roosevelt warned against.

Mr. JEFFERSON. I used to say that "I steer my bark with hope ahead and fear astern."

Mr. ADAMS. We were God-fearing people though.

Mr. MADISON. We have already touched briefly on the need for the regulation of commerce, which existed prior to the Federal Convention of 1787. I want to spend more time on this key issue for two reasons: first, it served as the catalyst for originating the Federal Convention of 1787; second, it was a critical bargaining lever during the convention.

Article IX of the Articles of Confederation provided, in part, that:

"The United States in Congress assembled . . ."

Dr. FRANKLIN. (To the spectators) It is most significant that the *Biographical Dictionary of the American Congress* published by the Government Printing Office in the 1980s treats both the Continental Congress and the Congress of the United States as the American Congress.

Mr. MADISON. (Continuing) ". . . shall have the sole and exclusive right and power of . . . entering into treaties and alliances . . . provided that no treaty of commerce shall be made whereby the legislative power of the respective states shall be restrained from imposing such imposts and duties on foreigners, as their own people are subjected to, or from prohibiting the exportation or importation of any species of goods or commodities whatsoever. . . ."

So, for all practical purposes, Congress had no effective control over commerce. We have already noted in the records of this session the devastating impact of this failure to empower Congress to regulate commerce. On April 30, 1784, Congress adopted and sent to the states, for their approval, a report of a committee it had appointed to consider a grant of temporary power to Congress to regulate commerce. Mr. Jefferson was on that committee. Mr. Jefferson, would you kindly read the report to the committee, as sent to the states.

Mr. JEFFERSON. The report read as follows:

"The trust reposed in Congress renders it their duty to be attentive to the conduct of foreign nations and to prevent or restrain as far may be all such proceedings as might prove injurious to the United States. The situations of commerce at this time claim the attention of the several states, and few objects of greater importance can present themselves to their notice. The fortune of every citizen is interested in the success thereof; for it is the constant source of wealth and incentive to industry; and the value of our produce and our land must ever rise or fall in proportion to the prosperous or adverse state of trade. . . ."

Dr. FRANKLIN. They could have said that in 1984 instead of 1784, considering the foreign cars and other wares coming to American shores.

Mr. JEFFERSON. (Continuing) "Already Great Britain has adopted regulations destructive of our commerce with her West India Islands. There was reason to expect that measures so unequal and so little calculated to promote mercantile intercourse would not be persevered in by an enlightened nation. But these measures are growing into system. It would be the duty of Congress, as it is their wish, to meet the attempts of Great Britain with similiar restrictions on her commerce; but their powers on this head are not explicit, and the propositions made by the legislatures of the several states render it necessary to take the general sense of the Union on this subject.

"Unless the United States in Congress assembled shall be vested with powers competent to the protection of commerce, they can never command reciprocal advantages in trade; and without these, our foreign commerce must decline and eventually be annihilated. Hence it is necessary that the states should be explicit and fix on some effectual mode by which foreign commerce not founded on principles of equality may be restrained."

Thus came resolutions to recommend that the United States be given powers of embargo and regulation of imports for fifteen years; it was recommended that nine states approve the trade restriction empowerment resolution.

The request for a grant of temporary power to Congress to regulate commerce was not approved by the states.

Mr. MADISON. As the postwar commercial depression deepened, many merchants, mostly in the Northern states, were convinced that the request of Congress of April 30, 1784, for temporary commercial powers would be inadequate even if the states ratified it. Merchants demanded an amendment to the Articles of Confederation extending and making permanent Congress's power over commerce.

Congress responded on December 6, 1784, by appointing a committee consisting of John Jay, Elbridge Gerry, James Monroe, Richard Dobbs Spaight, and William Houston to consider investing Congress with the power to regulate trade. On February 17, 1785, the Committee reported an amendment to the Articles of Confederation. Congress considered the amendment on March 28 and debated it again on July 13 and 14, but there was so much opposition that the amendment was never sent to the states.

The proposed amendment to the Articles of Confederation granting commercial power to Congress read in part as follows:

"The United States in Congress assembled shall have the sole and exclusive right and power of . . . entering into treaties and alliances — of regulating the trade of the states as well with foreign Nations, as with each other, and of laying such imposts and duties, upon imports and exports, as may be necessary for the purpose; provided that the Citizens of the States, shall in no instance be subjected to pay higher imposts and duties than those imposed on the subjects of foreign powers; . . . provided also that all such duties as may be imposed, shall be collected under the authority and accrue to the use of the State in which the same shall be payable...."

The proposed amendment revived the antagonism between the "Carrying states" of the North and the "Planting states" of the South over the issue of trade regulation, an issue which had surfaced during the writing of the Articles of Confederation. It aroused, too, those who feared a powerful central government. James Monroe, a member of Congress summarized the arguments of the opponents of the amendment by observing "1. That is was dangerous to concentrate power, since it might be turned to mischievous purposes; that independent of the immediate danger of intoxication in those entrusted with it and their attempts on the government, it put us more in the power of other nations. 2. That the interests of the different parts of the Union were different from each other, and that the regulations which suited the one would not the other part. That eight states, for example, the Northern States, were of a particular interest whose business it would be to combine to shackle and fetter the others; for example, the southern states. 3. That all attacks upon the Confederation were dangerous and calculated, even if they did not succeed, to weaken it."

The widespread public debate over the issue of more power for the central government led to extended debates in Congress during the spring of 1786. Some members argued that a convention should be called, but the majority insisted that the proper method was for Congress to propose amendments to the Articles of Confederation.

On May 3, 1786, Congress, upon a motion of Charles Pinckney, agreed to sit as a "committee of the whole" to take into consideration the state of public affairs. On July 3, Congress appointed a "grand committee" to report such amendments to the Confederation and a draft of resolutions needed to obtain from the states the powers required by the federal government to function.

The grand committee reported seven amendments on August 7, 1786. I cite only one of them — that related to commerce — since this is the only amendment appropriate to our session and sequence.

"The United States in Congress assembled shall have the sole and exclusive power of regulating the trade of the States as well with foreign nations as with each other and of laying such prohibitions and such imposts and duties upon imports and exports as may be necessary for the purpose; provided the citizens of the States shall in no instance be subjected to pay higher duties and imposts than those imposed on the subjects of foreign powers, provided also, that all such duties as may be imposed shall be collected under such regulations as the United States in Congress assembled shall establish consistent with the Constitutions of the States respectively and to accrue to the use of the State in which the same shall be payable; provided also that the Legislative power of the several states shall not be restrained from laying embargoes in times of scarcity — and provided lastly that every Act of Congress for the purpose shall have the assent of Nine States in Congress assembled, and in that proportion which there shall be more than thirteen in the Union."

Congress set August 14, 1786, for consideration of the amendments. There is no record that Congress discussed the amendments on the 14th or any other day. The adoption of the amendments by Congress was blocked by a quarrel between the North and the South over a treaty with Spain which Secretary for Foreign Affairs John Jay proposed to negotiate with the Spanish minister, Don Diego de Gardoqui.

Thus, Congress never considered the amendments or submitted them to the states.

Mr. ADAMS. For the record, Mr. Madison, did any of the proposed amendments pertain to a change in the office of the President of Congress?

Mr. MADISON. No. Rufus King summed the dire state of our affairs in 1786 when he wrote: "The situation of the federal Government is now critical; the authority of the confederation is found to be inadequate. . . . No commercial nation will regret our disjointed condition or wish the states to unite in any system of commerce. Every partisan of France or England residing among us uses his utmost exertions to inspire the people of the different states with jealousies of each other; and some of them have even sounded the alarm that the liberties of the People were endangered by the plan of delegating additional powers to Congress.

"I fear that the commercial convention proposed to be held in Maryland in September will go but a little way in effecting those measures essentially necessary for the prosperity and safety of the States. Georgia and South Carolina have not appointed Delegates; and their legislatures will not be in session before the winter. Maryland has not appointed, although the convention is to be in that State. The assembly of North Carolina has not elected Delegates, but it is said that the executive of that State has nominated persons for the office. It is doubtful what the real sentiments of Virginia are on the question of commercial powers. This is certain, that the proposition for the Annapolis convention, which originated in the Assembly of Virginia, did not come from the persons favorable to a commercial system common to all the States, but from those who in opposition to such a general system have advocated the particular regulations of individual states. The merchants through all the States are of one mind and in favor of a national system. The planters in the southern states are divided in their opinions, and it is to be feared that the majority is against the only plan which can insure the prosperity and honor of the confederacy. . . ."

The Annapolis Convention, to which Mr. King refers, I will discuss in a moment.

Also, in 1786, Mr. David Ramsay, Chairman of Congress in the absence of President John Hancock, wrote to the unrepresented states, "I forbear to mention . . . that even in private life where two persons agree to meet at a given time and place for the adjustment of their common concerns, the one who attends has a right to complain that he is not treated with common politeness by the other who breaks his appointment. I say nothing of the unequal burden imposed on the States who are present: They incur a heavy expense to maintain their delegates. . . .

"The remissness of the States in keeping up a representation in Congress naturally tends to annihilate our Confederation. That once dissolved, our State establishments would be of short duration. Anarchy or intestine wars would follow till some future Caesar seized our Liberties, or we would be the sport of European politics and perhaps parcelled out as appendages to their several Governments. . . ."

Also in 1786, Nathan Miller, a member of Congress from Rhode Island, wrote: "I think I find a disposition in many of our new faces in the Legislature to not send any Members to Congress; but they are small men — they have heads and so have board nails."

Now — back to the Annapolis Convention. The real action had already shifted from the Congress to certain states early in 1786. It culminated with the Annapolis Convention in September, 1786, which was the forerunner of the Constitutional Convention of 1787.

The Annapolis Convention derived its origin directly from an effort on the part of Virginia and Maryland to adjust their own problems relating to commerce of the Potomac; indirectly the convention was an outgrowth of the movement for a general regulation of trade by Congress. At a convention of commissioners of those two states at Alexandria and Mount Vernon in March, 1785, the issues were satisfactorily adjusted; then, in order to achieve a fuller consummation of the purposes of the agreement, Maryland invited the accession of Delaware and Pennsylvania.

In the autumn of 1785, when this proposition came before the Virginia legislature, I embraced the opportunity to promote the larger plan of a convention of commissioners from all the states "for the purpose of digesting and reporting the requisite augmentation of the power of Congress over trade." On January 21, 1786, just as the legislative session was closing, a Resolution of the General Assembly of Virginia proposing a joint meeting of commissioners from the states to consider and recommend a Federal plan for regulating commerce was adopted.

The representatives, Edmund Randolph, James Madison, Walter Jones, Saint George Tucker, and Meriwether

Smith, were to meet with other states' representatives "at a time and place to be agreed on." The purpose of the convention was to consider "the trade of the United States; to examine the relative situations and trade of the said States; to consider how far a uniform system in their commercial regulations may be necessary to their common interest and their permanent harmony; and to report to the several States such an act relative to this great object, as, when unanimously ratified by them, will enable the United States in Congress effectually to provide for the same."

Annapolis was chosen as the place for the meeting and the first Monday in September as the time. It was thought prudent to avoid the neighborhood of Congress and the large commercial towns in order to disarm the adversaries of the project of insinuations of influence from either of these quarters. Considering that the states must first agree to the proposition for sending deputies, that the deputies must then agree to a plan to be sent back to the states, and that the states must agree unanimously in a ratification of it, I almost despaired of success.

The question, whether it be possible and worthwhile to preserve the Union of the States, had to be speedily decided some way or other. Those who were indifferent to its preservation, I thought, would do well to look forward to the consequences of its extinction. The prospect to my eye was a gloomy one indeed.

Well, only a handful of delegates appeared at the Annapolis Convention — those of New York, New Jersey, Pennsylvania, Delaware, and Virginia. The Commissioners met in Annapolis on Monday, September 11, 1786, with Mr. John Dickinson of Delaware elected as chairman.

Mr. ADAMS. John Dickinson! — he changed his colors, from Pennsylvania to Delaware!

Gen. WASHINGTON. Mr. Adams, order please! Continue, Mr. Madison.

Mr. MADISON. I was a member of the Virginia delegation. After deliberate consideration of the proper tasks of the commissioners, it was unanimously agreed that a committee be appointed to prepare a draft of a report to be made to the states attending, and on September 14 the report was agreed upon. The report recognized that most states attending had granted, in nearly the same terms, authority to their respective commissioners "to take into consideration the trade and commerce of the United States, to consider how far a uniform system in their commercial intercourse and regulations might be necessary to their common interest and permanent harmony. . . ."

But it was noted that the state of New Jersey had enlarged that authority, empowering its commissioners, "to consider how far a uniform system in their commercial regulation and other important matters might be necessary to the common interest and permanent harmony of the several states. . ." The words "other important matters" were to become significant.

The report observed that New Hampshire, Massachusetts, Rhode Island, and North Carolina had appointed commissioners, but none had attended and that no appointment had been made by Connecticut, Maryland, South Carolina, or Georgia. Thus the "Commissioners did not conceive it advisable to proceed on the business of their mission, under the circumstance of so partial and defective a representation." The report continued:

"Deeply impressed however with the magnitude and importance of the object confided to them on this occasion, your Commissioners cannot forbear to indulge an expression of their earnest and unanimous wish that speedy measures may be taken to effect a general meeting of the States in a future Convention for the same, and such other purposes as the situation of public affairs may be found to require. . . .

"In this persuasion, your Commissioners submit an opinion, that the idea of extending the powers of their deputies to other objects than those of Commerce, which has been adopted by the State of New Jersey, was an improvement on the original plan and will deserve to be incorporated into that of a future Convention. . . ."

They were led to the conclusion that "the power of regulating trade is of such comprehensive extent . . . that to give it efficacy . . . may require a correspondent adjustment of other parts of the Federal System. . . . There are important defects in the system of the Federal Government. . . . The defects upon a closer examination may be found greater and more numerous than even these acts imply. . . . The embarrassments which characterize the present State of our national affairs, foreign and domestic . . . merit a deliberate and candid discussion, in some mode, which will unite the sentiments and Councils of all the States. In the choice of the mode, your Commissioners are of opinion that a Convention of Deputies from the different States, for the special and sole purpose of entering into this investigation and digesting a plan for supplying such defects as may be discovered to exist, will be entitled to a preference. . .

"Under this impression, your Commissioners, with the most respectful deference, beg leave to suggest their unanimous conviction that it may essentially tend to advance the interests of the union if the States, by whom they have been respectively delegated, would themselves concur and use their endeavours to procure the concurrence of the other States in the appointment of Commissioners to meet at Philadelphia on the second Monday in May next to take into consideration the situation of the United States to devise such further provisions as shall appear to them necessary to render the constitution of the Federal Government adequate to the exigencies of the Union; and to report such an Act for that purpose to the United States in Congress assembled, as when agreed to, by them, and afterwards confirmed by the Legislatures of every State, will effectually provide for the same.

"Though your Commissioners could not with propriety address these observations and sentiments to any but the States they have the honor to represent, they have nevertheless concluded from motives of respect to transmit copies of this Report to the United States in Congress assembled and to the executives of the other States. By order of the Commissioners. Dated at Annapolis September 14th, 1786."

And so was begun the first major step toward a Federal Convention.

Mr. ADAMS. Who drafted the report?
Mr. MADISON. I believe it was Mr. Hamilton.

Mr. ADAMS. Who signed the report?

Mr. MADISON. It was "Resolved, that the Chairman sign the aforegoing Report in behalf of the Commissioners."

Mr. ADAMS. By Chairman, you mean Mr. Dickinson?

Mr. MADISON. Yes.

Mr. ADAMS. But he did not sign pursuant to the resolution, did he?

Mr. MADISON. No, all the Commissioners signed.

Mr. ADAMS. Do you know why?

Mr. MADISON. I do not recall — if I ever knew.

Mr. ADAMS. Did Mr. Dickinson sign his own name or was his name signed by proxy, as was his signature to the Constitution?

Mr. MADISON. Offhand, I do not know, but I would suspect it was his own signature. On second thought, I believe copies of the report, but not the proceedings, were signed only by Mr. Dickinson and sent with covering letters from Mr. Dickinson to Congress and the executives of the states.

Mr. ADAMS. Thank you.

Gen. WASHINGTON. Mr. Adams, I have recently received telegrams from students of Dickinson College in Carlisle, Pennsylvania, protesting your attack on Mr. John Dickinson. This current line of questioning is typical of the pattern you have followed. Is this a pattern you intend to continue to pursue, and if so, why?

Mr. ADAMS. Mr. Chairman. Mr. Dickinson has told me that he did not intend to let any man impugn his character and that he stood ready to vindicate his position on any question that might arise concerning his conduct. There are several issues concerning the conduct of Mr. Dickinson that should be considered by this Commission:

First, that he opposed the Declaration of Independence.

Second, that he disapproved the constitution of his state.

Third, that he deserted his battalion.

Fourth, that he endeavored to injure the continental money.

Fifth, that he refused to call the militia to protect Congress during a mutiny which threatened Congress.

Since Mr. Dickinson was a delegate to the Federal Convention in 1787 that formed the Constitution of the United States, and since he sat on key committees, particularly a committee which made substantive changes in the office of the president within two weeks prior to its signing, and since he has stated that he stands ready to vindicate his position on any question that might arise concerning his conduct, I am of the opinion that Mr. Dickinson should be free to testify here, as he has before, to vindicate himself, if he sees fit.

I do not believe that I should be singled out for commenting on Mr. Dickinson's conduct, since Mr. Dickinson himself made his conduct an issue before this Commission. Furthermore, insofar as Dickinson College students are concerned, I would call their attention to the following observations concerning Mr. Dickinson, as stated in a letter dated December 10, 1784, from Dr. Benjamin Rush to John Montgomery, both trustees of Dickinson College.

The letter was occasioned by Dickinson College's need for funds and Mr. Dickinson's obstructionist tactics. Dr. Rush's letter said that: "The Assembly passed a report to pay the interest on all kinds of certificates, but Mr. Dickinson has thrown in a remonstrance against it from council which we are afraid will prevent its passing into a law. . . . Thus has he attempted to cut off the last hopes and dependence of his College. . . . The professorship of divinity which Mr. Dickinson promised to endow must for a while fall to the ground. . . . Our poor friend Mr. Dickinson is alas! steady in nothing but in his instability. This is the only fixed trait in his character." The confidence of potential donors to Dickinson College had vanished in the bickering. Dickinson was moving closer to Friendly ideals. He would not again give directly to Dickinson College. His final large benefaction was in support of a Quaker School.

Mr. Chairman, I hope this answers your question to

your satisfaction.

Gen. WASHINGTON. I will be carefully monitoring your statements in this regard, Mr. Adams. As to Mr. Dickinson's testifying before this Commission, the matter will be held in abeyance. Mr. Madison, will you please continue.

Mr. THOMSON. (To the spectators.) From those who are not aware of Mr. Dickinson's background, he was born on his father's estate, "Crosiadore," near Trappe, Maryland, on November 8, 1732. He moved with his parents in 1740 to Dover, Delaware, where he studied under a private teacher and later he studied law in Philadelphia and at the Middle Temple in London. Admitted to the bar in 1757, he commenced practice in Philadelphia. He was a member of the Pennsylvania Assembly in 1762 and 1764, a delegate to the Colonial Congress in 1765, a member from Pennsylvania to the Continental Congress from 1774 to 1776 and from Delaware in 1776, 1777, 1779, and 1780. A brigadier general of the Pennsylvania Militia, Mr. Dickinson served as pesident of the state of Delaware in 1781; he returned to Philadelphia and served as president of Pennsylvania from 1782 to 1785, then returned to Delaware and was a delegate from that state to the Federal convention of 1787 which framed the Constitution; he was one of the signers of the Constitution.

Dr. FRANKLIN. If I may, Mr. Chairman, I, too, have had the experience of casting invectives at my fellow man. Glass, china, and reputation, I suppose, are easily crack'd, and never well mended. When Lord Howe, commander of the British fleet in America, tried to negotiate peace with the colonies after the Declaration of Independence, I wrote to him:

"It is impossible we should think of submission to a Government that has with the most wanton barbarity and cruelty burnt our defenseless towns in the midst of winter, excited the savages to massacre our farmers and our slaves to murder their masters, and is even now bringing foreign mercenaries to deluge our settlements with blood. These atrocious injuries have extinguished every remaining spark of affection for that parent country we once held so dear. Long did I endeavour with unfeigned and unwearied zeal to preserve from breaking that fine and noble china vase — the British Empire; for I knew that being once broken, the separate parts could not retain even their share of the strength or value that existed in the whole and that a perfect re-union of those parts could scarce even be hoped for."

By the way, John Adams and I were two of the three commissioners who met with Lord Howe on September 13, 1776. When his Lordship asked in what capacity he was to receive us, Mr. Adams replied "In any capacity your Lordship pleases except in that of British subjects." His Lordship said that nothing could mortify him more than to witness the fall of America and that he would weep for her as for a brother. "I hope," I said, "your Lordship will be saved that mortification. America is able to take care of herself."

As to Mr. Adams's impatience with and lack of tolerance of Mr. Dickinson, I am reminded of a parable I wrote some time ago. An old traveller, hungry and weary, applied to the patriarch Abraham for a night's lodging. In conversation, Abraham discovered that the stranger differed with him on religious points, and turned him out of doors. In the night, God appeared unto Abraham and said, "Where is the stranger?" Abraham answered, "I found that he did not worship the true God, and so I turned him out of doors." The Almighty thus rebuked the patriarch: "Have I borne with him threescore and ten years, and couldst thou not bear with him one night?"

Gen. WASHINGTON. Thank you Dr. Franklin, but we must attend to the subject at hand. Mr. Madison?

Mr. MADISON. The report of the Annapolis Convention was laid before Congress on September 20, 1786, and was referred to a committee on October 11. On February 21, 1787, Congress debated the recommendation of the Annapolis Convention and on the same day adopted a resolution calling for a Constitutional Convention. The committee after considerable difficulty and discussion had agreed, by a majority of only one, on a report that coincided with the Annapolis report suggesting amendments to the Articles. The prevailing objections to a convention were: (1) that it tended to weaken the federal authority by lending its sanction to an extraconstitutional mode of proceeding, and (2) that the interposition of Congress would be considered an ambitious wish to get additional power into its hands.

The reserve of many of the members made it difficult to decide their real wishes and expectations. All agreed and owned that the federal government in its existing shape was inefficient and could not last long. The members from the Southern and Middle states seemed generally anxious for some republican organization of the system which would preserve the Union and give due energy to its government. Mr. William Bingham alone avowed his wishes that the Confederacy might be divided into several distinct confederacies, its great extent and various interests being incompatible with a single government. The Eastern members were suspected by some of leaning towards some anti-republican establishment, or of being less desirous or hopeful of preserving the unity of the empire. For the first time the idea of separate confederacies had gotten into the newspapers. Whatever the views of leading men in the Eastern states may have been, it seemed that the great body of the people were equally indisposed either to dissolve or divide the Confederacy or to submit to any anti-republican innovations.

Mr. JEFFERSON. Mr. Madison, what type of matter was being published in the newspapers?

Mr. ADAMS. I can answer that. For example, this item appeared in the *Boston Independent Gazette* on February 15, 1787:

"How long, asks a correspondent, are we to continue in our present inglorious acquiescence in the shameful resistance that some of the states persist in against federal and national measures? How long is Massachusetts to suffer the paltry politics, weak jealousy, or local interests of New York and Pennsylvania, to distract our own government, and keep up holden to those wretched measures which have so long made America the pity or contempt of Europe? How long are we to distress our own numerous citizens with the weight of continental taxes and support our delegation in an assembly which has no powers to maintain the reputation or advance the real interest of our commonwealth? . . . It is therefore now time to form a new and stronger union. The five states of New England, closely confederated, can have nothing to fear. Let then our General Assembly immediately recall their being a useless and expensive establishment. Send proposals for instituting a new congress, as the representative of the nation of New England, and leave the rest of the continent to pursue their own imbecile and disjointed plans, until they have experimentally learned the folly, danger and disgrace of them, and acquired magnanimity and wisdom sufficient to join a confederation that may rescue them from destruction."

How many times had this nation been on the verge of separation? I like a statement Franklin Delano Roosevelt once made: "The men who wrote the Constitution were the men who fought the revolution . . . when these men planned a new government, they drew the kind of agreement men make when they really want to work together under it for a very long time. For the youngest of nations they drew what is today the oldest written instrument under which men have continuously lived as a nation."

Mr. MADISON. Following the debates in Congress on the call for a Constitutional Convention on February 21, 1787, it was "Resolved that in the opinion of Congress it is expedient that on the second Monday in May next a convention of delegates who shall have been appointed by the several states be held at Philadelphia for the sole and express purpose of revising the Articles of Confederation and reporting to Congress and the several legislatures such alterations and provisions therein as shall when agreed to in Congress and confirmed by the states render the federal constitution adequate to the exigencies of government and the preservation of the Union."

The second Monday in May was May 14, 1787.

Mr. THOMSON. This resolution I sent to the states the same day it was adopted.

Gen. WASHINGTON. Thank you Mr. Madison and Mr. Thomson. The hour is late. This session is adjourned until tomorrow, Friday, June 19, 1987 at 10 o'clock a.m.

FRIDAY, JUNE 19, 1987

COMMISSION DISCUSSES PREFERENCES ON GOVERNMENT STRUCTURE

The Committee met pursuant to notice, at 10 a.m. in the Assembly Room of Independence Hall, Gen. George Washington presiding.

Present: Mr. John Adams, Dr. Benjamin Franklin, Mr. Thomas Jefferson, Mr. James Madison and Gen. George Washington.

Mr. THOMSON (To the spectators) "George Washington Slept Here" is an aphorism having its origin perhaps in the diaries Washington kept of where he slept on his various treks or in the commercial claims of east coast, old house proprietors. "A concise Act. of my journey to Philadelphia," Washington wrote as he prepared to leave Mount Vernon to attend the Federal Convention of 1787.

On Thursday, May 3, 1787, he rode to his various plantations — Ferry, French's, Dogue Run, and Muddy Hole Plantation — with his nephew, George Augustine Washington, to explain to him the nature and the order of the business at each as he wanted it carried on during his absence at the Convention in Philadelphia.

On Wednesday, May 9, Washington left Mt. Vernon, crossed the Potomac a little after sunrise, and pursuing the route by the way of Baltimore, dined at Mr. Richard Henderson's in Bladensburg and lodged at Maj. Thomas Snowden's at Elk Ridge Landing, "where, feeling very severely a violent headache and sick stomach," he "went to bed early."

On Thursday, May 10, 1787, he was recovered enough to set off and at one o'clock he arrived at Baltimore. He "dined at the Fountain, and supped and lodged at Doctor James McHenry's." Dr. McHenry served as a surgeon in the Continental Army and later as a secretary to General Washington. He represented the state of Delaware at the Federal Convention in 1787 and was Secretary of War from 1796 to 1800. Fort McHenry, that bastion of American military success against the British in the War of 1812 that inspired Francis Scott Key to compose our national anthem, bears his name.

On Friday, May 11, Washington "set out before breakfast, rode twelve miles to Skerrett's Tavern for it; baited there, and proceeded without halting, weather threatening to the Ferry at Havre de gras," on the Susquehanna River "where he dined but could not cross, the wind being turbulent and squally." He lodged there.

On Saturday, May 12, with difficulty, because of the wind, he crossed the Susquehanna. He "breakfasted at the Ferry House on the East Side, dined at the Head of Elk, Hollingsworth's Tavern, and lodged in Wilmington at Patrick O'Flins, at the 'Sign of the Ship.'" At the Head of Elk he was overtaken by Mr. Francis Corbin, a member of the Virginia Assembly, who took a seat in his carriage to Wilmington.
and dined in Chester, Pennsylvania, at Mrs. Withy's, where he was met by Thomas Mifflin, then Speaker of the Pennsylvania Assembly; generals Henry Knox and James Mitchell Varnum; colonels David Humphreys and Francis Mentges, and Major William Jackson and Francis Nicholas, with whom, after dinner, he proceeded to Philadelphia. At Gray's Ferry, outside Philadelphia, the city light horse, commanded by Col. Samuel Miles, met him, and, while the artillery officers stood arranged and saluted him as he passed, escorted him to the entrance of the city. He alighted through a crowd at Mrs. Mary House's, whose boarding house was at Fifth and Market streets; but being "warmly and kindly pressed by Mr. and Mrs. Robert Morris to lodge with them" he did so.

And so it came to pass that "George Washington Slept

Here" and there.

Washington then recorded that he "Waited on the President, Doctor Franklin, as soon as I got to Town." Franklin, also a delegate to the Convention, was concerned about his gout. "My malady does not grow perceptibly worse and I hope it may continue tolerable to my life's end, which cannot be far distant, being in my 82nd year." Washington thought his "rheumatic complaint" had "very much abated."

There were many establishments of "good repute" where a delegate could stay during the Convention. There was the Indian Queen Tavern run by Mrs. Sidney Paul, which was situated at the east side of Fourth Street, between Market and Chestnut. There was the City Tavern, under the management of Edward Moyston; the Indian King, below Third Street; the George, run by Michael Dennison, at the southwest corner of Second and Arch Street; the Black Horse, run by Isaac Connelly, at Market Street between Fourth and Fifth; Cross Keys, run by Israel Israel, at the northeast corner of Third and Chestnut streets; and the Conestoga Wagon, run by Samuel Nicholas, at Market Street between Fourth and Fifth. George Mason wrote his son, "We found travelling very expensive — from eight to nine dollars per day. In this city the living is cheap. We are at the old Indian Queen in Fourth Street, where we are very accommodated, have a good room to ourselves, and are charged only twenty-five Pennsylvania currency per day, including our servants and horses. . ."

On Monday, May 14, at the State-House in the City of Philadelphia, deputies appointed by the various states began to appear — but, a majority of the states not being represented, the members present adjourned.

That night, George Washington "dined in a family way at the Robert Morris's and drank tea." By Wednesday there was still no quorum. He "dined at the President, Dr. Franklin's, and drank tea, and then spent the evening at Mr. John Penn's." By Thursday, the 17th, there was still no quorum and he "dined at Mr. Samuel Powell's and drank tea there."

On Friday, the representation from New York appeared, but still no quorum. Washington "dined at the Club at Gray's Ferry, over the Schuylkill, and drank tea at Mr. Morris's; after which accompanied Mrs. Morris and some other ladies to hear a Mrs. O'Connell read at a charity affair; the lady being reduced in circumstances had had recourse to this expedient to obtain a little money. Her performance was tolerable at the College Hall."

On Friday, May 25, another Delegate, coming in from New Jersey, gave it a representation and increased the number to seven, which, forming a quorum of the thirteen, the members present resolved to organize the body.

It is of interest to note that delegates from the state of Rhode Island never appeared. But George Washington did receive a letter from certain citizens of Rhode Island — merchants and tradesmen — dated May 11, 1787, which I thought of interest: "The Honorable the Chairman of the General Convention, Philadelphia.

"Since, the Legislature of this State have finally declined sending Delegates to meet you in Convention . . . the merchants, tradesmen, and others of this place, deeply affected with the evils of the present unhappy times, have thought proper to communicate in writing their approbation of your meeting, and their regret that it will fall short of a complete representation of the Federal Union. . .

The majority of the administration is composed of a licentious number of men, destitute of education, and many of them void of principle. From anarchy and confusion they derive their temporary consequence; and this they endeavour to prolong by debauching the minds of the common people, whose attention is wholly directed to the abolition of debts, public and private. With these are associated the disaffected of every description, particularly those who were unfriendly during the war. Their paper money system, founded in oppression and fraud, they are determined to support at every hazard; and rather than relinquish their favorite pursuit, they trample upon the most sacred obligations. As a proof of this they refused to comply with a requisition of Congress for repealing all laws repugnant to the treaty of peace with Great Britain and urged as their principal reason that it would be calling in question the propriety of their former measures."

So we lost Rhode Island for the duration — with appropriate explanation.

By a unanimous vote George Washington was called up to the Chair as president of the body. Major William Jackson was appointed secretary. Major Jackson had previously been assistant secretary of war under the Continental Congress. And, of course, the Major is serving as assistant secretary to our present Commission. Major Jackson prepared the Journal, which was the official record of the Convention of 1787. As we have pointed out, other members kept some records, but the most important and accurate were those kept by Mr. Madison. Mr. Madison is now describing his method. Let's listen.

Mr. MADISON. . . . In pursuance of the task I had assumed, I chose a seat in front of the presiding member, with the other members on my right and left hands. In this favorable position for hearing all that passed, I noted, in terms legible and in abbreviations and marks intelligible to myself, what was read from the Chair or spoken by the members; and losing not a moment unnecessarily between the adjournment and reassembling of the Convention, I was enabled to write out my daily notes during the session, or within a few finish-days after its close.

In the labor and correctness of this I was not a little aided by practice and by a familiarity with the style and the train of observation and reasoning which characterized the principal speakers. It happened, also, that I was not absent a single day, nor more than a casual fraction of an hour in any day, so that I could not have lost a single speech, unless a very short one.

It may be proper to remark, that, with a very few exceptions, the speeches were neither furnished, nor revised, nor sanctioned, by the speakers, but written out from my notes, aided by the freshness of my recollections. A further remark may be proper, that views of the subject might occasionally be presented, in the speeches and proceedings, with a latent reference to a compromise on some middle ground, by mutual concessions.

The speeches of Doctor Franklin, excepting a few brief ones, were copied from the written ones read to the Convention by his colleague, Mr. Wilson, it being inconvenient to the Doctor to remain long on his feet. I was not unaware of the value of my notes to the fund of materials for the history of a Constitution on which would be staked the happiness of a people great even in its infancy, and possibly the cause of liberty throughout the world.

Of the ability and intelligence of those who composed the Convention, the debates and proceedings may be a test as to the character of the work which was the offspring of their deliberations, that had to be tested by experience.

But whatever may be the judgment pronounced on the competency of the architects of the Constitution, or whatever may be the destiny of the edifice prepared by them, I feel it a duty to express my profound and solemn conviction, derived from my intimate opportunity of observing and appreciating the views of the Convention, collectively and individually, that there never was an assembly of men charged with a great and arduous trust who were more pure in their motives or more exclusively or anxiously devoted to the object committed to them than were the members of the Federal Convention in 1787; to the object of devising and proposing a constitutional system which should best supply the defects of that which it was to replace and best secure the permanent liberty and happiness of their country.

Gen. WASHINGTON. Thank you, Mr. Madison.

Mr. ADAMS. As we have already indicated at these sessions, neither Mr. Jefferson nor I knew of the existence of Mr. Madison's notes until about 1815. In fact, I understand the notes were not published until 1840. Mr. Jefferson had written to me from Monticello on August 10, 1815 saying: "Do you know that there exists in manuscript the ablest work of this kind ever yet executed, of the debates of the constitutional convention of Philadelphia in 1787? The whole of everything said and done there was taken down by Mr. Madison with a labor and exactness beyond comprehension."

Therefore, no member of this Commission, excepting Mr. Madison, had read the notes until this year — 1987. I also want to remind the Commission that both Mr. Jefferson and I were in foreign countries during the entire Federal Convention of 1787 — Mr. Jefferson in France, and I in Britain.

Gen. WASHINGTON. There are only two rules of procedure of the Federal Convention that I want to mention. First, nothing spoken in the House was permitted to be printed, or otherwise published, or communicated without leave — thus, the injunction of a rule of secrecy was imposed upon the members. Second was a rule which has been quoted at a previous session of this Commission, but which I consider sufficiently important to repeat: "a motion to reconsider a matter, which had been determined by a majority, may be made, with leave unanimously given, on the same day in which the vote was passed, but otherwise, not without one day's previous notice; in which last case, if the House agree to the reconsideration, some future day shall be assigned for that purpose." This rule meant that no vote was to be taken as final and that any question could be reopened for further debates and votes at any time. Thus it generated endless repetition of arguments, but more importantly, the rule made it possible for men to change their minds and to compromise issues in the course of the debates.

I wish to advise the Commission that I have invited all delegates to the Federal Convention of 1787 to attend these sessions as spectators, and if necessary, as participants. On the same basis I have invited all past presidents of the United States to so attend.

Mr. THOMSON. (Aside to the Spectators) Dr. Franklin appeared at the Convention on Monday, May 28; stormy weather had kept him away until this day. The Doctor suffered greatly from gout and stone; he came to the State House in a sedan chair which he had brought from Paris, as the only mode of transportation that did not jostle him painfully. The Doctor's chair was the first such vehicle in Philadelphia and one of the city's sights. There were glass windows on both sides. The poles, ten or twelve feet long, were pliant, allowing the chair to give a little with the bearer's footsteps — vibrate gently, a contemporary said. Four husky prisoners from the Walnut Street jail bore the cheerful cargo, measuring their pace as smoothly as they could. Up five steps to the State House went the little procession and into the east room, where the bearers sat down their burden beside the bar. The Doctor was helped out and made his way through the gate to his nearby armchair at the Pennsylvania delegates' table. The prisoners, having placed the sedan close by the west wall, took their leave until the afternoon.

Dr. FRANKLIN. If I alone had been responsible for writing the Constitution, the federal form of government might have been vastly different. But I was not alone. The players of the game were so many, their ideas so different, their prejudices so strong and so various, that not a move could be made that was not contested. The numerous objections confounded the understanding; the wisest had to agree to some unreasonable things, that reasonable ones of more consequence may be obtained.

Thus, chance has its share in many of the determinations, so that the play was more like . . . with a box of dice.

I want to state my position here, and I hope others will follow, so that we can narrow the areas of discussion and analysis to a manageable group of ideas. I was, and am, of the opinion that the two Chambers in the Constitution were not necessary, and I disliked some other articles that are in it, and wished for some that are not in it.

I was also of the opinion that the president of the United States should have a constitutional council — a Council of State — instead of the willy-nilly cabinet system which has prevailed since General Washington's administration. I do not mean to imply that the cabinet is an unconstitutional council; it is simply a council not provided for in the Constitution. In fact, for reasons I will give later, it is a misplaced council, since there was a constitutional council established by law, but nobody knows or recognizes its existence.

Mr. JEFFERSON. As Dr. Franklin has stated his position, so will I do the same. In my case also, I have given my thoughts in a previous session, and therefore I will be brief in my recapitulation. I thought that the Constitution should have divided the powers of government into two distinct departments, the leading characters of which were domestic and foreign. I also thought the Constitution should have designated a distinct set of functions for each. My thoughts on the Constitution have not emerged in practice. We have contaminated the Constitution to such an extent that it has lost its original flavor.

I am for a domestic affairs department that places great emphasis on cooperation with the states; and I am for a foreign affairs department which is reduced to foreign concerns only. This process perhaps presumes the creation of two vice-presidents — working vice-presidents — one for domestic affairs and one for foreign affairs. I believe this would go far toward eliminating or at least assuaging the plight of our presidents as depicted by their own statements in our sessions. I am for a government vigorously frugal and simple, applying all the possible savings of the public revenue to the discharge of the national debt and not for a multiplication of officers and salaries merely to make partisans and for increasing, by every device, the public debt, on the principle of its being a public blessing.

Gen. WASHINGTON. Mr. Madison, would you care to state your position at this time?

Mr. MADISON. While I was involved in the debates respecting most provisions of the Constitution, I intend to restrict my opinion to one provision. I am of the opinion that the term for members of the House of Representatives be extended from two to three years, and I will consider recommending that one third of the House be elected annually.

Mr. JEFFERSON. Did you actually vote for a three-year term at the Federal Convention?

Mr. MADISON. I not only voted in favor of the proposal, I seconded the motion.

Mr. ADAMS. Do you recall the vote?

Mr. MADISON. I refer that question to Major Jackson.

Major JACKSON. The vote was in the affirmative:

seven states, aye; four states, no.

Mr. ADAMS. What transpired to change the term from three to two years?

Gen. WASHINGTON. Mr. Adams, we are at the point of stating opinions and not at the point of examining detail. I would therefore ask you to defer this line of questioning until the appropriate time. Do you have anything further to state, Mr. Madison?

Mr. MADISON. No, Mr. Chairman.

Gen. WASHINGTON. Mr. Adams, we are now ready for your opinion.

Mr. ADAMS. In the year 1774, a certain British officer, then at Boston, was often heard to say, "I wish I were Parliament. I would not send a ship or troop to this country; but would forthwith pass a statute, declaring every town in North America a free, sovereign, and independent commonwealth. This is what they all desire, and I would indulge them. I should soon have the pleasure to see them all at war with one another, from one end of the continent to the other." When I was vice-president of the United States, in 1790, I said in a similar vein, "Our new Government is a new attempt. . . . It cannot be expected to be very stable or very firm. It will prevent us, for a time, from drawing our swords upon each other.

"The difficulty of bringing millions to agree in any measure, to act by any rule, can never be conceived by him who has not tried it. It is incredible how small the number in any nation who comprehend any system of Constitution or Administration; and those few it is wholly impossible to unite."

Richard Henry Lee once was polite enough to ask me for a model of government I thought appropriate. It was in November 1775, twelve years before the Federal Convention. I told him then that if such a trifle would be of any service to him or any gratification of curiosity, he would have it, and here you have it, as I gave it to him:

"Dear Sir. The course of events naturally turns the thoughts of Gentlemen to the subjects of Legislation and jurisprudence, and it is a curious problem what form of Government is most readily and easily adopted by a Colony upon a sudden emergency. Nature and experience have already pointed out the solution of this problem, in the choice of Conventions and Committees of Safety. Nothing is wanting in addition to these to make a complete Government but the appointment of Magistrates for the due Administration of Justice.

"Taking nature and experience for my guide I have made the following sketch, which may be varied in any one particular an infinite number of ways so as to accommodate it to the different genius, temper, principles, and even prejudices of different people.

"A Legislative, an Executive and a Judicial Power, comprehend the whole of what is meant and understood by Government. It is by balancing each one of these powers against the other two that the effort in human nature towards tyranny can alone be checked and restrained and any degree of freedom preserved in the Constitution.

"Let the House choose by ballot twelve, sixteen, twenty-four or twenty-eight persons, either Members of the House or from the people at large as the elections please for a Council.

"Let the House and Council by joint ballot choose a governor, annually, triennially or septennially as you will.

"Let the Governor, Council and House be each a distinct and independent Branch of the Legislature and have a negative on all laws.

"Let the Lieutenant Governor, Secretary, Treasurer, Commissary, Attorney General and Solicitor General be chosen annually by joint ballot of both Houses.

"Let the Governor with Seven Councillors be a quorum.

"Let all officers and magistrates, civil and military, be nominated and appointed by the governor, by and with the advice and consent of his council.

"Let no officer be appointed but at a General Council and let notice be given to all the Councillors, seven days at least before a General Council.

"Let the Judges, at least of the Supreme Court, be incapacitated by law from holding any share of the Legislative or Executive Power, let their commissions be during good behaviour and their salaries ascertained and established by law.

"Let the Governor have the Command of the army, the militia, forts, etc.

"Let the Colony have a seal and affix it to all Commissions.

"In this way a single month is sufficient without the least convulsion or even animosity to accomplish a total revolution in the Government of a Colony.

"If it is thought more beneficial, a law may be made by this new Legislature leaving to the people at large the privilege of choosing their Governor and Councillors annually, as soon as affairs get into a more quiet course.

"In adopting a plan, in some respects similar to this, human nature would appear in its proper glory asserting its own moral dignity, pulling down tyrannies at a single exertion, and erecting such new fabrics as it thinks best calculated to promote its happiness.

"As you were the last evening polite enough to ask me for this model, if such a trifle will be of any service to you or any gratification of curiosity, here you have it, from, sir your friend and humble servant. John Adams."

Yes, I said all that twelve years in advance of the Federal Convention which drafted the Constitution.

Mr. THOMSON. (Aside to spectators) John Adams in person is rather short and thick; his manner somewhat cold and reserved, as the citizens of Massachusetts, his native state, are said generally to be. His presence caused a general feeling of respect, but the modesty of his demeanor and the tolerance of his opinions placed all in convenient restraint. He was generally dressed in a light or drab-colored coat and had the appearance of an English country gentleman who had seen much of public life.

When he became president he appeared before both Houses of Congress wearing a sword. He would receive gifts of cigars and graciously write each donor thanking him for the "good segars."

Mr. ADAMS. (Continuing) To my mind, the most important resolution ever taken in America was passed by Congress on May 15, 1776. It read: "Resolved, that it be recommended to the respective assemblies and Conventions of the United Colonies, where no Government sufficient to the exigencies of their affairs has been hitherto established, to adopt such government as shall in the opinion of the Representatives of the people best conduce to the happiness and safety of their Constituents in particular, and America in general."

The states went on to draft their own Constitutions. Mr. Thomson kindly collected copies for me.

On the basis of this collection and my study of the structure of foreign governments, I wrote a three-volume book entitled *A Defence of the Constitutions of the Government of the United States of America*. A portion of my writings were available before the Federal Convention. While I want to reserve for later review the material I then wrote, a few paragraphs are appropriate now:

"If there is one certain truth to be collected from the history of all ages, it is this: That the people's rights and liberties and the democratical mixture in a constitution can never be preserved without a strong executive, or, in other words, without separating the executive power from the legislative. If the executive power, or any considerable part of it, is left in the hands either of an aristocratical or a democratical assembly, it will corrupt the legislature as necessarily as rust corrupts iron, or as arsenic poisons the human body; and when the legislature is corrupted the people are undone.

"Among every people, and in every species of republics, we have constantly found a first magistrate, a head, a chief, under various denominations indeed, and with different degrees of authority, with the title of stadtholder, burgomaster, avoyer, doge, confalloniero, president, syndick, mayor, alcalde, capitaneo, governor, or king. In every nation, we have met with a distinguished officer. If there is no example in any free government, any more than those which are not free, of a society without a principal personage, we may fairly conclude that the body politic cannot subsist without one any more than the animal body without a head. . . .

"Let us compare every constitution we have seen, with those of the United States of America, and we shall have no reason to blush for our country; on the contrary, we shall feel the strongest motives to fall upon our knees, in gratitude to heaven, for having been graciously pleased to give us birth and education in that country and for having destined us to live under her laws! We shall have reason to exult, if we make our comparison with England and the English constitution. Our people are undoubtedly soveriegn. All the landed and other property is in the hands of the citizens. Their senators and governors are annually chosen. There are no hereditary titles, honours, offices, or distinctions. The legislative, executive, and judicial power are carefully separated from each other. The powers of the one, the few, and the many are nicely balanced in their legislatures. Trials by jury are perservered in all their glory . . . The habeas corpus is in full force. The press is the most free in the world — and where all these circumstances take place, it is unnecessary to add that the laws alone can govern."

Well, I went on to become vice-president of the United States under President Washington. In the light of this experience it is my opinion that the position of vice-president, as presently constituted in the Constitution, be eliminated. If this is accomplished it may be necessary to reassess and revise other facets of the Constitution as well.

Gen. WASHINGTON. We will take a ten-minute recess.

A SPECTATOR. (To Mr. Jacques Dupois, a Frenchman who travelled the American Continent in 1777) Sir, in your travels through America two hundred years ago, what did you think of the American woman?

Mr. DUPOIS. You will find the good and the bad everywhere. There were in Philadelphia girls just as chaste and others just as wanton as those you would find in Paris, London, or any other large city. . . . One may say, without deviating from at least three quarters of the truth, that Anglo-American women were all pretty, either in the general impression they gave or in the delicacy of their features. They were extremely graceful, had very fair complexions, blue eyes, well modeled arms, and good figures. Their youthful freshness, which they do not lose for many years, they owed to their way of dressing. Usually they were shy when you met them in their homes, or they felt self-conscious without their hats, which kept them from being stared at — and also practically kept them from seeing anything themselves. Those hats came in an infinite variety of shapes and, were I an artist, I could give you descriptions of at least twenty or thirty different styles. What a treat that would have been for our French coquette and what an advantage for our modistes!

All the women, young and old, wore gowns which hung to the ground without trailing and were just short enough not to touch, so that they did need not have to be picked up in crossing a street, except barely enough to reveal the shoe and no more. On the front of the dress an apron of muslin was worn, so like those of our French chambermaids one would take all the Anglo American women for servants out on errands or as hairdressers on their way to a customer. They wore mantels as in France and all the riches and adornments which French women put around their necks.

If the dress of Anglo American Women suffered on weekdays — by comparison, nothing was more elegant, more splendid or more beautiful than their Sunday gowns. You would not recognize them though they were dressed in the same style as during the week. Hair, ribbons, hats, aprons, everything was so carefully chosen and looked so neat that a French woman decked out in all her finest silks and pompons could not compare with an Anglo American in her ordinary Sunday dress. And for what and for whom was the show of finery? She put it on to leave her house, go straight to church, come home, go back to church, return home again, and then finished the day in the deadly boredom of an evening spent all alone in pious meditation.

Girls were brought up carefully, though this varied with the wealth of their parents. Most of them went to schools where they were taught all that was proper to learn: studies, writing, keeping accounts, geography, grammer, religion, and history.

They also had, as in France, teachers to instruct them in dancing, singing, and music. Generally speaking, there was little difference between the education of a rich heiress and that of the daughter of a simple citizen. They all stayed at home a great deal, never went out alone, and were raised to be diligent, patient, and modest. One can well believe that they adopted themselves to marriage as easily as French girls and that they made their husbands just as happy.

ANN LANDERS (Approaches General Washington.) General, I'm so pleased to meet you at last! My name is Ann Landers.

Gen. WASHINGTON. Yes. You are a journalist, I believe?

ANN LANDERS: You could say that. I've always admired your reputation for honesty, respectability, and good sense. I wonder, would you tell me — for my readers, of course — what advice you would give to a woman getting married?

Gen. WASHINGTON. I never did, nor do I believe I shall, give advice to a woman who is setting out on a matrimonial voyage; first because I never could advise one to marry without her own consent; and, secondly, because I know it is to no purpose to advise her to refrain, when she has obtained it. A woman very rarely asks an opinion or requires advice on such an occasion, till her resolution is formed; and then it is with the hope and expectation of obtaining a sanction . . . that she applies.

ANN LANDERS. Would you advise a woman *not* to get married?

Gen. WASHINGTON. It has never been a maxim with me through life, neither to promote nor to prevent a matrimonial connection, unless there should be something indispensably requiring interference in the latter. I have always considered marriage as the most interesting event of one's life, the foundation of happiness or misery.

ANN LANDERS. Can I print that?

Gen. WASHINGTON. As you wish. If you will pardon me, I see that the Commission is reassembling.

ANN LANDERS. Of course.

Gen. WASHINGTON. This session will resume. In retrospect of this session:

Dr. Franklin has retained his long-standing concept of a unicameral legislature and a constitutional council to the president.

Mr. Jefferson originally conceived and remains convinced that there should be two major departments in government; one for domestic affairs and the other for foreign affairs. In the domestic affairs department he would place emphasis on cooperation with the states; the foreign affairs department he would reduce to foreign concerns only.

Mr. Madison was for extending the term of House of Representative members from two to three years — he had voted for a three-year term at the Federal Convention — and he would possibly have a one-third rotation annually in the House, meaning annual elections.

Mr. Adams, as the first vice-president of the United States, was desirous of eliminating the post.

Gentlemen, beginning with the next session we will discuss and assess the concepts of the members of this Commission as stated at today's session.

It is my intention to set the order of discussion, since each member appears to have a vested interest in his own topic. It would be to our best interest to take the simple one . . .

Dr. FRANKLIN. Eh? Did you say "simpleton"?

Gen. WASHINGTON. No, Doctor, I said "simple one."

Dr. FRANKLIN. Oh, thank you.

Gen. WASHINGTON. I said it would be to our interest to take the simple one first, and by making this decision I have no intention of casting any aspersions upon the originator of the thought. The simplest one for us to handle first would be the subject proposed by Mr. Adams — namely, the elimination of the office of vice-president of the United States.

In order to allow sufficient time for preparation we

will adjourn until Monday, June 29 at 10 a.m. But, before we do so, I want to mention one thing. It might seem peculiar to anyone among the spectators — our audience — that not one of the members of this Commission made a recommendation today directly affecting the presidency of the United States. I am advised by the other members of the Commission that a recommendation directly affecting the presidency is under consideration and will be presented for discussion at an appropriate time.

Gentlemen, this session is adjourned.

MONDAY, JUNE 29, 1987

THE "UNNECESSARY" VICE PRESIDENT

The Committee met pursuant to notice, at 10 a.m. in the Assembly Room of Independence Hall, Gen. George Washington presiding.

  Present: Mr. John Adams, Dr. Benjamin Franklin, Mr. Thomas Jefferson, Mr. James Madison and Gen. George Washington.

  Gen. WASHINGTON. The number of words in the Constitution we sent to the states for ratification in 1787 was 4,528. The number of words added during my administration as president of the United States was 499. And America since my time has added to and subtracted from the total. Eleven amendments to the Constitution were made during my presidential term. Only fifteen amendments have been made since. Now, from colonial times, in colloquial terms, the old gang is back again, so to say: the founding fathers, to make amends, perhaps, and to make amendments for their amends.

  We begin this session with Mr. John Adams's suggestion that we consider, discuss, and assess the desirability of preparing an amendment eliminating the office of vice-president.

  Major Jackson, I call upon you to summarize key provisions of the Constitution applying to the office of the vice-president.

  Major JACKSON. I welcome the opportunity, sir.

  The vice-president is chosen, along with the president, for a term of four years.

The vice-president is president of the Senate.

He has no vote unless the Senate is equally divided.

The Senate chooses a president pro tempore in the absence of the vice-president.

In case of the removal of the president from office or his death or resignation, the vice-president becomes president.

Whenever there is a vacancy in the office of the vice-president, the president nominates a vice-president who takes office upon confirmation by a majority vote of both Houses of Congress.

Whenever the president transmits to the president pro tempore of the Senate and the Speaker of the House of Representatives his written declaration that he is unable to discharge the powers and duties of his office, and until he transmits to them a written declaration to the contrary, such powers and duties are to be discharged by the vice-president as acting president.

Dr. FRANKLIN. Pardon me, but isn't Mr. Ronald Reagan an acting president?

Gen. WASHINGTON. Dr. Franklin, the president was formerly an actor, not an acting president.

First SPECTATOR. (To Second SPECTATOR) What is the difference between an actor and a president?

Second SPECTATOR. (To First SPECTATOR) One stands before a camera and says things he does not mean, and the other makes movies.

Major JACKSON. I have not presented the mode of election of the vice-president, which is the same as that of the president. If there is further detail needed, I shall be pleased to furnish it.

Mr. MADISON. Does anyone on this Commission believe it necessary to summarize or restate provisions of the Constitution either for our purposes or for the record? Can we not presume that we and any reader of our records knows the provisions of the Constitution?

Mr. ADAMS. I do not think this Commission should presume anything of the like. We can look back just a few years to the time when President Ronald Reagan was shot in

Washington, D.C.; vice-president George Bush was out of town and Secretary of State Alexander Haig announced on television, from Washington, something like "I am now in charge," a statement contrary to the order of succession under the Constitution. We can and should presume nothing.

Gen. WASHINGTON. Mr. Adams will initiate the questions on this matter of the vice-presidency.

Mr. ADAMS. Mr. Madison, since your notes on the debates are somewhat more detailed than Mr. Jackson's, I will direct this question to you: When was the subject of a vice-president first introduced at the Convention?

Mr. MADISON. On Monday, June 18, 1787, Mr. Alexander Hamilton read a sketch of his ideas which included the following:

"On the death, resignation or removal of the Governor"—he used the title governor instead of president, since titles had not yet been determined—"his authorities to be exercised by the President of the Senate till a successor be appointed."

Mr. WILLIAM PIERCE. (Aside to spectators.) I clearly remember Hamilton's reading of those ideas. You see, I was a delegate from Georgia to the Federal Convention of 1787. Allow me to introduce myself. My name is William Pierce. Perhaps you know of me?

SPECTATOR. Uh, I'm afraid I . . .

Mr. PIERCE. No matter. My name does not carry such fame as those of this Commission, but I, too, was one of that august assemblage of Founders. Let me tell you a little about myself. I am conscious of having discharged my duty as a soldier through the course of the revolution with honor and propriety; and my services in Congress and the Convention were bestowed with the best intention towards the interest of Georgia and towards the general welfare of the Confederacy. I possessed ambition, and it was that, and the flattering opinion which some of my friends had of me, that gave me a seat in the wisest Council in the world and furnished me with an opportunity of giving short sketches of the characters who composed it. Would you find them of interest?

SPECTATOR. Of course. Please tell us.

Mr. PIERCE. Gladly. Colonel Alexander Hamilton, for example, was deservedly celebrated for his talents. He was a practitioner of the law and reputed to be a finished scholar. To a clear and strong judgment he united the ornaments of fancy. He was able, convincing, and engaging in his eloquence. Yet there was something too feeble in his voice to be equal to the strains of oratory. It is my opinion that he was rather a convincing speaker than a blazing orator. Colonel Hamilton required time to think. He enquired into every past of his subject with the searchings of philosophy, and when he came forward he came highly charged with interesting matter. There was no skimming over the surface of a subject with him; he sank to the bottom to see what foundation it rested on. His language was not always equal, sometimes didactic like Bolingbroke's, at other times light and tripping like Stern's. His eloquence was not so delusive as to trifle with the senses, but he rambled just enough to strike and keep up the attention. He was about thirty-three years old then, of small stature, and lean. His manners were tinctured with stiffness and sometimes with a degree of vanity that was highly disagreeable.

Mr. ADAMS. . . . but, the term "vice-president" was not used in Mr. Hamilton's sketch. When was the term first introduced?

Mr. MADISON. In my notes the title first appears on Tuesday, September 4, 1787. A Committee of Eleven had been appointed on August 31 to consider such parts of the Constitution as had been postponed and such parts of reports as had not been acted on by the Convention.

On September 4, the Committee of Eleven reported among other items that in their opinion the following addition and alteration be made to a section applying to the president: that the president "shall hold office during the term of four years, and together with the Vice-President, chosen for the same term, be elected in the following manner. . . ."

The Committee of Eleven also recommended that "The Vice-President shall be ex officio President of the Senate, except when they sit to try the impeachment of the President, in which case the Chief Justice shall preside, and excepting also when he shall exercise the powers and duties of President, in which case and in case of his absence, the Senate shall choose a President pro tempore. The Vice-President when acting as President of the Senate shall not have a vote unless the House be equally divided.''

Mr. ADAMS. Major Jackson, does this correspond with your Journal?

Major JACKSON. It does, sir.

Mr. ADAMS. And what was the vote, Major?

Major JACKSON. There was no vote. It was moved and seconded to postpone consideration of this clause.

Mr. ADAMS. Why?

Mr. MADISON. In order to decide first on the mode of electing the President. I do want to call your attention to the fact, Mr. Adams, that while the term "vice-president" was not introduced on the floor of the Convention until September 4, the person to succeed to the office of the president on the death, resignation, or removal of the president was first mentioned on the floor . . .

Mr. ADAMS. Mr. Madison, is it not true that the order of succession to the presidency could have been established without creating the office of a vice-president?

Mr. MADISON. It is.

Mr. ADAMS. The point is that the first mention on the floor of a person to be elected along with the president— namely, a vice-president — was not until September 4, 1787. The Convention first met on May 14, 1787—without a quorum, I acknowledge. In a total of eighty-eight sessions of the Convention, the office of a vice-president was first mentioned on the floor on the seventy-eighth day! That was thirteen days before the Convention adjourned permanently, and only ten sessions were held in that thirteen-day period.

Major Jackson, who were the members of that Committee of Eleven, which established the office of the vice-president?

Major JACKSON. The Committee of Eleven consisted

of a member from each state and included

    Mr. Nicholas Gilman of New Hampshire
    Mr. Rufus King of Massachusetts
    Mr. Roger Sherman of Connecticut
    Mr. David B. Brearley of New Jersey
    Gouverneur Morris of Pennsylvania
    Mr. Daniel Carroll of Maryland
    Mr. James Madison of Virginia
    Mr. Hugh Williamson of North Carolina
    Mr. Pierce Butler of South Carolina
    Mr. Abraham Baldwin of Georgia
    Mr. John Dickinson of Delaware

Mr. ADAMS. Mr. Dickinson!

Dr. FRANKLIN. Incredible!

Gen. WASHINGTON. Mr. Adams!

Mr. THOMSON. (Aside to the spectators). One might wonder why only eleven states were represented on this Committee. The two missing states are accounted for by the fact that Rhode Island never did appoint delegates to the Convention, and that at this stage of the Convention, the State of New York was represented only by Mr. Alexander Hamilton, thereby not entitling the state to a vote since a minimum of two delegates were necessary for that purpose.

Mr. MADISON. Mr. Adams, let me explain the sequence of events leading to the final approval. Mr. James McHenry's notes from September 5, 1787 state: "The greatest part of the day spent in desultory conversation on that part of the report respecting the mode of chusing the President—adjourned without coming to a conclusion." Since the mode of electing the president was directly tied in with the election of the vice-president, a decision was not reached on September 5.

My own notes for September 6 read: "The Report relating to the appointment of the Executive stands as amended, as follows:

"He shall hold his office during the term of four years, and together with the Vice-President, chosen for the same term, be elected in the following manner...."

And that vote in the Journal reads: "To agree to the

clause respecting President and Vice President. Ayes—10; noes—1." South Carolina voted no.

On September 8th a motion to appoint a committee of five to revise the style of and arrange the Articles agreed to by the House passed. On September 12 the Committee of Style reported its draft of the Constitution as revised and arranged. The language relating to the vice-president, as Major Jackson and I have cited, remained unchanged in the committee drafts. To my knowledge there was no further vote on this clause until the Constitution was agreed to in its entirety on Saturday, September 15, 1787.

Mr. PIERCE. (Aside to Spectators) Mr. Madison was a character who had long been in public life; and what was very remarkable was that every person seemed to acknowledge his greatness. He blended together the profound politician with the scholar. In the management of every great question he evidently took the lead in the Convention, and though he cannot be called an orator, he was a most agreeable, eloquent, and convincing speaker. From a spirit of industry and application which he possessed in a most eminent degree, he always came forward as the best informed man of any point in debate. Of the affairs of the United States he perhaps had the most correct knowledge of any man in the Union. He had been twice a member of Congress and was always thought one of the ablest members that ever sat in that Council. Mr. Madison was about thirty-seven years of age at the time he served, a gentleman of great modesty, with a remarkable sweet temper. He was easy and unreserved among his acquaintances and had a most agreeable style of conversation.

Mr. ADAMS. What we have discussed so far has been the sequence of drafts leading to the formal draft, which finalized the establishment of the office of the vice-president. Now let us review the debates, discussions and letters associated with the establishment of this office.

Mr. MADISON. Mr. George Mason was one of three who declined to sign the Constitution and apparently entertained many objections to it. Mr. Mason, on the blank pages of your copy of the September 12th draft, you wrote your objections.

Will you please state those that you think touch on our current discussion of the office of the vice-president?

Mr. MASON. Certainly. One of my objections relating to the issue of the vice-president was that the president of the United States had no Constitutional Council, a thing unknown in any safe and regular government. He would therefore be unsupported by proper information and advice, and generally be directed by minions and favorites; or he would become a tool to the Senate—or a Council of State would grow out of the principal officers of the great departments, the worst and most dangerous of all ingredients for such a council in a free country for they may be induced to join in any dangerous and oppressive measures, to shelter themselves, and prevent an inquiry into their own misconduct in office.

Mr. MADISON. And what actually happened?

Mr. MASON. Exactly what I feared. Had a constitutional council of six members been formed, as was proposed—two from the eastern, two from the middle, and two from the southern states, to be appointed by vote of the states in the House of Representatives, with the same duration and rotation of office as the Senate—the executive would always have had safe and proper information and advice; the president of such a council might have acted as vice-president of the United States pro tempore upon any vacancy or disability of the chief magistrate. From this fatal defect has arisen the improper power of the Senate in the appointment of public officers and the alarming dependence and connection between that branch of the legislature and the supreme executive.

Hence sprung that unnecessary and dangerous officer, the vice-president, who for want of other employment is made president of the Senate, thereby dangerously blending the executive and legislative powers, besides always giving to some one of the states an unnecessary and unjust preeminence over the others. . . . I think, that in the course of human affairs, he will be made a tool of in order to bring about his own interest, and aid in overturning the liberties of his country. Thus, the Vice-President appears to me to be not only an unnecessary but a dangerous officer.

Dr. FRANKLIN. (Aside to Mr. Adams) Perhaps Mr. Mason heard of Mr. Spiro Agnew.

Mr. ADAMS. Mr. Mason, for the record, do these constitute some of the reasons why you declined to sign the Constitution on September 17, 1787?

Mr. MADISON. Yes.

Mr. ADAMS. Thank you.

Mr. PIERCE. (Aside to spectators) Mr. George Mason was a gentleman of remarkable strong powers and possessed a clear and copious understanding. He was able and convincing in debate, steady and firm in his principles, and undoubtedly one of the best politicians in America. Mr. Mason was about sixty years of age when he attended, and he had a strong constitution.

Gen. WASHINGTON. Mr. William R. Davie is present and has requested the floor. Mr. Davie was a delegate to the Federal Convention from the State of North Carolina. The chair will recognize Mr. Davie.

Mr. DAVIE. Thank you. I would like to state to this commission the reasons upon which the office of vice-president was introduced. It was in the Senate that the several political interests of the states were to be preserved and where all their powers were to be perfectly balanced. The commercial jealousy between the eastern and southern states had a principal share in this business. It might happen, in important cases, that the voices would be equally divided. Indecision might be dangerous and inconvenient to the public. It would then be necessary to have some person who should determine the question as impartially as possible. Had the vice-president been taken from the representation of any of the states, the vote of that state would have been under local influence. It is true he must be chosen from some state; but, from the nature of his election and office, he represents no one state in particular, but all the states. It is impossible that any officer could be chosen more impartially. He is, in consequence of his election, the creature of no particular district or state, but the officer and representative of the Union. He must possess the confidence of the states in a very great degree, and consequently be the most proper person to decide in cases of this kind. These, I believe, are the principles upon which the Convention formed this officer.

Mr. ADAMS. Mr. Davie, Section 3 of Article I of the Constitution, as it existed in your time and mine, provided that "The Senate of the United States shall be composed of two senators from each state, chosen by the Legislature thereof, for six years, and each Senator shall have one vote." This provision as it exists today, by virtue of the Seventeenth Amendment to the Constitution, provides that "The Senate of the United States shall be composed of two Senators from each State, elected by the people thereof, for six years; and each Senator shall have one vote." Thus, in the 1787 Constitution, senators were chosen by the state legislatures; in the 1987 Constitution, senators are elected by the people. If what you say is valid, and I have no reason to doubt your veracity, that the states were literally in control of the senators, then the change in the Constitution whereby the states no longer choose the senators, removes the foundation, the reasoning, upon which the office of the vice-president was constituted.

Is that not true, Mr. Davie?

Mr. DAVIE. It would appear so, Mr. Adams.

Mr. ADAMS. Thank you, Mr. Davie.

MR. THOMSON. (Aside to spectators) Mr. Davie was a lawyer of some eminence in his state of North Carolina. He was said to have a good classical education and was a gentleman of considerable literary talents. He was generally silent in the Convention, but his opinion when given was always respected. Mr. Davie was about thirty years of age when he attended the Convention.

Gen. WASHINGTON. The Chair now recognizes Mr. Thomas McKean, former president of the Continental Congress.

Mr. MCKEAN. It has been said before this Commission that "The vice-president is a useless officer." Perhaps the government might be executed without him, but there is a necessity of having a person to preside in the Senate to continue a full representation of each state in that body. The chancellor of

England is a judicial officer, yet he sits in the House of Lords.

Mr. ADAMS. I agree with your statement that "Perhaps the government might be executed without him," but I do not subscribe to the remainder. However, I do have one question. If the number of senators were increased from two to three per state would there be any rationale for the continuance of a vice-president as president of the Senate?

Mr. MCKEAN. Absolutely not, since each state would then have at least two out of three functioning senators. Under such circumstances, a vice-president as president of the Senate would definitely be a useless officer.

Mr. ADAMS. Mr. McKean, were you not solicited to become a candidate for the vice-presidency in 1804?

Mr. MCKEAN. Yes, but I declined, responding that the honor of being "President of the United States in Congress assembled in the year 1781 equalled any merit or pretensions of mine and cannot now be increased by the office of Vice-President."

Mr. ADAMS. Thank you, Mr. McKean.

Gen. WASHINGTON. Our next speaker will be Mr. James Monroe. Mr. Monroe is a former president of the United States, was a Senator from the state of Virginia and a delegate from that state to the Continental Congress. Mr. Monroe.

Mr. MONROE. I must agree that the vice-president is an unnecessary officer. I can see no reason for such an officer. The Senate might of their own body elect a president who would have no dangerous influence. He is to succeed the President in case of removal, disability, etc., and is to have the casting vote in the Senate. This gives undue advantage to the state he comes from and will render foreign powers desirous of securing his favor, to obtain which they will exert themselves in his behalf. I am persuaded that the advantage of his information will not counterbalance the disadvantages attending his office.

Gen. WASHINGTON. The Chair recognizes Mr. Alexander Hamilton.

Mr. HAMILTON. The appointment of an extraordinary person, as vice-president, has been objected to as superfluous, if not mischievous. It has been alleged that it would have been preferable to have authorized the Senate to elect out of their own body an officer answering that description. But two considerations seem to justify the ideas of the Convention in this respect. One is, that to secure at all times the possibility of a definite resolution of the body, it is necessary that the president should have only a casting vote. And to take the senator of any state from his seat as senator, to place him in that of president of the Senate, would be to exchange, in regard to the state from which he came, a constant for a contingent vote. The other consideration is that as the vice-president may occasionally become a substitute for the President, in the supreme executive magistracy, all the reasons which recommend the mode of election prescribed for the one apply with great if not with equal force to the manner of appointing the other. It is remarkable that in this, as in most other instances, the objection which is made would lie against the constitution of this State—New York. We have a lieutenant-governor, chosen by the people at large, who presides in the Senate and is the constitutional substitute for the governor, in casualties similar to those which would authorize the vice-president to exercise the authorities and discharge the duties of the president.

Gen. WASHINGTON. The Chair now recognizes Mr. Richard Henry Lee, former president of the Continental Congress and senator in the United States Congress from the state of Virignia. Mr. Lee.

Mr. LEE. I will use but a moment of your time. Shortly after the Constitution was signed, I wrote a letter to Mr. George Mason recommending certain changes in it. That part of my letter dated October 1, 1787, applying to the vice-president, reads as follows:

"That it be further amended so as to omit the creation of a Vice President, whose duties as assigned by the Constitution, may be discharged by the Privy Council (except in the instance of presiding in the Senate, which may be supplied by a Speaker chosen from the body of Senators by themselves as usual) and thus render unnecessary the establishment of a Great

Officer of State who is sometimes joined with the Legislature and sometimes to administer the Executive power, rendering responsibility difficult and adding unnecessarily to the Aristocratic influence; besides giving unjust and needless preeminence to the State from whence this officer may come"

Mr. JEFFERSON. I have been sitting here listening intently to these discussions concerning the vice-president. I was the second vice-president of the United States, serving when Mr. Adams was president. I have gathered a few letters I wrote during that time. I believed that the vice-presidency was solely a legislative position, and I wrote to Mr. Madison in that vein on January 22, 1797, from Monticello: "As to my participating in the administration, if President Adams meant the executive cabinet, both duty and inclination shut that door to me. I do not wish to . . . descend daily into the arena like a gladiator to suffer martyrdom in every conflict. As to duty, the constitution knows me only as the member of a legislative body; and its principle is that of a separation of legislative, executive and judiciary functions."

The office of vice-president was ideal for me. I once commented to Dr. Benjamin Rush, "I have no wish to meddle again in public affairs. . . . If I am to act however, a more tranquil and unoffending station could not have been found for me. . . . It will give me philosophical evenings in the winter, and rural days in the summer."

As vice-president, I had planned to be away from Monticello only a few weeks of the year for four years. I wished not to leave home at all. However, since I was called from it, the shortest absences and most tranquil station suited me best.

Dr. FRANKLIN. It seems to me that the vice-presidency was like "waiting for the Robert E. Lee." Mr. John Nance Garner, who was vice-president for two terms under President Franklin Delano Roosevelt, once described the vice-presidency as the spare tire on the automobile of government. I would suppose that by the time you get to use it, it's run out of air.

Mr. ADAMS. From my point of view, the point has

been adequately established at this session that the office of the vice-president of the United States, insofar as it relates to the function of president of the Senate, is useless.

Gen. WASHINGTON. That is a logical point at which to suspend our discussion. This session is adjourned until tomorrow, June 30, at 10 a.m.

TUESDAY, JUNE 30, 1987

THE HOUSE OF REPRESENTATIVES

The Committee met pursuant to notice, at 10 a.m. in the Assembly Room of Independence Hall, Gen. George Washington presiding.

>Present: Mr. John Adams, Dr. Benjamin Franklin, Mr. Thomas Jefferson, Mr. James Madison and Gen. George Washington.

Gen. WASHINGTON. On Friday, June 19, Mr. Madison stated that he was of the opinion that the term for members of the House of Representatives should be extended from two to three years. He also stated that he would consider recommending that one third of the House be elected annually. The subject of a change in the term of Representatives in the House of Representatives is on the agenda for our session today. Mr. Madison, will you please initiate the discussion?

Mr. MADISON. With respect to the term of members of the House of Representatives, the Constitution, as in effect in 1987, provides that "The House of Representatives shall be composed of members chosen every second year by the People of the Several States . . ."

The genesis of the term of two years is important toward an understanding of my recommendation of a three-year term.

On May 29, 1787, Mr. Edmund Randolph of Virginia proposed certain resolutions in the Convention. The one applying to our discussion today reads: "Resolved that the members of the first branch of the Legislature"—today known as the House of Representatives—"ought to be elected by the people of the several states every (blank) for the term of (blank). . . ." On June 12, it was moved and seconded to fill up the second blank in the resolution with the words "three years."

Major Jackson, would you please give us the detail of that vote?

Major JACKSON. On the queston to fill up the term of members for the first branch with "three years," the vote was in the affirmative: Ayes—7, noes—4.

Voting "Aye" were the states of New York, New Jersey, Pennsylvania, Delaware, Maryland, Virginia, and Georgia.

Voting "No" were the states of Massachusetts, Connecticut, North Carolina, and South Carolina.

Mr. ADAMS. Did you not keep the votes of the individual delegates of the states?

Major JACKSON. I did not, sir.

Mr. MADISON. I can fill in some of the detail—particularly the debates. Mr. Robert Sherman and Mr. Oliver Ellsworth, both of Connecticut, moved to fill the blank left in the Resolution for the periods of electing the members of the first branch with the words, "every year." Mr. Sherman observed that he did it in order to bring on some question.

Mr. John Rutledge, of South Carolina, proposed "every two years."

Mr. Daniel of St. Thomas Jenifer of Maryland proposed "every three years," observing that too great frequency of elections rendered the people indifferent to them, and made the best men unwilling to engage in so precarious a service.

I seconded the motion for three years. Instability was one of the great vices of our republics to be remedied. Three years was necessary, in a government so extensive, for members to form any knowledge of the various interests of the states to which they do not belong, and of which they can know but little from the situation and affairs of their own. One year would be almost consumed in preparing for and travelling to and from the seat of national business.

Mr. Elbridge Gerry said that the people of New England would never give up annual elections; that they knew of the transition made in England from triennial to septennial elections and would consider such an innovation as the prelude to a like usurpation. He considered annual elections as the only defense of the people against tyranny. He was as much against a triennial House as against a hereditary executive.

On June 18, Mr. Alexander Hamilton of New York sketched a three-year term for representatives, though the Convention had already approved the three-year term.

On June 21, the election of the first branch "for the term of three years," was reconsidered. Mr. Randolph of Virginia, moved to strike out "three years" and insert "two years"—he was sensible that annual elections were a source of great mischief in the states, yet it was the want of such checks against the popular intemperance as were now proposed that rendered them so mischievous. He would have preferred annual to biennial but for the extent of the United States and the inconvenience which would be imposed on representatives from the extreme parts of the empire. The people were attached to frequency of elections. All the Constitutions of the states, except that of South Carolina, had established annual elections.

Mr. Dickinson said . . .

Mr. ADAMS. Mr. Dickinson!

Gen. WASHINGTON. Mr. Adams!

Mr. MADISON. Mr. Dickinson of Delaware said that the idea of annual elections was borrowed from the ancient usage of England, a country much less extensive than ours. He supposed biennial would be inconvenient. He preferred triennial; and in order to prevent the inconvenience of an entire change of the whole number at the same moment suggested a rotation, by an annual election of one third.

Mr. ADAMS. (Aside to Dr. Franklin) That is undoubtably the best idea Mr. Dickinson ever had.

Dr. FRANKLIN. (Aside to Mr. Adams) Indubitably.

Mr. ADAMS. Mr. Madison, isn't Mr. Dickinson's idea

of 1787 about a three-year term for representatives, with a one-third rotation, the same as yours today in 1987?

Mr. MADISON. It is. More of that later. But, continuing, Mr. Ellsworth of Connecticut was opposed to three years, supposing that even one year was preferable to two years. He said the people were fond of frequent elections and might be safely indulged in one branch of the legislature. He moved for one year.

Mr. James Wilson of Pennsylvania was for making the first branch an effectual representation of the people at large and preferred an annual election. This frequency was most familiar and pleasing to the people. It would not be more inconvenient to them than triennial elections, as the people in all the states had annual meetings with which the election of the National representatives might be made to coincide. He did not conceive that it would be necessary for the national legislature to sit constantly; perhaps not half—perhaps not one-fourth of the year.

Mr. ADAMS. And your own idea, Mr. Madison?

Mr. MADISON. I was persuaded that annual elections would be extremely inconvenient, and apprehensive that biennial would be too much so. I did not mean inconvenient to the electors but to the representatives. They would have to travel seven or eight hundred miles from the distant parts of the Union and would probably not be allowed even a reimbursement of their expenses. Besides, none of those who wished to be reelected would remain at the seat of government. It must be supposed that the members from the most distant states would travel backwards and forwards at least as often as the elections would be repeated. Much was to be said also on the time requisite for new members, who would always form a large proportion of the House, to acquire that knowledge of the affairs of the States without which their trust could not be usefully discharged.

Mr. Sherman of Connecticut said that he preferred annual elections but would be content with biennial. He thought the representatives ought to return home and mix with the people. By remaining at the seat of government they would acquire the habits of the place which might differ from those of their constituents.

Colonel Mason of Virginia observed that the states being differently situated throughout the country, a rule ought to be formed as would put them as nearly as possible on a level. If elections were annual, the middle States would have a great advantage over the extreme ones. He wished them to be biennial; thus they would coincide with the periodical elections of South Carolina as well as of the other states.

Colonel Hamilton urged the necessity of three years. There ought to be neither too much nor too little dependence on the popular sentiments. The British House of Commons were elected septennially, yet the democratic spirit had not ceased. Frequency of elections tended to make the people listless to them and to facilitate the success of little cabals. This evil was complained of in all the states. In Virginia it had been lately found necessary to force attendance and voting of the people by severe regulations.

The question of striking out "three years" was then put to vote on June 21, 1787: "Ayes—7; noes—3; divided—1.

The motion for two years was then inserted without further discussion.

Mr. JEFFERSON. There appears to be an inconsistency here. Mr. Madison, your notes indicate that the motion for "two" years was inserted without contradiction but does not show or even indicate a vote was taken. Major Jackson's Journal, on the other hand, indicates that there was a unanimous vote on the insertion of "two" years. Mr. Robert Yates's notes state "Two years duration agreed to." However, his notes do not show a vote was taken. Major Jackson, will you read the Journal on this question?

Major JACKSON. "It was moved and seconded to insert the word 'Two'. . . which passed unanimously in the affirmative."

Mr. JEFFERSON. Did you record this vote in the detailed chart of Ayes and Noes?

Major JACKSON. Apparently not. I never noticed that.

Mr. JEFFERSON. You should have noticed that vote number 73 on the chart of Ayes and Noes for June 21 shows the vote for striking out the "three" year duration, while the next vote—Vote number 74—appears on June 22, and the subject matter of that vote has no connnection with the subject at hand.

Major JACKSON. It may be that there were only a few instances where I recorded a unanimous vote on the chart.

Mr. JEFFERSON. Is it possible then that no vote was taken on the motion to insert "two"?

Major JACKSON. That is possible. I just do not recall.

Mr. THOMSON. (To the spectators) Whether Mr. Jefferson's point is valid or not is not so significant as the point it raises on the completeness of notes taken by Major Jackson. Jared Sparks, the historian, had written to James Madison complaining that Major Jackson "was a very stupid secretary, not to take care of those things better and to make a better journal than the dry bones which now go by that name."

James Madison took exception to Robert Yate's notes; "Mr. Yates's notes are very inaccurate; they are, also, in some respects, grossly erroneous."

Mr. MADISON. On July 24, a Committee of Detail was chosen for the purpose of reporting a Constitution conforming to the proceedings. On August 6, the Committee of Detail brought forth its draft. The section on the term of members of the House read: "The members of the House of Representatives shall be chosen every second year. . ." and on August 8, this section was agreed to unanimously.

One month later, on Saturday, September 8, a Committee of Style was chosen to revise the style and arrange the articles which had been agreed to by the Convention. On Wednesday, September 12, the Committee on Style reported their draft, which included the phraseology "The House of Representatives shall be composed of members chosen every second year," which is as the present Constitution reads. Thus, it appears that the two-year provision was not reconsidered for debate between June 21 and September 17, the day the Constitution was signed.

We now turn to opinions on this provision which were

expressed during the ratification process.

Gen. WASHINGTON. Mr. Madison, let us first recess for ten minutes.

Mr. THOMSON. (To several Spectators) There were thirteen state legislatures that called conventions to consider the ratification of the Constitution. In these conventions 1,071 men voted to ratify the Constitution and 577 voted to reject it—a total of 1,648 men. The ratification of the Constitution was debated, for the most part, in ignorance of the proceedings of the Federal Convention. However, many of the men debating the ratification of the Constitution had been debating the issue of a central government best suited for the United States ever since the Declaration of Independence, and even before. Some had helped write the first constitution of the United States, the Articles of Confederation. The First Continental Congress met in 1774. All told, ten of forty-one surviving members of the First Continental Congress were elected to the Federal Convention which drafted the Constitution, although Richard Henry Lee, Patrick Henry, and Richard Caswell refused to serve. The seven members of the First Congress who did serve in the Federal Convention of 1787 were John Dickinson, William Livingston, Thomas Mifflin, George Read, John Rutledge, Roger Sherman and George Washington. All signed the Constitution and suggested its ratification. Twenty of the surviving members of the First Congress were elected to the state conventions in 1787 and 1788, and the majority of them voted to ratify the Constitution.

It was my understanding that all state constitutions in 1787, other than that of South Carolina, provided for a one-year term for representatives to the legislature, South Carolina having a two-year provision.

Gen. WASHINGTON. This session will resume. I think it useful to this Commission to hear additional debate on this subject, this time from members of state legislatures as they discussed ratification of the Constitution. The Chair will recognize Mr. Archibald Maclaine, delegate to the North Carolina Convention debating the ratification of the Constitution.

Mr. MACLAINE. Mr. Chairman, while many objections were made to biennial elections, I stated their superiority to annual elections. Our elections had been annual for some years. People are apt to be attached to old customs. Annual elections may have been proper in our state governments but not in the general government. The seat of government is at a considerable distance; and in case of a disputed election it would be so long before it could be settled that the state would be totally without representation. There is another reason, still more cogent, to prefer biennial to annual elections. The objects of state legislation are narrow and confined, and a short time will render a man sufficiently acquainted with them; but those of the general government are infinitely more extensive and required a much longer time to comprehend them. The representatives to the general government must be acquainted not only with internal situations and circumstances of the United States but also with the state of our commerce with foreign nations and our relative situation to those nations. They must know the relative situation of these nations to one another and be able to judge with which of them, and in what manner, our commerce should be regulated. I still think that perhaps biennial elections are better for this country. Our laws are less fluctuating.

Mr. MADISON. Your statement supporting biennial elections is reasonable. However, is it not conceivable that the same reasoning can apply to triennial elections?

Mr. MACLAINE. Conceivably so.

Gen. WASHINGTON. The Chair will recognize Dr. John Taylor, delegate to the Massachusetts Convention debating the ratification of the Constitution. Dr. Taylor.

Dr. TAYLOR. Mr. Chairman, I was opposed to biennial and was in favor of annual elections. Annual elections had been the practice of our state of Massachusetts and no objections to such a mode of electing had ever been made in my time. Annual elections were considered as the safeguard of the liberties of the people; and the annihilation of it was considered to be the avenue through which tyranny will enter. In the Articles of Confederation, annual elections were provided for, though we had additional securities in a right to recall any or all of our members from Congress and a provision for rotation. In the present Constitution, there is no provision for rotation and no right to recall our delegates. These considerations and others made me favor annual elections; and the further we deviate therefrom, the greater is the evil.

Gen. WASHINGTON. The Chair recognizes Mr. T. Sedgwick, also a delegate to the Massachusetts Convention. Mr. Sedgwick.

Mr. SEDGWICK. It appeared necessary, Mr. Chairman, that federal representatives should be chosen for two years. Annual elections, in a single state, may be the best for a variety of reasons; but when the great affairs of thirteen states are to be the objects of deliberation, is not such a period too short? Can a man, called into public life, divest himself of local concerns and instantly initiate himself into a general knowledge of such extensive and weighty matters?

Mr. ADAMS. Again, Mr. Sedgwick, is it not true that your statement can be applied equally to a three-year term?

Mr. SEDGWICK. It can be.

Gen. WASHINGTON. Thank you, Mr. Sedgwick. The Chair recognizes Mr. Moses Ames, also of the Massachusetts Convention.

Mr. AMES. The term of election must be so long that the representative may understand the interest of the people, and yet so limited, that his fidelity may be secured by a dependence upon their approbation.

Before I proceed to the application of this rule, I cannot forbear to premise my remarks.

Much is said about the people divesting themselves of power when they delegate it to representatives; and that all representation is to their disadvantage, because it is but an image, a copy, fainter and more imperfect than the original, the people, in whom the light of power is primary and unborrowed, which is only reflected by their delegates. I cannot agree to either of these opinions. The representation of the people is something more than the people. I know, sir, but one purpose the people can effect without delegation, and that is to destroy government.

That they cannot erect a government directly, is evinced by our delegates assembling on their behalf. The people must govern by a majority, those with whom all power resides. But how is the sense of this majority to be obtained?

I think it will not be denied that the people are gainers by the election of representatives. They may destroy, but they cannot exercise, the powers of government in person, but by their servants they govern; they do not renounce their power; they do not sacrifice their rights; they become the true sovereigns of the country when they delegate that power to their trustees.

I know, sir, that the people talk about the liberty of nature and assert that we divest ourselves of a portion of it when we enter into society. This is declamation against matter of fact. We cannot live without society; and as to liberty, how can I be said to enjoy that which another may take from me when he pleases? The liberty of one depends not so much on the removal of all restraint from him as on the due restraint upon the liberties of others. Without such restraint, there can be no liberty. Liberty is so far from being endangered or destroyed by this that it is extended and secured. For I said that we do not enjoy that which another may take from us. But civil liberty cannot be taken from us when anyone may please to invade it; for we have the strength of the society on our side. . . .

They who commend annual elections ought to consider that the question is whether biennial elections are a defect in the Constitution; for it does not follow that because annual elections are safe, biennial are dangerous; for both may be good. . . . I thought that we ought to prefer, in this article, biennial elections to annual; and my reasons for this opinion were drawn from these sources: from the extent of the country to be governed; the objects of their legislation; and the more perfect security of our liberty.

It seemed obvious that men who are to collect in Congress from this great territory, perhaps from the Bay of Fundy, or from the banks of the Ohio, and the shore of Lake Superior, ought to have a longer term in office than the delegates of a single state in their own legislature. It was not by riding post to and from Congress that a man could acquire a just knowledge of the true interests of the Union. . . .

Every citizen grows up with a knowledge of the local circumstances of the state. But the business of the federal government was very different. At least two years in office were necessary to enable a man to judge of the trade and interests of the state which he never saw. The time, I hoped, would come when this excellent country would furnish food and freedom—which is better than food, which is the food of the soul—for fifty millions of happy people. Will any man say that the national business can be understood in one year?

I consider biennial elections as a security that the sober, second thought of the people shall be law. To provide for popular liberty, we must take care that measures shall not be adopted without due deliberation. The member chosen for two years has time for due deliberation.

The people are proportionably attentive to the merits of a candidate. Two years affords opportunity to the member to deserve well of them, and the people require evidence that he has done it.

For these reasons, I am clearly of opinion that the article is entitled to our continued approbation as it stands. It has been asked why annual elections were not preferred to biennial. Permit me to retort the question and to inquire, in my turn, what reason can be given, why, if annual elections are good, biennial elections are not better

Mr. ADAMS. Under your train of thought, am I straining the issue if I ask, why, if annual elections are good, and biennial elections better, are not triennial elections best?

Mr. AMES. It is possible.

Gen. WASHINGTON. The Chair will now recognize the Reverend Samuel Stillman, delegate to the Massachusetts Convention. Reverend Stillman.

Reverend STILLMAN. Elections ought to be so frequent as to make the representatives feel they are dependent on and amenable to the people. Under the Constitution, every two years there is a revolution in the general government in favor of the people. At the expiration of the first two years, there is a new choice of representatives; and at the expiration of the second two years, there is a new choice of president and representatives; and at the expiration of the third term, making six years from the commencement of the Congress, there is a new choice of senators and representatives. We all know, sir, that power thus frequently reverting to the people proves a security to their liberties, and a most important check to the power of the general government. Viewing the Constitution in this light, I stood ready to give my vote for it without any amendments at all.

Mr. MADISON. I have a few words to add to these discussions on the lengthening of the term for members of the House of Representatives.

During the ratification process, Mr. Alexander Hamilton, Mr. John Jay, and I wrote a series of eighty-five letters to the public. They appeared at short intervals in the newspapers of New York City beginning on October 27, 1787, and are collectively known as *The Federalist Papers*. It was Mr. Hamilton's idea that he had to marshal all forces to the task of winning his state—New York—to the cause of the new Constitution.

Gen. WASHINGTON. In the summer of 1788, I wrote to Mr. Hamilton saying, "When the transient circumstances and fugitive performances which attended this crisis shall have disappeared, that work will merit the notice of posterity, because in it are candidly and ably discussed the principles of freedom and the topics of government—which will be always interesting to mankind so long as they shall be connected in civil society."

Mr. MADISON. A few quotes from the *Federalist* are in order. However, bear in mind that our object was to support the Constitution as it was agreed to at the Federal Convention—with a two-year term for the House members—whereas Mr. Hamilton and I opted for a three-year term in the Federal Convention. I now quote parts of the *Federalist* on the question of term of office.

"Frequent elections are unquestionably the only policy by which . . . dependence . . . can be effectually secured. But what particular degree of frequency may be absolutely necessary for the purpose does not appear to be susceptible of any precise calculation and must depend on a variety of circumstances. . . . Let us consult experience. . . . In Connecticut and Rhode Island, the periods are half-yearly. In the other States, South Carolina excepted, they are annual. In South Carolina they are biennial—as is proposed in the federal government. Here is a difference, as four to one, between the longest and shortest periods; and yet it would not be easy to show that Connecticut or Rhode Island is better governed or enjoys a greater share of national liberty, than South Carolina; or that either the one or the other of these States is distinguished in these respects, and by these causes, from the States whose elections are different from both.

"Happily for mankind, liberty is not, in this respect, confined to any single point of time but lies within extremes, which afford sufficient latitude for all the variations which may be required by the various situations and circumstances of civil society.

"In a single State, the requisite knowledge relates to the existing laws which are uniform throughout the State and with which all the citizens are more or less conversant; and to the general affairs of the State, which lie within a small compass, are not very diversified, and occupy much of the attention and conversation of every class of people. The great theatre of the United States presents a very different scene. The laws are so far from being uniform that they vary in every State; whilst the public affairs of the Union are spread throughout a very extensive region and are extremely diversified by the local affairs connected with them and can with difficulty be correctly learnt in any other place than in the central councils to which a knowledge of them will be brought by the representatives of every part of the empire. Yet some knowledge of the affairs, and even of the laws, of all the States ought to be possessed by the members from each of the States. How can foreign trade be properly regulated by uniform laws without some acquaintance with the commerce, the ports, the usages, and the regulations of the different States? How can the trade between the different States be duly regulated without some knowledge of their relative situations in these and other respects? How can taxes be judiciously imposed and effectually collected, if they be not accommodated to the different laws and local circumstances relating to these objects in the different States? How can uniform regulations for the militia be duly provided without a similar knowledge of many internal circumstances by which the States are distinguished from each other? These are the principal objects of federal legislation and suggest most forcibly the extensive information which the representatives ought to acquire. . . .

"The business of federal legislation must continue so far to exceed, both in novelty and difficulty, the legislative business of a single State, as to justify the longer period of service assigned to those who are to transact it.

"A branch of knowledge which belongs to the acquirements of a federal representative and which has not been mentioned is that of foreign affairs. In regulating our own commerce he ought to be not only acquanted with the Treaties between the United States and other nations but also with the commercial policy and laws of other nations. He ought not to be altogether ignorant of the law of nations; for that, as far as it is a proper object of municipal legislation, is submitted to the federal government. And although the House of Representatives is not immediately to participate in foreign negotiations and arrangements, yet from the necessary connection between the several branches of public affairs, those particular branches will frequently deserve attention in the ordinary course of legislation and will sometimes demand particular legislative sanction and cooperation. Some portion of this knowledge may, no doubt, be acquired in a man's closet; but some of it also can only be derived from the public sources of information; and all of it will be acquired to best effect by a practical attention to the subject during the period of actual service in the legislature . . .

"All these considerations taken together warrant us in affirming that biennial elections will be as useful to the affairs of the public as we have seen that they will be safe to the liberty of the people."

It appears to me, from today's session, that on the basis of functional logic, looking at the issue in 1987, we would have to resolve the matter on the basis of a three-year term. However, on the basis of proverbial logic—that "where annual elections end, tyranny begins"—we would have to resolve the matter on the basis of a one-year term. Essentially the crux is to have public participation in the politics of their nation on a regular annual basis. This is important, and is a condition which exists nowhere in federal politics in 1987. The people have a right to be heard—not every two, three or four or six years, but every year. Otherwise, people lose contact, get frustrated, and sometimes act outside the realm of Constitutional processes.

It has been said that "all government is an evil." It would be more proper to say that the necessity of any government is a misfortune. This necessity, however, exists; and the problem to be solved is not what form of government is perfect but which of the forms is least imperfect.

In my judgment, the "least imperfect" in this issue is not the average of "one" and "three" producing "two," but rather that answer which best satisfies the requirements for annual elections **and** a three-year term for members of the House. It is with this in mind that I recommend a three-year term for members of the House of Representatives, with an annual election of one-third of the House. I believe this to be sober reasoning.

I am reminded of a speech made on June 20, 1788, by Mr. Melancton Smith in the debates in the Convention of the state of New York, in Poughkeepsie, on the ratification of the Federal Constitution, in which he said: "We may wander in the fields of fancy without end and gather flowers as we go. It may be entertaining, but it is of little service to the discovery of truth. We may, on one side, compare the scheme advocated by our opponents to golden images, with feet part of iron and part of clay; and on the other, to a beast dreadful and terrible, and strong exceedingly, having great iron teeth, which devours, breaks in pieces, and stamps the residue with his feet; and after all, we shall find that both these allusions are taken from the same vision; and their true meaning must be discovered by sober reasoning."

Gen. WASHINGTON. Gentlemen, we will adjourn until tomorrow, Wednesday, July 1, at 10 a.m.

WEDNESDAY, JULY 1, 1987

NEED FOR CONSTITUTIONAL COUNCIL TO PRESIDENT

*T*he Committee met pursuant to notice, at 10 a.m. in the Assembly Room of Independence Hall, Gen. George Washington presiding.

    Present: Mr. John Adams, Dr. Benjamin Franklin, Mr. Thomas Jefferson, Mr. James Madison and Gen. George Washington.

    Gen. WASHINGTON. Today we will begin discussion of ideas posed to this Commission by Dr. Franklin—ideas which he has maintained since time immemorial, so to say Dr. Franklin.

    Dr. FRANKLIN. Today, it is my intention to discuss the need for a constitutional council to the president of the United States. Mr. Wilson Nicholas, delegate to the Virginia Convention considering ratification of the Constitution, said: "No powers ought to be vested in the hands of any who are not representatives of the people and amenable to them."

    Who are these persons who act the part of representatives but are not really elected representatives of the people?

    There was a Mr. H. R. Halderman, aide to President Richard Milhouse Nixon, who, a White House tape tells us, suggested to President Nixon in 1971 that "thugs" and "murderers" be used against antiwar protesters to "knock their heads off." And who can forget the other members of the Watergate fraternity?

    And there was a Mr. Bert Lance, director of the Office of Management and Budget in President Jimmy Carter's administration, who was indicted by a federal grand jury on charges that he and three of his business associates conspired to obtain $20 million in loans for their own benefit from forty-one banks from 1970 to 1978. The grand jury alleged that Lance and his associates continued the conspiracy after Lance entered the Carter administration. Lance resigned his office in September 1977.

Then there was the David Stockman snafu, in which he criticized an economic program he helped design an action he later called "poor judgment" and a "grievous error."

And when the House Budget Committee began hearings on President Reagan's 1983 budget and its projected $91.5 billon deficit, Congressman David Obey, Democrat from Wisconsin, zeroed in on Mr. Stockman: "There is nothing funny about what happens to the country when people who run the government don't level with Congress. . . . I have no questions for you because, very frankly, I would not believe the answers you would give me."

There was Mr. Edwin Meese, counselor to President Reagan, about whom Mr. James McCarney, a *Washington Herald* bureau reporter, said, "President Reagan's own staff did not allow him until recently to make decisions on important foreign and defense policy matters. . . . The principal decision maker in these policy areas during Reagan's first year in office was presidential counselor Edwin Meese; final decisions were made by cabinet members on their own—mainly Secretary of State Alexander Haig and Defense Secretary Casper Weinberger. . . . Meese had no foreign policy background and . . . relied on specialists to educate him on substantive issues. . . . One official said that there is no clear administrative concept of foreign policy objectives for the next few months, the next year, or the next two or three years."

For good or bad, others in this category are:

Hamilton Jordan, of "stuff like snuff" fame, assistant to President Carter.

Richard V. Allen, former assistant to the president for national security affairs, forced out of the Reagan administration after a $1,000 "misunderstanding" that arose when three

Japanese tried to hand the cash to Nancy Reagan after an interview Allen helped to arrange.

And then came the discord between bureaucrats which sometimes led them to discard each other, such as the cases of:

Secretary of State William Rogers and National Security Advisor Henry Kissinger under the Nixon administration.

Secretary of State Cyrus R. Vance and National Security Advisor Zkigniew Brzezinski under the Carter administration.

Secretary of State Alexander Haig and Secretary of Defense Casper Weinberger and other associates under the Reagan administration.

The common thread connecting all these persons is that they were "not representatives of the people, and amenable to them." Yet they held incredibly responsible positions—positions to give advice to the president for action or positions from which action could be taken in the name of the president, without even the knowledge of the president. In many cases they were personal friends of the president. In some cases they were presidential appointees. In some cases they had the "consent" of the Senate. In some cases they were in positions not requiring the "consent" of the Senate.

My contention is that advice to the president should come from a Constitutional Council, from persons who truly are "representatives of the people, and amenable to them."

That is not to say that all representatives of the people are square. "I must hasten to the square Room where I often meet many crooked things." So said President Henry Laurens, talking about the Assembly Room in Independence Hall, where the Continental Congress and the Federal Convention met. And history since then can attest to similar thoughts.

If you recall, at a prior session of this Commission, Mr. Madison reported that I had submitted a plan of government for the United States on June 21, 1775, which provided for an Executive Council. In my draft, the council was to be appointed by Congress out of their own body, consisting of twelve persons, one third of whom were to be changed annually. Each person was to serve three years as counsellor and was to have a respite of three years before he could be elected again. My plan was not even taken into consideration, as you recall, and it would be another year—1776—before Congress authorized that proposed articles of confederation be drafted. I did, however, assist in the drafting of the Pennsylvania Constitution adopted in 1776. I was president of the Pennsylvania Constitutional Convention called to draft a frame of government. The constitution so drafted vested the executive power in a president and a council. It also provided for a unicameral legislature. The Council was to be called the Supreme Executive Council and consisted of twelve persons to serve as counsellors for three years, with a rotation of one third every year. The section creating the council had a purpose clause which read as follows: "By this mode of election and continual rotation, more men will be trained to public business, there will in every subsequent year be found in the Council a number of persons acquainted with the proceedings of the foregoing years, whereby the business will be more consistently conducted and moreover the danger of establishing an inconvenient aristocracy will be effectually prevented."

Mr. ADAMS. Did John Dickinson play any part in the formation of the Pennsylvania Constitution?

Dr. FRANKLIN. I believe Mr. Dickinson was personna non grata, at the time, in Pennsylvania and perhaps throughout the thirteen colonies, since he had declined to sign the Declaration of Independence. By September 28, 1776, a convention had confirmed and ratified a constitution. But in October 1776, Dickinson and others opposed the convention and attempted to devise methods for setting aside what they called "sundry improper and unconstitutional rules laid down by the late convention."

Dickinson failed in this endeavor, but as a member of the Pennsylvania Legislature he proposed to the Assembly that he would assist in organizing the government, provided the Assembly would agree to a measure seeking to call a convention to revise the objectionable features of the Constitution drafted by the late convention. Mr. Dickinson's proposition was not accepted and he resigned his legislative post. Does that answer your question, Mr. Adams?

Mr. ADAMS. Yes, it does. Thank you.

Dr. FRANKLIN. So, as you see, Pennsylvania had a council but Pennslyvania was not alone. With the influx of new constitutions after the Declaration of Independence, many states adopted provisions calling for councils, among them Delaware, New Hampshire, New Jersey, North Carolina, South Carolina, and Virginia. New York had what they called a Council of Revision and a Council of Appointment.

The Constitution of the United States did not in its origin in 1787, and does not today, in 1987, include any provision for a council!

Let us now trace the question through the Federal Convention. Mr. Adams has kindly consented to carry the brunt of the questioning. . . .

Mr. ADAMS. (Aside, soliloquizing softly). . . Abigail . . . What will become of this Labour, time will discover. I shall get nothing by it, I believe, because I never get any thing by any thing that I do. I am sure the public or posterity ought to get something. I believe my children will think I might as well have thought and labored a little night and day for their benefit. But I will not bear the reproaches of my children. I will tell them that I studied and laboured to procure a free Constitution of Government for them to solace themselves under, and if they do not prefer this to ample fortune, to ease and elegance, they are not my children, and I care not what becomes of them. They shall live upon thin diet, wear mean clothes, and work hard, with cheerful hearts and free spirits or they may be the children of the earth or of no one, for me.

John has genius and so has Charles. Take care that they don't go astray. Cultivate their minds, inspire their little hearts, raise their wishes. Fix their attention upon great and glorious objects, root out every little thing, weed out every meanness, make them great and manly. Teach them to scorn injustice, ingratitude, cowardice, and falsehood. Let them revere nothing but religion, morality and liberty.

Nabby and Tommy are not forgotten by me altho I

did not mention them before. The first by reason of her sex requires a different education from the two I have mentioned. Of this you are the only judge. I want to send each of my little pretty flock some present or other. I have walked over this City twenty times and gaped at every shop like a countryman to find something, but could not. Ask every one of them what they would choose to have. From this I shall judge of their taste and fancy and discretion. . . .

Gen. WASHINGTON. I beg your pardon, Mr. Adams? You will have to speak up. Mr. Adams? Mr. *Adams*!

Mr. ADAMS. Excuse me, General, my mind was elsewhere for the moment. What was the question?

Gen. WASHINGTON. Dr. Franklin has turned the issue of the council over to you.

Mr. ADAMS. Of course. Let us proceed. Major Jackson, can you give us the first date on which a proposal was made or question raised in the Federal Convention relative to the establishment of a council to the president, in the nature of a privy council?

Major JACKSON. The first reference to a council to assist and advise the president is in the Journal for Monday, August 20, 1787.

Mr. ADAMS. Mr. Madison, was not this subject brought up before August 20?

Mr. MADISON. It was. Let me review my notes . . . On June 1, Mr. Elbridge Gerry stated that he favored a policy of annexing a council to the executive—the president—in order to give weight and inspire confidence.

Mr. Rufus King, too, had recorded the testimony of Mr. Gerry on that date. His records show that Mr. Gerry said, "I am in favor of a council to advise the Executive. They will be the organs of information of the persons proper for offices. Their opinions may be recorded. They may be called to account for their opinions and be impeached; if so, their responsibility will be certain, and in case of misconduct their punishment certain."

Mr. William Pierce's records likewise confirm Mr.

Gerry's introduction of a council. His notes show that Mr. Gerry was of the opinion that a council ought to be the medium through which the feelings of the people could be communicated to the executive. The next reference to a council in my notes occurred on June 4, when Mr. Roger Sherman of Connecticut said he thought a council necessary to make the establishment acceptable to the people, pointing out that in all the states there was a council of advice, without which the first magistrate could not act. Even in Great Britain, he said, the king had a council, and though he appointed it himself, the advice had its weight with him and attracted the confidence of the people. Mr. Hugh Williamson of North Carolina then asked Mr. James Wilson of Pennsylvania whether he would annex a council to the executive. Mr. Wilson stated that he would have no council which more often served to cover than to prevent malpractices.

At about this time in the Federal Convention, George Mason prepared the draft of a speech to be made in the Convention, in which he said: "It is not yet determined how the Executive is to be regulated, whether it is to act solely from its own judgment, or with the advice of others; whether there is, or is not, to be a Council annexed to it; and if a Council, how far their advice shall operate in controlling the Judgment of the supreme magistracy . . ."

On August 18, Mr. Oliver Ellsworth of Connecticut observed that a council had not yet been provided for the president, and there ought to be one. His proposition was that it should be composed of the president of the Senate, the chief justice, and the ministers from the departments of foreign and domestic affairs, war, and finance, who should advise but not rule the President. Mr. Pinckney of South Carolina thought that the president should be authorized to call for advice or not as he might choose. Give him an able council and it will thwart him, he observed; a weak one and he will shelter himself under their sanction.

August 20, you will recall, was the first day on which the Journal had a reference to a proposed council. Major Jackson's Journal and my notes are substantially identical, except that mine identifies the persons direcly involved with the proposals. In my notes for that day, therefore, it was moved by Gouverneur Morris and seconded by Mr. Pinckney that the following propositions be referred to a Committee of Detail:

"To assist the President in conducting the Public affairs there shall be a Council of State composed of the following officers—1. The Chief Justice of the Supreme Court, who shall from time to time recommend such alterations of and additions to the laws of the United States as may in his opinion be necessary to the due administration of justice, and such as may promote useful learning and inculate sound morality throughout the Union: He shall be President of the Council in the absence of the President.

"2. The Secretary of Domestic Affairs who shall be appointed by the President and hold his office during pleasure. It shall be his duty to attend to matters of general police, the state of agriculture and manufacturers, the opening of roads and navigation, and the facilitating communications through the United States; and he shall from time to time recommend such measures and establishments as may tend to promote those objects.

"3. The Secretary of Commerce and Finance, who shall also be appointed by the President during pleasure. It shall be his duty to superintend all matters relating to the public finances, to prepare and report plans of revenue and for the regulation of expenditures, and also to recommend such things as may in his judgment promote the commercial interests of the United States.

"4. The Secretary of foreign affairs who shall also be appointed by the President during pleasure. It shall be his duty to correspond with all foreign Ministers, prepare plans of Treaties, and consider such as may be transmitted from abroad; and generally to attend to the interests of the United States in their connections with foreign powers.

"5. The Secretary of War who shall also be appointed by the President during pleasure. It shall be his duty to superintend everything relating to the War-Department, such as the raising and equipping of troops, the care of military stores—public fortifications, arsenals and the like—also in time of war to prepare and recommend plans of offense and defense.

"6. The Secretary of the Marine who shall also be appointed during pleasure. It shall be his duty to superintend every thing relating to the Marine-Department, the public ships, dockyards, naval-stores and arsenals—also in the time of war to prepare and recommend plans of offense and defense.

"The President shall also appoint a Secretary of State to hold his office during pleasure; who shall be Secretary to the Council of State, and also public Secretary to the President. It shall be his duty to prepare all public dispatches from the President which he shall countersign.

"The President may from time to time submit any matter to the discussion of the Council of State, and he may require the written opinions of any one or more of the members: But he shall in all cases exercise his own judgment and either conform to such opinions or not as he may think proper; and every officer abovementioned shall be responsible for his opinion on the affairs relating to his particular Department.

"Each of the officers abovementioned shall be liable to impeachment and removal from office for neglect of duty, malversation, or corruption."

On August 22, the Committee of Detail reported that in their opinion the following addition should be made to the draft of the Constitution then before the Convention:

"The President of the United States shall have a privy-council which shall consist of the President of the Senate, the Speaker of the House of Representatives, the Chief-Justice of the Supreme-Court, and the principal officer in the respective departments of foreign affairs, domestic-affairs, War, Marine and Finance, as such departments of office shall from time to time be established—whose duty it shall be to advise him in matters respecting the execution of his Office, which he shall think proper to lay before them. But their advice shall not conclude him, nor affect his responsibility for the measures which he shall adopt."

It was then moved, seconded, and approved to postpone consideration of this report, in order that the members might furnish themselves with copies of it.

On August 27, during the course of discussions on presidential successors, I suggested that the Executive powers during a vacancy be administered by the persons composing the Council to the President.

Mr. ADAMS. You say "composing the Council to the President." Had any action been taken on the proposal for a council?

Mr. MADISON. No. However, on August 31, nothing having been accomplished in many respects, including the subject of the proposed council, the convention decided to refer such parts of the Constitution as had been postponed and such parts of reports as had not been acted on, to a committee of one member from each state. The committee appointed by ballot consisted of the honorable Mr. Gilman, Mr. King, Mr. Sherman, Mr. Brearley, Mr. G. Morris, Mr. Dickinson, Mr. Carrol, Mr. Madison, Mr. Williamson, Mr. Butler, and Mr. Baldwin. I will refer to this Committee as the Committee of Eleven.

On this day too, I recorded anger and impatience rising. We were considering the method by which the new Constitution should be approved. Mr. Elbridge Gerry moved to postpone the issue of approval. Colonel Mason seconded, declaring that he would sooner chop off his right hand than put it to the Constitution as it stood. He wished to see the issue of a council, not yet decided, brought to a decision before being compelled to give a final opinion. Should this point and some other points be improperly settled, his wish was then to bring the whole subject before another general convention.

Mr. Gouverneur Morris was also ready for a postponement. He had long wished for another convention that would have the firmness to provide a vigorous government, which we were afraid to do.

The question for postponing was negated.

All this just seventeen days away from the last day of the Convention. I could almost see the Convention enmeshed in obscurities descending into oblivion. What I did not know until long after the Convention had ended was that Colonel Mason had given a memorandum to the Maryland delegates requesting their "concurrence and assistance to carry them"—that is, approve his suggestions for a council and certain other matters. His idea was that "the Council of State, instead of being formed out of the offices of the Great Departments, consist of not less than five nor more than seven members to be constituted and appointed by law." In other words, a constitutional Council.

Mr. THOMSON. (To the Spectators) On this day, too, August 31, 1787, the *Pennsylvania Packet* contained an editorial on the Federal Convention: "It is laughable says a correspondent, to observe the strange whims and ideas of people in respect to the grand convention and their proceedings. It is taken for granted by the generality that something is accidentally wrong in our political machines which a little skill and contrivance may at once put to right by the magic of a few resolves upon paper; not considering that the evils and confusions we experience have originated in a great measure with the people themselves and by them only can be eventually rectified. A long course of frugality, disuse of foreign luxuries, encouragement of industry, application to agriculture, attention to home manufactures, and a spirit of union and national sobriety can alone place us in the respectable rank of rich and flourishing nations, a situation which we all pant for, but the price of which very few are willing to pay."

Mr. MADISON. On September 4, the Committee of Eleven recommended that, among other clauses, there be added to the powers of the president that he "may require the opinion in writing of the principal officer in each of the Executive Departments, upon any subject relating to the duties of their respective offices."

The previous recommendation of the Committee of Detail was thus buried.

Mr. ADAMS. Were any of the members of the Committee of Detail on the later appointed Committee of Eleven?

Mr. MADISON. Not one. The issue of a council next arose on September 7, ten days before the signing of the Constitution. Colonel Mason had stated . . .

Mr. JEFFERSON. Mr. Madison, Colonel Mason is

present, shall we let him present the testimony he then gave?

Mr. MADISON. I yield to Colonel Mason.

Col. MASON. Thank you. The subject under discussion on that September 7 was the question of where the power to make federal appointments should lie.

The section of the draft of the Constitution under consideration read as follows: "The President by and with the advice and consent of the Senate shall have power to make treaties; and he shall nominate and by and with the advice and consent of the Senate shall appoint Ambassadors and other public Ministers, Judges of the Supreme Court, and all other officers of the United States whose appointments are not otherwise herein provided for. But no Treaty shall be made without the consent of two-thirds of the Members present."

I was averse to granting the power of appointments to either branch of the Legislature. On the other hand, I was averse to vest so dangerous a power in the president alone. As a method for avoiding both, I suggested that a privy council of six members to the president should be established; to be chosen for six years by the Senate, two out of the southern quarters of the Union, and that two should go out in rotation every second year, the concurrence of the Senate to be required only in the appointment of Ambassadors and in making treaties, which are more of a legislative nature. This would prevent the constant sitting of the Senate, which I thought dangerous, and would keep the departments separate and distinct. It would also save the expense of constant sessions of the Senate. I always considered the Senate as too unwieldy and expensive for appointing officers, especially the smallest.

Mr. MADISON. Mr. James Wilson objected to any mode of appointing that would blend a branch of the legislature with the executive. Good laws are of no effect without a good executive, he said, and there can be no good executive without a responsible appointment of officers to execute. Responsibility is in a manner destroyed by blending the executive and the Senate. He preferred the council proposed by Colonel Mason, provided its advice should not be made obligatory on the president.

Col. MASON. The Committee of Eleven had recommended that the president "may require the opinion in writing of the principal officer in each of the Executive Departments, upon any subject relating to the duties of their respective offices."

I said that in rejecting a council to the president we were about to try an experiment on which the most despotic governments had never ventured. The Grand Signor himself had his Divan. I moved to postpone the consideration of the clause in order to take up the following: "That it be an instruction to the Committee of the States to prepare a clause or clauses for establishing an Executive Council, as a Council of State for the President of the United States, to consist of six members, two of which from the Eastern, two from the Middle, and two from the Southern States, with a Rotation and duration of office similar to those of the Senate; such Council to be appointed by the Legislature or by the Senate."

Dr. FRANKLIN. I seconded that motion. We seemed, I said, to have too much fear of cabals in appointments of a number of persons and to have too much confidence in those of a single person. Experience showed that caprice, the intrigues of favorites and mistresses, and so on, were nevertheless the means most prevalent in monarchies where a single person reigned. Among instances of abuse in such modes of appointment, I mentioned the many bad governors appointed in Great Britain for the Colonies. I thought a council would not only be a check on a bad president but be a relief to a good one.

Mr. MADISON. Mr. Wilson approved of a council, in preference to making the Senate a party to appointments. Mr. Dickinson was for a council, saying that it would be a singular thing if the measures of the executive were not to undergo some previous discussion before the president. I was in favor of the instruction of the committee proposed by Colonel Mason.

Major Jackson, will you please let us have the vote on Mr. Mason's motion?

Major JACKSON. The motion of Mr. Mason was negatived.

Mr. ADAMS. Was there then a vote on the question

"authorizing the President to call for the opinions of the Heads of Departments in writing"?

Major JACKSON. There was.

Mr. ADAMS. Will you state the vote?

Major JACKSON. It was passed in the affirmative—unanimously.

Mr. ADAMS. Was the question of a council discussed again or was it lost at this point?

Mr. MADISON. On September 8, a Committee of Style was appointed to revise the style and arrange the articles agreed to by the House. The provision stating that the president "may require the opinion in writing of the principal officer in each of the executive departments" was included in the proceedings referred to the Committee of Style.

On September 12, the Committee of Style reported the Constitution as revised and arranged. The provision for the president to require the opinion of the principal officer in each of the executive departments, in his discretion, remained intact in this draft and in the draft signed on September 17, 1787.

Colonel Mason said on Saturday, September 15, just two days before the Constitution was signed, that as the Constitution stood, he could neither give it his support nor vote for it in Virginia and that he could not sign here what he could not support there.

Mr. MASON. On the blank pages of my copy of the draft of September 12, I wrote my objections to this Constitution. Among them, I wrote that "The President of the United States has no Constitutional Council, a thing unknown in any safe and regular government. He will therefore be unsupported by proper information and advice and will generally be directed by minions and favorites; or he will become a tool to the Senate—or a Council of State will grow out of the principal officers of the great departments, the worst and most dangerous of all ingredients for such a council in a free country; for they may be induced to join in any dangerous or oppressive measures, to shelter themselves, and prevent an inquiry into their own misconduct in office."

And that's exactly what happened. Had a Constitutional Council been formed, as I proposed, of six members, to be appointed by vote of the states in the House of Representatives, with the same duration and rotation in office as the Senate, the executive would always have had proper information and advice.

This, among other things, was not included in the Constitution.

Thus, I did not sign it.

First SPECTATOR. (To second Spectator) I was reading an article by James J. Kilpatrick on Mason back in 1981. He said something like, "We now have a stamp honoring the most neglected of the Founding Fathers, George Mason of Gunston Hall. . . . All the other Founding Fathers long ago won philatelic recognition—Washington, Jefferson, Franklin, Hamilton, the whole pantheon—but a Postal Service that could honor George Gershwin and George Eastman never thought of George Mason. . . ."

Second SPECTATOR. (To first Spectator) You know, Mason said in the Federal Convention that under the new Constitution the government would end either in a monarchy or a tyrannical aristocracy. Benjamin Franklin pleaded that the Constitution be signed by all of the delegates. Mason and two others refused. If there were more men like Mason maybe there never would have been a United States.

You know, he was never a member of the Continental Congress or of the United States Congress.

First SPECTATOR. (To second Spectator) But we do have to give Mason credit for one thing. He had drafted the Bill of Rights for the Virginia Constitution and one of his main objections to the U.S. Constitution was that it did not contain a Declaration of Rights. As things turned out, the First Congress adopted a Bill of Rights—the first ten Amendments to the Constitution. So he deserves some credit.

Second SPECTATOR. (To First Spectator) Well, then, maybe George Mason's stamp should be smaller than George Gershwin's and larger than George Eastman's.

Mr. ADAMS. Mr. Gouverneur Morris is present and

I would like to address a few questions to him.

Mr. Morris, you were a member of the committee of Eleven appointed by the Federal Convention on August 31, 1787, to make recommendations with respect to certain matters remaining before the Convention. Is that correct?

Mr. MORRIS. I was a member of that committee.

Mr. ADAMS. Was not the question of a council considered by such Committee?

Mr. MORRIS. It was.

Mr. ADAMS. What was the outcome?

Mr. MORRIS. On September 7, I reported to the Convention that the question of a council was considered in the Committee, where it was judged that the president, by persuading his council to concur in the wrong measures, would acquire their protection for them.

Mr. ADAMS. Is it not true that while you were in France in 1791 you drafted a proposed constitution for France?

Mr. MORRIS. I did.

Mr. ADAMS. Did that proposed constitution include a plan for a Constitutional Council of State in France composed of nine officials—the chancellor, the president of the council, and ministers of the interior, finance, commerce, foreign affairs, war, marine, besides a secretary of state?

Mr. MORRIS. It did.

First SPECTATOR. (To Second Spectator) I once read that Gouverneur Morris enjoyed intrigue and was a "person of no principle, a downright Machiavellian politician."

Second SPECTATOR. (To First Spectator) I heard that he was probaby the man who issued illegal orders that contributed to the Philadelphia Mutiny debacle in 1783.

First SPECTATOR. (To Second Spectator) Did you know George Washington pointed to him as the man who had built the "groundwork of the superstructure" that became the Newburgh Conspiracy?

Second SPECTATOR. (To First Spectator) No, but I *do* know that during the ratification period Morris was referred to as "Gouvero the cunning man." Also, it was sarcastically said of him, "blessed art thou amongst men, O Gouvero! for thy strategems are wise, thy councils deep, and thy cunning exceedeth all things!"

First SPECTATOR. (To Second Spectator) Hah! I can top that. I was reading Morris's diary, and listen to **this**: "While sitting one evening with a friend in the Palais Royal, drinking lemonade and tea, the waiter comes to tell me that two ladies are without who wish to speak to me. These, I find, are Madame de Boursac and Madame d'Espanchall, whom we had met before at the Tuileries. A good deal of light, trivial conversation, in which these ladies intimate to me that their nuptial bonds do not at all straighten their conduct, and it would seem that either would be content to form an intrigue. As they can have no real want of lovers, and as they can have no prepossession in my favor, this conduct evidently resolves itself into some other motive—probably a view to some jolis cadeaux . . ."

Oh, the rest of the page is torn, there's more.

"Today, November 13th, 1789, I am . . . at Madame de Flahaut's . . . Madame being ill goes into the bath, and when placed there sends for me. It is a strange place to receive a visit, but there is milk mixed with the water, making it opaque. She tells me that it is usual to receive in the bath, and I suppose it is, for otherwise I should have been the last person to whom it would have been permitted."

Mr. ADAMS. Just one more question, Mr. Morris. Do I understand correctly that you were on the Committee of Style for the Constitution and that you were credited with most of the final draft form?

Mr. MORRIS. That is true.

Mr. ADAMS. That is all the questioning I have of Mr. Morris.

Dr. FRANKLIN. "Approve not of him who commends all you say" I printed a long, long time ago. And yet this statement characterizes what Colonel Mason prophetically said, that a "Council of State"—our present-day cabinet—"will grow out of the principal officers of the great departments"—the president's appointees—his "minions and favorites . . . the worst and most dangerous of all ingredients for such a Council in a free country."

I suppose the country slowly drifted into "minions and favorites." In President Washington's first administration there was only one cabinet member out of seven who had not served in the Continental Congress. In his second term, there were two non-Congressional members out of ten. By the time we reach President Madison's second term, seven out of fourteen cabinet members never had Congressional experience. Buy the time we reach President Franklin Roosevelt's third and fourth terms, no member of his cabinet had any Congressional experience. It was just as Mason said.

A couple of centuries ago I wrote, "The first Degree of Folly, is to conceit one's self wise; the second to profess it; the third to despise Counsel." Take heed.

Gen. WASHINGTON. This session will adjourn until tomorrow, Thursday, July 2 at 10 a.m.

THURSDAY, JULY 2, 1987

THE SENATE

The Committee met pursuant to notice, at 10 a.m. in the Assembly Room of Independence Hall, Gen. George Washington presiding.

  Present: Mr. John Adams, Dr. Benjamin Franklin, Mr. Thomas Jefferson, Mr. James Madison and Gen. George Washington.

  Gen. WASHINGTON. At our last session we discussed Dr. Franklin's thoughts on a constitutional council to the president of the United States. Today, Dr. Franklin discusses the manner in which such a council should be established. Dr. Franklin.

  Dr. FRANKLIN. My thought is that the Senate should be made the constitutional council to the president of the United States.

  I claim that there is no justification for the continued existence of the Senate in its present capacity and that its purpose, composition, structure, and legal functions should be overhauled. This claim, I maintain, lies mainly in this chain:

  First, in the Federal Convention the states gained control of the Senate by providing in the Constitution for the selection of senators by the state legislatures.

  Second, in the Federal Convention the states gained control of the president by providing for the sharing of powers between the Senate and the president.

  Third, by the sharing of powers, the Senate became an imperfect council to the president for certain powers.

  Fourth, the entire chain collapsed when the main link

broke—when ratification of the Seventeenth Amendment was completed on April 8, 1913. By virtue of this amendment the state legislatures no longer chose the senators—the senators are now elected by the people.

Thus, the main reason for the creation of the Senate—to serve the states—has long vanished.

Is there a reason, then, for the continuance of the Senate? Technically, no, yet in my opinion the Senate should remain in existence for three purposes:

First, to serve as council to the president. But since it is too weak in its present structural relationship to the president, it should be restructured. It should be made a true "Constitutional Council," as I always wanted.

Second, the Senate seems to temper legislation by the House of Representatives. As General Washington told Mr. Jefferson, "we pour legislation into the senatorial saucer— to cool it" for the same reason "you pour that coffee into your saucer." For this reason, it should retain its legislative character.

Third, the Senate seems to be the proper body to monitor the activities of the executive branch. Montesquieu said in 1748 that "the legislative power . . . has a right and ought to have a means of examining in what manner its laws have been executed."

Two hundred and thirty three years later, on January 5, 1981, Congress made a feeble attempt to implement Montesquieu's concept by introducing a "Joint Resolution proposing an amendment to the Constitution of the United States requiring a review by the Congress of each rule and regulation issued to carry out any law and allowing the Congress to approve, modify, or disapprove such rule or regulation." It was referred to the Committee of the Judiciary.

Mr. THOMSON. (To spectators) During the Constitution's ratification process Dr. Franklin wrote to M. Le Veillard: "It is very possible, as you suppose, that all the Articles of the proposed new Government will not remain unchanged after the first meeting of the Congress. I am of the opinion with you that the two chambers were not necessary; and I disliked some other

Articles that are in and wished for some that are not in the proposed plan:—I nevertheless hope it may be adopted, though I shall have nothing to do with the execution of it, being determined to quit all public business with my present employment. . . ."

Mr. PIERCE. (To spectators) Dr. Franklin was well known to be the greatest philosopher of his age; all the operations of nature he seemed to understand:—the very heavens obeyed him, and the clouds yielded up their lightning to be imprisoned in his rod. But what claim he had to the politician, posterity had to determine. It is certain that he did not shine much in public Council;—he was no speaker, nor did he seem to let politics engage his attention. He was, however, a most extraordinary man and told a story in a style more engaging than anything I ever heard. He was eighty-two years old when he attended the Federal Convention, and possessed activity of mind equal to a youth of twenty-five years of age.

Dr. FRANKLIN. (Continuing) The Senate was designed with the states in mind. Its counterpart in Europe was, in Montesquieu's words, "a separate upper chamber hereditary in nature"—a "hereditary nobility"—a status outlawed in the Constitution: "No Title of Nobility shall be granted in the United States." So in Europe the upper house was designed with "nobility" in mind. Montesquieu's *The Spirit of Laws* was very present in the political thought of those times, especially in regard to the theory of the separation of powers. "The people in whom the supreme power resides," he wrote "ought to do of themselves whatever conveniently they can; and what they cannot well do, they must commit to the management of ministers.

"The ministers are not properly theirs, unless they have the nomination of them: 'tis therefore a fundamental maxim in this government, that the people should choose their ministers, that is, their magistrates. . . .

Political liberty . . . is a tranquility of mind, arising from the opinion each person has of his safety. In order to have this liberty, it is requisite the government be so constituted as one man need not be afraid of another.

When the legislative and executive power are united in the same person, or in the same body of magistracy, there can be then no liberty; because apprehensions may arise, lest the same monarch or senate should enact tyrannical laws, to execute them in a tyrannical manner.

Again, there is no liberty, if the power of judging be not separated from the legislative and executive powers. Were it joined with the legislative, the life and liberty of the subject would be exposed to arbitrary control; for the judge would be then the legislator. Were it joined to the executive power, the judge might behave with all the violence of an oppressor.

"Miserable indeed would be the case were the same man or the same body, whether of the nobles or of the people, to exercise those three powers, that of enacting laws, that of executing the public resolutions, and that of judging the crimes or differences of individuals."

Who in America read Montesquieu? Many. In 1760, John Adams noted in his diary that he had begun to read *The Spirit of Laws.* Fifteen years later, Thomas Jefferson devoted twenty-eight pages of his "Commonplace Book" to extracts from Montesquieu. And James Madison in *The Federalist Papers* wrote extensively about Montesquieu. Many founders came to the Federal Convention in 1787 with a knowledge of the concept of "separation of powers," and many had their own ideas about it. Did the sharing of powers of the Senate with the President as included in the Constitution help or defeat the purpose of the Constitution? Some said yes; some said no. I wanted only one branch of Congress—the House of Representatives. So the fact that there was a sharing of powers between the Senate and the president did not affect good government in my mind. At least the House of Representatives was separate, and that was sufficient. Mr. Madison in *The Federalist Papers* wrote that separation of powers "can amount to no more than this, that where the 'whole' power of one department is exercised by the same hands which possess the 'whole' power of another department, the fundamental principles of a free constitution are subverted." Montesquieu "did not mean that these departments ought to have no 'partial agency' in, or no 'control' over the acts of each other," wrote Madison.

This is consistent with my thoughts. It was sufficient that there was a complete separation of power between the president, the House of Representatives, and the judiciary without having to consider the Senate.

Of a constitutional council in Britain, Mr. Madison wrote that "On the slightest view of the British Constitution, we must perceive that the legislative, executive and judiciary departments are by no means totally separate and distinct from each other. . . . One branch of the legislature department also forms a great constitutional council to the executive chief. . . .

But we were in no mood in the Federal Convention to duplicate the British form of government. James Wilson in the Convention oft repeated that "he was not governed by the British Model which was inapplicable to the situation of this country." Our scorn of British inhumanity had not abated. I wrote that King George had destroyed not less than forty thousand of his subjects in America "by battles on land or sea, or by starving them, or poisoning them to death, in the unwholesome air, with the unwholesome food of his prisons. . . . His base-bought parliaments, too, who sell him their souls and extort from the people the money with which they aid his destructive purposes, as they share his guilt will share his infamy,—parliament, who, to please him, have repeatedly, by different votes year after year, dipped their hands in human blood . . . that me thinks . . . if they could wash it off in the Thames, which flows under their windows, the whole river would run red to the ocean."

Is it any wonder, then, that less than a decade later we were so unwilling to consider the British form of government—or its constitutional council?

Mr. ADAMS. Most of us unwilling except Mr. John Dickinson.

Gen. WASHINGTON. Mr. Adams!

Dr. FRANKLIN. Before we change, disengage, exchange, or rearrange any provisions in the Constitution pertaining to the Senate, it is essential that the concepts attaching to how we arrived at the provisions be known—before we eulogize its demise.

Let us therefore examine the validity of my claims:
- That the states gained control of the Senate.
- That by a sharing of power between the president and the Senate, the Senate became an imperfect council to the president.
- That the powers of the states collapsed upon passage of the Seventeenth Amendment, by virtue of which the state legislatures no longer chose the Senators.
- That, therefore, the main reason for the creation of the Senate vanished, leaving it to this Commission to recommend a new purpose for its existence.

Let us begin with my first contention—the states gained control of the Senate by providing in the Constitution for the selection of Senators by the state legislatures, and let's take it through the Federal Convention. Now, historians would not put it that way, but being a printer, I see it as an excellent headline—"States Gain Control of Senate."

Possibly one-third of the debates and time in the Federal Convention was devoted to issues of representation and voting in the House of Representatives and the Senate. In forming the Senate, the great anchor of government, the questions turned mostly on the mode of appointment of senators and on suffrage.

The different modes of appointment of senators proposed were:
1. By the House of Representatives.
2. By the President.
3. By electors chosen by the people for that purpose.
4. By the state legislatures.

On the matter of suffrage in the Senate, the questions revolved about two modes: 1. Proportional representation, and 2. Equal Suffrage. The subject matter of appointments and voting, in the House of Representatives particularly, was so crucial to the success of the Convention that failure to reach a decision by compromise or otherwise would have precipitated the Convention to a dissolution. Recognizing this, on June 28 on the floor of the Convention I said:

"Mr. President, the small progress we have made after four or five weeks' close attendance and continual reasonings with each other—our different sentiments on almost every question, several of the last producing as many noes as ayes, is methinks a melancholy proof of the imperfection of the human understanding. We indeed seem to feel our own want of political wisdom, since we have been running about in search of it. We have gone back to ancient history for models of government and examined the different forms of those Republics which, having been formed with the seeds of their own dissolution, now no longer exist. And we have viewed Modern States all round Europe but find none of their Constutitions suitable to our circumstances.

In this situation of this Assembly, groping as it were in the dark to find political truth, and scarce able to distinguish it when presented to us, how has it happened, Sir, that we have not hitherto once thought of humbly applying to the Father of lights to illuminate our understandings? In the beginning of the contest with Great Britain, when we were sensible of danger we had daily prayer in this room for the divine protection. Our prayers, Sir, were heard, and they were graciously answered. All of us who are engaged in the struggle must have observed frequent instances of a superintending providence in our favor. To that kind providence we owe this happy opportunity of consulting in peace on the means of establishing our future national felicity. And have we now forgotten that powerful friend? Or do we imagine that we no longer need his assistance? I have lived, Sir, a long time, and the longer I live, the more convincing proofs I see of this truth—that God governs in the affairs of men. And if a sparrow cannot fall to the ground without his notice, is it probable that an empire can rise without his aid? We have been assured, Sir, in the sacred writings, that 'except the Lord build the House they labor in vain that build it.' I firmly believe this; and I also believe that without his concurring aid we shall succeed in this political building no better than the Builders of Babel:

We shall be divided by our little partial local interests; our projects will be confounded, and we ourselves shall become a reproach and bye word down to future ages. And what is worse, mankind may hereafter from this unfortunate instance, despair of establishing Governments by human wisdom and leave it to chance, war and conquest.

I therefore beg leave to move that henceforth prayers imploring the assistance of Heaven and its blessings in our deliberations be held in this Assembly every morning before we proceed to business, and that one or more of the Clergy of this City be requested to officiate in that service."

Gen. Jonathan DAYTON. (To the spectators) I was there. The doctor sat down, and never did I behold a countenance at once so dignified and delighted as was that of Washington, at the close of this address! Nor were the members of the Convention, generally less affected. The words of the venerable Franklin fell upon our ears with a weight and authority, even greater than we may suppose an oracle to have had in a Roman senate! A silent admiration superseded, for a moment, the expression of that assent and approbation which was strongly marked on almost every countenance; I say almost, for one man was found in the Convention . . . saying that . . . he did not see the necessity of calling in foreign aid!

Washington fixed his eye upon the speaker, with a mixture of surprise and indignation, while he uttered this impertinent and impious speech, and then looked around to ascertain in what manner it affected others. They did not leave him a moment to doubt; no one deigned to reply or take the smallest notice of the speaker. . . .

Mr. ADAMS. How was Dr. Franklin's request for a Chaplain disposed of?

Mr. MADISON. Mr. Sherman seconded the motion. But Mr. Wiliamson observed that the convention had no funds. After several unsuccessful attempts for silently postponing the matter by adjourning, the adjournment was at length carried without any vote on the motion.

Mr. THOMSON. (To the Spectators) It is perhaps

significant to note how distinguished persons viewed the seriousness of this critical point in the Convention. For example, General Washington wrote to David Stuart on July 1, 1787 just a few days after Dr. Franklin's speech, "As the rules of the Convention prevent me from relating any of the proceedings of it, and the gazettes contain more fully than I could detail other occurrences of public nature, I have little to communicate to you on the article of news. Happy indeed would it be if the Convention shall be able to recommend such a firm and permanent Government for this Union, as all who live under it may be secure in their lives, liberty and property; and thrice happy would it be, if such a recommendation should obtain. Everybody wishes—everybody expects something from the Convention—but what will be the final result of its deliberation, the book of fate must disclose. Persuaded I am that the primary cause of all our disorders lies in the different State governments and in the tenacity of that power which pervades the whole of their systems. Whilst independent sovereignty is so ardently contended for, whilst the local views of each State and separate interests by which they are too much governed will not yield to a more enlarged scale of politics; incompatibility in the laws of different States and disrespect to those of the general government must render the situation of this great Country weak, inefficient and disgraceful. It has already done so, almost to the final dissolution of it—weak at home and disregarded abroad is our present condition, and contemptible enough it is. . . .

I have had no wish more ardent than that of knowing what kind of Government is best calculated for us to live under. No doubt there will be a diversity of sentiment on this important subject; and to inform the judgment, it is necessary to hear all arguments that can be advanced. To please all is impossible, and to attempt it would be vain; the only way therefore is . . . to form such a government as will bear the scrutinizing eye of criticism and trust it to the good sense and patriotism of the people to carry it into effect. Demagogues—men who are unwilling to lose any of their state consequence . . . will oppose any general government; but let these be regarded rightly, and justice it is to be hoped will at length prevail."

Mr. Alexander Hamilton left the Convention after Dr. Franklin's speech—not on account of it, of course—and on July 3 he wrote to General Washington, "I owe to you, Sir, that I am seriously and deeply distressed at the aspects of the Councils which prevailed when I left Philadelphia—I fear that we shall let slip the golden opportunity of rescuing the American empire from disunion and anarchy and misery. No motley or feeble measure can answer the end or will finally receive the public support. Decision is true wisdom and will be not less reputable to the Convention than salutory to the community.

I shall of necessity remain here ten or twelve days; if I have reason to believe that my attendance at Philadelphia will not be mere waste of time, I shall after that period rejoin the Convention." And as the "I shall return" of another great was fulfilled, so too was Hamilton's.

Then there was Mr. Stephan M. Mitchell, who wrote to me at about that time, "The Clergymen begin to omit poor old Congress in their prayers and substitute instead thereof, the Convention. You know many of our political ideas on New England have their birth in the pulpit."

Dr. FRANKLIN. Section 3 of Article I of the Constitution of 1787 read as follows:

"The Senate of the United States shall be composed of two Senators from each State, chosen by the Legislature thereof, for six years, and each Senator shall have one vote."

As I have pointed out, there were two questions to debate concerning this clause: First, the mode of appointment; second, the suffrage. Mr. Madison, what do your notes show with respect to these debates?

Mr. MADISON. Mr. Edmund Randolph, governor of Virginia, and delegate to the Convention, on May 29, 1787, proposed the so-called "Randolph Plan" or "Virginia Plan" as it was sometimes called.

Provision five of the Randolph Plan "Resolved that the members fo the second branch of the National Legislature ought to be elected by those of the first out of a proper number of persons nominated by the individual Legislatures. . . ."

Mr. Randolph thought the second branch—the Senate—ought to be much smaller than the first—the House, so small as to be exempt from the passionate proceedings to which numerous assemblies are liable. The general object was to provide a cure for the evils under which the United States labored, which, he thought, had their roots in the turbulence and follies of democracy. Some check therefore was sought against this tendency, and a good Senate seemed most likely to answer the purpose.

Gen. WASHINGTON. The chair will recognize Mr. John Dickinson.

Mr. DICKINSON. On June 7, the following resolution was submitted by me and seconded by Mr. Sherman, namely, "Resolved that the members of the second branch of the national Legislature ought to be chosen by the individual Legislatures."

I had two reasons for this motion. First, because the sense of the states would be better than that of the people at large. Second, because I wished the Senate to consist of the most distinguished characters, distinguished for their rank in life and their weight of property, and bearing as strong a likeness to the British House of Lords as possible. I thought such characters more likely to be selected by the state legislatures than in any other mode. The greatness of the number was no objection to me. I hoped there would be eighty and twice eighty of them. If their number should be small, the popular branch could not be balanced by them. The legislature of a numerous people ought to be a numerous body.

The preservation of the states was indispensible. To attempt to abolish the states altogether would have degraded the councils of our country, would have been impracticable, and would have been ruinous. The proposed national system could have been compared to the solar system in which the states were the planets, and left to move freely in their proper orbits. The gentleman from Pennsylvania, Mr. Wilson, wished, I believe to extinguish these planets . . .

Mr. ADAMS. Mr. Dickinson, are these your opinions or are you speaking in conformity with the dictates of your state credentials?

Gen. WASHINGTON. Mr. Dickinson, you do not have to respond to that question.

Mr. MADISON. It will throw light on Mr. Dickinson's comments to remark that an election by the state legislature involved discarding the principle of proportional representation in the Senate, insisted on by the large states and dreaded by the small ones. Proportional representation would have made the Senate too numerous since the smallest state must elect one member at least. Mr. Rufus King thought that the Senate would have to have eighty or a hundred members to entitle Delaware to the choice of one of them.

With respect to Mr. Adams's question of Mr. Dickinson, it is true, as has been sometimes suggested, that in the course of discussions in the conventions, where so much depended on compromise, the patrons of different opinions often set out on negotiating grounds more remote from each other than the real opinions of either were from the point at which they finally met.

Mr. THOMSON. (To the spectators) On the question of "real opinions," one may ask whether the mere presence of General Washington at the Federal Convention "limited" the conduct and voting of the delegates. To illustrate, the Journal of the Convention for May 25 contains the following paragraph:

"Mr. Robert Morris informed the members assembled that by the instruction and in behalf of the deputation of Pennsylvania, he proposed George Washington, Esq., late Commander-in-Chief, for President of the Convention. Mr. John Rutledge seconded the motion; expressing his confidence that the choice would be unanimous and observing that the presence of General Washington forbade any observations on the occasion which might otherwise be proper."

Yes, it gives us something to think about as to what influence the mere presence of General Washington had on the delegates.

On June 25 Robert Morris wrote to his sons in Leipzig: "General Washington is now our guest, having taken up his abode at my house during the time he is to remain in the city.

He is President of a Convention of Delegates from the Thirteen States of America, who have met here for the purpose of revising, amending, and altering the Federal Government. There are gentlemen of great abilities employed in this Convention, many of whom were in the first Congress, and several that were concerned in forming the Articles of Confederation now about to be altered and amended. You, my children, ought to pray for a successful issue to their labours, as the result is to be a form of Government under which you are to live, and in the administration of which you may hereafter probably have a share. . . ."

On the other hand, William Grayson, delegate from Virginia to the Continental Congress in 1787, wrote to James Monroe on May 29, 1787, "What will be the result of their meeting I cannot with any certainty determine, but I hardly think much good can come of it. The people of America don't appear to me to be ripe for any great innovations, and it seems they are ultimately to ratify or reject. The weight of General Washington as you justly observe is very great in America, but I hardly think it is sufficient to induce the people to pay money or part with power.

Did Gen. Washington's presence influence "real opinions?"

Gen. WASHINGTON. The chair will recognize Mr. James Wilson, delegate from Pennsylvania.

Mr. PIERCE. (Aside to Spectators) Mr. James Wilson ranked among the foremost in legal and political knowledge. He was well acquainted with Man and understood all the passions that influence him. Government seems to have been his peculiar study; all the political institutions of the world he knew in detail and could trace the cause and effect of every revolution from the earliest states of the Grecian commonwealth down to the present time. No man was more clear, copious, and comprehensive than Mr. Wilson, yet he was no great orator. He drew attention not by the charm of his eloquence but by the force of his reasoning. He was about forty-five years old when he attended the Convention.

Mr. WILSON. The question before us was whether the second branch of the general legislature should or should not be appointed by the state legislatures. In every point of view it was an important question. When we are laying the foundation of a building, which is to last for ages and in which millions are interested, it ought to be well laid. In laying a stone amiss we may injure the superstructure; and what would be the consequence, if the cornerstone should be loosely placed? It was improper that the state legislatures should have the power comtemplated to be given them. A citizen of America may be considered in two points of view—as a citizen of the general government and as a citizen of the particular state in which he may reside. We had to consider in what character he acts in forming a general government. I was both a citizen of Pennsylvania and of the United States. I therefore had to lay aside my state connections and act for the general good of the whole. The general government was not an assemblage of states, but of individuals for certain political purposes. The individuals, therefore, not the States, should have been represented in it. I therefore moved that the second branch of the legislature of the national government be elected by electors chosen by the people of the United States, which was not seconded.

Mr. ADAMS. Mr. Wilson, do you have any comment on Mr. Dickinson's statement that the Senate should bear a likeness to the British House of Lords?

Mr. WILSON. The British government could never be our model. Our manners, our laws, the abolition of entails and of primogeniture, the whole genius of the people were opposed to it.

Mr. ADAMS. Mr. Madison, do you care to comment?

Mr. MADISON. I found great differences of opinion in this convention on the clause now under consideration. I thought that the true question was in what mode the best choice should be made.

I thought that if the motion of Mr. Dickinson should be agreed to, we must either depart from the doctrine of proportional representation or admit into the Senate a very large number of members. The first was inadmissable, being evidently unjust. The second was inexpedient. The Senate was expected to conduct its proceedings with more coolness, with more system, and with more wisdom, than the popular branch. Enlarge their number and you communicate to them the vices which they are meant to correct. I differed from Mr. Dickinson who thought that the additional number would give additional weight to the body. On the contrary it appeared to me that their weight would be in an inverse ratio to their number.

The more the representatives of the people were multiplied, the more they partook of the infirmities of their constituents, the more liable they became to be divided among themselves either from their own indiscretions or the artifices of the opposite factions, and of course the less capable of fulfilling their trust. When the weight of a set of men depends merely on their personal characters, the greater the number the greater the weight. When it depends on the degree of political authority lodged in them, the smaller the number the greater the weight. The latter was the material consideration, in my judgment.

Gen. WASHINGTON. The chair will recognize Mr. Elbridge Gerry, delegate from Massachusetts.

Mr. GERRY. Four modes of appointing the Senate had been mentioned. First, by the first branch of the national legislature. This would have created a dependence contrary to the end proposed. Second, by the national executive. This would have been a stride towards monarchy that few would consider. Third, by the people. The people had two great interests: the landed interest and the commercial interest including the stockholders. To draw both branches from the people would leave no security to other interests. Fourth, by the individual legislatures. The elections being carried through this refinement would be most likely to provide some check in favor of the commercial interest against the landed, without which oppression would take place, and no free government can last long when that is the case. I was therefore in favor of this last—appointment of senators by the individual legislatures.

Gen. WASHINGTON. The chair recognizes Mr. Oliver Ellsworth of Connecticut.

Mr. ELLSWORTH. I thought the state legislatures

more competent to make a judicious choice than the people at large. Instability pervades the peoples' choice. In the second branch of the general government we wanted wisdom and firmness. As to balances, I thought that where nothing could be balanced a perfect utopian scheme existed. Great advantages, I conceived, would result in having a second branch. Their weight and wisdom may check the inconsiderate and hasty proceedings of the first branch.

I could not see the force of the reasoning in attempting to detach the state governments from the general government. Without a standing army, you cannot support the general government but on the pillars of the state governments. Were the larger states more energetic than the smaller? Massachusetts could not support a government at the distance of one hundred miles from her capital, without an army. Were we to proceed like unskillful workmen and make use of timber which was too weak to build a first-rate ship? We knew that the people of the states were strongly attached to their own constitutions. If you held up a system of general government, destructive of their constitutional rights, they would oppose it. Some were of the opinion that if we could not form a general government so as to destroy state governments, we ought at least to balance the one against the other. On the contrary, the only chance we had to support a general government was to graft it on to the state governments. I wanted to proceed on this ground as the safest, and I believed no other plan practicable. In this way, and in this way only, could we rely on the confidence and support of the people.

Gen. WASHINGTON. The chair recognizes Mr. George Read, delegate from the state of Delaware.

Mr. READ. I proposed that the Senate "should be appointed by the Executive Magistrate—the President—out of a proper number of persons to be nominated by the individual Legislatures." Nothing short of this approach towards a proper model of government would answer the purpose. My proposition was not seconded nor supported.

Mr. THOMSON. (To the spectators) George Read— this is the man who signed John Dickinson's name to the Constitution, in addition to his own!

Dr. FRANKLIN. And then, on June 25, 1787, on the question to agree "that the members of the second branch of the Legislature of the United States be chosen by the individual Legislatures," the vote was taken.

Ayes—9; noes—2, with Pennsylvania and Virginia voting "no." This was the eighty-seventh vote of the Convention.

Mr. MADISON. It must be kept in view that the largest states, particularly Pennsylvania and Virginia, always considered the choice of the second branch—the Senate—by the state legislatures as opposed to a proportional representation, as a fundamental principle of just government.

Dr. FRANKLIN. We turn now to the debates on the basis of voting in the Senate—shall it be by proportional representation or by equal vote of the states, or some other procedure?

Mr. MADISON. A sampling of these debates should be sufficient for our purposes.

On June 11 it had been moved by Mr. Robert Sherman and seconded by Mr. Oliver Ellsworth, both of Connecticut, "That in the second branch of the National Legislature each State have one vote." This resolution did not pass. It was then moved by Mr. Wilson and seconded by Mr. Hamilton to adopt the following resolution, namely, "Resolved that the right of suffrage in the second branch of the National Legislature ought to be according to the rule established for the first." It passed in the affirmative: Ayes—6, noes—5.

Mr. THOMSON. (To the spectators) Roger Sherman's proposal lost that day, but it probably saved the Convention shortly thereafter when Sherman's proposal became the basis for a major compromise. Sherman was a New Englander who looked and acted the part. At sixty-six he was tall, lean, and sharp-nosed. His dark hair, streaked with gray and cut straight across the forehead, hung to his collar; he was plainly dressed. His hands and feet were big; his gestures, someone noted, "rigid as buckram." Yet in the craggy face was dignity, the widespaced brown eyes had depth behind them. "That old Puritan, honest as an angel," John Adams said of Sherman. Jefferson, pointing him out to a visitor in Congress, had remarked, "That is Mr. Robert Sherman of Connecticut, who never said a foolish thing in his life." The son of a shoemaker and in youth apprenticed to his father, Sherman had risen through farming and the law and had been a signer of the Declaration of Independence. People liked to tell stories about him, how as a young politician he used to advise his colleagues, "When you are in a minority, talk; when you are in a majority, vote." How, when he was asked one time to make a speech at the opening of a new bridge, he walked onto the bridge, turned around and came back. "I don't see but it stands steady," he told a waiting audience—and that was all he said.

Mr. MADISON. By June 30 the rules for voting in the first branch—the House of Representatives—had been established on the principle of proportional representation. Mr. James Wilson of Pennsylvania supported this principle and argued against an equal vote in the second branch—the Senate.

Gen. WASHINGTON. The chair will recognize Mr. James Wilson.

MR. WILSON. I would like to read the statement I made then. "Gentlemen have said, that if this amendment is not agreed to, a separation to the north of Pennsylvania may be the consequence. This neither staggers me in my sentiments or my duty. If a minority should refuse their assent to the new plan of a general government, and if they will have their own will, and without it, separate the union, let it be done; but we shall stand supported by stronger and better principles. The opposition to this plan is as 22 is to 90, in the general scale—not quite a fourth part of the union. Shall three-fourths of the union surrender their rights for the support of that artificial being, called state interest? . . . I cannot consent that one-fourth shall control the power of three-fourths.

If the motion is adopted, seven States will control the whole, and the lesser seven compose 24 out of 90. One-third must control two-thirds—24 overrule 66. For whom do we form a constitution, for men, or for imaginary beings called States, a mere metaphysical distinction? If we proceed on any other foundation than the last, our building will neither be solid nor lasting. Weight and numbers is the only true principle—every other is local, confined or imaginary. Much has been said of the danger of the three larger States combining together to give rise to monarchy, or an aristocracy. Let the probability of this combination be explained, and it will be found that a rivalship rather than a confederacy will exist among them. Is there a single point in which this interest coincides? Supposing that the Executive should be selected from one of the larger States, can the other two be gratified? Will not this be a source of jealousy amongst them, and will they not separately court the interest of the smaller States to counteract the views of a favorite rival? How can an aristocracy arise from this combination more than amongst the smaller States? On the contrary, the present claims of the smaller States lead directly to the establishment of an aristocracy, which is the government of the few over the many. . . . There are only two kinds of bad governments—the one which does too much, and is therefore oppressive, and the other which does too little, and is therefore weak. Congress partakes of the latter, and the motion will leave us in the same situation and as much fettered as ever we were. The people see its weakness, and would be mortified in seeing our inability to correct. . . . We all aim at giving the general government more energy. The state governments are necessary and valuable. No liberty can be obtained without them. On this question depend the essential rights of the general government and of the people."

Mr. MADISON. Mr. Ellsworth, do you wish to respond to Mr. Wilson?

Mr. ELLSWORTH. Indeed. I said then that "I have the greatest respect for the gentleman who spoke last. I respect his abilities, although I differ from him on many points. He asserts that the general government must depend on the equal suffrage of the people. But will not this put it in the power of few states to control the rest? It is a novel thing in politics that the few control the many. . . . Where is, or was a confederation ever formed, where equality of voice was not a fundamental principle? Mankind are apt to go from one extreme to another, and because we have found defects in the Confederation, must we therefore pull down the whole fabric foundation and all, in order to erect a new building totally different from it, without retaining any of its materials?

What are its defects? It is said equality of votes has embarrassed us; but how? Would the real evils of our situation have been cured, had not this been the case? Would the proposed amendment in the Virginia Plan, as to representation, have relieved us? I fancy not. Rhode Island has been often quoted as a small State and by its refusal once defeated the grant of the impost. Whether she was right in so doing is not the question; but was it a federal requisition? And if it was not, she did not in this instance defeat a federal measure.

"If the larger States seek security, they have it fully in the first branch of the general government. But can we turn the tables and say that the lesser States are equally secure? In commercial regulations they will unite. In the disposition of lucrative offices, they would unite. But I ask no surrender of any of the rights of the great States, nor do I plead duress on the makers of the old confederation, nor suppose they soothed the dangers in order to resume their rights when the danger was over. No; small states must possess the power of self defense or be ruined. Will anyone say there is no diversity of interests in the states. And if there is, should not those interests be guarded and secured? But if there is none, then the larger states have nothing to apprehend from an equality of rights. And let it be remembered, that these remarks are not the result of partial or local views. The State I represent is respectable and in importance holds a middle rank."

Mr. MADISON. I responded by saying: "Notwithstanding the admirable and close reasoning of the gentlemen who spoke last . . . I apprehend he is mistaken as to the facts on which he builds one of his arguments. . . . He . . . appeals to our good faith for the observance of the confederacy. We know we have found it inadequate to the purposes for which it was made—why then adhere to a system which is proved to be so remarkably defective? I have impeached a number of states for the infraction of the confederation, and I have not even spared my own state, nor can I justly spare his. Did not Connecticut refuse her compliance to a federal requisition? Has she paid, for the last two years, any money into the continental treasury? And does this look like government, or the observance of a solemn compact? Experience shows that the confederation is radically defective, and we must in a new national government guard against such defects. Although the large states in the first branch have a weight proportionate to their population, . . . if the smaller states have an equal vote in the second branch, they will be able to control and leave the larger without any essential benefit...."

Mr. ELLSWORTH. My state, Connecticut, had always been strictly federal. The muster rolls showed that she had more troops in the field than even the state of Virginia. We strained every nerve to raise them; and we spared neither money nor exertions to complete our quotas.

This extraordinary exertion greatly distressed and impoverished us, and it accumulated our state debts. But we defied any gentleman to show that we ever refused a federal requisition. We constantly exerted ourselves to draw money from the pockets of our citizens, as fast as it came in; and it was the ardent wish of the state to strengthen the federal government. If she proved delinquent through inability only, it was not more than others had been, without the same excuse.

Gen. WASHINGTON. The chair recognizes Mr. Jonathan Dayton, delegate from the state of New Jersey.

Mr. DAYTON. In this debate I observed that "Declamation has been substituted for argument. Have gentlemen shown, or must we believe it, because it is said, that one of the evils of the old confederation was unequal representation? We, as distinct Societies, entered into the compact. Will you now undermine the thirteen pillars that support it?"

Mr. MADISON. I questioned whether experience had evinced any good in the old confederation. I knew that question could never be answered, and I therefore made use of bold language against it.

Gen. WASHINGTON. The chair recognizes Mr. Gunning Bedford, delegate from Delaware.

MR. PIERCE. (To the spectators) Mr. Bedford was educated for the bar, and in his profession, I am told, had merit. He was a bold and nervous speaker, and had a very commanding and striking manner; but he was warm and impetuous in his temper, and precipitate in his judgment. Mr. Bedford was about thirty-two years old when he attended the Federal Convention, and very corpulant.

Mr. BEDFORD. On this issue I stated: "That all the states at present are equally sovereign and independent has been asserted from every quarter of this house. Our deliberations here are a confirmation of the position; and I may add to it, that each of them act from interested, and many from ambitious, motives. Impartiality, with them, is already out of the question . . . the three great states form nearly a majority of the people of America. . . . I do not, gentlemen, trust you. If you possess the power, the abuse of it could not be checked. . . . 'The larger states,' you say, 'all differ in productions and commerce; and experience shows that instead of combinations, they would be rivals, and counteract the views of one another.' This, I repeat, is language calculated only to amuse us. Yes, sir, the larger states will be rivals, but not against each other—they will be rivals against the rest of the States. . . . Has it come to this, then, that the sword must decide this controversy and that the horrors of war must be added to the rest of our misfortunes? . . . And are we to be told, if we won't agree to it, it is the last moment of our deliberations? I say, it is indeed the last moment if we do agree to this assumption of power. The states will never again be entrapped into a measure like this. The people will say the small states would confederate and grant further powers to Congress; but you, the large states, would not. Then the fault will be yours, and all the nations of the earth will justify us. But what is to become of our public debts if we dissolve the union? Where is your plighted faith? Will you crush the smaller states or must they be left unmolested? Sooner than be ruined, there are foreign powers who will take us by the hand. I say this not to threaten or intimidate, but that we should reflect seriously before we act. If we once leave this floor, and solemnly renounce your new project, what will be the consequence? You will annihilate your federal government, and ruin must stare you in the face. Let us then do what is in our power—amend and enlarge the confederation but not alter the federal system. The people expect this and no more. We all agree in the necessity of a more efficient government—and cannot this be done? Although my state is small, I know and respect its rights, as much, at least, as those who have the honor to represent any of the larger states."

Mr. Rufus KING. I was concerned for what fell upon the gentleman from Delaware to say—"Take a foreign power by the hand!" I was sorry he mentioned it, and I hoped he was able to excuse it to himself on the basis of passion. Whatever may have been my distress, I never would have courted a foreign power to assist in relieving myself from it.

Mr. ADAMS. When a great question is first stated there are very few, even of the greatest minds, who suddenly and instinctively comprehend it in all its consequences.

Dr. FRANKLIN. And so, it went on and on and on—increasing anger, passion—without conclusion—without decision. Is it any wonder, then, that I proposed prayers?

MR. THOMSON. (To the spectators) At this time, William R. Davie wrote to the governor of his state, North Carolina, "We move slowly in our business; it is indeed a work of great delicacy and difficulty, impeded at every step by jealousies and jarring interest." And James McHenry of Maryland wrote to his wife, "We are beginning to enter seriously upon the business of the convention, so that I shall have but little time to give my Peggy."

Dr. FRANKLIN. The diversity of opinions turned on two points. If a proportional representation took place, the small states contended that their liberties would be in danger. If an equality of votes was to be put in its place, the large states said their money would be in danger. I said, when a board table is to be made, and the edges of planks do not fit, the artist takes a little from both, and makes a good joint. In like manner, I said, both sides must part with some of their demands, in order that they may join in some accommodating proposition.

Well, on July 2, 1787, we hit a blue note by a bad vote. It was moved and seconded to agree to the following resolution: "Resolved that in the Second Branch of the legislature of the United States each State shall have an equal vote." It failed to pass.

General Pinckney proposed that a committee consisting of a member from each state should be appointed to devise and report some compromise. It was so moved, seconded, and passed, and I was one of the members of the committee. On July 3 the grand committee met, and on July 5 submitted its report to the Convention:

"That the subsequent propositions be recommended to the Convention, on condition that both shall be adopted. First, that . . . all Bills for raising or appropriating money and for fixing the salaries of the officers of the Government of the United States, shall originate in the first Branch of the Legislature, and shall not be altered or amended by the Second Branch—and that no money shall be drawn from the public Treasury but in pursuance of appropriations to be originated by the first Branch.

"Secondly, that in the second Branch of the Legislature each State shall have a equal vote."

Mr. Nathanial Gorham called for an explanation of the principles on which the decision was grounded.

Mr. James Wilson thought the Committee has exceeded their powers, saying, "I do not choose to take a leap in the dark."

Mr. Madison said: "I must confess I see nothing of concession in it. The originating of money bills is no concession on the part of the smaller States. . . . When we satisfy the majority of the people in securing their rights, we have nothing to fear; in any other way, everything. The smaller States, I hope will at last see their true and real interest."

They then called on me, as a committee member, to defend the compromise. I did not mean to go into a justification of the report; but as it had been asked what would be the use of restraining the second branch from meddling with money bills, I could not but remark that it was always of importance that the people should know who had disposed of their money and how it had been disposed of. It was a maxim that those who feel, can best judge. This end, I thought, would be best attained, if money affairs were confined to the immediate representatives of the people. This was my inducement to concur in the report. As to the danger or difficulty that might arise from a negative in the second branch, where the people would not be proportionally represented, I said that it might easily be got over by declaring that there should be no such negative or, if that would not do, by declaring that there shall be no second Branch at all—no Senate.

Finally, on July 16, the report of the grand committee, with some changes, was voted on. The result:

Ayes	Noes	Divided
Connecticut	Pennsylvania	Massachusetts
New Jersey	Virginia	
Delaware	South Carolina	
Maryland	Georgia	
North Carolina		

The tally: Ayes—5; noes—4; divided—1.

The resolution that in the second branch of the legislature of the United States each state should have one vote had been approved.

Mr. ADAMS. Let us look at the aftermath of opinions and then have Dr. Franklin summarize his position.

In March 1836 Mr. Madison looked back and summarized the situation in the Convention: "It is well known that the equality of the States in the Federal Senate was a compromise between the larger and the smaller States, the former claiming a proportional representation in both branches of the Legislature, as due to their superior population; the latter an equality in both as a safeguard to the reserved sovereignty of the States, an object which obtained the concurrence of members from the larger States." As early as October 1787, Mr. Madison explained that the issue "created more embarrassment and a greater alarm for the issue of the Convention than all the rest put together. The little States insisted on retaining their equality in both branches. ... It ended in the compromise ... very much to the dissatisfaction of several members from the larger States."

Two days after the Constitution was signed, Nicholas Gilman wrote to Joseph Gilman, "it was done by bargain and compromise, yet notwithstanding its imperfections, on the adoption of it depends, in my feeble judgment, whether we shall become a respectable nation or a people torn to pieces by intestine commotions and rendered contemptible for ages."

During the ratification debates in Pennsylvania, Mr. James Wilson said of the system, "the Senators, sir, those tyrants that are to devour the legislatures of the States, are to be chosen by the State Legislatures themselves. Need anything more be said on this subject? So far is the principle of each state's retaining the power of self-preservation from being weakened or endangered by the general government that the Convention went further, perhaps, than was strictly proper, in order to secure it; for, in this Second Branch of the legislature, each State, without regard to its importance, is entitled to an equal vote. And in the articles respecting amendments of this Constitution, it is provided 'that no State, without its consent, shall be deprived of its equal suffrage in the Senate.'

"Does it appear, then, that provision for the continuance of the State governments was neglected, in framing this Constitution? On the contrary, it was a favorite object in the Convention to secure them."

And to this day, some two hundred years later, Article V of the Constitution still provides "that no State, without its Consent, shall be deprived of its equal suffrage in the Senate."

But back then the matter was hotly contested. In the ratification debates in North Carolina, Mr. James Iredell stated: "Our senators will not be chosen by a King, nor tainted by his influence. They are to be chosen by different legislatures in the Union. Each is to choose two. It is to be supposed that, in the exercise of this power, the utmost prudence and circumspection will be observed. We may presume that they will select two of the most respectable men in the State; two men who had given the strongest proofs of attachment to the interests of their country. The senators are not to hold estates for life in the legislature nor to transmit them to their children. Their families, friends, and estates will be pledges for their fidelity to their country. Holding no other office under the United States, they will be under no temptation of that kind to forget the interest of their constituents."

In the ratification debates in the state of New York, Mr. R. R. Livingston observed, "consider but a moment the purposes for which the Senate was instituted. . . . The Senate are designed to represent the State governments. . . . They, together with the President, are to manage all our concerns with foreign nations. . . ." Mr. Alexander Hamilton added, "Sir, the Senators will constantly be attended with a reflection that their future existence is absolutely in the power of the states. Will not this form a powerful check? It is a reflection which applies closely to their feelings and interest; and no candid man, who thinks deliberately, will deny that it would be alone a sufficient check. The State Legislatures are to provide the mode of electing the President and must have a great influence over the electors. Indeed, they convey their influence, through a thousand channels, into the general government."

Mr. Moses Ames, in the Massachusetts debates on ratification, said that "the Senators represent the sovereignty of the States; in the other house, individuals are represented. The Senate may not originate bills. It need not be said that they are principally to direct the affairs of wars and treaties. They are in the quality of ambassadors of the states."

Mr. William R. Davie, in the ratification debates in North Carolina observed: "The Senators represent the sovereignty of the States; they are directly chosen by the state legislatures, and no legislative act can be done without their concurrence. The election of the executive is in some measure under the control of the legislatures of the states, the electors being appointed under their direction."

Mr. MADISON. Let me read my notes on Mr. Gouverneur Morris's statements in the Federal Convention on

July 5, 1787. Mr. Morris thought state importance had been the bane of our country.

He conceived the whole apsect of it to be wrong. He came here as a Representative of America; he flattered himself that he came here in some degree as a Representative of the whole human race; for the whole human race will be affected by the proceedings of this Convention. He wished gentlemen to extend their views beyond the present moment of time; beyond the narrow limits of place from which they derive their political origin. If he were to believe some things which he had heard, he should suppose that we were assembled to truck and bargain for our particular States. We cannot descend to think that any gentlemen are really actuated by these views. We must look forward to the efforts of what we do. These alone ought to guide us. Much has been said of the sentiments of the people. They were unknown. They could not be known. All that we can infer is that if the plan we recommend be reasonable and right, all who have reasonable minds and sound intentions will embrace it, notwithstanding what had been said by some gentlemen. . . .

The Country must be united. If persuasion does not unite it, the sword will. He begged that this consideration might have its due weight. The scenes of horror attending civil commotion can not be described, and the conclusion of them will be worse than the term of their continuance. . . . As the second branch is now constituted, there will be constant disputes and appeals to the States which will undermine the General Government and Control and annihilate the first branch. . . . State attachments and State importance have been the bane of this Country. We cannot annihilate; but we may perhaps take out the teeth of the serpents. He wished our ideas to be enlarged to the true interest of man, instead of being circumscribed within the narrow compass of a particular spot. And after all how little can be the motive yielded by selfishness for such a policy? Who can say whether he himself, much less whether his children, will the next year be an inhabitant of this or that State?"

Mr. ADAMS. Mr. Morris failed in his objective here. Is it possible that this type of thinking was perpetuated by him in other matters before the Convention?

Gen. WASHINGTON. Mr. Adams, these sessions are factual, not fictional. We are here to evaluate, not speculate. The question is out of order.

Dr. FRANKLIN. At the beginning of today's session I claimed that there was no justification for the existence of the Senate in its present capacity and that its purpose, composition, structure, and legal functions should be overhauled. I cited links of a chain of events on which I based my claim and then set out in today's session to discuss the first claim: that the states gained control of the Senate by providing for the selection of senators by the state legislatures. I am of the opinion that we have entered upon the records of the session today sufficient testimony to justify my first claim.

The second link in my chain of events I expect will be discussed tomorrow; that the states gained control of the president by providing in the Constitution for the sharing of powers between the president and the Senate.

Lest we lose sight of our ultimate objective, let us remember that the entire chain collapsed when the Seventeenth Amendment broke the main link by providing that Senators be chosen by the people, not the state legislatures. Yet all other provisions in the chain of state powers remained in existence, but without the power of the state to act or influence. They still remain today, without purpose.

Before this session adjourns for the day I would like to read to you a speech given by the Honorable Mr. Josiah Smith in the debates in Massachusetts on the ratification of the Federal Constitution.

"Mr. President, I am a plain man and get my living by the plough. I am not used to speaking in public, but I beg your leave to say a few words to my brother plough joggers in this house. I have lived in a part of the country where I have known the worth of good government by the want of it. . . . Now, Mr. President, when I saw this Constitution, I found that it was a cure for these disorders. It was just such a thing as we wanted. I got a copy of it and read it over and over. I had been a member of the Convention to form our own State constitution and had learnt something of the checks and balances of power, and I found them all here. I did not go to any lawyer to ask his opinion; we have no lawyer in our town, and we do well enough without. I formed my own opinion and was pleased with this Constitution. My honorable old daddy there won't think that I expect to be a Congressman and swallow up the liberties of the people. I never had any post, nor do I want one. But I don't think the worse of the Constitution because lawyers, and men of learning, and moneyed men, are fond of it. I don't suspect that they want to get into Congress and abuse their power. I am not of such a jealous make. They that are honest men themselves are not apt to suspect other people. I don't know why our constituents have not a good right to be as jealous of us, as we seem to be of the Congress; and I think those gentlemen, who are so very suspicious that as soon as a man gets into power he turns rogue, had better look at home.

"We are by this Constitution allowed to send ten members to Congress. Have we not more than that number fit to go? I dare say, if we pick out ten, we shall have another ten left, and I hope ten times ten; and will not these be a check upon those that go? Will they go to Congress, and abuse their power, and do mischief, when they know they must return and look the other ten in the face and be called to account for their conduct? Some gentlemen think that our liberty and property are not safe in the hands of moneyed men and men of learning. I am not of that mind.

"Brother farmers, let us suppose a case, now: Suppose you had a farm of 50 acres, and your title was disputed, and there was a farm of 5,000 acres joined to you that belonged to a man of learning, and his title was involved in the same difficulty; would you not be glad to have him for your friend, rather than to stand alone in the dispute? Well, the case is the same. These lawyers, these moneyed men, these men of learning, are all embarked in the same cause with us, and we must all swim or sink together; and shall we throw the Constitution overboard because it does not please us alike? Suppose two or three of you had been at the pains to break up a piece of rough land and sow it with wheat; would you let it lie waste because you could not agree what sort of a fence to make? Would it not be better to put up a fence that did not please every one's fancy, rather than not fence it at all, or keep disputing about it until the wild beasts came in and devoured it? Some gentlemen say, Don't be in a hurry; take time to consider, and don't take a leap in the dark. I say, take things in time; gather fruit when it is ripe. There is a time to sow and a time to reap; we sowed our seed when we sent men to the Federal Convention; now is the harvest, now is the time to reap the fruit of our labor; and if we won't do it now, I am afraid we never shall have another opportunity."

Thank you gentlemen, for letting me read this to you.

Gen. WASHINGTON. This session is adjourned until tomorrow, Friday, July 3, at 10 a.m.

FRIDAY, JULY 3, 1987

THE CHADHA CASE

The Committee met pursuant to notice, at 10 a.m. in the Assembly Room of Independence Hall, Gen. George Washington presiding.

Present: Mr. John Adams, Dr. Benjamin Franklin, Mr. Thomas Jefferson, Mr. James Madison and Gen. George Washington.

Mr. THOMSON. (To the spectators) While we wait for the Commission to assemble, let me describe the way in which the seat of the government was determined. The Constitution says that "The Congress shall have power . . . to exercise exclusive Legislation in all cases whatsoever, over such District (not exceeding ten miles square) as may, by Cession of particular States, and the Acceptance of Congress, become the Seat of the Government of the United States . . ."

The location was reached in a peculiar manner during General Washington's term as president. Thomas Jefferson, Alexander Hamilton, and James Madison worked out an arrangement whereby in return for the Southerners accepting assumption of state debts, there would be Northern support for locating the permanent capital of the country in the South, at a site on the banks of the Potomac River, to be selected by General Washington. As a sop to Pennsylvania politicians, the capital was to be moved from New York City to Philadelphia until the new city on the Potomac was ready. Within a few weeks the bills to move the capital and to approve the funding measures were passed by Congress.

It took years to build the new city, and although General Washington never lived in the White House, he once said: "I had rather be at Mount Vernon with a friend or two about me than to be attended at the Seat of Government by the Officers of State and the Representatives of every Power in Europe."

Gen. WASHINGTON. This session will come to order. Dr. Franklin.

Dr. FRANKLIN. We have observed some difficulty among the delegates in the Federal Convention to maintain a reasonable degree of civility among themselves. In this connection, I am reminded of a story I once told.

A Swedish minister, having assembled the chiefs of the Susquehanah Indians, made a sermon to them, acquainting them with the principal historical facts on which our religion is founded, such as the fall of our first parents by eating an apple, the coming of Christ to repair the mischief, his miracles and suffering. When the minister had finished, an Indian orator stood up to thank him. "What you have told us," says he, "is all very good. It is indeed bad to eat apples. It is better to make them all into cider. We are much obliged by your kindness in coming so far to tell us these things which you have heard from your mothers. In return, I will tell you some of those we have heard from ours. In the beginning, our fathers had only the flesh of animals to subsist on; and if their hunting was unsuccessful, they were starving. Two of our young hunters, having killed a deer, made a fire in the woods to broil some part of it. When they were about to satisfy their hunger, they beheld a beautiful young woman descend from the clouds and seat herself on that hill, which you see yonder among the Blue Mountains. They said to each other, it is a Spirit that has smelt our broiling venison and wishes to eat of it; let us offer some to her. They presented her with the tongue; she was pleased with the taste of it, and said, 'Your kindness will be rewarded; come to this place after thirteen moons, and you shall find something that will be of great benefit in nourishing you and your children to the latest generations.' They did so and, to their surprise, found plants they had never seen before but which from the ancient time have been constantly cultivated among us, to our great advantage. Where her right hand touched the ground, they found maize; where her left hand touched it, they found kidney-beans; and where her backside had sat on it, they found tobacco." The good missionary, disgusted with this idle tale, said, "What I delivered to you were sacred truths, but what you tell me is mere Fable, Fiction, and Falsehood." The Indian, offended, replied, "My brother, it seems your friends have not done you justice in your education; they have not well instructed you in the rules of common civility. You saw that we, who understood and practice those rules, believed all your stories, why do you refuse to believe ours?" Let us, then, listen with some care to each other's stories as we continue here today.

Lest we lose track of my objective, at our last session I claimed that there was no justification for the continued existence of the Senate in its present capacity, that the purpose for which the Senate was established ceases to exist. I claimed the Senate was established to serve the states—that the states gained control of the Senate by providing for the selection of Senators by the state legislature—and this was evidenced by testimony at our last session.

Let us remember that the entire chain of control collapsed when the main link was broken by the Seventeenth Amendment, which provided that the Senators were to be chosen by the people, not the state legislature. Hence, the original purpose for its establishment no longer exists.

It is therefore my contention that the Senate can best serve the nation by being converted into a Constitutional Council to the president of the United States.

Today, it is my intention to establish that the states gained control of the president by providing for the sharing of powers between the Senate and the president.

The applicable portion of the Constitution reads in part:

"The President . . . shall have Power, by and with the Advice and Consent of the Senate, to make Treaties provided two-thirds of the Senators present concur; and he shall nominate, and by and with the Advice and Consent of the Senate, shall appoint Ambassadors, other public Ministers and Consuls, Judges of the Supreme Court, and all other officers of the United States, whose Appointments are not herein otherwise provided for and which shall be established by Law . . ."

Thus, three key functions of government are shared by the Senate and the president; first, the making of treaties; second, the appointment of judges; and third, the appointment of certain officers of government.

Mr. Madison, you kept the notes. Would you kindly take the floor?

Mr. MADISON. Again, instead of burdening the record with day-to-day matters on this subject, let us place the bits of information in a kaleidoscope and look at the endless variety of patterns of thought on this question of shared powers.

On June 1, 1787, I moved that, in Mr. Edmund Randolph's Plan, after the words "a National Executive ought to be instituted," there be inserted the words "with power to carry into effect the national laws, to appoint to offices in cases not otherwise provided for, and to execute such other powers, not legislative or judiciary in their nature, as may from time to time be delegated by the National Legislature." It was then moved by Mr. Pinckney that the words "not legislative or judiciary in their nature" be delegated. My motion was approved, as was Mr. Pinckney's. Clearly, the inclusion of the deleted phrase would have emphasized a proposition already discussed before this Commission, that regulations drafted by any of the executive departments could not include substantive provisions—provisions which would encroach upon the legislative prerogatives of Congress—and would have more clearly restricted the executive departments to what they should have been doing, namely, administering the laws. I clearly had in mind then the concept of the legitimate scope of delegation of authority by Congress.

Mr. Alexander Hamilton, on June 18, proposed an intertwining of the senate's and the president's powers: "The authorities and functions of the Executive to be as follows: . . . to have, with the advice and approbation of the Senate, the power of making all treaties; to have the sole appointment of the heads or chief officers of the departments of Finance, War, and Foreign Affairs; to have the nomination of all other officers (Ambassadors to foreign Nations included) subject to the approbation or rejection of the Senate. . . ."

Mr. ADAMS. Mr. Madison, you referred before to the Randolph Plan—can you elaborate?

Mr. PIERCE. (Aside to spectators) Mr. Edmund Randolph was governor of Virginia—a young gentleman in whom was united all the accomplishments of the scholar and the statesman. He came forward with the postulate, or first principles, on which the Convention acted, and he supported them with a force of eloquence and reasoning that did him great honor. He had a most harmonious voice, a fine person and striking manners. Mr. Randolph was about thirty-two years of age when he attended the Convention.

Mr. MADISON. The propositions of Mr. Randolph were the result of a consultation among the seven Virginia deputies, of which I was one, and of which he, being at the time governor of the state, was the organ. The propositions were prepared on the supposition that, considering the prominent agency of Virginia in bringing about the Federal Convention, some initiative step might be expected from that quarter. It was meant that they should sketch a real and adequate government for the union but without committing the parties against the freedom of discussion and decision. The Journal shows that the Randolph Plan was in fact the basis of the deliberations and proceedings of the Convention.

Continuing, on July 17, I said that if it be essential to the preservation of liberty that the legislative, executive and judiciary powers be separate, it was essential to a maintenance of the separation that they should be independent of each other. A dependence of the executive on the legislature would render it the executor as well as the maker of laws and, as Montesquieu observed, tyrannical laws may be made that they may be executed in a tyrannical manner.

Mr. THOMSON. (To the spectators) On Saturday, July 21, 1787, the *Pennsylvania Journal* published the following: "So great is the unanimity, we hear, that prevails in the Convention, upon all great Federal subjects, that it has been proposed to call the room in which they assemble—Unanimity Hall."

"Unanimity Hall?" It was more like an oratorical brawl!

Mr. ADAMS. The thought of unsettled matters in the 1780s still being unsettled in the 1980s is unsettling. Two thoughts have just been posited, which I place in juxtaposition for our benefit:

First, Mr. Madison stated that the had moved that, in Mr. Edmund Randolph's Plan, after the words "a National Executive ought to be instituted," there be inserted the words "with power to carry into effect the national laws . . . and to execute such other powers, not legislative or judiciary in their nature, as may from time to time be delegated by the National Legislature." Mr. Pinckney then moved that the words "not legislative or judiciary in their nature" be deleted. This proposition would have granted powers to the president expressly "not legislative or judiciary in their nature." In essence, the power to execute laws—not make laws.

Second, Mr. Madison then noted that on July 17 he stated "if it be essential . . . that the legislative, executive and judiciary powers be separate, it is essential to a maintenance of the separation, that they should be independent of each other . . . a dependence of the executive on the legislative would render it the executor as well as the maker of laws." This proposition expressed concern that a dependence of the president on Congress would make Congress the executor of laws as well as the maker of laws. In essence, Congress should make the laws—not execute them.

I sensed an everlasting problem in an intertwining of powers. Remember, I was not at the Federal Convention. I was in Britain at the time. But on March 1, 1789, I wrote Mr. Jefferson from Braintree:

"In four days the new Government is to be erected. . . . Amendments to the Constitution will be expected and no doubt discussed. . . . That greatest and most necessary of all Amendments [is] the separation of the Executive Power from the legislative. . . . Without this our government is in danger of being a continual struggle. . ."

Mr. THOMSON. (To the spectators) Mr. Adams just stated that "In four days the new Government is to be erected." Actually the first House of Representatives did not secure a quorum until April 1, nor the first Senate until April 6. President Washington and Vice-President Adams were inaugurated on April 30.

Mr. ADAMS. (Continuing) Yes, all that took place in the 1780s. Let's move forward two hundred years. On June 23, 1983, the Supreme Court of the United States decided one of its most significant cases—bearing totally on matters we have been discussing—the separation of powers. I call it the "The Chadha Case." The opinion of the Supreme Court is important for our purposes here.

The facts are these: The Immigration and Nationality Act authorized either house of Congress, by resolution, to invalidate the decision of the executive branch to allow a particular deportable alien to remain in the United States. In effect, the Act granted Congress a "legislative veto."

Mr. JEFFERSON. (To the spectators) If I may explain, under the "legislative veto" Congress drafts a statute broadly but incorporates a provision reserving a right to review the executive branch's implementation of the law. The provision permits one or both houses of Congress—or even a single committee—to block any actions with which they disagree. It grants Congress a great deal of power, as you will see.

Mr. ADAMS. (Continuing) Ragdish Rai Chadha, an alien who had been lawfully admitted to the United States on a nonimmigrant student visa, remained in the United States after his visa had expired and was ordered by the Immigration and Naturalization Service (INS) to show cause why he should not be deported. Chadha applied for suspension of the deportation and, after a hearing, an immigration judge ordered the suspension and reported the suspension to Congress as required by law.

Thereafter, the House of Representatives vetoed the suspension, and the immigration judge reopened the deportation proceedings. Chadha moved to terminate the proceedings on the ground that the Act, to the extent that it authorized either house of Congress to invalidate the decision of the executive branch, was unconstitutional. The judge held that he had no authority to rule on its constitutionality and ordered Chadha deported pursuant to the House Resolution. Chadha then filed a petition for review of the deportation order in the Court of Appeals, and the INS joined him in arguing that the Act was unconstitutional. The Court of Appeals held that the applicable section of the Act violated the constitutional doctrine of separation of powers and, accordingly, directed the attorney general to cease taking any steps to deport Chadha based on the House Resolution.

The Supreme Court granted certiorari and held that the Congressional veto provision of the Immigration and Nationality Act was unconstitutional by a 7 to 2 decision. Chief Justice Warren E. Burger delivered the opinion of the Court, Justices Byron Raymond White and William Hubbs Rehnquist dissenting.

The majority and dissenting opinions both contain statements relating to the Federal Convention of 1787 and to the work of this Commission. It is appropriate, therefore, that we review the Supreme Court decision in the Chadha case. For this purpose Chief Justice Burger and Justice White have kindly consented to participate in this session and share their respective views on this landmark case. Gentlemen, we welcome you, and express our thanks for the time you have taken from your heavy schedule. Mr. Jefferson, will you initiate the questioning?

Mr. THOMSON. (To the Spectators.) Immediately to the east of the Pennsylvania State House, in which we now sit, is the Supreme Court building which was occupied by the Supreme Court of the United States between 1791 and 1800. At its first session John Jay presided as chief justice. Here the court began its active work, laying the foundation for the development of the judicial branch of the Federal government. John Marshall and Alexander Hamilton each presented one case before the Supreme

Court in this building.

The Supreme court building is a two-story brick structure approximately fifty feet wide by sixty feet deep, with a peaked roof and a cupola in the middle of the roof. The building contained six rooms. When Philadelphia became the national capital, the new city hall became the seat of the Supreme Court of the United States. The funds for the erection of the new city hall were raised mainly from a lottery auuthorized by the Assembly on March 27, 1789. The lottery was to raise ten thousand dollars, of which eight thousand was to go to the City of Philadelphia and two thousand to Dickinson College, believe it or not!

Mr. JEFFERSON. Justice White, would you give us a sort of capsule history of the "legislative veto?"

Justice WHITE. I thank you for the compliment— that a judge can give a capsule history of anything. However, I will try. The legislative veto developed initially in response to the problems of reorganizing the sprawling government structure created in response to the Depression. The Reorganization Acts established the chief model for the legislative veto. When President Hoover requested authority to reorganize the government in 1929, he coupled his request with a proposal for legislative review. Congress followed President Hoover's suggestion and authorized reorganization subject to legislative review.

Over the years, the provision was used extensively. Presidents submitted 115 reorganization plans to Congress, of which 23 were disapproved by Congress pursuant to legislative veto provisions.

During World War II, Congress enacted over thirty statutes conferring powers on the executive with legislative veto provisions. President Roosevelt accepted the veto as the necessary price for obtaining exceptional authority.

Over the quarter century following World War II, presidents continued to accept legislative vetoes by one or both Houses as constitutional, while regularly denouncing provisions by which Congressional committees reviewed executive activity. The legislative veto balanced delegations of statutory authority in new areas of governmental involvement: the space program, international agreements on nuclear energy, tariff arrangements, and adjustment of federal pay rates.

During the 1970s the legislative veto was important in resolving a series of major constitutional disputes between the president and Congress over claims of the president to broad impoundment, war, and national emergency powers. The key provisions of the War Powers Resolution authorized the termination, by concurrent resolution, of the use of armed forces in hostilities. A similar measure resolved the problem posed by presidential claims of inherent power to impound appropriations.

In the energy field, the legislative veto served to balance broad delegations in legislation emerging from the energy crisis of the 1970s. In the trade regulation area the veto preserved Congressional authority over the Federal Trade Commission's broad mandate to make rules to prevent businesses from engaging in "unfair or deceptive acts or practices in commerce."

Justice BURGER. The "convenience" of the legislative veto was not a legal avenue for government. The fact that a given law or procedure is efficient, convenient, and useful in facilitating functions of government, standing alone, will not save it if it is contrary to the Constitution. Convenience and efficiency are not the primary objectives—or the hallmarks—of democratic government and our inquiry is sharpened rather than blunted by the fact that Congressional veto provisions are appearing with increasing frequency in statutes which delegate authority to executive and independent agencies.

Justice WHITE. I disagree. You see, the legislative veto is more than "efficient, convenient and useful." It is an important if not indispensable political invention that allows the President and Congress to resolve major constitutional and policy differences, assures the accountability of independent regulatory agencies, and preserves Congress's control over lawmaking. Perhaps there are other means of accommodation and accountability, but the increasing reliance of Congress upon the legislative veto suggests that the alternatives to which Congress must now turn are not entirely satisfactory.

Justice BURGER. But I must point out that the veto

power legally belongs to the President, not to Congress. Explicit and unambiguous provisions of the Constitution prescribe and define the respective functions of the Congress and of the executive in the legislative process. These provisions are integral parts of the constitutional design for the separation of powers. We have recently noted that the principle of separation of powers was not simply an abstract generalization in the minds of the Framers; it was woven into the documents that they drafted in Philadelphia in the summer of 1787.

The records of the Constitutional Convention reveal that the requirement that legislation be presented to the president before becoming law was uniformly accepted by the Framers. Presentment to the president and the presidential veto were considered so imperative that the draftsmen took special pains to assure that these requirements could not be circumvented.

Justice WHITE. It is true that the purpose of separating the authority of government is to prevent unnecessary and dangerous concentration of power in one branch. For that reason, the Framers saw fit to divide and balance the powers of government so that each branch would be checked by the others. Virtually every part of our constitutional system bears the mark of this judgment.

But the history of the separation of powers doctrine is all a history of accommodation and practicality. Apprehensions of an overly powerful branch have not led to undue prophylatic measures that handicap the effective working of the national government as a whole. The Constitution does not contemplate total separation of the three branches of government. A hermetic sealing off of the three branches of government from one another would preclude the establishment of a nation capable of governing itself effectively.

I do not suggest that all legislative vetoes are necessarily consistent with separation of powers principles. But the legislative veto device here—and in many other settings—is far from an instance of legislative tyranny over the executive. It is a necessary check on the unavoidably expanding power of the agencies, both executive and independent, as they engage in exercising authority delegated by Congress.

The history of the legislative veto makes clear that it has not been a sword with which Congress has struck out to aggrandize itself at the expense of the other branches—the concerns of Madison and Hamilton. Rather, the veto has been a means of defense, a reservation of ultimate authority necessary if Congress is to fulfill its designated rule under Article I as the nation's lawmaker. While the president has often objected to particular legislative vetoes, generally those left in the hands of congressional committees, the executive has more often agreed to legislative review as the price for a broad delegation of authority. To be sure, the president may have preferred unrestricted power, but that could be precisely why Congress thought it essential to retain a check on the exercise of delegated authority.

The reality of the situation is that the constitutional question posed here is one of immense difficulty over which the executive branches—as well as scholars and judges—have understandably disagreed. That disagreement stems from the silence of the Constitution on the precise question: The Constitution does not directly authorize or prohibit the legislative veto.

If the veto devices so flagrantly disregarded the requirements of Article I as the Court suggests, I find it incomprehensible that Congress, whose members are bound by oath to uphold the Constitution, would have placed these mechanisms in nearly 200 separate laws over a period of 50 years.

Our task should be to determine whether the legislative veto is consistent with the purposes of Article I and the principles of separation of powers which are reflected in the Article and throughout the Constitution. We should not find the lack of a specific constitutional authorization for the legislative veto surprising, and I would not infer disapproval of the mechanism from its absence. From the summer of 1787 to the present, the government of the United States has become an endeavor far beyond the contemplation of the Framers. Only within the last half century has the complexity and size of the Federal government's responsibilities grown so greatly that the Congress must rely on the legislative veto as the most effective if not the only means to insure their role as the nation's lawmakers. But the wisdom of the Framers was to anticipate that the nation would grow and new problems of governance would require different solutions. Accordingly, our Federal government was intentionally chartered with the flexibility to respond to contemporary needs without losing sight of fundamental democratic principles.

In my view, neither Article I of the Constitution nor the doctrine of separation of powers is violated by this mechanism by which our elected representatives preserve their voice in the governance of the nation.

Justice BURGER. I disagree. Once a power is delegated to the Executive Branch it cannot be altered except by new legislation. Congress must abide by its delegation of authority until that delegation is legislatively altered or revoked.

Justice WHITE. The Court's holding that all legislative-type action must be enacted through the lawmaking process ignores that legislative authority is routinely delegated to the executive branch, to the independent regulatory agencies, and to private individuals and groups.

By virtue of congressional delegation, legislative power can be exercised by independent agencies and executive departments without the passage of new legislation. For some time, the sheer amount of law made by the agencies has far outnumbered the lawmaking engaged in by Congress through the traditional process. There is no question but that agency rulemaking is lawmaking in any functional or realistic sense of the term. Mr. Willard A. Weiss, who testified before this Commission, provided a blatant example of agency lawmaking in his discussion of the way regulations inconsistent with law are issued by the executive branch.

If Congress may delegate lawmaking power to independent and executive agencies, it is most difficult to understand Article I as forbidding Congress from also reserving a check on legislative power for itself. Absent the veto, the agencies receiving delegations of legislative or quasi-legislative power may issue regulations having the force of law without bicameral approval and without the president's signature. It is thus not apparent why the reservation of a veto over the exercise of that legislative power must be subject to a more exacting test.

The prominence of the legislative veto mechanism in our contemporary political system and its importance to Congress can hardly be overstated. It has become a central means by which Congress secures the accountability of executive and independent agencies. Without the legislative veto, Congress is faced with a Hobson's choice: either to refrain from delegating the necessary authority, leaving itself with a hopeless task of writing laws with the requisite specificity to cover endless special circumstances across the entire policy landscape, or in the alternative, to abdicate its lawmaking function to the executive branch and independent agencies. To choose the former leaves major national problems unresolved; to opt for the latter risks unaccountable policy-making by those not elected to fill that role. The device is know in every field of governmental concern: reorganization, budgets, foreign affairs, war powers, and regulation of trade, safety, energy, the environment and the economy.

Dr. FRANKLIN. I call your attention to one statement Justice White made that we have repeated many times before this Commission. Without the legislative veto, Congress leaves policy making to "those not elected to fill that role."

On July 1, 1987, before this Commission, I quoted Mr. Wilson Nicholas, delegate to the Virginia Convention considering the ratification of the Constitution in 1788, as saying: "No powers ought to be vested in the hands of any who are not representatives of the people, and amenable to them."

In July, 1983, Rep. Elliot H. Levitas of Georgia penned a letter to the *New York Times* deploring the Supreme Court's legislative veto decision as "simplistic."

The Congressman claimed that the legislative veto was an attempt by Congress to counter the explosion of administrative lawmaking in the 1970s. He wrote: "The Framers of our Constitution would be most surprised to find that regulations that have the force and effect of law are today actually developed and put into effect by unelected officials in the executive branch and in independent agencies rather than in Congress. . . . As this practice developed over the years, Congress attempted to redress the balance with the legislative veto."

Justice BURGER. The bicameral requirement, the president's veto, and Congress' power to override a veto, as provided in the Constitution, were intended to erect enduring checks on each branch and to protect the people from the improvident exercise of power by mandating certain prescribed steps. To preserve those checks, and maintain the separation of powers, the carefully defined limits on the power of each branch must not be eroded.

The Congressional veto doubtless has been in many respects a convenient shortcut, a "sharing" of authority. There is no support in the Constitution or decisions of the Supreme Court for the proposition that the cumbersomeness and delays often encountered in complying with explicit Constitutional standards may be avoided, either by the Congress or by the president. With all the obvious flaws of delay, untidiness, and potential for abuse we have not yet found a better way to preserve freedom than by making the exercise of power subject to the carefully crafted restraints spelled out in the Constitution.

We therefore held that the Congressional veto provision was unconstitutional.

Justice WHITE. With this decision the Court sounded the death knell for nearly 200 statutory provisions in which Congress reserved a 'legislative veto.'

I regret that I am in disagreement with my colleagues on the fundamental question that this case presents. But even more, I regret the destructive scope of the Court's holding. It reflects a profoundly different conception of the Constitution than that held by the Courts which sanctioned the modern administrative state. This decision strikes down in one fell swoop provisions in more laws enacted by Congress than the Court has cumulatively invalidated in its history. I fear it will now be more difficult "to insure that the fundamental policy decisions in our society will be made not by an appointed official but by the body immediately responsible to the people." I must dissent.

Mr. ADAMS. Thank you, Justice Burger and Justice White, for your valuable contributions to the work of this Commission. In my opinion this Commission would be remiss if it did not put to rest this "continual struggle" by recommending to the Congress of the United States an amendment to the Constitution allowing the Congress to exercise a "legislative veto" and at the same time preventing regulations drafted by any agency of the executive branch from including substantive provisions encroaching upon the legislative prerogatives of Congress; such an amendment would thereby require that such regulations drafted by agencies contain only such provisions as allow the laws to be faithfully executed. It is also reasonable to require that the Senate monitor compliance therewith for the Congress. In this manner, as Justice White suggested, "the fundamental policy decisions in our society will be made not by an appointed official but by the body immediately responsible to the people." To further prevent the executive branch from being a "lawmaker" it would be well to consider Mr. Randolph's original proposal to the Federal Convention to the effect that the president's powers not include any matter "legislative or judicial."

Dr. FRANKLIN. The Chadha case is an important addition to our perspective on government power. But as in my *Poor Richard's Almanack*, "like different clocks," the executive, legislative and judicial branches "may be . . . near the matter 'tho they don't quite agree."

Gen. WASHINGTON. Gentlemen, this session is adjourned until Monday, July 6 at 10 a.m.

MONDAY, JULY 6, 1987

THE PRESIDENT AND THE SENATE: SHARING OF POWERS

The Committee met pursuant to notice, at 10 a.m. in the Assembly Room of Independence Hall, Gen. George Washington presiding.

> Present: Mr. John Adams, Dr. Benjamin Franklin, Mr. Thomas Jefferson, Mr. James Madison and Gen. George Washington.

Gen. WASHINGTON. We ought not to look back, unless it is to derive useful lessons from past errors, and for the purpose of profiting by dear bought experience. To inveigh against things that are past and irremediable is unpleasing; but to steer clear of the shelves and rocks we have struck upon, is the part of wisdom.

Without a continuing aim to derive useful lessons, I ask Dr. Franklin to resume his discussion.

Dr. FRANKLIN. In a similar vein, I wrote in my *Poor Richard's Almanack*: "Experience keeps a dear school, yet Fools will learn in no other." Isn't 200 years of this "experience" stuff enough? Get wise America, before America is turned otherwise.

Mr. Madison wrote in 1835: "Our history, short as it is, has already disclosed great errors . . . and it may be expected to throw new lights on problems still to be decided." The Chadha case revealed a great error in history and an opportunity for the 1980s. It focused on the whole issue of laws that are handed down by non-elected lawmakers.

From Paris, Mr. Jefferson wrote to Mr. Adams on September 28, 1787:

"It is a misfortune that . . . our countrymen . . . do not sufficiently know the value of their constitutions and how much happier they are rendered by them than any other people on earth by the governments under which they live." Mr. Jefferson included state constitutions. He continued, "The first principle of a good government is certainly a distribution of its powers into executive, judiciary, and legislative, and a subdivision of the latter into two or three branches."

This brings us back on the track of the facts I am presenting. As far as Mr. Jefferson's division of the legislative branch goes, my ultimate objective is to leave the House intact but to let the Senate perform its legislative functions and also become the source of a Constitutional Council to the president. In pursuance of this objective, at our last session I was presenting the steps taken in the Federal Convention by the states to gain control of the president, only to lose that control by the Seventeenth Amendment, which eventually removed the original purpose for which the Senate was established. Let us return to my premise that the states gained control of the president by providing for a sharing of powers between the Senate and the president.

We were discussing the three key functions of government which are shared by the Senate and the president; first, the making of treaties; second, the appointment of judges; and third, the appointment of certain officers of government.

Mr. Madison will now discuss the sharing of powers between the Senate and the president insofar as it relates to the appointment of judges, based on the notes he took in the Federal Convention of 1787. Mr Madison.

Mr. MADISON. Thank you Dr. Franklin. Under Mr. Randolph's plan, judges were to be appointed by the Senate. The debate ran as follows.

Mr. Ghorum of Massachusetts preferred an appointment of the judges by the Senate to an appointment by the whole legislature, but he thought even the Senate was too numerous, and too little personally responsible, to ensure a good choice. He suggested that the judges be appointed by the president with the advice and consent of the Senate, in the mode prescribed by the Constitution of Massachusetts. This mode had been long practiced in the country, and was found to answer perfectly well.

Mr. Martin of Maryland was strenuous for the appointment of judges by the Senate. The Senate, being of all the states, would be best informed of characters and most capable of making a fit choice.

Mr. Mason thought the mode of appointing the judges should depend in some degree on the mode of trying an impeachment of the president. If the judges were to form a tribunal for that purpose, they surely ought not to be appointed by the president. He had other objections against referring the appointment to the president. One was that, as the seat of government must be in some one state, and the president would remain in office for a considerable time, he would insensibly form local and personal attachments within the particular state that would deprive outlying parts of the country of equal merit of appointment.

Mr. Ghorum argued that as the president will be responsible, in point of character at least, for a judicious and faithful discharge of his trust, he will be careful to look through all the states for proper characters. Senators would be as likely as the president to form local attachments. If they could not get the man of their particular state, they would probaby be indifferent to the rest. Public bodies feel no personal responsibility and give full play to intrigue and cabal. Rhode Island, he suggested, was a full illustration of the insensibility to character produced by a participation of numbers, in dishonorable measures, and of the length to which a public body could carry wickedness and cabal.

I suggested that the judges might be appointed by the president with the concurrence of at least one-third of the Senate. This would unite the advantage of responsibility in the president with the security afforded in the Senate against any incautious or corrupt nomination by the president.

Mr. Sherman of Connecticut was clearly for an election of judges by the Senate, which would be composed of men nearly equal to the president and would, of course, have on the whole more wisdom. They would bring into their deliberations a more diffusive knowledge of characters. It would be less easy for candidates to intrigue with them, than with the president.

Mr. Randolph of Virginia said that when the appointment of the judges was vested in the Senate an equality of votes had not been given to it. Yet he had rather leave the appointment there than give it to the president. He thought the advantage of personal responsibility might be gained in the Senate by requiring the respective votes of the members to be entered on the Journal. He thought too that the hope of receiving appointments would be more diffusive if they depended on the Senate, the members of which would be diffusively known, than if they depended on a single man who could not be personally known to a very great extent.

Mr. Ghorum moved that "the Judges be nominated and appointed by the President, by and with the advice and consent of the Senate." This mode he said had been ratified by the experience of 140 years in Massachusetts. If the appointment should be left to either branch of the Legislature, it would be a mere piece of jobbing. Mr. Gouverneur Morris seconded and supported the motion.

Mr. Ghorum's motion failed to pass.

I moved that the judges should be nominated by the president and such nomination should become an appointment if not disagreed to within a specified number of days by two-thirds of the Senate. Mr. Gouverneur Morris seconded the motion. By common consent the consideration of it was postponed.

Three days later the Convention resumed discussion of my motion.

I stated as my reasons, first, that it secured the responsibility of the president, who would in general be more capable and likely to select fit characters than the legislature, or even the Senate, who might hide their selfish motives in the appointment. Second, that in case of any flagrant partiality or error in the nomination, it might be fairly presumed that two-thirds of the

Senate would join in putting a negative on it. Third, that as the Senate was very differently constituted when the appointment of the judges was formerly referred to it, and was now to be composed of equal votes from all the states, the principle of compromise which had prevailed in other instances required in this that there should be a concurrence of two authorities, in one of which the people, in the other the states, should be represented. The president would be considered as a national officer, acting for and equally sympathizing with every part of the United States. If the Senate alone should have this power, the judges might be appointed by a minority of the people, though by a majority of the states.

Mr. Pinckney was for placing the appointment in the Senate exclusively, arguing that the president would possess neither the requisite knowledge of characters nor the confidence of the people for so high a trust.

Mr. Ellsworth preferred an absolute appointment by the Senate. The president, he said, might be regarded by the people with a jealous eye. Every power for augmenting unnecessarily his influence would be disliked. As he would be stationary, it was not to be supposed he could have a better knowledge of characters. He would be more open to intrigues than the Senate. The right of the Senate to supersede his nomination would be ideal only. A nomination by the president under such circumstances would be equivalent to an appointment.

Mr. Gouverneur Morris supported my motion that the president make judicial appointments, that the states would frequently have an interest staked on the determination of judges, and since the states control the vote in the Senate, the judges ought not to be appointed by that house. Second, it had been said the president would be uninformed of characters. The reverse was the truth. The Senate would be so. They must take the character of candidates from the flattering pictures drawn by their friends. The president in the necessary intercourse with every part of the United States required by the nature of his administration would have the best possible information. Third, it had been said that a jealousy would be entertained of the president. If the president could be safely trusted with the command of the army, there surely could not be any reasonable ground of jealousy in the appointment of judges.

Mr. Gerry said that the appointment of the judges, like every other part of the Constitution, should be so modeled as to give satisfaction both to the people and to the states, and the current motion would satisfy neither. He could not conceive that the president could be as well informed of characters throughout the Union as the Senate. It also appeared to him as a strong objection that two-thirds of the Senate were required to reject a nomination of the executive.

Colonel Mason found it his duty to differ from his colleagues. He considered the appointment by the president as a dangerous prerogative. It might even give him an influence over the judiciary department itself.

And the vote? The motion "that the President should nominate, and such nominations should become appointments unless disagreed to by the Senate" failed.

The clause as it stood, by which the judges were to be appointed by the Senate, passed.

Dr. FRANKLIN. In the time which elapsed from July 26 to August 6, the Committee of Detail worked on a draft of the Constitution, based on what had been approved to date. Fifty-three Convention days had elapsed. Thirty-five Convention days remained.

Up to this point, the states, through the Senate, remained in control of foreign affairs and most appointments.

Mr. JEFFERSON. I was in Paris at this time. On August 4 I wrote: "My general plan would be to make the States one as to everything connected with foreign nations, and several as to every thing purely domestic. I think it very material to separate in the hands of Congress the Executive and Legislative powers, as the Judiciary already are in some degree. This I hope will be done. The want of it has been the source of more evil than we have ever experienced from any other cause. Nothing is so embarrassing nor so mischievous in a great assembly as the details of execution. The smallest trifle of that kind occupies as long as the most important act of legislation and takes place of everything else. Let any man recollect, or look over the files of Congress, he will observe the most important propositions hanging over from week to week and month to month, till the occasions have past them, and the thing never done. I have ever viewed the executive details as the greatest cause of evil to us, because they in fact place us as if we had no federal head, by diverting the attention of that head from great to small objects; and should this division of power not be recommended by the Convention, it is my opinion Congress should make it itself by establishing an Executive Committee.''

Mr. THOMSON. (To the spectators) Earlier in the Convention General Washington had written to Mr. Jefferson, "The business of this convention is as yet too much in embryo to form any opinion of the conclusion. Much is expected from it by some; not much by others; and nothing by a few. That something is necessary, none will deny; for the situation of the general government, if it can be called a government, is shaken to its foundation, and liable to be overturned by every blast. In a word, it is at an end; and, unless a remedy is soon applied, anarchy and confusion will inevitably ensue.''

Mr. MADISON. On August 6, the Committee of Detail reported a draft which provided that the Senate "shall have the power to make treaties." By August 15, Colonel Mason was saying that the Senate "could already sell the whole country by means of Treaties." Thus, the debate continued over powers shared by the president and the Senate.

Mr. John Francis Mercer of Maryland observed, according to my notes, that the Senate ought not to have any power in the making of treaties. This power belonged to the Executive department; he added that treaties should not be final until ratified by legislative authority, as this was the case of Treaties in Great Britain; particularly the late Treaty of Commerce with France.

Colonel Mason responded that he "did not say that a Treaty would repeal a law but that the Senate by means of treaty might alienate territory without legislative sanction. The cessions of the British Islands in the West Indies by treaty alone were an example. If Spain should possess herself of Georgia, therefore, the Senate might by treaty dismember the Union."

The subject was not resumed until August 23. On this late date the provision still read, "The Senate of the United States shall have power to make treaties and to appoint Ambassadors and Judges of the Supreme Court."

I observed that the Senate represented the states alone, and that for this reason as well as others it was proper that the president should be an agent in treaties.

Mr. Gouverneur Morris was undecided but for the present would add as an amendment to the section, "but no Treaty shall be binding on the United States which is not ratified by a law."

I suggested the inconvenience of requiring a legal ratification of treaties of alliance for the purposes of war.

Mr. Ghorum said that many other disadvantages may be experienced if treaties of peace and all negotiations were required to be previously ratified. And yet, if not previously ratified, the ministers would be at a loss how to proceed. What would be the case in Great Britain if the king were to proceed in this manner? Are American Ministers to go abroad not instructed by the same authority which is to ratify their proceedings?

Mr. Morris then said that as to treaties of alliance, they will oblige foreign powers to send their ministers here. Treaties could not be otherwise made, if his amendment should succeed. In general he was not solicitous to multiply and facilitate treaties. He wished none to be made with Great Britain, till she should be at war. Then a good bargain might be made with her. So with other foreign powers. The more difficulty in making treaties, the more value will be set on them.

Dr. Johnson thought there was something of solecism in saying that the acts of a minister with plenipotentiary powers from one body should depend for ratification on another body.

Mr. Ghorum in answer to Mr. Morris said that negotiations on the spot were not to be desired by us, especially if the whole legislature were involved with Treaties. In such a government as ours, it is necessary to guard against the government itself being seduced.

Mr. Randolph observed that almost every speaker had made objections to the clause as it stood. The subject was referred to the Committee of Five.

Mr. ADAMS. Again, who were the Committee of Five?

Mr. MADISON. This was actually the Committee of Detail, consisting of Mr. Gorham of Massachusetts, Mr. Ellsworth of Connecticut, Mr. Wilson of Pennsylvania, Mr. Randolph of Virginia, and Mr. Rutledge of South Carolina.

On August 31, matters still not being resolved, a committee of a member from each state was appointed to consider and make recommendations with respect to such parts of reports as had not been acted on by the Convention. On September 4 this Committee of Eleven recommended that the section on treaties and appointments read as follows:

"The President by and with the advice and consent of the Senate, shall have power to make Treaties; and he shall nominate and by and with the advice and consent of the Senate shall appoint ambassadors, and other public Ministers, Judges of the Supreme Court, and all other Officers of the United States, whose appointments are not otherwise herein provided for. But no Treaty shall be made without the consent of two-thirds of the members present."

Mr. ADAMS. Mr. Madison, who was on the Committee of Eleven?

Mr. MADISON. The members were Mr. Gilman of New Hampshire, Mr. King of Massachusetts, Mr. Sherman of Connecticut, Mr. Brearley of New Jersey, Mr. Carroll of Maryland, Mr. Madison of Virginia, Mr. Williamson of North Carolina, Mr. Butler of South Carolina, Mr. Baldwin of Georgia, Mr. G. Morris of Pennsylvania, and Mr. Dickinson of Delaware.

Mr. ADAMS. So, on July 24, a Committee of Detail was appointed to report a Constitution conformable to the resolutions which had been passed up to that time by the Convention. And on August 31, a Committee of Eleven was appointed to whom were referred such parts of reports as had not then been acted upon by the Convention. Mr. Madison, not one person on the Committee of Detail was on the Committee of Eleven.

It appears as though there was a shift in power as evidenced by the change in committee composition.

On September 4 with only ten sessions remaining the Committee of Eleven recommended a complete change in certain provisions which had held a certain course for seventy-eight Convention sessions. By September 4, 114 days had already elapsed since the Convention met and 13 days were remaining to its end.

Mr. MADISON. Mr. Adams, you are correct in your assumption. The struggle, which occasioned a shift in power, was attributable to the debates on slave trade and navigation laws, and the compromises resulting from those issues. If I may indulge your patience, Mr. Adams, I would like to introduce your question at a later point in these sessions, and for the moment, just complete the record on the issue at hand.

Mr. ADAMS. I am of the opinion that such a transition in power is part and parcel of the issue at hand.

Mr. MADISON. I agree, but I merely request that the discussion of it be deferred, not abandoned.

Mr. ADAMS. So be it.

Mr. MADISON. On the recommendation of the Committee of Eleven, Mr. Wilson, who was not on that committee, objected to the suggested mode of appointing officers, as blending a branch of the legislature with the executive. Good laws are of no effect without a good executive, he contended, and there can be no good executive without a responsible appointment of officers to execute. Responsibility is in a manner destroyed by such an agency of the Senate. He preferred a Council, provided its advice should not be made obligatory on the president.

Mr. Morris, who was on the Committee of Eleven, said that as the president was to nominate, there would be responsibility, and as the Senate was to concur, there would be security.

Mr. Gerry, who was not on the Committee, said that the idea of responsibility on the nomination to offices was chimerical—the president cannot know all characters and can therefore always plead ignorance.

On the subject of treaties, Mr. Wilson thought it objectionable to require the concurrence of two-thirds, which puts it in the power of a minority to control the will of a majority. If a majority cannot be trusted, it is a proof that we are not fit for one society.

Mr. Morris responded that if a two-thirds vote of the Senate should be required for peace, the legislature will be unwilling to make war. Besides, if a majority of the Senate supports peace and are not allowed to make it, they might effect their purpose in the more disagreeable mode of opposing the supplies for the war.

Mr. Williamson remarked that treaties are to be made in the branch of the government where there may be a majority of the states without a majority of the people, and Mr. Wilson said that if two-thirds are necessary to make peace, the minority may perpetuate war, against the sense of the majority.

Mr. Gerry enlarged on the danger of putting the essential rights of the Union in the hands of so small a number as a majority of the Senate, representing, perhaps, not one-fifth of the people. The Senate might be corrupted by foreign influence.

On September 8 a Committee of Style was appointed "to revise the style of and arrange the articles agreed to. . . ."

Mr. ADAMS. And who was on the Committee, Mr. Madison?

Mr. MADISON. Mr. Johnson of Connecticut, Mr. Hamilton of New York, Mr. G. Morris of Pennsylvania, Mr. Madison of Virginia, and Mr. King of Massachusetts.

Mr. ADAMS. In other words, the four largest states plus one. And what was the power play?

Mr. MADISON. I trust the question is rhetorical.

Mr. ADAMS. I suppose so.

Mr. MADISON. The section under consideration was reported by the Committee on Style as follows:

"The President . . . shall have power, by and with the advice and consent of the Senate, to make treaties, provided two-thirds of the senators present concur; and he shall nominate, and by and with the advice and consent of the Senate, shall appoint ambassadors, other public ministers and consuls, judges of the Supreme Court, and all other officers of the United States, whose appointments are not herein otherwise provided for."

On Saturday, September 15, two days before the Constitution was signed, my notes show that Mr. Gouverneur Morris moved to add at the end of the provision just read: "but the Congress may by law vest the appointment of such inferior Officers as they think proper, in the President alone, in the Courts of law, or in the heads of Departments." Mr. Sherman seconded the motion.

On the motion the vote was: Ayes—5; noes—5, divided—1.

My notes then read: "The motion being lost by the equal division of votes, it was urged that it be put to a vote a second time, since such provision was too important to be omitted, and on a second vote it was agreed to. . . ."

At this same time, Mr. Mason wrote: "The Senate have the power of altering all money bills and of originating appropriations of money and the salaries of the officers of their own appointment, in conjunction with the President of the United States, although they are not the representatives of the people or amenable to them.

These with their other great powers, their power in the appointment of ambassadors and all public officers, in making treaties, and in trying all impeachments, their influence upon and connection with the supreme Executive from these causes, their duration of office and their being a constantly existing body, almost continally sitting, joined with their being one complete branch of the legislature will destroy any balance in the government and enable them to accomplish what usurpations they please upon the rights and liberties of the people."

One man's view; many men's views. . .

And despite all, the provision for sharing powers entered the Constitution. It reads now as it did in 1787:

"The President . . . shall have Power, by and with the Advice and Consent of the Senate, to make Treaties, provided two-thirds of the Senators present concur; and he shall nominate and by and with the Advice and Consent of the Senate shall appoint Ambassadors, other public Ministers and Consuls, Judges of the Supreme Court, and all other Officers of the United States whose Appointments are not herein otherwise provided for and which shall be established by Law; but the Congress may by Law vest the Appointment of such inferior officers as they think proper, in the President alone, in the Courts of Law, or in the Heads of Departments.''

Gen. WASHINGTON. Gentlemen, we will take a ten-minute recess.

Mr. JEFFERSON. I would like to tell a story about one of the members of the Continental Congress. The man was Henry Wisner. He was born in Orange County, New York in 1720. He had early invested in real estate and built a gristmill near Goshen, New York. Henry Wisner was a member of the Continental Congress from 1774 to 1776. You were not in Congress at the time, Mr. Madison, so this story should be all new to you. Henry Wisner voted for the Declaration of Independence but was absent at the time it was signed since he was attending the Provincial Congress in New York, to which he had just been elected. Wisner erected three powder plants in the vicinity of Goshen and supplied powder to the Continental Armies during the revolution. He was a member of the Commission to provide for fortifying the Hudson River, which constructed forts at West Point and placed a chain across the Hudson River in 1777 and 1778. He was a member of the state convention that ratified the Federal Constitution in 1788. He was an honorable man, indeed. Wisner's penchant for detail, however, was remarkable. From Philadephia on December 21, 1775, Mr. Wisner wrote to Mr. Benjamin Towne explaining the art of making gun powder, telling him everything from how to mix saltpetre, brimstone, charcoal and water to how to strain explosive stuff out.

And who was Benjamin Towne? Oddly, Benjamin Towne was the printer of the *Pennsylvania Evening Post*. He was noteworthy for his unstable political allegiances in the revolutionary era. He supported the American patriot cause until the British occupied Philadelphia; he then adopted a loyalist position during the British occupation and returned to the American side after the British evacuated the city.

Interestingly, two days later, on December 23, 1775, Samuel Adams sent a copy of Wisner's plan of a powder mill with a short covering letter to Paul Revere.

Dr. FRANKLIN. I suppose Paul Revere wanted to find out how to get a charge for his charger for his next midnight ride. Y' know, it was the search for "powder" which brought the British to Lexington and Concord on April 18 and 19, 1775.

Mr. ADAMS. And that's how we fought the Revolutionary War. Nobody objected to the construction of a powder mill. Of course, it wasn't a nuclear plant.

Gen. WASHINGTON. This session will resume.

Mr. ADAMS. Mr. Madison, if you recall, you deferred the question of a change in power or a new coalition among the members of certain key committees. I wonder whether you can dispose of that question now?

Mr. MASON. If I may interrupt, Mr. Chairman, I ask for permission to respond to Mr. Adams' question—if Mr. Madison will yield and you grant permission.

Mr. MADISON. I yield to the gentleman from my home state, Virginia.

Gen. WASHINGTON. The chair recognizes Mr. Mason.

Mr. MASON. Thank you. The Constitution, as agreed to till a fortnight before the Convention ended, was such a one as I would have set my hand and heart to. Under its terms, the president was to be elected for seven years, then be ineligible for seven more; there was rotation in the Senate; there was a vote of two-thirds in the legislature on particular subjects, and expressly on that of navigation. The three New England states—New Hampshire, Massachusetts, and Connecticut—were constantly with us Virginians in all questions. Rhode Island was not there, and New York, seldom, so that it was these three states with the five southern ones against Pennsylvania, New Jersey, and Delaware. The question of the importation of slaves had been left to Congress. This disturbed the two southernmost states, who knew that Congress would immediately suppress such importation. Therefore, those two states struck up a bargain with the three New England states; if they would join to admit slaves for some years, the two southernmost states would join in changing the clause which required two-thirds of the legislature in any vote. It was done. These articles were changed accordingly, and from that moment the two southern states and the three northern ones joined Pennsylvania, New Jersey, and Delaware and made the majority 8 to 3 against us, instead of 8 to 3 for us, as it had been through the whole Convention. Under this coalition, the great principles of the Constitution were changed in the last days of the convention.

Mr. ADAMS. So those states not in the coalition were Virginia, Maryland, and North Carolina. Is that correct?

Mr. MASON. That is correct.

Mr. ADAMS. And the slavery question was thereby left to posterity?

Mr. MASON. That is correct.

Mr. ADAMS. Is it not conceivable then, Mr. Mason, that the compromise involving the origination of money bills in the House of Representatives and the equal vote of the states in the Senate, on the one hand, and the compromise involving slavery and the navigation laws, on the other hand, created an environment in the Convention under which the true wishes of the delegates could not have been attained?

Gen. WASHINGTON. Mr. Adams, the question is out of order.

Mr. ADAMS. Mr. Mason, I have a sheet of paper before me which I would like to read and ask if you can validate the incidents recited.

Mr. MASON. I will try.

Mr. ADAMS. The document reads: "The Constitution as agreed at first was such that amendment to the Constitution might be proposed either by Congress or the State Legislatures. A Committee was appointed to digest and redraw. Gouverneur Morris and Rufus King were on the Committee. One morning Morris moved an instruction for certain alterations. Not one half the members of the Committee had yet come in. In a hurry and without understanding, it was agreed to. The Committee reported that Congress should have the exclusive power of proposing amendments. George Mason observed it on the report and opposed it. King denied the construction. Mason demonstrated it and asked the Committee by what authority they had varied what had been agreed. Morris then impudently got up and said—by authority of the Convention—and produced a blind instruction which was unknown by one-half of the house and not till then understood by the other. They then restored it as it originally stood."

Mr. Mason, will you examine this document?

Mr. MASON. Yes.

Mr. ADAMS. Is the information contained in that document valid to your best information and belief?

Mr. MASON. It is. The document is in the handwriting of Mr. Thomas Jefferson and is an account of certain proceedings of the Federal Convention as I related them to him on September 30, 1792.

Mr. ADAMS. Mr. Jefferson. Will you again examine this document and state whether it is in your own handwriting and whether it is correctly recorded to your best information and belief.

Mr. JEFFERSON. It is in my handwriting and correctly recorded as Mr. Mason related the incident to me.

Mr. ADAMS. Mr. Chairman, I submit that Mr. Gouverneur Morris, when a member of the Committee on Style, deliberately attempted to deceive the Convention by varying the intended meaning of provisions of the Constitution. I offer this document as an exhibit.

Gen. WASHINGTON. It will be so entered.

Mr. ADAMS. Mr. Mason, is there any further substantiation of the facts stated in the exhibits I just read?

Mr. MASON. I . . .

Mr. MADISON. Perhaps I can help. There was a paralleling discussion in the House of Representatives in 1798, by Representative Albert Gallatin. The Annals of Congress contains his remarks:

"Mr. Gallatin said he was well informed that those words had originally been inserted in the Constitution as a limitation to the power of laying taxes. After the limitation had been agreed to, and the Constitution was completed, a member of the Convention—he was one of the members who represented the State of Pennsylvania—being one of a committee of revisal and arrangement, attempted to throw these words into a distinct paragraph, so as to create not a limitation but a distinct power. The trick, however, was discovered by a member from Connecticut . . . and the words restored as they now stand."

Mr. ADAMS. For the record, Mr. Gouverneur Morris was from the state of Pennsylvania. The incident is very significant in that it makes clear the terrible intrigue that plagued the Federal Convention in the closing days of its sessions.

Major Jackson, with respect to the Committee of Eleven appointed on August 31 to report on matters previously postponed, were not Mr. Gouverneur Morris and Mr. John Dickinson members of that committee?

Major JACKSON. They were.

Mr. ADAMS. Major Jackson, was Mr. Morris a member of the Committee of Five appointed on September 8, 1787, nine days before the Constitution was signed, to "revise the style of and arrange the articles agreed to."

Mr. JACKSON. He was.

Mr. ADAMS. Major Jackson, is there anything in the Journal of the Federal Convention, general or specific, relating to either or both of these matters concerning Gouverneur Morris?

Major JACKSON. Not to my knowledge, sir.

Mr. ADAMS. Mr. Madison, is there anything in your notes of debates in the Federal Convention, general or specific, relating to either or both of these matters concerning Gouverneur Morris?

Mr. MADISON. Not to my recollection.

Mr. ADAMS. That is all the questioning I have on this particular point at this time.

Gen. WASHINGTON. We will take a ten-minute recess.

Susan B. ANTHONY. (Among the spectators) Mrs. Adams, did you ever take a stand against your husband on woman's rights?

Abigail ADAMS. I certainly did. In March, 1776, I wrote Mr. Adams, "I have sometimes been ready to think that the passion for Liberty cannot be Equally Strong in the Breasts of those who have been accustomed to deprive their fellow Creatures of theirs . . . I am certain that it is not founded upon that generous and christian principle of doing to others as we would want others should do unto us . . .

"I long to hear that you have declared an independency—and by the way in the new Code of Laws which I suppose it will be necessary for you to make I desire you would Remember the Ladies and be more generous and favorable to them than your ancestors. Do not put such unlimited power into the hands of the Husbands. Remember all Men would be tyrants if they could. If particular care and attention is not paid to the Ladies, we are determined to foment a Rebellion and will not hold ourselves bound by any Laws in which we have no voice, or Representation.

"That your Sex are Naturally Tyrannical is a Truth so thoroughly established as to admit of no dispute, but such of you as wish to be happy willingly give up the harsh title of Master for the more tender and endearing one of Friend. Why then not put it out of the power of the vicious and the Lawless to use us with cruelty and indignity with impunity? Men of Sense in all Ages abhor those customs which treat us only as the vassals of your Sex. Regard us then as Beings placed by providence under your protection and in imitation of the Supreme Being make use of that power only for our happiness."

Susan B. ANTHONY. What did he say to that?

Mrs. ADAMS. Well, he wrote back in April, 1776, "As to your extraordinary Code of Laws, I cannot but laugh. We have been told that our Struggle has loosened the bands of Government every where. That Children and Apprentices were disobedient—that schools and Colleges were grown turbulent— that Indians slighted their Guardians, and Negroes grew insolent to their Masters. But your Letter was the first Intimation that another Tribe more numerous and powerful than all the rest were grown discontented. This is rather too coarse a compliment but you are so saucy, I won't blot it out.

"Depend on it. We know better than to repeal our Masculine systems. Although they are in full Force, you know they are little more than Theory. We dare not exert our Power in its full Latitude. We are obliged to go fair, and softly, and in Practice you know We are the subjects. We have only the Name of Masters, and rather than give up this, which would completely subject Us to the Despotism of the Petticoat, I hope General Washington and all our Heroes would fight. I am sure every good Politician would plot . . . as he would against Despotism, Empire, Monarchy, Aristocracy, Oligarchy or Ochlocracy."

Susan B. ANTHONY. And, of course, you responded?

Mrs. ADAMS. I certainly did! On May 7, I wrote, "I can not say that I think you very generous to the Ladies for whilst you are proclaiming peace and good will to Men, Emancipating all Nations, you insist upon retaining an absolute power over Wives. But you must remember that Arbitrary power is like most other things which are very hard, very liable to be broken—and notwithstanding all your wise Laws and Maxims, we have it in our power not only to free ourselves but to subdue our Masters and without violence throw both your natural and legal athority at our feet."

Susan ANTHONY. He certainly must have reacted to that.

Abigail ADAMS. No, he was unmoved.

[Commission members return.]

Gen. WASHINGTON. This session will resume.

Mr. ADAMS. Mr. Madison, what was the reaction in the ratification debates in the states to this sharing of powers created between the Senate and the president?

Mr. MADISON. There were many reactions to the relationship created. Let me cite a few of them.

In the Virginia ratification debates Mr. Mason said:

"It has been wittily observed that the Constitution has married the President and Senate—has made them man and wife. I believe the consequence that generally results from marriage will happen here. They will be continually supporting and aiding each other: they will always consider their interest as united. We know the advantage the few have over the many. They can with facility act in concert and on a uniform system: they may join, scheme, and plot against the people without any chance of detection. The Senate and President will form a combination that cannot be prevented by the representatives. The executive and legislative powers, thus connected, will destroy all balances: this would have been prevented by a constitutional council to aid the President in the discharge of his office, vesting the Senate, at the same time, with the power of impeaching them. Then we should have real responsibility. In its present form, the guilty try themselves. The President is tried by his counsellors. He is not removed from office during his trial. When he is arraigned for treason, he has the command of the army and navy and may surround the Senate with thirty thousand troops. But I suppose that the cure for all evils—the virtue and integrity of our representatives—will be thought a sufficient security. On this great and important subject, I am one of those (and ever shall be) who object to it."

Mr. Wilson, in the Pennsylvania ratification debates said:

"I am not a blind admirer of this system. Some of the powers of the senators are not with me the favorite parts of it, but as they stand connected with other parts, there is still security against the efforts of that body: it was with great difficulty that security was obtained, and I may risk the conjecture, that if it is not now accepted, it never will be obtained again from the same States. Though the Senate was not a favorite of mine, as to some of its powers, yet it was a favorite with a majority in the Union; and we must submit to that majority or we must break up the Union. It is but fair to repeat those reasons that weighed with the Convention: perhaps I shall not be able to do them justice; but yet I will attempt to show why additional powers were given to the Senate rather than to the House of Representatives. These additional powers, I believe, are that of trying impeachments, that of concurring with the President in making treaties, and that of concurring in the appointment of officers. These are the powers that are stated as improper. It is fortunate, that, in the extent of every one of them, the Senate stands controlled. If it is that monster which it is said to be, it can only show its teeth; it is unable to bite or devour. With regard to impeachments, the Senate can try none but such as will be brought before them by the House of Representatives.

"The Senate can make no treaties: they can approve of none, unless the President of the United States lays it before them. With regard to the appointment of officers, the President must nominate before they can vote; so that, if the powers of either branch are perverted, it must be with the approbation of some one of the other branches of government. Thus checked on each side, they can do no one act of themselves."

At a later point in the debates, Mr. Wilson said:

". . . by combining those powers of trying impeachments and making treaties, in the same body, it will not be so easy, as I think it ought to be, to call the senators to an account for any improper conduct in that business. . . . when two-thirds of the Senate concur in forming a bad treaty, it will be hard to procure a vote of two-thirds against them, if they should be impeached . . .

"When a member of the Senate shall behave criminally, the criminality will not expire with his office. The senators may be called to account after they shall have been changed, and the body to which they belonged shall have been altered. There is a rotation; and every second year one third of the whole number go out. Every fourth year two thirds of them are changed. In six years the whole body is supplied by a new one. Considering it in this view, responsibility is not entirely lost. There is another view in which it ought to be considered, which will show that we have a greater degree of security. Though senators may not be convicted on impeachment before the Senate, they may be tried by their country, and if their criminality is established, the law will punish. A grand jury may present, a petty jury may convict, and the judges will pronounce the punishment. This is all that can be done under the present Confederation, for under it there is no power of impeachment: even here, we gain something. Those parts that are exceptionable, in this Constitution, are improvements on that concerning which so much pains are taken, to persuade us that it is preferable to the other.''

The foregoing remarks of Mr. Wilson should be of special interest to those who followed the Abscam debates in Congress.

And Mr. Wilson continued.

"The next objection that I mean to take notice of is, that the powers of the several parts of this government are not kept as distinct and independent as they ought to be. I admit the truth of this general sentiment. I do not think that, in the powers of the Senate, the distinction is marked with so much accuracy as I wished, and still wish; but yet I am of the opinion that real and effectual security is obtained, which is saying a great deal. I do not consider this part as wholly unexceptionable; but even where there are defects in this system, they are improvements upon the old. I will go a little further; though, in this system, the distinction and independence of power is not adhered to with entire theoretical precision, yet it is more strictly adhered to than in any other system of government in the world.

Mr. THOMSON. (To the spectators) Before Mr. Madison leaves the Pennsylvania debates I want to call your attention to a quip which appeared at the time in the *Pennsylvania Gazette*: "as perfection is not the lot of human nature, we are not to expect it in the new Federal Constitution. Candor must confess however that it is a well-wrought piece of stuff."

Dr. FRANKLIN. On November 28, Mr. Wilson stated: "The President and the Senate cannot exist without the existence of state legislatures." This is precisely what I have been saying—that the state legislatures controlled the president and the senate.

Mr. MADISON. Mr. King in the Massachusetts ratification debates argued that "the state legislatures, if they find their delegates erring, can and will instruct them. Will not this be a check? When they hear the voice of the people solemnly dictating to them their duty, they will be bold men indeed to act contrary to it. These will not be instructions sent them in a private letter, which can be put in their pockets; they will be public instructions, which all the country will see, and they will be hardy men indeed to violate them."

Mr. Oliver Wolcott observed during the ratification debates in Connecticut, "The Constitution effectually secures the states in their several rights. It must secure them for its own sake; for they are the pillars which uphold the general system. The Senate, a constituent branch of the general legislature, without whose assent no public act can be made, are appointed by the States and will secure the rights of the several states."

During New York's ratification debates Mr. John Jay said: "The Senate is to be composed of men appointed by the state legislatures; they will certainly choose those who are most distinguished for their general knowledge. I presume they will also instruct them, that there will be a constant correspondence supported between the senators and the state executives, who will be able, from time to time, to afford them all that particular information which particular circumstances may require."

Mr. R. R. Livingston in the ratification debates in New York said: "The Senate are indeed designed to represent the state governments . . ."

Before the same assemblage Mr. Hamilton stated: "There are certain social principles in human nature, from which we may draw the most solid conclusion with respect to the conduct of individuals and of communities. We love our families more than our neighbors; we love our neighbors more than our countrymen in general. The human affections, like the solar heat, lose their intensity as they part from the center, and become languid in proportion to the expansion of the circle in which they act. On these principles, the attachment of the individual will be first and forever secured by the state governments; they will be mutual protection and support.

"I insist that it never can be the interest or desire of

the national legislature to destroy the state governments. It can derive no advantage from such an event; but, on the contrary, would lose an indispensable support, a necessary aid in executing the laws and conveying the influence of government to the doors of the people. The Union is dependent on the will of the state governments for its chief magistrate and for its Senate."

Mr. THOMSON. (To the spectators) The resolutions calling the State Convention in Georgia contained a provision unlike any adopted by the other state legislatures. The Convention was empowered "to adopt or reject any part of the whole" Constitution, thus opening the way for partial ratification.

When General Washington learned of it, he commented that "Georgia has accompanied her act of appointment with powers to alter, amend and whatnot. But, if a weak state, with powerful tribes of Indians in its rear and the Spaniards on its flank, do not incline to embrace a strong general government there must, I should think, be either wickedness or insanity in their conduct."

Mr. MADISON. In my state of Virginia, Mr. Edmund Randolph, who was one of the three who declined to sign the Constitution, supported it nonetheless in the ratification debates: "I have labored for the continuance of the Union—the rock of our salvation. I believe that, as sure as there is a God in heaven, our safety, our political happiness and existence, depend on the union of the states; and that without this union, the people of this and the other states will undergo the unspeakable calamities which discord, faction, turbulence, war, and bloodshed have produced in other countries. The American spirit ought to be mixed with American pride, to see the Union magnificently triumphant. Let that glorious pride, which once defied the British thunder, reanimate you again. Let it not be recorded of Americans, that, after having performed the most gallant exploits, after having overcome the most astonishing difficulties and after having gained the admiration of the world by their incomparable valor and policy, they lost their acquired reputation, their national consequence and happiness by their own discretion. Let no future historian inform posterity that they lacked wisdom and virtue to concur in any regular, efficient government. Catch the present moment—seize it with avidity and eagerness—for it may be lost, never to be regained! If the Union be now lost, I fear it will remain so forever. I believe gentlemen are sincere in their opposition and actuated by pure motives; but, when I maturely weigh the advantages of the Union and dreadful consequences of its dissolution; when I see safety on my right and destruction on my left; when I behold respectability and happiness acquired by the one but annihilated by the other, I cannot hesitate to decide in favor of the former."

In the *Federalist Papers*, on the subject of intertwining powers, I wrote:

"One of the principal objections inculcated by the more respectable adversaries to the Constitution is its supposed violation of the political maxim that the legislative, executive, and judiciary departments ought to be separate and distinct. . . . The oracle who is always consulted and cited on this subject is the celebrated Montesquieu. . . . [He] did not mean that . . . departments ought to have no partial agency in, or no control over the acts of each other. His meaning . . . can amount to no more than this, that where the 'whole' power of one department is exercised by the same hands which possess the whole power of another department, the fundamental principles of a free constitution are subverted. . . . If we look into the Constitutions of the several States we find that, notwithstanding the emphatical and, in some instances . . . unqualified terms in which this axiom has been laid down, there is not a single instance in which the several departments of power have been kept absolutely separate and distinct." We have discussed this matter, too, in the Chadha case.

Dr. FRANKLIN. It has been my intention today to establish, for the record, the existence of a sharing of powers between the Senate and the president, and that by this link the States gained control of the president. It should be evident from the presentation that under the 1787 Constitution the states controlled the election of Senators and that in exercising that control through only one-third of the senators, our relationship with all foreign nations could be controlled. And, in exercising that control through only one-half of the Senators all major appointments could be controlled.

Before this session concludes for the day, and before I proceed to the third link in my chain, I would like to discuss further the Senate's role in treaty ratification, which is, of course, a shared power. Mr. Alexander Hamilton is with us today and I ask him to initiate the discussion.

Mr. HAMILTON. Thank you, Dr. Franklin. The president was to have power, "by and with the advice and consent of the Senate, to make treaties, provided two-thirds of the Senators present concur." Though this provision has been assailed on different grounds, and with no small degree of vehemence, I scruple not to declare my firm persuasion that it is one of the best digested and most unexceptionable parts of the plan. One ground of objection is the trite topic of the intermixture of powers; some contending that the president ought alone to possess the power of making treaties; and others, that it ought to have been exclusively deposited in the Senate. Another course of objection is derived from the small number of persons by whom a treaty may be made. Of those who espouse this objection, a part are of the opinion that the House of Representatives ought to have been associated in the business, while another part seem to think that nothing more was necessary than to have substituted two-thirds of all the members of the Senate to two-thirds of the members present. I shall here content myself with offering only some supplementary remarks, principally with a view to the objections which have been just stated.

The power of making treaties relates neither to the execution of the subsisting laws nor to the enaction of new ones; and still less to an exertion of the common strength. Its objects are contracts with foreign nations which have the force of law but derive it from the obligations of good faith. They are not rules prescribed by the sovereign to the subject, but agreements between sovereign and sovereign. The power in question seems therefore to form a distinct department and to belong, properly, neither to the legislative nor to the executive. The qualities, indispensable in the management of foreign negotiations, point out the executive as the most fit agent in those transactions, while the vast importance of the trust and the operation of treaties as laws plead strongly for the participation of the whole or a portion of the legislative body in the office of making them. It would be utterly unsafe and improper to intrust that power to an elective magistrate of four years' duration. A man raised from the station of a private citizen to the rank of chief magistrate, possessed of but a moderate or slender fortune, and looking forward to a period not very remote when he may probably be obliged to return to the station from which he was taken, might sometimes be under temptations to sacrifice his duty to his interest, which it would require superlative virtue to withstand. An avaricious man might be tempted to betray the interests of the state to the acquisition of wealth. An ambitious man might make his own aggrandizement, by the aid of a foreign power, the price of his treachery to his constituents. The history of human conduct does not warrant that exalted opinion of human virtue which would make it wise in a nation to commit interests of so delicate and momentous a kind, as those which concern its intercourse with the rest of the world, to the sole disposal of a magistrate created and circumstanced as would be a President of the United States.

To have intrusted the power of making treaties to the Senate alone would have been to relinquish the benefits of the constitutional agency of the president in the conduct of foreign negotiations.

It must indeed be clear to a demonstration that the joint possession of the power in question, by the president and Senate, would afford a greater prospect of security than the separate possession of it by either of them.

The remarks apply with conclusive force against the admission of the House of Representatives to a share in the formation of treaties. The fluctuating and, taking its future increase into the account, the multitudinous composition of that body forbid us to expect in it those qualities which are essential to the proper execution of such a trust. Accurate and comprehensive knowledge of foreign politics; a steady and systematic adherence to the same views; a nice and uniform sensibility to national character; decision, secrecy, and dispatch are incompatible with the genius of a body so variable and so numerous. The very complication of the business, by introducing a necessity of the concurrence of so many different bodies, would of itself afford a solid objection. The greater frequency of the calls upon the House of Representatives and the greater length of time which it would often be necessary to keep them together when convened to obtain their sanction in the progressive stages of a treaty would be a source of so great inconvenience and expense as alone ought to condemn the project.

Mr. ADAMS. Mr. Hamilton, you first proposed the "advice and consent" clause, did you not?

Mr. HAMILTON. On June 18, 1787, I presented a plan in which the chief executive, the "governor" was the term I used, would have "with the advice and approbation of the Senate the power of making all Treaties." The word "approbation" was used instead of "consent."

Mr. ADAMS. To your knowledge, do you believe that the advice and consent provision—this sharing of power—has been adhered to?

Mr. HAMILTON. The question you raise has long been an issue with respect to which Mr. Madison and I have taken opposite sides. My claim has been that the president possesses implied powers in foreign policy not written into the Constitution. Mr. Madison has not supported my contention.

Mr. ADAMS. And yet you originated the concept of the sharing of this power of the president with the Senate.

Mr. HAMILTON. At least insofar as the making of treaties is concerned.

Mr. ADAMS. Mr. Madison, what is your thought on the treaties?

Mr. MADISON. My opinion is that the president violates his constitutional duty when he does not seek the advice and consent of the Senate in connection with treaties and that the Senate violates its constitutional duty when it does not insist on its right and duty to render advice in connection with treaties.

Mr. ADAMS. To what extent do you believe this format or pattern of violation has occurred?

Mr. MADISON. It appears that presidents, since 1940 particularly, have been conducting foreign affairs by means of executive agreements and not by means of treaties. It appears that it is the submission or nonsubmission of an international instrument to the Senate which makes the difference between a "treaty" and an "executive agreement." Any international agreement which is not submitted to the Senate, be it called a protocol, convention, treaty, agreement, articles, or some other name is considered a treaty.

As of January 1, 1979, there were 966 treaties and 5,946 international agreements other than treaties in force.

Since 1946, the use of executive agreements has increased dramatically. With the chair's permission, I would like to introduce into the testimony the following chart which provides statistics on the treaties and executive agreements concluded in selected years.

Gen. WASHINGTON. Please distribute copies among the commission members.

Mr. MADISON. Thank you. As the members can see for themselves, the numbers of executive agreements has increased thirty-fold in some fifty years. To wit . . .

Year	Treaties	Executive Agreements	Year	Treaties	Executive Agreements
1930	25	11	1970	20	183
1935	25	10	1971	17	214
1940	12	20	1972	20	287
1944	1	74	1973	17	241
1945	6	54	1974	13	229
1946	19	139	1975	13	264
1950	11	157	1976	13	402
1955	7	297	1977	17	424
1960	5	266	1978	15	417
1965	14	204	1979	30	360

This is certainly not what was intended.

It is my opinion that the Convention defined precisely what role it intended for the Senate in the treaty-making process. The Senate was to share fully with the president in the power to make treaties; this sharing was to begin early in the treaty-making process, with the Senate helping to formulate instructions to the negotiators and acting as counsel to the president on decisions which might be necessary during the course of the negotiations, as well as approving each treaty entered into by the United States. That's the "advice" function.

In the Continental Congress, all instructions to negotiators of treaties emanated from that body, and the negotiators were always in contact with the Congress for further instructions. Under the Constitution, the president, in effect, became the negotiator of treaties for the Congress. Nothing more. Nothing less.

Within several years, however, problems were encountered in treaty-making which led the president to abandon the practice of getting the Senate's advice and consent on detailed questions or on a regular basis prior to the negotiations.

It has been contended that the Constitution does not define the term "treaty" nor provide any procedure to be followed by the president and the Senate. In addition, it is contended that the Constitution provides no guidelines which would distinguish an executive agreement from a treaty, either in definition or in scope. Thus it is claimed that the relationship between the executive and legislative branches in this area remains unidentified and unsettled. These are mere excuses.

Gen. WASHINGTON. Dr. Franklin, it would appear to me that your premise—a link, as you call it—namely, that the states gained control of the president by providing for the sharing of power between the Senate and the president—has already been established. The course of testimony being conducted now no longer has a bearing on the premise at issue. What is transpiring now is leading to a discussion of periods in which the sharing of powers had its strengths and periods in which it had its weaknesses. While collateral to the subject matter, it is perhaps too digressive. I therefore suggest that at our next session you proceed with your next "link."

Dr. FRANKLIN. This reminds me of a story, which I will read:

> A town fear'd a Siege, and held Consultation,
> What was the best method of fortification:
> A skillful Mason declar'd his opinion,
> That nothing but Stone could secure the Dominion.
> A Carpenter said, Tho' that was well spoke
> Yet he'd rather advise to defend it with Oak.
> A Tanner much wiser than both these together,
> Cry'd, try what you please, but nothin's like leather.

The point you raise is between author and authority. I am the author, but you are the authority. With due respect General, I strive not with my superiors in argument, but always submit my judgment to others with modesty.

Gen. WASHINGTON. Whose saying was the last, Dr. Franklin?

Dr. FRANKLIN. Yours, General.

Mr. THOMSON. (To the spectators) It would be my impression that General Washington cut short Mr. Madison's discussion of Dr. Franklin's subject in order to avoid discussion of an embarrassing incident which occurred early in his administration. On August 10, 1789, President Washington made clear his belief that the Senate was to be consulted in advance of making a treaty. Accordingly, on August 21, 1789, the Senate adopted a rule on the procedure to be followed when the president met with the Senate. The rule said: "Resolved. That when the President of the United States shall meet the Senate in the Senate Chamber, the President of the Senate shall have a chair on the floor . . . and his chair shall be assigned to the President of the United States."

The same day President Washington gave notice of his intention to meet with the Senate to consider the terms of a treaty to be negotiated with the southern Indians. The next day, Saturday, August 22, 1789, President Washington came into the Senate chamber and presented a paper giving an explanation of the proposed treaty and then asked the Senate for their advice and consent on specific questions related to the treaty. The Senate voted on one of the questions but postponed the others until the following Monday, August 24, 1789, when the president again returned to the Senate chamber and votes were taken on the rest of the questions.

These meetings between the Senate and the president are famous as the first and last times that a president personally appeared before the Senate to seek its advice and consent, meetings which apparently were unsatisfactory to both sides. While the Executive Journal of the Senate does not record the debate, William Maclay, a senator from Pennsylvania, recorded in his journal the difficulty of hearing, the seeming haste for decisions, and Washington's "violent fret" and statement that "this defeats every purpose of my coming here."

The dissatisfaction on the president's side is often illustrated with the following quotation from the memoirs of John Quincy Adams:

"Mr. Crawford told twice over the story of President Washington's having at an early period of his administration gone to the Senate with a project of a treaty to be negotiated and been present at their deliberations upon it. They debated it and proposed alterations so that when Washington left the Senate Chamber he said he would be d-d if he ever went there again."

Amidst these passions, was a legitimate requirement of the Constitution discarded?

Gen. WASHINGTON. Gentlemen, this session is adjourned until Tuesday, July 7 at 10 a.m.

TUESDAY, JULY 7, 1987

THE SENATE AS COUNCIL TO THE PRESIDENT

The Committee met pursuant to notice, at 10 a.m. in the Assembly Room of Independence Hall, Gen. George Washington presiding.

  Present: Mr. John Adams, Dr. Benjamin Franklin, Mr. Thomas Jefferson, Mr. James Madison and Gen. George Washington.

  Gen. WASHINGTON. This session will come to order. Dr. Franklin.

  Dr. FRANKLIN. At our last session, I attempted to show that the states gained control of the president by providing for a sharing of powers between the Senate and the president.

  Today I want to show that by the sharing of powers, the Senate became a council to the president, or at least was recognized, as such at the time.

  At our session on Wednesday, July 1, I showed that my proposal and that of others for a constitutional council to the president was turned down by the Federal Convention. Today, I want to show that the Senate itself was considered as a council to the president by many who participated in its creation.

  In order that we not lose sight of the object of our present course of discussion, let me emphasize that we are tracing the controls established by the states in the Federal Convention; the states, it should be remembered, controlled the Senate by virtue of the fact that they chose the senators, and thus the states controlled the president by a sharing of powers between the president and their representative in the Senate. All these objects failed when the right to select senators was taken away from the states, at which time the purpose underlying the existence of the Senate was thereby voided and became meaningless.

Let us now turn to the third link in my chain—by the sharing of powers, the Senate became a council to the president.

Several of the ratification conventions dwelt on this very subject. Mr. G. Livingston in New York, when referring to the Senate, remarked on "their capacity of council to the President. . . ." Mr. Boundinot in Massachusetts observed that "the Federal Senate, having not only legislative, but executive powers" was a "legislating and, at the same time, an advising body to the executive."

Mr. THOMSON. (To the spectators) In those same debates in Massachusetts—I think even on the same day—Maj. Samuel Nason blasted the Constitution: "Great Britain, sir, first attempted to enslave us by declaring her laws supreme and that she had a right to bind us in all cases whatever. What, sir, roused the Americans to shake off the yoke preparing for them? It was this measure, the power to do which we are now about giving to Congress. . . . Gentlemen ask, 'Can it be supposed that a Constitution so pregnant with danger could come from the hands of those who framed it?' Indeed, sir, I am suspicious of my own judgment when I contemplate this idea—when I see the list of illustrious names annexed to it; but, sir, my duty to my constituents obliges me to oppose the measure they recommend as obnoxious to their liberty and safety.

When, sir, we dissolved the political bands which connected us with Great Britain, we were in a state of nature. We then formed and adopted the Confederation, which must be considered as a sacred instrument. This confederates us under one head as sovereign and independent states. Now, sir, if we give Congress power to dissolve that Confederation, to what can we trust? If a nation consent thus to treat their most solemn compacts, who will ever trust them? Let us, sir, begin with this Constitution and see what it is. And first, 'We, the people of the United States, do' etc. If this, sir, does not go to an annihilation of the state governments and to a perfect consolidation of the whole Union I do not know what does. What! Shall we consent to this? Can ten, twenty, or a hundred persons in this state who have taken the oath of allegiance to it dispense with this oath? Gentlemen may talk as they please of dispensing, in certain cases, with oaths but, sir, with me they are sacred things. We are under oath: We have sworn that Massachusetts is a sovereign and independent state. How, then, can we vote for this Constitution that destroys that sovereignty? . . .

The term, sir, for which the Senate is chosen, is a grievance. It is too long to trust any body of men with power. It is impossible but that such men will be tenacious of their places; they are to be raised to a lofty eminence, and they will be loath to come down; and, in the course of six years, may, by management, have it in their power to create officers and obtain influence enough to get in again, and so for life. When we felt the hand of British oppression upon us, we were so jealous of rulers as to declare them eligible but for three years in six. In this constitution, we forget this principle. I, sir, think that rulers ought, at short periods, to return to private life, that they may know how to feel for and regard their fellow-creatures. In six years, sir, and at a great distance, they will quite forget them; 'For time and absence cure the purest love.'

We are apt to forget our friends, except when we are conversing with them."

Dr. FRANKLIN. (Continuing) Then there was Mr. Spencer, in North Carolina, who saw the Senate as a body "who are to advise the President and who in effect are possessed of the chief executive powers."

Luther Martin, in a letter to the House of Delegates in Maryland wrote: "The Senate, sir, is so constituted that they are not only to compose one branch of the legislature but . . . are to compose a privy council for the President." Martin stated before the Maryland House of Delegates that senators "are not only Legislative but make a part of the Executive, which all wise Governments have thought it essential to keep separated. They are the National Council. . . ."

And you, Mr. Madison, in the House of Representatives of the United States; on May 19, 1789, said: "But why, it may be asked, was the Senate joined with the President in appointing to office if they have no responsibility? I answer, merely for the sake of advising, being supposed, from their nature, better acquainted with the characters of the candidates than an individual. . . ."

Mr. Rufus King declared in the Senate on January 12, 1818: ". . . in respect to foreign affairs, the President has no exclusive binding power except that of receiving the Ambassadors and other foreign ministers. . . ; to the validity of all other definitive proceedings in the management of the foreign affairs, the Constitutional advice and consent of the Senate are indispensable.

In these concerns the Senate are the Constitutional and the only responsible counsellors of the President. And in this capacity the Senate may, and ought to, look into and watch over every branch of the foreign affairs of the nation; they may, therefore, at any time call for full and exact information respecting the foreign affairs and express their opinion and advice to the President respecting the same, when, and under whatever other circumstances, they may think such advice expedient.

There is a peculiar jealousy manifested in the Constitution concerning the power which shall manage the foreign affairs and make treaties with foreign nations; hence the provision which requires the consent of two-thirds of the Senators to confirm any compact with a foreign nation that shall bind the United States; thus putting it in the power of a minority of the Senators or States to control the President and a majority of the Senate; a check on the Executive power to be found in no other case.

To make a treaty includes all the proceedings by which it is made; and the advice and consent of the Senate being necessary in the making of treaties must necessarily be so touching the measures employed in making the same. The Constitution does not say that treaties shall be concluded, but that they shall be made, by and with the advice and consent of the Senate; none therefore can be made without such advice and consent; and the objections against the agency of the Senate in making treaties, or in advising the President to make the same, cannot be sustained but by giving to the Constitution an interpretation different from its obvious and most salutary meaning."

Note especially Mr. King's statement that the two-thirds consent provision puts "it in the power of a minority of the senators or states to control the President and a majority of the Senate. . . ." This is what I have been saying right along.

In the process of ratification of the Constitution there were many proposals for amendments to include a constitutional council to the president.

Richard Henry Lee's suggested that, "whereas it is necessary for the good of society that the administration of government be conducted with all possible maturity of judgment; for which reason it hath been the practice of civilized nations, and so determined by every State in this Union that a Council of State or Privy Council should be appointed to advise and assist in the arduous business assigned to the Executive power—therefore, that the New Constitution be so amended as to admit the appointment of a Privy Council to consist of Eleven Members. . . ." George Mason's resolution before the Virginia ratifying convention read in part, "there shall be a constitutionally responsible Council to assist in the administration of Government . . ." And Mr. Robert Whitehill proposed in the ratification debates in Pennsylvania "that the legislative, executive, and judicial powers be kept separate and, to this end, that a constitutional council be appointed to advise and assist the President, who shall be responsible for the advice they give. . . ."

Mr. William Stephen Smith wrote to Mr. Thomas Jefferson on December 2, 1787, "where Government is committed to the hands of a few, the human mind under those circumstances is apt to be inflated with pride, disposed to keep up what they call the dignity of their station and instead of nourishing a superior degree of benevolence and attention to those who placed them there, they feel themselves on the high horse of power and expect every knee to bend to their station. I should grieve for my Country if, in any degee, the engines of power should be permitted to move to the injury of the rights and Liberties of the people properly defined and well founded.

I should have been much better pleased if the President was furnished with a Constitutional Council.

I note that my own ideas, which this Commission is well aware of, were expressed in Ezra Stiles's diary for December 21, 1787: "Dr. Franklin's idea was that the American Policy be one Branch only, . . . proportioned to the number of inhabitants and property—often elected—with a President assisted with an executive Council. . . ."

In essence, he that won't be counsell'd can't be help'd.

Mr. MADISON. My position with respect to counselling may be obtained from the following portion of a letter I once sent to Mr. James Monroe: "A Government cannot long stand which is obliged, in the ordinary course of its administration, to court a compliance with its constitutional acts from a member not of the most powerful order, situated within the immediate verge of authority. . . ."

I am certain my colleagues will understand what I mean.

Mr. THOMSON. (To the spectators) Examples of nonelected persons—including cabinet members—as direct and close advisors are easy to find among modern presidents. Such men as Harry Hopkins in Franklin D. Roosevelt's administration, Sherman Adams in Dwight D. Eisenhower's, Hamilton Jordan in Jimmy Carter's, H. R. Haldeman and John Ehrlichman, both in the administration of Richard M. Nixon, and others. Such men might be called "all the President's 'Yes' men". Dr. Franklin always said, "Approve not of him who commends all you say."

Dr. FRANKLIN. Today the state's power is gone—the chain is broken, the links long rusted. Perhaps Mr. Gouverneur Morris said it best in the year 1811, when he spoke of that demise: "Those who formed our Constitution were not blind to its defects. They believed a monarchial form to be neither solid nor durable. Fond, however, as the framers of our national Constitution were of Republican government, they were not so much blinded by their attachment as not to discern the difficulty, perhaps impracticability, of raising a durable edifice from crumbling materials. History, the parent of political science, had told them that it was almost as vain to expect permanency from democracy as to construct a palace on the surface of the sea.

But it would have been foolish to fold their arms and sink into despondency because they could neither form nor establish the best of all possible systems.

What has been and what is now the influence of the State governments on the Federal system? The States . . . were made electors of the Senate; and so long as the State governments had considerable influence and the consciousness of dignity which the influence imparts, the Senate felt something of the desired sentiment and answered in some degree the end of its institution. But that day is past.

This opens to our view a dilemma, which was not unperceived when the Constitution was formed. If the State influence should continue, the union could not last; and, if it did not, the utility of the Senate would cease.

I once avowed 'that, if Aaron's rod could not swallow the rods of the magicians, their rods would swallow his.' It is one thing to perceive a dilemma, and another thing to get out of it. In the option between two evils, that which appeared to be the least was preferred and the power of the union provided for. At present the influence of the general government has so thoroughly pervaded every State that all the little wheels are obliged to turn according to the great one."

The Seventeenth Amendment to the Constitution provided that "The Senate of the United States shall be composed of two Senators from each State, elected by the people thereof" instead of being chosen by the state legislatures. The Amendment was proposed by Congress on May 13, 1912, and ratification was completed on April 8, 1913. Thus died state power.

With the demise of state power I raise the question, as others have, "What purpose does the Senate now serve?"

State control of the Senate through the selection of senators by the state legislatures is gone.

State control of the president through the sharing of

powers between the Senate and the president is gone.

The Senate, though it shares powers with the president, did not become a Constitutional Council to the president.

Thus, did not the Seventeenth Amendment eliminate every vestige of state control? Mr. Chairman, I have concluded my statements.

Gen. WASHINGTON. We will recess for ten minutes.

James SULLIVAN. (A spectator) Mr. Adams, as you know, the Nineteenth Amendment to the Constitution gave women the right to vote in 1920. In your time, did you ever consider this possibility?

Mr. ADAMS. Yes, it was of concern to me. As I thought of it then, "It is certain in Theory that the only moral Foundation of Government is the Consent of the People. But to what an Extent Shall We carry this Principle? Shall We Say that every Individual of the Community, old and young, male and female, as well as rich and poor, must consent expressly to every Act of Legislation? No, you will say, this is impossible. How then does the right arise in the Majority to govern the Minority against their Will? Whence arises the Right of the Men to govern Women, without their Consent? Whence the Right of the old to bind the Young without theirs?

But let us first Suppose that the whole Community of every Age, Rank, Sex, and Condition has a Right to vote. This Community is assembled—a Motion is made and carried by a Majority of one Voice. The Minority will not agree to this. Whence arises the Right of the Majority to govern and the obligation of the Minority to obey? From Necessity, you will Say, because there can be no other Rule. But why exclude Women? You will say because their delicacy renders them unfit for Practice and Experience in the great Businesses of Life and the hardy Enterprises of War, as well as the arduous Cares of State. Besides, their attention is so much engaged with the necessary Nurture of their Children that Nature has made them fittest for domestic Cares. And Children have not Judgment or Will of their own. True. But will not these Reasons apply to others? . . .

The Same Reasoning, which will induce one to admit all Men who have no Property to vote with those who have, will prove that you ought to admit Women and Children: for generally Speaking, Women and Children have as good Judgment and as independent Minds as those Men who are wholly destitute of Property. . . .

Society can be governed only by general Rules. Government cannot accommodate itself to every particular Case, as it happens, nor to the Circumstances of particular Persons. It must establish general, comprehensive Regulations for Cases and Persons. The only Question is which general Rule will accommodate most Cases and most Persons.

Depend upon it, it is dangerous . . . to alter the Qualifications of Voters. There will be no End of it. New Claims will arise. Women will demand a Vote. Lads from 12 to 21 will think their Rights not enough attended to, and every Man who has not a Farthing will demand an equal Voice with any other in all Acts of State. It tends to confound and destroy all Distinctions and prostrate all Ranks to one common Level."

[Commission members reenter the Hall]

Gen. WASHINGTON. This session will resume. Mr. Jefferson.

Mr. JEFFERSON. It appears to me that before we consider changes in the office of the president we ought to consolidate and consider the testimony already before this Commission and determine whether there are amendments which we deem necessary or advisable to render the Constitution of the United States more adequate to the exigencies of this nation—which, after all, is the purpose for which we were commissioned by Congress.

During the 198-year period during which the Constitution has been in operation, approximately three thousand proposals for constitutional change have been introduced in Congress. Only twenty-six amendments have been ratified by the required three-fourths of the states, however. Five others have been submitted but have failed to obtain ratification by the required three-fourths of the states. Is there an obstacle to Constitutional revision? Is Congress too absorbed in the immediate details of government to be a suitable forum for the origination of fundamental changes in government? Or is the Constitution too sacred to be touched? I believe that document must progress with the times.

Dr. FRANKLIN. I agree. The Constitution cannot be put in mothballs like many a government ship stilled in its slip. We cannot allow its mandate to stagnate in a cobweb of congressional inactivity.

Mr. MADISON. I have long observed that the Constitution of the United States may doubtless disclose, from time to time, faults which call for the pruning of overgrown or vestigial limits. But remedies ought to be applied, not in the paroxysms of party and popular excitements but with leisure and reflection, as the great departments of power, according to experience, may move successively and alternately in and out of public favor. Changes hastily accommodated to these vicissitudes would destroy the symmetry and the stability aimed at in our political system.

We owe it to ourselves, and to the world, to watch, to cherish, and as far as possible, to perfect a new modification of the powers of government, which aims at the better security against external danger and internal disorder, a better provision for national strength and individual rights.

Gen. WASHINGTON. It has long been my opinion that the established government, being the work of our own hands with the seeds of amendment implanted in the Constitution, may by wisdom, good dispositions, and mutual allowances, aided by experience, bring it as near to perfection as any human institution ever approximated.

In all the changes which we consider, remember that time and habit are at least as necessary to fix the true character of governments as of other human institutions; that experience is the surest standard by which to test the real tendency of the existing constitution of a country; that changes upon mere hypothesis and opinion expose government to perpetual change, from an endless variety of hypothesis and opinion; and remember especially that for the efficient management of common interests in a country so extensive as ours, a government of as much vigor as is consistent with the perfect security of liberty is indispensable. Liberty itself will find in such a government, with powers properly distributed and adjusted, its surest guardian.

This government, the offspring of our own choice, uninfluenced and unawed, adopted upon full investigation and mature deliberation, contains within itself a provision for its own amendment and has a just claim to your confidence and your support. The basis of our political system is the right of the people to make and to alter their constitutions of government. However, till changed by an explicity and authentic act of the whole people, the constitution which at any time exists is sacredly obligatory upon all.

Mr. ADAMS. The difficulty of bringing millions to agree in any measure, to act by any rule, can never be conceived by him who has not tried it. It is incredible how small the number in any nation who comprehend any system of Constitution or administration—and those few it is wholly imposible to unite.

Some people must have time to look around them, before, behind, on the right hand, and on the left, then to think and after all this to resolve. Others see at one intuitive glance into the past and the future and judge with precision at once. But remember you can't make thirteen or fifteen clocks strike precisely alike at the same second.

Gov. Samuel Huntington once said in the ratification debates in Connecticut, "The best way to learn the nature and effects of different systems of government is not from theoretical dissertations but from experience—from what has actually taken place among mankind. From this same source it is that mankind have obtained a more complete knowledge of the nature of government than they had in ages past."

I believe this is what we have attempted to accomplish before this Commission.

Mr. James Wilson's observation in the Pennsylvania ratification debates is indeed appropriate: "Time, reflection, and experience will be necessary to suggest and mature the proper regulations on this subject; time and experience were not possessed by the Convention; they left it therefore to be particularly organized by the legislature—the representatives of the United

States—from time to time as should be most eligible and proper. . . . Let the experiment be made; let the system be fairly and candidly tried before it is determined that it cannot be executed."

The experiment has been made. It has been fairly and candidly tried.

Mr. Gouverneur MORRIS. (Among the spectators) I suspect I am personna non grata here. I get no respect. But, I do have my thoughts on constitutional amendments. Mankind are not disposed to embark the blessings they enjoy on a voyage of syllogistic adventure to obtain something more beautiful in exchange. They must feel before they will act. When misfortunes press hard, and not before, the people will look for that wisdom and virtue in which formerly they found safety. They will then listen to the voice which in the wantonness of prosperity they despised. Then, and not till then, can the true patriot be of any use.

Mr. ADAMS. It is time for decision making here. I am going to make a suggestion to this Commission which I trust will be accepted in the genuine spirit in which it is offered.

I suggest that we ask Dr. Franklin to prepare his thoughts as to the recommendations this Commission should make under the authority vested in it by the Congress of the United States.

General Washington, history knows you as the father of your country. Mr. Madison, history knows you as the father of the Constitution. Mr. Jefferson, history knows you as the author of the Declaration of Independence. Dr. Franklin, history knows you for your experiments in electricity, the stove, and perhaps as the author of *Poor Richard's Almanack*. Our posterity has little knowledge of the real Dr. Franklin.

Probably no man in the Western world so personified the eighteenth century as did Benjamin Franklin, who lived through that whole remarkable age from the beginning to nearly the end. How many really know that Dr. Franklin signed both the Declaration of Independence and the Constitution of the United States of America! No member of this Commission can lay claim to that honor. Harry S. Truman said of Dr. Franklin, "I don't think that Franklin has found his real place in American history yet—he was one of the great ones of his time and of all American history." Horace Greeley, that dedicated radical who fought monopolies and opposed slavery, publisher of the *New York Tribune* said, "I think I inadequately appreciate the greatness of Washington; yet I must place Franklin above him as the consummate type and flowering of human nature under the skies of colonial America."

The tributes to Dr. Franklin are innumerable. Herman Melville, best known for his novel *Moby Dick*, called him the "wit-jack of all trades, master of each and mastered by none—the type and genius of his land," while John F. Fitzgerald, mayor of Boston and grandfather of President John F. Kennedy, dubbed Franklin "our first great democrat." Victor Riquete, French author and political economist saw in him "the genius that freed America and poured a flood of light over Europe," while Jaques Turgot, minister of finance under King Louis XVI, said, "He snatched the thunder from Heaven, the sceptre from tyrants."

Perhaps the greatest summation of Dr. Franklin's character came from Thomas Carlyle, Scottish philospher, essayist and historian: "Franklin was the father of all the yankees."

Thus it is that I suggest that Dr. Franklin prepare his thoughts as to the recommendations this Commission should make pursuant to its authority.

Gen. WASHINGTON. Do you want to put this in the form of a motion?

Mr. ADAMS. I so move.

Mr. JEFFERSON. I second the motion.

Gen. WASHINGTON. Any discussion? . . . All in favor . . .

Dr. Franklin is unanimously chosen.

Dr. Franklin, will you accept the honor?

Dr. FRANKLIN. Gentlemen, friends, I accept the

honor fully aware that you may give a man an office, but you cannot give him discretion. I trust I have the discretion to man the office.

Permit me to digress for a moment with a philosophical thought, in a space age. Our comfort on earth is that the whole machine of nature is in the hands of one who knows how to conduct and manage all its vast and unwieldly parts. If we consider the immense distance of the fixed stars, and consequently, the magnitude they must be of, to be visible by us at this distance, we can hardly suppose the divine wisdom, which does nothing in vain, has created such numbers of luminous bodies, of magnitudes inconceivable, and at distances almost infinite, for no other purpose but to afford us a little glimmering light in the night, which could have been done more effectually, and with infinitely less exertion of creating power, by one single additional moon. For what purpose then shall we suppose such a profusion of stupendous luminaries was created?

If each of those innumerable millions and myriads of luminaries be in fact, as is highly probable, a glorious sun, a stupendous world of light and heat, with its system of planets, moons and comets going round it; and if all those planets and moons be worlds inhabited by various orders of beings, enjoying or preparing themselves for such degrees of happiness as the divine wisdom and goodness has appointed for them; the Universe, considered in this manner, is a theater truly fit for a God to display his infinite power, wisdom, and goodness. Were an angelic being to take his flight from this part of the universe and to proceed in a direct course with the swiftness of light, it is certain that, should he continue his flight to all eternity, he must still find himself in the center of the divine presence.

I published that thought back in 1754, in my *Poor Richard's Almanack*. I mention it now because I was impressed with a similar thought expressed by Harvard Professor Henry A. Kissinger more than 225 years after mine. I would like to read it: "We are clearly living through one of the most difficult periods of our history.... Throughout our history we have believed that effort was its own reward. Partly because so much has been achieved here in America, we have tended to suppose that every problem must have a solution and that good intentions should somehow guarantee good results. . . . Our generation is the first to have found that the road is endless, that in traveling it, we will not find our Utopia, but only ourselves."

Gentlemen, I thank you for the honor. I am privileged.

Gen. WASHINGTON. And we are grateful. How much time should be allowed to enable you to complete your task?

Dr. FRANKLIN. Since my maxim is "never put off to tomorrow what . . ."

Gen. WASHINGTON. Dr. Franklin, just the time you need, please.

Dr. FRANKLIN. One week, General.

Gen. WASHINGTON. This session is adjourned until Moday, July 13 at 10 a.m.

Mr. ADAMS. (Aside to Dr. Franklin) Ben, though you may not be the "father" of anything, perhaps you will wind up as the grandfather of the Constitution.

Dr. FRANKLIN. (Aside to Mr. Adams) I would have preferred to have a state named after me.

Mr. ADAMS. (Aside to Dr. Franklin) You almost did.

MONDAY, JULY 13, 1987

BENJAMIN FRANKLIN PROPOSES EIGHT AMENDMENTS TO CONSTITUTION

The Committee met pursuant to notice, at 10 a.m. in the Assembly Room of Independence Hall, Gen. George Washington presiding.

  Present: Mr. John Adams, Dr. Benjamin Franklin, Mr. Thomas Jefferson, Mr. James Madison and Gen. George Washington.

  Gen. WASHINGTON. Dr. Franklin, are you prepared to report to the Commission?

  Dr. FRANKLIN. I am, General.

  Gen. WASHINGTON. Please proceed.

  Dr. FRANKLIN. In presenting my report I will from time to time resort to the transcript and statements already made before this Commission. As a basic premise, I believe we have accepted the fact that the Constitution ought to be amended to render it more adequate to the exigencies of this nation.

  Each of us here, under the guidance of our chairman, General Washington, has contributed positive and creative thoughts and solutions to this Commission. Many of these thoughts and solutions are inbedded in the framework of testimony given before the Federal Convention in 1787. I have explored the maze of testimony before this Commission, the Journals of the Federal Convention, James Madison's notes of the debates in the Federal Convention and the compromises made in 1787. With those facts, reports, and testimony in mind, and fully cognizant of the gravity of my task and that of this Commission, I am recommending that eight amendments be made to the Constitution of the United States of America.

Gentlemen, my proposals follow:

I. PROPOSED RESOLUTION NUMBER ONE

A. Resolution

It is recommended that it be RESOLVED that:

1. The Constitution shall be amended so as to establish two offices of vice-president. Each vice-president shall be chosen by Congress from among its own members, for the same term and period as the president of the United States.
2. Each such vice-president chosen shall have the same political affiliation as the president.
3. One such vice-president shall head an executive department to be known as the Department of Domestic Affairs, and the other vice-president shall head an executive department to be known as the Department of Foreign Affairs.
4. Each such vice-president shall be directly responsible and subject to the authority of the president of the United States, other than removal from office, and upon appointment shall cease to be a member of Congress.
5. Each such executive department shall consist of such subsidary agencies as shall be established by law and headed by such officers as shall be nominated by the president and, with the advice and consent of the Senate, appointed by the president.

B. Rationale

This resolution is based almost entirely on Mr. Jefferson's concepts. Mr. Jefferson stated in his time and before this Commission that "Our country is too large to have all its affairs directed by a single government. . . . The people, to whom all authority belongs, have divided the power of government into two distinct departments, the leading characters of which are foreign and domestic. . . . I am for a domestic affairs department that places great emphasis on cooperation with the States, and I am for a foreign affairs department which is reduced to foreign concerns only."

Mr. Jefferson's ideas presume, and in fact justify, the creation of two vice-presidents—that is, *working* vice-presidents—one for domestic affairs and one for foreign affairs. This would go far toward eliminating or at least assuaging the plight of our presidents as depicted in their own statements before these sessions. The evidence clearly indicates that the rigors of the office of the president are intolerable. The powers of the president are not changed by virtue of the creation of two vice-presidents. The president retains the power "by and with the advice and consent of the Senate" to appoint certain officers of the United States.

The vice-presidents chosen by Congress shall be subject to the authority of the president in the same manner as the authority of the president currently extends over officers of the United States appointed by him, except, however, as to removal. Such vice-presidents shall be removable from office in the same manner as the president, as, for example, by impeachment.

It is anticipated that Congress will divide and assign the various agencies of government among these departments, reserving to the president the direct supervision of those agencies most appropriate to his immediate authority.

For example, it is anticipated that Congress would assign the following agencies to the Department of Domestic Affairs:

Department of Agriculture
Department of Commerce
Department of Education
Department of Health and Human Services
Department of Housing and Urban Development
Department of Labor
Department of Transportation

Federal Bureau of Investigation

It is anticipated that the following agencies would be assigned to the Department of Foreign Affairs:

Department of State
Department of National Security
Central Intelligence Agency

Because of the comprehensive and complex nature of foreign affairs, it is contemplated that Congress will consider an expansion of agencies within the Department of Foreign Affairs with particular emphasis on global problems and the need to assess areas of responsibility.

As to those agencies reserved to the president's direct supervision, it is contemplated, for example, that the following agencies would fall in this category:

Department of Defense
Department of the Air Force
Department of the Army
Department of the Navy
Department of the Treasury

Gentlemen, this resolution is just one of several intended to make inroads on the presence of all the president's "Yes" men. Lest we forget, it's difficult to soar with the American eagle when you work with turkeys.

Gentlemen, we now reach the least controvertible resolution regarding the "spare tire" for the wheels of government.

II. PROPOSED RESOLUTION NUMBER TWO

A. Resolution

It is recommended that it be RESOLVED that:

1. The office of vice-president of the United States, as presently provided for under the Constitution, be eliminated.
2. The Senate shall choose its own president of the Senate.

B. Rationale

Mr. Adams made this suggestion before this Commission. The term "vice-president" did not appear before the Convention until September 4, 1787, which was the 78th Convention day, the 114th elapsed day and just 13 days before the Constitution was signed, and never received substantial debate. The introduction of such an officer came about only after a major change in committee membership occurred owing to a major compromise in matters unrelated to the creation of a vice-president but related to power politics.

The office of vice-president had been created to (a) ensure a person was available in the Senate to break a tie vote; (b) ensure a successor to the president.

George Mason, who declined to sign the Constitution, called the vice-president "that unnecessary and dangerous officer," who "for want of other employment is made president of the Senate."

James Monroe said, "The Vice President is an unnecessary office. I can see no reason for such an office. . . . I am persuaded that the advantage of his information will not counterbalance the disadvantages attending his office. . . . The Senate might of their own body elect a president who would have no dangerous influence."

Richard H. Lee recommended that the Constitution be "amended so as to omit the Creation of a Vice President. . . ."

Thomas Jefferson, second vice-president of the United States, said of the vice-presidency: "a more tranquil and unoffending status could not have been found for me. . . . It will give me philosphical evenings in the winter and rural days in the summer."

In my judgment it has been adequately established that the office of vice-president of the United States is "useless." The proposal before this Commission to establish two working vice-presidents clearly removes any necessity or justification for the retention of the single office of vice-president as presently established.

Gentlemen, on June 1, 1787, in the Federal Convention, Mr. Elbridge Gerry, who also declined to sign the Constitution, stated his position, positively and firmly: "I am in favor of a Council to advise the executive. They will be the organs of information of the persons proper for offices. Their opinions may be recorded. They may be called to account for their opinions, and impeached. If so, responsibility will be certain and, in case of misconduct, their punishment certain."

That brings us directly to the next resolution.

III. PROPOSED RESOLUTION NUMBER THREE

A. Resolution

It is recommended that it be RESOLVED that:

1. The Constitution shall be amended so as to create a Constitutional Council for Domestic Affairs to consult with and advise the vice-president heading the Department of Domestic Affairs; a Constitutional Council for Foreign Affairs to consult with and advise the vice-president heading the Department of Foreign Affairs; a Constitutional Council for National Affairs to consult with and advise the president of the United States.
2. Each such Council shall consist of sixteen senators chosen by the Senate, on a bipartisan basis.
3. Each such senator chosen shall serve on such Council during his term as senator, at the will of the Senate, for such period as the Senate shall specify, and the status of any such senator as a senator shall not be affected by virtue of such service on any such Council.
4. The Councils shall be the Constitutional and the only responsible counsellors to the vice-presidents and the president. No source of advice shall be created or interposed between any such Council and a vice-president or between

any such Council and the president.
5. The advice rendered by any such council shall not "conclude" or be binding upon any vice-president or the president, nor affect their respective responsibilities for the measures which they may adopt.

B. Rationale

It should be evident from these resolutions that the Senate thus becomes a Constitutional Council to the president. For all time past I recommended a Constitutional Council, in my Albany Plan in 1754, in my draft of the Articles of Confederation in 1775, and finally in the Federal Convention in 1787. Well, they didn't listen to me then. But perhaps, after a lapse of two hundred years, my opponents have collapsed. Perhaps.

I do not believe that the use of the Senate as a Council violates the principles of separation of powers. I always favored a unicameral legislature. A House of Representatives is fully and unequivocably separated from the executive and judicial. The Senate is still there to "cool it" as General Washington told Mr. Jefferson. The Senate and the president cannot connive to the detriment of the public, since the House of Representatives controls the purse strings. But these are my opinions, what did the others think? Much testimony has been presented before this Commission to evidence the fact that many thought the Senate as originally created—sharing powers with the president—was a Council to the president. Many thought a Council should have been created.

On August 22, 1787, the Committee of Detail reported that in its opinion the following additions should be made to matters then before the Convention:

"The President of the United States shall have a Privy Council ... whose duty it shall be to advise him in matters respecting the execution of his office, which he shall think proper to lay before them: But their advice shall not conclude him, nor affect his responsibilities for the measures which he shall adopt."

The proposal was rejected.

We have heard Mr. George Mason say that "in rejecting a Council to the President we were about to try an experiment on which the most despotic governments has never ventured."

We have shown that the states gained control of the Senate by providing for the selection of senators by the state legislatures and of the president by providing for a sharing of powers between the Senate and the president.

We have shown that, by the sharing of powers, the Senate became an imperfect Council to the president.

We have shown that the entire chain of power collapsed with the passage of the Seventeenth Amendment, which changed the mode of appointment of senators from selection by state legislatures to election by the people.

The Senate had been designed with the states in mind.

The Senate lost its justification for existence when the original reasons for establishment were undermined.

The connection between the Senate and the states was expressed by many in our sessions.

Mr. Madison said: "The Senate will represent the States in their political capacity; the other House will represent the people of the States in their individual capacity."

Mr. William R. Davie said, "The senators represent the sovereignty of the states; they are directly chosen by the state legislatures, and no legislative act can be done without their concurrence. The election of the Executive is in some measure under the control of the legislature of the states, the electors being appointed under their direction."

Mr. Livingston said, "The Senate is indeed designed to represent the state governments."

Many thought the Senate was a council to the president, as did Mr. Mason who saw "the substitution of the Senate in place of an Executive Council," and Mr. Elias Boudinot, who spoke of "The second branch of the legislature . . . an advisory body to the Executive," or Mr. Luther Martin who envisioned "This Senate being constituted a privy council to the President . . . the Senators . . . are the National Council."

Many did not believe the Senate was a council to the president, but thought it should be, including such as Mr. Richard Henry Lee who thought "a Council of State or Privy Council should be appointed to advise and assist in the arduous business assigned to the Executive power," or Mr. William Stephen Smith who wrote, "I should have been much better pleased if the President was furnished with a Constitutional Council."

These men spoke my language.

But the man who said it best was Mr. George Mason. He said it before this Commission, and he said it two hundred years ago in the Federal Convention just a few days before the Constitution was signed:

"The President of the United States has no Constitutional Council, a thing unknown in any safe and regular government. He will therefore be unsupported by proper information and advice and will generally be directed by minions and favorites . . . or a Council of State will grow out of the principal officers of the great departments the worst and most dangerous of all ingredients for such a Council in a free country for they may be induced to join in any dangerous or oppressive measures, to shelter themselves, and prevent an inquiry into their own misconduct in office." And, as I have stated before this Commission, this is exactly what happened.

I realize that we cannot impose the function of a council upon the Senate without making provision for the personnel to carry out the task. After all, we cannot take forty-eight Senators and place them in Councils and expect the Senate to perform its regular duties. And that brings me to my next proposal.

IV PROPOSED RESOLUTION NUMBER FOUR

A. Resolution

It is recommended that, in order to implement the creation of Constitutional Councils, it be RESOLVED that the Constitution be amended so that:

1. The number of Senators shall be increased by one per state, making the total number from each state three, and the total number in the Senate one hundred and fifty.
2. Each such Senator added shall be elected and shall serve in the Senate in the same manner as is provided for in the present Constitution, and with like rotation.

B. Rationale

On July 23, 1787, it was resolved in the Federal Convention that "the representation in the second Branch of the Legislature of the United States consist of (blank) Members from each State, who shall vote per capita."

Mr. Gouverneur Morris moved to fill the blank with the word "three," wishing the Senate to be a numerous body. "If two members only should be allowed to each state," he said "and a majority be made a quorum, the power would be lodged in 14 members, which was too small a number for such a trust."

The vote was in the negative.

I mention this simply to remind us that the possibility of three senators per state was considered in the Federal Convention. If we were not ready for it then, we should be now. Mathematically the addition of fifty new senators fits our requirements very well. A total of forty-eight senators would be required in the Councils (three times sixteen), in addition to two members of Congress, possibly originating from the senate, as vice-presidents, making a total of fifty. A small price to pay for a big solution to America's problems.

We now come to the fifth proposal.

V. PROPOSED RESOLUTION NUMBER FIVE

A. Resolution

It is recommended that it be RESOLVED that the Constitution be amended so that:

1. The Supreme Court, or its specially created impeachment court, shall have the sole power to try all impeachments.
2. When the president or any vice-president is tried, the trial shall be conducted by the Supreme Court.
3. Any Impeachment Court specially created by the Supreme Court shall consist of not less than nine federal judges.
4. No person shall be convicted without the concurrence of two-thirds of the full court.

B. Rationale

Under the present Constitution the power is given to the Senate to *try* all impeachments, while the House of Representatives, of course, has the sole power of impeachment.

It should be evident that if the senate is to become the Constitutional Council to the president, it can no longer try impeachments because many of its leading and influential members may have advised or concurred in the very measures for which a person may be impeached and for which the senate, under the present Constitution, would try the impeachment. Therefore, the trial of an impeachment should be conducted by another body. The most practical and capable body for trying such impeachments is the Supreme Court.

Actually, in the Federal Convention, the Supreme Court was the first choice for the trial of impeachments.

Gen. WASHINGTON. Dr. Franklin, you recognize that the subject of impeachment has not yet been examined in any detail by the Commission. Its introduction, therefore, is subject to questioning by any member of this Commission.

Dr. FRANKLIN. I realize that. On August 6, 1787 The Committee of Detail reported to the Convention the detail of the

Constitution to date. Under its terms, it was reported that the House of Representatives "shall have the sole power of impeachment," and that the "jurisdiction of the Supreme Court shall extend . . . to the trial of impeachments of officers of the United States." As originally conceived, therefore, the Supreme Court was to try impeachments.

On September 4, 1787, however, the Committee of Eleven, to whom sundry resolutions had been referred on August 31, reported that in its opinion the section on the trial of impeachments should be altered to read, "The Senate of the United States shall have power to try all impeachments, but no person shall be convicted without the concurrence of two-thirds of the members present."

So the impeachment trial was moved from the Supreme Court to the Senate at that late date.

Mr. ADAMS. Dr. Franklin, was either Mr. Morris or Mr. Dickinson a member of the Committee of Detail which reported on August 6, 1787, that the function of the Supreme Court shall extend to the trial of impeachments?

Dr. FRANKLIN. Neither Mr. Morris nor Mr. Dickinson was a member of the Committee of Detail.

Mr. ADAMS. Dr. Franklin, was either Mr. Morris or Mr. Dickinson a member of the Committee of Eleven which recommended that the Senate has the power to try impeachments?

Dr. FRANKLIN. Both Mr. Morris and Mr. Dickinson were members of the Committee of Eleven.

Mr. ADAMS. For the record, was any member of the Committee of Eleven a member of the Committee of Detail?

Dr. FRANKLIN. No.

Mr. ADAMS. Mr. Chairman, I ask that the secretary summarize a statement by Mr. Mason on the change in power which caused many changes in the Constitution in the final days of the Federal Convention.

Gen. WASHINGTON. Mr. Thomson, will you please locate the subject and refresh our minds?

Mr. THOMSON. Yes sir . . . here it is. Mr. Mason said in effect that the Constitution as agreed to up to a fortnight before the Convention ended was such as he could have set his "hand and heart" to. Up to that time Pennsylvania, New Jersey, and Delaware tended to vote as a block against the remaining states present. Rhode Island was not there, and New York, seldom, so that it was these three states against eight. The question of the importation of slaves had been left to Congress. This disturbed the two southernmost states who knew that Congress would immediately suppress the importation of slaves. Therefore, those two states struck up a bargain with the three New England states; if they would join to admit slaves for some years, the two southernmost states would join in changing the clause which required two-thirds of the legislature in any vote. These articles were changed accordingly and from that moment the two southern states and the three New England states joined Pennsylvania, New Jersey, and Delaware and made the majority eight to three against us, instead of eight to three for us as it had been through the whole convention. Under this coalition the great principles of the Constitution were changed in the last days of the Convention.

Mr. ADAMS. Dr. Franklin, during what period of the Federal Convention did the compromise encompassing the importation of slaves and the navigation acts occur?

Dr. FRANKLIN. My recollection is that the compromise was reached during the month of August.

Mr. ADAMS. So that the action of the Committee of Detail in reporting the Supreme Court as having jurisdiction over the trial of impeachments could not have been influenced by the compromise?

Dr. FRANKLIN. That is true. . . .

Mr. ADAMS. And the action of the Committee of Eleven could have been influenced by the compromise?

Dr. FRANKLIN. It is possible.

Mr. ADAMS. What reason did Mr. Morris give for the change?

Dr. FRANKLIN. Mr. Morris gave this as his reason: "A conclusive reason for making the Senate instead of the Supreme Court the Judge of Impeachments was that the Supreme Court was to try the President after the trial of the impeachments." Mr. Morris thought "no other tribunal than the Senate could be trusted. The Supreme Court were too few in number and might be warped or corrupted." He was against "a dependence of the Executive on the Legislature, considering the Legislative tyranny the great danger to be apprehended; but there could be no danger that the Senate would say untruly on their oaths that the President was guilty of crimes. . . ."

Mr. ADAMS. Mr. Madison, you were there; did you agree?

Mr. MADISON. I objected to a trial of the president by the Senate, especially as he was to be impeached by the other branch of the legislature, and for any act which might be called a misdemeanor. The president under these circumstances was made improperly dependent. I preferred the Supreme Court for the trial of impeachments, or rather a tribunal of which that should form a part.

Mr. ADAMS. Dr. Franklin, at that point in the session of the Federal Convention, when Mr. Morris and Mr. Dickinson proposed trials of impeachment by the Senate, was the provision already in the proposed Constitution that the Senate would be elected by the state legislatures?

Dr. FRANKLIN. It was.

Mr. ADAMS. Thank you. These are all the questions I have on this point, at this point.

Dr. FRANKLIN. Mr. Luther Martin before the Maryland House of Representatives on November 29, 1787, anticipated that the "impeachment can rarely come from the Second Branch, who are his council and will be under his influence."

The Hamilton Plan provided that impeachments "shall be tried by a Council consisting of Judges of the Supreme Court and the Chief Justice or the first Senior Judge of the Supreme Court of Law in each state of whom twelve shall constitute a court."

Gentlemen, I urge that we return to the thinking of the Convention before the compromise; namely, that the jurisdiction of the Supreme Court shall extend over to the trial of impeachment.

I come now to my sixth proposal.

VI. PROPOSED RESOLUTION NUMBER SIX

A. Resolution

It is recommended that it be RESOLVED that the Constitution be amended so as to require the ratification of treaties by a majority vote of both Houses of Congress.

B. Rationale

The present provision of the Constitution requiring a two-thirds vote of the Senate for the ratification of treaties is obsolete. This provision was based on a conception of the states as sovereign powers whose individual consent must be obtained to any material agreement with a foreign power, through the Senate as conduit. The provision as it stands permits the representation of a small minority of the people to defeat the will of a large majority on issues that may involve the survival of this nation. This matter has already been discussed before this Commission. However, it becomes essential that this change be made if the Senate is to become council to the president. In this case, the Senate cannot recommend foreign policy and at the same time be the sole legislative body approving that policy. The concept of separation of powers requires that the House of Representatives and the Senate approve treaties by a majority vote.

As for my next proposal . . .

VII. PROPOSED RESOLUTION NUMBER SEVEN

A. Resolution

It is recommended to this Commission that it be RESOLVED that the Constitution be amended so that:

1. Rules and regulations drafted and promulgated by any agency of the government to implement federal law shall not

include substantive provisions encroaching upon the legislative prerogatives of Congress, but shall contain only such provisions as allow the laws to be faithfully executed.

2. The Senate shall monitor compliance therewith for the Congress.

3. The Congress shall have the power to approve, modify, or disapprove any such rule or regulation.

B. Rationale

Testimony has been given before this Commission to illustrate the manner in which governmental agencies develop regulations inconsistent with law. Under the Constitution the executive departments are to execute the laws, not make the laws. Restrict the executive departments to what they should be doing, namely, administering the laws.

Testimony has also been presented on the Chadha case, in which the Supreme Court decided on June 23, 1983, that the "legislative veto" was unconstitutional. The proposed amendment places legislative authority back where it belongs—in the Congress.

It is about time this government of the people, by the people, and for the people stop doing it *to* the people.

It is to be recalled that in the Federal Convention Mr. Madison proposed that the president have powers "not legislative or judiciary in their nature." The words "not legislative or judiciary in their nature" were never inserted in the Constitution. I therefore recommend that the Constitution be amended to add a Section 5 to Article II thereof, to read as follows:

"Section 5. The executive power of the president shall not include any matter legislative or judicial in its nature, except as specified in Section 7 of Article I and Section 2 of Article II."

The next recommendation is the last for today and was proposed by Mr. Madison.

VIII. PROPOSED RESOLUTION NUMBER EIGHT

A. Resolution

It is recommended to this Commission that it be RESOLVED that:

1. The Constitution shall be amended so that the term of members of the House of Representatives shall be extended from two to three years.

2. Beginning with the first election in the House after ratification of the amendment, members of the House shall be divided as equally as possible into three classes. The seats of the members of the first class shall be vacated at the expiration of the first year, of the second class at the expiration of the second year, and of the third class at the expiration of the third year, so that one-third may be elected every year.

B. Rationale

Under the proposed amendments the Senate retains its legislative powers as a body and, in addition, serves as council to the president. To strengthen, stabilize, and provide greater continuity in the House of Representatives, the term of its members should be extended from two to three years, with a rotation of one-third annually.

Mr. Madison kept extensive notes on this subject, many of which have already been discussed before this Commission. Mr. Daniel of St. Thomas Jenifer proposed that members of the first branch of the legislature should be chosen every three years. Mr. Madison stated that a three year term would produce stability and allow representatives sufficient time to learn their jobs. I stated that "instability is one of the great vices of our republic."

The question of triennial election in the first branch passed, and on June 18, Mr. Alexander Hamilton sketched a plan for the three-year term for representatives.

But on June 21, the election of the first branch "for the term of three years" was reconsidered, with Mr. Randolph moving for a two-year term.

Mr. Madison's notes indicated that Mr. John Dickinson preferred triennial elections and that in order to prevent the inconvenience of an entire change of the whole House at the same time suggested a rotation, by an annual election of one-third. His idea was right, but we weren't bright enough then to buy it. The idea is still right. Have we brightened?

  Mr. ADAMS. (Murmuring) It had to be him!

  Dr. FRANKLIN. (Continuing) Mr. Madison beieved that annual elections would be extremely inconvenient and reiterated that members needed sufficient time "to acquire that knowledge of the affairs of the states without which their trust could not be usefully discharged."

Mr. Hamilton again "urged the necessity of three years," but the question for striking out "three years" passed, the motion for "two years" was then inserted, without further debate, and the concept of the two-year term was not revised thereafter.

On the basis of functional logic, looking at the issue in 1987, we would have to resolve the matter as a three-year term. However, on the basis of proverbial logic—"where annual elections end, tyranny begins"—we would have to resolve the matter as a one-year term. Essentially the ideal is to have both.

It has been said that all government is an evil. It is more proper to say that the necessity of any government is a misfortune. This necessity, however, exists; and the problem to be solved is not what form of government is perfect but which of the forms is least imperfect.

  In my judgment the least imperfect solution of this issue is not the average of "one" and "three" producing "two," but rather that answer which best satisfies the requirements of annual elections and yet at the same time satisfies the longer-term requirement for understanding both the job and the wishes of the people. With this in mind, I recommend a three-year term for members of the House of Representatives, with an annual election of one-third of the House.

Mr. Chairman, I have concluded my recommendations. You will observe, however, that I have made no specific recommendation covering the office of the president. While all recommendations are on the periphery of this subject, they do ease the rigors of the presidency. Therefore, what has been recommended to date moves toward a solution of the problems residing in the structure of the American government. However, I am of the opinion that we should examine the debates in the Federal Constitution to determine whether any changes in the structure of the office of the president are exigent to the interests of our nation.

Gentlemen, I thank you.

Gen. WASHINGTON. Dr. Franklin, we thank you. In order that we may consider Dr. Franklin's recommendations, these public sessions will adjourn until Monday, July 27, 1987 at 10 a.m.

MONDAY, JULY 27, 1987

COMMISSION ACCEPTS BENJAMIN FRANKLIN'S PROPOSALS

The Committee met pursuant to notice, at 10 a.m. in the Assembly Room of Independence Hall, Gen. George Washington presiding.

Present: Mr. John Adams, Dr. Benjamin Franklin, Mr. Thomas Jefferson, Mr. James Madison and Gen. George Washington.

Gen. WASHINGTON. The Commission met in closed session during the period beginning Monday, July 20, and ending Friday, July 25, to consider Dr. Franklin's recommendations. After considerable discussion and debate it was unanimously agreed to accept Dr. Franklin's recommendations.

The Commission has also unanimously agreed to accept Dr. Franklin's recommendations that this Commission continue its sessions so as to examine documents applicable to the Federal Convention applying to the creation of the office of the president. In order to allow time for preparation, discussions and testimony on this matter will begin August 6 at 10 a.m.

Accordingly, this session is adjourned until such date and time.

THURSDAY, AUGUST 6, 1987

ORIGIN OF PRESIDENTIAL FOUR YEAR TERM

The Committee met pursuant to notice, at 10 a.m. in the Assembly Room of Independence Hall, Gen. George Washington presiding.
>Present: Mr. John Adams, Dr. Benjamin Franklin, Mr. Thomas Jefferson, Mr. James Madison and Gen. George Washington.

Mr. THOMSON. (To the spectators) While we wait for General Washington to arrive for today's session, I thought I would give you some inkling as to the functions of the presidents before General Washington.

There were sixteen presidents of the Continental Congress—John Hancock having been elected to two terms. As you know, I served as secretary to the Continental Congress from 1774 to 1789, which covered the terms of all the presidents. I even presided over Congress for brief periods as acting president.

While the Congress provided for by the Constitution in 1787 is in a real sense the successor of the Congress of 1774, the president of the United States is not in a real sense the successor of the presidents of the old Congress. The presidents of Congress were solely presiding officers, whereas the president of the United States is an executive officer, with no presiding duties at all. The duties of the presidents of the Continental Congress were largely those of presiding in Congress, looking after certain official correspondence, and entertaining Americans and foreigners of distinction. During the urgencies of Government business, John Hancock once turned to Mr. Robert Morris with a request: "I must ask the favour of you to send me by the next Express, half a ream of good writing paper, two pounds of the best sealing wax, a box of wafers and three hundred of the best quills."

Of course, we must not lose sight of the fact that the president was a delegate from some state and that his first duty, as viewed at the time, was to his constituency. He had the right to serve on committees, to participate in debate, and to vote, though he had no casting vote in case of a tie. Though President Henry Laurens did so, it appears that it was not customary for the president to participate in a debate as a delegate and then in the character of a chairman to hear himself replied to.

The duty of presiding when combined with other duties made the president's position not a particularly enviable one. Richard Henry Lee was compelled to sit in Congress from eleven in the morning till four in the afternoon, during the summer months of 1785, and found his total load almost too much for him to bear.

There was no vice-president in the Continental Congress, and sometimes when the president was unable to attend to his duties, I, who was not even a delegate, or a temporary chairman, presided. During the illness of President Hanson in April and May 1782, an effort was made to create a temporary vice-presidency, and a motion looking toward that end was defeated by a close vote. It was decided that a chairman should serve but that official papers must be signed by the president. David Ramsay and Nathaniel Gorham served as chairmen in the place of John Hancock for something more than six months—President John Hancock, you will recall, never attended his second term.

Quite different was the presidential task of taking care of official correspondence. Letters to and from state officials, military and naval officers, and American representatives abroad passed through the presidential office. Letters received were reported by the president to Congress where they were disposed of by reference to a special or standing committee or, later, to one of the executive departments. The presidents also framed letters in accordance with Congressional resolutions, to be sent to various officials hither and yon. To be sure, the whole burden of official correspondence did not rest upon the presidential office; much of it was discharged by the secretary of Congress—me—and by committees or departments. Furthermore, many letters, especially circular ones to the states, were prepared by the committees, though they went out over the president's signature.

Early in 1777, Hancock wrote: "I am almost hurried out of my life, but I will bear up"; and again, "I am almost hurried to death but must keep at it." He was so rushed with business, he said, that he scarcely had time to write to a friend. He looked upon his letter-books as private property and carried them away with him when he left Congress in October 1777, though they were later restored to The Papers of the Continental Congress by the Massachusetts Historical Society. There are no presidential libraries for presidents of the Continental Congress.

The amount of labor required to discharge the presidential correspondence varied according to the letter-writing qualities of the occupants of the office. Some were far more prolific and verbose than others, the letters of John Laurens being noted for length and those of John Jay and Samuel Huntington for brevity and terseness. A president's private correspondence when added to the official correspondence made the task a considerable one, even with secretarial assistance. Richard Henry Lee wrote, "I am from all parts of the U.S. written to in my private capacity, so I am at this moment at least 20 letters in arrears to my correspondents—To answer them all punctually would at once destroy my health and prevent all attention to public business. I do assure you that the business and the ceremonies of my office are too much for my feeble state of health." So the president was overworked, even then.

But exactly who was the first president of the United States?

John Hanson has been referred to as the first president of the United States and at times as the president of the United States in Congress Assembled, having been elected president in November 1781. Two hundred years later, in November

1981, the Postal Service issued a twenty-cent stamp in his honor, the Postal Service having previously issued a postcard honoring him in the "Patriots Series." So time has either elevated his importance in history or inflated his value in an inflated economy.

Perhaps the honor of being first rests with Mr. Peyton Randolph, who was elected the first president of the Continental Congress in 1774, when the Congress was a revolutionary Congress. Or perhaps the honor goes to Gen. Thomas Mifflin of Pennsylvania, who was the first president of Congress elected after the treaty of peace was signed with Britain in 1783. Or, perhaps it was Mr. Richard Henry Lee of Virginia, who was elected the first president of Congress after Congress ratified the treaty in 1784. Or, perhaps the honor goes to Gen. George Washington of Virginia, who was the first president under the second Constitution of the United States, which became effective March 4, 1789.

Gen Washington has arrived.

Gen. WASHINGTON. This session will come to order. Today we will examine documents applicable to the Federal Convention applying to the creation of the office of the president. Before we proceed, however, I have a word.

The foundation of our Empire was not laid in the gloomy age of ignorance and superstition but at an epoch when the rights of mankind were better understood and more clearly defined than at any former period. During that auspicious period, the United States came into existence as a Nation.

The United States is making great progress towards national happiness; and, if it is not attained here in as high a degree as human nature will admit, I think we may then conclude that political happiness is unattainable.

Such is our situation, and such are our prospects; but notwithstanding the cup of blessing is thus reached out to us, notwithstanding happiness is ours if we have a disposition to seize the occasion and make it our own; yet it appears to me there is an option still left to the United States of America, that it is in its choice and depends upon its conduct, whether it will be respectable and prosperous or contemptible and miserable as a Nation.

Mr. MADISON. I agree. Of the ability and intelligence of those who composed the Convention, the debates and proceedings may be a test; as to the character of the work which was the offspring of their deliberations, it must be tested by the experience of the future.

Gen. WASHINGTON. In pursuance of our task here today, Mr. Jefferson will conduct the course of discussion. Mr. Jefferson.

Mr. JEFFERSON. Our nation, kindly separated by nature and a wide ocean from the exterminating havoc of one quarter of the globe; possessing a chosen country, with room enough for our descendants to the thousandth and thousandth generation, entertaining a due sense of our equal right, honesty, truth, temperance, gratitude, and the love of man; acknowledging and adoring an overruling Providence; with all these blessings, what more is necessary to make us a happy and prosperous people? Still one thing more, gentlemen, a wise and frugal government, which shall restrain men from injuring one another, shall leave them otherwise free to regulate their own pursuits of industry and improvement, and shall not take from the mouth of labor the bread it has earned. This is the sum of good government; and this is necessary to close the circle of our felicities.

The wisdom of our sages and blood of our heroes have been devoted to their attainment; they should be the creed of our political faith, the text of civic instruction, the touchstone by which to try the services of those we trust; and should we wander from them in moments of error or of alarm, let us hasten to retrace our steps and to regain the road which alone leads to peace, liberty and safety.

And that brings us to our task today, our discussion of the office of the president.

I was the third president of the United States, and I learned to expect that it will rarely fall to the lot of imperfect man to retire from this station with the reputation and the favor which brought him into it.

What, therefore, is the character of the office that can so affect the character of the one who occupies the seat of that office?

I have asked Major Jackson to prepare a chronology of the voting on two subjects debated in the Federal Convention: first, on the length of the term of the president; second, on the mode or manner of electing the president. What I want to illustrate, in both issues, is the emormous amount of uncertainty, indecision, vacillation, and, in fact, intrigue, that prevailed in the process of debating the issue. Major Jackson will be using the Journals of the Convention, which he kept, and Mr. Madison will be using his notes.

Let me not forget to remind you that the term for the president in our time was for a period of four years, with unlimited opportunity for reeligibility. The Twenty-second Amendment to the Constitution changed this provision so no person today can be elected more than twice.

Please proceed, Major Jackson.

Major JACKSON. I hope that within the time allotted me during the past few days I have gathered adequate material. I say this because just before the Constitution was signed Mr. Rufus King suggested that the Journals of the Convention should either be destroyed or deposited in the custody of the president. He thought that if made public they might be put to bad use by those who would wish to prevent the adoption of the Constitution. Mr. James Wilson preferred depositing the Journals in the custody of the president. A question was then put on depositing the Journals and other papers of the Convention in the hands of the president, which question passed. General Washington then asked what the Convention meant should be done with the Journals, whether copies were to be allowed to the members if applied for. It was resolved that he "retain the Journal and other papers, subject to the order of Congress, if ever formed under the Constitution."

That evening, after the Constitution was signed, I did something I regret to this day. Let me read you a note I wrote to General Washington:

"Major Jackson presents his most respectful compliments to General Washington. . . . Major Jackson, after burning all the loose scraps of paper which belong to the Convention, will this evening wait upon the General with the Journals and other papers which their vote directs to be delivered to His Excellency. [Endorsed:] From Major Wm. Jackson 17th September, 1787."

Yes, I delivered the Journals "after burning all the loose scraps of paper." At the time I did not realize the value of those scraps of paper.

The issue before the Convention, which I will attempt to trace, was the length of the term of the president.

On May 29, 1787, Mr. Randolph proposed a resolution which in part suggested "that a National Executive be instituted; to be chosen by the National Legislature for the term of [blank] years . . . and to be ineligible a second time." The debates, votes and re-votes that accompanied the filling in of that blank characterized that same power struggle, already discussed before this Commission, which resulted in massive changes in policy within the Constitution. One cannot say that there was at any point of the discussion of the issue of the presidential term any one clear call for a term of "four" years or, for that matter, any other length of term. For example,

> —On June 1, Mr. Wilson moved to fill in the blank with "three years," Mr. Mason was for seven, and Mr. Bedford was for three with ineligibility after nine; the vote for seven years passed, 5 to 4, with one divided vote.
>
> —On July 19 a repeat vote for a seven-year term failed to pass, while a term of six years did pass, 9 to 1.
>
> —On July 24 Mr. Wilson suggested going back to a term of seven years, Mr. Martin was for eleven years, Mr. Gerry suggested fifteen, Mr. King proposed twenty, and Mr. Davie, eight. Action was postponed this day, no doubt to allow the delegates an opportunity to consult their calculators on the matter of these mathematical possibilities.

But at this time a Committee of Detail was appointed—the same committee we have spoken of earlier—to report a drafting of the Constitution, conforming to the resolutions already acted upon. On July 26, the matter of the presidential term was reconsidered, and this time the seven-year term passed once again, 7 to 3, with the president "to be ineligible a second time."

On August 6, the Committee of Detail reported a draft of the Constitution which included the phrase, "He shall hold his office during the term of seven years; but shall not be elected a second time." On August 31, such parts of the Constitution as had been postponed were referred to the Committee of Eleven. On September 4, the Committee of Eleven recommended that the provision for the term of the president read, "He shall hold his office during the term of four years." The following day it was moved to postpone consideration of the Committee of Eleven's report in order to take up the question of reinstating the seven-year term. The next day the seven-year term once again failed, 3 to 8, as did a six-year, 2 to 9. It was then agreed to retain the word "four," 10 to 1, and the question did not arise again. That, Mr. Jefferson, is my report on the chronology of the consideration of the presidential term.

Mr. JEFFERSON. Thank you, Major Jackson. I have been sitting here tallying the number of votes you recorded in the Journals on this issue, and if my tally is correct, there was only one vote for a four-year term and that occurred on September 6, eleven days before the Constitution was signed.

Debates before September 4 on the question of "term" included three, six, seven, eight, eleven, fifteen, and twenty years, and also a term during the "good behaviour" of the president, but never "four" years. The preponderance of voting before September 4 favored a term of "seven" years.

It was the Committee of Eleven that recommended "four" years . . .

Mr. ADAMS. You mean, Mr. Gouverneur Morris and Mr. John Dickinson of that Committee . . .

Gen. WASHINGTON. Mr. Adams!

Mr. JEFFERSON. If I may interject a thought—I strongly disliked the perpetual re-eligibility of the president. I thought it would be productive of cruel distress to our country in your day and mine. My later wish was that the president should be elected for seven years and be ineligible afterwards. This term I thought sufficient to enable him, with the concurrence of the legislature, to carry through and establish any system of improvement he should propose for the general good. But the practice adopted, I think, is better, allowing his continuance for eight years, with a liability to be dropped at half way of the term, making that a period of probation. That his continuance should be restrained to seven years was the opinion of the Convention at an earlier stage of its session, when it voted that term by a majority of eight against two and by a simple majority that he should be ineligible a second time. This opinion was confirmed by the House so late as July 26, referred to the Committee of Detail, reported favorably by them, changed to the present form by final vote on the last day but one only of their session. Of this change, three states expressed their disapprobation; New York, by recommending an amendment that the president should not be eligible a third time, and Virginia and North Carolina that he should not be capable of serving more than eight, in any term of sixteen years; and though this amendment has not been made in form, yet practice seems to have established it, except as to President Franklin Roosevelt whose longer term generated the Twenty-second Amendment to the Constitution.

Gen. WASHINGTON. I confess I differed widely from Mr. Jefferson on the question of reeligibility of the president. There cannot, in my judgment, be the least danger that the president will by any practicable intrigue ever be able to continue himself one moment in office, much less perpetuate himself in it—but in the last stage of corrupted morals and political depravity. Though, when a people shall become incapable of governing themselves and fit for a master, it is of little consequence from what quarter he comes.

Miss Catherine COLE. (Among the spectators, to Mrs. James Madison) Dolley, do you remember I wrote to you before you married Mr. Madison, "Madison told me I might say what I pleas'd to you about this. To begin with, he thinks so much of you in the day that he has lost his tongue. At night he dreams of you and awakes in his sleep calling on you to relieve his flame, for he burns to such an excess, that he will shortly be consumed. He hopes that your heart will be callous to every other swain but himself. He has consented to everything that I have written about him with sparkling eyes.''

Mrs. Dolley MADISON. (To Miss Cole) I could not fail to remember that letter. And then Jemmy and I were married at Harwood, in Virginia, on September 15, 1794.

Mr. Jonathan TRUMBULL, JR. (Overhearing; to Mr. John Trumbull) Madison got married in the summer of '94 and that event or some other relieved him of much bile and rendered him much more open and conversant than I had ever seen him before.

Mr. John TRUMBULL (To Mr. Jonathan Trumbull, Jr.) Be careful, she might overhear you. She's turning around now . . .

Mr. Jonathan TRUMBULL. Well, Hello, Dolley . . .

Mr. JEFFERSON. I asked Mr. Madison a few days ago if he would kindly prepare from his notes what he considers the key debates on the subject of the term of the president. Mr. Madison.

Mr. MADISON. There is perhaps a paucity of debate in the Convention specifically on the term of the president. Much of what was said was tied in with the mode of the election or appointment of the president.

Early in the debates, Mr. Wilson moved for a term of three years, with a provision for reeligibility, but Mr. Mason was for seven years at least and for prohibiting a reeligibility as the best expedient both for preventing the effect of a false complaisance on the side of the legislature towards unfit characters and temptation on the side of the executive to intrigue with the legislature for a reappointment. This premise, of course, presumed that the president would be chosen by the legislature.

Mr. Gunning Bedford opposed so long a term, begging the Committee to consider what the situation of the country would be in case the first magistrate did not possess the qualifications ascribed to him, or should lose them after his appointment. Impeachment would be no cure for this evil; it would reach misfeasance only, not incapacity. He was for a triennial election and for ineligibility after a period of nine years.

Mr. Broom was for a shorter than seven-year term if the executive magistrate was to be reeligible. If he were to remain ineligible a second time, he preferred a longer term.

Doctor McClurg desired the term to be "during good behavior." Reeligibility put the chief executive into a situation that would keep him dependent forever on the legislature. He believed the independence of the executive to be equally essential with that of the judiciary department. This presumed appointment of the executive by the legislature.

Mr. Gouverneur Morris agreed. He thought this was the way to get a good government. He was indifferent how the executive should be be chosen, provided he held his place "during good behavior."

Mr. Broom liked the idea, but Mr. Sherman considered such a tenure as by no means safe or admissible. If the executive magistrate were reeligible, he would be on good behavior in order to be reelected.

As I look back on this debate, the probable object was merely to enforce the argument against the reeligibility of the executive magistrate by holding out a tenure during good behavior as the alternative for keeping him independent of the legislature.

Colonel Mason thought it impossible to define misbehaviour and perhaps still more impossible to compel so high an offender to submit to a trial. He considered "Executive during good behavior" as a softer name only for "Executive for life," an easy step to hereditary monarchy.

I was not apprehensive of being thought to favor any step towards monarchy. The real object with me was to prevent its introduction. Experience had proved a tendency on our governments to throw all power into the legislative vortex. The executives of the states were, in general, little more than cyphers, the legislatures omnipotent. If no effectual check could have been devised for restraining the instability and encroachments of the legislatures, a revolution of some kind or other would be inevitable. The preservation of republican government was, therefore, essential.

Mr. Gouverneur Morris concurred that the way to keep out monarchial government was to establish such a republican government as would make the people happy and prevent a desire of change. while Dr. McClurg was not so much afraid of the shadow of monarchy as to be unwilling to approach it, nor so wedded to republican government as not to be sensible of the tyrannies that had been and might be exercised under that form. It was an essential object with him to make the executive independent of the legislature, and the only mode left for effecting it was to appoint him during good behavior.

It is of interest to note the close vote: Inserting "during good behavior" in place of "seven years" with an ineligibility clause failed to pass, 4 votes to 6 against. The debate continued.

Mr. Randolph was for making the executive ineligible for a second term. If he were reappointable by the legislature, obviously he would be no check on it. The fear that a constitutional bar to reappointment might inspire unconstitutional endeavors to perpetuate the executive's term might be answered that such endeavors can have no effect unless the people be so corrupt as to render all precautions hopeless; this argument supposes the executive to be more powerful and dangerous than other arguments which have been used, and consequently calls for stronger fetters on his authority. Mr. Randolph supported an election by the legislature with an incapacity to be elected a second time.

Again, it is evident that most of the debate presumed appointment of the president by the legislature.

Mr. King liked neither an ineligibility clause nor a short term. He thought that one who had proven most fit for an office ought not be excluded from holding it, that the term should be twenty years, the medium life of princes.

Mr. Morris was for a short term, in order to avoid impeachments which would be otherwise necessary.

Mr. Butler opposed the difficulties of frequent elections, and Mr. Ellsworth was for six years, because if the elections be too frequent, the executive would not be firm enough.

Mr. Williamson thought that if the elections were too frequent, the best men would not undertake the service and those of an inferior character would be liable to be corrupted.

And so it went—utter confusion. No real direction. An untimely time to be deciding on a term. "We seem to be entirely at a loss on this head," Mr. Gerry said, and suggested referring the clause relating to the executive to the Committee of Detail. "Perhaps they will be able to hit on something that may unite the various opinions which have been thrown out."

Mr. ADAMS. It must have been boring.

Dr. FRANKLIN. It was boring. It is boring.

Mr. JEFFERSON. Whether it was boring, fatiguing, tiring, or annoying, it all brings out several points:

First, the debates on the term of the president were primarily based on the premise that the national legislature would appoint him: an incorrect premise in the light of what transpired.

Second, the weakness of argument in the debates kept the door open for the Committee of Eleven to act, and kept the Convention unable to react.

Third, this nation has gone through two hundred years living with a myth, the myth that the "term" of the president is inviolate, untouchable. This is far from the truth—it was, in fact, an unsolvable dilemma, decided at last almost out of desperation rather than cogitation and consideration.

My own impressions of the Constitution when I first read it in November 1787, were varied. I was in Paris as minister to France. Mr. Adams was minister to Britain. Displeased with my first review, I did not hesitate to write of my dissatisfaction to Mr. Adams.

"How do you like our new constitution? I confess there are things in it which stagger all my dispositions to subscribe to what such an assembly has proposed. The house of federal representatives will not be adequate to the management of affairs either foreign or federal. Their President seems a bad edition of a Polish king. He may be reelected from four years to four years for life. Reason and experience prove to us that a chief magistrate, so continuable, is an officer for life. . . . Once in office, and possessing the military force of the union, without either the aid or check of a council, he would not be easily dethroned, even if the people could be induced to withdraw their votes from him. I wish that at the end of the four years they had made him forever ineligible a second time. Indeed I think all the good of this new constitution might have been couched in three or four new articles to be added to the good, old, and venerable fabric, which should have been preserved even as a religious relique."

I must admit that I had previously expressed my view on the tenure of the chief executive during the time the Federal Convention was still in session, while I was still in Paris: "I am sensible that there are defects in our federal government; yet they are so much lighter than those of monarchies that I view them with much indulgence. I rely too on the good sense of the people for remedy. If any of our countrymen wish for a King, give them Aesop's fable of the frogs who asked a King; if this does not cure them, send them to Europe: they will go back good republicans. . . ."

Mr. THOMSON. (To the spectators) Mr. Jefferson's remark about the frogs is most appropriate. The fable, as you may already know, concerns a group of frogs who were discontented because they had no one to rule over them, so they sent a deputation to Jupiter to ask him to give them a king. Jupiter, despising the folly of their request, cast a log in the pool where they lived and said that that should be their king. The frogs were terrified at first by the splash and scuttled away into the deepest parts of the pool; but by and by, when they saw that the log remained motionless, one by one they ventured to the surface again, and before long, growing bolder, they began to feel such contempt for it that they even took to sitting upon it. Thinking that a king of that sort was an insult to their dignity, they sent to Jupiter a second time and begged him to take away the sluggish king he had given them and to give them another and a better one. Jupiter, annoyed at being pestered in this way, sent a stork to rule over them, who no sooner arrived among them than he began to catch and eat the frogs as fast as he could.

Mr. JEFFERSON. It would appear that the decision regarding the presidential term was a contorted one for the delegates. Mr. Madison's notes of debates seemingly denote moments of defeat, frustration, blundering, fruitlessness—just a hobbling bunch of founders, floundering and foundering in seas of ideas.

The fact is, the subject continues to be debated to this very day. President Andrew Jackson in all eight of his annual messages to Congress advocated a single term of either four or six years. President William H. Harrison in his inaugural address in 1811 spoke for a single term. In 1844, the Whig platform contained a single-term provision. President Buchanan supported the principle of a single term of six years during the campaign of 1856. In 1864, the Confederacy adopted the single term of six years for its president. Samuel Tilden in 1876 and President Hayes in his inaugural address in 1877 both advocated a single six-year term.

Grover Cleveland, in accepting the Democratic nomination in 1884, expressed his opposition to the reeligibility of the president. The platforms of the People's Party in 1888 and 1892 and the Democratic Party in 1912 favored a single term but did not specify the length of the term. The Prohibition Party in 1912 and 1916 favored a single six-year term. Ex-President William Howard Taft in a lecture at Columbia University in 1915 supported a single term of six or seven years. In more recent years, Wendell Willkie in his 1940 campaign favored a single term of eight years or less. The National Negro Council, Governor (later Senator) John Bricker of Ohio, Sen. Harry Byrd of Virginia, Sen. W. Lee O'Daniel, and other prominent people have all expressed approval of the proposal for a single term of six years. Gallop polls in 1939, 1943, and 1945, however, during the Franklin Roosevelt era, showed that the public opposed, approximately three to one, changing the presidential tenure to a single term of six years.

Still, since the adoption of the Constitution, hundreds of amendments have been proposed to alter the tenure of the president, among them nearly 160 offering to change the term from four to six years. The great majority of the proposed amendments would also have made the president ineligible for reelection. During the Constitution's first hundred years over 125 amendments were submitted, fifty-two of them advocating a six-year term. Thirty-eight proposed ineligibility for reelection, while fourteen proposed reeligibility. An amendment providing for a six-year term was first introduced by Congressman Hemphill of Pennsylvania in 1826 and has been advocated at different periods ever since. The majority of the proposals offered during the time stipulated that the president should be ineligible to reelection.

In this period only one six-year term amendment was reported to the full House. In 1875, the Committee on the Judiciary reported H.R. 147 introduced by Congressman Potter of New York and providing for a six-year term with the incumbent ineligible for two successive terms of office. The measure, however, failed of the necessary two-thirds vote, 134 to 104. In the First Session of the next Congress the question was called up again by a majority and minority report of the House Committee on the Judiciary on H.R. 41. Both the reports concurred that the president should not be eligible to reelection, but differed as to tenure, the majority favoring the present term of four years, the minority one of six years. In a vote taken on the majority view, an amendment failed of passage by a vote of 145 to 108. A second vote on the minority proposal of six years was rejected by a vote of 72 ayes to 184 nayes.

In 1876, H.R. 117 of the 43rd Congress embodying the single six-year term proposal was reported from the House Judiciary Committee and was read twice. The motion to read the bill for the third time was defeated by a vote of 134 to 104. An attempt to pass the bill during the next Congress failed after disagreement developed on whether the length of the single term should be four years or six years.

Two proposals were made to extend the period to another term of years. In 1881, Congressman Tucker proposed a term of five years; and in 1888, Representative Hudd proposed a term of eight years. Only one proposal was introduced to reduce the length of terms as fixed by the Constitution: an amendment sponsored by Senator Hillhouse in 1808 for a term of one year. A large number of the amendments did not propose to change the term but to limit the number of terms the same person could serve.

From 1889 to 1926, eighty-five proposals to restrict the president's incumbency to one term, prohibiting a longer tenure than two terms, and restricting the president to one term, but lengthening that term, were introduced. Nine resolutions were introduced providing for a single term of four years: four in 1894 and five in 1889, 1893, 1908, 1909, and 1912. A total of sixty-three resolutions were introduced calling for a six-year term. On February 1, 1913, one of the proposals, S. J. Res. 78 was passed in the Senate by a vote of 47 to 23. The debate on the resolution began on March 11, 1912, and continued to February 1, 1913, through the election of 1912. The question arose as to whether President Taft and ex-President Roosevelt should be exempted from the provisions of the amendment should it take effect. On January 30, 1913, Senator Clarke introduced an amendment to S.J. Res. 78 excluding Taft and Roosevelt from the provisions. The amendment subsequently was defeated in fear that an exemption might allow the two men to occupy office for as long as thirteen and ten years respectively.

Other amendments, making the term a single one of four years, including a provision for the direct vote of the president, and making two terms of four years each the limit, were defeated.

In the two-year period of 1892-93 and 1912-13, an unusual number of amendments were introduced suggesting the controversy created by one ex-president running for election after an absence of four years from office and another seeking a third term after a similar intervening hiatus. During 1892 and 1893, fourteen amendments were submitted, seven providing for a six-year term with no eligibility to a second term, four providing a president could not succeed himself in office, two making two consecutive terms of office the limit, and one providing one term as the limit. During 1912 and 1913, twenty-two bills were offered, fifteen providing for six-year terms with ineligibility for a second term, three prohibiting a third term, two providing for a single seven-year term, and one prohibiting any more than two consecutive terms in office. In 1913, the Senate approved a proposed amendment providing a single six-year term; President-elect Woodrow Wilson objected, however, and the amendment died in the House Judiciary Committee.

From 1926 through 1963, a total of forty-three proposed amendments calling for a six-year term were introduced, three sponsored limiting the president to one four-year term, thirty-four proposals limited the president to two terms, and one provided for a term of eight years. Hearings were held during the 76th Congress on S.J. Res. 15 and during the 79th Congress on S.J. Res. 21, both bills providing for a six-year term.

In 1947, after the Roosevelt era, a constitutional amendment limiting the president to two terms of four years each was proposed. At that time a minority of the House Judiciary Committee favored no change in the present system but, if there had to be a change, expressed preference for a single term of six years. During the debate on the subject, Senator O'Daniel offered an amendment, defeated by a vote of 823 to 1, to limit all elected officials to a single term of six years.

The Twenty-Second Amendment, providing that "No person shall be elected to the office of the president more than twice" was finally passed by Congress and submitted to the states; ratification was completed on February 21, 1951.

It is significant that the House stated that "By reason of the lack of a positive expression upon the subject of the tenure of the office of president, and by reason of a well-defined custom which has risen in the past that no President should have more than two terms in that office, much discussion has resulted upon this subject. Hence, it is the purpose of this . . . [proposal] . .
to submit this question to the people so they, by and through the recognized processes, may express their views upon this question, and if they so elect, they may . . . thereby set at rest this problem."

But the problem was not set at rest by the Twenty-Second Amendment. The period 1963 to 1971 contained still more attention to the question. One proposed amendment was introduced by Senator Mike Mansfield as S.J. Res. 178 on June 17, 1968, in the Second Session of the 90th Congress. Four resolutions were introduced calling for a three-year term: H.J. 630, introduced by Mr. Herbert Tenzer August 17, 1965, in the First Session of the 89th Congress; H.J. Res. 909, introduced by Mr. Henry Smith II (New York), on March 17, 1966, in the Second Session of the 89th Congress; H.J. Res. 526, introduced by Mr. Benjamin Rosenthal March 6, 1969, in the First Session of the 91st Congress.

On October 28 and 29, 1971, hearings were held before the Subcommittee on Constitutional Amendment of the Committee on the Judiciary, United States Senate, on S.J. Resolution 77 proposing to amend the Constitution by providing for a single six-year term for the president.

Mr. THOMSON. (To the spectators) I have before me those hearings on S.J. Resolution 77. Listen, "Mr. Thomas Corcoran. It took a depression to repeal the 18th and I am sure you and I are glad it was repealed.

"Senator Birch Bayh. Are there any other amendments to the Constitution that you would repeal?

"Mr. Corcoran. Well, now that I am beginning to make money I would like to get rid of the 16th, income tax...."

Mr. JEFFERSON. On September 28, 1973, hearings were held before the Sub-Committee on Crime—I repeat, Subcommittee on Crime—of the Committee on the Judiciary, House of Representatives, on a single six-year presidential term.

On August 15, 1974, in the House of Representatives, Mr. Henry Reuss introduced Joint Resolution H.J. Res. 1111, proposing an amendment to the Constitution relative to a congressional vote of no confidence in the president.

And on July 21, 1975, in the House of Representatives, Mr. Reuss introduced an amendment to the Constitution which would create an Office of Chief of State to separate the roles of Chief of State and Chief Executive.

Fruitless? Frustrating? A sea of ideas—yet no other solution appears. The stream of ideas is like a stream of water. Congress may step into the stream and stir up the water galore, but let them step out and the stream will look just as it did before.

Gentlemen, for today, I thank you.

Gen. WASHINGTON. Thank you, Mr. Jefferson.

Today we have discussed the term of the president.

At our next session, we will discuss the mode or manner of appointment of the president. I hope that we may conclude this discussion tomorrow, which will then enable us to then discuss possible solutions.

This session is adjourned until Monday, August 10, 1987, at ten a.m.

MONDAY, AUGUST 10, 1987

ORIGIN OF METHOD OF ELECTION OF PRESIDENT

The Committee met pursuant to notice, at 10 a.m. in the Assembly Room of Independence Hall, Gen. George Washington presiding.

Present: Mr. John Adams, Dr. Benjamin Franklin, Mr. Thomas Jefferson, Mr. James Madison and Gen. George Washington.

Mr. THOMSON. (To the spectators) Suppose you saw a newspaper headline that said "President Held Hostage in Tower of London." Would you think such a thing could happen? Well, it did happen in the 1780s. While we wait for Mr. Jefferson to arrive, let me tell the incredible tale.

Henry Laurens was president of the Continental Congress from November 1, 1777 to December 9, 1778. During the Revolutionary War—in fact it was on Monday, November 1, 1779—Congress appointed Laurens "to negotiate a treaty of amity and commerce with the United Province of the low countries. . . ."

Laurens had barely begun his voyage to Europe when he was captured by the British. His destination was accordingly altered from the court of the Netherlands to the Tower of London.

From October 1780 to November 1781, he remained a close prisoner in the Tower, without hearing of any steps taken for his release or receiving consolation in that distressful state, either from Congress or from any of their servants. Mr. Edmund

Burke, at one point, applied to Dr. Franklin to effect an exchange of Lieutenant-General Burgoyne for Laurens. The Doctor had replied that he had in his possession a resolution of Congress for that purpose, a copy of which he then transmitted to Mr. Burke. About the same time, a letter from Dr. Franklin was slipped into Laurens' hands in the Tower. In this letter, the Doctor expressed some satisfaction in having heard from "high authority" that Laurens was well satisfied with the treatment he had received during his imprisonment—the contrary was evidently known to the whole world—and Franklin directed the pittance of one hundred pounds to be paid to the prisoner if he should stand in need. The Doctor had been misinformed by the "high authority," and after thirteen months imprisonment, the one hundred pounds would have been like a drop of water from the very tip of Lazarus' little finger. But Laurens heard no more from Dr. Franklin while he was in confinement, and he received no money from him at any time.

The British ministry determined against accepting Lieutenant-General Burgoyne in exchange for Laurens, but an inquiry was made by them as to whether Dr. Franklin had power to exchange Lord Cornwallis for Laurens, to which no positive answer could be given, and there the subject was dropped. On December 31, 1781, Laurens, who was extremely ill and unable to rise from his bed, was carried out of the Tower to the presence of the Lord Chief Justice of England and admitted to bail "to appear at the court of king's bench on the first day of the Easter term and not to depart thence without leave of the court." He was discharged on April 27, 1782.

It is of interest to note that on June 14, 1781, immediately following a vote on a resolution for the exchange of Lieutenant General Burgoyne for Henry Laurens, the Journals of Congress read as follows:

"Resolved, that . . . more persons be joined to the honorable John Adams in negotiating a treaty of peace with Great Britain. Mr. Henry Laurens was put in nomination by Mr. Theodorick Bland. Congress proceeded to the election and the ballots being taken; The Honorable Benjamin Franklin, The

Honorable Henry Laurens and the Honorable Thomas Jefferson were elected."

And so it was that the Honorable Henry Laurens, a former president of the Congress of the United States, was elected one of the commissioners to negotiate a treaty of peace with Great Britain—while in the Tower of London!

Dr. FRANKLIN. (To the spectators) I have been sitting here, listening and doodling, while Mr. Thomson told you this tale. I think you should know that after Laurens's release from the Tower of London in 1781 he was exchanged for Lt. Gen. Charles Earl Cornwallis. Think of it now—exactly two hundred years later, in 1981, the American hostages were released by Iran. There is an incredible relationship—perhaps you never thought of it—between the release of the hostages in Iran and the Declaration of Independence on July 4, 1776. It is as simple as adding, dividing, and multiplying. It goes this way.

First. The hostages sought their freedom from Iran. The Americans sought their freedom from Britain. The words "hostage" and "freedom" each contain seven letters. July is the seventh month of the year. So we have "July."

Second, There were 52 hostages in Iran. There were 13 American colonies. 52 divided by 13 equals 4. We now have "July 4."

Third. The hostages were held for 444 days. The Declaration was signed on the 4th. 4 times 444 equals 1776!

We now have "July 4, 1776."

You know, when I do doodle-things like that sometimes I think I should've been an actuary. I'm just a Yankee doodle doodler.

Gen. WASHINGTON. This session will come to order. We proceed today with the debates in the Federal Convention on the mode of election of the president. As a matter of background, the final provision respecting the mode of election of the president in the Constitution as adopted on September 17, 1787 provided for his election by "electors" chosen, in effect, by the people.

Altogether more than sixty ballots were needed before

the method of selecting the president was decided. At least five times the Convention voted in favor of having Congress appoint the president, and this remained the choice until the last two weeks of the Convention, when the mode was changed to elect the president by electors chosen by the people.

Mr. THOMSON. (To the spectators) Jefferson and Adams shared the experiences of debates surrounding this issue, though neither attended the Federal Convention. Jefferson wrote to Adams in 1813: "Whether the power of the people or that of the aristocracy should prevail were questions which kept the states of Greece and Rome in eternal convulsions; as they now schismatize every people whose minds and mouths are not shut up by the gag of a despot. . . . To come to our country and to the times when you and I became first acquainted, we well remember the violent parties which agitated the old Congress, and their bitter contests. There you and I were together, and the Jays, and the Dickinsons, and other anti-independents were arrayed against us. . . . When our present government was in the mew, passing from Confederation to Union, how bitter was the schism between the Feds and Antis. Here you and I were together again . . . But as soon as it was put into motion, the line of division was again drawn; we broke into two parties, each wishing to give a different direction to the government; the one to strengthen the most popular branch, the other the more permanent branches, and to extend their permanence. Here you and I separated for the first time; and as we had been longer than most others on the public theatre, and our names therefore were more familiar to our countrymen, the party which considered you as thinking with them placed your name at their head; the other for the same reason selected mine. But neither decency nor inclination permitted us to become the advocates of ourselves or to take part personally in the violent contests which followed. We suffered ourselves, as you so well expressed it, to be the passive subjects of public discussion. And these discussions, whether relating to men, measures, or opinions, were conducted by the parties with an animosity, a bitterness, and an indecency which had never been exceeded. . . . Shall we, at our age, become the Athletae of party and exhibit ourselves, as gladiators in the Arena of the newspapers? Nothing in the universe could induce me to it. My mind has been long fixed to bow to the judgment of the world, who will judge me by my acts and will never take counsel from me as to what that judgment shall be. . . ."

Mr. Jefferson knew whereof he spoke, for he had distinguished himself in all the branches of knowledge. The French language he had learned when very young and became very familiar with it, as he did with the literary treasures which it contains. He read, and at one time spoke, the Italian, also, with a competent knowledge of the Spanish; adding to both the Anglo-Saxon, as a root of the English and an element in legal philology. The law itself he studied to the bottom, and in its greatest breadth, of which proofs were given at the Bar, which he attended for a number of years and occasionally throughout his career. For all the fine arts he had a more than common taste; and in that of architecture, which he studied both in its useful and its ornamental characters, he made himself adept. . . . Over and above these acquirements, his miscellaneous reading was truly remarkable; for which he derived leisure from the methodical and indefatigable application of the time required for indispensable objects, and particularly from his rule of never letting the sun rise before him. His relish for books never forsook him. He was certainly one of the most learned men of the age. It may be said of him, as has been said of others, that he was a walking library and, what can be said but of few of such prodigies, that the genius of philosophy ever walked hand in hand with him.

First SPECTATOR. (To second spectator) He did it the old-fashioned way—he *learned* it.

Mr. JEFFERSON. Mr. Madison, can you give us a report from your notes on what you consider were the major points on the mode of selecting the president?

Mr. MADISON. I can.

Mr. JEFFERSON. Please proceed.

Mr. MADISON. This was a thorny issue and was, as I wrote to Jared Sparks in 1831, "The last department of government that received its full and final discussion." Perhaps we saved the worst for last.

The reason for establishing an office of the president was best summarized by Mr. Sherman of Connecticut. He considered the executive magistracy as nothing more than an institution for carrying the will of the legislature into effect, and thus that person ought to be appointed by and accountable to the legislature only, which was the depository of the supreme will of the society. As the members of the legislature were the best judges of the business to be done by the executive department, and consequently of the number of executives necessary for doing it, he wished the number of chief magistrates might not be fixed; the legislature should be at liberty to appoint one or more as experience and needs might dictate.

Mr. Sherman's statement lead to the question of a single or multiple executive, a question which in itself was cause for debate.

Mr. Randolph of Virginia strenuously opposed a unity in the executive magistracy, regarding it as the "foetus of monarchy." We had, he said, no motive to be governed by the British government as our prototype; the fixed genius of the people of America required a different form of government. He could not see why the great requisites for the executive department—vigor, dispatch, and responsibility—could not be found in three men, as well as in one.

Mr. Wilson of Pennsylvania, on the other hand, believed that a single executive instead of being the fetus of monarchy, would be the best safeguard against tyranny. It gave most energy, dispatch, and responsibility to the office. The British model was inapplicable to the situation of this country; the prerogatives of the British monarch were not a proper guide in defining the executive powers here because some of these prerogatives were of a legislative nature. The only powers that were strictly executive were those of executing the laws and appointing officers not appointed by the legislature.

Likewise, Mr. Rutledge of South Carolina was for vesting the executive power in a single person, except for the power to declare war and peace. A single man, he thought, would feel the greatest responsibility and administer the public affairs best. And Mr. Butler of South Carolina also contended for a single magistrate as most likely to answer the purpose of the remote parts of the country because a single executive would be responsible for the whole and would be impartial to its interests. If three or more should be taken from as many districts, there would be a constant struggle for local advantages. In military matters this would be particularly mischievous.

Mr. Randolph responded with renewed opposition to a single executive. He urged: 1. that the people were permanently averse to the very semblance of monarchy. 2. that a "unity was unnecessary because a plurality would be equally competent to execute the duties of the department. 3. that the necessary confidence would never be reposed in a single magistrate, and 4. that the appointment of a single executive would generally be in favor of some inhabitant near the center of the community, and consequently the remote parts would not be on an equal footing. He was in favor of three members of the executive to be drawn from different portions of the country.

I thought it would be proper, before a choice should be made between a unity and a plurality in the executive, to fix the extent of the executive authority.

Mr. Gerry favored the policy of annexing a Council to the executive in order to give weight and inspire confidence.

And, of course, this was Dr. Franklin's idea, then and now, and it is the position this Commission has taken. In addition, our Commission has resolved the matter of unity versus plurality in the executive by the creation of posts for two vice-presidents without affecting the responsibilities of the president.

Now, back to the positions taken on the issue of the mode of selecting the president.

The arguments on this issue fall into two major categories: namely, those who argued for election of the president by the national legislature and those who desired elections by the people directly, or by the people through their electors. As we thread our way through the debates on the Constitution, is there any idea embedded that can assist our Commission?

Let me share my own general thinking as I expressed it in the Convention. I stated that, in order to judge of the form to be given to this institution, it will be proper to take a view of the ends to be served by it. These were first to protect the people against their rulers. Secondly, to protect the people against the transient impressions into which they themselves might be led. A people deliberating in a temperate moment, and with the experience of other nations before them, on the plan of government most likely to secure their happiness, would first be aware that those charged with the public happiness might betray their trust. An obvious precaution against this danger would be to divide the trust between different bodies of men, who might watch and check each other. In this they would be governed by the same prudence which has prevailed in organizing the subordinate department of government where all business liable to abuses is made to pass through separate hands, the one being a check on the other.

It would next occur to such a people that they themselves were liable to temporary errors, through want of information as to their true interest, and that men chosen for a short term, and employed but a small portion of that in public affairs, might err. This reflection would naturally suggest that the government be so constituted that it might have an opportunity of acquiring competent information about the public interest.

Another reflection equally becoming a people on such an occasion would be that they themselves, as well as a numerous body of representatives, were liable to err also, from fickleness and passion. A necessary fence against this danger would be to select a portion of enlightened citizens whose limited number and firmness might seasonably interpose against impetuous counsels.

It ought finally to occur to a people deliberating on a government for themselves that as different interests necessarily result from the liberty meant to be secured, the major interest might under sudden impulses be tempted to commit injustice on the minority. In all civilized countries the people fall into different classes having a real or supposed difference of interests. These will be creditors and debtors, farmers, merchants, and manufacturers. There will be particularly the distinction of rich and poor.

We cannot be regarded as one homogeneous mass in which everything that affects a part will affect in the same manner the whole. In framing a system which we wish to last for ages, we should not lose sight of the changes which ages will produce. An increase of population will of necessity increase the proportion of those who will labor under all the hardships of life and secretly sigh for a more equal distribution of its blessings. These may in time outnumber those who are placed above the feelings of indigence. According to the equal laws of suffrage, the power will slide into the hands of the former. No agrarian attempts have yet been made in this country, but symptoms of a leveling spirit, as we have understood, have sufficiently appeared in certain quarters to give notice of the future danger. How is this danger to be guarded against on republican principles? How is the danger in all cases of interest coalitions to oppress the minority to be guarded against? Among other means, by the establishment of a body in the government sufficiently respectable for its wisdom and virtue, to aid on such emergencies, the preponderance of justice, by throwing its weight into that scale.

I observed then that as it was more than probable we were digesting a plan which in its operation would decide forever the fate of republican government; we ought not only to provide every guard to liberty that its preservation could require but be equally careful to supply the defects which our own experience had particularly pointed out.

Mr. Hamilton concurred in thinking we were now to decide forever the fate of republican government; and that if we did not give to that form due stability and wisdom, it would be disgraced and lost among ourselves, disgraced and lost to mankind forever.

Mr. Gerry wished we could be united in our ideas concerning a permanent government. All aim at the same end, but there are great differences as to the means. One circumstance he thought should be carefully attended to. There were not one one-thousandth part of our fellow citizens who were not against every approach toward monarchy. Would they ever agree to a plan which seems to make such an approach? The Convention ought to be extremely cautious in what they hold out to the people. Whatever plan may be proposed would be espoused with warmth by many out of respect to the quarter it proceeds from as well as from an approbation of the plan itself. And if the plan should be of such a nature as to rouse a violent opposition, it was easy to forsee that discord and confusion would ensue, and it was even possible that we might become a prey to foreign powers. He did not deny that the majority would generally violate justice when they have an interest in so doing; but he did not think there was any such temptation in this country.

I thought the only remedy was to enlarge the sphere, and thereby divide the community into so great a number of interests and parties, that in the first place, a majority will not be likely at the same moment to have a common interest separate from that of the whole or of the minority; and in the second place, that in case they should have such an interest, they may not be apt to unite in the pursuit of it. I thought it was incumbent on us then to try this remedy and with that view to frame a republican system on such a scale and in such a form as would control all the evils which had been experienced.

The key question facing the Convention during these debates was, what was the nature of the presidency in a republic such as ours? I myself observed that the great difficulty in rendering the executive competent to its own defense arose from the very nature of republican government, which would not give to an individual citizen that same settled pre-eminence in the eyes of the rest, that weight of property, that personal interest against betraying the national interest, which appertain to a hereditary magistrate. In a republic, personal merit alone earned political exaltation, but this merit would rarely be so preeminent as to produce universal acquiescence. The executive magistrate would be envied and assailed by disappointed competitors. His firmness therefore would need support. He would not possess those great emoluments from his station, nor that permanent stake in the public interest which would place him out of the reach of foreign corruption. He would stand in need therefore of being controlled as well as supported.

Thus the founders had much to consider as they discussed the best way to elect a president. Let us first hear those favoring selection by the legislature, the selection method which predominated the convention during most of its existence.

Colonel Mason of Virginia began his comments by reviewing what had already been done. It has been proposed, he said, that the election should be made by the people at large; that is, that an act which ought to be performed by those who know most of eminent characters and qualifications should be performed by those who know least. 2. That the election should be made by the legislatures of the states. 3. By the executives of the states. Against these modes strong objections had been urged. 4. It had been proposed that the election should be made by electors chosen by the people for that purpose. 5. Another expedient was proposed by Mr. Dickinson, which was liable to so palpable an inconvenience that Mr. Dickinson had little doubt of its being rejected by himself. It would have excluded every man who happened not to be popular within his own state; though the causes of his local unpopularity might be of such a nature as to recommend him to the states at large. Finally, among other expedients, a lottery had been introduced. But as the tickets did not appear to be in much demand, nothing more need be said on that subject.

After reviewing all these various modes, Colonel Mason was led to conclude that an election by the national legislature as originally proposed was the best. If it was liable to objections, he said, it was liable to fewer than any other. He held it as an essential point, as the very palladium of civil liberty, that the great officers of the state, and particularly the executive, should at fixed periods return to that mass from which they were at first taken, in order that they may feel and respect those rights of interests which are again to be personally valuable to them.

Mr. Sherman of Connecticut agreed that the appointment should be absolutely dependent on that body, as it was the will of the legislature which was to be executed. An independence of the executive from the supreme legislative was in his opinion the very essence of tyranny and the national legislature should have power to remove the Executive at its pleasure. The sense of the nation would be better expressed by the legislature than by the people at large because the people could never be sufficiently informed of characters, and besides would never give a majority of votes to any one man. They would generally vote for some man in their own state, and the largest state would have the best chance for the appointment.

Mr. THOMSON. (To the spectators) Jeremiah Wadsworth wrote Rufus King at the beginning of the Convention telling him that he was satisfied with the appointments—"except Sherman, who I am told, is disposed to patch up the old scheme of Government. This was not my opinion of him, when we chose him. He is as cunning as the Devil, and if you attack him, you ought to know him well; he is not easily managed, but if he suspects you are trying to take him in, you may as well catch an eel by the tail."

Mr. MADISON. (Continuing) Mr. Randolph of Virginia argued for an election by the legislature with an incapacity to be elected a second time. The executive should not be left under a temptation to court a reappointment. If he should be reappointable by the legislature, he would be no check on it, his veto power of no avail. If the executive be appointed by the legislature, he would probably be appointed either by joint ballot of both houses or nominated by the House and appointed by the Senate. In either case the largest states would preponderate.

Mr. Pinckney of South Carolina did not expect this question would have been brought forward again and again. An election by the people was liable to the most obvious and striking objections. The people would not have sufficient knowledge of the fittest men and would be swayed by an attachment to the eminent men of their respective states. They might be led by a few active and designing men. The most populous states by combining in favor of the same individual would be able to carry their points. But the national legislature, being most immediately interested in the laws they made, would be most attentive to the choice of a fit man to carry them into execution.

Mr. Houston of New Jersey had moved that the president be appointed by the national legislature instead of "Electors appointed by the State Legislatures" because it was improbable that capable men would undertake the service of electors from the more distant states. He urged the extreme inconvenience and the considerable expense of drawing together men from all the states for the single purpose of electing the president.

Mr. Rutledge of South Carolina was opposed to the plan reported by the Committee of Eleven, the election of the president by electors. He wanted the original plan: "He shall be elected by joint ballot by the Legislature to which election a majority of the votes of the members present shall be required. He shall hold his office during the term of seven years; but shall not be elected a second time."

For the other side of the picture, the election of the president by the people, directly or through electors, Gouverneur Morris of Pennsylvania set the pace:

"Of all possible modes of appointment, that by the Legislature is the worst. . . . The Legislature is worthy of unbounded confidence in some respects, and liable to equal distrust in others. When their interest coincides precisely with that of their Constituents, as happens in many of their acts, no abuse of trust is to be apprehended. When a strong personal interest happens to be opposed to the general interest, the Legislature can not be too much distrusted. In all public bodies there are two parties. The Executive will necessarily be more connected with one than with the other. There will be a personal interest therefore in one of the parties to oppose as well as in the other to support him. Much has been said of the intrigues that will be practiced by the Executive to get into office. Nothing has been said on the other side of the intrigues to get him out of office. Some leader of party will always covet his seat, will perplex his administration, will cabal with the Legislature, till he succeeds in supplanting him.

This was the way in which the King of England was got out . . . the real King, the Minister. Our President will be the British Minister, yet we are about to make him appointable by the Legislature. Something had been said of the danger of monarchy. If a good government should not now be formed, if a good organization of the executive should not be provided," he warned, we would "have something worse than a limited monarchy."

Then he continued: "In order to get rid of the dependence of the Executive on the Legislature, the expedient of making him ineligible a second time had been devised. This was as much as to say we should give him the benefit of experience and then deprive ourselves of the use of it. But make him ineligible a second time—and prolong his duration even to fifteen years, will he by any wonderful interposition of providence at that period cease to be a man? No, he will be unwilling to quit his exaltation, the road to his object through the Constitution will be shut; he will be in possession of the sword, a civil war will ensue, and the Commander of the victorious army on whichever side will be the despot of America. This consideration renders me particularly anxious that the Executive should be properly constituted. It is the most difficult of all rightly to balance the Executive. Make him too weak, the legislature will usurp his powers. Make him too strong, he will usurp on the Legislature." Mr. Morris preferred a short period, a re-eligibility, but a different mode of election.

Mr. THOMSON. (To the spectators) This man, Gouverneur Morris—an enigma, a puzzlement—a Machiavellian. Here was one man filled with love, anger, intelligence.

To Madame De Stael he wrote, "Happy the man who can enjoy your society!" when responding to her letter: " 'If I were only twenty-five instead of thirty-five years old, I think that I would visit you.' You believe me, then, to be only fit for the society of young ladies. Kindly persuade yourself of the contrary. Believe, also, that the age of reason is the best age for travelling; one derives greater profit, one risks less.

To build castles in Spain is an amusing folly; to build castles in the United States would be a ruinous one, for labor is too expensive. But to organize a small summer establishment in a country that develops rapidly; to stay there during three to five months of the fair season; then to sojourn four months in Philadelphia or New York, and devote the rest of one's time to travelling—that constitutes a mode of life which lacks not in commonsense, especially in our times. . . ."

As late as the year 1815, Mr. Morris was asked how, with his known impressions, could he have been an advocate of the Federal Constitution, to which he responded. "To this I answer, first, that I was warmly pressed by Hamilton to assist in writing the *Federalist*, which I declined; secondly, that nothing human can be perfect; thirdly, that the obstacles to a less imperfect system were insurmountable; fourthly, that the old confederation was worse; and fifthly, that there was no reason, at that time, to suppose our public morals would be so soon and so entirely corrupted. Mr. Mason, a delegate from Virginia, constantly inveighing against aristocracy, labored to introduce aristocratic provisions. Some of them might have been wholesome, but they would have been rejected by public feeling in the form proposed; and if modified to render them acceptable, by detracting proportionately from executive authority, which was his plan, we should have risked less, indeed, from the flood of democracy, but we should have had a president unable to perform the duties of his office. Surrounded by difficulties, we did the best we could, leaving it with those who should come after us to take counsel from experience and exercise prudently the power of amendment which we had provided."

After the Constitution was amended twelve times, Mr. Morris was asked, "How far have the Amendments to the Constitution altered its spirit?" "These amendments are, generally speaking, mere verbiage," he responded. "It has been said that our Constitution is remarkable for the perspicuity of its language, and, if so, there was some hazard in attempting to clothe any of its provisions by the so-called amendment in different terms. It would be a tedious work of supererogation to show that the original Constitution contained those guards which form the apparent object of the amendments."

In the year 1811, he answered one question which this Commission has asked itself: How far has the Senate answered the end of its creation? "I answer, further than was expected, but by no means so far as was wished. . . . To obtain anything like a check on the rashness of democracy, it was necessary not only to organize the Legislature into different bodies, but to endeavor that these bodies should be animated by a different spirit. To this end the States, in their corporate capacity, were made electors of the Senate, and, so long as the State governments had considerable influence and the consciousness of dignity which that influence imparts, the Senate felt some of the desired sentiment and answered in some degree the end of its institution. But that day is past. This opens to our view a dilemma which was not experienced when the Constitution was formed. If the State influence should continue, the Union could not last; and if it did not, the utility of the Senate would cease. . . . The influence of the General Government has so thoroughly pervaded every State that all the little wheels are obliged to turn according to the great one."

In January 1802, in the United States Senate, Gouverneur Morris said: "There are some honorable gentlemen now present, who sat in the Convention which formed this Constitution. I appeal to their recollection, if they have not seen the time when the fate of America was suspended by a hair? . . . Never, in the flow of time, was there a moment so propitious, as that in which the Convention assembled. The States had been convinced, by melancholy experience, how inadequate they were to the management of our national concerns. The passions of the people were lulled to sleep; State pride slumbered; the Constitution was promulgated; and then it awoke, and opposition was formed; but it was in vain. The people of America bound the States down by this compact."

Mr. MADISON. Mr. Morris thought the president would be the mere creature of the legislature if appointed and impeachable by that body. He thought the president ought to be elected by the people at large, by the freeholders of the country. The people as electors would never fail to prefer some man of distinguished character or services; some man of continental reputation. If the legislature should elect, it might be influenced by intrigue, cabal, and faction, like the election of a pope by a conclave of cardinals; real merit would rarely be the title to the appointment. Appointments made by large bodies of people are always worse than those made by single responsible individuals.

On July 19, in the Convention, Mr. Morris said: "It has been a maxim in Political Science that Republican Government is not adapted to a large extent of Country, because the energy of the executive Magistrate cannot reach the extreme parts of it. Our Country is an extensive one. We must either then renounce the blessing of the Union, or provide an Executive with sufficient vigor to pervade every part of it. . . . One great object of the Executive is to control the Legislature. The Legislature will continually seek to aggrandize and perpetuate themselves and will seize those critical moments produced by war, invasion or convulsion for that purpose. It is necessary then that the Executive Magistrate should be the guardian of the people, even of the lower classes against Legislative tyranny, against the great and the wealthy who in the course of things will necessarily compose the Legislative body. Wealth tends to corrupt the mind and to nourish its love of power and to stimulate it to oppression. History proves this to be the spirit of the opulent. The check provided in the Senate was not meant as a check on Legislative usurpations of power but on the abuse of lawful powers, on the propensity in the House to legislate too much, to run into projects of paper money and similar expedients. It is no check on Legislative tyranny. . . . The Executive therefore ought to be so constituted as to be the great protector of the mass of the people. . . .

He added, "If he is to be the Guardian of the people let him be appointed by the people. If he is to be a check on the Legislature let him not be impeachable. Let him be of short duration, that he may with propriety be re-eligible. It has been said that the candidates for this office will not be known to the people. If they be known to the Legislature, they must have such a notoriety and eminence of Character that they cannot possibly be unknown to the people at large. It cannot be possible that a man shall have sufficiently distinguished himself to merit this high trust without having his character proclaimed by fame throughout the Empire."

He suggested that "an election by the people at large throughout so great an extent could not be influenced by those little combinations and those momentary lies which often decide popular elections within a narrow sphere." He saw "no alternative for making the Executive independent of the Legislature but either to give him his office for life or make him eligible by the people."

Mr. THOMSON. (To the spectators) And, here is Morris, extolling the public vaingloriously. Of the people, Morris wrote in 1811: "Montesquieu said tritely, he did not write to make people read, but to make them think. Did he live in our day and our country he would find it no easy matter to make them read.... Ignorant as the mass of mankind must of necessity and forever be of the great political subjects, it is not so much the ignorance as the depravity of our citizens which causes their misfortunes."

First SPECTATOR. (To Mr. Thomson) And this is the man who wrote the final draft of the Constitution. . . ?

Mr. THOMSON. Yes, Mr. James Madison wrote to Mr. Jared Sparks, a historian, on April 8, 1831: "The finish given to the style and arrangement of the Constitution fairly belongs to the pen of Mr. Morris; the task having, probably, been handed over to him by the chairman of the Committee, himself a highly respectable member, and with the ready concurrence of the others. A better choice could not have been made, as the performance of the task proved. It is true that the state of the materials consisting of a reported draft in detail and subsequent resolutions accurately penned, and falling easily into their proper places, was a good preparation for the symmetry and phraseology of the instrument, but there was sufficient room for the talents and taste stamped by the author on the face of it. . . ."

And, despite the incongruities of the man, we must give him credit for *some* of his political views. "Forget party and think of country," he said, stressing that "the interest of our country must be preferred to every other interest." He sensed the ennobling within us—"what is it that renders a nation respectable?—power, courage, wisdom"—but also the bestial: "Must we wait till the claws of a human tiger tear us to pieces to look for a heart? We once had hearts—hearts that beat high with the love of liberty. But 'tis over." He knew well our human frailties but seemed to believe that our strengths would win the day: "The engine by which a giddy populace can be most easily brought on to do mischief is their hatred of the rich. If any of these supposes he can climb into power by civil commotions, he will find himself mistaken." In our country, he said, "we have indeed a set of madmen in the administration, and they will do many foolish things, but there is a vigorous vegetative principle at the root which will make our tree flourish, let the winds blow as they may." Perhaps Morris saw this contradiction of the noble and the bestial more clearly than other men because of his insights into his own character. Perhaps he was merely a shrewd observer of human nature. Perhaps he only enjoyed paradox. In 1803, after the United States acquired the Louisiana Territory, Morris wrote to a Frenchman, "We have at present the misfortune to be ruled by that spirit of vertigo which this ridiculous century calls by the name of philosophy. Do you realize, monsieur, that this philosophy is a hussy who lavishes her caresses without ever having felt love? Well, this wretch can boast that, by flattering the selfishness of the rich and the pretensions of the rabble, with her Tartuffian ways and her wheedling language, she has benumbed our soul and our minds. Yes, America is asleep, while they are whetting the dagger that may strike the mortal blow. But they are mistaken. The waves of an immense sea roll and roar between the project and its execution. Those great arbiters of human affairs, Time and Fate, have pronounced for the separation of the two worlds. And what are politics against the decrees of the Everlasting! But who am I to speak thus? No, I respect these decrees and remain silent."

And finally, in 1803, Morris drafted these words: "The Constitution is . . . in my opinion, gone."

First SPECTATOR. (To Second spectator) I should

ask, will the real Mr. Morris please stand up?

Mr. MADISON. On June 2, in Convention, Mr. Gerry of Massachusetts opposed the election of the president by the national legislature. He thought there would be a constant intrigue kept up for the appointment, the legislature and the candidates bargaining and playing into one another's hands. But by July 19, he had changed his position. Now he was against a popular election, saying the people are uninformed and would be misled by a few designing men. He urged the appointment of the executive by electors to be chosen by the state executives. The people of the state would then choose the first branch; the legislatures of the states, the second branch of the national legislature; and the executives of the states, the national executive. This would form a strong attachment of the states to the national system.

But on July 24, he changed his mind again and moved that the legislatures of the states should vote for the executive in the same proportions as it had been proposed they should choose electors; if a majority of the votes should not center on the same person, the first branch of the national legislature should choose two out of the four candidates having most votes, and out of these two, the Senate should choose the Executive.

By September 5, he was off on another tack, suggesting that the eventual election should be made by six senators and seven representatives chosen by joint ballot of both Houses.

Then, on the following day he proposed that the president should be elected by the Senate out of the five highest candidates; if he should not at the end of his term be reelected by a majority of the electors and no other candidate should have a majority, the eventual election should be made by the legislature. This would relieve the president from his particular dependence on the Senate for his continuance in office.

Finally Mr. Gerry's confusion overcame him, and he observed that the Convention seemed to be entirely at a loss on the issue. Would it not be advisable to refer the clause relating to the executive to the Committee of Detail? Perhaps they would be able to hit on something that may unite the various opinions.

And thus the debate went, a tennis match of endless rallying with no point won and no advantage gained. On June 1, Mr. Wilson of Pennsylvania declared in favor of an appointment by the people, wishing to derive not only both branches of the legislature from the people, without intervention of the state legislatures, but also the executive, in order to make them as independent as possible of each other, as well as of the states. The next day he repeated his arguments in favor of an election without the intervention of the states, adding that this mode would produce more confidence among the people in the first magistrate than if he were elected by the national legislature. By July 19, Mr. Wilson was saying that the idea of an election mediately or immediately by the people was gaining ground.

On July 24, Mr. Wilson said his opinion remained unshaken that we ought to resort to the people for the election, but he pointed out that at a certain advance in life, a continuance in office would cease to be agreeable to the officer as well as desirable to the public. Experience had shown in a variety of instances that both a capacity and inclination for public service existed in very advanced stages. He mentioned the instance of a Doge of Venice who was elected after he was eighty years of age. The Popes had generally been elected at very advanced periods, and yet in no case had a more steady or a better concerted policy been pursued than in the Court of Rome. If the executive should come into office at thirty-five years of age, which he presumed may happen, and his continuance should be fixed at fifteen years, at the age of fifty in the very prime of life, and with all the aid of experience, he must be cast aside like a useless hulk. What an irreparable loss would the British jurisprudence have sustained had the age of fifty been fixed as the ultimate limit to serve the public! The great luminary, Lord Mansfield, held his seat for thirty years after his arrival at that age.

Mr. THOMSON. (To the spectators) . . . And then, of course, there is the Ayattollah Khomeini, President of Iran, an octogenarian; and our own President Ronald Reagan, a septaugenarian.

Mr. MADISON. (Continuing) Notwithstanding what

had been done, Mr. Wilson could not but hope that a better mode of election would yet be adopted; and one that would be more agreeable to the general sense of the Convention. "We should consider that we are providing a Constitution for future generations, and not merely for the peculiar circumstances of the moment," he said.

The business of the executive was so important that it drew from Mr. Dickinson a discourse of some length, the sum of which was that the legislative, executive, and judiciary departments ought to be made as independent as possible; but that such an executive as some seemed to have in contemplation was not consistent with a republic; that a firm executive could only exist in a limited monarchy. In the British government itself the weight of the executive arose from the attachments which the Crown drew to itself, and not merely from the force of its prerogatives. In place of these attachments we must look out for something else. One source of stability is the double branch of the legislature. The division of the country into distinct States formed the other principal source of stability. This division ought therefore to be maintained and considerable power to be left with the states.

Mr. Dickinson at one point moved "that the executive be made removable by the national legislature on the request of the majority of the legislatures of individual states." It was necessary, he said, to place the power of removing somewhere, and his provision seemed the best because the happiness of this country required considerable powers to be left in the hands of the states.

Mr. King of Massachusetts was of opinion that an appointment by electors chosen by the people for the purpose would be liable to fewest objections, since people at large would probably choose wisely. He thought we ought to be governed by reason, not by chance. As nobody seemed to be satisfied, he wished the matter to be postponed. And so we deferred and deferred and deferred the issue until the very end.

And finally, what did I enter upon my notes as to my own thinking on this quandary? I had said in the convention that if it be a fundamental principle of free government that the legislative, executive, and judiciary powers should be separately exercised, it is equally so that they be independently exercised. There is the same and perhaps greater reason why the executive should be independent of the legislature than why the judiciary should. A coalition of the two former powers would be more immediately and certainly dangerous to public liberty. It is essential then that the appointment of the executive should either be drawn from some source, or held by some tenure, that will give him a free agency with regard to the legislature. This could not be if he was to be appointable from time to time by the legislature. I was disposed for these reasons to refer the appointment to some other source. The people at large was in my opinion the fittest in itself. It would be as likely as any that could be devised to produce an executive magistrate of distinguished character. The people generally could only know and vote for some citizen whose merits had rendered him an object of general attention and esteem. One serious difficulty with the immediate choice by the people was the much more diffusive suffrage in the Northern than the Southern states; and the latter could have no influence in the election on the score of the Negroes. The substitution of electors obviated this difficulty and seemed on the whole to be liable to fewest objections.

Mr. JEFFERSON. Major Jackson, will you kindly summarize for us the chronology of the voting in the Federal Convention on the subject of the mode or manner of electing the president?

Major JACKSON. Certainly, although I trust you will bear in mind what I said yesterday about burning all the loose scraps of paper which belonged to the Convention before I delivered the Journal to General Washington in September, 1787.

The first resolution was by Mr. Edmund Randolph on May 29; he proposed "that a National Executive be instituted; to be chosen by the National Legislature," and on June 2, the resolution was agreed to 8 votes to 2.

The matter was not taken up again, I believe, until July 17, when it was moved and seconded to change the resolution to read "That a National Executive . . . be chosen by the Citizens of the United States," but that resolution failed to pass, with only 1 vote for and 9 against. It was then moved and seconded that the resolution be altered so that the national executive "be chosen by Electors to be appointed by the several Legislature of the individual States." Again the vote was negative, 8 to 2. Then it was moved and seconded to agree again that the national executive "be chosen by the national Legislature," which passed unanimously.

Two days later it was moved, seconded and unanimously agreed upon to reconsider the mode of appointment of the national executive. A proposition that the executive "be chosen by Electors appointed for that purpose by the Legislatures of the States" was set forth and seconded, but on July 24th, it was moved and seconded to strike the very same words and to insert instead the words "by the national Legislature," which passed 7 to 4.

It was then resolved that "the supreme Executive shall be chosen . . . by Electors to be taken by lot from the national Legislature; the Electors to proceed immediately to the choice of the Executive and not to separate until it be made." A question of order was taken on the motion; it was determined the motion was in order and the motion passed 7 to 4.

On July 26, the whole resolution respecting the supreme executive was called, namely: "Resolved that a national Executive be instituted to consist of a single person to be chosen by the national Legislature for the term of seven years, to be ineligible a second time, with power to carry into execution the national Laws and to appoint to offices in cases not otherwise provided for; to be removable on impeachment and conviction of malpractice or neglect of duty; to receive a fixed compensation for the devotion of his time to public service; to be paid out of the public Treasury," passed, 6 votes for, 3 against, and one divided.

On August 6, the Committee of Detail, to whom were referred the proceedings of the Convention, reported in its draft of the Constitution that "The Executive Power of the United States shall be vested in a single person. His stile shall be 'The

President of the United States of America;' and his title shall be, 'His Excellency.' He shall be elected by ballot by the legislature. He shall hold his office during the term of seven years but shall not be elected a second time."

On August 24 the motion to strike the word "Legislature" in the sentence "he shall be elected by ballot by the Legislature" and to replace it with the word "People" was defeated, 9 to 2. It was then moved to agree that the president "shall be chosen by electors to be chosen by the People of the several States," which also failed, 6 to 5.

Mr. ADAMS. Who made that motion, Major?

Major JACKSON. Mr. Gouverneur Morris, sir.

Mr. ADAMS. Thank you.

Major JACKSON. A motion to refer the issue to a committee of a member from each state also failed, 5 votes for, 5 against, and 1 divided. A vote was then taken on the first part of Mr. Morris's motion, to wit, "shall be chosen by electors," as an abstract question, and it failed, the states being equally divided, 4 votes for, 4 against, 2 divided.

On August 31, Mr. Morris moved to strike out the words "choose the President of the United States" in the paragraph reading "To introduce this government . . . the Members of the Legislature should meet at the time and place assigned by Congress, and should, as soon as may be, after their meeting, choose the President of the United States and proceed to execute this Constitution," since the method of choosing the president had not yet finally been determined. The motion passed, 9 to 1, with 1 vote divided.

It was then agreed to refer such parts of the Constitution as had been postponed and such parts of reports as had not been acted on, to the Committee of Eleven.

Mr. ADAMS. So Mr. Gouverneur Morris placed the mode of election in issue so as to get it before the committee of Eleven, of which he was a member.

Gen. WASHINGTON. Mr. Adams, Major Jackson does not have the authority to respond to that question, if it is a question, and if it is addressed to Major Jackson.

Mr. ADAMS. It is not a question, General.

Major JACKSON. On September 4, the Committee of Eleven reported partially. Included in its report was a proposal for the election of the president by "electors" chosen, in effect, by the people.

Mr. ADAMS. Mr. Chairman, I consider it imperative that we insert at this point in our records just why the mode of electing the president was changed.

Gen. WASHINGTON. Mr. Madison, do you have your notes on this question available?

Mr. MADISON. I do.

Gen. WASHINGTON. Would you kindly furnish the pertinent information from your notes.

Mr. MADISON. According to my records, Mr. Randolph and Mr. Pinckney had asked the same question as Mr. Adams and the discussion was as follows:

Mr. Morris said he would give the reasons of the Committee and his own. The first was the danger of intrigue and faction if the appointment should be made by the legislature. Second was the inconvenience of ineligibility for reappointment, necessary to lessen the evils of appointment by the legislature. Third, the difficulty of establishing a Court of Impeachment other than the Senate or the other branch; neither could try their own appointee. Fourth, nobody had appeared to be satisfied with an appointment by the legislature. Fifth, many were anxious even for an immediate choice by the people. Sixth was the indispensable necessity of making the executive independent of the legislature. As the electors would vote at the same time throughout the United States and at so great a distance from each other, the great evil of cabal and corruption was avoided.

Mr. Pinkney objected that, first, the electors would be strangers to the several candidates and of course unable to decide on their comparative merits, and second, the executive would be reeligible, which might endanger the public liberty.

This subject, Mr. Wilson said "is in truth the most difficult of all on which we have had to decide." He thought the Committee's plan on the whole a valuable improvement on the former because it got rid of cabal and corruption, and he believed that continental characters would multiply as the nation more and more coalesced, so as to enable the electors in every part of the union to know and judge of them. The Committee's plan also cleared the way for a discussion of the question of reeligibility on its own merits, which the former mode of election seemed to forbid.

These statements are from my notes of September 4, 1787.

Gen. WASHINGTON. Major Jackson, will you kindly continue?

Major JACKSON. On September 5, it was moved and seconded to postpone the consideration of the report in order to take up the following with respect to the president: "He shall be elected by joint ballot by the Legislature. . . . He shall hold his office during the term of seven years but shall not be elected a second time." The question to postpone was defeated.

Mr. THOMSON. (To the spectators) This was probably the last thrust to restore the provisions for election of the president by the legislature.

Mr. ADAMS. Mr. Chairman, I ask that Mr. Madison's notes on this point be read into the record.

Gen. WASHINGTON. Mr. Madison.

Mr. MADISON. My notes for September 5 read as follows:

"The Report made yesterday as to the appointment of the Executive was then taken up. Mr. Pinckney renewed his opposition to the mode, arguing that: First, the electors will not have sufficient knowledge of the fittest men and will be swayed by an attachment to the eminent men of their respective states. Second, the dispersion of the votes would leave the appointment with the Senate, and as the President's reappointment will thus depend on the Senate he will be the mere creature of that body. Third, he will combine with the Senate against the House of Representatives. Fourth, this change in the mode of election was meant to get rid of the ineligibility of the President a second time, whereby he will become fixed for life under the auspices of the Senate.

Mr. Gerry did not object to this plan of constituting the Executive in itself but said his final vote would be governed by the powers that may be given to the President.

Mr. Rutledge was much opposed to the plan reported by the Committee. It would throw the whole power into the Senate. He was also against a reeligibility. He moved to postpone the Report under consideration and take up the original plan of appointment by the Legislature. To wit. 'He shall be elected by joint ballot by the Legislature to which election a majority of the votes of the members present shall be required. He shall hold his office during the term of Seven years; but shall not be elected a second time.' "

This motion to postpone failed, 8 to 2, with one divided vote. On this motion, the appointment of the president by the national legislature was lost forever.

Mr. ADAMS. Thank you.

Mr. THOMSON. (To the spectators) As Mr. McHenry recorded in his own notes, "The greatest part of the day was spent in desultory conversation on that part of the report respecting the mode of choosing the president. Adjourned without coming to a conclusion."

Gen. WASHINGTON. Major Jackson, please continue.

Major JACKSON. On September 6, just eleven days before the end of the Convention, the mode of election of the president as reported by the Committee on Detail was agreed upon by a 9 to 2 vote.

Mr. THOMSON. (To the spectators) Mr. Spaight thought an election by electors was being "crammed down."

Mr. ADAMS. Mr. Thomson, I overheard that remark. "Crammed down," eh? A legitimate question, I suppose, one that leads to still another: is there any evidence to indicate that the Convention was being hurried to close its sessions? After all, the Convention was meeting in the Assembly Room, which was normally occupied by the General Assembly of Pennsylvania. Can anyone shed any light?

Mr. MADISON. Perhaps I can. You must keep in

mind that the difficulty of finding an unexceptionable process for appointing the executive organ of the government was deeply felt by the Convention; still, as the final arrangement of it took place in the latter stage of the session, it was not exempt from a degree of the hurrying influence produced by fatigue and impatience in all such bodies, though the degree was much less than usually prevails in them.

Major JACKSON. Perhaps I can respond on this question also. The minutes of the General Assembly of Pennsylvania for September 5, 1787, are germane here: "Mr. Speaker informed the House that the Honorable Convention of the United States, during the recess of the House, had met in the room appropriated to the use of the General Assembly and that the session of the Convention would probably not be closed before the end of next week and requested to know what order the House would be pleased to take on the subject, thereupon. Resolved, That This House do adjourn, to meet in the chamber above stairs, tomorrow, at half past nine, AM."

Mr. MADISON. It is possible that Mr. Spaight may indeed have thought himself rushed, since he wrote this note to Mr. John Gray Blount on Sunday, September 2, 1787: "The Convention will I imagine finish their business by next Saturday," which would have been September 8.

Dr. FRANKLIN. Since I was a printer, all I know is what I read in the papers. The *Pennsylvania Herald* on Saturday, September 8, 1787, which was the date Mr. Spaight imagined the Convention would adjourn, published this notice: "We hear that the Convention propose to adjourn next week, after laying America under such obligations to them for their long, painful and disinterested labours, to establish her liberty upon a permanent basis, as no time will ever cancel."

Mr. ADAMS. Of course, the Convention did not adjourn until Monday, September 17. But it would appear that the Convention may have been under pressure to close its session in order to give the Assembly Room back to the General Assembly of Pennsylvania.

Mr. THOMSON. Gentlemen, it is my recollection that

the Pennsylvania General Assembly reconvened "above stairs" on September 4, 1787.

Major JACKSON. Yes. And below stairs, a Committee of Detail was appointed by ballot on September 8 to revise and arrange the articles which had been agreed to by the House. The Committee consisted of Mr. William Samuel Johnson, Mr. Alexander Hamilton, Mr. Gouverneur Morris, Mr. James Madison, and Mr. Rufus King.

Mr. ADAMS. Major Jackson, was September 6 the day on which the appointment of the president by electors, as opposed to appointment by the legislature, was finalized?

Major JACKSON. I believe so.

Mr. ADAMS. It appears that the change away from an election of the president by the legislature originated with the Committee of Eleven, of which Mr. Dickinson was a member. We have already discussed the change in power in the Convention that existed by the time the Committee of Eleven met. At this time, I would like to place in the record a letter which appears to be in the handwriting of John Dickinson.

Gen. WASHINGTON. Unless it can be definitely ascertained that the letter referred to is in the handwriting of Mr. Dickinson, the letter is inadmissable.

Mr. ADAMS. Since I have no basis for authentication today, I withdraw my request.

Mr. THOMSON. (To the spectators) The letter Mr. Adams referred to was found on a single sheet with no identification. It appears to be in handwriting of John Dickinson and internal evidence suggests it as part of other letters in the same folder, written to Sen. George Logan, Dickinson's "kinsman," dealing with Constitutional questions. The letter in question is dated November 4, 1802.

Of the activities of the Committee of Eleven on choosing the president, Mr. Dickinson wrote to Sen. Logan: "One morning the Committee met in the Library Room of the State House, and went upon the business. I was much indisposed during the whole time of the Convention. I did not come into The Committee till late and found the members upon their feet.

"When I came in, they were pleased to read to me their minutes, containing a report to this purpose, if I remember rightly—That the President should be chosen by the Legislature. The particulars I forget. I observed that the powers which we had agreed to vest in the President were so many and so great that I did not think the people would be willing to deposit them with him, unless they themselves would be more immediately concerned in his Election - - - That from what had passed in Convention respecting the magnitude and accumulation of those powers, we might easily judge what impressions might be made on the public mind, unfavorable to the Constitution we were framing—That if this single article should be rejected, the whole would be lost, and the States would have the work to go over again under vast disadvantages—That the only true and safe principle on which these powers could be committed to an Indidivual, was—that he should be in a strict sense of the expression, The Man of the People—besides, that an election by the Legislature would form an improper dependence and connection.

"Having thus expressed my sentiments, Gouverneur Morris immediately said—'Come Gentlemen, let us sit down again, and converse further on this subject.'

"We then all sat down and, after some conference, James Madison took a pen and paper and sketched out a mode for electing the President agreeably to the present provision. To this we assented and reported accordingly. These two gentlemen, I dare say, recollect these circumstances."

It appears, then, from Mr. Dickinson's own words that he shared a major responsibility in changing the concept of the office of the president in the final days of the Convention.

Mr. JEFFERSON. We cannot point to the establishment of the office of the president in the Convention with any assurance that it was the real opinion of a majority. At best, it was a method least objectionable at that critical moment. And because of situations like this I have said time and again that we cannot look upon the Constitution with sanctimonious reverence.

Does anyone here believe there is a thread embedded

in the history of the Convention that would satisfy our inquiry?

Mr. ADAMS. Gentlemen, we are reaching the point when the Commission must come to a decision, if any can be made on the reconstitution of the office of the president. We have already made recommendations which meet the needs of this nation; but, as we pointed out, these were all on the periphery of the office itself. I think we ought to leave ourselves time to reflect on this.

Did the Convention founders flounder on an answer to the presidential riddle?

Will the public be dumbfounded by our indecision? Will we be remembered only as the dumb founders? Two hundred years of history have not yielded a satisfactory answer. I trust that any change made in the office will be real and not illusory and that posterity will not say, as Sen. Timothy Pinckney did, in the United States Senate on December 2, 1803: "I hoped, after so long a course of pork that our diet would be changed, but I find it is pork still with only a change of sauce."

I suggest we leave adequate time to allow all of us to consider this important matter. And there are contiguous matters which should be touched upon. For example, what about the cost of presidents to the taxpayers? I would also implore the Chair to agree to a session on matters related to Mr. Dickinson.

Mr. MADISON. And I would suggest a session on the war powers of the president, Mr. Chairman.

Gen. WASHINGTON. Mr. Adams, on the cost of presidents to taxpayers could you be prepared to discuss this subject on, let's see, as soon as Monday, August 24?

Mr. ADAMS. Yes, I will ask Mr. Fairhill to return here for questioning.

Gen. WASHINGTON. Mr. Madison, could you be prepared to discuss "war powers" on the following Monday?

Mr. MADISON. Yes, I would ask that Gen. Douglas MacArthur be invited to testify on that day.

Gen. WASHINGTON. That can be done. Now Mr. Adams, on the subject of a session concerning Mr. Dickinson, I will not allow such a session to be conducted.

Our agenda, then, should allow us to discuss the cost of presidents to the taxpayers on August 24th; the war powers of the president on August 31st; adequate time to resume the discussion of the office of the president on September 7. Are we agreed?

(Members nod assent.)

Gen. WASHINGTON. Good. Gentlemen, this session is adjourned until Monday, August 24 at 10 a.m.

Mr. THOMSON. (To the spectators) I think it's high time we cleared the air about Mr. Dickinson. General Washington has rejected a session on matters related to John Dickinson, but that does not prevent you and me from chatting about this. We've already seen that Mr. Adams and Dr. Franklin, and many others had problems with Dickinson, who, Mr. Adams once said, had "fallen like grass before the scythe" because he had opposed independence and was, as a result, "in total Neglect and Disgrace."

Dickinson was quite sensitive to attacks on his character and responded to political opponents in *Freeman's Journal* on January 1, 1783, "Let those who were witnesses of my behaviour declare whether throughout my whole life I have been the warm, disinterested friend of the people, the zealous and industrious asserter and maintainer of their rights and liberties, or the artful pursuer of private advantages.

"I challenge my enemies to point out a single instance, where, either as a lawyer or as a member of assembly, I ever took a part in the least degree unfavorable to those rights and liberties. I go farther. I challenge them to point out instances while I practiced at the bar or had a seat in legislation where questions of moment to the public arose, and I was not found on the side of my country. . . . Justice remains to be enquired."

In his "vindication" letter Dickinson cited four charges brought against him: first, that he opposed the Declaration of Independence in Congress; second, that he highly disapproved the Constitution of Pennsylvania; third, that he deserted his battalion when it went into the field in December 1776, and in so doing deserted the American cause; and fourth, that he injured or endeavored to injure the continental money, specifically by writing a letter to his brother, Philemon Dickinson.

To which we can add a fifth, which occurred less than six months after his statement of "vindication": fifth, that he refused to call the militia to protect Congress during a mutiny which threatened it.

Dickinson denied the first charge but quibbled, "I confess that I opposed the making of Declaration of Independence at the time when it was made. . . . . The policy of then making it I disputed. . . . I knew, and told Congress, that I was acting an unpopular part in the debate upon the declaration; and I desired that illustrious assembly to witness the integrity, if not the policy, of my conduct."

Dickinson had received his legal education in London in the Middle Temple, one of England's Inns of Court.

One may be led to the suggestion that his English training in law influenced his decisions and trend of thinking in connection with the American Revolution. There were about 115 American students who were admitted to the Inns of Court from 1760 to the close of the Revolution, among them Mr. Edward Rutledge, who also opposed to the last the Declaration of Independence.

Dr. FRANKLIN. (To the spectators) Not to be omitted from this illustrious group, I daresay that I attended Boston Grammar School for one year, though I signed the Declaration of Independence.

Mr. THOMSON. (Continuing to the spectators) The second charge against Dickinson was that he "highly disapproved" the Constitution of Pennsylvania. Dickinson's answer: "So I did; for I thought it unnecessarily expensive, and not as well calculated as it might have been, for permanently securing and advancing the happiness of the people." What Dickinson failed to mention was that Franklin had drafted the Constitution he "highly disapproved"!

We now come to the third charge brought against Dickinson—that he deserted his battalion and the American cause. Wrote Dickinson: "When the associated militia of Pennsylvania was formed for the defense of the liberties of America . . . I had the honour of being elected Colonel of the first battalion, and thereby held the indisputed honor of commanding the whole militia. . . . My adversaries found a new mode for degrading me from the command of the militia of Pennsylvania. A meeting of officers and privates was held at Lancaster; and while I was consulting with a committee of Congress, the committee of safety, and some officers, and forming plans for the public defense, two Brigadiers General were put over my head."

Dickinson then stated that: "On the 28th of September, 1776, the Convention that had been summoned for the express purposes of forming a new government . . . stepped unnecessarily beyond the purposes marked out for them, by those who called them, and confirmed two Brigadiers over me. The next day, I resigned my command of the first battalion.

"My enemies were now in full possession of power in Pennsylvania, and her former favourite was reduced to a disregarded thing.

"I could not consent to stand like a chopping-block before them, to be hack'd by their tomahawks into such shape as might gratify their capricious fancy. I resolved, in the first place, never to be accountable to such men for any military command—secondly, to seek my fortune and a kinder usage in another state."

There was still another front Dickinson had to contend with. In his own words: "My persecutors in Philadelphia remembered me . . . I had not been but ten days in camp when I was turned by them out of Congress.

"Yes! While I was exposing my person to every hazard, and lodging every night within half a mile of hostile troops that the members of the convention at Philadelphia might slumber and vote in quiet and safety, they ignominiously voted me, as unworthy of my seat, out of the national senate. . . .

"This shock I also bore—and 'faultered not on the approach of danger' to face my 'foreign enemies,' for the protection of my 'domestic enemies.' "

The fourth charge, concerning his injury of the Continental money by a letter he wrote to his brother, he denied also. The letter in question was in these words: "Receive no more continental money on your bonds and mortgages—The British troops have conquered the Jerseys, and your being in camp are sufficient reasons—Be sure you remember this—It will end better for you." This letter was sealed and directed "To Brigadier General Philemon Dickinson, at the American camp." It was unsigned.

In his defense Dickinson presented what he thought "were solid reasons then that would have justified my brother's refusal of continental money." Dickinson expressed concern that "some men wished the public to believe that I contemplated, when I wrote the letter, a great depreciation of the continental money—and that this contemplation was the sole cause of my writing it. . . . I acknowledged that I did apprehend such a depreciation and that this apprehension had weight with me in inducing me to write the letter. But I totally deny and still deny that this consideration would have moved me to write, if my brother had not been in so uncommon a situation as he then was."

As to his not signing the letter, Dickinson said: "There seems to be a consciousness that I was writing something blameable, from the letter not being signed.

"It was a common way of writing to my brother. The writing proved the writer. In the present case, it could not possibly be my intention to conceal my being the author from any persons in Pennsylvania if the letter should get into their possession; for any one acquainted with my writing would know on seeing the letter that it was written by me as well as if my name was subscribed to it."

Thus, he answered the charges. But Mr. Dickinson sat on important committees at the Federal Convention, and appears to have been present whenever important decisions were made. Thus, the question arises, to what extent do these prior incidents affect his credibility?

Perhaps we can find an answer in the fifth charge, that Dickinson refused to call the militia to protect Congress during a mutiny which threatened Congress, on June 21, 1783, during the presidential term of the Honorable Elias Boudinot, tenth president of the Continental Congress. Dickinson was president of Pennsylvania at the time.

The event clearly symbolizes the power struggle between Congress and the states, as well as the incapacity of Congress and its president under the Articles of Confederation; in addition, it depicts the power play of one man—John Dickinson—against Congress; and finally, it marked the departure of the Continental Congress from Philadelphia, never again to return to the place where it debated and created the Declaration of Independence.

The events leading to this incident were as follows: on April 15, 1783 Congress ratified a peace treaty with Great Britain officially ending the Revolutionary War. With assurance of peace, the soldiers became eager for their discharge, and Congress was eager to disband the army. General Washington advised Congress that at least three months' pay would be necessary before disbandment, a total sum estimated at $750,000. But where was the money to come from? The Rhode Island delegates wrote to their Governor, William Greene, "those enlisted during the war are already impatient to be discharged. The want of money in the public Treasury to satisfy their moderate claims on being discharged is a perplexing circumstance, and throws Congress into a very disagreeable dilemma," while Richard Peters wrote to Baron Steuben, "The difficulty which heretofore oppress'd us was how to raise an Army. The one which now embarrasses us is how to dissolve it. . . . But an empty purse is a bar to the execution of our best intentions. We have under consideration a plan for establishing a mint. All we want to put it in execution is the necessary metal. . . . But I fear we have not yet found the vein in which these precious ores are lodged."

The events of June 21, 1783, constituted a most dangerous insurrection that President Boudinot described in detail: "About three or four hundred soldiers in the barracks here in Philadelphia surrounded Congress and the Supreme Executive Council of Pennsylvania and kept us prisoners, in a manner, near three hours. Tho' they offered no insult personally, to my great mortification, not a citizen came to our assistance. The President of Pennsylvania, Mr. John Dickinson, and Council had not the firmness enough to call out the militia and alleged as a reason that the militia would not obey them. In short, the political maneuvers entirely unhinged government. This handful of mutineers, with arms in their hands, I thought would make us all prisoners in a short time."

Three days later President Boudinot issued a proclamation: "Whereas the said Soldiers still continue in a state of open mutiny and revolt, so that the dignity and authority of the United States would be constantly exposed to a repetition of insult, while Congress shall continue to sit in this City. I do therefore, by and with the advice of the said Committee and according to the powers and authorities in me vested for this purpose, hereby summon the honorable The Delegates composing the Congress of the United States, and every of them, to meet in Congress, on Thursday the twenty-sixth day of June instant, at Princeton, in the State of New Jersey, in order that further and more effectual measures may be taken for suppressing the present revolt, and maintaining the dignity and authority of the United States. . . ."

I myself heard said at the time that had John Dickinson called up the militia, Philadelphia would possibly have remained the capital of the United States; America would have saved the millions it spent on building Washington, D.C.

Mr. Oliver Ellsworth observed, "I am fully persuaded that no honest, disinterested man in the World who was acquainted with the circumstances could be of the opinion that we could with propriety have staid longer in the City after having been surrounded by an armed and menacing Banditti and after having applied in vain to the Executive Authority for protection. I cannot help thinking that if the militia had been called out, or if application had been made to the most virtuous and respectable part of the Citizens, such a dishonour would never have been suffered."

Alexander Hamilton reported to Governor George Clinton of New York: "The conduct of the executive of this State—John Dickinson—was to the last degree weak and disgusting. In short, they pretended it was out of their power to bring out the militia. without making the experiment."

But on the other hand Dr. Benjamin Rush wrote to

President Boudinot that "Congress is called the 'little' Congress, and in many places no Congress at all. . . . our whole state have taken side with the Council and the City of Philadelphia. . . . Congress is angry—at what?—a few drunken soldiers insulted them as they walked the streets. Three wrongs will not make one right. The soldiers did wrong in revolting—The Council did wrong in not calling out the militia—and the Congress did wrong in remaining at Princeton. Congress alone persevered in the wrong."

Mr. John Montgomery, a delegate to Congress from Pennsylvania, knew of Dr. Rush's opinion and responded that he was astonished at the assertion that Congress was the aggressor in the dispute. Montgomery thought the charge lay with more propriety against the states, who had withheld their taxes and defeated every measure proposed by Congress to establish revenues in order to pay to the soldiers. Montgomery wondered why "those fellows had a right to complain since many of them were not more than five months in service. They received a nine pound bounty, a suit of clothes and their arms. They were fellows who had never been in action. They were the off-scourings and filth of the earth. Were these the men to draw down the vengeance of the army on Congress?"

Montgomery flattered himself "into thinking that in a short time things would come to rights again, men's tempers would cool and their fears subside, and Congress would strut on the pavements of the grand metropolis and congratulate each other on the marvelous escape it made to Princeton and the great Wisdom and prudence in conducting affairs to a happy ending." But it never happened.

Alexander Hamilton "viewed the departure of Congress a delicate measure, including consequences important to the national character with respect to the state of Pennsylvania and in particular the city of Philadelphia. The triumph of a handful of mutinous soldiers, permitted in a place which was considered as the capital of America, surrounding and in fact imprisoning Congress without the least effort on the part of the citizens to uphold their dignity and authority, obliging Congress to move from the place which had been their residence during the revolution, was a general disaffection of the citizens to the federal government, and discredited and affected the national interests."

He continued, "I was fully convinced Congress would in reality be justified in withdrawing from a place where such an outrage to government had been with impunity perpetrated by a body of armed mutineers who were for several days in complete command of the city. The feebleness of public councils of the indisposition of the citizens afforded no assurance of protection and support.

"Congress left the city because they had no forces at hand, no jurisdiction over the militia and no assurances of effectual support. The Council and the Executive of the state, of necessity, were required to remain on the spot. Soon after Congress removed, the mutineers were deserted by their leaders and surrendered at discretion. . . .

"The rights of government are as essential to be defended as the rights of individuals. The security of the one is inseparable from that of the other. And indeed in every new government, especially of the popular kind, the great danger is that public authority will not be sufficiently respected. . . . The insult was not to Congress personally, it was to the government, to public authority in general; and was very properly put upon that footing. The regular forces which Congress could command were at a great distance, and could not but in a length of time be brought to effectuate their purpose. The disorder which continued to exist on the spot where they were, was likely to increase by delay and might be productive of sudden and mischievous effects by being neglected. The city and the bank were in immediate danger of being rifled and perhaps of suffering other calamities. The citizens, therefore, were the proper persons to make the first exertion. . . .

"The best apology for the government of Pennsylvania in this case is that they could not command the services of their citizens. But so improper a disposition in the citizens, if admitted, must operate as an additional justification to Congress in their removal.

"The call for the militia was made the day after it had been pronounced ineligible by the Council. When the Supreme Executive Council learned, on June 24, that the soldiers were planning an attack on the Bank of North America, it ordered that a guard be placed there. On June 25, fearing that the mutinous troops would engage in violence, the Council finally ordered the state militia into service. There could have been little change in that time, either in the temper or preparation of the citizens. The truth is that the departure of Congress brought the matter to a crisis and that the Council were compelled by necessity to do what they ought to have done before through choice.

"It is to be lamented that they did not by an earlier decision prevent the necessity of Congress taking a step which had many disagreeable consequences."

Such was Mr. Hamilton's assessment. James Madison is the only one on this current Commission who was present at the evacuation of Congress from Philadelphia in 1783 and of the government from Washington, D.C. in 1814. In 1814, he beat a fast retreat from Washington, alone, on horseback, first to Georgetown, then from place to place on both sides of the Potomac. The British entered Washington, burned his house— now the White House—put a torch to every public building except the Patent Office, and after twenty-four hours Mr. Madison returned unscathed. Congress returned to Washington, but the Continental Congress never returned to Philadelphia.

To Governor Edmund Randolph of Virginia Madison wrote, "Philadelphia will ever be obnoxious while it contains and respects an obnoxious character!"

Mr. Madison—since you are still here—can you tell us what you thought of the mutiny of '83?

Mr. MADISON. All incidents that occurred in the political life of Mr. Dickinson before the Federal Convention should be important to us in evaluating the influence he may have had in the making of the Constitution. My opinion may be singular, but any man who refuses to sign the Declaration of Independence and refuses to call out the militia to protect the Congress of the United States—and then serves on committees responsible for drafting the Constitution of the United States—merits further investigation, as has been done here today.

Dr. Franklin, do you have any thoughts on the mutiny of '83?

Dr. FRANKLIN. There is a thought with which I once prefixed my *Poor Richard's Almanack*.

A little neglect may breed mischief,
For the want of a nail, the shoe is lost,
For the want of a shoe, the horse is lost,
For the want of a horse, the rider is lost.

Perhaps I can say this differently:
For the want of money, the bounty is lost,
For the want of bounty, respect is lost,
For the want of respect, Congress is lost.

And as to a title for this sad episode in American history, let's just call it:

Mutiny - on the Bounty.

MONDAY, AUGUST 24, 1987

COST OF PRESIDENTS TO TAXPAYERS

The Committee met pursuant to notice, at 10 a.m. in the Assembly Room of Independence Hall, Gen. George Washington presiding.

Present: Mr. John Adams, Dr. Benjamin Franklin, Mr. Thomas Jefferson, Mr. James Madison and Gen. George Washington.

Gen. WASHINGTON. At the request of Mr. Adams, today's session will be devoted to the cost of presidents to United States taxpayers. Mr. Adams.

Mr. ADAMS. We have asked Mr. William S. Fairhill to appear before our Commission again. Mr. Fairhill, as you may recall, was formerly deputy director in the office of Management and Budget.

The presidency is an important office and it is not our purpose to tarnish it or engage in any partisan politics. However, it is also an area of government expenditure that has grown remarkably in recent years. Mr. Fairhill, what can you tell us about the amounts spent by the government for the executive office of the president?

Mr. FAIRHILL. In 1980, which is the year I will use as a base, the expenditure was just over $100 million.

Mr. ADAMS. Now, just what did that cover?

Mr. FAIRHILL. Well, it covered the compensation of the president, the White House Office, the executive residence at the White House, the official residence of the vice-president, special assistance to the president . . .

Mr. ADAMS. Let us restrict our discussion just to the areas where federal funds are used for the president. What is the compensation of the president?

Mr. FAIRHILL. $200,000 a year . . .

Dr. FRANKLIN. Mr. Chairman, it is with reluctance that I rise to express a disapprobation. In this particular of salaries to the executive branch I happen to differ; and as my opinion may appear new and chimerical, it is only from a persuasion that it is right and from a sense of duty that I hazard it. The Commission will judge my reasons when they have heard them, and their judgment may possibly change mine. I think I see inconveniences in the appointment of salaries; I see none in refusing them, but on the contrary, great advantages.

Sir, there are two passions which have a powerful influence on the affairs of men. These are ambition and avarice: the love of power and the love of money. Separately each of these has great force in prompting men to action; but when united in view of the same object, they have in many minds the most violent effects. Place before the eyes of such men a post of honor that shall at the same time be a place of profit, and they will move heaven and earth to obtain it . . .

Mr. THOMSON. (To the spectators) Ladies and gentlemen, Dr. Franklin's speech is already familiar to me, for it is the same one he gave before the Federal Convention on June 2, 1787, the day he opposed paying salaries to the officials of the federal government. Because it pained him to stand on his feet then, his few speeches were read by his colleague James Wilson. His speech given here bespeaks his principal contribution at the Constitutional Convention; he sought to persuade his co-workers that compromise, a sense of fallibility, and a willingness to trust men in the management of their own affairs were the requisites of free, republican government.

Dr. FRANKLIN. (Continuing) The struggles for them are the true sources of all those factions which are perpetually dividing the Nation, distracting its councils, hurrying sometimes into fruitless and mischievous wars, and often compelling a submission to dishonorable terms of peace.

And of what kind are the men that will strive for this profitable pre-eminence, through all the bustle of cabal, the heat of contention, the infinite mutual abuse of parties, tearing to pieces the best of characters? It will not be the wise and moderate, the lovers of peace and good order, the men fittest for the trust. It will be the bold and the violent, the men of strong passions and indefatigable activity in their selfish pursuits. These will thrust themselves into your government and be your rulers. And these too will be mistaken in the expected happiness of their situation; for their vanquished competitors will perpetually be endeavoring to distress their administration, thwart their measures, and render them odious to the people.

Besides these evils, Sir, though we may set out in the beginning with moderate salaries, we shall find that such will not be long in continuance. Reasons will never be wanting for proposed augmentations. And there will always be a party for giving more to the rulers, that the rulers may be able in return to give more to them. Hence as all history informs us, there has been in every State and Kingdom a constant kind of warfare between the Governing and Governed: the one striving to obtain more for its support and the other to pay less. And this has alone occasioned great convulsions, actual civil wars, ending either in dethroning of the Princes or enslaving of the people. Generally, indeed the ruling power carries its point, the revenues of princes constantly increasing, and we see that they are never satisfied, but always in want of more. The more the people are discontented with the oppression of taxes the greater need the prince has of money to distribute among his partisans and pay the troops that are to suppress all resistance and enable him to plunder at pleasure. There is scarce a king in a hundred who would not, if he could, follow the example of Pharoah, get first all the people's money, then all their lands, and then make them and their children servants forever. . . . But this Catastrophe I think may be long delayed if in our proposed system we do not sow the seeds of contention, faction and tumult, by making our posts of honor, places of profit. If we do, I fear that though we do employ at first a number, and not a single person, the number will in time be set aside; it will only nourish the fetus of a King . . . and a King will the sooner be set over us.

It may be imagined by some that this is a Utopian Idea and that we can never find men to serve us in the Executive department, without paying them well for their services. I conceive this to be a mistake . . . have we not seen the great and most important of our officers, that of General of our armies, serve for eight years without the smallest salary, by a Patriot whom I will not now offend by any other praise; and this through fatigues and distresses in common with the other brave men, his military friends and companions, and the constant anxieties peculiar to his station? And shall we doubt finding three or four men in all the United States with public spirit enough to bear sitting in peaceful Council for perhaps an equal term, merely to preside over our civil concerns and see that our laws are duly executed. Sir, I have a better opinion of our country. I think we shall never be without a sufficient number of wise and good men to undertake and execute well and faithfully the Office in question.

Sir, I must be contented with the satisfaction of having delivered my opinion frankly and done my duty.

Mr. ADAMS. Thank you, Dr. Franklin. Mr. Fairhill, what does the White House Office cost the taxpayers?

Mr. FAIRHILL. A little over $20 million a year.

Mr. ADAMS. And the cost of the executive residence at the White House?

Mr. FAIRHILL. That runs $3.2 million a year.

Mr. ADAMS. Please compare that figure to the cost of maintaining the official residence of the vice-president.

Mr. FAIRHILL. The cost of the residence of the vice-president is about $200,000 a year.

Mr. ADAMS. What about the cost of the Secret Service and special protection for the president?

Mr. FAIRHILL. The Executive Protective Service, which is the uniformed branch of the Secret Service, is regularly charged with the protection of the Executive Mansion and grounds, protection of the president and members of his immediate family, protection of the residence of the vice-president, as well as the vice-president and members of his immediate family, and . . .

Mr. ADAMS. What is the cost of this protection?

Mr. FAIRHILL. The cost of protecting the president and other protectees is included in other activities of the Secret Service such as suppressing counterfeiting and forgery.

Mr. ADAMS. Why?

Mr. FAIRHILL. We felt revealing the budget would jeopardize the security provided for the president and others. If we were to break out protection separately, a reasonably astute accountant, through deductions, could arrive at, or come pretty close to arriving at, the number of people we have assigned to a particular detail, to the president, for example. As you know, our cost accounting system is designed so that we can supply the Commission any figure it needs with respect to the cost of any particular item in our activities. However, since these sessions are open to the public . . .

Mr. ADAMS. I understand, Mr. Fairhill. I remember when I was president—and I didn't have an Executive Protection Service. In April 1798, I received a letter informing me that some wretches intended setting fire to the city in four places at once, and then blowing up my house. Then on April 30, I received a letter informing me that it was planned to set fire to the city on May 9. Now, May 9 was the day I had declared to be a day of fasting and prayer.

On May 9, as a newspaper reported, "about 40 young men, in a body, wearing the French cockade . . . came down the streets . . . and went directly to the President's house; where they were observed to be loitering about and seeming to have no particular object. They soon attracted the public attention and a crowd of people assembled about them. A magistrate came and enquired of them their business and, receiving an evasive reply, he desired them to go away; they answered it was a land of liberty, and they should go where they pleased. Very soon they came to blows with the people about them, who, in obeisance to the magistrate attempted to seize some of them. One of the rioters was apprehended and sent to gaol; . . . they threatened their assailants with vengeance and said they expected several hundred of butchers and carpenters . . . to join them, and they would pull out all the black Cockades. . . ."

Mr. THOMSON. (To the spectators) I should explain that the National Cockade of France had been long considered as the badge of an open avowed attachment to that country. The black Cockade, which was strictly American, evidencing attachment to our own country and government, was chiefly worn by young citizens.

Mr. ADAMS. The newspaper account continued, "The citizens flew to arms, and the villains were dispersed. Several other squads of fellows with French Cockades were observed in different parts of the city, which increased the alarm; but no further disturbance took place. A large body of horses paraded in front of the President's house all evening; and a vast number of citizens assembled. Several bodies of volunteer horse and foot patrolled the streets all night. A strict look out is kept for them; and it is probable that the next appearance of the French Cockade in the hats of Americans will not pass off so quietly. The citizens discovered a noble solicitude for the safety of the President and the support of the government."

Now I do not want to convey the wrong impression. That was my situation then, and I understand the necessity of protecting the president and others. My protection came not only from the good graces of citizens but also from the agencies of government. For example, on November 8, 1798, the following note appeared in *Claypoole's American Daily Advertiser*: "Mr. Luther Baldwin, of Newark, was arrested, on Saturday last, by the Marshall of the state of New Jersey, under the late Sedition Act, for expressing a wish that the President of the United States was dead."

Well, so much for that.

Mr. Fairhill, what pension does a former president receive?

Mr. FAIRHILL. Sixty-nine thousand dollars a year, using my base year, 1980.

Mr. ADAMS. What expenses do the taxpayers have for former presidents?

Mr. FAIRHILL. Former presidents receive office allowances, Secret Service protection, and the government pays for the maintenance of and additions to presidential libraries.

Mr. ADAMS. What was the total cost of former presidents to the United States taxpayers in 1980?

Mr. FAIRHILL. I would say in the area of $18 million.

First SPECTATOR. (To second spectator) Do you think that in the near future we might be treated to one of those American Express Card commercials which will begin with a shot of an ex-president saying, "Hi, do you know me?"

Mr. ADAMS. Do former presidents work?

Mr. FAIRHILL. Benjamin Harrison wrote a book *This Country of Ours*. Herbert Hoover and Dwight D. Eisenhower wrote articles for the *Saturday Evening Post*. Paid television interviews began with Harry Truman and Dwight Eisenhower. These practices have been carried on by more recent former presidents.

Mr. ADAMS. Let's discuss the subject of the office allowances.

Mr. FAIRHILL. The Former Presidents Act of 1958 provided former Presidents with retirement benefits, office space, office staff, and franking privileges.

Mr. ADAMS. What about travel?

Mr. FAIRHILL. The act did not mention travel as an authorized expense, but the fiscal year 1969 Supplemental Appropriations Act states that a former president and no more than two members of his staff are authorized to use the Former President's Act fund to pay travel expenses.

Mr. ADAMS. What were the total funds expended in 1980 for office allowances for former presidents?

Mr. FAIRHILL. About $800,000.

Mr. ADAMS. I understand the General Accounting Office only does a periodic audit and is not required by law to audit the former presidents' account annually, is that correct?

Mr. FAIRHILL. That is correct. I might just say, since

the first report was issued in 1970, the audits that we have done have been at the request of committee chairmen.

Mr. ADAMS. I made such a request of you.

Mr. FAIRHILL. That is correct.

Mr. ADAMS. And I do have the Comptroller General's report pursuant to that request. Now, this is the first audit that has been done since 1975.

Mr. FAIRHILL. That's correct. Actually, the last report we issued was 1977, but it covered expenditures through 1975.

Mr. ADAMS. According to page 8 of your report, one of the former presidents charged his account for car washes, minor auto repairs, leased cars, gasoline. Those sound a little more like personal items to me.

Then we see water softeners, swimming pool services, silver coffee service. Do you think that is the kind of thing Harry Truman had in mind when he said, "I need some help to keep the hounds away from the door?"

Mr. FAIRHILL. No sir, I do not think so. They are unusual items, if you will. But considering the legislative guidelines that are presently available to the General Services Administration, they don't have a lot to go on.

Mr. ADAMS. I agree that there is a problem in that. On the subject of Secret Service protection for former presidents, what is the extent of that protection?

Mr. FAIRHILL. Authority for the Secret Service to protect our former presidents was first enacted in 1962. At that time protection was provided for only a "reasonable time" after the president requested such protection. In 1965, the statute was changed to extend the protection provided to a former president for his lifetime. Protection for former First Ladies was later provided in legislation. When first enacted, the legislation applied only to Mrs. Kennedy and her children and only authorized protection for two years. In late 1965, however, the wife, widow, and minor children of a former president were added to the list of those entitled to protection on a permanent basis.

Mr. ADAMS. What was the cost of providing all these protections in 1980?

Mr. FAIRHILL. About $7.9 million.

Mr. ADAMS. What was it in 1965?

Mr. FAIRHILL. About $100,000.

Mr. ADAMS. So the cost of providing that protection has escalated seventy-nine times in a fifteen-year period.

Mr. FAIRHILL. That is correct.

Mr. ADAMS. Now let us move over to the subject of presidential libraries. What was spent by the taxpayers of the United States for presidential libraries in 1980?

Mr. FAIRHILL. About $9.5 million.

Mr. ADAMS. Under what authority are these payments made?

Mr. FAIRHILL. The Presidential Libraries Act was enacted on August 12, 1955. The purpose of the Presidential Libraries Act was to provide a library system capable of providing for the care and preservation of the papers and mementoes of presidents of the United States after they leave office. The historical value of presidential papers and records along with the governmental interest require that these records be preserved and made available to officials and scholars alike.

The Presidential Libraries Act authorizes the administrator of the General Services Administration, when he considers it to be in the public interest, to accept for deposit the papers and other historical materials of a president or former president. He may also accept other papers and collections of documents assembled by others in the presidential administration or contemporary and relevant to the administration. To complement these collections, the adminstrator is authorized to accept, subject to congressional approval, land, buildings, and equipment, which have been funded and constructed by public and private interests close to the president, to house these collections as a presidential library.

Once accepted by the administration and the Congress, the burden of maintaining and servicing the library falls on the government.

Mr. ADAMS. Is there a library for my papers and mementoes?

Mr. FAIRHILL. Well, you see, sir . . .

Mr. ADAMS. All I see is $9.5 millon spent for presidential libraries, and I don't see where my papers are!

Gen. WASHINGTON. Easy, Mr. Adams.

Mr. FAIRHILL. The Library of Congress has custody of a body of papers for twenty-three presidents beginning with George Washington and ending with Calvin Coolidge. The Library of Congress does not hold the papers of all presidents through Coolidge. The papers of John and John Quincy Adams are at the Massachusetts Historical Society. James Buchanan's papers are at the Historical Society of Pennsylvania; those of Millard Fillmore are at the Buffalo and Erie County Historical Society; Rutherford B. Hayes' papers are in the Hayes Library, Fremont, Ohio; and the Warren G. Harding papers are in the custody of the Ohio Historical Society. With the exception of the Hayes papers, the Library of Congress holds a microfilm edition of the presidential papers located in these repositories.

All presidents beginning with President Hoover have or will have presidential libraries maintained by the government under the Act.

Mr. ADAMS. What were the original cost estimates for this project?

Mr. FAIRHILL. During the hearings on the Libraries Act in 1955, considerable discussion was given to the annual operating costs for presidential libraries. Based on the costs at the Roosevelt Library, it was estimated that the annual net maintenance and operating cost for fifteen presidential libraries would grow to $1.5 million. This assumed that the $150,000 operating and maintenance cost for each library would be offset by $50,000 in fees from visitors to the museums.

Mr. ADAMS. Was that a General Accounting Office study?

Mr. FAIRHILL. No, I think these were . . .

Mr. ADAMS. You don't want to take responsibility for that projection in cost, do you?

Mr. FAIRHILL. No sir, it was not my projection. I was not there.

Mr. ADAMS. I am glad I don't have to take responsibility for that projection, either. Go ahead.

Mr. FAIRHILL. The testimony on that projection was given by Dr. Wayne G. Grover, then Archivist of the United States.

Mr. ADAMS. Is he still working for the government?

Mr. FAIRHILL. I don't believe so.

Mr. ADAMS. So the net cost of each library to the taxpayer was, in 1955, projected to be $100,000. Now, Mr. Fairhill, in fact the estimated cost in 1979 for the Johnson library alone was $1.8 million, for the Eisenhower, $1.3 million, for the Truman, $1.1 million, and so on.

Mr. FAIRHILL. I want to note that income from fees or donations was expected to offset about one-third of the annual costs of the libraries. In fiscal year 1979, the offset was estimated to be $732,000, or 10 percent of the costs of the seven libraries. It should also be noted that the offset does reduce the amount of appropriated funds that might otherwise be required by the libraries.

Mr. ADAMS. I didn't realize the General Services Administration was paying for added space to these libraries. I was under the impression that funds for the space were to be raised by private contributions and the government just had maintenance and upkeep expenses after the libraries were built. I see, in fact, that space has been added to most of the libraries. The Truman, the Hoover, almost all of the libraries have built additions. So is not the taxpayer paying for that?

Mr. FAIRHILL. That is right.

Mr. ADAMS. What are some of these costs for additions?

Mr. FAIRHILL. The Truman addition in 1968 cost $312,000. The Hoover addition in 1969 cost $1,074,000. The Eisenhower addition in 1971 cost $1,610,000. The Roosevelt addition in 1972 cost $882,000, and the second Truman addition in 1979 cost $2,667,000.

Mr. ADAMS. Do you see anything in the Act that provides for these funds?

Mr. FAIRHILL. It is difficult to pin that question down on the basis of information in the act. It appears that there is a recognition that the function could expand. We discussed this with our general counsel. Their opinion is that once the building is donated to the federal government and we accept title to it, then it is our responsibility to pay for any expansions.

Mr. ADAMS. Bearing in mind that the cost for the presidential libraries under the Presidential Libraries Act in fiscal year 1980 was approximately $9.5 million, let us now turn our attention to the cost of maintaining presidential works in the Library of Congress. Mr. Fairhill, you stated earlier in your testimony that the Library of Congress has custody of a body of papers for twenty-three presidents beginning with George Washington and ending with Calvin Coolidge. We understand, too, that the Library of Congress does not hold the papers of all presidents through Coolidge. Those that are not in the Library of Congress are privately maintained by historical societies?

Mr. FAIRHILL. That is correct.

Mr. ADAMS. In your view, are there any major problems in the way the Library of Congress operates its program, particularly from the point of view of the various researchers who want to use the papers?

Mr. FAIRHILL. Well, we are not aware of difficulties.

Mr. ADAMS. What is the annual operating cost of the presidential papers activities of the Library of Congress?

Mr. FAIRHILL. That is a very difficult figure to come up with, Mr. Adams. The annual direct cost for the manuscript division as a whole is approximately $1.2 million.

Mr. ADAMS. That is the entire manuscript division?

Mr. FAIRHILL. That is correct. We have no way of breaking out a particular figure that would apply just to the presidential papers. If you took a percentage based on possible usage, perhaps 10, 15 percent of that.

Mr. ADAMS. Well, we were told by someone over there that there is approximately $50,000 in direct cost and approximately $200,000 in indirect cost annually for presidential papers. Would that be a fair estimate?

Mr. FAIRHILL. Well, as I say, it is difficult to say what the indirect cost would be since we don't have a cost analysis basis for that. I think I would prefer to state a somewhat lower figure, perhaps $125,000 to $150,000.

Mr. ADAMS. Well, $200,000 should cover it.

Mr. FAIRHILL. Yes. As part of a larger operation.

. . .

Mr. ADAMS. That is for twenty-three presidents. Now I understand microfilming would be in addition to that, that is, the first microfilming of those papers.

Mr. FAIRHILL. Yes, that's right.

Mr. ADAMS. And you spent about $1.5 million for all your microfilming?

Mr. FAIRHILL. Those were the direct appropriations. There was approximately another $15,000 in other kinds of expenses.

Mr. ADAMS. Mr. Fairhill, do you believe the Library of Congress operates an adequate program for making presidential papers available for scholarly research?

Mr. FAIRHILL. I certainly do.

Mr. ADAMS. Do you receive any complaints or criticisms from scholars, historians, or others who have needed use of presidential papers maintained by the Library of Congress?

Mr. FAIRHILL. I am not aware of any complaints specifically on that point.

Mr. ADAMS. Would it be fair to say then that what costs $9.5 million to do under the Presidential Libraries Act would cost only $200,000 if done by the Library of Congress?

Mr. FAIRHILL. That is substantially correct.

First SPECTATOR. (To second spectator) Seems like a lot of egomaniacs.

Second SPECTATOR. (To first spectator) Seems more like an egomoneyac problem.

Mr. ADAMS. I have just one or two further questions. Is it true that there is a bikini-clad statue of Raquel Welch in the Lyndon Baines Johnson Library?

Mr. FAIRHILL. Well, let me explain about that.

There was a traveling exhibit by the Smithsonian Institution titled "The Time of Our Lives" which was temporarily displayed at the Johnson Library. This exhibit included the original artwork for *Time* magazine covering the 1960s and 1970s, and one cover did picture a sculpture of Raquel Welch. The sculpture itself was exhibited along with the other original artwork. All rental and installation fees for this exhibit were paid by the Lyndon B. Jonnson Foundation fron nonfederal funds. This exhibit was previously at the National Portrait Gallery.

Mr. ADAMS. Oh, I see. What relationship does this display have to the mission of the Lyndon Baines Johnson Library as an archival depository of presidential papers?

Mr. FAIRHILL. As a part of its mission each presidential library maintains exhibits on the history of the respective presidential administrations. These exhibits draw heavily from the archival holdings of the libraries. In this case the Johnson Library determined that the Smithsonian exhibit provided a valuable retrospective look at the 1960s and 1970s by focusing on the public personalities who appeared on the cover of *Time*.

Mr. ADAMS. Mr. Fairhill, I want to commend you on the way you handled yourself here. The Commission extends its thanks to you for your extensive efforts. That is all the questions we have.

Gen. WASHINGTON. Gentlemen, next Monday we will have the honor of an appearance here by Gen. Douglas McArthur. We look forward to his testimony. We will now adjourn until Monday, August 31st, at 10 o'clock a.m.

Mr. JEFFERSON. (To Dr. Franklin, on exiting) Ben, if you are not busy Wednesday evening, perhaps we can have supper at the City Tavern?

Dr. FRANKLIN. (To Mr. Jefferson) It so happens I am meeting Will Rogers that night. How about tomorrow night?

Mr. JEFFERSON. (To Dr. Franklin) Fine.

WEDNESDAY EVENING, AUGUST 26, 1987

BENJAMIN FRANKLIN MEETS WILL ROGERS

(Dr. Benjamin Franklin and Will Rogers are dining at the City Tavern, located at Second Street near Walnut, in Philadelphia. Supper is in progress.)

Dr. FRANKLIN. . . . Will, you were born on the last frontier as it was passing out of existence. You were "the big Honest Majority." Your humor, your comments, your sarcasm were just as much a part of America as your big ears, your shuffling gait, your grin, and your unruffled good nature. You were as real as a mule wiggling its ears on a hot summer day. You were America.

Will ROGERS. You sure you've got the right guy?

Dr. FRANKLIN. Well, all I know is what I read in the papers.

Will ROGERS. That's my line, Ben.

Dr. FRANKLIN. You just don't know how important you are. It may interest you to know that five of your articles have been read on the floor of Congress and printed in the Congressional Record as representing a typical American view of important public subjects.

Will ROGERS. Yes, I know.

When a gentleman quoted me on the floor of Congress the other day, another member took exception and said he objected to the remarks of a Professional Joke Maker going in to the Congressional Record.

Excerpts from *Autbiography of Will Rogers*, edited by Donald Day. Copyright © 1949 by Rogers Company. Copyright © renewed 1977 by Donald and Beth Day. Reprinted by permission of Houghton Mifflin Company.

Now can you beat that for jealousy among people in the same line? Calling me a Professional Joke Maker! He is right about everything but the Professional. THEY are the Professional Joke Makers. Read some of the bills that they have passed, if you think they ain't Joke makers. I could study all my life and not think up half the number of funny things they can think of in just one session of Congress. Besides, my jokes don't do anybody any harm. You don't have to pay any attention to them. But every one of the jokes those birds make is a LAW and hurts somebody.

And, by the way, I have engaged counsel and if they ever put any more of my material in that "Record of Inefficiency" I will start suit for "deformation of character." I don't want my stuff buried away where nobody ever reads it. I am not going to lower myself enough to associate with them in a literary way.

Dr. FRANKLIN. I do not think you or the public realize just how important your views are on public subjects. And that's why I am here with you tonight. You see, Gen. Douglas MacArthur is going to testify before our Commission tomorrow, and I have to evaluate what the situation was just before World War II—before we get into a World War III. And I understand that you were probably the greatest prophet of the times.

Will ROGERS. Was I?

Dr. FRANKLIN. You certainly were. Did you ever stop to think that there are an infinite number of worlds under the divine government, and if ours was annihilated it would scarce be missed in the universe? You see,

>"God sees with an equal eye, as Lord of all,
>A Hero perish, or a Sparrow fall.
>Atoms, or Systems, in Ruin hurl'd,
>And now a Bubble burst,—and now a World!"

Will ROGERS. When did you write that? Looks like you were a prophet, too.

Dr. FRANKLIN. I wrote that 230 years ago, in my *Poor Richard's Almanack*. But y'know, I may have to change my mind.

Will ROGERS. Why?

Dr. FRANKLIN. Well, we have been exploring space for many years now and haven't found another peopled world like ours. Maybe we are the only one. Maybe we are the chosen one. Maybe we really will be missed in the universe if we blow up His world here. Maybe there is a dearth of earths like ours.

Will, tell it to me as it was then . . .

Will ROGERS. It was May 3, 1932, when I wrote: "See where two English scientists were able, headlines said, 'to split the atom.' The world is not bad enough off as it was, now they go and split up the atom. That's the last straw . . . we always felt that the old 'atom' would remain intact. It was certainly a big disappointment to me."

Dr. FRANKLIN. All we think about today is guns, guns, and missiles. How did you see it then?

Will ROGERS. You can't say civilization don't advance, for in every war they kill you a new way.

Well, one day Austria said they wanted a gun. Then it was Germany. England had a gun. France had a gun. Italy had a gun. Germany wanted a gun. Austria wanted a gun. All God's children wanted guns—going to put on the guns, going to buckle on the guns, and smear up all of God's Heaven.

Dr. FRANKLIN. What about disarmament?

Will ROGERS. That's a good question, Ben. Around 1924, we called a disarmament conference. We were building a lot of battleships and we had plenty of money to do it on, and it looked like in a couple of years we might have the largest navy in the world. Charles Evan Hughes, who was secretary of state, happened to think of an idea: "Let us confer on sinking battleships." Well, the idea was so original that they immediately made him the Toastmaster. You see, up to then, battleships had always been sunk by the enemy, and when he proposed to sink our ships ourselves it was the most original thought that had ever percolated the mind of a statesman. So, when we communicated the idea to England and Japan that we had an idea whereby we would sink some of our own battleships, why they come over so fast, even the butler wasn't dressed to receive them when they arrived.

England was willing to tear her blueprints on planned building into half, Japan was willing to give up her dreams of having more ships on the seas than any nation and stop building up to three-fifths of the size of England and America, and Secretary Hughes met that with, "Now, Gentlemen, I will show you what America is prepared to do. FOR EVERY BATTLESHIP YOU FELLOWS DON'T BUILD AMERICA WILL SINK ONE."

Then they were talking of having another Naval Disarmament Conference. We could only stand one more. If they ever had a second one we would have had to borrow a boat to sink it.

You see, we don't like to ever have the start on any nation in case of war. We figure it looks better to start late and come from behind. If we had a big navy some nation would just be kicking on us all the time. Sinking your own boats is a military strategy that will always remain in the sole possession of America.

Then we sent our fleet to Australia to impress Japan with the size of it. That was not necessary. Japan knew more about our war strength than either of our secretaries of War or Navy.

In 1932, I attended the disarmament Conference in Geneva. There was a hash of nations. There was sixty-five nations represented there. Every nation with railroad fare and a gun was there. The smaller the nation the bigger the delegation. If you disarmed the delegates you would have disarmed over half the countries represented. Turkey was not there to disarm but to try and book some wars for the coming season. There was lots of nations willing to throw away two spears and a shield for every battleship we sank.

You see, to reduce your navy in those times was exactly like a man not doing well financially who cancels all his life insurance, figuring it's a dead loss because he hasn't died yet.

Well, we got a treaty signed for the limitation of naval vessels. We held a conference and decided to sink some vessels that would sink themselves if the conference was postponed for another year. England was to sink three battleships that competed against the Spanish Armada. Japan was to raise two that the Russians sunk and resink them for the treaty. We were building two to sink.

And speaking of treaties, y'know, America and Britain signed a treaty that they wouldn't fight each other. Then America and France signed a treaty they wouldn't fight each other. Now, if we could just sign with some nation that there is a chance of having war with, why it would mean something.

Dr. FRANKLIN. And what about our foreign policy?

Will ROGERS. America has a great habit of always talking about protecting American interests in some foreign country. How many Americans spend the summer trying to get to some places where there is no development—no street cars, elevators, Fords, telephones, radios, and a million and one other things that you just like to get away from once in a while? Well, suppose they don't want 'em at all down there. Why don't you let every nation do and act as they please?

America and England, especially, are regular old busybodies when it comes to telling somebody else what to do. But you notice, England and America never tell each other what to do. You bet your life they don't.

Big nations are always talking about Honor. Yet England promised to protect France against Germany—if France would pay them what they owed them.

Dr. FRANKLIN. When did you say that?

Will ROGERS. In 1925. Then, in 1930, I said: "So you think we are doing bad in the United States, do you? Well, let's look around and see what our companions are doing. China is in a mess, not only again, but yet. Russia is starving her own people to feed propaganda to the rest of the world. A guy named Hitler has Germany like Capone has Chicago. France has plenty of gold, but is short on friendship. England has her fine diplomats but no world markets. Spain is trying to get a Republic; they think one is great. That shows their ignorance. Italy has black shirts, but no pants to go with 'em. Brazil has got coffee, but no president, so before you think of giving up your citizenship here, you better think it over.

Did you ever kinder stop to figure it out, this old world

of ours as a whole is not sitting so pretty just at the present time? Did you know that there is an awful lot of parts of Europe that is just sitting on what the old time Orator used to call a powder keg? Well, it is. We can't pick up a paper that from one to a hundred don't prophesy that prosperity is just around the corner. But let me tell you that war is nearer around the corner than prosperity is.''

Dr. FRANKLIN. What incredible foresight!

Will ROGERS. That's not all. In 1932 I said: "If you want to know when a war is coming, just watch the U.S. and see when they start cutting down on their defense. It's the surest barometer in the world . . . We are going to get into a war some day either over Hololulu or the Philippines."

Dr. FRANKLIN. What a visionary you were!

Will ROGERS. We are the only nation in the world that waits till we get into a war before we start getting ready for it. Pacifists say that, "If you are ready for war, you will have one." I bet no man insulted Jack Dempsey after he was champion.

Dr. FRANKLIN. In any war, what would be the safest country to be in?

Will ROGERS. Switzerland is the most independent country in the world. When nations get ready to make peace or war, why, they always go to Switzerland. Geneva and Locarno are the principal conference towns. Switzerland has a corner on all conferences. It has had fewer wars and has been the starting place of more of them than any nation that ever lived. They just sit around and remain neutral during these wars and then collect from all ends. It's the only country where both sides can go and meet and have a drink.

Dr. FRANKLIN. Well, there never was a good war or a bad peace. Let's get off that subject for the moment. Will, what did you think of General Washington?

Will ROGERS. There wasn't any Republicans in Washington's day. No Republicans, no income tax, no cover charge, no disarmament conferences, no luncheon clubs, no stop lights, no static, no headwinds. Liquor was a companion, not a problem; no margins, no ticket speculators, no golf balls or

Scotch jokes.

My Lord, living in those times, who wouldn't be great? What do you think of him, Ben?

Dr. FRANKLIN. To me he was George Washington, Commander of the American Armies, who, like Joshua of old, commanded the sun and the moon to stand still, and they obeyed him.

Will ROGERS. Amen.

Dr. FRANKLIN. Will, did you have an oil cartel problem in your time?

Will ROGERS. The oil people? Why, they got rich so quick they were millionaires before they had time to get the grease off their hands. They'd jump from a Ford to a Rolls Royce so fast that they tried to crank the Rolls through force of habit.

Dr. FRANKLIN. Well, the world found out about inflation and credit trouble when the oil people in the Middle East decided to squeeze the tap shut a little.

Will ROGERS. That's right, and it caught people by surprise. In my time we spent years buying everything under the sun on credit, whether we needed it or not. We had to pay for 'em under Mr. Hoover and we howled like a pet coon. This would be a great world to dance in, if we didn't have to pay the fiddler.

If there ever was a time to save it's now. When a dog has a bone he don't go out and make the first payment on anything. First payments is what made us think we were prosperous, and the other nineteen is what showed us we were broke.

I believe in your saying, a penny saved is a penny earned.

No, it's not politics that is worrying this country; it's the second payment and it ain't taxes that is hurting this country; it's interest.

Dr. FRANKLIN. Yep, he that goes a borrowing goes a sorrowing. Americans are still suffering from high interest rates, unemployment. . . .

Will ROGERS. Unemployment! That one really gets me riled. Why if you live under a government and it don't provide some means of you getting work when you really want it and will do it, why then there is something wrong. You can't just let the people starve, so if you don't give 'em work, and you don't give 'em food or money to buy it, why, what are they to do? What is the matter with our country, anyhow? With all our brains in high positions and all our boasted organizations, why can't there be some means of at least giving everybody all the bread they wanted anyhow? —instead of selling it to Russia.

But the main thing is we just ain't doing something right; we are on the wrong track somewhere. We shouldn't be giving people money and them not do anything for it. No matter what you have to hand out for necessities, the receiver should give some kind of work in return. Cause he has to eat just the same when he is laying off as when he is working.

Dr. FRANKLIN. Yes, unemployment and welfare are ways to reduce a great country to a little one, but so is odious taxation with a collection company composed of the "indiscreet, ill-bred, and insolent"—so I wrote in 1773.

Will ROGERS. Taxes! Now, when I tell you that if I was running the government, there would be no lowering of taxes, you know now a comedian is crazy.

President Coolidge said that we were approaching an era of prosperity. Everybody generally admitted that we were better off than we ever were in our lives, yet we owed a national debt of thirty billions of dollars.

We owed more money than any nation in the world, and we were lowering taxes. When is the time to pay off a debt if it is not when you are doing well? All government statistics said that 70 percent of every dollar paid in the way of taxes went to just the keeping up our interest and a little dab of amortization of our national debts. In other words, if we didn't owe anything our taxes would have been less than one-third what they were. Well, if two-thirds of what you pay goes to keeping up just interest, why don't we do our best to try and cut down the principal, so it will lower that tremendous interest?

Now, here is what I can't savvy. Why is it that one of us, in fact all of us, will work and save and stint all our lives. For what? Why, to leave something to our children. When we die we want everything we have left clear and unencumbered. We will break our necks to leave them without a single debt. In fact we won't die if we can help it till we get out of debt for their sake. Now that is what we will do as individuals, *but*, when it comes to us *collectively*, why it looks like we will break our neck to see how much we can leave them owing.

Dr. FRANKLIN. You just reminded me of something. In 1788, when the debates on the ratification of the Constitution were in progress in the convention of the state of New York, the Honorable Mr. Melancton Smith rose: "We are now come to a part of the system which requires our utmost attention and most careful investigation. It is necessary that the powers vested in government should be precisely defined, that the people may be able to know whether it moves in the circle of the Constitution. It is the more necessary in governments like the one under examination because Congress here is to be considered as only a part of a complex system. . . . The power of the general government extends to the raising of money. . . . It is a general maxim that all governments find a use for as much money as they can raise. Indeed, they have commonly demands for more. Hence it is that all, as far as we are acquainted, are in debt. I take this to be a settled truth, that they will all spend as much as their revenue; that is, will live at least up to their income. Congress will ever exercise their powers to levy as much money as the people can pay. They will not be restrained from direct taxes by the consideration that necessity does not require them. If they forbear, it will be because the people cannot answer their demands."

Will ROGERS. That's my point, all right. Too bad nobody listened to that fellow back then. Why, our crazy spending doesn't stop at home, either. There's the one thing no nation can ever accuse us of and that is secret diplomacy. Our foreign dealings are an open book, generally a check book.

Dr. FRANKLIN. Speaking of foreign affairs, I wonder if Gen. MacArthur will address the issue of Communism when he testifies tomorrow.

Will ROGERS. Don't get me started on those fellers. Why, a conservative communist in Russia is a fellow that thinks you only ought to divide with him what you have, while a real communist believes that you ought to give it all to him; in exchange, you get to call him Comrade.

Russia is a country that is burying its troubles. Communism is like Prohibition; it's a good idea but it won't work.

Dr. FRANKLIN. What do you think of our Chief Diplomats? I mean the ones who've inhabited the White House.

Will ROGERS. Well, in my time, there was Coolidge, Hoover, and Roosevelt. Those are the ones that I know the most about. I've got a few opinions on those fellas, all right.

Dr. FRANKLIN. I thought you might.

Will ROGERS. I remember when President Coolidge made a good speech. He didn't say that he would do anything, but on the other hand, he didn't say that he would not do anything. So it was what you might call a conservative speech. Dwight Morrow, Ambassador to Mexico, once told me that Cal Coolidge told him: "Dwight, I am not going to try and be a great president." That's all he said. That will stand in my memory as the greatest remark any office-holder ever made.

Then there was the presidential election in 1932. I'll tell you, Al Smith and Franklin Roosevelt didn't make up a day too soon. They made up, decided to bury the hatchet. Decided to bury it in Hoover.

Dr. FRANKLIN. What about the Roosevelt era?

Will ROGERS. All we had was codes and codes and codes—you know, regulations. The minute a thing is long and complicated it confuses. Whoever wrote the Ten Commandments made 'em short. They may not always be kept, but they can be understood. They are the same for all men. Some industry can't come in and say, "Ours is a special and unique business. You can't judge it by the others." Well no committee come into Jerusalem looking for Moses and saying, "Ours is a special business." Moses just went up on the mountain with a letter of credit and some instructions from the Lord, and He just wrote em out, and they applied to the steel men, the oilmen, the bankers, the farmers, and even the United States Chamber of Commerce. And he said, "Here they are, Brothers, you take 'em and live by 'em, or else."

Well that's where Moses had it on Hugh Johnson. He managed the National Recovery Administration under Franklin Roosevelt. Hugh had as good intentions, but Hugh Moses Johnson went up on Capitol Hill and come down with twenty-four truckloads full of codes. He just couldn't come out plain and say, "Thou shalt pay so much. And thou shalt work thy men only so much, and if thou canst not, getteth thee some more, but payeth them likewise." Hugh should have been born B.C.—before codes.

Course, that was not all our troubles. It wouldn't have solved everything any more than the Commandments have solved human weaknesses, but they did stop all arguments as to whether they were good and fair to all concerned, and they left no argument as to whether they would work if you kept them. I expect there is a lot of lessons in the Bible that we could learn and profit by and help us out, but we are just so busy doing nothing we haven't got time to study 'em out. But in Moses' time the rich didn't gang up on you and say, "You change that Commandment or we won't play."

Well, now that George Washington is back in town, he sees our system is working so smoothly that over seven million are without a chance to earn a living. He is seeing rations in peace time that should remind him of Valley Forge. In fact, we have reversed the old system; we all get fat in war times and thin during peace.

I'll bet if he hangs around for a while he'll sue us for calling him "father."

Dr. FRANKLIN. Will, your insight was remarkable; your foresight, unforseeable—by others! T'is easy to see, hard to foresee. I see the hour is late. Can we get together again?

Will ROGERS. Sure. But first I got to go see that Alaska. Y'see, I'm off on a little sight-seeing trip with Wiley Post. When my wife knew it was Wiley, it didn't matter where it was we was going—and she was mighty fine about it. Well, she is about everything. You can't live with a comedian long without being mighty forgiving.

Well, we'll get together when I get back.
Goodnite Ben. Y'know early to bed and early to . . .
Dr. FRANKLIN. That's my line, Will. Goodnight.

THURSDAY, AUGUST 31, 1987

GENERAL DOUGLAS MACARTHUR TESTIFIES

The Committee met pursuant to notice, at 10 a.m. in the Assembly Room of Independence Hall, Gen. George Washington presiding.

  Present: Mr. John Adams, Dr. Benjamin Franklin, Mr. Thomas Jefferson, Mr. James Madison and Gen. George Washington.

  Gen. WASHINGTON. Gentlemen, today we are privileged to have with us Gen. Douglas MacArthur.

  General MacArthur was born on an army post near Little Rock, Arkansas, on January 26, 1880. He was the son of Capt. Arthur MacArthur, who rose to become a lieutenant general and the ranking officer of the army. Douglas MacArthur graduated from West Point, first in his class of 1903. He was aide to President Theodore Roosevelt in 1906-07, and took part in the occupation of Vera Cruz in April 1914. He helped organize the 42nd (Rainbow) Division when the United States entered World War I and served in France with the temporary rank of brigadier general.

  From 1928 to 1936, he held various posts: he commanded the Department of the Philippines and was chief of staff of the army and field marshall of the Philippines. In 1937, rather than be transferred to other duties, he resigned from the army only to be recalled to active duty in 1941, when he was placed in command of the combined U.S. Army Forces in the Far East. When the Japanese forces invaded the Philippines, MacArthur withdrew his forces to the Bataan peninsula and finally to the fortified island of Corregidor. In February 1942, he was ordered to leave the Philippines for Australia. He was appointed supreme commander of the Allied Forces in the Southwest Pacific Area and began his counter-offensive in an island-hopping strategy that led the Allied forces slowly through New Guinea and the smaller islands toward Japan. On September 2, 1945, General MacArthur, as supreme commander of Allied Powers, accepted the surrender of Japan aboard the battleship *Missouri*. For the next six years, as commander of the Allied Occupation Forces in Japan, he oversaw the reorganization of the government and the economy of the nation. In June 1950, North Korea launched an invasion of South Korea that began the Korean War. General MacArthur was ordered to provide assistance to South Korea. Differences of opinion over the conduct of the action led President Truman to relieve him of his command on April 11, 1951. MacArthur returned to the United States and retired to private life, retaining active status and his five-star rank as general of the army.

Gentlemen, our copatriot, Gen. Douglas MacArthur.

Gen. MACARTHUR. I appear before you with a sense of deep humility and great pride; humility, in the presence of you, the great architects of our history; pride, in the reflection that this debate represents human liberty in the purest form yet devised.

At the turn of the century, when I entered the army, the target was one enemy casualty at the end of a rifle or bayonet or sword. Then came the machine gun, designed to kill by the dozen. After that, the heavy artillery, raining death by the hundreds. Then the aerial bomb, to strike by the thousands, followed by the atom explosion to reach the hundreds of thousands. Now, electronics and other processes of science have raised the destructive potential to encompass millions. And with restless hands we work feverishly in dark laboratories to find the means to destroy all at one blow.

I know war as few other men know it, and nothing to me is more revolting. I have long advocated its complete abolition, as its very destructiveness on both friend and foe has rendered it useless as a means of settling international disputes.

Men since the beginning of time have sought peace. Various methods through the ages have been attempted to devise an international process to prevent or settle disputes between nations. From the very start workable methods were found insofar as individual citizens were concerned, but the mechanics of an instrumentality of larger international scope have never been successful.

Military alliances, balances of powers, leagues of nations, all in turn failed, leaving the only path to be by way of the crucible of war. The utter destructiveness of war now blocks out this alternative. We have had our last chance. If we will not devise some greater and more equitable system, our Armageddon will be at our door.

Gen. WASHINGTON. I share your thoughts, General. My first wish is to see this plague to mankind banished from all the earth and the sons and daughters of this world employed in more pleasing and innocent amusements than in preparing implements and exercising them for the destruction of mankind.

Dr. FRANKLIN. I, too, agree with you perfectly in your disapprobation of war, General. Abstracted from the inhumanity of it, I think it wrong in point of human prudence; for, whatever advantage one nation would obtain from another, whether it be part of their territory, the liberty of commerce with them, free passage on their rivers, it would be much cheaper to purchase such advantage with ready money than to pay the expense of acquiring it by war. An army is a devouring monster, and when you have raised it, you have, in order to subsist it, not only the fair charges of pay, clothing, provisions, arms, and ammunition, with numberless other contingent and just charges to answer and satisfy, but you have all the additional knavish charges of the numerous tribes of contractors to defray, with those of every other dealer who furnishes the articles wanted for your army and takes advantage of that want to demand exorbitant prices. It seems to me that, if statesmen had a little more arithmetic or were more accustomed to calculation, wars would be much less frequent. I am confident that Canada might have been purchased from France in my time, for a tenth part of the money

England spent in the conquest of it. And if, instead of fighting with us for the power of taxing us, she had kept us in good humor by allowing us to dispose of our own money and now and then give us a little of hers, by way of donation to colleges, or hospitals, or for cutting canals, or fortifying ports, she might have easily drawn from us much more by our occasional voluntary grants and contributions than ever she could be taxes.

Sensible people will give a bucket or two of water to a dry pump that they may afterwards get from it all they have occasion for. England's ministry were deficient in that little point of common sense. And so they spent one hundred millions of her money and after all lost what they contended for. The expenses required to prevent a war are much lighter than those that will, if not prevented, be absolutely necessary to maintain it. As I told Will Rogers last night, there never was a good war or a bad peace.

Mr. MADISON. Your suggestion of purchased peace troubles me. As I said long ago, the United States, whilst they wish for war with no nation, will buy peace of none. It is a principle incorporated into the settled policy of America, that as peace is better than war, war is better than tribute.

Mr. THOMSON. (To the spectators) It is interesting to know why that remark of Mr. Madison's was made. President Madison had received a letter in August 1816, from the Dey of Algiers claiming that two vessels of war captured by the American squadron were not restored according to the promise of its Commander, Decatur, inferring that this failure violated the peace treaty. The Dey of Algiers proposed a renewal of the former treaty made many years previously, or a withdrawal of our consul from Algiers.

President Madison answered the Dey in this way:

"The United States being desirous of living in peace and unity with all nations, I regret that an erroneous view of what has passed should have suggested the contents of your letter.

Your predecessor made war without cause on the United States driving away their Counsul and putting into slavery the Captain and crew of one of their vessels, sailing under the faith of an existing treaty. The moment we had brought to an honorable conclusion our war with a nation the most powerful in Europe on the seas, we detached a squadron from our naval force into the Mediterranean to take satisfaction for the wrongs which Algiers had done to us. Our squadron met yours, defeated it, and made prize of your largest ship and of a smaller one. Our Commander proceeded immediately to Algiers, offered you peace, which you accepted, and thereby saved the rest of your ships, which it was known had not returned into port and would otherwise have fallen into his hands. Our Commander, generous as brave, altho' he would not make the promise a part of the Treaty, informed you that he would restore the two captured ships to your officer. They were accordingly restored. The frigate, at an early day, arrived at Algiers. But the Spanish government, alleging that the capture of the Brig was so near the Spanish shore as to be unlawful, detained it at Carthagena, after your officer had received it into his possession. Notwithstanding the fulfillment of all that could be required from the United States, no time was lost in urging on that government a release of the Brig, to which they would have no right whether the capture were or were not agreeable to the law of nations. The Spanish government promised that this Brig should be given up; and altho' the delay was greater than was expected, it appears that the Brig, well as the frigate, has been actually replaced in your possession.

"It is not without great surprise, therefore, that we find you, under such circumstances, magnifying an incident so little important as it affects the interests of Algiers, and so blameless on the part of the United States, into an occasion for the proposition and threat contained in your letter. I cannot but persuade myself that a reconsideration of the subject will restore you to the amicable sentiments towards the United States which succeeded the war so unjustly commenced by the Dey who reigned before you. I hope the more that this may be the case, because the United States, whilst they wish for war with no nation, will buy peace of none. It is a principle incorporated in the settled policy of America, that as peace is better than war, war is better than tribute. . . ."

Secretary of State John Quincy Adams, during the administration of President James Monroe, kept true to the policy of withholding recognition until a new nation had earned it, though he was a sincere well-wisher to all those states in their struggles for liberty. Mr. Adams wrote to the United States minister to England on May 20, 1818, "The time is probably not remote when the acknowledgement of the South American independence will be an act of friendship towards Spain herself; when it will be kindness to her to put an end to that self-delusion under which she is wasting all the remnant of her resources in a war, infamous by the atrocities with which it is carried on and utterly hopeless of success."

On June 19, 1822, Mr. Manual Torres from the Republic of Columbia was presented by Mr. Adams as the charge d'affaires from that country, an event Mr. Adams refers to in his diary as "chiefly interesting as being the first formal act of recognition of an independent South American Government." The point is of historical interest only, but worthy of note because of our vacillating attitudes and unclear policies in regard to the revolutions in the Western hemisphere during the 1980's.

And it is significant to recognize that the United States was at one time a revolutionary country.

Mr. ADAMS. General MacArthur, as you are aware, our examination of the president's war powers is necessarily precipitated by a world situation far different from the one we knew when we first met in this Hall. As I see it the United States as a whole is chiefly concerned with one major external threat—communism, with the Soviet Union as chief proponent of that ideology. Can you comment on this situation?

Gen. MACARTHUR. I can certainly speak from my own experience. On August 6, 1945, an American airplane dropped one bomb on Hiroshima. Two days later, with the world still reeling from this shattering experience, the Soviet Union formally declared war on Japan—following four years of pretentious neutrality that had allowed Japanese forces to move against and occupy New Guinea and the Philippines, instead of being tied down to guarding the Siberian frontier. The Russians attacked the Japanese Kwangtung Army in Manchuria and sent a military mission to my headquarters in Manila. It was headed by General Kuzma Derevyanko, an officer of considerable ability who later became the Soviet diplomatic representative in Tokyo.

On August 9, a second atomic bomb destroyed the city of Nagasaki amid a cloud of dust and debris that rose 50,000 feet and was visible for more than 175 miles. The bombs which fell on Hiroshima and Nagasaki were dropped by the 509th Composite Bomb Group based on Tinian and belonged to General Arnold's strategic command. The selection of Nagasaki as the second objective of the atomic bomb was caused by unfavorable weather conditions. After circling for fifty minutes above the smoke-obscured city of Kokura, which was the primary target, the bombing plane flew on to drop the bomb over Nagasaki, the alternate target. Kokura was spared by a blind miracle of chance, but in Nagasaki 100,000 inhabitants died within seconds.

By August 10, Japan had had enough; and on August 15, Emperor Hirohito broadcast to his people the announcement that he would accept the surrender terms.

This sequence of events is significant. Here Russia comes into the war with Japan a few days before the war ends and appoints General Derevyanko head of a military mission to my headquarters in Manila. I was then commander of the Allied Occupation Forces in Japan. Five years later, in June, 1950, after a long series of provocations, I temporarily suppressed the Communist Party and its newspaper in Japan. Their relief from suspension was made dependent on their future responsible behavior. This action drew a violent protest from General Derevyanko, the Soviet member of the Allied Council, which I answered with a firm rejection, calling his letter "a conglomeration of misstatement, misrepresentation and prevarication of fact. Without new or constructive thought, it is but a labored repetition of the line of fantastic propaganda which for some time had been emanating from centers within the orbit of Communist totalitarian imperialism. So complete is the unrealism of its premise that it offers no basis for rational discussion. Its plain purpose to support and encourage those few irresponsible

Japanese bent upon creating mass confusion and social unrest leading to violence and disorder is a shameful misuse of diplomatic privilege which ill-becomes the representative of a nation charged with a measure of responsibility in the democratic reorganization of Japan. I am accordingly left no other alternative than to disapprove its intemperate proposals, and indeed to reject the complete context of the document itself."

What happened in Japan may very well be a pattern throughout the world. In Japan, Communism became "the other minority."

On the third anniversary of the Japanese Constitution, May 3, 1950, I said, "The checks and balances established to safeguard against abuse of the powers conferred by the Japanese Constitution have firmly served their purpose during this period of political reorientation and democratic growth, and issues of interpretation and application have found their peaceful solution in the forum of public debate or under the established judicial process rather than in the crucible of social violence. Above all, there has been an increasingly healthy awareness and acceptance of that individual political responsibility which exists where sovereignty rests with the people. In this, indeed, lies the best assurance for Japan's continued advance as an exponent and practitioner of representative democracy. And as Japan goes, so in due time may go all of Asia. For men will come to see in Japan's bill of rights and resulting social progress the antidote to many of Asia's basic ills. If Japan proceeds firmly and wisely upon the course now set, its way may well become the Asian way, leading to the ultimate goal of all men—individual liberty and personal dignity—and history may finally point to the Japanese Constitution as the Magna Charta of free Asia. . . .

"Established in the immediate postwar era as a political party under constitutional protection and dedication to the advance of certain political, economic and social theories, the Japanese Communist Party proceeded initially in moderation and thereby enlisted some public support. In its endeavor to press this advantage, however, it went the way of all Communist movements, becoming increasingly intemperate in political and social activity, and in due course aroused a popular revulsion which in turn relegated the party into virtual political eclipse. More latterly its shattered remnant, in frustration born of this failure, has cast off the mantle of pretended legitimacy and assumed instead the role of an avowed satellite of an international predatory force and a Japanese pawn of alien power policy, imperialistic purpose and subversive propaganda. . . . Thus while here, as in the other democracies of the world, it professes championship of the workers' rights in order to enlist support within labor's ranks, events abroad demonstrate that the worker loses all rights under Communist political rule; where here as elsewhere it poses as an ardent advocate of freedom of speech and peaceful assembly, of freedom to worship in accordance with conscience, and of the other freedoms which flow from the universally recognized fundamental human rights, events irrefutably disclose the complete suppression of all freedom with the ascendancy of Communist political power. Indeed, history offers no slightest evidence of increase in social stability, preservation of social justice or continuation of social progress in the spiritual vacuum which lies in the wake of Communism's advance. . . .

"Experience, the great teacher, indeed points to no greater hypocrisy than the perorations of those who thus align themselves with this form of international political perfidy, social deception, and territorial fraud and seek an alliance of expediency with the fundamental human rights, giving lip service to their preservation solely to provide a screen of respectable plausibility to mask a sinister subversive design to destroy liberty as the obstacle to personal power."

Mr. THOMSON. (To the spectators) Listen, my friends, to these exhortations—think of Cuba, Afganistan, Poland and other lands . . .

Gen. MACARTHUR (Continuing). "There is involved no question of the privilege extended to all free people constitutionally to advocate evolutionary change, for Communism now makes but a shallow pretense of seeking such an objective. Its tactics are almost entirely confined to such as are conducive to arousing social unrest and public hysteria as the means toward establishing a more favorable base for ascendancy to political power. Its pressure is by no means localized to within national or regional borders as through a high degree of centrally controlled direction and coordination of policy and tactic at the international level; it is able at will, from the principal capitals within the Communist orbit, to bring to bear upon individual areas of freedom the full power of its subversive attack. It employs this coordinated force with ruthlessness and cunning and seeks to reduce the spirituality which bulwarks modern civilization by exploiting weaknesses in detail as they appear. The problem thus rapidly confronting Japan, as other countries throughout the world, is how locally to deal with this anti-social force in order to prevent, without impairment of the legitimate exercise of personal liberty, such an abuse of freedom as to imperil the national welfare. Thus far, here as elsewhere, reliance has been placed in the counter-pressure of an aroused public opinion finding its expresson at the ballot box where people of right have the opportunity to pass upon the responsibilty of all aspirants for elective leadership. While this safeguard serves to arrest the danger of the emergence through constitutional means of a lawless and irresponsible leadership, it less adequately protects against the danger that the abusive use of freedom may create conditions of unrest and lawlessness favorable to the emergence of just such a leadership through intimidation and force.

"The issue is therefore clear and unequivocal—how far may the fundamental rights be exercised unabridged without becoming the instrument of their own destruction? It is an issue which confronts all free peoples, forewarned that others have lost their liberties because, blindly following an ideal, they have failed to see the dangers inherent in reality."

Dr. FRANKLIN. Well said, General MacArthur. Communism—that long-standing riddle—about which the free world can no longer stand by and diddle. I advise—get wise, free world, before the world gets otherwise.

Mr. ADAMS. (Aside to Dr. Franklin) When did you say that, Ben?

Dr. FRANKLIN. Just now.

Gen. MACARTHUR. Well said, Dr. Franklin. I am no seer who can predict whether or not the Soviet aims at ultimately provoking and engaging in a global struggle. I give him infinitely more credit, however, than to believe he would embark upon so reckless and ill-conceived a course. Up to now, there is no slightest doubt in my mind but that he has been engaging in the greatest bulldozing diplomacy that history has ever recorded. Without committing a single soldier to battle, other than in Afganistan, he has assumed direct or indirect control over a large part of the population of the world. His intrigue has found its success, not so much in his own military strength nor, indeed, in any overt threat of intent to commit that strength to battle but in the moral weakness of the free world. It is a weakness which has caused many free nations to succumb to and embrace the false tenets of Communist propaganda.

Of this we may be sure. The Soviet's moves, should it actually want war, will be dictated by its own assessment of the relativity of military force involved, actual and potential. It will not be so much influenced by the destruction it believes itself capable of inflicting upon us as by the punishment it knows it itself would have to accept should it embark upon so reckless an adventure.

In 1951 I said: "I believe the free world has the strength to meet the enemy wherever he may threaten, be it on one front, two fronts, or many fronts. To hold the contrary—to say that freedom has not strength enough to meet Communism wherever its predatory forces may attack is an admission, even before the battle starts, of defeatism, without historical parallel. Can anyone seriously believe that as we now build our own normal military strength, the Soviet will not do all in its power to match our increase with a corresponding one of its own?

"Time is not, as some would have us believe, invincibly on our side, as in the field of atomic development where we now so predominantly lead; the gap between the Soviet and ourselves may well decrease with each passing year."

And so it has.

On September 2, 1945, after accepting the surrender

of Japan in Tokyo Bay, I warned of the need for a "spiritual recrudescense and improvement of human character that will synchronize with our almost matchless advances in science, art, literature and material and cultural development." Such an improvement is slow to come to pass. To the contrary, there is unmistakable evidence of a tendency toward moral deterioration throughout the free world. This moral deterioration does not occur through evolutionary change in human thought but rather from the relentless war being waged by a fifth column within the ranks of every free society. This is a far greater threat to the free world than is the advance of predatory force. Its very purpose is to destroy faith in moral values, to introduce cynicism in human thought and to transform tranquility into confusion, disorder and dismay. Our own people harbor a strong spiritual urge in their hearts, but many leaders have become absorbed in the demands of political expediency and have lost the traditional American patriot's touch. Such a leadership offers no panacea for freedom's festering wounds.

  I see a growing lack of faith by a large segment of our population in the responsibility and moral fiber of our own process of government. Truth has ceased to be the keystone to the arch of our national conscience, and propaganda has replaced it as the rallying medium for public support. Corruption and rumors of corruption have shaken the people's trust in the integrity of those administering the civil power. Government has assumed progressively the arrogant mantle of obligarchic power as the great moral and ethical principles upon which our nation grew strong have been discarded or remolded to serve narrow political purposes. The cost of government has become so great and the consequent burden of taxation so heavy that the system of free enterprise which built our great material strength has become imperiled. The rights of individuals and communities have rapidly been curtailed in the advance toward centralized power, and the spiritual and material strength, amassed through our original concept of a federation—erected upon the local responsibilty and autonomy of its several components—shows marked deterioration. Possibly these adverse factors account for our inability to advance a vigorous and courageous leadership at a time when the world never more needed such a leadership. Whatever the cause, the facts are undeniable. Our prestige abroad has reached a tragically low ebb and our leadership is little wanted.

Mr. ADAMS. General MacArthur, you are now touching upon a subject which is at the core of our own discussions. We would like you to expand upon this subject of leadership for the United States.

Gen. MACARTHUR. First, let me give a classic case of the disintegration of leadership.

The panorama of events which contributed so decisively to the downfall of our wartime ally, the Republic of China, has never been told to the American people. After the surrender of Japan, events and actions transpired that now seem almost incredible, brought about by ignorance, misinterpretation, and errors of judgment. One of the most accurate comments on this period was made on January 30, 1949, by a young veteran of the war in the Pacific, a Congressman, in an address at Salem, Massachusetts.

"Our relationship with China since the end of the Second World War has been a tragic one, and it is of the utmost importance that we search out and spotlight those who must bear the responsibility for our present predicament.

"It was clearly enunciated on November 26, 1941, that the independence of China and the stability of the national government was the fundamental object of our Far Eastern policy. That this and other statements of our policies in the Far East led directly to the attack on Pearl Harbor is well known.

"During the postwar period began the great split in the minds of our diplomats over whether to support the Government of Chiang Kai-shek or force Chiang Kai-shek as the price of our assistance to bring Chinese Communists into his government to form a coalition.

"Our policy in China reaped the whirlwind. The continued insistence that aid would not be forthcoming unless a coalition government was formed was a crippling blow to the national government. So concerned were our diplomats and their advisors

... with the imperfections of the diplomatic system in China after twenty years of war and the tales of corruption in higher places that they lost sight of our tremendous stake in a non-Communist China.

"This is the tragic story of China whose freedom we once fought to preserve. What our young men had saved, your diplomats and our president frittered away."

Those were the words of Congressman John Fitzgerald Kennedy.

Leadership. Daniel Webster once said on the floor of the Senate, "Our security is in our watchfulness of executive power. It was the constitution of this department which was infinitely the most difficult part in the great work of creating our present government; to give to the executive department such power as should make it useful, and yet not such as should render it dangerous; to make it efficient, independent and strong, and yet to prevent it from sweeping away everything by its union of military . . . force. I do not wish to impair the power of the President as it stands written down in the Constitution. But . . . I will not trust executive power, vested in the hands of a single magistrate, to keep the vigils of liberty."

He spoke those words years ago; but they could as well have been spoken today.

The object and practice of liberty lies in the limitation of government power. Through the ages the constantly expanding grasp of government has been liberty's greatest threat.

Mr. ADAMS. General, will you please repeat what Daniel Webster said about executive power?

Gen. MACARTHUR. He said, "I will not trust executive power, vested in the hands of a single magistrate, to keep the vigils of liberty."

Mr. ADAMS. Thank you.

Gen. MACARTHUR. I might add that there are many today who have lost faith in the early American ideal and believe in a form of socialistic, totalitarian rule, a sort of big brother deity to run our lives for us. They no longer believe that free men can successfully manage their own affairs. Their thesis is that a handful of men, centered in government, largely bureaucratic, not elected, can utilize the proceeds of our toil and labor to greater advantage than those who create it. Nowhere in the history of the human race is there justification for this reckless faith in political power. It is the oldest, most reactionary of all forms of social organization. It was tried out in ancient Babylon, ancient Greece and ancient Rome; in Mussolini's Italy, and Hitler's Germany, and in all communist countries. Wherever and whenever it has been attempted, it has failed utterly to provide economic security and has generally ended in national disaster. It embraces an essential idiocy that individuals who, as private citizens, are not able to manage the disposition of their own earnings, become in public office supermen who can manage the affairs of the world.

Mr. ADAMS. Is that not in essence what prevails today—a government that is largely bureaucratic and not elected?

Mr. JEFFERSON. It certainly appears to me that there exists a large non-elected bureaucracy. I have long said that we must endeavor to reduce the government to the practice of rigid economy to avoid burdening the people and arming the magistrate with a patronage of money which might be used to corrupt the very principle of government. The multiplication of public offices, increase of expense beyond income and growth of the public debt are indications soliciting the employment of the pruning knife. It is incumbent on every generation to pay its own debt as it goes.

Mr. ADAMS. I may agree with your point but it is somewhat off the issue. The main point being made is not that we have a large bureaucracy but that it is a largely *non-elected* bureaucracy. If, then, there be those who do not trust executive power in the hands of a single magistrate; from your statement, Mr. Jefferson, we would have to extend that mistrust to a largely non-elected bureaucracy. That is the essence.

Dr. FRANKLIN. Mistrust by whom, Mr. Adams—the Congress?

Mr. ADAMS. The Public, Doctor.

Dr. FRANKLIN. It would seem to me that our recommendation establishing Constitutional Councils, being councils of first resort by the president, and creating offices for two vice-presidents represent far-reaching steps in alleviating public mistrust. I certainly believe that our recommendations satisfy the admonition of Daniel Webster when he said "Our security is in our watchfulness of executive power."

I think we ought to look at some of the antecedents of this question of executive power vested in a single rather than a multiple executive. Mr. Madison, you have that information at hand. Would you kindly review it briefly?

Mr. MADISON. Much of this matter we have already covered in conjunction with other subjects. The constitutional debates on this issue occurred primarily on June 1, 2, and 4, 1787, and my notes indicate the following:

On June 1, Mr. Wilson of Pennsylvania moved that the executive consist of a single person. Mr. Pinckney of South Carolina seconded the motion "that a National Executive, to consist of a single person, be instituted." A considerable pause ensued. Doctor Franklin observed that it was a point of great importance, and he wished that the gentlemen would deliver their sentiments on it before the question was put to a vote.

Mr. Pinckney was for a vigorous executive but was afraid the executive powers of the existing Congress might extend to peace and war, which would render the executive a monarchy of the worst kind, to wit, an elective one. Mr. Rutledge of South Carolina said he was for vesting the executive power in a single person, though he was not for giving him the power of war and peace. A single man would feel the greatest responsibility, and administer the public affairs best.

Mr. Sherman of Connecticut considered the executive magistrate as nothing more than an institution for carrying the will of the legislature into effect, and thus the legislature, as they were the best judges of the business which ought to be done by the executive department, should be at liberty to appoint one or more as experience might dictate.

Mr. Wilson preferred a single magistrate, and Mr. Gerry of Massachusetts favored the policy of annexing a council to the executive, in order to give weight and inspire confidence.

Mr. Randolph of Virginia strenuously opposed a unit in the executive magistracy, regarding it as the fetus of monarchy. The vigor, dispatch, and responsibility required for the position could be found in three men as well as in one. The executive ought to be independent and, in order to support that independence, should consist of more than one. Mr. Wilson responded that unity in the executive, instead of being the fetus of monarchy, would be the best safeguard against tyranny.

On June 2, Mr. Randolph strongly opposed the establishment of a unity in the executive, arguing that a single magistrate would never receive the confidence of his country and would tend to be a local, not a national, figure. He was in favor of three members of the executive, to be drawn from different portions of the country.

Mr. Butler of South Carolina contended strongly for a single magistrate as most likely to answer the purpose of the remote parts. If one man should be appointed, he would be responsible to the whole, and he would be impartial to its interests. If three or more should be taken from as many districts, there would be a constant struggle for local advantages. In military matters this would be particularly mischievous. He said his opinion on this point had been formed under the opportunity he had had of seeing the manner in which a plurality of military heads distracted Holland when threatened with invasion of the imperial troops. One man was for directing the force to the defense of this part, another to that part of the country, just as he happened to be swayed by prejudice or interest.

On June 4, Mr. Wilson argued for a single person for the office of the executive. On examination he could see no evidence of Mr. Randolph's alleged antipathy of the people. On the contrary, he was persuaded that it did not exist. All knew that a single magistrate is not a king. One fact had great weight with him. All the thirteen states, though agreeing in scarce any other instance, agreed in placing a single magistrate at the head of the government. The idea of three heads had taken place in none. The degree of power is indeed different, but there are no co-ordinate heads. In addition to his former reasons for preferring a Unity, he would mention another. The tranquility not less than the vigor of the Government he thought would be favored by it. Among three equal members, he foresaw nothing but uncontrolled, continued and violent animosities which would be disruptive and harmful.

Mr. Sherman observed that, as Mr. Wilson had pointed out, in each state a single magistrate had been placed at the head of the government. He wished the same policy to prevail in the federal government. But then it should be also remarked that in all the states there was a council of advice, without which the first magistrate could not act: a Council he thought necessary to make the establishment acceptable to the people.

Mr. Gerry believed the policy of three members for the executive would be extremely inconvenient in many instances, particularly in military matters, whether relating to the militia, an army, or a navy. It would be a general with three heads.

Mr. Mason of Virginia stated that the chief advantages which had been urged in favor of unity in the executive were secrecy, dispatch, vigor and energy, especially in time of war. "I am inclined to think a strong executive necessary," he said, but if "strong and extensive powers are vested in the executive, and that executive consists only of one person, the government will of course degenerate into a monarchy; a government so contrary to the genius of the people that they will reject even the appearance of it. If the executive is vested in three persons, one chosen from the northern, one from the middle, and one from the southern states, will it not contribute to quiet the minds of the people and convince them that there will be proper attention paid to their respective concerns?"

The question for a single executive was called to a vote and passed 7 votes to 3.

Mr. ADAMS. Who were the states voting "nay?"

Mr. MADISON. Delaware, Maryland, and New York.

Dr. FRANKLIN. It appears to me that some of the thoughts expressed at the Convention on this subject of mistrust of a single executive coincided with the thinking of Mr. Daniel Webster and Gen. Douglas MacArthur. This Commission has already resolved this issue in its recommendations: first, for the establishment of a Constitutional Council; second, for the establishment of offices for two working vice-presidents chosen by the Congress. I am firmly of the opinion that the opinions of Mr. Webster and General MacArthur are valid and that the solutions offered by this Commission reinforce their position.

Gen. WASHINGTON. I agree. Collective judgment, under the Constitution, should be given more weight than singular judgment.

General MacArthur, is there any closing statement you would like to make?

Gen. MACARTHUR. The present tensions with their threat of national annihilation are kept alive by two great illusions. The one, a complete belief on the part of the Soviet world that the capitalist countries are preparing to attack them, that sooner or later we intend to strike. And the other, a complete belief on the part of the capitalistic countries that the Soviets are preparing to attack us; that sooner or later they intend to strike. Both are wrong. Each side, so far as the masses are concerned, is equally desirous of peace. For either side war with the other would mean nothing but disaster. Both equally dread it. But the constant acceleration of preparation may well, without specific intent, ultimately produce a spontaneous combustion.

Almost fifty years ago, the shadow of mounting violence overhung the earth, and men and races and continents desperately struggled to resolve the issues of war. Then over Hiroshima was launched a yet mightier weapon, and warfare assumed a new meaning in deadliness and destruction, and the agonies of that fateful day serve as warning to all men of all races that the harnessing of nature's forces in furtherance of war's destructiveness will progress until the means are at hand to exterminate the human race and destroy the material structure of the modern world. This is the lesson of Hiroshima. God grant that it be not ignored.

First SPECTATOR. (To Second Spectator) Y'know,

the twenty-one gun salute has got to go. This "royal salute" is a mockery, paradoxical and obsolete in our present world. The time is now to have this custom eliminated from international protocol.

It is highly irrational, if not almost irreverent, to have a barrage of twenty-one deafening, war-related blasts of gunfire spitting out over the countryside to herald the arrival of a visiting head of state. Words are exchanged by host and visitor proclaiming the lofty aspirations of each, that his country craves peace for all the nations of the world. The assurances are pronounced; the diplomatic entourage stands at rigid attention; faces are full of emotion while the shattering sound of the twenty-one guns tears through the air.

What does this signify? What vibrations are we to respond to? What symbolism is there in the theme that, while we earnestly pray for peace, the war sounds crack the atmosphere in the background?

Second SPECTATOR. (To First Spectator) Ruffles and flourishes on the drums, with the playing of the national anthems of the countries involved, would be a more dignified and meaningful salute of recognition to arriving heads of state.

Sure, the twenty-one gun salute has got to go!

Gen. MACARTHUR. Let us regain some of the courage and faith of the architects who charted the course to our past greatness. Let us look up as befits the most powerful nation on earth, both spiritually and physically. Let us tell all, that while firmly and invincibly dedicated to the course of peace, we will not shrink from defending ourselves if the alternative is slavery or some other form of moral degradation. Let us proudly reassume our traditional role of readiness to meet and vanquish the forces of evil at any time and any place they are hurled against us. Let us make clear our eagerness to abolish the scourge of war from the face of the earth just as soon as others are willing to rise to so noble a stature with us. And above all else let us regain our faith in ourselves, and rededicate all that is within us to the repair and preservation of our own free institutions and the advance of our own free destiny. Our history still lies ahead.

Our finest hours are yet to come.

Gen. WASHINGTON. General MacArthur, we have been delighted with and are grateful for your presence. This session will adjourn and resume its hearings on Monday, September 7, at 10 a.m.

Gen. WASHINGTON. (On exiting with General MacArthur) May I invite you to dine with me tonight? I would like to talk to you about Valley Forge.

Gen. MACARTHUR. I accept with pleasure, General. Perhaps we can also talk about Major Harry S Truman.

MONDAY, SEPTEMBER 7, 1987

BENJAMIN FRANKLIN PROPOSES "NO CONFIDENCE VOTE" BY THE PEOPLE

The Committee met pursuant to notice, at 10 a.m. in the Assembly Room of Independence Hall, Gen. George Washington presiding.

Present: Mr. John Adams, Dr. Benjamin Franklin, Mr. Thomas Jefferson, Mr. James Madison and Gen. George Washington.

Mr. THOMSON. (To the spectators) Perhaps you are not aware that John Hancock and I were the first and only signers of the Declaration of Independence for a period of almost thirty days. Mr. Hancock was the fourth and thirteenth president of the Continental Congress, although Mrs. Hancock often spoke of her husband's reluctance, from natural modesty, to accept the office. Once, while he hesitated, one of the members clasped him around the waist, lifted him from his feet, and placed him in the chair of state.

Anyway, on July 4, 1776, I wrote in the Journals of the Continental Congress that Congress had "Ordered, that the declaration be authenticated and printed . . . [and] . . . sent to the several assemblies . . . and . . . that it be proclaimed in each of the United States. . . ." John Dunlap printed the Declaration that night, and on July 5 and 6, we sent the printed documents to the states—authenticated with John Hancock's name and mine, attesting his. No other signature was on the document.

New York had "abstained" from voting on July 4th and it was not until July 15, that I recorded in the Journals that

New York had approved "the same and will, at the risk of our lives and fortunes, join with the other Colonies in supporting it." That made it unanimous. Four days later, on July 19th, Congress "Resolved, That the Declaration, passed on the 4th, be fairly engrossed on parchment, with the title and stile of 'The unanimous declaration of the thirteen United States of America,' and that the same, when engrossed, be signed by every member of Congress." If I recall correctly, it was my assistant, Timothy Matlack, who engraved the Declaration. It was not until August 2, that I recorded in the Journals, "The declaration of Independence being approved and compared at the table was signed by the members."

One more episode must be told in the story of the Declaration.

Abraham Clark, a member of Congress, foresaw the possibility that Congress might "be exalted on a high gallows" since the Declaration was, in fact, an act of treason, likely to incur the penalty meted out to traitors. This fear led Congress to withhold publicizing the names of the signers until January 18, 1777, when I recorded in the Journals that Congress had "Ordered, That an authenticated copy of the Declaration of Independency, with the names of the members of Congress subscribing the same, be sent to each of the United States."

And so it was that John Hancock and I were the only publicly known signers of the Declaration of Independence until January 18, 1777.

It should be of interest to note that during Mr. Hancock's presidency—on Saturday, June 14, 1777, to be exact—Congress "Resolved, that the flag of the thirteen United States be thirteen stripes, alternate red and white: that the union be thirteen stars, white in a blue field, representing a new constellation."

It is fitting and proper for me to close my remarks about John Hancock by reciting a little of an oration he rendered in Boston on March 5, 1774, in memory of those Americans who lost their lives in the Boston Massacre of 1770. In the Address at Gettysburg in 1863, Abraham Lincoln said "The world will little note, nor long remember what we say here, but it can never forget what they did here." The speech, of course, became as famous as the battlefield. But, while we have not forgotten the Boston Massacre of 1770, we have forgotten Hancock's oration—words that could be equally applied to the killing of students at Kent State University two hundred years later in 1970:

"Let this sad tale of death never be told without a tear; let not the heaving bosom cease to burn with a manly indignation at the barbarous story through the long tracts of future time; let every parent tell the shameful story to his listening children until tears of pity glisten in their eyes, and boiling passions shake their tender frames; and whilst the anniversary of that ill-fated night is kept a jubilee in the grim court of pandemonium, let all America join in one common prayer to Heaven, that the inhuman, unprovoked murders of the fifth of March, 1770, may ever stand in history without a parallel. . . ."

And then, in closing, John Hancock, the champion of American colonists in their struggle against Britain oppression, said:

"Ye dark designing knaves, ye murderers, parricides! how dare you tread upon the earth which has drunk in the blood of slaughtered innocents shed by your wicked hands? How dare you breathe that air which wafted to the ear of Heaven the groans of those who fell a sacrifice to your accursed ambition? But if the laboring earth doth not expand her jaws; if the air you breathe is not commissioned to be the minister of death; yet, hear it and tremble! The eye of Heaven penetrates the darkest chambers of the soul, traces the leading clue through all the labyrinths which your industrious folly has devised; and you, however you may have screened yourselves from human eyes, must be arraigned, must lift your hands, red with the blood of those whose death you have procured, at the tremendous bar of God!"

Dr. FRANKLIN. (To the spectators) Isn't it eerie to note that the Boston Massacre occurred on March 5, 1770, and that the Kent State Massacre—if it be called that—occurred two hundred years later on May 4, 1970; that five persons were murdered on the fifth of March and four persons on the fourth of May; and that the letter "M" is in both March and May -

the only two months in the year starting with an "M"; and that "M" also stands for Murder and Massacre. Is it not eerie? History just repeats and repeats and repeats—in some Manner, with a capital "M".

Mr. THOMSON. (To the spectators) Here comes the General!

Gen. WASHINGTON. This session will come to order. Our session today will explore the possibility of making a specific recommendation to Congress concerning the presidency. Eight resolutions have already been approved by this Commission as recommendations to the Congress. While all the proposals will enable this nation "to form a more perfect union," it behooves us to consider whether there is any specific and direct recommendation affecting the presidency which may better meet the exigencies of this nation. Mr. Jefferson.

Mr. JEFFERSON. We are faced with certain facts which militate against a solution. We must recognize that in the Federal Convention more than sixty ballots were taken with respect to the office of the president. We must also recognize that since 1789 more than 250 amendments affecting the office have been proposed in Congress. Nearly 160 amendments have been proposed just to change the term from four to six years.

We cannot even point to the establishment of the office or its continuance with any assurance that the provisions attaching to it represent the true opinion of the founders.

Dr. FRANKLIN. Perhaps the "guy" at the helm has us overwhelmed.

On September 17, 1787, the last day of the Federal Convention—in fact, it was the very day the Constitution was signed—I said: "I confess that there are several parts of this Constitution which I do not at present approve, but I am not sure that I will ever approve them . . . In these sentiments, sir, I agree to the Constitution with all its faults, if they are such; because I think a general Government necessary for us, and there is no form of Government but what may be a blessing to the people if well administered. . . . I doubt too whether any other Convention we can obtain may be able to make a better Constitution. For when you assemble a number of men to have the advantage of their joint wisdom, you inevitably assemble with those men, all their prejudices, their passions, their errors of opinion, their local interests, and their selfish views. From such an Assembly can a perfect production be expected? It therefore astonishes me, sir, to find this system approaching so near to perfection as it does. . . . Thus I consent, sir, to the Constitution because I expect no better, and because I am not sure that it is not the best."

And so, we had our doubts. We were not certain. Certainly not.

Is there a thread imbedded in two hundred years of history? If so, it is like finding a needle in a stack of history.

What is the common denominator of all our efforts concerning this office?

It seems to me that you may give a man an office, but you cannot give him discretion. You know, glass, china, and reputation are easily cracked and never well mended. The same with presidents. Many a man when he votes for a president thinks he is buying "life, liberty, and the pursuit of happiness," for four years, when in reality he is making himself a slave to it for four years, a slave because if the administration of the president is faulty, the citizen can do nothing about it.

Mr. MADISON. But there is the impeachment process.

Dr. FRANKLIN. The individual voter has no control over the impeachment process, and thus I think we should briefly discuss that process. But, before we do so, let me mention one more thought.

Let's reduce the situation down to two people. You make a friend. You break with your friend. You break up with your friend. The same with the president. It isn't important whether the president be elected for four, six, nine, fifteen, twenty years, or even for life. It isn't important whether the president is eligible or ineligible for another term. What **is** important is that when we break with the president for any reason, how do we "break up"? Virtually all of the hundreds of amendments proposed over the last two hundred years have related to the making of the presidency—not the breaking or the unmaking of the presidency.

Mr. JEFFERSON. Dr. Franklin, that is an excellent observation. Suppose you collect your thoughts further while we discuss the impeachment process.

Mr. Madison, will you please initiate this discussion?

Mr. MADISON. Certainly. The Constitution deals with the subject of impeachment and conviction at several places. The scope of the power is stated as follows:

"The President, Vice President and all civil officers of the United States shall be removed from Office on Impeachment for, and Conviction of, Treason, Bribery, or other High Crimes and Misdemeanors."

Other relevant provisions dealing with procedures and consequences state:

"The House of Representatives . . . shall have the sole Power of Impeachment."

"The Senate shall have the sole Power to try all Impeachments. When sitting for that Purpose, they shall be on Oath or Affirmation. When the President of the United States is tried the Chief Justice shall preside: And no persons shall be convicted without the Concurrence of two-thirds of the Members present."

The consequences of adverse judgment in cases of impeachment is stated as follows:

"Judgment in Cases of Impeachment shall not extend further than to removal from Office and disqualification to hold and enjoy any Office of Honor, Trust or Profit under the United States: but the Party convicted shall nevertheless be liable and subject to Indictment, Trial, Judgment and Punishment, according to law."

Of lesser significance is the provision that "The President . . . shall have Power to grant Reprieves and Pardons for Offences against the United States, except in cases of impeachment."

Alexander Hamilton wrote in *The Federalist* that Great Britain had served as the model from which impeachment had been borrowed. Parliament developed the process as a means to exercise some measure of control over the power of the king. An impeachment proceeding in England was a direct method of bringing to account the king's ministers and favorites—men who might otherwise have been beyond reach. Impeachment, at least in its early history, has been called "the most powerful weapon in the political armoury short of civil war." It played a continuing role in the struggles between king and Parliament that resulted in the formation of the unwritten English constitution. In this respect impeachment was one of the tools used by Parliament to create more responsive and responsible government and to redress imbalances when they occurred.

At the time of the Constitutional Convention the phrase "high crimes and misdemeanors" had been in use for over 400 years in impeachment proceedings in Parliament. Two points emerge from the 400 years of English parliamentary experience with that phrase. First, the particular allegations of misconduct alleged damage to the state in such forms as misapplication of funds, abuse of official power, neglect of duty, encroachment on Parliament's prerogatives, corruption, and betrayal of trust. Second, the phrase "high crimes and misdemeanors" was confined to parliamentary impeachments.

The debates on impeachment at the Constitutional Convention in Philadelphia focused principally on its applicability to the president. We hoped, in the words of Eldridge Gerry of Massachusetts, that "the maxim would never be adopted here that the chief Magistrate could do no wrong." Impeachment was to be one of the central elements of executive responsibility in the framework of the new government as we conceived it.

On August 6, 1787, in the Federal Convention the elements of impeachment in the drafting of the Constitution to that date were "treason, bribery, or corruption," but on September 4, the Committee of Eleven reduced the elements of impeachment to "treason or bribery" in their recommendation.

On September 8, just nine days before the Consitution was signed, Mr. George Mason moved to add the word "maladministration" to the other two grounds. Maladministration was a term in use in six of the thirteen state constitutions including Mr. Mason's home state of Virginia, as a ground for impeachment.

I objected, stating that "so vague a term will be equivalent to a tenure during pleasure of the Senate." Mr. Mason withdrew "maladministration" and substituted "high crimes and misdemeanors" which was adopted, 8 votes to 3, with no further debate on the elements of impeachment.

Well, fourteen officers have been impeached by the House since 1787: one president, one cabinet officer, one United States senator, and eleven federal judges. In addition there have been numerous resolutions and investigations in the House that did not result in impeachments. Twelve of the thirteen impeached officers were tried in the Senate. Articles of impeachment were presented to the Senate against a thirteenth, but he resigned shortly before the trial. The fourteenth resigned before articles could be drawn. Only five of the fourteen impeachments—all involving judges—have resulted in conviction in the Senate and removal from office.

On February 6, 1974, the House of Representatives by a vote of 410 to 4 "authorized and directed" the Committee on the Judiciary "to investigate fully and completely whether sufficient grounds exist for the House of Representatives to exercise its constitutional power to impeach Richard M. Nixon, President of the United States of America." Mr. Nixon resigned the office of President of the United States on August 9, 1974. This was but the second time in our history that the House of Representatives resolved to investigate the possibility of impeachment of a president. Some 107 years earlier the House had investigated whether President Andrew Johnson should be impeached.

It must be concluded that impeachment is a constitutional remedy addressed to serious offenses against the system of government and that history demonstrates a congressional reluctance to implement such a powerful weapon.

Mr. THOMSON. (To the spectators) Did you ever see a car built without a reverse gear? What about the lesser-than-impeachable offenses? Just among the twentieth-century presidents, how did the nation handle the physical incapacity of

Wilson, the incompetence of Harding, the ill-health of Roosevelt, the heart attacks of Eisenhower, the weaknesses of Carter, and so on?

One thing this country needs is a reverse gear.

Mr. ADAMS. There are several questions that arise on the impeachment issue:

First, if the impeachment provision is addressed to the serious offenses against government, what are the less serious offenses?

Second, what are the available constitutional means for removing a president, other than by impeachment?

Third, what are the available non-constitutional means for dislodging a president?

Fourth, if, as Dr. Franklin suggested, our attention should be directed to the "unmaking" of the president rather than the "making" of the president, just what are our options in this area?

Mr. MADISON. As to your first question, Mr. Adams, in the category of "less serious offenses" are the more common things that affect public interests, such as a high level of unemployment, high interest rates, enlarged federal spending, a growing Federal deficit, rising taxes, responsibility for an economic depression, unauthorized expansion of a war, or a high defense budget—in other words, matters which singly or collectively serve to lessen the public confidence.

As to your question about the constitutional means for removing a president, the most prominent, of course, is the election process. But the remaining period of a president's term may be too long and too frustrating to the general public. Another means is resignation of the president, which occurred one time in this century. As to the question relative to the non-constitutional means for dislodging a president, I suppose assassination has been the prevalent mode.

As to what our options for "unmaking" the president are, I can only say at the moment that there should be some way other than the massive blunderbuss of impeachment to enable the American people to remove some Chief Executive who has lost their confidence. Impeachment is too ponderous, too clumsy, too time-consuming.

Mr. JEFFERSON. With respect to Mr. Adams' first question, I can perhaps identify several "less serious" offenses.

Among them are abuse of power that violates the spirit, if not the letter of the laws.

Another circumstance is mental or emotional breakdown. Physical disability was, almost half a century after Woodrow Wilson's incapacitation, finally taken care of—perhaps not fully satisfactorily—by the Twenty-Fifth Amendment, which allows the vice-president and the cabinet, with the assent of the Congress, to declare a president incapable of fulfilling his duties. This power may be easy to exercise in a clear case of physical incapacitation—a stroke or a heart attack, for instance. But while a mental or emotional disability would also be covered by the amendment, it is a far more subtle ailment, much more difficult to diagnose with certainty. A president who suddenly went "raving mad" presumably would be removable, but in the case of a mental disorder short of obvious insanity it is difficult to conceive of the vice-president and a majority of the cabinet, all of whom are the president's men, selected by him, and, in the case of the cabinet, removable by him, taking the unprecedented step of initiating the president's removal.

The presidency is the country's very symbol of solidarity and certitude, and so one shrinks from even admitting the possibility that a president might go mad gradually and quietly—become impulsive or obsessive and erratic in his judgments, lose some of his grip on reality, suffer delusions of grandeur or persecution, conduct himself in a myriad of eccentric ways that are harmless enough in the ordinary citizen but are unacceptably risky in a president. But it could happen. It has happened to the prime ministers of other countries. It has happened to governors, to members of Congress, to cabinet officers. Pressures upon the president exceed those on almost any other human being. Under immeasurably less severe stress than that to which a president is daily subjected, men have "nervous breakdowns" of one type or another. The fact that our Constitution ignores the possibility that this could happen to a president has been a hazard since the founding of the Republic, but in an age when the possibility of thermonuclear war is never absent, the need for assurance that the "finger on the button" is a stable one becomes even more compelling.

Another identifiable circumstance is loss of public confidence, to which we have already referred. Under any of the preceding circumstances, public confidence in a resident may be destroyed, but he may lose the public confidence for many other reasons as well. He may simply lack the capacity to handle a domestic or foreign crisis. He may make policy decisions that visit disaster upon the country, and then stick with those decisions after the consequences have become clear. He may be egregiously bad in the selection of people in whom he imposes trust and retain those advisors and subordinates after their incapacity has been exposed. This list is endless.

The United States needs at all times an effective government. It cannot afford to wait for as long as three or three-and-a-half years if its president loses his ability to lead and govern for any reason. It does not take high crimes or misdemeanors to destroy the capacity of a president to lead, inspire, and unify the country as he must. Misfeasance that is not malfeasance in the impeachable sense can fatally impair the presidency. The people need to be safeguarded not just against a president who commits or tolerates crime but against the one who is incompetent, or negligent, or rash, and against the one who loses his stability, his capacity to make sound judgments. For all these kinds of circumstances, short of obvious incapacitation, the Constitution now provides no remedy. The question is how much the present constitutional arrangements can be modernized to provide for presidential accountability. The procedures for replacing a president can fall at many different points on the spectrum between impeachment and replacement by a vote of no confidence.

We have the rules about impeachment, but what of the possibility of a vote of no confidence?

The British system comes closest to the model; there a prime minister normally serves a full five-year term, but when he botches his job and loses the confidence of the country, the governing majority of the House of Commons has the means to force him out and get the country off to a fresh start under a leader who can lead and a government that can govern. Neville Chamberlain was forced to give way to Winston Churchill. Under 14, 1974, he proposed a no-confidence amendment, which em- his full term even if that meant losing a war and the very freedom of the nation.

A basic device for removing leaders who have discredited themselves, or suffered personal incapacitation, or lost public confidence and leadership capacity for any other reason is the no-confidence vote. In countries having a no-confidence procedure, the highest political office in the land is not considered, as it is here, as some kind of property right that, once won, cannot be taken away short of a criminal conviction. The right to lead must be continuously sustained through performance. The people who confer the right to lead can at any time, through their elected representatives, withdraw that right. This does not mean that, as in Great Britain, for example, the power to remove rulers is often exercised. But it is always present and available as a measure of last resort.

The mere existence of a no-confidence procedure could not help but have a continuously desirable influence on presidents.

A power reserved for the people, acting through their representatives, to remove the chief executive is a principle difficult to fault. The American system, however, is a compromise between representative democracy and monarchy, against which the colonists revolted. Every four years we elect a president through democratic processes. Between elections, however, he reigns out of reach of any sanctions, as long as he avoids getting caught committing an indictable felony. Outside of such a mistake, no matter how outrageously he defaults in the exericise of the presidential powers nor what the consequences are to the country, he remains in office. A president could embroil the country in a war or lose a war through lack of leadership, or he could plunge the contry into a depression or fail to take the initiative to get it out of one, and nothing could be done about it. In a sense, we have an untouchable executive.

Dr. FRANKLIN. Two resolutions proposing an amendment to the Constitution of the United States relative to a congressional vote of no confidence in the president were made by congress Henry S. Reuss in the 93rd Congress. On February 14, 1974 he proposed a no-confidence amendment, which embodied a variation of the parliamentary system, vesting in Congress the power to initiate the removal of the president from office. By an extraordinary three-fifths majority vote of both Houses, the Congress would have been empowered to compel a special election which would allow the electorate to select a new president and vice-president. In an amended version, on August 15, 1974, Mr. Reuss added two provisions: the incumbent president and vice-president would be allowed to remain in office during a 90- to 110-day interim period between the no-confidence vote and a special election, and as a safeguard against capricious use of the procedure, all members of Congress would also be required to stand for reelection in the special election.

While I am inclined toward a "no-confidence" vote, I am not inclined toward the procedures set forth in Mr. Reuss's amendment. While I commend him for instituting the "no-confidence" concept, I am concerned that his proposal would grant to the Congress a new and constitutionally undefined power, one which far exceeds any of the express powers of the Constitution. The extent to which the adoption of this resolution would alter the present balance of governmental powers is evident. In essence, Congress would have the power to dissolve the existing government by the passage of a vote of no confidence. Such a power would clearly subordinate the executive to the discretion of the legislature, thus undermining the basic constitutional principle of the separation of powers between discrete but equal branches of government. The overall effect of tilting the balance of power in favor of the legislature would be to supplant the constitutional system of checks and balances with a political format analogous to the parliamentary system in Great Britain.

Further, I am concerned that any procedure whereby Congress would be required to stand for reelection if it opts for a no-confidence vote would be dangerous to the nation and traumatic to the public.

The president is popularly elected. The public relates directly to him as its national leader and has allegiance to him. He is either its "good guy" or its "bad guy." Given American tradition, for the "lesser offenses" I believe it is feasible to remove the president without hearings, without showing that he has done something wrong, and without creating a national trauma—a sort of "no-fault" divorce.

The one principle that is fundamental to every aspect of the constitutionally established Republican form of government is that the ruling elite must be accountable to the People as a whole. The fallacy in all efforts to date has been the assumption that the president is accountable to the Congress for his position as president. The president is accountable to the Congress solely for what the Constitution says he is to be accountable for and nothing more. The president does not owe his position to the Congress. He owes his position to the public. How many times have presidents testifying before this Commission stated that they are the president of all the people? If I may paraphrase a line from the divine and apply it to the presidency, "The public giveth and the public taketh away."

I am firmly in favor of a no-confidence vote, but I am equally in favor of seeing that vote emanate from the public and not from the Congress.

Mr. JEFFERSON. I think your ideas are excellent. The people cannot do through their representatives in Congress what Congress itself cannot do with respect to the president. At this point in our sessions I would like us to review and discuss what our original attitude was toward public participation. I would also like to see Dr. Franklin develop his no-confidence concept and present us with suggestions for some acceptable procedure for its implementation. Mr. Madison, you have the notes on attitudes toward "the People's" participation—suppose you initiate the discussion.

Mr. MADISON. Remember that for most of the duration of the Federal Convention, the president was to be elected by ballot by the legislature. But the delegates did express their ideas about the capability of the people to make decisions on government affairs. For example, Mr. Mason said: "Some mode of displacing an unfit magistrate is rendered indispensable by the fallibility of those who choose, as well as by the corruptibility of the man chosen." Mr. James Wilson was of the opinion that "the national legislative powers ought to flow immediately from the people, so as to contain all their understanding and to be an exact transcript of their minds." Mr. Gouverneur Morris stated: "It is said that people will be led by a few designing men. This might happen in a small district. It can never happen throughout the continent. . . . It is said the multitude will be uninformed . . . they will not be uninformed of those great and illustrious characters which have merited their esteem and confidence."

On July 19, I recorded myself as saying: "If it be a fundamental principle of free government that the Legislative, Executive and Judiciary powers should be separately exercised; it is equally so that they be independently exercised. . . . It is essential then that the appointment of the Executive should either be drawn from some source, or held by some tenure, that will give him a free agency with regard to the Legislature." The people at large were in my opinion the fittest in itself. Finally, Mr. Morris added that the magistrate is not a king but the prime-minister, and that "The people are the King."

Mr. THOMSON. (To the Spectators) Was Gouverneur Morris truthful unto himself or did he have an inherent duplicity? Here in Mr. Madison's notes it is reported that Mr. Morris said, "The people are the King." Yet in his diary many years later, Mr. Morris said "experience, that wrinkled matron which genius condemns and youth abhors—experience, the mother of wisdom— will tell us that the man destined from the cradle to act an important part will not, in general, be so unfit as those who are objects of popular choice."

Are these thoughts inconsistent?

Mr. MADISON. (Continuing) On August 7, the question "to agree to the Preamble to the constitution as reported from the Committee of Detail, to whom were referred the proceedings of the Convention" passed unanimously, although the Preamble then read: "We the People of the States of New Hampshire, Massachusetts, Rhode Island and Providence Plantations, Connecticut, New York, New-Jersey, Pennsylvania, Delaware, Maryland, Virginia, North Carolina, South Carolina and Georgia do ordain, declare, and establish the following Constitution for the Government of Ourselves and our Posterity."

This Preamble was later changed by the Committee on Style to: "WE, the People of the United States, in Order to form a more perfect Union, establish Justice, insure domestic Tranquility, provide for the common defence, promote the general Welfare, and secure the Blessings of Liberty to ourselves and our Posterity do ordain and establish this Constitution for the United States of America."

The key is the use of the word "People" in the Constitution. The Articles of Confederation did not include this word in its Preamble since it was only an association *between* the states, established *by* the states. The Constitution was established by the *People* and for the people.

Dr. FRANKLIN. I remember on that same day I stated that it is of great consequence that we should not depress the virtue and public spirit of our common people; of which they displayed a great deal during the revolutionary war and of which contributed principally to the favorable issue of it. I did not think that the elected had any right in any case to narrow the privileges of the electors.

Mr. MADISON. I thought then that "under every view of the subject, it seems indispensable that the mass of citizens should not be without a voice in making the laws which they are to obey and in choosing the magistrates who are to administer them."

Let us now turn to the immediate aftermath of the Federal Convention.

Gen. WASHINGTON. I suggest that we first take a twenty-minute recess. (Leaves the Hall.)

Mr. THOMSON. (To the spectators) General Washington's exits are never without dignity. When he resigned his commission on December 23, 1783, for example, Mr. James McHenry, a delegate to Congress, wrote his fiance, Miss Margaret Caldwell, that "Today my love, the General at a public audience made a deposit of his commission and in a very pathetic manner took leave of Congress. It was a solemn and affecting spectacle; such a one as history does not present. The spectators all wept, and there was hardly a member of Congress who did not drop tears. The general's hand which held the address shook as he read it. When he spoke of the officers who had composed his family, and recommended those who had continued in it to the present moment to the favorable notice of Congress, he was obliged to support the paper with both hands. But when he commended the interests of his dearest country to almighty God and those who had the superitendence of them to his holy keeping, his voice faultered and sunk and the whole house felt his agitations. After the pause which was necessary for him to recover himself, he proceeded to say in the most penetrating manner, 'Having now finished the work assigned me, I retire from the great theatre of action and bidding an affectionate farewell to this august body under whose orders I have so long acted I here offer my commission and take leave of all the employments of public life.' So saying he drew out from his bosom his commission and delivered it up the the President of Congress. He then returned to his station, when the President read the reply that had been prepared—but I thought without any shew of feeling, tho' with much dignity.

"This is only a sketch of the scene. But, were I to write you a long letter I could not convey to you the whole. So many circumstances crowded into view and gave rise to so many affecting emotions. The events of the revolution just accomplished—the new situation into which it had thrown the affairs of the world—the great man who had borne so conspicuous a figure in it, in the act of relinquishing all public employments to return to private life—the past—the present—the future—the manner—the occasion—all conspired to render it a spectacle inexpressibly solemn and affecting."

And the General's entrances can be equally impressive.

Here he comes now.

Gen. WASHINGTON. This session will resume. Mr. Jefferson.

Mr. JEFFERSON. We have established that within the Federal Convention there was a significant question as to who would be the best keeper of Liberty in America. Outside the convention, *The Pennsylvania Evening Herald* thought the people might be duped: "There is little reason to apprehend danger, for the people will hardly be induced to make a voluntary surrender of their rights; but they may indeed be deceived by the flattery of outward shew into a passive and destructive acquiescence." But Mr. James Wilson in the Pennsylvania Convention argued that "if there are errors in government, the people have the right not only to correct and amend them but likewise totally to change and reject its form; and under the operation of that right, the citizens of the United States can never be wretched beyond retrieve, unless they are wanting to themselves." Mr. Wilson concluded that the president will "under this Constitution, be placed in office as the President of the whole Union and will be chosen in such a manner that he may be justly styled the man of the people, but in this plan they are represented. . . . all authority, of every kind, is derived by representation from the people."

The preamble to the ratification in the New York Convention stated, "We the Delegates of the People of the State of New York, Do declare and make known:

"That all Power is originally vested in and consequently derived from the People, and that Government is instituted by them for their common interest, protection and security.

"That the Powers of Government may be reassumed by the People, whensoever it shall become necessary to their Happiness. . . ."

In the Virginia debates on ratification, Mr. Edmund Pendleton said: "As a republican, sir, I think that the security of the liberty and happiness of the people, from the highest to the lowest, being the object of government, the people are consequently the fountain of all power."

Mr. THOMSON. (To the Spectators) Mr. Nathaniel Barrell in the Massachusetts debates made a statement you will probably be interested in hearing: "I attempt to speak my mind of the federal Constitution as it now stands. I wish, sir, to give my voice for its amendment before it can be salutary for our acceptance; because, sir . . . I fear it is pregnant with baneful effects, although I may not live to feel them.

Because, sir, as it now stands, Congress will be vested with more extensive powers than ever Great Britain exercised over us; too great, in my opinion, to intrust with any class of men, let their talents or virtues be ever so conspicuous, even though composed of such exalted, amiable characters as the great Washington; for, while we consider them as men of like passions, the same spontaneous, inherent thirst for power with ourselves, great and good as they may be, when they enter upon this all-important charge, what security can we have that they will continue so? And, were we sure they would continue the faithful guardians of our liberties, and prevent any infringement on the privileges of the people what assurance can be have that such men will always hold the reins of government—that their successors will be such? History tells us Rome was happy under Augustus, though wretched under Nero, who could have no greater power than Augustus; and yet this same Nero, when young in government, could shed tears on signing a death-warrant, though afterwards he became so callous to the tender feelings of humanity as to behold, with pleasure, Rome in flames."

Mr. MADISON. General Washington, can you share your thoughts with us on the part people should play, or not play, in the affairs of government?

Gen. WASHINGTON. Whatever my own opinion may be on this or any other subject interesting to the community at large, it always has been and will continue to be my earnest desire to learn, and, as far as is consistent, to comply with, the public sentiment; but it is on great occasions only, and after time has been given for cool and deliberate reflection, that the real voice of the people can be known.

Mr. Madison, who are the best keepers of the People's Liberties?

Mr. MADISON. The people themselves, General. The sacred trust can be nowhere so safe as in the hands of those most interested in preserving it. And Mr. Adams, what are your thoughts?

Mr. ADAMS. There is no country upon earth where the maxims that all power ought to reside in the great body of the people and all honors and authorities are to be frequently derived from them are so universally and sincerely believed as in America. The fountain of all just power and government is in the People.

Mr. Jefferson?

Mr. JEFFERSON. I wrote in the Declaration of Independence that "We hold these Truths to be self-evident, that all Men are created equal, that they are endowed by their Creator with certain unalienable Rights, that among these are Life, Liberty, and the Pursuit of Happiness—That to secure these rights, Governments are instituted among Men, deriving their just Powers from the Consent of the Governed . . ."

I repeat these last words—"deriving their just Powers from the Consent of the Governed . . ."

I then continued by writing that "whenever any Form of Government becomes destructive of those Ends, it is the Right of the People to alter or abolish it and to institute new Government, laying its foundation on such Principles and organizing its Powers in such Form as to them shall seem most likely to effect their Safety and Happiness."

In every government on earth is some trace of human weakness, some germ of corruption and degeneracy, which cunning will discover and wickedness insensibly open, cultivate, and improve. Every government degenerates when trusted to the rulers of the people alone. The people themselves therefore are government's only safe depositories. The influence over government must be shared among all the people. If every individual participates in the ultimate authority, the government will be safe.

Dr. Franklin, have you found a solution?

Dr. FRANKLIN. Gentlemen, I propose as Resolution Number Nine, that this Commission recommend to the Congress of the United States that the Constitution of the United States be amended so that:

At each annual national election, other than a regularly scheduled national election for the office of the president:

1. There shall appear on each national ballot the words "Shall a special national electon for the office of president of the United States be held on _____, _____ _____ _____, _____," with the day of the week, month, date of month, year, and the words of choice "Yes" and "No," properly adjoined thereto.

2. Prior to each such national balloting, Congress shall fix a date falling not less than sixty days and not more than ninety days from the date of such national ballot, to be inserted in the blank spaces above.

3. A majority vote shall be necessary to cause such special national election to be held for the office of the president.

4. In the event of a special national election, the clerk of the House of Representatives shall notify the chief executive of each state and of the District of Columbia of the date of the special election, and each State and the District of Columbia shall provide for the choosing of electors on that date. The convening and balloting of electors at a date specified by Congress and the transmittal of the ballots to Congress which shall count them shall be in the manner specified in the twelfth and twentieth articles of amendment of the Constitution.

5. In the event a special election occurs, the president chosen pursuant to such special election shall enter upon his term of office on such date as shall be specified by Congress, which date shall be not less than thirty and not more than sixty days following the date of election. The term of office for the president shall be whatever remains of the term of the predecessor.

6. Notwithstanding the twenty-second article of amendment, the incumbent of the office of president at the time a special election is voted shall be eligible to stand for election at the election herein provided for and to serve the terms commencing thereafter. Such incumbent shall be entitled to remain in office until a president chosen pursuant to such special elec-

tion shall enter upon his term of office.

Gentlemen, the rationale underlying this recommendation should be evident. It is thoroughly consistent with what has been discussed throughout our sessions, and particularly at today's session.

In Resolution Number Eight this Commission approved a recommendation to Congress that the term of members of the House of Representatives be extended from "two" to "three" years, with a one-third rotation so that one-third of the House is elected annually. This means, then, that we have created an annual national election basis which renders Proposed Resolution Number Nine entirely feasible, as the people will go to the polls once a year instead of every two years under our current structure.

This resolution does not create an annual election for the office of the president, but it does enable the people, as the ultimate arbiter of the effectiveness of a president, to cause a special "no-fault" presidential election to be held.

I say "no-fault" election because, as I said in our first session, there is nothing in which mankind reproach themselves more than in their diversity of opinions. Every man sets himself above another in his own opinion and there are not two men in the world whose sentiments are alike in everything; like lawyers, who with equal force of argument, can plead either for the plantiff or defendant. Much of the strength and efficiency of any government in processing and securing happiness to the people depends on the opinion of the people. But to assess "fault" in a special election would simply "fault" the people for having made the election in the first instance. It is in effect a no-confidence vote of the people which gives rise to a special election.

Allow me to summarize. We have seen that virtually all of the hundreds of amendments proposed to the Constitution over the last two hundred years related to the "making" of the presidency and not the "unmaking" of the presidency.

We have seen that impeachment is a constitutional remedy addressed to "serious offenses" against the system of government and that history demonstrates a reluctance by Congress to implement such a powerful weapon.

We have seen that there are "less serious" offenses to which the Constitution does not address itself and yet they may well affect life, liberty, and the pursuit of happiness.

We have determined that the United States needs at all times an effective government and that it cannot afford to wait long if the president loses his ability to lead and govern for any reason.

We must take note, therefore, that in a sense we have an untouchable president.

Given the American sense of justice and the truism that no two people are equally affected by the actions of our chief magistrate it is essential that when a majority of the people are adversely affected by any such action, they have at least opportunity to show a vote of no confidence and call for a special election without assessing a reason therefore. That is exactly what is accomplished by Resolution Number Nine.

Many presidents in testifying before this Commission took pride in stating that they were the president of all the people. As a corollary they must be accountable to all the people.

And so, in Resolution Number Nine, the question of whether a president shall continue in office is referred to the people.

Mr. Thomas Jefferson has here reminded us that the Declaration of Independence states that "Governments are instituted among Men, deriving their just Powers from the Consent of the Governed. . . ." The proposed resolution insures that balance.

Gen. WASHINGTON. Thank you, Dr. Franklin. Gentlemen, the Commission will meet in closed session on Monday, September 14 at 10 a.m., to consider Dr. Franklin's recommendation. This session is adjourned.

THURSDAY, SEPTEMBER 17, 1987

COMMISSION MAKES RECOMMENDATIONS TO CONGRESS

The Committee met pursuant to notice, at 10 a.m. in the Assembly Room of Independence Hall, Gen. George Washington presiding.

Present: Mr. John Adams, Dr. Benjamin Franklin, Mr. Thomas Jefferson, Mr. James Madison and Gen. George Washington.

Gen. WASHINGTON. The Commission met in closed session on Monday, September 14, to consider Dr. Franklin's proposed Resolution Number Nine. Mr. Thomson, would you report the results of that session?

Mr. THOMSON. The report is as follows: Resolution Nine was approved unanimously by the Commission with the exception that there was appended a recommendation to the Congress of the United States that consideration be given to amending the electoral college concept and adopting an amendment to the Constitution providing for the election of the president by direct popular vote.

The Chairman, General Washington, requested that Mr. Jefferson draft a letter of transmittal of its recommendation to the Congress of the United States.

Gen. WASHINGTON. Thank you, Mr. Thomson. Let us proceed with our agenda for today.

Gen. WASHINGTON. Two hundred years ago thirty-eight men, including Dr. Franklin, Mr. Madison, and I, met in this Assembly Room and signed the Constitution. Today we will conclude the sessions of this Commission by transmitting to the Congress of the United States nine proposed amendments to that Constitution. This Commission was established by Congress for the purpose of considering and recommending amendments to the Constitution of the United States on the occasion of that document's bicentennial so as to render such Constitution more adequate to the exigencies of this nation.

We are of the opinion that we have fulfilled this mandate.

At the time of our closed session Mr. Jefferson was asked to draft a transmittal letter for our recommendations. He has done so and I now ask him to read that letter and the final recommendations to be transmitted to Congress. Mr. Jefferson.

Mr. JEFFERSON. My colleagues, this letter from the Bicentennial Constitutional Commission is dated September 17, 1987, and addressed to the Congress of the United States:

> We have now the honor to submit to the consideration of the Congress of the United States proposed amendments to the Constitution which appear to us the most advisable.
>
> In all our deliberations on this subject we kept steadily in our view that which appears to us the greatest interest of every true American, our prosperity, felicity, safety, perhaps our national existence.
>
> The proposed amendments to the Constitution which we now present are the result of a spirit of amity and of that mutual deference and concession which the peculiarity of our political situation renders indispensible.
>
> That the proposed amendments will meet the full and entire approbation of every state is not perhaps to be expected; that they are liable to as few exceptions as could reasonably have been expected, we hope and believe; that they may promote the lasting welfare of that country so dear

to us all, secure her freedom and happiness, is our most ardent wish.

With respect, we have the honor to be

Your most obedient and humble servants,

/s/ _____
George Washington, Chairman
By unanimous Order of the Commision

/s/ _____
John Adams, Member

/s/ _____
Dr. Benjamin Franklin, Member

/s/ _____
Thomas Jefferson, Member

/s/ _____
James Madison, Member

Gentlemen, I read now the recommendations of this Commission to be transmitted to the Congress of the United States, pertaining to proposed amendments to the Constitution.

I. RESOLUTION NUMBER ONE

Be it Resolved that this Commission recommends to the Congress of the United States that the Constitution be amended so as to:

1. Establish two offices of vice-president. Each vice-president shall be chosen by Congress from among its own members, for the same term and period as the president of the United States.

2. Provide that each such vice-president chosen shall be chosen from among those having the same political affiliation as the president.

3. Provide that one such vice-president shall head an executive department to be known as the Department of Domestic Affairs and the other vice-president shall head an executive department to be known as the Department of Foreign Affairs.

4. Provide that each such vice-president shall be directly responsible to and subject to the authority of the president of the United States, other than for removal from office, and shall upon entering the office and duties of vice-president cease to be a member of Congress.

5. Provide that each such executive department shall consist of such subsidiary agencies as shall be established by law, and headed by such officers as shall be nominated by the president, and with the advice and consent of the Senate, appointed by the president.

II. RESOLUTION NUMBER TWO

Be it Resolved that this Commission recommends to the Congress of the United States that the Constitution be amended so as to eliminate the office of vice-president of the United States as presently constituted therein.

III. RESOLUTION NUMBER THREE

Be it Resolved that this Commission recommends to

the Congress of the United States that the Constitution be amended so as to:

1. Establish a Constitutional Council for Domestic Affairs to consult with and advise the vice-president heading the Department of Domestic Affairs.

2. Establish a Constitutional Council for Foreign Affairs to consult with and advise the vice-president heading the Department of Foreign Affairs.

3. Establish a Constitutional Council for National Affairs to consult with and advise the president of the United States.

4. Provide that each such Council consist of sixteen senators chosen by the Senate, on a bipartisan basis.

5. Provide that each such senator chosen serve on such Council during his term as senator, at the will of the Senate, for such period as the Senate shall specify, the status of any such senator as a senator not to be affected by virtue of such service on any such Council.

6. Provide that the Council be the sole Constitutional Counsellor to the vice-presidents and the president.

7. Provide that no source of advice shall be interposed between any such Council and a vice-president or between any such Council and the president.

8. Provide that the advice rendered by any such Council shall not conclude any vice-president or the president, nor affect their respective responsibilities for the measures which they may adopt.

IV. RESOLUTION NUMBER FOUR

Be it Resolved that this Commission recommends to the Congress of the United States that, in order to implement the creation of Constitutional Councils within the structure of the Senate, the Constitution be amended so as to:

1. Increase the number of senators in the Senate by one per state, making the total number of senators from each state three and the total number of senators one hundred and fifty.

2. Provide that each such senator added shall be elected and serve in the Senate in the same manner as is provided for in the present Constitution, and with like rotation.

V. RESOLUTION NUMBER FIVE

Be it Resolved that this Commission recommends to the Congress of the United States that the Constitution be amended so that:

1. The Supreme Court, or a court especially created by it, shall have the sole power to try impeachments.

2. When the president or any vice-president is tried, the trial shall be conducted by the Supreme Court.

3. Any Impeachment Court, so created by the Supreme Court, shall consist of not less than nine Federal Judges.

4. No person shall be convicted without the concurrence of two-thirds of the full court.

VI. RESOLUTION NUMBER SIX

Be it Resolved that this Commission recommends to the Congress of the United States that the Constitution be amended so as to require the ratification of treaties by a majority of each House of Congress.

VII. RESOLUTION NUMBER SEVEN

Be it Resolved that this Commission recommends to the Congress of the United States that the Constitution be amended so that:

1. Regulations drafted and promulgated by any agency of the government to implement federal law shall not be permitted to include substantive provisions encroaching upon the legislative prerogatives of Congress, but shall contain only such provisions as allow the laws to be faithfully executed.

2. The Senate shall monitor compliance therewith for the Congress.

3. The Congress shall have the power to approve, modify or disapprove any such rule or regulation.

Be it further Resolved that this Commission recommends to the Congress of the United States that the Constitution be amended by adding a Section 5 to Article II thereof, to read as follows:

"Section 5. The executive power of the president shall not include any matter legislative or judicial in nature, except as specifically provided in Section 7 of Article I and Section 2 of Article II."

VIII. RESOLUTION NUMBER EIGHT

Be it Resolved that this Commission recommends to the Congress of the United States that the Constitution be amended so that:

1. The term of members of the House of Representatives shall be extended from two to three years.

2. Beginning with the first election in the House after ratification of the amendment, members of the House shall be divided as equally as may be into three classes. The seats of the members of the first class shall be vacated at the expiration of the first year, of the second class at the expiration of the second year, and of the third class at the expiration of the third year, so that one-third may be elected every year.

IX. RESOLUTION NUMBER NINE

Be it Resolved that this Commission recommends to the Congress of the United States that the Constitution be amended so that:

1. At each national annual election, other than a regularly scheduled national election for the office of the president, there shall appear on the national ballot the words:

"Shall a special national election for the Office of the president of the United States be held on _____ _____,
(day of week)   (month)
_____, _____," with the words
(date of month) (year)
of choice "Yes" and "No" properly adjoined thereto.

2. Prior to each such national balloting, Congress shall fix a date falling not less than sixty days and not more than ninety days from the date of such national ballot, to be inserted in the blank spaces above.

3. A majority vote shall be necessary to cause such special national election to be held for the office of the president.

4. In the event of a special national election, the clerk of the House of Representatives shall notify the chief executive of each state and the District of Columbia of the date of the special election, and each state and the District of Columbia shall provide for the choosing of electors on that date. The convening and balloting of electors at a date specified by Congress, and the transmittal of the ballots to Congress which shall count them, shall be in the manner specified in the Twelfth and Twentieth articles of amendment to the Constitution.

5. In the event a special national election occurs, the president chosen pursuant to such special election shall enter upon his term of office on such date as shall be specified by Congress which date shall not be less than thirty and not more than sixty days following the date of election. The term of office for the president shall be whatever remains of the term of the predecessor.

6. Notwithstanding the Twenty-second article of amendment, the incumbent of the office of president at the time a special national election is called for shall be eligible to stand for election at the election herein provided for and to serve the term commencing thereafter. Such incumbent shall be entitled to remain in office until a president chosen pursuant to such special national election shall enter upon his term of office.

The Commission further recommends to the Congress that it consider the abandonment of the electoral college and the election of the president by direct popular vote.

Dr. FRANKLIN. I move that the instrument of transmittal be signed by all the members.

Mr. MADISON. I second the motion.

Gen. WASHINGTON. All in favor? (Affirmative response.) The motion is carried. Gentlemen, we will proceed with the signing of the document. (He signs and hands pen to Mr. Adams.)

Mr. ADAMS. (He signs.)

Dr. FRANKLIN. (He signs.)

Mr. JEFFERSON. (He signs.)

Mr. MADISON. (He signs.)

It is done.

Gen. WASHINGTON. (Soliloquizing) It is now a child of fortune, to be fostered by some and buffeted by others.

(Continuing) Today, gentlemen, is the two-hundredth anniversary of the signing of the Constitution. Before we conclude our sessions, I pay homage to you of today and you of yesterday.

Although there were some few things in the Constitution recommended by the Federal Convention to the determination of the people which did not fully accord with my wishes; yet, having taken every circumstance seriously into consideration, I was convinced it approached nearer to perfection than any government hitherto instituted among men. I was also convinced that nothing but a genuine spirit of amity and accommodation could have induced the members to make those mutual concessions and to sacrifice, at the shrine of enlightened Liberty, those local prejudices which seemed to oppose an insurmountable barrier, to prevent them from harmonizing in any system whatsoever.

It appears to me, then, little short of a miracle, that the delegates from so many different states should unite in forming a system of national government so little liable to well-founded objections.

Dr. FRANKLIN. I said then as I say today, "We have ... done our best, and it must take its chance."

Mr. THOMSON. (To the spectators) Of course, all did not think that way. William Grayson wrote to William Short on November 10, 1787, "Upon the whole I look upon the new system as a most ridiculous piece of business—something like the leg of Nebuchadnezar's image. It seems to have been formed by jumbling or compressing a number of ideas together, something like the manner in which poems were made in Swift's flying Island. However, bad as it is, I believe it will be crammed down our throats rough and smooth with all its imperfections."

Dr. FRANKLIN. (Continuing) I could hardly conceive that a transaction of such momentous importance to the welfare of millions then existing and to exist in the posterity of a great nation should be suffered to pass without being in some degree influenced, guided, and governed by that omnipotent, omnipresent, and beneficent Ruler, in whom all inferior spirits live and move and have their being.

Mr. MADISON. I was there on September 17, 1787. Whatever may be the judgment pronounced on the competency of the architects of the Constitution or whatever may be the destiny of the edifice prepared by them, I feel it a duty to express my profound and solemn conviction, derived from my intimate opportunity of observing and appreciating the views of the Convention, collectively and individually, that there never was an assembly of men charged with a great and arduous trust who were more pure in their motives or more exclusively or anxiously devoted to the object committed to them than were the members of the Federal Convention of 1787, to the object of devising and proposing a constitutional system which should best supply the defects of that which it was to replace and best secure the permanent liberty and happiness of their country.

Mr. THOMSON. (To the spectators) Cyrus Griffin was the sixteenth and last president of the Continental Congress. It was for him to witness the last gasp of the old Congress in preparation for the new government under the Constitution. His last day as the last president of the Continental Congress was on Saturday, November 15, 1788. Congress did not expire on that date. However, October 10, 1788, was the last day on which Congress could muster a quorum—seven states. I remained faithfully and hopefully on the watch, recording the attendance of states and individual delegates as from day to day they made their appearance. By March 4, 1789, the Old Congress had departed, destined never again to assemble.

Dr. FRANKLIN. Maybe old Congresses never die . . . they just resemble that condition; or should the expression be, Old Congresses never die, they just reassemble? As did the

First Congress of the United States of America, born on the fourth of March, 1789, in New York City . . . clothed in a new Constitution.

    Gen. WASHINGTON. Gentlemen, this session is adjourned sine die.

MONDAY, JUNE 15, 1988

CONGRESS APPROVES AND TRANSMITS PROPOSED AMENDMENTS TO STATES FOR RATIFICATION

Mr. THOMSON. On this day, June 15, 1988, the amendments to the Constitution recommended by the Bicentennial Constitutional Commission to the Congress of the United States were proposed to the states for ratification by the One Hundredth Congress, Second Session, having passed the House of Representatives on May 3, 1988, and having previously passed the Senate on April 27, 1988.

The members of the Commission and their ladies attended sessions of the House and the Senate. On leaving the House on May 3, 1988, a Mrs. Powel of Philadelphia asked Dr. Franklin, "Well, Doctor, what have you got, a republic or a monarchy?" The Doctor replied, "A republic, if you can keep it."

Abraham Lincoln attended the Senate sessions. He sat with the people in the balcony. His countenance rose to the Heavens. He looked like God—if anyone can look like God. At least he looked more like God than George Burns did.

John Adams observed of General Washington that "if he was not the greatest president he was the best Actor of Presidency we have ever had."

MONDAY, JULY 4, 1988

CONCERT ON INDEPENDENCE MALL IN PHILADELPHIA: JOHN PHILLIP SOUSA CONDUCTING

Mr. WILLARD A. WEISS. A concert is being held today on Independence Mall in the City of Philadelphia honoring the Commission members: George Washington, John Adams, Benjamin Franklin, Thomas Jefferson, and James Madison.

Independence Mall is situated between Independence Hall and the Liberty Bell Pavilion, between Chestnut and Market Streets and between Fifth and Sixth Streets.

Mr. THOMSON. (To a group of spectators on the Mall) Two hundred years ago today, here in Philadelphia, there was The Great Federal Procession. It had a double purpose: to celebrate the adoption of the Constitution and to commemorate the Declaration of Independence on July 4, 1776. Francis Hopkinson, a signer of the Declaration and a delegate to the Federal Convention in 1787, said of the event, "It was to celebrate a nation's freedom and a people's system of self-government—a people recently made free by their desperate efforts, the remembrances of which then powerfully possessed every mind. They then all felt the deep importance of the experiment of self-government to which their hearts and voices were then so imposingly pledged. The scene ought not to be forgotten. We should impress the recollections of that day and of the imposing pageantries upon the minds of our children and of our children's children. This has been already too much neglected; so that even now, while I endeavour to recapitulate some of the most striking incidents of the day, I find it is like reviving the circumstances of an almost obliterated dream."

On that memorable day, the rising sun was saluted with a full peal from the Christ Church steeple and a discharge of cannon from the ship *Rising Sun*, commanded by Capt. Philip Brown, anchored off Market Street, and superbly decorated with the flags of various nations. Ten vessels, in honor of the Ten States of the Union, those which had by this time solemnly adopted and ratified the new Constitution, were dressed and arranged through the whole length of the harbor. The ratification of only nine states had been sufficient to establish the Constitution. Each vessel bore a broad white flag at the mast-head inscribed with the names of the states respectively in broad gold letters, in the following order: New Hampshire, Massachusetts, Connecticut, New Jersey, Pennsylvania, Maryland, Virginia, South Carolina, and Georgia.

About half after nine o'clock, The Grand Procession began to move. First came twelve axmen representing pioneers, dressed in white frocks with black girdles round their waists, and ornamented caps, headed by Maj. Philip Pancake. Then came the First City Troop of Light Dragoons, commanded by Captain Miles.

Then John Nixon, Esq. on horseback bearing the staff and cap of Liberty. Under the cap was a silk flag with the words, "Fourth of July, 1776," in large gold letters. Col. John Shee was also on horseback, carrying a flag, blue field, with a laurel and an olive wreath over the words, "Washington, the friend of his country," in silver letters, the staff adorned with olive and laurel.

There was a train of artillery, troops of dragoons and companies of light infantry.

There were the professions, decorated and bearing emblematic flags: Shipjoiners, ropemakers, merchants, and traders—one carrying a ledger; cordwainers had a shop, drawn by four horses and six men in it at work; coachpainters, cabinet and chairmakers, brickmakers, painters, draymen, clock and watchmakers, bricklayers, tailors, carvers and gilders—these had an elegant car and men at work; coopers, planemakers, whip and canemakers—these had a carriage and lads at work; blacksmiths had a shop drawn by nine horses and men at work, making plough-irons out of old swords; coachmakers had a shop, drawn by four horses and men at work; potters—a shop and men at work; hatters, wheel-wrights, had a stage and men at work; tinplate workers, glovers, tallowchandlers, victuallers with two fat oxen; printers and bookbinders had a stage and executed printing and cast out an ode among the people. Ten of these odes to the states were dispatched by carrier pigeons which issued from the Mercury cap worn by the printer, dressed as Mercury. Fourteen different trades then followed; then lawyers, physicians, clergy, and a troop of dragoons, concluded the whole.

About the "clergy" Dr. Benjamin Rush wrote, "The clergy formed a very agreeable part of the procession. They manifested by their attendance their sense of the connection between religion and good government. They amounted to seventeen in number. Four and five of them marched arm in arm with each other to exemplify the Union. Pains were taken to connect ministers of the most dissimilar religious priciples together, thereby to show the influence of a free government in promoting Christian charity. The Rabbi of the Jews locked in the arms of two ministers of the gospel was a most delightful sight. There could not have been a more happy emblem contrived of that section of the new Constitution which opens all its power and offices alike not only to every sect of Christians but to worthy men of every religion."

All in all, eighty-eight groups were in the procession, which started at the intersection of Third and Cedar Streets; the line moved up Third to Callowhill, to Fourth, down Fourth to High, and out that street across the commons to the lawn, known as Union Green, in front of Bush-hill, which place was reached in three hours. The length of the line was about a mile and a half. It was estimated that five thousand men were in the procession. A notable oration was delivered at Bush-hill by James Wilson, Esq., to upwards of 20,000 people, following which the members of the procession sat down to dinner.

The supplies were abundant; no wine or ardent spirits were present, but porter beer, and cider flowed for all who would receive them; and of these liquors, the casks lined all the innercircles of the tables. They drank ten toasts in honor of the then ten confederated states. As the names of the states were announced, they were responded to from the ship **Rising Sun** laying in the Delaware, off High Street, decorated with numerous flags. The same ship, at night, was highly illuminated. This great company withdrew to their homes by six o'clock in the morning, all sober.

And perhaps all was quiet on the Philadelphia waterfront, for among the regulations of the state of Pennsylvania was one which read, "Any boys or others who disturb the citizens by throwing Squibs or Crackers or otherwise will be immediately apprehended and sent to the Work-House."

A song, attributed to Dr. Franklin, had been written for the Procession of Trades. A few stanzas may be appropriate at this time:

> Ye coach makers, must not by tax be controll'd,
> But ship off our coaches, and fetch us home gold;
> The roll of your coach made Copernicus reel,
> And fancied the world to turn round like a wheel.
>
> Ye printers! who give us our learnings and news,
> And impartially print for Turks, Christians, and Jews,
> Let your favorite toasts ever bound in the streets,
> The freedom of speech and a volume in sheets.
>
> Each Tradesman turn out with his tools in his hand,
> To cherish the arts and keep peace through the land:
> Each 'Prentice and Journeyman join in my song,
> And let the brisk chorus go bounding along.

Today, two hundred years later, on July 4, 1988, we are at Independence Mall.

The United States Marine Corps Band is performing. John Philip Sousa is bandmaster.

Mr. SOUSA. Ladies and Gentlemen, our national anthem.

Mr. JEFFERSON. (Singing.)

Oh! Say, can you see the broad stripes and bright stars
So gallantly streaming, so proud to our hearts.

Catch the gleam of the banner,
And by Heaven praise the power
That hath made and preserved our nation
From generation to generation.

'Tis the star spangled banner.
Oh! long may it wave
O'er the land of the free
And the home of the brave!

For America's cause is just
And its motto, "In God is our trust."

Mr. MADISON. Great SCOTT, Tom, those are not the words of the Star Spangled Banner, and you are singing off KEY!

Mr. JEFFERSON. You are correct, I re-versed it.

Mr. SOUSA. Ladies and Gentlemen, for the South, a medley consisting of "Dixie Land" and "Carry Me Back to Old Virginny."

Mr. ADAMS. On July 3, 1776, I wrote Abigail that "The Second Day of July, 1776, will be the most memorable Epocha, in the History of America. I am apt to believe that it will be celebrated, by succeeding Generations, as the great anniversary festival. It ought to be commemorated as the Day of Deliverance by solemn Acts of Devotion to God Almighty. It ought to be solemnized with Pomp and Parade, with Shews, Games, Sports, Guns, Bells, Bonfires and Illuminations from one end of this Continent to the other from this Time forward forever more."

Either I misjudged the date by two days or America did. It was on July 3, 1776, that I wrote Abigail, "Yesterday, the greatest question was clenched which ever was debated in America, and a greater perhaps never was or will be decided among men. . . . You will see in a few days a Declaration setting forth the causes which have impelled Us to this mighty Revolution. . . ."

It was July 2, 1776, not July 4, that we resolved in the Continental Congress "That these United Colonies are, and, of right ought to be, Free and Independent States; that they are absolved from all allegiance to the British Crown and that all political connexion between them and the state of Great Britain, is and, ought to be, totally dissolved."

I went on to tell Abigail, "I am well aware of the Toil and Blood and Treasure that it will cost Us to maintain this Declaration and support and defend these States. Yet through all the Gloom I can see the Rays of ravishing Light and Glory. I can see that the End is more than worth all the means. And that Posterity will tryumph in that Day's Transaction . . ."

Mr. SOUSA. And for our next selection, we do honor to the North—"Yankee Doodle Dandy."

Mr. ADAMS. I recall writing on July 9, 1776, "the River is past and the bridge cut away. The Declaration was yesterday published and proclaimed from that awful stage in the State House Yard; by whom do you think? By the Committee of Safety, the Committee of Inspection, and a great crowd of people.

Three cheers rendered the Welkin. The Battalion paraded the common and gave a Feu de joy notwithstanding the scarcity of powder. The bells rang all day and almost all night. Even the cimers chimed away."

Today, there stands the Liberty Bell. It is mute. Its voice is still. Its sound is nil. But then, on July 8, 1776, it played its most dramatic role in history when it was tolled to bring Philadelphians to the State House Yard where the Declaration of Independence was first read publicly, and the story was told. Yes, today it is mute. I suppose, if I wrote about it today, I would say: -

> Of thee I sing, Bell.
> Summer, Autumn, Winter, Spring, Bell,
> You're my silver lining.
> You're my sky of blue;
> There's light shining,
> Just because of you.
> Of thee I sing, Bell,

You've got that certain thing Bell!
Shining star and inspiration
Worthy of a mighty nation.
Of thee I sing.

Dr. FRANKLIN. Haven't I heard that before . . . ?

Mr. SOUSA. . . . and now, "Give My Regards to Broadway."

Mr. MADISON. How did you hear about the Declaration, General?

Gen. WASHINGTON. On July 6, 1776, the President of Congress John Hancock wrote me:

"The Congress, for some time past, have had their attention occupied by one of the most interesting and important subjects that could possibly come before them; or any other assembly of men.

"Altho it is not possible to foresee the consequences of human actions, yet it is nevertheless a duty we owe ourselves and posterity, in all our public counsels, to decide in the best manner we are able and to leave the event to that Being who controls both causes and events to bring about his own determinations.

"Impressed with this sentiment and at the same time fully convinced, that our affairs may take a more favorable turn the Congress have judged it necessary to dissolve the connection between Great Britain and the American Colonies and to declare them free and independent States as you will perceive by the enclosed Declaration, which I am directed to transmit to you and to request you will have it proclaimed at the Head of the Army in the way you shall think most proper. . . ."

Mr. SOUSA. Ladies and Gentlemen, a toast to the West—"San Francisco."

Mr. ADAMS. Tom, do you recall, you, Ben, and I were appointed to a Committee of Five on June 11, 1776, to prepare a Declaration? You proposed that I make the draft.

Mr. JEFFERSON. Let's see, just how did that conversation go?

Mr. ADAMS. I said, "I will not."

Mr. JEFFERSON. I remember now! I said, "You should do it!"

Mr. ADAMS. "Oh! no."

Mr. JEFFERSON. "Why will you not? You ought to do it."

Mr. ADAMS. "I will not."

Mr. JEFFERSON. Why?"

Mr. ADAMS. "Reasons enough."

Mr. JEFFERSON. "What can be your reasons?"

Mr. ADAMS. "Reasons first—You are a Virginian, and a Virginian ought to appear at the head of this business. Reason second—I am obnoxious, suspected, and unpopular. You are very much otherwise. Reason third—You can write ten times better than I can."

Mr. JEFFERSON. "Well, if you are decided, I will do as well as I can."

Mr. ADAMS. "Very well. When you have drawn it up, we will have a meeting."

Dr. FRANKLIN. I was recovering from a severe fit of the gout, which had kept me from Congress so that I knew little of what passed there, except that a Declaration of Independence was preparing.

Mr. MADISON. I was not even in Congress then—I was only twenty-five years old.

Dr. FRANKLIN. Next thing I knew, I received a note from Tom along with an enclosure!

"The enclosed paper has been read and with some small alterations approved of by the committee. Will Doctor Franklin be so good as to peruse it and suggest such alterations as his more enlarged view of the subject will dictate? The paper having been returned to me to change a particular sentiment or two, I proposed laying it again before the committee tomorrow, if Doctor Franklin can think of it before that time."

Mr. SOUSA. . . . and now, to the Midwest—"The Saints Go Marching In."

Dr. FRANKLIN. So the Saints Go Marching In—I can

recall, in the early days, just before the revolution, my neighbor Mr. A. Mackraby wrote to his brother, in England, Sir Philip Francis,

"My dearest brother, - - - Would you think that in a city with twenty thousand inhabitants we should find difficulty in collecting twenty native Englishmen to celebrate St. George Day yesterday? . . . got drunk, sang 'God Save the King,' Your ever faithful, A. Mackraby."

Mr. ADAMS. The Saints . . . I wrote to Abigail about them on April 23, 1776: "This is St. George's Day, a Festival celebrated by the English, as Saint Patrick's is by the Irish, St. David's by the Welch, and St. Andrew's by the Scotch. The Natives of old England in this City heretofore formed a Society which they called Saint George's Club or Saint George's Society. Upon the twenty-third of April annually, they had a great Feast. But the times and politicks have made a schism in the society so that one part of them are to meet and dine at the City Tavern and the other at the Bunch of Grapes, Israel Jacob's, and the third party go out of town.

One set are staunch Americans, another staunch Britons I suppose, and a Third half way men, neutral beings, moderate men, prudent folks—for such is the division among men upon all occasions and every question."

Dr. FRANKLIN. Where did you get all that information, John?

Mr. ADAMS. From my barber.

Mr. SOUSA. . . . and now a tribute to America.

Mr. ADAMS. (speaking) America. Beautiful for spacious skies. Amber waves of grain. Purple mountain majesties above the fruited plain. America—God shed his grace on thee, and crown thy good with brotherhood from sea to shining sea.

Dr. FRANKLIN. (speaking) My country, 'tis of thee I sing. Sweet land of liberty, land of the noble free. Long may our land be bright with freedom's light. From every mountain side, let freedom ring.

Mr. JEFFERSON. (speaking) America, the home of the brave and the free. The shrine of each patriot's devotion.

The ark of freedom's foundation. Thy banners make tyranny tremble. Three cheers for the red, white, and blue!

Mr. MADISON. (speaking) God bless America, land that we love. Stand beside her and guide her through the night with the light from above. From the mountains to the prairies, to the oceans white with foam, God bless America, my home sweet home.

Gen. WASHINGTON. It is not easy to be wise for all times, not even for the present—much less for the future; and those who judge of the past must recollect that, when it was present, the present was future.

Mr. SOUSA. Ladies and gentlemen, will you please rise—"The Stars and Stripes Forever."

Mr. MADISON. Good-bye, John.

Mr. ADAMS. Good-bye, Jemmy, Tom, Ben.

Mr. JEFFERSON. Good-bye, my faithful friends.

Dr. FRANKLIN. Good-bye, my learned colleagues.

Gen. WASHINGTON. Good-bye, my fellow patriots.

Dr. FRANKLIN. And good-bye to you, General. By George, we did it!

BIBLIOGRAPHY

ADC   Adams, John. **A Defence of the Constitutions of the United States of America**. 3 vols. New York: DaCapo Press, 1971.

AGE   Austin, James. **The Life of Elbridge Gerry**. 2 vols. New York: Da Capo Press, 1970.

AJA   Adams, John and Abigail. **The Book of Abigail and John:** Selected Letters of the Adams Family 1762-1784. Edited by L.H. Butterfield, Marc Friedlaender and Mary-Jo Kline. Cambridge, Mass.: Harvard University Press, 1976.

AJD   Adams, John. **The Adams Papers: Diary and Autobiography of John Adams.** Edited by L.H. Butterfield. New York City: Antheneum, 1964.

AJL   Adams, John. **Letters from a Distinguished American: Twelve Essays** by John Adams on American Foreign Policy, 1780. Edited by James H. Hutson. Washington, D.C.: GPO, 1978.

BCC   Burnett, Edmund Cody. **The Continental Congress**. New York: Macmillan, 1941.

BLM   **Letters of Members of the Continental Congress.** 8 vols. Gloucester, Mass.: Peter Smith, 1963.

BMP   Bowen, Catherine Drinker. **Miracle at Philadelphia**. Boston: Little, Brown and Company, 1966.

CAJ   Carpon, Lester J., ed., **The Adams - Jefferson Letters**. 2 vols. Chapel Hill: University of North Carolina Press, 1959.

CFP   U.S. Congress. Senate. Committees on Appropriations and Government Affairs. **Cost of Former Presidents to U.S. Taxpayers**. 96th Cong., 1st Sess., November 6th, 7th and 8th, 1979. Washington, D.C.: GPO, 1980.

CFU   U.S. Congress House. Documents Illustrative of the Formation of the Union of the American States. 69th Congress, 1st Session., House Doc. 398 Washington, D.C.: GPO, 1927.

CGS   Copeland, Lewis and Lawrence W. Lamm, eds. **The World's Great Speeches**. New York: Dover Publications, 1973.

COC   Conway, Moncure Daniel. **Omitted Chapters of History Disclosed in the Life and Papers of Edmund Randolph**. New York: Da Capo. 1971.

CPI   U.S. Congress. House Committee of the Judiciary. **Constitutional Grounds for Presidential Impeachment**. 93rd Cong., 2nd Sess., Feb., 1974 Wash., D.C.: GPO, 1974.

CTR   U.S. Congress, Senate. The Role of the Senate in Treaty Ratification: A Staff Memorandum to the Committee on Foreign Relations, United States Senate. 95th Cong. 1st Sess., Washington, D.C.: GPO, 1977.

CUS   Congressional Research Service. Library of Congress. **The Constitution of America: Analysis and Interpretation**. Washington, D.C.: GPO, 1973.

DHR   The Documentary History of the Ratification of the Constitution Vols. 1, 2, 3, 13, 14. Madison: State Historical Society of Wisconsin; Vol. 1, 1976; Vol. 2, 1976; Vol. 3, 1978; Vol. 13, 1980; Vol. 14, 1983.

DJW Dickinson, John. **The Political Writings of John Dickinson**: 1764-1774. Edited by Paul Leicaster Ford. New York: Da Capo Press, 1970.

EDC Elliot, Jonathan, ed.. **The Debates in the Several State Conventions on the Adoption of the Federal Constitution as Recommended by the General Convention at Philadelphia in 1787**. 2 Vols. Charlottesville: The Michie Company, 1941.

FBA Franklin, Benjamin. **The Autobiography of Benjamin Franklin**. Edited by Leonard W. Labaree, Ralph L. Ketcham, Helen C. Boatfield, and Helen H. Fineman. New Haven: Yale University Press, 1964.

FBP Franklin, Benjamin. **The Political Thought of Benjamin Franklin**. Edited by Ralph L. Ketcham. New York: Bobbs-Merrill, 1965.

FBR Franklin, Benjamin. **Poor Richard's Almanacks**. Edited by Richard Saunders. New York: Bonanza Books, 1979.

FBW Franklin, Benjamin. **The Life and Writings of Benjamin Franklin**. 2 Vols. Philadelphia: M'Carty & Davis, 1834.

FRC Farrand, Max, ed. **The Records of the Federal Convention of 1787**. 4 Vols. New Haven: Yale University Press, 1966.

HAM Hodgson, Godfrey. **All Things to All Men**. New York: Simon and Shuster, 1980.

HAP Hamilton, Alexander. **The Papers of Alexander Hamilton**. Edited by Harold C. Syrett and Jacob E. Cooke. 29 Vols. New York: Columbia Univ. Press, 1961-1979.

HLR Hoover, Herbert Clark. Hoover Commission Reports. 01- for the years 1947-49; 02- for the years 1953-55. Washington, D.C.: GPO. 1949, 1955.

HHC Hoover, Herbert Clark. **Herbert Hoover's Challenge to America: His Life and Words**. Garden City: Country Beautiful Foundations, 1965.

HHM Hoover, Herbert Clark. **Memoirs of Herbert Hoover**. 3 Vols., 1951-1952. New York: Macmillan, 1951-52.

HMJ Hamilton, Alexander, James Madison, and John Jay. **The Federalist: A Commentary on the Constitution of the United States**. New York: Tudor Publishing, 1942.

HRR Rules of the House of Representatives of the United States. 95th Congress, 2nd Session House Document 95-403. Washington, D.C.: GPO, 1979.

HSP Historical Society of Pennsylvania. Philadelphia.

HTC Henricks, J. Edwin. **Charles Thomson and the Making of a New Nation: 1729-1824**. Cranbury, New Jersey: Associated University Presses, 1979.

JCC Journals of the Continental Congress, 1774-1789. Edited by Worthington C. Ford et al. 34 vols. Washington, D.C., 1904-37.

JTB Jefferson, Thomas. **The Founding Fathers: Biography in his Own Words**. New York: Newsweek, 1974.

JTP Jefferson, Thomas. **The Papers of Thomas Jefferson**. Edited by Julian P. Boyd. Vol. 12. Princeton: Princeton University Press, 1955.

LDC	Letters of Delegates to Congress, 1774-1789. 10+ vols. Washington, D.C.: GPO, 1976 et seq.
LHH	Lyons, Eugene. **Herbert Hoover: A Biography**. Garden City: Doubleday, 1964.
MAC	Manchester, William. **American Caesar: Douglas MacArthur 1880-1964**. New York City: Dell Publishing Co., Inc., 1978.
MAD	Madison, James. **Letters and Other Writings of James Madison**. 4 vols. Philadelphia: J. B. Lippincott, 1865.
MDR	MacArthur, Douglas. **Reminiscences**. New York: McGraw Hill, 1964.
MDS	MacArthur, Douglas. **A Soldier Speaks: Public Papers and Speeches Of General of the Army Douglas MacArthur**. Edited by Norin E. Whan, Jr. New York: Praeger, 1965.
MFC	Morris, Richard B. **The Framing of the Federal Constitution: Handbook 103, National Park Service**. Washington, D.C.: GPO, undated.
MGD	Morris, Gouverneur. **The Diary and Letters of Gouverneur Morris**. Edited by Ann Cary Morris. 2 vols. New York: Da Capo Press, 1970.
MGP	Mason, George. **The Papers of George Mason: 1725-1792**. Edited by Robert A. Rutland. 3 vols. Chapel Hill: The University of North Carolina Press, 1970.
MJB	Madison, James. **The Founding Fathers: James A. Madison, A Biography In His Own Words**. New York: Newsweek, 1974.
MJJ	Madison, James. **Journal of the Federal Convention**. Edited by E. H. Scott. Freeport, New York: Book for Libraries Press, 1970.
MJP	Madison, James. **The Papers of James Madison**. 3 vols. New York: Jeff G. Langley, 1841.
MTI	Milley, John C., ed. **Treasures of Independence**. New York: Mayflower Books, 1980.
PCP	Polsby, Nelson W. **Congress and the Presidency**. 3rd edition. Englewood Cliffs, New Jersey: Prentice-Hall, Inc., 1976.
PFF	Padover, Saul K. **World of the Founding Fathers**. New York: T. Yoseloff, 1960.
PHS	Pennsylvania Historical Society. Philadelphia.
PJT	Padover, Saul K. **Jefferson**. New York: Harcourt, Brace, 1942.
PJW	Padover, Saul K. **The Writings of Thomas Jefferson**. New York: Heritage Press, 1967.
PMH	Du Ponceau, Peter Stephen. **Autobiography of Peter Stephen Du Ponceau**. Philadelphia: Pennsylvania Magazine of History and Biography, vol. 63, pages 334, 335.
PPP	Public Papers of the Presidents of the United States: (President). Washington, D.C.: GPO.
RBL	Rush, Benjamin. **Letters of Benjamin Rush**. Edited by L.H. Butterfield. 2 vols. Princeton: Princeton University Press, 1951.

RCF	Research Note Card File. Philadelphia, Independence National Historical Park Library.
RWA	Rogers, Will. **The Autobiography of Will Rogers**. Edited by Donald Day. New York: Avon Books, 1975.
SDJ	**The Life and Times of John Dickinson: 1732-1808**. New York: Burt Frankin, 1969.
SEE	Sanders, Jennings B. **Evolution of Executive Departments of the Continental Congress: 1774-1789**. Gloucester, Mass.: Peter Smith, 1971.
SPC	Sanders, Jennings B., **The Presidency of the Continental Congress: 1774-1789**. Gloucester, Mass.: Peter Smith, 1971.
TAD	Tocqueville, Alexis De. **Democracy in America**. Edited by J.P. Mayer. Garden City: Doubleday, 1969.
TPP	Tourtellot, Arthur Benson. **The Presidents on the Presidency**. New York: Russell & Russell, 1964.
VFB	Van Dorn, Carl. **Benjamin Franklin**. New York: Viking Press, 1938.
WGW	Washington, George. **The Writings of George Washington**. Edited by John C. Fitzpatrick. 39 vols., Washington, D.C.: GPO 1931 et seq.
WGD	Washington, George. **The Diaries of George Washington: 1748-1799**. Edited by John C. Fitzpatrick. 4 vols. Boston: Houghton Mifflin, 1925.
WGB	Washington, George. **The Founding Fathers: George Washington, A Biography in His Own Words**. New York: Newsweek, 1972.
WEM	Weiss, Emanuel M. **The Recognition by the United States of the Independence of the South American Republics**. M.A. Thesis. New York University, 1912.
WFF	Whitney, David C., **Founders of Freedom in America**. Chicago: J. G. Ferguson, 1965.
WLR	The George Washington Law Review. Lincoln, Nebraska: Joe Christanson, Inc. January, 1975, Volume 43, Number 2.

SOURCE REFERENCES

As stated in the Foreword, in the use of documents researched, I strove to achieve an adaptation of the material used without changing the author's intent. In most instances material has been used without quotation marks. Editorial changes were silently made as required to modernize and clarify the text. For example, correct spelling has been inserted; omitted words have been inserted at appropriate places; obvious slips of the pen and inadvertent repetitions have usually been corrected; capitalization and punctuation have been standardized; tenses have been changed where necessary; doubtful cases have been resolved in favor of modern usage. Yet in many cases the material is preserved and presented as is.

Source references are presented in the following manner and order:
1. Each chapter is identified by month, day, and year.
2. Each page number is identified in the left column.
3. Text material for which source reference is given is generally denoted by quoting the first few words and the last word of the applicable material.
4. Reference to the bibliography is generally given in the following form.

(a) Three letter code reference to Bibliography

(b) Volume

(c) Page or Date

Page

Wednesday, May 13, 1987

25 "It was two hundred . . ": WGD:03:236,237.
26 "Mr. MADISON. Well. . .": EDC:01:128.
27 "The men who . . .": FRC:03:56,57.
27 "Mr. MADISON. No. Major William Jackson . . .": FRC:03:514.
27 "Gen. WASHINGTON . .": WGD:03:237,238.
28 "Mr. MADISON . . .": MGP:03:1007.
28 "I recall him saying . . .": MGP:03:1086.
28 "Anyway . . .": MGP:03:1002.
29 "Gen. WASHINGTON. I remember that . . .": MGP:03:1001.
29 "Mr. ADAMS. I recall . . .": AJD:02:97.
30 "And then . . .": BLM:01:1.
30 "The following morning . . .": AJD:02:122.
31 "Dr. FRANKLIN . . .": actually the words of the President of Congress, Thomas McKean, to George Washington, on October 31, 1781, BLM:06:252,253.
31 "Mr. ADAMS. Do you remember . . .": MTI:00:106,107.
31 "Mr. JEFFERSON. Aye, your Poor Richard . . .": JTB:00:23:24.
32 "Mr. MADISON. . .": MAD:01:432.
33 "Dr. FRANKLIN. In our time . . .": FBA:00:145.
33 "Mr. MADISON. Yes, in those times . . .": MTI:00:87-89.
34 "I remember that I approved . . .": as stated by C. Sherrill in French Memories of 18th Century America, pp. 85-88. RCF.
35 "Gen. WASHINGTON. So be it . . .": BLM:08:486.
35 "I violated . . .": MGP:03:1009:1010.

36	"Mr. MADISON: General . . .": EDC:04:431.
36	"Yet, when I . . .": EDC:04:431.
36	"If men were angels . . .": from The Federalist, No. 51. HMJ:00:354.
36	"Mr. ADAMS. . .": PMH:63:334,335.
37	"As for myself . . .": LDC:02:387.
37	"Mr. MADISON., I would personally. . .": AGE:01:130:131.
38	"Mr. JEFFERSON. . .": BLM:07:511,512.
39	"Dr. FRANKLIN. . . Jacob Hiltzheimer . . .": BLM:05:404.
39	"Mr. ADAMS. . .": AJD:02:132.
39	"Gen. WASHINGTON. . .": FRC:03:339,340.
40	"Dr. FRANKLIN. Yet . . .": BLM:04:137.
40	"Gen. WASHINGTON. True. It appears to me . . .": Washington to Lafayette, February 7, 1788.
40	"Mr. MADISON. And today . . .": MAD:04:1791-2.
40	"Mr. JEFFERSON. You . . .": Jefferson to Samuel Kercheval, July 12, 1816.
41	"Dr. FRANKLIN. The Constitution . . .": FBP:00:404.
41	"Dr. FRANKLIN. May I propose . . .": LDC:04:318.

Thursday, May 14, 1987

44,45	"On a personal note . . .": Derived from Washington's Inaugural Address. CGS:00:245-47.
45	"There is nothing . . .":FSP:00:10.
46	"I confess. . .": MJJ:00:741.
46	"A certain . . .": FBP:00:23,24.
47	"Much of the strength . . .": MJJ:00:743.
47	"Since presumption . . .": MJJ:00:743.
48	"For fifteen years. . .": HTC:00:129.
49	"Mr. Charles Thomson . . .": RCF.
51	"Mr. BURNETT. . .": BCC:00:724-6.
52	"Mr. JEFFERSON. . .": BLM:08:55,56.
52	"Mr. ADAMS. . .": RCF: Nicholas Biddle; Reminiscences of Bishop White, July 4, 1813.
53	"It is interesting . . .": HRR:00:109.
54	"Mr. Onslow . . .": HRR:00:109.
55	"Every member . . .": FRC:01:8.
55	"A member may . . .": FRC:01:9.
55	"That a motion . . .": FRC:01:16.
56	"So we wind up . . .": VFB:00:550,51.

Monday, May 25, 1987

65	"The Treasury . . .": BLM:06:109.
65	"No Journals . . .": BLM:06:142.
65	"We suggested . . .": BLM:08:246.
65	"Hugh Williamson . . .": BLM:07:46.
65	"Mr. MADISON. . .": BLM:08:205.
66	"Dr. FRANKLIN. . .": BLM:06:52.
66	"David Ramsay . . .": BLM:08:301.
66	"Mr. ADAMS. . .": BLM:08:264.
66	"Dr. FRANKLIN. . .": BLM:01:490.
67	"Mr. MADISON. . .": MAD:04:477.
67	"As an illustration . . .": MAD:04:477.
67	"Dr. FRANKLIN. . .": LDC:06:80.
68	"On May 29, 1775 . . .": SEE:00:153-158.
70	"Mr. ADAMS. . .": BLM:02:375.
70	"Dr. FRANKLIN. The word Excellency . . ." Letter, B. Franklin to his sister, Jane Mecom, August 3, 1789.

Thursday, May 28, 1987

71   "Gen. WASHINGTON. . .": From the Declaration of Independence.
74   "No man can . . .": PPP:HOOVER II:383.
74   "The Presidency . . ." PPP:HOOVER II:479.
74   "The nature of . . .": HHM:02:216.
75   "He said, I always felt . . .": RWA:00:210.
76   "Dr. FRANKLIN. . ." **Akron Beacon Journal**, July 21, 1981: "Time for Look at Federal Octopus." by James J. Kilpatrick.

Friday, May 29, 1987

82   "Dr. FRANKLIN. . .": BLM:05:430
83   "Dr. FRANKLIN. I would say. . .": Attributed to Saul Pett, Associated Press reporter.
83   "I realize . . .": FBW:01:247.

Monday, June 1, 1987

98   "Dr. FRANKLIN. . .": Congressional Record, July 21, 1975, page 23892.
107   "The Safety Commission's actions . . .": **Federal Register**, August 22, 1979, page 49,288.
108-9   "Just one illustration . . .": **Federal Register**, August 31, 1979, page 51,233.
112   "He is . . .": PJT:00:334.
113   "Never put off . . .": PJW:00:361:362.
113   "Dr. FRANKLIN. . . I have heard . . . to me.": FBP:00:237.
114   "It may be . . .": WFF:00:97.
115   "Mr. MADISON. . ." Mr. William S. Fairhill is the sole fictitious character in the book. However, the facts he relates are true.
122   "In 1979 . . .": **Federal Register**, August 22, 1979, page 49, 274.
123   "Here is another . . . **Federal Register**, August 27, 1979, page 50,104.
123   "Mr. FAIRHILL. In this particular . . .": **Federal Register**, August 10, 1979, page 47,039.
123   "Mr. FAIRHILL. Look at one more . . .": **Federal Register**, Proclamation 4676, August 29, 1979.

Tuesday, June 2, 1987

128   "I believed, then . . .": PJT:00:386.
129   "Mr. JEFFERSON. It is . . .": PJT:00:387.
130   "I was for . . .": PJT:00:262.
130   "Mr. MADISON. I was not unaware . . . experiment.": MAD:04:385.
130   "The ratification . . .": CUS:00:1565.
132   "At the time of . . .": FBP:00:414.
132   "As to . . .": FBP:00:416.
132   "Dr. FRANKLIN. . .": FBP:00:423.
133   "There is a story . . .": FRC:03:359.
133   "Mr. JEFFERSON. In it he advised me . . . by a vote only." PHS: Letter, John Dickinson to Thomas Jefferson, January 1, 1807.
133,134   "I have tired you . . .": PHS: Letter, Thomas Jefferson to John Dickinson, January 13, 1807.
134   "Mr. MADISON. In consequence of . . .": MAD:01:554 et seq.
140   "Gen. WASHINGTON . . .": WGB:02:338.
140   "Lastly . . .": WGB:02:329.
141   "The people . . .": TPP:00:78.
141   "At the mid-term. . .": TPP:00:348.
142   "Mr. MADISON. . .": MJB:00:407.
142   "Dr. FRANKLIN. (Aside to Mr. Jefferson) . . .": BLM:06:20.

Wednesday, June 3, 1987

145   "Mr. J. Q. ADAMS. No one knows . . .": TPP:00:349.

146	"I could never be sure . . .": TPP:00:349.
146	"But it was not . . .": TPP:00:349.
146	"Mr. John Q. ADAMS. I can scarcely. . .": TPP:00:349.
146	"Mr. John Q. ADAMS. I do. . .": TPP:00:349.
148	"Mr. JACKSON. I can with truth. . .": TPP:00:350.
148	"Mr. JACKSON. I thought that . . .': TPP:00:350.
148	"Mr. JACKSON. It was . . .": TPP:00:382.
149	"Dr. FRANKLIN. . .": FBP:00:37.
150	"Mr. VAN BUREN. . .": TPP:00:350,351.
150	"Mr. VAN BUREN. At the very . . .": TPP:00:351.
152	"Mr. POLK. . .": TPP:00:352.
153	"Mr. BUCHANAN. From the . . .": TPP:00:417.
153	"Mr. BUCHANAN. As I said . . .": TPP:00:417,418.
154	"Mr. BUCHANAN. I was . . .": TPP:00:352.
154	"Mr. BUCHANAN. Yes . . .": TPP:00:352.

Thursday, June 4, 1987

157-161	"Mr. DOUGLASS. . .": CGS:00:808-814.
162	"At this point . . .": PFF:00:604.
162	"At my point . . . offence cometh.": From Abraham Lincoln's Farewell Address at Springfield, Illinois, February 11, 1861.
167	"Mr. LINCOLN. I would save . . .": TPP:00:398.
167	"Mr. LINCOLN. It was . . .": TPP:00:353.
168	"From my boyhood . . .": TPP:00:353.
168	"In God's name . . .": TPP:00:353.
168	"I could not fly . . .": TPP:00:354.

Friday, June 5, 1987

170	"Mr. JOHNSON. . .": TPP:00:102 Andrew Johnson addressing U.S. Senate, March 2, 1867, Richardson VI, 447.
171	"Yet, during my term . . .": TPP:00:103.
171	"You no doubt . . .": TPP:00:225.
171	"The persons . . .": TPP:00:225,226.
173	"Mr. HAYES. Presidents in . . .": TPP:00:44.
173	"Mr. HAYES. I was not liked . . .": TPP:00:44.
173	"Nobody ever left . . .": TPP:00:356.
173-4	"The escape . . .": TPP:00:356.
174	"Mr. HAYES. Yes. . ." As times passes.": TPP:00:355.
174	"Mr. GARFIELD. On the personal side. . .": TPP:00:357.
175	"I did not know. . .": TPP:00:356.
175	"Once or twice . . .": TPP:00:357.
176	"Mr. CLEVELAND. In the scheme . . . office.": TPP:00:48.
176	"Thus will you . . . vouchsafed to man.": TPP:00:46
176	"The world . . .": TPP:00:47.
176	"It is a high office . . .": TPP:00:46.
176	"Mr. CLEVELAND. I believe. . .": TPP:00:111.
176-7	"Mr. CLEVELAND. Do you remember . . .": TPP:00:385.
177	"Mr. CLEVELAND. It has always . . . disposition.": TPP:00:421 ". . . No man . . . invites. ": TPP:00:48.
177	"Mr. CLEVELAND. The office . . . allurement.": TPP:00:358; "I suffered . . . end.": TPP:00:359; Sometimes I believed . . . grind.": TPP:00:358; "I often thought . . . mission.": TPP:00:357 "I was comforted . . . could rest.": TPP:00:358.
178	"And so . . .": TPP:00:360.
178	"Mr. HARRISON. The Presidency?": TPP:00:112.
179-80	"Mr. HARRISON. The fears . . .": TPP:00:50.
180	"Mr. HARRISON. A distinguished . . .": TPP:00:111.
180	"Mr. HARRISON. It was a rare. . .": TPP:00:360.

Monday, June 8, 1987

182	William McKinley: TPP:00:360
183	"A President. . . as I did.": TPP:00:362; "But even a President has feelings. . . and dangers": TPP:00:362; I was in . . . it all.": TPP:00:361; "Everyday . . . as a whole.": TPP:00:361.
183	"Mr. ROOSEVELT. I don't know. . .": TPP:00:385.
184	"Mr. ROOSEVELT. Any strong man . . . term": TPP:00:361; "The Presidency . . . terms.": TPP:00:386.
184	:"Mr. ROOSEVELT. If I . . . else.": TPP:00:386.
184	"Therefore . . . terms": TPP:00:387.
184-5	"I thoroughly . . . too long.": TPP:00:386.
185	"There inheres . . . sprang.": TPP:00:54.
185	"I think . . . power.": TPP:00:55.
185	"Mr. ROOSEVELT. While President . . . people.": TPP:00:116,117.
186	"To me. . . live up to it.": TPP:00:53.
187	"Dr. FRANKLIN. (Aside to Mr. Adams) . . .": TPP:00:361.
187	"Mr. TAFT. Gentlemen . . . interest.": PCP:00:64.
188	"Mr. ROOSEVELT. Thank you . . . prohibition.": PCP:00:64.
188	"Mr. TAFT. The Constitution . . . require.": TPP:00:58.
188	"But . . . predecessors.": TPP:00:58,59.
189-90	"Mr. TAFT. The President . . . existence.": TPP:00:336; "In my time . . . exercise.": TPP:00:337.
190	"Mr. TAFT. I hated . . .": PPT:00:176.
190	"In my judgment . . . departments.": TPP:00:177.
191	"Mr. Taft. The assassination . . . protection.": TPP:00:363.
191	"Mr. TAFT. I am strongly . . . duties.": TPP:00:387.
191-92	"I'll be damned . . . talk.": TPP:00:363; "One trouble . . . arose.": TPP:00:363; "I came to the conclusion . . . into town.": TPP:00:362.
192	"I thought . . . undergo.": TPP:00:363; "In the end . . . world.": TPP:00:363.
192	"Mr. WILSON. The office . . . Christian.": TPP:00:363; "It is not . . . it.": TPP:00:364.
192-93	"I was . . . incognito.": TPP:00:364; "The amount . . . preposterous. . .": TPP:00:365.
193	"I never dreamed . . . duty.": TPP:00:365; "The President is . . . superior.": TPP:00:364.
193	"When I thought . . . I had.": TPP:00:388.
193	"Mr. WILSON. I am confident. . . from it.": TPP:00:298.
194	"Mr. WILSON. I have read . . .": TPP:00:364,365.
195	"Mr. HARDING. Thank you . . .": TPP:00:365,366.
196	"Mr. COOLIDGE. The Presidency . . . own.": TPP:00:120;"An unofficial government.": TPP:00:121.
196	"Mr. COOLIDGE. The President . . . Providence. . .": TPP:00:367; "No one can . . . sovereign.": TPP:00:120,121.
197	"Mr. COOLIDGE. It is . . . institutions." : TPP:00:367.
197	"Mr. COOLIDGE. The President . . . needs.": TPP:00:60.
197-8	"Mr. COOLIDGE. The duties . . . days.": TPP:00:366.
198	"It is of course . . . done.": TPP:00:366.
198	"In the discharge . . . for you.": TPP:00:367.
198	"Mr. Coolidge. Ten years . . . President.": TPP:00:367.
198	"Mr. COOLIDGE. I know . . . diplomats.": TPP:00:299.
199	"Mr. HOOVER. The structure . . . not do.": TPP:00:251.
199	"The whole genius . . .": TPP:00:123.
199	"Mr. HOOVER. The first requisites. . .": TPP:00:63.
199	"Mr. HOOVER. There are . . .": TPP:00:368.
199	"Mr. HOOVER. Yes. . . for no man.": TPP:00:427.
200	"Many years ago . . .": TPP:00:368.
200	"Mr. HOOVER. A useless. . . ": TPP:00:369.

200	"Mr. HOOVER. Why yes . . . journey.": HHC:00:January 27, 1952.
200	"What in the world . . . freedom.": LHH:00:420,421.
200	"This nation . . . aggression.": LHH:00:423.
201	"Never after victory . . . government.": LHH:00:426.
205	"Mr. ROOSEVELT. I received . . . old.": From F.D.R.'s campaign address in Detroit, Michigan, October 2, 1932.
205	"I saw . . . ill nourished.": From F.D.R.'s second inaugural address, January 20, 1937.
206	"Mr. ROOSEVELT. The Presidency . . .": TPP:00:65.
206	"Mr. ROOSEVELT. To carry out . . . government.": TPP:00:390.
206	"Within this process . . . tradition.": TPP:00:252.
206	"Dr. FRANKLIN. (Aside to Mr. Jefferson) . . .": TPP:00:253.
207	"Mr. ROOSEVELT. History proves . . .": F.D.R.'s fireside chat on economic conditions, April 14, 1938.
208	"Arthur Schlesinger, Jr. said . . .": PCP:00:21.
208	"The genius of . . . house.": LHH:00:422.
208	"Mr. ROOSEVELT. Now see here . . .": TPP:00:126.
209	"Mr. ADAMS. Mr. Roosevelt . . .": TPP:00:125.
209	"Mr. ROOSEVELT. I honored these men . . . a lawyers contract.": F.D.R.'s address on Constitution Day, Washington, D.C., September 17, 1937.
209	"I have also said . . . go on.": Based on F.D.R.'s address at Fremont, Nebraska, September 28, 1935.
210	"Mr. ROOSEVELT. For many years . . . powers.": TPP:00:125.
210	"In my time . . . avoided.": TPP:00:124.
211	"It was common . . . again.": TPP:00:124.
211	"The plain fact . . . good.": TPP:00:124.
211	"Mr. ROOSEVELT. In 1899 . . . effort.": TPP:00:126.
212	"To the President . . . domain.": TPP:00:125.
212	"There were . . . followed me.": TPP:00:369.
212	"Mr. HOOVER. May I . . . one another.": LHH:00:427,428.
213	"The principal thing . . . Think about it.": LHH:00:426
213	"I have lived . . . civilization.": LHH:00:423.

Tuesday, June 9, 1987

216-18	"Mr. TRUMAN. There's never been . . . to the President.": CGS:00:592-594.
218	"Mr. TRUMAN. Let me just . . . significance.": TPP:00:302.
219	"Mr. TRUMAN. The presidency . . . themselves.": TPP:00:128.
219	"The difficulty . . . it at all.": TPP:00:129.
219	"Mr. TRUMAN. The President . . . worthless.": TPP:00:130.
219-220	"Mr. TRUMAN. As a practical . . .": TPP:00:256.
220	"Mr. TRUMAN. The President . . . confidence.": TPP:00:66.
220	"Mr. TRUMAN. I did not . . . successor.": TPP:00:130.
221	"Mr. TRUMAN. I felt as if . . . I learned . . . There is no exaltation . . . great decisions.": TPP:00:370.
221	"I have said . . . United States.": TPP:00:430.
221	"No one who has . . . I had learned . . . I do not know . . . are few.": TPP:00:371.
221-22	"Mr. TRUMAN. In my opinion . . .": TPP:00:371.

Tuesday, June 16, 1987

236-37	"Mr. MADISON. Mr. Jefferson. I favor . . . growing out of it.": MAD:03:442; "It would be wrong . . . Constitution.": MAD:04:15.
237	"The Constitution . . . period.": MAD:04:390.
237	"When we consider . . . lessons of experience.": MAD:04:388.
237	"Experience . . . determine.": MAD:00:99.

Wednesday, June 17, 1987

239-46	"Two hundred years . . . The Constitution still stands.": Based on speech by Senator Robert C. Byrd as entered in the Congressional

Record, Proceedings and Debates of the 96th Congress, Second Session, Vol. 126, No. 144, Wednesday, September 17, 1980.

248 "Dr. FRANKLIN. The General's . . . .": FRC:03:85.
248-49 "Mr. JEFFERSON. I do not . . . entangling foreign alliances.": From **The Pennsylvania Magazine of History and Biography**, Vol. LVI., 1932, No. 2; **Washington and Lincoln: The Father and the Saviour of the Country**, page 109.
249 "Dr. FRANKLIN. I believe . . . and folly.": FBP:00:387.
250 "As early as . . .": FBP:00:83.
251 "Dr. FRANKLIN. The Crown . . .": FBP:00:84.
251 "Mr. MADISON. It nevertheless . . . of the colonies.": FBP:00:84.
251 "The Grand Council . . . carried out.": FBP:00:85,86.
251 "The President General . . . Council.": FBP:00:86,87.
252 "Dr. FRANKLIN. The plan . . . each other.": Based on paper "The Public Career of Benjamin Franklin", **The Pennsylvania Magazine**, LV, 1931, No. 3, pages 199, 200.
253 Franklin's Articles Of Confederation are in: JCC:02:195-199.
254 "Well, Franklin concluded . . .": JCC:02:198,199
256 "On December 31, 1776 . . . whole island.": From **The Pennsylvania Magazine**, January, 1956, an article entitled "A British Editor Reports The American Revolution", pages 102-104.
257-8 "Mr. ADAMS. On the face . . . states.": BCC:00:213.
258 "On June 29, 1776 . . . made of it.": BLM:01:517:518.
259 "It was on November 12, 1813 . . .": CAJ:02:392,393.
260 "Mr. JEFFERSON. . . . Samuel Adams . . . virtue.": Samuel Adams to James Warren, December 12, 1776, Warren-Adams Letters, Vol. I, pages 279,280.
260 "He pleaded. . . rage.": John Dickinson to Thomas McKean, February 2, 1799. McKean Papers, Pennsylvania Historical Society.
260-2 "The situation . . . which I will explain.": AJD:03:314-318.
262 "On July 24, 1775. . . the soundest policy?": LDC:01:658.
262 "Then one day . . . Dickinson.": AJD:02:173.
263 Mr. JEFFERSON. "I must agree . . . countrymen.": CAJ:02:335.
263 "Finally . . . me.": CAJ:02:597.
268 "In olden time . . . expressed.": FBP:00:11.
270 "Mr. ADAMS. I had proposed . . .": JCC:05:691.
270 "Mr. JEFFERSON. I had proposed . . .": JCC:00:691.
271 "Dr. FRANKLIN. Mr. Chairman, . . . ": TFBP:00:361,362.

Thursday, June 18, 1987

273 "As we all recall. . . place. . .": BLM:06:12.
274 "Our political . . . requisitions. . .": BLM:05:397.
274-5 "Mr. Jefferson. . . one state. . .": BLM:06:41,24.
275 "Mr. Varnum's . . . people.": DHR:01:176.
275 Mr. MADISON. "What were . . . payment.": WFF:00:24.
275-77 "Mr. MADISON. . . The reiterated . . . The want of authority . . . In sundry instances. . . In certain cases. . . In the internal . . . Among the defects. . . As a natural consequence. . . It was known. . . such were. . . provided.": WFF:00:24-26.
280 "During Shay's rebellion . . .": BLM:08:516-518.
281 "Mr. JEFFERSON. I believe. . . poor.": JTB:00:178,179.
282 "Gen. WASHINGTON. I did not conceive. . .": MFC:00:37.
282-3 "First. . . Confederation?": MAD:01:320:322.
283 "Mr. MADISON. In answering. . . errors.": MAD:01:322.
284 "Mr. HAMILTON. I will just . . . authority.": HMJ:00:150,151.
284 "Mr. MADISON. What . . . together.": MAD:01:324.
284-5 "Ninth. . . Tenth. . . Eleventh. . . private rights.": MAD:01:324,325.
285 "The great desideratum. . . society.": MAD:01:327.
286 "Mr. ADAMS. . . states. . .": BLM:08:354,355.

654

287	"Mr. JEFFERSON. I was in France. . . of the laws.": RCF: Correspondence Political, Etats Unis. Min. Att. Etrang......., Paris, Vol. 31. Otto, New York 16 February 1786, to Vergennes.
287	"Mr. ADAMS. The British. . . policy.": BLM:08:556.
287	"Mr. JEFFERSON. I thought then. . . with us.": JTB:00:169,170.
288	"Mr. ADAMS. (Soliloquizing) . . .": LDC:01:278,279.
288	"Mr. JEFFERSON. (Soliloquizing) . . .": JTP:12:33.
288	"Gen. WASHINGTON. (Soliloquizing) . . .": BLM:05:336.
289	"Mr. MADISON. (Soliloquizing) . . .": MAD:04:480.
289	"Mr. ADAMS. (Soliloquizing) . . .": LDC:03:560.
290	"Mr. ADAMS. It appears . . . members.": BLM:08:292.
291	"Mr. THOMSON. On September 27, 1784. . .": BLM:07:593.
292	"Dr. FRANKLIN. Our Constitution. . .": FBP:00:375,376.
292-3	"Mr. HAMILTON. The insufficiency. . .": HMJ:00:____.
295	"The trust . . . trade. . .": DHR:01:153.
295	"Mr. JEFFERSON. (Continuing). . . shall be necessary.": DHR:01:153,154.
296-8	"Mr. MADISON. As the postwar. . .": DHR:01:154-164.
299	"Also, in 1786. . . several governments.": BLM:08:290,291.
300	"Also in 1786, Nathan Miller . . . nails.": BLM:08:367,368.
300	"The Annapolis . . . following words.": BCC:00:665.
300-1	"The representatives. . . same.": CFU:00:38.
301	"The question. . . indeed.": BCC:00:665,666.
302-4	Quoted portions from CFU:00:41-43.
305	"The letter . . . character.": RBL:01:345,346.
307	"By the way . . . herself.": LDC:05:168.
307	"As to Mr. Adams's . . .": EDC:04:410.
307	"On February 21, 1787 . . . innovations.": DHR:01:188-190.
308-9	"How long . . . destruction.": DHR:01:190.

Friday, June 19, 1987

310-13	"Mr. THOMSON. . . . the body.": WGD:03:211-219.
313	"Since . . . the Federal Union.": MJP:03:iv.
313-14	"The majority . . . former measures.": MJP:03:iii,iv.
314-15	"Mr. MADISON. In pursuance . . . country.": MJJ:00:50,51.
315	"Mr. ADAMS. . . . beyond comprehension.": FRC:03:421.
316-17	"Mr. THOMSON. . . . afternoon.": BMP:00:34,35.
317	"Dr. FRANKLIN. If I alone . . . box of dice.": WFF:00:95.
317-18	"Mr. JEFFERSON. . . . flavor.": PJT:00:387.
318	"I am for. . . blessing.": PJT:00:262.
319	"Mr. ADAMS. In the year . . . the other.": ADC:01:286.
319	"When I was vice-president . . . to unite.": RCF: John Adams to Dr. Price, dated New York, April 19, 1790; Waterston Autographs, Vol. I, n.p. (MHS).
319-21	"Dear Sir . . . humble servant. John Adams.": LDC:02:348.
321	"Mr. THOMSON. . . . public life.": RCF: Thomas Twining, Travels in America - 100 Years Ago, pages 38,39, April 9, 1796.
321	"When . . . sword.": RCF: Letter from Joseph H. Nicholson to Becky Bishop (Mrs. J. H. Nicholson), October 3, 1799, Letters to Mrs. Joseph H. Nicholson, Shippen Family of Pennsylvania Papers, MSS, Library of Congress.
321	"He would . . . segars.": RCF: John Adams to Thomas H. Perkins, Esq., September 14, 1804, Cote 676, No. 10, Biblio. Municipale de Nantes.
322	"If there is . . . undone.": ADC:01:xii.
322	"Among every people . . . without a head.": ADC:01:91.
323	"Let them compare . . . govern.": ADC:01:95,96.
323-25	"Mr. Dupois . . . happy.": RCF.

Monday, June 29, 1987

[Unless otherwise indicated, material applicable to dates cited in this chapter are to be found in FRC.]

- 330 "Mr. MADISON. On Monday, June 18, 1787 . . .": FRC:01:292.
- 330 "Mr. PIERCE. No matter . . .": FRC:03:97.
- 331 "Mr. PIERCE. Gladly. . .": FRC:03:89.
- 331 "Mr. MADISON. In my notes. . .": FRC:02:497,498.
- 334 "Mr. PIERCE. . . Mr. Madison. . .": FRC:03:94.
- 335 "Mr. MASON. Certainly. One of my objections. . .": FRC:02:638.
- 335 "Mr. MASON. Exactly what I feared. . . over the others.": FRC:02:639.
- 335-6 "I think, that in the course of human affairs. . . a dangerous officer.": MGP:03:1094.
- 336 "Mr. PIERCE. . . Mr. George Mason. . .": FRC:03:94.
- 336 "Mr. DAVIE. Thank you. . .": FRC:03:343,344.
- 337 "Mr. THOMSON. . . Mr. Davie. . .": FRC:03:95,96.
- 337 "Mr. MCKEAN. It has been said. . .": DHR:02:540.
- 338 "Mr. MCKEAN. Yes, but I declined. . .": Thomas McKean to Alexander J. Dalls, October 16, 1803. Henry Adams, The Life of Albert Gallatin, p. 313. Also, SPC:00:40,41.
- 338 "Mr. MONROE. I must agree. . .": EDC:03:489,490.
- 338-9 "Mr. HAMILTON. The appointment . . . of the President.": HMJ:00:No.68.
- 339 "Mr. Lee. . .": MGP:03:998,999.
- 340 "As to my. . . functions.": JTB:00:271,272.
- 340 "The office of Vice President. . .": JTB:00:272, As Vice President . . .": JTB:00:272.

Tuesday, June 30, 1987

[Unless otherwise indicated, material applicable to dates cited in this chapter are to be found in FRC.]

- 347 "Mr. THOMSON. . ." FRC:03:514.
- 347 "James Madison. . . erroneous.": FRC:03:537.
- 348-9 "Mr. MACLAINE. . . fluctuating.": EDC:04:28,29.
- 349 "Dr. TAYLOR. . . evil.": EDC:02:5.
- 350 "Mr. SEDGWICK. . . weighty matters?": EDC:02:4.
- 350-2 "Mr. AMES. The term. . . better.": EDC:02:7-11.
- 352 "Reverend STILLMAN. . .": EDC:02:168,169.
- 353-5 "Frequent elections. . . experience.": HMJ:00:No.52; "In Connecticut . . . liberty of the people.": HMJ:00:No.53; ". . . it appears . . . of them.": HMJ:00:No.52.
- 356 "It has been said . . . imperfect.": MAD:04:329.
- 356 "We may wander. . . reasoning.": EDC:02:225.

Wednesday, July 1, 1987

[Unless otherwise indicated, material applicable to dates cited in this chapter are to be found in FRC.]

- 357 "Dr. FRANKLIN. . .": EDC:03:19.
- 359 "That is not to say. . . thoughts.": RCF: Henry Laurens to R.H. Lee, September 28, 1779; R.H. Lee and Arthur Lee Correspondence, Vol. II, p. 184.
- 361-2 "Mr. ADAMS. Abigail. . . discretion." LDC:03:524,525.
- 363 "At about this time. . . magistracy. . .": FRC:04:15,16.
- 372 "Second SPECTATOR. . . I heard that. . . in 1783.": The Pennsylvania Magazine, October 1977; New Light on the Philadelphia. Mutiny of 1783: Federal-State Confrontation at the close of the War for Independence; pages 428,429.
- 372-3 "Second SPECTATOR. . . Gouverno the cunning man. . .": DHR:02:182: "blessed art thou. . . all things!" DHR:02:183.
- 373 "First SPECTATOR. . . I can top that . . . cadeaux. . .": MGD:01:85,86.
- 373 "Today, November 13, 1789. . . permitted.": MGD:01:226.

656

Thursday, July 2, 1987

[Unless otherwise indicated, material applicable to dates cited in this Chapter are to be found in FRC.]

376	"Mr. THOMSON. . .": FRC:03:297.
377	"Mr. PIERCE. . .": FRC:03:91.
379	"Of a Constitutional. . .": HMJ:00:330,331.
379	"I Wrote that King George. . . ocean.": FBP:00:328,329.
382	"General Jonathan DAYTON. . .": FRC:03:471,472. But see letter of James Madison to Thomas S. Grimke, FRC:03:531.
382-4	"Mr. THOMSON. . . at length prevail." FRC:03:51,52.
384	"Mr. Alexander Hamilton. . . rejoin the convention.": FRC:03:54.
384	"Then there was . . . in the pulput.": Letter, Stephen M. Mitchell to Charles Thomson, Weathersfield, June 6, 1787; Box: Charles Thomson Papers, Gratz Collection, Case 14, Box 31, HSP.
386	"With respect to . . . finally met.": FRC:03:449.
386	"On June 25th . . . have a share.": FRC:03:49.
387	"On the other hand . . . power.": FRC:03:30.
387	"Mr. WILSON. . .": FRC:01:413,414.
388	"Mr. WILSON. The British government . . .": FRC:01:153.
388-9	"Mr. MADISON. I found . . . consideration.": FRC:01:415; "I thought made?": FRC:01:154; I thought that . . . in my judgment.": FRC:01:151,152.
389	"Mr. GERRY. . .": FRC:01:152.
389-90	"Mr. ELLSWORTH. . .": FRC:01:414,415.
390	"Mr. READ. . . ": FRC:01:151.
391	"Mr. MADISON. It must be . . . government.": FRC:01:408.
391	"Mr. THOMSON. . .": BMP:00:92,93.
393	"Mr. ELLSWORTH. . .": FRC:01:495,496.
394	"Mr. MADISON. . .": FRC:01:496,497.
395	"Mr. ELLSWORTH. . .": FRC:01:497:498.
395	"Mr. DAYTON. . .": FRC:01:499.
395	"Mr. MADISON. . .": FRC:01:499.
396	"Mr. PIERCE. . .": FRC:03:92.
396	"Mr. BEDFORD. . .": FRC:01:500-502.
397	"Mr. Rufus KING. . .": FRC:01:502.
397	"Mr. ADAMS. . .": BMP:00:95.
397	"Mr. THOMSON. . . At this time . . . interest.": RCF Letter dated June 19, 1787; William R. Davie, P.R.C. 78, 1778-1817, North Carolina Department of Archives and History; "And James McHenry . . . Peggy.": RCF: Letter to his wife dated May 29, 1787; McHenry Papers, Vol. 2, LC, ALS, Photostat.
397-8	"Dr. FRANKLIN. . . proposition.": FRC: 01:488.
398	"They then called . . . at all . . .": FBP:00:397:398.
399-400	"In March 1836...States: MAD:04:429; "As early as . . . larger States.": FRC:03:135.
400	"Two days after . . . ages." FRC:03:82.
400	"During . . . them.": EDC:02:439.
400	"But back then...in the ratification debates.": EDC:04:40,41.
401	"In the ratification . . . nations. . .": EDC:02:291.
401	"In the ratification . . . nations. . .": EDC:02:291.
401	"Mr. Alexander Hamilton . . . government.": EDC:02:317,318.
401	Mr. Moses Ames. . .: EDC:02:46.
401	"Mr. William R. Davie. . . ": FRC:03:340.
403-5	"Mr. President. I am a plain man . . . opportunity.": EDC:02:102-104.

Friday, July 3, 1987

[Unless otherwise indicated, material applicable to dates cited in this chapter are to be found in FRC.]

- 407   "It took years. . . Europe.": WGB:00:313.
- 407-8   "Dr. FRANKLIN. . . believe ours?": FBP:00:371,372.
- 412   "Mr. ADAMS (continuing) Yes. . .": Case referred to in remaining portions of chapter is Supreme Court Opinion in re Immigration and Naturalization Service Appelant v. Jagdish Ral Chadha et al. (80-1832) on Appeal from the United States Court of Appeals for the Ninth Circuit; United States House of Representatives, Petitioner v. Immigration and Naturalization Service et al. (80-2170) United States Senate, Petitioner v. Immigration and Naturalization Service et al. (80-2171); on Writs of Certiorari to the United States Court of Appeals for the Ninth Circuit. Decided June 23, 1983.

Monday, July 6, 1987

[Unless otherwise indicated, material applicable to dates cited in this chapter are to be found in FRC.]

- 422   "Gen. WASHINGTON. . . wisdom.": PFF:00:573.
- 423   "It is a misfortune . . . .": CAJ:01:199.
- 423-5   "Mr. MADISON. . . it was postponed.": FRC:02:41-44.
- 425-7   "Three days later. . . Judiciary department itself.": FRC:02:80-83.
- 427   "Mr. JEFFERSON. . .": JTB:00:187,188.
- 428   "Mr. THOMSON. . .": FRC:03:31.
- 431-2   "Mr. MADISON. On the recommendation . . .": FRC:02:538-548.
- 434   "Mr. JEFFERSON. . .": LDC:02:504-506.
- 435-6   "Mr. MASON. Thank you . . . Convention.": FRC:03:367.
- 436   "Mr. ADAMS. The document reads. . .": FRC:03:367.
- 438   "Mr. Gallatin said. . .": FRC:03:379 in the House of Representatives June 19, 1798; Annals of Congress, Fifth Congress, 2nd and 3rd Session, II. 1976.
- 439   "Abigail ADAMS. I certainly did. . .": AJA:00:120,121.
- 439-40   "Mrs. ADAMS. Well. . .": AJA:00:122,123.
- 440   "Mrs. ADAMS. I certainly did. . .": AJA:00:127.
- 441   "It has been wittily. . . object to it.": EDC:03:493.
- 441-2   "I am not. . . act of themselves.": EDC:02:465.
- 442-3   ". . . by combining. . the other.": EDC:02:477.
- 443   "The next objection. . . in the world.": EDC:02:504,505.
- 443   "Mr. THOMSON. . . ": DHR:02:150.
- 443-5   "Mr. MADISON. Mr. King. . . violate them." EDC:02:47; "Mr. Oliver Wolcott. . . states.": EDC:02:202; "During New York's. . . may require.": EDC:02:283; "Mr. R. R. Livingston. . . governments.": EDC:02:291; "Before the. . . for its Senate.": EDC:02:354.
- 445   "Mr. THOMSON. . .": DHR:03:221.
- 445-6   "Mr. MADISON. . . of the former.": EDC:03:85.
- 447-9   "Mr. HAMILTON. . . the project.": HMJ:00:No. 75.
- 450   "Mr. MADISON. It appears that . . . treaty.": CTR:00:27.
- 451   "It is my opinion. . . States.": CTR:00:25.
- 451   "Within . . . negotiations.": CTR:00:25.
- 452   "Dr. FRANKLIN. . . like leather.": Poor Richard's Almanack.
- 452   "The point. . . modesty.": PFF:00:573.
- 452-3   "Mr. THOMSON . . . on August 10, 1789. . . there again.": CTR:00:33,34.

Tuesday, July 7, 1987

- 455-6   "Mr. THOMSON. . . with them.": EDC:02:133-135.
- 456-7   "Dr. FRANKLIN. . . executive powers. . .": EDC:04:117; "Luther Martin . . . for the President.": EDC:01:361; "Martin. . . National Council . . .": FRC:03:155; "And you, Mr. Madison. . . individual. . .": FRC:03:424.

458	"Richard Henry Lee. . . Members. . .": DHR:01:339.
458	"George Mason's . . . Government. . .": MGP:03:1056.
458	"And Mr. Robert Whitehill. . . give. . .": DHR:02:598.
458	Mr. William Stephen Smith. . . Council . . .": JTP:12:390,391.
459	I note that . . . Council. . .": FRC:03:170.
459	"Mr. MADISON. . . authority. . .": MAD:01:230.
459-60	"Dr. FRANKLIN. . . the great one.": FRC:03:418,419.
461	"Mr. ADAMS. . .": LDC:04:73-75.
463	"Mr. MADISON. . . system.": MAD:04:343.
463	"We owe. . . rights.": MAD:04:191.
463-4	"Gen. WASHINGTON . . . ever approximated.": PFF:00:563; In all. . . guardian.": PFF:00:564; "This government . . . upon all.": PFF:00:653.
464	"Mr. ADAMS. . . unite." RCF:John Adams to Dr. Price, dated New York, April 19, 1790, A.L.S., Waterston Autographs, Vol I.N.P., MHS. "Some people must . . . second.": LDC:04:290.
464	"Gov. Samuel Huntington. . . past.": EDC:02:198.
464-5	"Mr. James Wilson's. . . executed.": EDC:02:488.
465	"Mr. Gouverneur Morris. . .": MGD:02:531.
465	"Probably no man . . . the end.": PFF:00:157.
466	"The tributes. . . Yankees.": In the Telephone Exchange in Franklin Court in Philadelphia there is a large wall directory which lists numbers for famous people ranging from George Washington to Harry Truman. By dialing the appropriate number - including real life area codes - callers can hear each personage tell something about Franklin, Thomas Jefferson (area code 203 can be heard to say "I served with Washington and Franklin. . . I never heard either of them speak ten minutes at a time, nor to any but the main point which was to decide the question." The quotations cited here are from the Telephone Exchange, as furnished by the National Park Service.
466-7	"Dr. FRANKLIN. . . . . . him discretion.": FBR.
467	"Dr. FRANKLIN. . . divine presence.": FBR:00:235,236.

Monday, July 13, 1987

[Unless otherwise indicated, material applicable to dates cited in this chapter are to be found in FRC.]

480	"Mr. THOMSON. . .": FRC:03:367.
481-2	"Dr. FRANKLIN. . . inpeachments.": FRC:02:500.
482	"Mr. Morris. . . crimes. . .": FRC:02:551.
482	"Mr. MADISON. . . form a part.": FRC:02:551.
482	"The Hamilton Plan . . . court." FRC:03:626.

Thursday, August 6, 1987

489-90	"During. . . quills.": LDC:06:21,22.
490-1	"Of course. . . signature.": SPC:00:33-35.
491	"Early in 1777. . . Society.": SPC:00:35.
491	"The amount of labor. . . health.": SPC:00:36,37.
492	"Gen. WASHINGTON. . . The United States . . . unattainable.": PFF:00:595+ "Such is . . . Nation.": PFF:00:546.
493	"Mr. Madison. . .": MJJ:00:51.
493	"Mr. JEFFERSON. . . liberty and safety.": CGS:00:216; "I learned . . . into it.": SWG:00:262.
494	"Major JACKSON. . . Constitution.": FRC:02:648.
495	"Major Jackson presents. . . September, 1787.": FRC:03:82.
497	"Miss Catherine COLE. . .": RCF: Letter of Catherine Coles to Dolley P. Todd, Philadelphia, June 1, 1794.1614, Mass. Div. 1, University of Virginia Library.
	Hubbard Collection Vault 1, 920/IT 7721-1, Connecticut State Library, Hartford.

659

498-9 Testimony of Mr. Wilson, Mr. Mason and Mr. Bedford is in FRC:01:June 1, 1787.
499-500 Testimony of Mr. Morris, Mr. Broom, Doctor McClurg, Mr. Sherman, Colonel Mason and Mr. Madison is in FRC:02:July 17, 1787.
500 Testimony of Mr. Randolph and Mr. King is in FRC:02:July 19, 1787.
500-1 Testimony of Mr. Morris, Mr. Butler, Mr. Ellsworth and Mr. Williamson is in FRC:02:July 19, 1787.
501 "And so it went . . . thrown out.": FRC:02:July 24, 1787.
501-2 "How do you . . . relique.": CAJ:01:212.

Monday, August 10, 1987

[Unless otherwise indicated, material applicable to dates cited in this chapter are to be found in FRC.]

512-3 "Jefferson wrote to Adams . . . shall be . . .": CAJ:02:335-337.
514-5 Testimony of Mr. Sherman, Mr. Randolph, Mr. Wilson and Mr. Rutledge is in FRC:01:June 1, 1787.
515 Testimony of Mr. Butler and Mr. Randolph is in FRC:01:June 2, 1787.
515 Testimony of Mr. Gerry is in FRC:01:June 1, 1787.
517 Testimony of Mr. Hamilton is in FRC:01:June 6, 1787.
519 "Colonel Mason. . . . valuable to them.": FRC:02:July 26, 1787.
520 "Mr. Sherman. . . . appointment.": FRC:01:June 1, 1787.
520 "Mr. MADISON. . . . preponderate.": FRC:02:July 19, 1787.
520-1 "Mr. Pinckney. . . . objections.": FRC:02:July 17, 1787; "The people . . . respective states.": FRC:02:September 5, 1787; "They might be . . . into execution.": FRC:02:July 17, 1787.
521 "Mr. Houston. . . . distant states.": FRC:02:July 24, 1787; "He urged . . . president.": FRC:02:July 23, 1787.
521 "Mr. Rutledge. . . .": FRC:02:September 5, 1787.
521 "For the other side . . .": FRC:02:July 24, 1787.
522 "To Madame De Stael . . .": MGD:02:489.
523 "As late as . . . provided.": MGD:02:586,587.
523 "After the Constitution . . . amendments.": MGD:02:529.
524 "In the year 1811 . . . the great one.": MGD:02:528,529.
524 "In January, 1802 . . . compact.": FRC:03:390,391.
524-5 "Mr. MADISON. . . . individuals.": FRC:02:July 17, 1787.
525-6 "On July 19th, in Convention . . . mass of people . . .": CFU:00:408,409; "He added . . . Empire.": CFU:00:409,410; "He suggested . . . by the people.": CFU:00:410,411.
526 "Mr. THOMSON. . . . misfortunes.": MGD:02:522,523.
526 "Mr. THOMSON. . . . on the face of it.": FRC:03:498,499.
526-7 "Forget party . . . every other interest.": MGD:02:602.
527 "Must we wait . . . over.": MGD:02:564.
527 "The engine . . . mistaken.": MGD:02:429.
527 "In our country . . . may.": MGD:02:418,419.
527 "And finally, in 1803 . . .": MGD:02:442.
528-30 "Mr. MADISON. . . . he said.": FRC:02:July 26, 1787.
530 "Mr. Dickinson. . . . of the states.": FRC:01:June 2, 1787.
530 "Mr. KING. . . .": FRC:02:July 19, 1787.
530-1 "And finally . . . objections.": FRC:02:July 19, 1787.
537 "Mr. MADISON. It is possible . . .": RCF:Latter, Richard Dobbs Spaight to John Gray Blount, Philadelphia, September 2, 1787; The John Gray Blount Papers, A. B. Keith, editor, Raleigh, North Carolina, 1952, I, 342.
537-8 "Mr. THOMSON. . . .": RCF:John Dickinson's recollections in letter to Senator George Logan, November 4, 1802; Folder 18, Box 17-33, uncatalogued, Dickinson Papers, Ridgway.
540 "Will the public . . . sauce.": FRC:03:404.

541   "In his vindication . . .": Dickinson's Vindication on "four" charges are set forth in SDJ:00:364-414.
545-6   "The events . . . short time.": BLM:07:195.
546   "Three days later . . . United States.": BLM:07:195,196.
546   "Mr. Oliver Ellsworth. . . .": BLM:07:209.
546   "Alexander Hamilton . . .": BLM:07:203.
546-7   "But on the other hand . . .": RBL:01:307,308.
547   "Mr. John Montgomery . . .": BLM:07:215,216.
547-9   "Alexander Hamilton. . . . consequences.": HAP:03:438-458.
549   "To Governor Edmund Randolph . . .": MJP:01:568.

Monday, August 24, 1987

This chapter is based almost in its entirety on CFP: U.S. Congress. Senate. Committees on Appropriations and Governmental Affairs. Cost of Former Presidents to U.S. Taxpayer. 96th Cong., 1st Sess., November 6th, 7th and 8th, 1979. Washington, D.C.; GPO, 1980.

Wednesday Evening, August 26, 1987

565-6   "When a Gentleman. . . way.": RWA:00:March 1, 1925.
567   "Will ROGERS. You can't say. . . Heaven.": RWA:00:December 22, 1929.
567-8   "Will ROGERS. That's a good. . . of America.": RWA:00:December 7, 1924.
568   "Then we sent. . . War or Navy.": RWA:00:April 16, 1925.
568   "In 1932. . . we sank.": RWA:00:February 2, 1932.
568   "You see. . . yet.": RWA:00:October 27, 1930.
568-9   "Well, we got. . . sink.": RWA:00:June 23, 1930.
569   "And speaking. . . something.": RWA:00:February 7, 1928.
569   "WILL ROGERS. "America. . . them.": RWA:00:June 28, 1925.
569-70   "Will Rogers. In 1925. . . is.": RWA:00:October 16, 1930.
570   "Will Rogers. "That's not all. . . in the world. . .": RWA:00:May 16, 1932; "We are going. . . Phillipines.": RWA:00:May 1, 1932.
570   "Will Rogers. We are. . . champion.": RWA:00:August 10, 1924.
570   "Will Rogers. Switzerland. . . drink.":July 11, 1926.
570-1   "Will Rogers. There wasn't. . . be great?: RWA:00:February 21, 1929.
571   "Will Rogers. The oil. . . habit.": RWA:00:February 10, 1924.
571   "Will Rogers. That's right. . . fiddler.": RWA:00:June 27, 1930; "If there ever. . . broke.": RWS:00:July 9, 1930.
571   "No it's not. . . Interest.": RWA:00:January 6, 1924.
571-2   "Will ROGERS. Unemployment!. . . working.": RWA:00:January 18, 1931.
572   "Will ROGERS. Taxes! . . . owing.": RWA:00:117
573-4   "Will ROGERS. Don't get me started . . . Comrade.": RWA:00:152.
574   "Russia. . . won't work.": RWA:00:226.
574   "He didn't say. . . speech.": RWA:00:168.
574   "Dwight. . . made.": RWA:00:193.
574   "I'll tell you. . . Hoover.": RWA:00:284.
574-5   "The minute. . . play.": RWA:00:364.
575   "Well, now that . . . father.": RWA:00:234
575   "I'm off. . . forgiving.": RWA:00:383.

Thursday, August 31, 1987

[Unless otherwise indicated, material applicable to dates cited in this chapter are to be found in FRC.]

578-9   "Gen. MacArthur. . . devised.": CGS:00:594; "At the turn. . . at one blow.": MAC:00:829; "I know war. . . door.": MAC:00:596.
579   "Gen. WASHINGTON. . .": PFF:00:609.
579   "Dr. FRANKLIN. . .": PFF:00:403,404.

580   "Our future safety. . . maintain it.": PFF:00:356,357.
580   "Mr. MADISON. . .": MAD:03:17.
580   "Mr. THOMAS. . . Algiers.": MAD:03:16.
580-1 "President Madison. . . tribute.": MAD:03:16,17.
582   "Secretary of State. . . success.": WEM:00:42; "On June 19, 1822 . . . Government.": WEM:00:55.
582-3 "Gen. MacArthur. . . terms.": MDR:00:263.
583-4 "This sequence. . . itself.": MDS:00:210,211.
584-6 "On the third. . . reality.": MDS:00:205-209.
587-9 "Gen. MacArthur. . . is little wanted.": MDS:00:265-269.
589-90 "The panorama. . . frittered away.": MDR:00:320,321.
590   "Leadership. . . liberty.": MDR:00:417,418.
590-1 "Gen. MACARTHUR. . . world.": MDR:00:418.
591   "Mr. JEFFERSON. . . goes.": MDS:00:327.
595   "Gen. MACARTHUR. . . combustion.": MDS:00:317.
595   "Almost fifty. . . ignored.": MDS:00:190.
595-6 "First SPECTATOR" and "Second SPECTATOR": From letter to the editor, "The 21-Gun Salute has got to Go," by Lillian Miller, Washington, D.C., The Washington Post. Saturday, March 31, 1979
596-7 "Gen. MacArthur Let us. . . to come.": MDS:00:272.

Monday, September 7, 1987

[Unless otherwise indicated, material applicable to dates cited in this chapter are to be found in FRC.]

598   "Mr. Thomson. . . Once, while he. . . state.": Ellet, Queens of Society, May 24, 1975, p.115,116.
600   "Let this sad tale. . . God!": CGS:00:230,231.
603   "Alexander Hamilton. . . borrowed.!": HMJ:00:No. 65.
604   "Parliament. . . occurred.": CPI:00:04; "At the time. . . Parliament.,": CPI:00:05; "Two points. . . impeachments. . .": CPI:00:07; "The debates. . . conceived it.": CPI:00:07.
605   "Well, fourteen officers . . . impeachments.": CPI:00:17
605   "Only five . . . office.": CPI:00:17 (Note 85)
605   "On February 6, 1974. . . August 9, 1974.": CPI:00:02.
605   "This was . . . impeached.": CPI:00:02.
606-7 "As to what our. . . consuming.": WLR:43:414.
607-8 "Among them. . . no remedy.": WLR:43:474,475; "The question. . . accountability.": WLR:43:390.
608-9 "The British system. . . nation.": WLR:43:481:482.
609   "A basic device. . . last resort.": WLR:43:476.
609-10 "A power reserved. . . about it.": WLR:43:476; ". . . untouchable executive.": WLR:43:477.
610   "Dr. FRANKLIN. . . On February 14, 1974. . . special election.": WLR:43:328; H.J.Res. 903, February 14, 1974; H.J. Res. 1111, August 15, 1974.
610   "While I am inclined. . . Great Britain.": WLR: 43:343.
611   "The one principle. . . as a whole.": WLR:43:364.
612   "Mr. THOMSON. . . experience. . . choice.": MGD:02:475.
613-4 "Mr. THOMSON. . . affecting.": BLM:07:394,395.
615   "Mr. Jefferson. . . acquiescence.": Pennsylvania Evening Herald, Wednesday, June 13, 1787.
616   "Mr. THOMSON. . .": EDC:02:159,160.
616   "Gen. WASHINGTON. . .": PFF:00:602.
617   "Mr. MADISON. . .": PFF:00:353.
617   "Mr. ADAMS. . .": AJL:00:19.

Thursday, September 17, 1987

- 622 "Mr. JEFFERSON. . .": Based on letter from Federal Convention to Continental Congress, dated, September 17, 1787; FRC:02:666,667.
- 630 "Gen. WASHINGTON. . . others.": JTP:12:150.
- 630 "Although. . . whatsoever.": FRC:03:339,340.
- 630 "It appears. . . objections.": FRC:03:270.
- 630 "Dr. FRANKLIN. . .": FRC:03:98.
- 630-1 "Mr. THOMSON. . . imperfections. . .": BLM:08:678,679.
- 631 "Dr. FRANKLIN. . . being.": FRC:03:296,297.
- 631 "Mr. MADISON. . . country.": MJJ:00:51.
- 631 "Mr. THOMSON. . . assemble.": Based on BLM:08:Preface.

Monday, June 15, 1988

- 633 "The members . . . keep it.": RFC:03:85.
- 633 "John Adams. . . ever had.": Letter John Adams, June 21, 1811, Old Family Letters, A. p. 287.

Monday, July 4, 1988

- 634-7 Based on diverse sources; primarily RFC, Francis Hopkinson's "Account of the Grand Federal Procession, printed in his Miscellaneous Essays, Philadelphia, 1792, II, 349-401, and RBL:01:474.
- 638 "Mr. Adams. . . . forever more.": LDC:04:376; "Either I misjudged . . . Revolution . . .": LDC:04:374.
- 639 "Mr. Adams. I recall. . . chimed away. . .": LDC:04:414.
- 639 "Of thee I sing, Bell. . .": a slight parody on "Of Thee I sing," by George Gershwin.
- 640 "The Congress. . . most proper. . .": LDC:04:397.
- 640-1 Jefferson-Adams dialogue re Declaration of Independence: BCC:00:186.
- 641 "Dr. FRANKLIN. Next thing. . . time.": LDC:04:286.
- 642-3 "Dr. FRANKLIN. So the Saints. . .": PMHB:11:493; Letter A. Mackraby to Sir Philip Francis, April 24, 1770; RCF.
- 642 "Mr. ADAMS. The Saints. . . question.": LDC:03:572.
- 643 "Mr. ADAMS. From my barber.": LDC:03:572.
- 643 "Gen. WASHINGTON. "It is not easy. . .": MGD:02:527. These are the words of Gouverneur Morris, not Washington - perhaps in tribute to his genius in prose; not his conduct as a Machiavellian, as some supposed.

INDEX

Adams, Abigail, 439-40
Adams, John, xi, 19, 24,
  29-30-31, 39, 41
  biography, 20, 36-7, 361-62,
  555-56, 638-39-40, 642
  on the Continental Congress,
  52-3, 241
  on John Dickinson, 260-61
  on the government, 319-20
  on the presidency, viii
  on rules of the Commission,
  56
  on the vice-presidency, 323
  on separation of powers,
  411-12-13
  on women's rights, 461
Adams, John Quincy
  biography, 144, 582
  on the presidency, 8, 144-45-46
Adams, Sherman, x
Agricultural Stabilization and
  Conservation Service, 105
Agricultural Dept., see Dept. of
  Agriculture
Albany Plan, the, 250-51
Alden, Roger, 52
Allen, Richard V., x, 358
American Daily Advertiser, 140
Ames, Moses, 350-51-52, 401
Annapolis Convention,
  299-300-301, 303, 307-8
Article I, The Constitution, 337,
  417-18-19
Article II, The Constitution,
  216-17, 484
Article V, The Constitution, 44-5,
  400
Article VI, The Constitution, 268
Articles of Confederation,
  241-42-43, 253-60, 264-70,
  278-79, 291-92, 294-95,
  296-97-98
Atlantic, The, x
Autobiography of Will Rogers,
  565
Barrell, Nathaniel, 616
Bedford, Gunning, 396-97, 498-99
Beekeeper Indemnity Program,
  105

Begin, Menachim, 271-72
Bicentennial Constitutional Commission, 19, 42-5, 622, 633
  see Commission, the
Biographical Dictionary of the
  American Congress, 294
Boston Independent Gazette, 308
Boston Massacre, 599, 600
Boston Post, 173
Boudinot, Elias, 477, 544-45-46
Broom, Jacob, 499
Brzezinski, Zkigniew, 359
Buchanan, James
  biography, 152-53
  on the presidency, 153-54, 503
Bureau of Reclamation, 87
Bureau of National Debt, 112
Burger, Chief Justice Warren,
  413-21
Burnett, Edmund Cody, 51-52
Burr, Aaron, 281
Butler, Pierce, 500, 515, 593

Cabinet, the, 82, 179, 317
  see Constitutional Council
Carlyle, Thomas, 460
Carrington, Edward, 280-81
Carter, Jimmy, x
Chadha Case, 412-21, 484
Chapin, Dwight L., xi
City Tavern, 24-5
Cleveland, Grover
Civil Aeronautics Board, 89
Clark, Abraham, 600
Claypoole's American Daily
  Advertiser, 556
Cleveland, Grover
  biography, 175-76
  on the presidency, viii,
  176-77-78, 503
Code of Federal Regulations,
  118-19
Codex Vaticanus, 49
Commission, The
  Discussion on...amending the
  Constitution
  see Constitutional Congress
  domestic vs. foreign depts.,
  318

665

resolutions on, 478,
485-86-87
  terms of office, 318, 242-56
  two houses, 317
  see Constitutional Council
  resolution on, 474-77
  see Senate, the
Government agencies resolution on, 484
  see Government agencies
impeachments, 479-82
  resolution on, 479
"no confidence vote", 598-620
Presidency, the, 601-5
  see Presidency, The
separation of powers, 409-21, 423-53, 454,68
  see Judges
treaties, resolution on, 483
  see Treaties
vice-presidency, the 54, 318
  resolution on, 470-72, 472-74
  resolution as proposed amendments, 621-32
    approved by Congress, 633
    rules of, 53-57
Committee on Administrative Management, 210
Committee of Detail, 364-65, 428, 475-76, 481, 495-96, 532-33, 536
Committee of Eleven, 332-33, 366-69, 430, 480, 496, 534, 538
Committee of Five, 430
Committee of Style, 370
Commodity Credit Corp., 87
"Common Cause of America: A Study of the First Continental Congress, The" xvi
Communism, threat of
  see MacArthur
Congress
  see Grace Commission
  see Legislation
  see Legislative veto
  see Senate, the
  see Separation of Powers
Congressional Record, 13, 121-22
Continental Congress, 50-3, 240-43, 489-92

Constitution, the
  on amending it, 15, 19, 20, 235-37, 462-65, 469-70
  Constitutional Council 458-59
  origins, 239-48, 255-56, 265-66, 267, 294
  president, election of, 511
  president, term of, 494, 503-8
  ratification, 348
  Senate, the, 380, 384
  terms of Congressional members, 342, 347-48
  vice-president, office of, 328-29, 336-37
  see Great Federal Procession
Constitutional Convention
  see Federal Convention of 1787
Constitutional Council, ix, 266, 335-36, 357-75, 454
  see Cabinet, the
  see Senate, the
Consumer Products Safety Commission, 107
Coolidge, Calvin
  biography, 195-96
  on the presidency, 196-98
Cranston, Alan, 10
Cumberland Chronicle, 256

Daily Digest, 121
Davie, William R., 336-37, 401, 476
Dayton, Gen. Johnathan, 382, 395
Dean, John W. III, 11
Declaration of Independence, 50-1, 257-60, 268, 598-99, 617
Defense Dept.
  see Dept. of Defense
Defense of the Constitution of the Government of the United States of America, The, 322-23
Department of Agriculture, 62-3, 104, 110
  see Agricultural Stabilization and Conservation Service
Department of Defense, 59, 61, 85-86, 90-2
Department of Domestic Affairs, 471
Department of Education, 112

666

Department of Energy, 59
Department of Foreign Affairs, 472
Department of Housing and Urban Development, 112
Department of the Interior, 109, 123
Department of Justice, 91-3
Department of Labor, 110
Department of State, 80-123
Department of Transportation, 112
Dickinson, John, 27, 133, 243, 260-66, 301, 304-6, 344, 360, 385, 486, 530, 538-9
  Articles of Confederation, 257-59, 264-68
Douglas, Stephen A., 156
Douglass, Frederick, 156-57
Draper's Massachusetts Gazette, 262
Dupois, Jacques, 323-25
Du Simitiere, 271

ERA, 124-25
ERISA, xiii, 97, 111
Ehrlichman, John D., xi
Eisenhower, Dwight D., x, 189
  biography, 222
  on the presidency, 222-25
Ellsworth, Oliver, 363, 389-90, 393-94, 395, 423
Emergency Banking Act, 203-4
Employee Retirement Income Security Act
  see ERISA
Employment and Training Administration, 112
Environmental Protection Agency, 112
Equal Rights Amendment
  see ERA
Executive Protection Service
  see Secret Service
Exxon Corporation to the Federal Energy Agency, 111

FBI, 92
FDA, 108-9
FHA, 60
FTC, 89, 108, 412

Fairhill, William S., 115-126
Farmers Home Administration, 87
Fat City, 103
Federal Convention of 1787 (Constitutional Convention), 25-6, 39-40, 239, 243-48, 251, 300, 336-38, 379, 407, 537-38
  on a Constitutional Council, 362-71
  on impeachment, 604-5
  on method of election of president, 511-22, 528-41, 611-13
  need for, 275-86, 290, 307-11
  on power of the people, 615-16
  on role of the Senate, 375-76
  rules of, 55-6, 316
  on term of office of the president, 492, 494-503
  on terms of congressional members, 342
Federal Crop Insurance Corp., 87
Federal Highway Administration
  see FHA
Federal Housing Administration, 87
Federal Information Centers, 119
Federal Paperwork Commission, 110-11
Federal Register, 117, 120-24
Federal Regulations
  see Governmental Agencies
Federal Reserve Board
  see Government Agencies
Federal Trade Commission
  see Government Agencies
Federalist, The, 523, 603
Federalist Papers, The, 353, 378, 446
Fish and Wildlife Service, 109-10, 123
Food and Drug Administration
  see FDA
Ford, Gerald, 60, 189, 229
Former Presidents Act of 1958, 557
Franklin, Benjamin, xi, xv, 19, 27, 37-8, 62, 75-6, 98, 233, 249-50, 272
  Albany Plan, the, 251-53
  Articles of Confederation, 253-55, 264-68

667

Biography, 21-2, 34, 55, 56-7, 113-15, 256-57, 307-8, 377, 465-66, 631-32
on Congressional veto, 419-20
on The Constitution, 41, 45-47, 235
on a Constitutional Council, 257-61, 369
as delegate to the Federal Convention, 26, 43, 132-33, 316
on John Dickinson, 262-63
on the government, 83, 114-15, 253
on government in the 1700s, 65, 66-8
on paying public officials, 252-54
on paying public officials, 252-54
on prayer, 381-82
on the role of the Senate, 375-84, 397-401, 403-5, 407-09
on the structure of Congress, 132, 317
Franklin Delano Roosevelt Memorial Commission, 106
Freedom of Information Act, 116
Freemans Journal, 541

Gallatin, Albert, 432-33
Garfield, James
biography, 174
on the presidency, 8, 174-75
General Accounting Office, 557
General Services Administration, The, 62, 89, 119, 558-59
Gerry, Elbridge, 26, 245, 344, 362-63, 366, 515, 517-18, 528-29
Gorham, Nathaniel, 423, 425, 429
Government
see U.S. Government
The Government of the Living Dead, 58, 64
Governmental agencies
inconsistent with law, 97-125
relationship with president, 226
Grace Commission, The, 95-6
Grayson, William, 265-66, 630-31
Great Depression, The, 202-6
Great Federal Procession, The, 634-37

Griffin, Cyrus, 631

Haig, Alexander, 358
Haldeman, H. R., 9, ix, xi, 357
Hamilton, Alexander, 26, 41, 275, 284, 292-94, 303, 344, 384, 447-49, 485, 517
Hamilton Plan, 482
Hancock, John, 49, 66-7, 241, 598-60, 640
Hanson, John, 491
Harding, Warren
biography, 194-6
on the presidency, 8, 195
Harrison, Benjamin
biography, 178
on the presidency, 178-81
Hayes, Rutherford
biography, 174-5
on the presidency, viii, 173-4
Henry, Patrick, 50
Hoover, Commission, the, 72-4, 75-8, 80-94, 209-10, 211
Hoover, Herbert, 212-13
on the presidency, 74-5, 198-201
Howe, Louis McHenry, x
Hunt, E. Howard, xi

ICC, 89
INS, 60, 412-13
IRS, 98
Immigration and Nationality Act, 412
Immigration and Naturalization Service
see INS
Impeachment
see Commission
see Presidency
Independent regulatory agencies, 89-90
Internal Revenue Code, 103
Internal Revenue Service
see IRS
Interstate Commerce Commission
see ICC
Iredell, James, 400-1

Jackson, Andrew, 77
biography, 147

on the presidency, xiii, 148, 503
Jackson, Major William, 27, 48, 53, 245, 343-44, 346-47, 494-95
Jay, John, 413
Jefferson, Thomas, xi, 19, 39, 40-41, 52, 512-13
 on amending the Constitution, 15, 231, 234-35, 248-49
 on appointment of judges, 427-28
 biography, 22-3, 31-2, 53, 112-13, 287, 340, 641
 on domestic vs. foreign affairs, 318
 on government structure, 128-30
 on the presidency, viii, 133-34, 189, 496-97
 on rules for the Commission, 53-4
 on Shay's Rebellion, 281
 on the vice-presidency, 340, 470-1, 473-4
Johnson, Andrew
 biography, 169-70
 on the presidency, 170-72
Johnson, Lyndon B., 189
Johnson, Dr. William Samuel,, 429
Jordan, Hamilton, 10, 358
Journal of the Federal Convention, 27, 245, 494
Judges, appointment of, 423-27

Kennedy, John F., 59, 189
 biography, 225
 on the presidency, ix, 225-30
Kent State University Massacre, 600
King, Rufus, 286, 298-99, 500, 530
Kissinger, Henry, 359
Krough, Egil, Jr., xi

Labor Dept.
 see Dept. of Labor
Lambro, Dr. Donald, 103-12
Lance, Bert, ix, 357-58
Landers, Ann, 325-26
Laurens, Henry, 359, 509-11

Lee, Richard Henry, 35, 339-40, 473, 477
Legislation, public action on, 119-25
Legislative veto, 412-21, 484
Lemon Administrative Committee, 123
Lemon Regulation, 123
Liddy, G. Gordon, xi
Life of Lincoln, 183
Lincoln, Abraham, 35, 169-70, 157-65
 biography, 157-65, 186, 194
 on the presidency, 164-68
Livingston, R.R., 401, 444
Lodge Brown Act, The, 72

MacArthur, General Douglas, xv, 577-599
Maclaine, Archibald, 348-49
Madison, James, xi, 20, 32, 33, 40, 48
 on appointment of judges, 423-27
 biography, 23, 37, 38, 244-45, 301, 334, 580-81, 631, 641
 on congressional terms, 318, 345-46, 485, 486
 on the Constitution, 233-37
 on a Constitutional Council, 379, 459
 as delegate to Federal Convention, 26, 43, 130, 244-46, 314-15
 on the Executive Department, 79-80
 on the government, states vs federal, 130-31
 on government in the 1700s, 65-66, 67
 on the Hoover Commission, 72-4
 on impeachment, 482
 on the presidency, 499-500, 516-17, 518, 530-31, 612
 on rules of the Commission, 55-56
 on the Senate, 388-89, 394-95, 399-400, 476
 on separation of powers, 410-11

on Shay's Rebellion, 281-82
on treaties, 449-51
on Washington's presidency, 134-46
Magazine of American History, 174
Magruder, Jeb Stuart, xi
Manual of Parliamentary Practice, 53
Marbury vs. Madison, 127
Marion Star, 194
Marshall, John, 413
Martin, Luther, 477, 481
Mason, George, 28-9, 334, 336, 363, 366, 473
   on appointment of judges, 424
   on a Constitutional Council, 366-71, 476, 477
   as delegate to the Federal Convention, 25, 245, 435-36
   as delegate to the Virginia General Assembly, 36
   on the presidency, ix, 499, 500, 519, 612
   on separation of powers, 441
   on the vice-presidency, 335-36
McClurg, Dr. James, 499, 500
McHenry, Dr. James, 28-9, 333-34
McKean, Thomas, 337-38
McKinley, William, 182, 211
Meese, Edwin, 358
Melville, Herman, 466
Mercer, John Francis, 428
Military Air Transport Service, 88
Military Unification Act, 82
Moby Dick, 466
Monroe, James, 338, 473
Montesquieu, 376-79, 446
Montgomery, John, 547
Morris, Gouverneur, xiv, 248, 366, 371-74, 401-402, 425-26, 459-60, 481-83, 499, 500, 521-28, 533, 534, 612

NASA, 122-23
National Aeronautics and Space Administration
   see NASA
National Board for the Promotion of Rifle Practice, 106

National Flood Insurance Program, 125-26
National Labor Relations Board, 89
National Star, 157
New York Packet, 278
New York Post, 100
New York Times, 419
New York Tribune, 466
Nixon, Richard, ix, 60, 189, 229-30, 269, 605

OSHA, 104
Obey, David, x
Occupational Safety and Health Act of 1970, 104
Occupational Safety and Health Administration
   see OSHA
Office of Management and Budget, 85, 115
Office of Revenue Sharing, 112
Orders of the Commission
   see Commission, rules of

Panic of 1837, 151
Panic of 1893, 175-76
Pell, Philip, 51
Pennsylvania Constitution, 360-61
Pennsylvania Evening Herald, The, 615
Pennsylvania Evening Post, 434
Pennsylvania Gazette, 22, 115, 443
Pennsylvania Herald, 540
Pennsylvania Journal, 263, 411
Penthouse Magazine, 64-5
Pierce, William, 330-31
Pickney, Charles, 243, 247, 297, 363, 398, 409, 426, 520-21, 534-35, 592
Polk, James
   biography, 151-52
   on the presidency, 152
Poor Richard's Almanack, 22, 115, 143, 263, 421, 422, 465, 467, 550
Porter, Herbert L., xi
Post Office Department, 68, 70
Postal Service, 62
   see Post Office Dept.

Preamble to the Constitution, 613
Presidency, the, 601-2
   burdens of the office, viii, 133-46, 147-56, 165-69, 173-81, 184-216, 217-32
   cost to taxpapers, 551-64
   in Hoover's term, 74-5
   impeachment vs. "no confidence vote", 603-20
   in Johnson's term, 172-73
   method of election, 509-50
   term of office, 489-509
   war powers, 582, 590
   see Commission, separation of powers
Presidential Libraries Act, 559-64
Private Sector Survey on Cost Control, 95
Public Access to Information, 116-26
Public Housing Administration, 87

Ramsay, David, 299-30
Randolph, Gov. Edmund, 25, 245, 342-43, 425, 445-46, 485, 500, 514, 515, 520
   see Randolph Plan
Randolph, Peyton, 30, 241
Randolph Plan, 384-85, 409-11
Read, George, 27, 243, 390-91
Reader's Digest, 99, 103
Reagan, Ronald, x, 95-6, 189
Rehnquist, Justice William Hubbs, 413
Reorganization Act, The, 414
Reuss, Henry S., 610
Revenue Acts of 1942, 98-103
   see IRS
Revere, Paul, 24
Roosevelt, Franklin D., x
   biography, 201-4, 208
   on the presidency, ix, 206-13
   on his programs, 205-6
Roosevelt, Theodore
   biography, 182-83, 185, 187
   on the presidency, 183-87, 188
Rural Electrification Administration, 87
Rush, Dr. Benjamin, 546-47, 636
Rutledge, J. 514, 521, 536, 592

Saalfield Publishing Company vs. The Commissioner, 100-2
Saturday Evening Post, 557
Secret Service, 554-55, 558-59
Securities and Exchange Commission, 89
Sedgwick, T., 350-405
Senate, the role of, 375
   see Commission, separation of powers
Septuagint, 49
Seventeenth Amendment, 376
Seward, William H. 170
Shay's Rebellion, 281-82
Sherrill, Robert, 58-65, 67, 68, 70
Sherman, Roger, 391-92
Slip Laws, 118
Smith, Josiah, 403-5
Smithsonian Institute, 107
Sousa, John Philip, 637-42
Sparks, Jared, 27
Spirit of Laws, The, 377, 378
Stamp Act of Congress, 1765, 240
State Department
   see Dept. of State
States' rights, 128-31
Stillman, Rev. Samuel, 352-53
Stockman, David, x, 358
Sullivan, John, 273-74
Sunshine Act, 116-17
"Sunshine Act Meetings", 117
Supplemental Apropriations Act, 1969, 557

Taft, William Howard
   biography, 187
   on the presidency, 187-92, 503
Taylor, Dr. John, 349-50
This Country of Ours, 557
Thomson, Charles
   biography, 48-50, 598-99
   on rules of the Commission, 56
   Secretary of the Continental Congress, 50-51, 52, 255, 290-91
Time, 564
Treaties, 408-9, 428-33, 447-53, 457-58
Truman, Harry, 189
   biography, 215
   on the presidency, ix, 216-22

Twenty-Fifth Amendment, 607
Twenty-Second Amendment, 223, 497, 506-7, 618

U. S. Government
   condition of, in the 1700s, 65-70
   condition of, in the 1980s, 77-8
      Lambro, 103-12
      Sherrill, 58-62
United States Maritime Commission, 87
United States Statutes at Large, 118

Van Buren, Martin
   biography, 149
   on the presidency, 150-51
Vance, Cyrus R., 359
Varnum, James Mitchell, 274-75
Vice-presidency, office of the, 54, 318, 323, 328-29, 331-41
Virginia Plan
   see Randolph Plan

War
   see MacArthur
War Powers Resolution, 190, 415
Washington, George, xi, 19, 27-8, 43-4, 96, 112-13
   biography, 20-21, 35-36, 55, 61, 248, 273, 310-314, 386-87, 452-53, 640
   on the Constitution, 71-2, 235
   as delegate to the Federal Convention, 25-6, 40-41, 43, 244-46
   on the government, 127-28, 383
   on the presidency, 134-45, 497
   on rules for the Commission, 54-7
Weekly Compilation of Presidential Documents, 118
Weinberger, Casper, 358
Weiss, Willard A., 24
   credentials, xiii, xiv
   on governmental agencies, 97, 103
White, Bishop William, 52

White, Justice Byron R., 413-21
Willkie, Wendell, 271-72, 503
Wilson, James, 387-88, 392-93, 400, 441-43, 489, 514, 529-3
Wilson, Woodrow
   biography, 192
   on the presidency, viii, 192-94
Wisner, Henry, 434-35
Woman's Equality Day, 124